Handbook of International Health Care Systems

PUBLIC ADMINISTRATION AND PUBLIC POLICY

A Comprehensive Publication Program

Executive Editor

JACK RABIN
Professor of Public Administration and Public Policy
School of Public Affairs
The Capital College
The Pennsylvania State University—Harrisburg
Middletown, Pennsylvania

Annals of Public Administration

Handbook of International Health Care Systems

edited by

Khi V. Thai
Florida Atlantic University
Fort Lauderdale, Florida

Edward T. Wimberley
Florida Gulf Coast University
Fort Myers, Florida

Sharon M. McManus
Macon State College
Macon, Georgia

MARCEL DEKKER, INC.   NEW YORK · BASEL

ISBN: 0-8247-8829-X

This book is printed on acid-free paper.

Headquarters
Marcel Dekker, Inc.
270 Madison Avenue, New York, NY 10016
tel: 212-696-9000; fax: 212-685-4540

Eastern Hemisphere Distribution
Marcel Dekker AG
Hutgasse 4, Postfach 812, CH-4001 Basel, Switzerland
tel: 41-61-261-8482; fax: 41-61-261-8896

World Wide Web
http://www.dekker.com

The publisher offers discounts on this book when ordered in bulk quantities. For more information, write to Special Sales/Professional Marketing at the headquarters address above.

Current printing (last digit):
10 9 8 7 6 5 4 3 2 1

PRINTED IN THE UNITED STATES OF AMERICA

Preface

This book project was initiated at a time when rising expenditures for health care were of great concern and a precipitating factor in calls for health care reform in the United States. Many other developed countries that had experienced increases in health care expenditures also viewed these events with increasing alarm.

The concern over rising costs has prompted governments to examine the underlying factors and to take action. The role of government in health care usually incorporates two major dimensions: the financing of health care and other social programs, and the determination, to some extent, of how the delivery system is organized. Thus, government action occurs most often in the form of restructuring the health care system or altering the mechanisms for financing health care. How extensive this role is varies with the history and culture of each nation, which influence the philosophy and values concerning the appropriate parameters for government involvement in the affairs of its citizens.

The government's ability to finance services is limited by its ability to raise funding through taxation and then to manage and allocate these funds effectively and efficiently. In developed countries, taxpayers attempt to determine their willingness to be taxed through their voting behaviors for political parties and candidates with whose promised positions on taxation and government spending they agree. Voters who favor government spending on particular programs are usually willing to be taxed for the provision of those programs. Voters who are concerned with containing government spending are less likely to be willing to pay taxes, let alone tax increases.

As expenditures for health care have steadily risen, voters and governments have had to become more aware of the tradeoffs between spending for health care and spending for other desired programs, as well as the impact of reducing spending on health care. While the extent of government involvement in the financing and organization of health care does vary among countries, these concerns over steadily rising costs are common.

The intent of this book is to examine what various countries have done in the area of health care financing, what the role of the national government has been, how the health care system is financed, how the providers are organized and structured, and whether these activities have been successful in addressing rising costs and expenditures. The book is intended to provide policy makers, researchers, and students of health care policy and administration with valuable information about various health care systems.

This book is dedicated to the memory of Dr. Sharon M. McManus, co-editor of the book. Dr. McManus was a scholar and an advocate for her students. She will be missed by all who came in contact with her. Determined to complete this book in the memory of Dr. McManus, I invited a dear colleague, Dr. Terry Wimberley, to fill the void left by Dr. McManus. Without his participation, the book would not have been finished by this time. I appreciate his hard work and his willingness to join this book project.

I also appreciate the patience, understanding, and cooperation of all contributors of this book, particularly those who completed their chapters very early and had to spend time to revise and update their early drafts. Special thanks go to Dr. Jack Rabin, editor of the Public Administration and Public Policy series, and Marcel Dekker, for accepting the original proposal and offering valuable encouragement. I am especially grateful for the professional assistance of Ms. Paige Force, Production Editor, and other staff members at Marcel Dekker, Inc.

Khi V. Thai

Contents

Contributors

Michelle A. Angeletti   Interim Chair and Assistant Professor, Department of Interdisciplinary Studies, College of Health Professions, Florida Gulf Coast University, Fort Myers, Florida

Karen Bloor   Department of Health Sciences and Clinical Evaluation, University of York, Heslington, York, England

Elena A. Bourhanskaia   Office of Health Care Policy Research and Development, University of Nevada, Las Vegas, Nevada

Peter L. Cruise   Assistant Professor, Health and Community Services Department, California State University, Chico, California

Tevfik Dinçer   Professor, School of Health Administration, Hacettepe University, Ankara, Turkey

Tamás Evetovits   Health Services Management Training Center, Semmelweis University, Budapest, Hungary

Paul Gunnar Kaati   Professor, Community Medicine and Rehabilitation, Social Medicine, University of Umea, Umea, Sweden

Aren Kubataev   Office of Health Care Policy Research and Development, University of Nevada, Las Vegas, Nevada

Helen M. Lapsley   Economist, Faculty of Medicine, University of New South Wales, Sydney, New South Wales, Australia

Laurence Malcolm Professor Emeritus and Consultant, Aotearoa Health, Lyttelton, New Zealand

Alan Maynard Department of Health Economics, University of York, Heslington, York, England

Sharon M. McManus† Associate Professor and Chair, Division of Health Sciences, Macon State College, Macon, Georgia

Dimitris Niakas Associate Professor, Health Services Management, School of Social Sciences, Hellenic Open University, Patras, Greece

Kant Patel Professor, Department of Political Science, Southwest Missouri State University, Springfield, Missouri

Mary A. Paterson Office of Health Care Policy Research and Development, University of Nevada, Las Vegas, Nevada

Carole M. Pohl Associate Professor, Health Administration Program—Industry Studies, Florida Atlantic University, Boca Raton, Florida

Arthur J. Rubens Associate Professor, Department of Management, and Director, Sponsored Projects and Programs, Center for Leadership and Innovation, Florida Gulf Coast University, Fort Myers, Florida

Mark E. Rushefsky Professor, Department of Political Science, Southwest Missouri State University, Springfield, Missouri

Balu Swami Business Analyst, Risk Management (IT), AT&T Wireless Services, Inc., Bothell, Washington

Kazue Takayanagi Associate Professor, Department of Health Services Administration, Nippon Medical School, Tokyo, Japan

Fahreddin Tatar* Associate Professor, School of Health Administration, Hacettepe University, Ankara, Turkey

Khi V. Thai Professor, School of Public Administration, Florida Atlantic University, Fort Lauderdale, Florida

---

† Deceased
* *Current affiliation*: The Futures Group International/POLICY Project, Ankara, Turkey

Edward T. Wimberley Associate Professor, Division of Interdisciplinary Studies, College of Arts and Sciences, Florida Gulf Coast University, Fort Myers, Florida

Rieko Yajima Research Fellow, Department of Health Services Administration, Nippon Medical School, Tokyo, Japan

Handbook of International Health Care Systems

1

Introduction to International Health Care Systems
Themes and Variations on Themes

Edward T. Wimberley
Florida Gulf Coast University, Fort Myers, Florida

Khi V. Thai
Florida Atlantic University, Fort Lauderdale, Florida

I. OVERVIEW: HEALTH AND HEALTH CARE IN A GLOBAL MARKET

This book is devoted to issues relating to health care delivery, finance, and policy on an international scale. The international viewpoint provided within this text is intended to broaden the perspective of students, policymakers, lawmakers, health care providers, and administrators who assume that the health-related problems they are confronted with are somehow unique to their particular culture or market. There is little doubt that cultural, social, economic, and historical factors significantly shape health care policy and provision within any given nation. Nevertheless, it must be recognized that within the millennium health care will increasingly become an integral component of a global market in which nations compete for health-related technology, pharmaceuticals, human resources, programs and services, and financing (Lazarus, 1999; Medical Marketing and Media, 1999; Velasquez and Boulet, 1999).

A. Health Care Costs, Access, and Delivery

Access to affordable, effective, and quality health care is without doubt the dominant theme that unites all of the Organization for Economic Cooperation and

Development (OECD) nations discussed within this text. Access not only includes making health care available to the largest portion of a nation's population; it also involves providing the appropriate level or type of care. How the issue of access is approached depends upon current economic, cultural, and political characteristics of nations, as well as upon the historical pattern of health care delivery within nations, and the nature of the health care infrastructure that is currently in place.

The global nature of the world's health care market is clearly observable within the OECD nations included in this book. Nations with varying economic capacities for providing quality health care for their populations find themselves in a situation where increased global communications heightens consumer expectations regarding what constitutes optimal "quality" and "accessible" health care. Such communication allows providers and citizens to remain current with the latest available medical technologies, procedures, and pharmaceuticals, which in turn motivates practitioners and their patients to seek these latest approaches and technologies.

Since access to such resources is costly, nations either find themselves endlessly spending national resources to keep up with the most current medical technologies and approaches and/or seeking to limit (i.e., ration) access to expensive technologies, pharmaceuticals, and procedures. Australia and the United Kingdom are examples of nations where rationing has been employed for some period of time, with generally broad-based public support (Bloor and Maynard, 2000; Lapsley, 2000). In nations such as the United States (Wimberley and Rubens, 2000; Pohl, 2000) where access to care is largely associated with access to employer-based health insurance, skyrocketing health care costs driven by medical technologies and pharmaceutical developments can result in:

   A complete or partial lack of access to health care for those lacking insurance coverage or financial resources,
   Limited access to services for those who have access to health insurance or coverage, and
   Immediate and full access for those with comprehensive insurance coverage, or for those with access to sufficient cash resources to pay for services regardless of costs.

As will be seen throughout this text, health care costs have created international problems of access to health care insurance and services. In virtually every nation, citizens can be categorized as falling within a group of "haves," "have some," and "have nots," in regard to access to even basic health care services. In every case citizen demand for such coverage is high, and is increasingly linked to rising consumer and practitioner expectations of quality, accessibility, and costs. However, each nation is experiencing some degree of mismatch between citizen expectations and economic realities. In the end, each nation is in competition with every other nation for a greater share of health care resources.

Unfortunately, there is no real upper limit on health care costs, particularly if nations and their citizens continue to pursue the most up-to-date health care technologies, products, and services. Something has to give, and in most instances what is "giving" is the delivery and financing models utilized within nations. Today, virtually every nation is pursuing some form of "rationing," "reengineering," "revamping," or "restructuring," of its health care systems. Patterned upon cost-containment strategies developed in the United States and exported abroad, these strategies are increasingly subsumed under the concept of "managed care." As the managed care philosophy becomes more prevalent internationally, issues of quality, access, and cost are becoming a subject of virtually constant international debate and discussion.

B. Health-Related Human Resources

A related theme to the one discussed above is the issue of national access to and training of persons engaged in medical, nursing, and allied health professions. As will be seen throughout this text, there are significant variations in the supply, training, and quality of health care providers from nation to nation, despite a significant degree of continuity of caregiver roles across nations and cultures. Unavoidably, citizen satisfaction with their nation's health care system is related to the perceived quality of providers. Where health care providers are well trained and where they remain current with modern technologies and treatments, citizens seem to be uniformly pleased with the quality of care that they receive (Pohl, 2000; Patel and Rushefsky, 2000). However, where training is perceived to be inadequate or lagging, consumer confidence falls (Bourganskaia et al., 2000).

This issue is of particular importance since most nations experience a tendency on behalf of their citizens to proceed directly to tertiary-specialist-level care without initially going through primary-care providers. The result of such practices is an overutilization of specialty care that, in turn, overrelies on technological, procedural, and pharmaceutically based interventions, even when equally or more effective interventions can be accessed less expensively at the primary care level. To remedy the penchant of the public to overutilize tertiary and inpatient resources, nations around the globe are making access to primary-care resources more available, while limiting access to specialty medical providers. As a consequence, some providers report that they now feel that they are being asked to practice outside their levels of competency (Evetovits, 2000).

C. Public and Environmental Health

This book also addresses issues relating to public and environmental health issues, particularly those aspects of public and environmental health that can result in the prevention of diseases and disorders. While these issues apply to every nation discussed in this text, it is a particularly important issue for the former

"Soviet bloc" nations. Historically, these are the nations that have experienced some of the worst environmental and public health problems relating to unfettered industrial and weapons production during the Cold War era (Bourganskaia et al., 2000; Evetovits, 2000). However, having observed this, environmental and public health problems relating to disease prevention are common themes for all nations, particularly for those emerging nations that emulate the currently industrialized countries.

D. Disenfranchised Populations

The chapters to follow also uniformly reflect problems in providing access to disenfranchised populations and groups within their national borders. In some cases, these groups may be categorized by age (children and the elderly), working status (unemployed and underemployed), ethnic or cultural status (such as Native Americans or aboriginal peoples) (Lapsley, 2000; Malcolm, 2000), or by virtue of their lack of resources to access the health care system. Likewise most of the nations discussed in this book are experiencing geographical challenges in providing quality, affordable, and accessible services (Bourganskaia et al., 2000; Patel and Rushefsky, 2000; Angeletti, 2000; Niakas, 2000; Malcolm, 2000). In most instances these challenges involve providing services to rural areas, while in other cases, such as in Italy, equality of access varies with the region of the country within which one resides.

E. Demographics and Population Aging

Finally, this book discusses issues of demographics and aging that not only relate to current cost, consumption, delivery, and access issues, but also relate to the future demands and needs of the world's health care systems. In virtually every nation discussed in this text, the aging of the population, coupled with increases or decreases in the birthrate, has resulted in a variety of strains on national health care systems (Wimberley and Rubens, 2000; Rieko and Kazue, 2000). Such strains typically involve the capacity of a nation to pay for needed health care services for the elderly, the capacity to plan for future needs, and the willingness of the society to assume a larger role in caregiving as opposed to leaving this responsibility to individuals and families. Inherent to this discussion is the issue of intergenerational equity and fairness.

II. ORGANIZATION OF THE BOOK

This book addresses issues cited above and other substantive issues by looking at the experiences of a group of OECD nations representing a range of health care systems in various stages of development. In so doing, the authors have grouped nations into geographically contiguous regions that include:

The former Soviet bloc nations,
North and Central America,
Northern, Central, and Eastern Europe,
The Mediterranean coast,
The Pacific rim nations.

Upon completing an analysis of the health care systems in these geographical regions, the text ends with a chapter that compares health care financing across all OECD nations. In so doing it provides the reader with a clearer comparison of how the national health care systems discussed in this text compare with one another.

A.   Former Soviet Bloc Nations

Both former Soviet bloc nations featured in this textbook (Hungary and Russia) are in the process of undergoing dramatic social, political, economic, and cultural changes following the demise of the former Soviet Union and its affiliated nations. These nations are in the midst of experimenting with democratic governance models and principles, as well as with market capitalism. In both instances, these nations are struggling to adapt Western market and business concepts to their unique cultural and historical milieu.

These efforts are hampered to the extent to which their national economies have been decimated by policies and activities that occurred during the Cold War era. Both nations are currently dealing with weak and, in some cases, failed economic infrastructures and are experiencing serious fiscal shortfalls. Despite these circumstances, both are attempting to upgrade their health care systems to provide their citizens with the best access to the highest-quality health care resources and services available.

Unfortunately, both Russia and Hungary are finding it extremely difficult to provide access to the latest in medical technology, resources, and procedures. Many of these difficulties can be attributed to poorly organized bureaucratic health care systems and ill-prepared administrators and medical practitioners. These nations are also hampered in effecting meaningful health care reform by a limited supply of specialty physicians and an antiquated primary, secondary, and tertiary care infrastructure. It is within this context that health care reform is currently developing within both Hungary and Russia (Evetovits, 2000; Bourganskaia et al., 2000).

1.   Hungary

In Chapter 2, ''Reforms in the Hungarian Health Care System,'' Tamas Evetovits provides an overview of a health care system that he describes as ''one of the worst'' in Europe. Its problems include an inability to effectively promote public health, skyrocketing health care costs (driven by technology and pharmaceutical innovations), and serious difficulties involving gaining access to basic health care for most of its citizens. According to the author, the ''basic conflict in health care provision lies between the technically-medically possible and the financially affordable.'' While this statement is narrowly applied to circumstances in Hungary, it could be equally applied to any number of industrialized and preindustrialized nations worldwide.

The most pressing issues confronting Hungary involve:

An inability to effectively promote public health, and
Rising health care costs fueled by the rising costs of medical technology
    and pharmaceuticals.

Although these two issues are of the greatest significance to the Hungarian health care system, there are any number of other related problems that the nation must confront if it is to improve the health and health care of its populace. These other issues include:

Problems of access to rural regions and to some social groups,

Environmental health and safety issues that will be costly to contain and reverse,

A declining national economy,

An excessively bureaucratic and hierarchical system organization,

The relative absence of health care purchasers beyond the state,

A health infrastructure that is overly invested in hospital and tertiary care,

A poorly developed primary care system utilizing physicians who lack ''legitimacy'' from the public's perspective,

The widespread use of informal ''gratuity'' payment systems for physicians that encourages graft and undercuts efficiency,

Problems of moral hazard bred by a ''free'' health care system,

Easy access to tertiary care that undercuts the development of a functional primary care network.

According to Evetovits, despite policy to the contrary, Hungary has simply failed to transfer resources to the primary care level. In fact, so few resources have been invested in the primary care level that many practitioners complain that they are forced to practice a level of medicine that exceeds their competency levels. A measure of the extent to which the primary care system is limited can be seen in the extent to which specialty care is represented among the nation's supply of physicians. Currently, 80% of all physicians are specialists, leaving only 20% of practitioners to cover the bulk of the nation's primary care needs.

Clearly, much work needs to be done to broaden the base of health care in this post–Soviet bloc nation.

2. Russia

Russia is confronted with many of the same problems as Hungary. According to Elena A. Bourganskaia, Arsen Kubatev, and Mary A. Paterson, in Chapter 3, "Russia's Health Care System: Caring in a Turbulent Environment," the major issue confronting Russia includes efforts to move from a centrally administered and highly regulated health care system to a managed care model that relies upon increasingly sophisticated health administrators. Since the Russian system has been historically managed by former Soviet bureaucrats and party members, the nation's health care system is undergoing considerable strain as these administrators are being retooled and retrained for today's market-oriented health care system. This effort is confounded to the extent that the Russian people struggle over their willingness to embrace a Western-style market economy. Recent evidence suggests that the Russian people are less enamoured with the promise of market reforms than they were several years ago (Holmes et al., 1999). There appears to be a shift of political will back toward a more centrally managed state model (Cohen, 1997), and this shift will exert a significant influence upon Russia's health care system.

However, regardless of which economic and political direction Russia finally takes, the nation must deal with the same health-related problems confronting other industrialized nations. Citizens have lost confidence in the current health care system owing to what they perceive as poor-quality care and significant issues of access to modern technologies, pharmaceuticals, and medical procedures. The citizenry is also concerned regarding the preparedness of medical practitioners to provide top-quality care. Although the management and delivery of services has become relatively decentralized since the days of the Soviet Union, the effectiveness of this decentralization in improving health care outcomes has yet to be demonstrated.

Like Hungary, Russia has yet to clearly and effectively define the role of public health. Currently, public health responsibilities are assigned to hospitals throughout Russia. However, in light of the significant environmental and public health issues to be found in Russia in this post-Soviet era, the sufficiency of current public health efforts and initiatives is highly questionable. In a related vein, Russia has yet to effectively cope with huge variations in public and primary health care across the diverse regions of its national landscape. These variations are not simply defined culturally, geographically (particularly urban versus rural areas), and economically, but are also defined by the extent to which military actions and initiatives have occurred within particular areas and regions. Ongoing military conflicts within Russia continue to contribute to environmental and public health problems (Cohen, 1997).

B.   North and Central America

The North American nations included within this text are the geographically contiguous countries of Canada, the United States, and Mexico. Two of these three
nations (Canada and the United States) are strikingly similar in many aspects of
their health care delivery system, while Mexico is more representative of Central
and South American nations, whose health care systems are still in an emergent
form.

Of these three nations, the United States is the irrefutable world leader in
health care research, provision, and management. However, it is also the most
expensive system in the world, and a system comprised of many gaps to access
based upon eligibility and costs. Even so, it casts a long shadow on both of its
neighbors, as it does worldwide. Canada, who has operated a national health
system since the British North American Act of 1867, is encountering increased
difficulty in containing health care costs and maintaining broad access to services
given the ready availability of costly high-tech medical services found nearby in
the United States. More important, however, is the extent to which U.S. healthcare has become a ''benchmark'' of quality for Canadians who expect health
care services in Canada to be comparable to those in the United States but at
lower prices.

A somewhat comparable situation exists in Mexico, where U.S. practice
standards to a substantial extent define the level of care anticipated by Mexican
citizens. Proximity to the United States has allowed many practitioners from
Mexico to attend medical school or serve in residencies in the United States.
Similarly, any number of U.S. physicians have completed their medical education
in Mexico and have completed residencies in the United States, thereby resulting
in significant intermingling between the nation's two medical communities. Factors of geographical proximity, intermingling of medical students between and
among U.S. and Mexican medical schools, and the heavy marketing of U.S.-
manufactured pharmaceuticals and medical technologies to Mexico have created
significant linkages between the two nations. Even so, issues of cost, access, and
delivery of services varies widely within and between Mexico and the United
States.

Mexico is currently engaging in a significant reform of its health system,
especially its various Social Security institutions. Particular attention is being
directed toward the Special Basic Health Program for the nation's uninsured,
who represent 48% of the population (Infante and Larios, 1998). As is the case
with other nations, the issue of expanding access to basic health care services is
an ongoing struggle within this Central American nation.

1.   Canada

According to Kant Patel and Mark Rushefsky, in Chapter 4, entitled ''The Canadian Health Care System,'' politicians, policymakers, and citizens within the

United States often emulate Canada's national health system because it has succeeded in providing universal access to health care for all of its citizens. However, the nation's parliamentary government and its provincial organization makes the Canadian system much more decentralized than is the case with comparable U.S. systems like Medicare. Interestingly enough, the Canadian health system is also known as Medicare, but unlike its U.S. counterpart, Canadian Medicare is administered across all of the Canadian provinces and provides access to care for all Canadians, not just the elderly or handicapped.

Canadians have been quite happy with their health care systems, until recent years when escalating costs of medical technology, treatments, and pharmaceuticals have steadily (and in some cases dramatically) increased the cost of health care. The provinces have responded to these events by increasing access to primary care providers while restricting access to specialty and inpatient medical care. The result has been longer wait lists for citizens awaiting access to surgery and inpatient care. Canadians with resources have circumvented the system by purchasing their care in the United States, particularly in the northern tier of states. However, as wait lists increase in length and access to state-of-the-art services has become harder to achieve, Canadians have begun to express a growing degree of disgruntlement with the nation's health system. While they remain satisfied with the quality and access to primary care physicians and services, they are becoming increasingly frustrated with their lack of access to specialty and tertiary care.

2. The United States

The U.S. health care system is covered in two chapters. First, Carole Pohl's Chapter 5, entitled "United States's Health Care System," presents a brief historical outline of the U.S. health care system, which is in fact a "nonsystem" when compared to that of many other OECD nations. In so doing Pohl documents how health care needs have been transformed over the years from a system that primarily responded to epidemics and acute infections to a system that increasingly deals with issues of chronic illness and disability. The chapter also describes how health care is financed in the United States as well as describing how care is provided.

The key issues confronting the U.S. system include the following:

Access to quality care,	Gaps in health care coverage,
Managed care,	Technological innovations and impacts,
Shifting of resources from hospitals to outpatient settings,	Pharmaceutical costs and development.
Cost containment,	

Edward T. Wimberley and Arthur Rubens, in Chapter 6 entitled "Like Plugging the Holes in a Colander: Health Policy and Provision in the United

States Circa the Millennium,'' provide a somewhat different perspective on the U.S. health care system, taking a close look at problems associated with paying for what some claim is the best health care in the world. Lacking a unified national health care system, the United States relies upon employer/employee-paid premiums to finance health care services. This approach, along with fee-for-service reimbursement for physicians, hospitals, and other health care providers and services, created a crisis in health care finance in the United States that emerged as a serious problem in the 1970s.

Wimberley and Rubens document how the U.S. Congress enacted cost-control legislation in the early eighties, designed to reduce health care expenditures in federal and state government-sponsored health programs such as Medicare and Medicaid. While system reforms have progressed steadily throughout the seventies, eighties, nineties, and into the new millennium, advances in technology, research, and pharmaceutical development have steadily increased demand for new products and services, thereby exerting upward pressure upon health care costs. As these pressures increase, managed care approaches to health care provision has increasingly changed the orientation of the nation's health care system away from "quality of care" to "cost of care."

The ultimate result of this change in policy focus has been that access to health care remains a problem for several million citizens who are either uninsured or underinsured. Moreover, reimbursement for services to disabled persons and care for the chronically ill elderly has been dramatically decreased over the last decade, leaving those served (or formerly served by home health agencies, assisted living facilities, and in skilled nursing facilities) either uninsured or underinsured. Ironically, even those possessing insurance have learned that exclusions from coverage can dramatically decrease their effective access to appropriate care.

As will be seen throughout the text, medical technology and research products developed in the United States are widely exported throughout the world and have not exerted an upward pressure on the U.S. health care system alone. Consequently, the conflict between "what is possible in health care" versus "what is affordable" is one that has been both created within the United States and exported internationally. Chapter 6 takes an in-depth look at how the national government has responded to the ongoing effort to control costs, insure quality, and improve access. In so doing, the authors raise serious reservations regarding whether the U.S. Congress is the appropriate forum for solving the nation's health care problems. Given that the U.S. system is both expensive and fragmented, the authors compare it to a colander with too many holes in it, and suggest a less porous and more unified approach.

3. Mexico

Researchers from the Pan American Health Organization (PAHO) present a perspective of the Mexican health care system. The authors present an overview of how this growing Central American nation is facing the challenge of providing affordable and quality health care to its citizens. The chapter also describes how health care is organized, paid for, and disbursed across this nation of 31 sovereign states. Mexico's health care system is almost equally funded via publicly funded insurance and private health insurance. Services are provided via a three-tier health care system consisting of:

> The social security institutions: including the Mexican Social Security Institute (IMSS), the Social Security Institute for Government Employees (ISSSTE), and the Medical Services for Petroleos Mexicanos (PEMEX),
> The public health services: services provided under the Secretariat of Health (SSA), the IMSS-Solidarity Program (IMSS-Sol), and the National Indigenous Institute (INI),
> The private sector (through a limited number of private insurers).

Under the General Health Act, this three-pronged system is coordinated via the Secretariat of Health (SSA) that attempts to deliver care to some 94.2 million citizens, of whom 26.5% reside in rural areas and 73.5% reside in urban areas. Some 24 million citizens live in extreme poverty and another 40 million can be characterized as poor, yielding 64 million (or 68%) of the nation's citizens who require significant assistance in gaining access to necessary health care services. To meet the needs of so many impoverished citizens, the nation has increased its health manpower capacity in the area of physicians and nurses throughout the nineties, while decreasing its per capita health care expenditures over the same period.

In the interest of improving access to care for the nation's poor, the Health Sector Reform Program was initiated in 1996, with its primary objectives including:

> To develop the capacity of improving and promoting quality and cost-efficiency in the delivery of health care services,
> To expand health care coverage via the Social Security institutions,
> To finalize the process of decentralizing the nation's health care services to better serve the uninsured, and
> To expand coverage to all marginalized persons residing in both rural and urban areas.

Central to the process of reform has been the transfer of health-related human resources, finances, and infrastructure to every state within the Mexican republic. These resources were effectively transferred to the states in 1997, and efforts are currently underway to implement the Program for Expanded Coverage, which will provide more health care coverage for the uninsured.

The Health Sector Reform Program has sought to implement system change in two ways:

1. By promoting voluntary affiliation with the Social Security system via the provision of health care insurance for families;
2. By creating a package of essential health care services that can be made available to all impoverished citizens.

As of 1998 the reform program has made health care services available to some seven million children who had lacked any coverage whatsoever as of 1995. Efforts continue to expand such access to every state, with the most needy remaining citizens (some three million in number) residing in the states of Chiapas, Guerrero, Hidlago, and Oaxaca.

C.   Northern, Eastern, Western, and Central Europe

This section of the book looks at the European nations that have long been engaged in providing broad-based health care coverage to their citizens. It begins with a look at the French health care system. While this system enjoys a very high rate of satisfaction among its consumers, it has nevertheless been forced to consider reform efforts that will aid the system in better controlling costs, consolidating control of the system, and improving health care quality.

From France, this section moves to the world-renowned health system in the United Kingdom. This chapter takes a close look at perhaps the most successful universal health care system in the world and studies the extent to which so-called market changes initiated under the Thatcher administration (Thatcher, 1983, 1994) have introduced market reform in the National Health Service (NHS).

Sweden, on the other had, while also recognized as having one of the most complete health care systems in Europe, is also looking toward increasing access to primary care providers, while controlling costs by curtailing access to higher-cost tertiary providers. Of particular interest is the extent to which some in Sweden believe that its welfare model should be replaced with a more market-oriented approach to health care provision.

Finally, Germany provides an interesting contrast to the other two European nations in that it relies upon an insurance model that provides various insurance plans to cover its entire population. This German model has drawn considerable interest in the United States and is clearly one of the most functional health care systems in the world. However, even here, issues of access and cost control remain high on the list of areas for improvement.

1.   France

An overview of health care provision if France is provided in Chapter 8 by Peter Cruise. This chapter, entitled ''France's Health Care System,'' describes a health care system in which the government assumes the primary responsibility for the health of its citizens whose participation in the system is mandatory. This system is characterized by a strong commitment to:

Intergenerational equity,
Patient choice of physician and hospital, and
Intergroup subsidization of health care costs.

As is the case with all OECD nations, France has been confronted with escalating health care costs that are high even by OECD standards. The nation has controlled these costs in a number of ways, to include a U.S.-style DRG system, and by limiting enrollment in the nation's medical schools. Part of the difficulty confronting France is that its health insurance system was originally designed to cover catastrophic care. However, as technological and pharmaceutical breakthroughs dramatically improve the quality of care and increase prices, French citizens increasingly demand that their health insurance cover these additional costs. Despite advances in technology, broad technological diffusion across the geographical expanse of France has not yet occurred. Consequently, technology is concentrated in urban areas but is less available in other areas. Cost escalation is also exacerbated by the government's commitment to broad access to care and choice of physician for all citizens.

The French health system's finance issues revolve around a number of factors currently under review. These factors include:

Ineffectiveness of centrally controlled system to contain costs and channel access to care,
Fragmentation in budget and finance authority geographically and across agencies,
Inadequate control in the outpatient and private hospital/provider sector,
Accreditation bodies that primarily focus upon reimbursable services,
Uncontrolled pharmaceutical prices,
Failure of cost-containment measures given French insistence upon having freedom of choice of health care providers,
Reform limitations given the overall satisfaction of the French people with their nation's health care system.

Indeed it may be the very satisfaction with the French system that serves as the greatest impediment to cost control and reform. The French are particularly avid about their system since it provides:

Near-universal coverage,
Moderate per capita spending,
A uniform benefit package,
A unified financing system that allows for substantial private sector services, and

Superb access to care, which is again based upon the principle of high levels of citizen choice of provider.

2. The United Kingdom

Karen Bloor and Alan Maynard, in Chapter 9, "Universal Coverage and Cost Control: The United Kingdom National Health Service," describe a well-regarded health care system that began after World War II ended (1948) and was reformed during the administration of former Prime Minister Margaret Thatcher. Reforms began in 1988 and 1989 with the Publication of two "White Papers": "Working for Patients" and "Caring for People." These papers preceded the passage of the National Health Service and Community Care Act of 1990 that was implemented in 1991.

The Prime Minister's intent in introducing this legislation was not to destroy the single (tax) "pipe" of finance, but rather to introduce market incentives into the system that would compel physicians (who heretofore had exercised complete control over the National Health Service) to incorporate economic incentives in delivering care. At issue is whether these "market incentives" have proved to be effective in controlling costs and guaranteeing quality care on the basis of prospective global budgets and an essentially single-source finance system.

The architect of system reform in the United Kingdom was ironically an American economist from Stanford University: Alain Enthoven. While Enthoven has historically argued for a larger market role in health care delivery (Enthoven, 1991), the British public was well satisfied with the system in its current form. Their major complaint had to do with the lines that must be endured to gain access to specialty care. This issue was addressed just prior to the Thatcher-led health reforms of the late 1980s and resulted in the creation of waiting-list funds that provided funds for targeted expenditures to reduce wait list length.

The United Kingdom joins the Netherlands, Australia, and New Zealand as countries that have become accustomed to rationing. The Thatcher initiatives were designed to introduce more market and economic incentives in rationing considerations. The jury is still out as to how effective these "market-oriented" reforms have been in changing the behavior of physicians and consumers. In fact, as Bloor and Maynard assert in their chapter, it would appear that the most fundamental concept of market competition was virtually written out of the design and implementation of the 1990 health reforms. Indeed, the authors question whether increased competition among providers actually contains costs and creates equity of access as well as a centrally administered, universal system like that found in the United Kingdom and in other regions of the globe. This argument, questioning the efficacy of market competition in containing costs, insuring access, and quality of care, is challenged by several authors throughout this book.

3. Sweden

Gunnar Kaati, in Chapter 10, "Sweden's Health Care System," looks at the Swedish health care system, one of Europe's most notable national health care systems. The Swedish system is more regional than national, with counties assuming the dominant role in the system. The so-called "constitution" of the Swedish health care system is the Health and Medical Care Act (HMCA), since it dictates where authority for finance and provision occurs, and delineates the guiding principles of the system. Included in these principles are the following stipulations (Sahlin, 1986):

1. "Every citizen is entitled to good health care."
2. The goal of the health care system is to secure good health and care equitably provided to all citizens.
3. The delivery of health care must meet the requirements of good care.
4. Every county is responsible for the provision of good health care to its inhabitants; an obligation that also applies to the municipalities that currently function outside the nation's counties.

In Sweden, counties and municipalities have the autonomy to raise their own revenue and to manage their own affairs, including health care. Likewise, local governments in Sweden include 288 municipalities and 26 counties. Counties typically have authority to provide health care under the HMCA. The HMCA docs proscribe certain binding requirements upon counties, but nevertheless allows significant latitude in designing their health care systems. As a consequence, there has been a great deal of innovation in health care delivery between counties, while still maintaining continuity in terms of programs and services.

Counties, in turn, are divided into health districts. Chapter 10 focuses on the health district in Umea to illustrate how the typical county delivers health care in Sweden. The chapter takes a particularly close look at health reform efforts that have sought to increase access to primary care while reducing demand for services in district hospitals.

Interestingly, care is delivered in a decentralized fashion at the county and municipal levels, and is funded through an array of county taxes and national income transfers, fees, and premiums. It is characterized by broad coverage and easy access. However, these characteristics of the system have resulted in high costs, especially to the extent that the system includes an upper liability limit for patients, allowing them to have easier access to primary care without placing an unduly heavy strain upon family budgets.

While costs for care in the Swedish health care system are not as elevated as elsewhere in Europe, they have only recently declined from even higher rates over the last few years. These rate reductions have been achieved via a series of government efforts designed to downsize the system. Despite effective cost-containment efforts on the part of the Swedish government, the chapter describes how further cost containment is being pursued. Central to this effort is the process by which the roles of the nation's health care centers, hospitals, and outpatient services are being rewritten and clarified. Many believe that the system remains ineffective and that the welfare model system should be dismantled and turned over to the proprietary interests of the market. At issue is whether the forces of privatization will dominate or whether the existing system will be made more inefficient. Chapter 10 discusses these concerns at length.

4. Germany

Whereas the French health care system is centrally administered to achieve near-universal coverage, the German system is more akin to that found in the United States, where a variety of insurance plans provide coverage to the population. In this sense, the German system, like that in the United States, is essentially a "nonsystem," as described by Balu Swaminathan in Chapter 11, entitled "The German Health Care System."

The German government, rather than providing health care services, primarily serves a regulatory role [similar to the Health Care Financing Administration (HCFA)] in the United States. Virtually 90% of the German public are enrolled in one of a number of sickness funds that fall in the categories of company-based funds, trade-based funds, or profession-based insurance plans. The remaining 10% of the public who are not covered under one of these funds pay for their care via private insurance.

The institutional configuration of the German health care infrastructure includes outpatient care, inpatient care, pharmaceuticals, public health, and occupational health. Financing of the system is complex with two-thirds of all health care funded by so-called "statutory funds" that include geographically based funds, craft funds dedicated to a specific trade or craft, and funds linked to specific companies and dedicated to the employees of the company.

Swaminathan asserts that the strengths of the German healthcare system include:

Ability to provide comprehensive, uniform, and universal coverage,
Ability to cover almost every German citizen,
Access to virtually cost-free outpatient, inpatient, and preventive care,
The right to freely select a health care provider of choice or any physician located within a given geographical area.

Other strengths attributable to the German system include:

A high degree of satisfaction with the system among citizens,
Remarkably high standards in the area of maternal and child health,
A simplified claims process, and
An extremely patient-oriented health care system.

Despite the many positive attributes associated with the German health care system, there are a number of notable weaknesses. These weaknesses include:

Generous benefit packages, which contribute to the overconsumption of health care resources,

Harmful divisions between inpatient and outpatient care, leading to the underutilization of outpatient care and significant inefficiency within the nation's health care system,

A dual financing system in which hospitals finance operational costs and the state governments finance capital costs,

Unresolved and ongoing tension between the forces of centralization and decentralization within the health care system,

Cost shifting of escalating health care costs upon the employers and employees.

D. The Mediterranean Coast

In this section, three nations along the Mediterranean coast are analyzed: Italy, Greece, and Turkey. Italy and Greece share a number of common characteristics, including geographical problems of access to care between their southern and northern regions. Italy's health care system is attempting to move from an historically centralized health care system to a decentralized model. Comparatively, Greece is attempting to move from an historically bureaucratic and centralized system to a welfare state approach reminiscent of that found in Great Britain. Turkey, on the other hand, is struggling to improve basic access to its citizens. Compared to Italy and Greece, Turkey is clearly a system under significant distress.

1. Italy

In Chapter 12, entitled "Italy's Health Care System," Michelle Angeletti describes a health care system in which access differs dramatically from north to south, and one in which black market health care services tend to undercut the implementation of an efficient and fair health care system.

The Italian system, like that in a number of other European nations, is government-operated in a decentralized locally administered model. The Italian system is also similar to that of other nations in that it is confronted with a common set of issues and problems. The major challenges facing the Italian health care system include the following:

An aging population,

Health care expenditures spiraling out of control,

Ongoing issues in providing quality and accessible health care,

Inflexible bureaucratic regulations that block access to primary care,
Profound regional variations involving access, quality, and cost of care,
Inequitable distribution of medical technology,
Corruption of the system involving the Mafia in the South of Italy, and
Ongoing political intrusion into the health care system.

Reform efforts have imposed a decentralized delivery model coupled with central government financing. These reform efforts (initiated in 1978) have proved to be inefficient and ineffective given the general lack of accountability for governmental entities and an absence of competition among service and product providers. The delivery model also tends to undercut efforts at spending controls and has ultimately resulted in the misallocation of resources.

Chapter 12 discusses how Italy's national debt contributes to its problems in controlling health care costs, and also discusses how health reform impacted the nation's physicians, hospitals, clinics, pharmacies, and public health efforts. Interestingly, Italy has introduced a DRG system modeled after the one used in the United States. Current data indicate that a variety of cost-control efforts have resulted in modest reduction in the escalation of health care costs. Since the nation's health care system is now decentralized, it is the regional governments that are now responsible for cost containment, not the national health budget. In this way, responsibility for health care costs has been delegated locally.

While headway has been made in Italy in regard to increasing access and operating more effectively at the regional and local level, there remain areas for improvement. Chief among these is the need to increase the accountability of physicians, to improve preventive and public health services, and to further improve services in the South of Italy. These issues must be immediately addressed in the interest of reducing patient migration to the North for needed services.

2. Greece

Dimitrios Niakas, in Chapter 13 entitled "The Political Economy of Health Care in Greece," provides an overview of the Greek health care system, and addresses issues confronting the health care system in Greece. The Greek health care system was formed between 1989 and 1990 and included the following features:

Comprehensive health care for all,
Access at point of use,
State-owned facilities,
Central governmental planning and control,
Salaried physicians, and
Restricted private sector providers.

This system, which also includes compulsory contributions from employers and employees and a cafeteria array of sickness packages with a variety of benefits (numbering 40), has not been fully implemented. The current system is referred to by the author as "an unmanned ship without fuel or a compass." Problems with the system include:

A scarcity of funds,

Lack of alternate sources for finance,

Unwillingness of the system to adjust and compensate for finance problems, and

Ignorance of the private health care system that typically fills gaps in national health care systems.

Niakas describes the dynamics of the current difficulties of the Greek health care system by reminding the reader that the Greek system reflects a transition from the era of Bismarck (which was a very hierarchical and bureaucratic era) to a comparatively social welfare–oriented model. This transition reflects a political movement toward welfare state–styled health care such as can be seen in the British National Health Service, and has been initiated by the Greek Socialist Party. The party took control in the eighties following a comparatively conservative era of government during the 1960s that favored developing and utilizing the private health care sector. Young physicians participated in this political transformation, pushing a British-style National Health System to replace the excessively bureaucratic model that previously existed. Unfortunately, the national intent to create a welfare state health care model was hampered by the prior authoritarian regime that had bequeathed to its Socialist successors:

A weak infrastructure, particularly in rural regions,

Fragmented social insurance,

Inadequate physical, clinical, and management resources, and

Social and geographical inequalities in access to health care.

As was the case with Italy, the southern region of Greece has endured greater shortages of resources than has the north, in part because of its predominantly more rural environment.

Niakas presents a detailed picture of how the new reform effort is attempting to transform the nation's health care system into a functional welfare state model. In so doing, he focuses upon reform efforts underway involving hospitals and managerial and financial problems in outpatient care as they relate to providing better access to quality care in rural areas.

3. Turkey

Chapter 14, "The Health Care System in Turkey," written by Fahreddin Tatar, and Tevfik Dýnçer, describes a system in serious distress. The most obvious problem confronting the Turkish system is the issue of access. Forty-five percent of citizens have no health insurance whatsoever, despite the presence of numerous public and private health care institutions and insurers that finance and/or provide care. In this setting, the private sector is growing, fed by out-of-pocket payments from those who can afford care.

Turkey's health care system operates around one of six health care schemes:

1. Active civil service: Providing free care for civil service employees.
2. Active and retired members of social insurance organizations: Premiums paid for health care costs, including 10–20% coverage of pharmaceuticals.
3. Government Employee Retirement Fund: Members receive free health care via public hospitals and providers that are paid for via payroll deductions.
4. Bao-Kur: Merchants and artisans obtain health insurance through this insurance fund, as do the self-employed and housewives.
5. The Green Card: Indigent persons receive their care through public hospitals and clinics, with funding following each person. Unfortunately, the public system is very hierarchical and indigents often encounter difficulty accessing the care they need.
6. Private insurance: Employees of banks and some insurance companies primarily utilize private insurance.

Currently, there is a plan afoot in Turkey to create a General Health Insurance Scheme (GHIS) that will subsume all of these plans into one. This proposal is expected to primarily focus upon restructuring the primary health care system, especially in rural areas, as well as reforming and improving the utilization of health centers. Under GHIS family practitioners would assume the main responsibility for primary care and patient follow-up in secondary and tertiary care settings. Public sector hospitals would be transformed into health enterprises, which would exercise considerable power in the system, having been granted significant autonomy over financial and managerial issues. Beyond these structural changes, it is anticipated that the GHIS will include the following features:

Incorporating the principles of social insurance,
Maintaining open membership to include uninsured Turkish citizens,
Guaranteeing enrollees a package of comprehensive benefits,
Indexing the contributions of citizens to their ability to pay while providing free care for the medically indigent,
Transferring premium income to Provincial Health Directorates who will assume direct responsibility for contracts with providers in both the public and private sectors, and

Utilizing a copayment in the interest of raising revenue and limiting unnecessary utilization.

Tatar and Dýnçer discuss the dynamics of the Turkish system and their understanding of what will be required to truly reform the nation's health care system.

E. The Pacific Rim: Japan, Australia, and New Zealand

The final section of the book tells the stories of three Pacific Rim nations that have each chosen very different approaches to health care delivery and reform. Two of these nations, Australia and New Zealand, have British colonial roots, while Japan has its own distinctive Asian cultural heritage. Australia has distinguished itself as having a national health care system that has exhibited remarkable self-discipline in terms of sticking to a rationing model that has held health care costs stable for a decade. New Zealand, on the other hand, is heading in a very different policy direction by moving toward a more market-oriented system. Comparatively, the Japanese system, which relies on health insurance plans, is undergoing its own efforts at reform as consumer expectations regarding quality and access continue to rise.

1. Japan

While the Japanese health care system, with its compulsory national health insurance and its uniformed fee schedule, appears from the outside to be one of the most efficient and accessible systems in the world, it is in fact experiencing a growing number of citizen complaints and concerns. This insight is reported by Rieko Yajima and Kazue Takayanagi in Chapter 15, entitled "The Japanese Health Care System: Citizen Complaints and Citizen Possibilities."

Yajima and Takayanagi evaluate a national health system that has been in place since 1961 and that has historically provided uniform medical benefits via a set of three basic health care insurance plans:

Employee health insurance,
Community health insurance, and
Health and medical services for the aged.

These three insurance plans (organized on a nonprofit basis) finance the costs of medical care that is delivered throughout Japan's three-tiered health care system of clinics, general hospitals, and special function hospitals (large university hospitals). While this three-plan model provides comprehensive coverage for the nation's citizens, it has nevertheless become a point of contention for many who desire a greater degree of choice in selecting a plan. In effect, the Japanese citizenry have become increasingly consumer-oriented in their values and reflect this orientation in their desire for greater variety and choice in health care providers and services.

Yajima and Takayanagi explore the extent to which the Japanese health care system contributes to access problems for the nation's citizenry. Of particular concern is the extent to which clinics and hospitals compete among one another for patients. One casualty of this competition has been the uniformity of the costs of care and the comparability of benefits across plans, and many of these inequities involved the copayment obligations of patients, which have varied from plan to plan. It is this perceived "inequity" in the Japanese system that is responsible for a large portion of citizen complaints.

The competition between clinics and hospitals is not surprising since citizens in Japan (as elsewhere) tend to shop around for their physicians. While such behavior is completely understandable, it tends to compromise continuity of care in a relatively regimented health care system using a defined referral system.

Beyond these issues of access and uniformity of services, Japan is also confronted with a number of other pressing issues, including:

The aging of the population,
Rapid social transformation,
Environmental hazards, and
Continual socioeconomic change.

As has been seen in other nations, Japan's health care system is also struggling to contain costs associated with medical technology and pharmaceuticals. Indeed, the Japanese system was designed with the intent of preventing the inappropriate use of either of these resources by requiring patients to access care through a defined referral system. Unfortunately, this model is proving to be ineffective, given the increased degree of autonomy demonstrated by Japanese citizens. Tertiary hospitals are a case in point, where any citizen can immediately access specialty physicians and technology for the cost of a nominal copayment fee. Given such ready access to tertiary care, clinic physicians often resist referring patients out of their clinics to tertiary care settings, realizing that once the referral is made patients are unlikely to return. The predicament of clinic physicians is further compromised by their lack of access to the high-technology resources that attract patients. Consequently, they find themselves in a competitive situation in which all the financial and professional incentives point toward practicing in tertiary as opposed to primary care settings.

In 1993, reforms were made to the medical care law that imposed a uniform fee schedule and redirected patient flow through the three-tier model. Unfortunately, the uniform fee system created inequities among physicians practicing in hospital and clinic settings. Moreover, the uniform fee system has exacerbated nonprice rationing, including the practice of financial gift giving to physicians in return for care. It is within this milieu that Yajima and Takayanagi examine the evolving health care system of Japan.

2. Australia

H. M. Lapsley provides a glimpse of Australia's health care system in Chapter 16, "The Health Care System in Australia." This tax-funded national health care system is confronted with the same kinds of issues confronting other OECD nations, including:

The aging of the population,
The rapid proliferation of costly medical technologies and pharmaceuticals,
Steady pressure to increase health care consumption and costs,
Increased problems of access,
Gaps in services,
Special needs of an indigenous population,
Divided responsibilities between federal and state governments that lead to cost shifting, and
Increasing expectations of health care consumers.

Cost containment issues are of ongoing concern, despite the fact that health care services in Australia have remained constant at 7.5–8.5% of the nation's GDP over the previous 10 years.

Another major agenda within the Australian health care system involves quality improvement in health care outcomes; that in turn can be linked to health care costs. Indeed, it is the linkage of cost and quality that serves as the major catalyst in creating an environment of change and transformation within this well-established national health care system. According to Lapsley, financing for health care in Australia has vacillated between "collectivism and individualism." The system, also known as Medicare, is basically a tax-funded system that includes free public hospital care for citizens and a fee-for-service reimbursement system for both specialty and primary care. As in the United States and elsewhere, this system is supplemented by private insurance that has actually decreased in popularity over recent years.

Australia has contained health care costs over the decade by rationing services. According to Lapsley, rationing is widely accepted as a basic necessity in Australia, thereby providing a measure of public support for containing health care costs. Cost controls are maintained in a variety of fashions, including restricting access to the most costly medical technologies and pharmaceuticals, and by utilizing the purchasing power of state and federal governments to procure technology and drugs at the most competitive price. Australia has also created a Pharmaceutical Benefits Scheme that includes an approved formulary that provides incentives for physicians and patients to use generic drugs by instituting a two-price fee schedule. Lapsley reports that the health care system also includes a safety net of services for the needy, as well as providing access to rural regions of the nation via the Royal Flying Doctor Service.

Despite the general acceptance among the public that rationing is a necessity, public expectations in regard to health care quality and access are on the rise. Such increased expectations naturally result in increased health care costs. Unfortunately, many in the population are increasingly reluctant to accept rising costs. Lapsley describes how this general sense of reluctance can be seen in the ongoing national "privatization" debate. This debate has also involved the nonprofit sector of health care providers, who are incrementally increasing the range of services that they offer in response to the reluctance of the public system to incur more costs by offering a greater variety of services and products. The problems facing Australia are consistent with those discussed throughout the book in regard to a host of other nations. Nevertheless, it will be particularly interesting to see whether Australia can continue to control costs while responding to the rising expectations of consumers, and the impact that these consumers are making on the nation's nonprofit and proprietary health care entities.

3.   New Zealand

In Chapter 17, entitled "A Health Care System in Radical Transition: The Experience of New Zealand," Laurence Malcolm describes a health care system that has been involved in significant system reform since 1993. He asserts that reform in New Zealand has been the most radical of any such movement within OECD nations. New Zealand has been moving away from a centralized national health care system, and in the direction of an internal health care market utilizing managed care approaches developed in the United States and in the United Kingdom.

Unfortunately, efforts at reform in the direction of a market-oriented health care system have been largely unsuccessful. To some degree, the process has been confounded by a political shift from the right to a more centrist position during recent elections. As a result, the emphasis has shifted from a profit orientation to one in which quality, as measured by meaningful health outcomes, is the overall focus of the system.

Perhaps the most interesting feature of the current reform movement is the extent to which system integration and managed care approaches have been initiated by primary care physicians working through independent practice associations (IPAs). With 70% of the nation's primary care physicians working through IPAs, the impact of these physicians upon the nation's health care system is truly remarkable.

As Malcolm discusses throughout this chapter, the key features of the emerging New Zealand health care system (beyond moving toward managed care) include the following:

A shift toward improved health status for the entire population,
An emphasis upon system equity in regard to disadvantaged and aboriginal
      peoples,

A commitment toward integrating primary, secondary, and tertiary care,
Regionally shifting health care financing and decision making to reflect
population needs, and
Improving access to the health care system for all citizens.

Malcolm describes the various steps the nation has undertaken in the interest of making this radical transition from a welfare- to a market-oriented system. He particularly emphasizes how reform efforts in New Zealand have been more broadly based than have similar efforts in the United States and elsewhere. While health care financing is of vital importance, as it is with every other OECD nation, it is a priority that is balanced with concerns over quality, access, and the appropriateness of services. Of particular interest is the discussion of how issues of system organization have become a priority in this Pacific Rim nation.

Malcolm also discusses the extent to which public health considerations have shaped the discussion regarding the future of the New Zealand health care system. In this regard, the primary focus of public health efforts has been in the areas of immunization and cancer-screening initiatives. Primary and public health initiatives among New Zealand's aboriginal population, the Maori, are also a major priority in improving the nation's health.

Finally, Malcolm discusses the extent to which purchasers and providers have been able to work effectively together to improve the cost-effectiveness of the nation's health care system. Malcolm's terse response to the question of how effectively purchasers and providers have worked together (answer: "no") belies an ongoing process that is still in need of resolution.

Throughout this chapter, it is clear that the problems confronted within New Zealand are very similar to those of other nations looking to apply managed care solutions to the ills of their nation's health care systems. In confronting barriers to a more efficient system, New Zealand's reorganization efforts attempt to transform the utilization of existing organizations and facilities (such as hospitals) into new forms that can be used to improve access and quality of care without breaking the bank.

F. International Health Care Finance

In the final chapter (Chapter 18) of the book, "Health Care Financing: A Comparative Analysis," Sharon M. McManus, Khi V. Thai, and Terry Wimberley provide a comparative analysis of health care financing for OECD member nations. This chapter compares and analyzes health care financing in the OECD countries. It does so across two dimensions:

1. Revenue sources and overall expenditures for health care, and
2. The mechanisms for reimbursement of hospitals and physicians.

Comparisons of health care financing data and health care reimbursement systems in these industrialized countries reveal several findings that should interest policymakers who are considering health reforms.

This chapter develops its analysis around a framework developed and modified by the OECD in 1999. This framework utilizes the following conceptual approach that integrates sources of health care finance and reimbursement method.

A Conceptual Approach for Integrating Sources of Financing and Reimbursement Methods

Model 1	Voluntary financing with out-of-pocket payment to providers by consumers, where consumers pay providers directly and do not have health insurance
Model 2	Compulsory financing with out-of-pocket payment to providers by consumers, where consumers are taxed and pay providers directly
Model 3	Voluntary financing with reimbursement of consumers, where consumers who have health insurance pay providers and are reimbursed from the insurance source
Model 4	Public financing with reimbursement of consumers, where there is publicly funded insurance and consumers pay the providers and are then reimbursed by the insurance
Model 5	Voluntary financing and third-party payers or insurers contract with providers for direct payment, where services are usually free to the consumer and providers are reimbursed through contracts with voluntary insurance programs
Model 6	Public financing and insurers contract with providers for reimbursement, where services are usually free to the consumer and providers are reimbursed through contracts with the publicly funded insurance programs
Model 7	Voluntary financing with integrated insurance and provision of services within the same organization, where there are typically global budgets for hospitals and salaried physicians, services free of charge to the consumers, and financing is through voluntary insurance (as in a health maintenance organization)
Model 8	Public financing with integrated insurance and service delivery, where there are usually global budgets for hospitals and salaried physicians, services are free of charge to the consumer, and financing is through a publicly funded insurance program

The OECD approach incorporates a set of 8 conceptual models into a framework that can be used to categorize the health care systems of all OECD nations. The framework itself is depicted in Table 1.

McManus et al. utilize the OECD framework to study the health care systems of OECD nations, paying particular attention to changes in financing sources over time. The chapter describes how health care spending as a percentage of GDP has risen for many OECD nations as the cost of health care has increased internationally. The chapter also looks at issues of patient satisfaction, quality,

Table 1   OECD Framework for Health Care Financing and
Reimbursement

	Financing	
Reimbursement	Private/ voluntary	Public/ compulsory
Out-of-pocket	Model 1	Model 2
Out-of-pocket with insurance reimbursement	Model 3	Model 4
Third-party contract	Model 5	Model 6
Third-party budgets and salaries	Model 7	Model 8

Source: OECD, 1992, 1994.

and changes in the way that health care is being delivered. This informative
overview provides a broader perspective from which the health care systems of
individual nations presented in this book can be compared and reconsidered.

REFERENCES

Angeletti, M. A survey of the Italian health care system. In: McManus, S., Thai, K., Wimberley, T., eds. The Handbook of International Health Care Systems. New York: Marcel Dekker, 2000, Chapter 11.

Bloor, K., Maynard, A. Universal coverage and cost control: the United Kingdom National Health Service. In: McManus, S., Thai, K., Wimberley, T., eds. The Handbook of International Health Care Systems. New York: Marcel Dekker, 2000, Chapter 8.

Bourganskaia, E.A., Kubatev, A., Paterson, M.A. Russia's health care system: caring in a turbulent environment. In: McManus, S., Thai, K., Wimberley, T., eds. The Handbook of International Health Care Systems. New York: Marcel Dekker, 2000, Chapter 2.

Cohen, A. A new paradigm for U.S.-Russian relations: facing the post–Cold War reality. Policy Backgrounder, No. 1105, The Heritage Foundation, March 6, 1997.

Cruise, P.L. France's health care system. In: McManus, S., Thai, K., Wimberley, T., eds. The Handbook of International Health Care Systems. New York: Marcel Dekker, 2000, Chapter 7.

Enthoven, A. Internal market reform of the British NHS. Health Affairs 3:60–71, 1991.

Evetovits, T. Reforms in the Hungarian health care system. In: McManus, S., Thai, K., Wimberley, T., eds. The Handbook of International Health Care Systems. New York: Marcel Dekker, 2000, Chapter 1.

Experts predict growing revenue, greater expense in global market. Med Market Media 34(2):18–20, 1999.

Holmes, K.R., Winberger, C.W., Woolsey, R.J., Cohen, A. Who lost Russia? Heritage Lecturs, No. 699, Washington, DC: The Heritage Foundation, January 8, 1999.

Infante, A., Larios, J.A.R. The health services system of Mexico. In: McManus, S., Thai,

K., Wimberley, T., eds. The Handbook of International Health Care Systems. New York: Marcel Dekker, 2000, Chapter 6.

Kaati, J. The Swedish health care system: change and reform. In: McManus, S., Thai, K., Wimberley, T., eds. The Handbook of International Health Care Systems. New York: Marcel Dekker, 2000, Chapter 9.

Lapsley, H.M. The health care system in Australia. In: McManus, S., Thai, K., Wimberley, T., eds. The Handbook of International Health Care Systems. New York: Marcel Dekker, 2000, Chapter 15.

Lazarus, I.R. Providing local care on an international scale. Managed Care 9(6):16–21, 1999.

Malcolm, L. A health system in radical transition: the experience of New Zealand. In: McManus, S., Thai, K., Wimberley, T., eds. The Handbook of International Health Care Systems. New York: Marcel Dekker, 2000, Chapter 16.

Niakas, D. The political economy of health care in Greece. In: McManus, S., Thai, K., Wimberley, T., eds. The Handbook of International Health Care Systems. New York: Marcel Dekker, 2000, Chapter 12.

Patel, K., Rushefsky, M. The Canadian health care system. In: McManus, S., Thai, K., Wimberley, T., eds. The Handbook of International Health Care Systems. New York: Marcel Dekker, 2000, Chapter 3.

Pohl, C.M. United States' health care system. In: McManus, S., Thai, K., Wimberley, T., eds. The Handbook of International Health Care Systems. New York: Marcel Dekker, 2000, Chapter 4.

Sahlin, J. Hälso-och sjuvårdslagen, Statens nämnd for utgivande av förvaltningsrättsliga publikationer, Stockholm, 1986.

Swaminathan, B. The German health care system. In: McManus, S., Thai, K., Wimberley, T., eds. The Handbook of International Health Care Systems. New York: Marcel Dekker, 2000, Chapter 10.

Tatar, F., Dýnçer, T. The healthcare system in Turkey. In: McManus, S., Thai, K., Wimberley, T., eds. The Handbook of International Health Care Systems. New York: Marcel Dekker, 2000, Chapter 13.

Thai, K., McManus, S.M., Wimberley, T. Health care financing: a comparative analysis. In: McManus, S., Thai, K., Wimberley, T., eds. The Handbook of International Health Care Systems. New York: Marcel Dekker, 2000, Chapter 17.

Thatcher M. Speech to the Conservative Party Conference, 1983.

———. The Downing Street Years. London: Harper Collins, 1994.

U.S.-Mexico Border Health Association (USMGHA) (1999) Home Page, *http://www. usmbha.org/* El Paso, TX.

Velasquez, G. Essential drugs in the new international economic environment. Bull WHO 77(3):288–291, 1999.

Wimberley, E.T., Rubens, A. Like plugging holes in a colander: health policy and provision in the United States circa the millennium. In: McManus, S., Thai, K., Wimberley, T., eds. The Handbook of International Health Care Systems. New York: Marcel Dekker, 2000, Chapter 5.

Yajima, R., Takayanagi, K. The Japanese health care system: citizen complaints, citizen possibilities. In: McManus, S., Thai, K., Wimberley, T., eds. The Handbook of International Health Care Systems. New York: Marcel Dekker, 2000, Chapter 14.

2

Reforms in the Hungarian Health Care System

Tamás Evetovits
Semmelweis University, Budapest, Hungary

I. INTRODUCTION

The health status of the Hungarian population is one of the worst in Europe. Among the factors contributing to this condition is the ineffectiveness of health care services in promoting health and preventing diseases. Remarkably, such poor health status persists despite the fact that the nation's health sector consumes around 7% of the GDP.

The structural and functional imbalances of the inherited socialist health care system reflect a skewed allocation of resources between primary and secondary care, and between preventive and curative services. Low-quality primary care and free access to a comprehensive range of secondary and tertiary services, including the expensive high-tech facilities, resulted in the dominance of specialist-centered, institution-based care provision. Primary care has weakened in terms of both human and technical resources.

The government is reorganizing health sector financing and provision in an attempt to achieve higher allocation efficiency and to reestablish the balance of care level structure. This chapter aims to describe the characteristics of the Hungarian health care system prior to the reforms. It examines the need for reforms in a wider context and then discusses the reforms themselves with special attention to the changes in primary care services.

Most of the major changes in the Hungarian health sector took place between 1990 and 1992. Analysis of the system prior to the reforms uses data from the years between 1970 and 1990. Data used for international comparisons are from the years of 1990–1992. The discussion of the reforms follows most of the relevant data up until 1994 and in some respects until 1996.

II. NEED FOR A CHANGE—A BROADER CONTEXT

A. The Basic Dilemma of Health Care Systems in the 1990s

The costs of health services are rising everywhere in the world, putting great pressure on the economies of both developed and developing nations. Among the primary reasons for escalating costs is the growth of medical technology. The high-technology component of health care costs accounts for 50–60% of the increase, while increasing service volume and the change in age structure (steady growth in the elderly) account for another 30% and 5–10%, respectively (Jávor, 1994). The basic conflict in health care provision lies between the technically medically possible and the financially affordable. Medical science and its technical support have reached a level of development where almost anything is possible as far as curative services are concerned. Because supply typically defines demand in the health care market, the cost of all possible services would be far greater than what is affordable even for the richest countries in the world.

The underlying problem is not the economic recession that can be observed in many countries but the fact that medical-technical research and its cost consequences are growing much faster than the economy. The growth of scientific knowledge and medical capability is exponential but the growth of the economy is at best linear. This and the other trend of aging populations threaten the achieved level of access to health services. The "everything to everyone at any time" principle, which was sought by both the Soviet socialist and the Swedish or British type of health care system, cannot be realized. The gap between the promise and the reality is greater in the so-called ex-communist countries. The promise of high-quality, full range of services for free to all citizens cannot be met in the reality of a crisis of the health services in a collapsing (or collapsed) economy.

Two points stand out. First, a new social contract is needed concerning health services in terms of priorities and access to services. Second, the medical professionals and the recipients of their services have to acknowledge the fact that a "National Health Service" is part of a national economy and as such has to fit into a macroeconomic environment. This calls for the introduction of cost-containment strategies and giving priority to those cost-effective services where the most health gain can be expected at the least cost.

B. Health Status of the Hungarian Population

The health status of the Hungarian population has been declining since the 1970s. Life expectancy at birth has been decreasing for men and stagnating for women during the past decades, despite improved infant and child mortality rates. According to the Ministry of Welfare (1995), life expectancy was 73.8 years for women and 64.5 years for men in 1992 (Table 1). In comparison, the average

Table 1 Life Expectancy at Birth in Selected Countries

Country	Life expectancy at birth		Year
	Males	Females	
Austria	72.9	79.5	1992
France	73.5	82.0	1991
Greece	74.5	80.0	1991
Netherlands	74.1	80.4	1991
Sweden	74.9	80.6	1991
United Kingdom	73.7	79.2	1992
United States	71.9	79.1	1991
Hungary	64.5	73.8	1992

Source: Ministry of Welfare, Hungary, 1995.

Western European life expectancy was around 80 years for women and 73 years for men. We have to stress that in the 1970s the health status of the Hungarian population was about the same as the health status of the Western European populations.

Figure 1 shows the five main disease groups responsible for mortality in Hungary. Mortality rates are among the highest in Europe. Infant mortality rates have fallen from 35.9 per thousand live births in 1970 to 12.5 in 1993, but remain

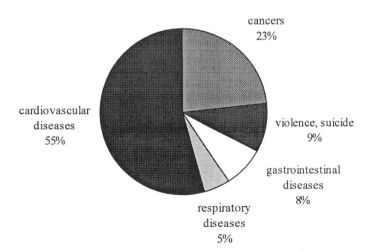

Figure 1 Main causes of death in Hungary. (From: Statistical Yearbook of Hungary, 1992.)

Table 2 Age-Specific Mortality Rates in
Selected Countries (1991)

	Adult mortality rates for ages 15–59[a]	
Country	Males	Females
Austria	162	76
France	159	66
Greece	133	71
Netherlands	141	72
Sweden	135	71
United Kingdom	156	87
United States	157	75
Czech Republic	243	98
Poland	263	102
Hungary	305	133

[a] Per 100,000 inhabitants (aged 15–59).
Source: World Bank, 1993.

around double the Western European average (Ministry of Welfare, 1995). Mortality rates of the middle-aged population (productive years of life) are seriously increasing. Table 2 shows a comparison of age-specific mortality rates in selected countries. Disease-specific mortality rates for all ages are also about 50–90% higher in Hungary than in the Western European countries.

Within the country data differences between social classes are substantial, with higher mortality rates observed among people of lower socioeconomic status. The geographical distribution shows differences between the western and eastern parts of the country, with lower mortality rates in the west (Table 3).

Table 3 Regional Differences in Mortality
Rates (1989)

Region	Standard mortality ratios[a]
Western region	90.5
Northeastern region	107.5
Country	100.0
Budapest (the capital)	94.0

[a] For ages 0–64.
Source: Ministry of Welfare, Hungary, 1995.

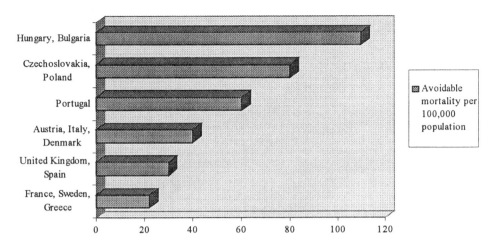

Figure 2 Avoidable mortality for men in selected European countries (1989). (From: Ministry of Welfare, 1995.)

This is also true to a certain degree in north-south comparisons, with lower rates documented in the south. Lifestyle-related mortality plays an increasing role due to the growing proportion of smokers and high alcohol consumption. The rate of suicide is the highest in Europe, although a slight decrease has been observed since 1992. Unhealthy life-styles and irresponsible health behavior are widespread, although there are great differences between socioeconomic groups. Smoking can be associated with a high percentage of all deaths. The quantity of cigarettes smoked is almost double the mean of other European countries (2700 vs. 1500 cigarettes per inhabitant per annum). However, what is of most concern is the increased smoking rate in Hungary, despite the fact that smoking rates are decreasing throughout most other European countries.

The avoidable mortality, which is considered a good measure of the effectiveness of health services, is again one of the highest in Europe. Figure 2 groups selected European countries according to the avoidable mortality data.

Within the country, the distribution of doctors and effective medical technology does not reflect actual needs and demands for services. Table 4 illustrates that more physicians are working in the national capital and in the more-developed western region of the country as compared to the less-developed eastern regions. The fact that most of the national centers and institutes of expertise and two of the five medical schools are in Budapest only partly explains the very high figure for the capital city. The average number of physicians per 10,000 population in the country is 33.2 for all physicians (including research and teaching positions), but there are shortages in general practitioners in remote, underde-

Table 4 Regional Differences in the Number
of Physicians (1993)

Region	Physicians per 10,000 inhabitants
Western region	28.9
Northeastern region	23.7
Country average[a]	25.4
Budapest (the capital)	56.8

[a] Without the physicians employed by medical schools
  in teaching and research positions.
Source: Ministry of Welfare, 1995.

veloped areas. Health care facilities are also in better condition in the west and
in Budapest.

Environmental health problems are again of major importance. In the previous political system a rapid buildup of factories and heavy industry was favored
without any awareness of the health damages caused. Environmental and health
protection measures have been neglected. Some improvements in recent years
can be identified, but high air pollution emission rates are still far above acceptable levels. There are higher incidence rates of respiratory and cardiovascular
diseases in these heavily industrialized areas.

C.   The Macroenvironment of Health System's Reforms: Spending on Health Care

Although the health sector in Hungary consumed 6.0% of the GDP in 1990, the
health system has been remarkably ineffective in health promotion and disease
prevention. It is very difficult to determine the extent to which the health system
contributes to the health status of the population. The Lalonde model of the World
Health Organization (WHO) (1994) suggests that the provision of medical care
is typically less important compared to other factors such as individual lifestyles,
biological factors, and the environment.

Table 5 provides information on health expenditures in selected countries.
The official rate for Hungary from 1991 is 6.7%, a rate higher than that reported
by the established economies of Europe, such as Greece and Great Britain (Ministry of Welfare, 1995). International comparison shows that Hungary's spending
on health care as a percentage of the GDP conforms to trends among other Organization for Economic Cooperation and Development (OECD) countries. It is
even more so in respect to the public expenditure component of the total spending,
as shown in Figure 3. The absolute amount of spending is the statistic that is

Table 5   Health Expenditures in Selected Countries

Country	As a percentage of GDP (1991)	Per capita at official exchange rates U.S. dollars (1990)	Per capita PPP-adjusted U.S. dollars (1990)
Austria	8.4	1710	1200
France	9.1	1870	1380
Greece	5.5	350	400
Netherlands	8.3	1500	1180
Sweden	8.6	2340	1420
United Kingdom	6.6	1040	910
United States	13.4	2570	2570
Hungary	6.7	190	400

Source: Ministry of welfare, Hungary, 1995, and Bondár, 1993.

substantially less than the average OECD data. This is the case even if one takes the purchasing power parities (PPP) into consideration, which puts Hungary in a comparatively better position (Table 5). For instance, the PPP-adjusted, per capita spending in Hungary is comparable to Greek spending on health care (Bondár, 1993). The rationale behind such a comparison is that the Greeks have

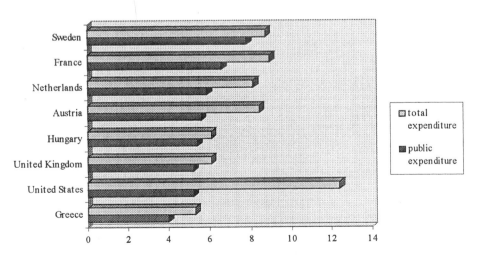

Figure 3   Health expenditures as a percent of GDP in selected countries (1990). (From: World Bank, 1993.)

one of the highest life expectancies at birth in Europe and the Hungarians have one of the lowest (see Table 1). The same relationship can be found when comparing the avoidable mortality figures of the two countries, with Greece having the best and Hungary the worst rates in Europe (see Fig. 2).

The comparison with the former socialist economies of Europe in Table 6 clearly illustrates that Hungary spends the most on health care (both per capita and as a percentage of the GDP) and has the worst health status among its population (see Fig. 2 and Table 2). The avoidable mortality in the Czech Republic and in Poland is three-quarters of the Hungarian figure (Ministry of Welfare, 1995).

It is also interesting to consider the structure of total spending. Hungary spends a higher proportion of its health care budget on pharmaceuticals, equipment, and investments, as compared to some other European countries, while spending less on salaries, which represents the major component of health care expenditures in most countries (Bondár, 1993). The primary reason for this disparity revolves around the fact that Hungary primarily purchases imported pharmaceuticals and equipment at inflated Western European prices. These costly purchases constitute an attempt on the part of the national government to compensate for the government's historical neglect in modernizing health care technology. Consequently, the nation finds itself saddled with high current medical technology investment costs without realizing an appreciable increase in access to such technology for most citizens.

On the other hand, the nation pays much lower salaries to health care professionals as compared to other Western countries. The low salaries of physicians are partly compensated for by the so-called gratitude payment system (extra direct costs on the part of the patients). This practice has exerted a significant influence on every level of Hungarian health care, and will be discussed later in more depth. The amount of the total gratitude payment is not exactly known but it is

Table 6   Health Expenditure in Selected Formerly Socialist Countries (1990)

Country	Per capita spending in U.S. dollars (at official exchange rate)	Health expenditure as a percentage of GDP
Bulgaria	130	5.4
Czechoslovakia	170	5.9
Poland	85	5.1
Romania	65	3.9
Russia	160	3.0
Hungary	190	6.1

Source: World Bank, 1993.

inevitable that this gratuity further increases total expenditures on health care, resulting in an even higher percentage of GDP devoted to health care expenses.

The preceding discussion on health expenditures suggests that it is not only the level of spending on health care that determines the health status of a population or even the performance of the health care delivery system. The structure of expenditure (allocation of resources) at both the macro and micro levels seems to be more important in understanding the problems of the Hungarian health services. Simply spending more will not solve the problems.

The current state of the Hungarian economy is critical. The GDP of the country decreased between 1989 and 1995 (except in 1994), and the purchasing power of the money spent on health care shows an even more serious decrease. As discussed above, the state spends around 7% of GDP on health care. Given the nation's current economic situation, it is very unlikely that additional financial resources will be allocated to health. On the contrary, cuts in the health budget can be certainly expected. Even if the nation manages to contain health expenditures at the current level, it still means that the real value of these investments will decrease yearly. More rational approaches to resource allocation within the health sector are the only fiscal way to improve the performance of the health care delivery system. The rising costs of health care unavoidably call for the introduction of cost-containment strategies.

D. The Type of System Required

After comparing the wide variety of national health care systems (Kincses, 1994), one can reasonably assert that a publicly financed national health service system offers the best approach to implementing a cost-effective, efficient, and universally accessible delivery model. However, problems with quality and efficiency are common in the state-run systems. Typically, such social health insurance–based systems tend to provide more choice and better quality for the insured consumers, but at higher costs.

The solidarity principle is the basis of many health care systems. Providers might be public and private. Private health insurance companies play only a partial role, usually by offering supplementary insurance packages for special services, i.e., access to services of higher quality without limitations or rationing. Systems based on the principle of self-responsibility for health are usually dominated by private health insurance offering good access to high-quality services to those who can afford it. The rationing device is the price of services. These systems are the most costly compared with the previous ones at given access to and range of services provided.

The most important factor influencing the cost of running a system is whether a collective buyer exists (the state or the social insurance scheme) for health services or whether the system operates on the basis of individual purchasing under privatized conditions. The fragmentation of organizational and financial arrangements leads to costs that are much higher than those in better-organized systems of care.

Problems of access to health care services and rationing (which is another form of limited access) persist regardless of whether the system provides universal access to a defined range of services or offers more choices among a broad range of health care services (but not for everyone). Low- and middle-income nations, such as Hungary, do not have many choices regarding the system they will utilize to provide health services, assuming they seek to secure equal access to a reasonable range of services for the entire population.

Hungary is particularly limited in its choice of health care delivery system given its political history. Prior to 1990 the Hungarian health care system was a centrally administered, state-run socialist system. Services were financed by the state budget and provided by public institutions. These institutions were owned by the state and operated by local councils. Private businesses were not encouraged or even allowed. Consequently, private insurance models linked to employers are not readily available for implementation in Hungary.

The basic structure of health services in Hungary is described in Table 7. Primary care was provided by salaried general practitioners (GPs). The government created geographical districts and assigned GPs to these districts. Patients had no choice of doctors to visit; they had to go to their district GP. These primary care physicians then referred patients to outpatient clinics or hospitals where specialists continued the patients' care.

The method of reimbursement for specialists was also salary. Local councils operated and budgeted for the GP offices, outpatient clinics, and hospitals of the national health care system. There were no financial barriers to access to care; patients had universal access to services. A rigid planning system was developed to identify what kind of services were to be provided for the patients. Like-

Table 7 The Basic Structure of Health Services Delivery in Hungary

Level of care	Description	Provider
Primary care	General practice	General practitioners and pediatricians
Secondary care (acute and chronic care)	Outpatient services by specialties	Polyclinics and outpatient departments of hospitals
	Inpatient services by specialties	General hospitals (acute and chronic care)
Tertiary care (highly specialized care)	Inpatient services by specialties	University teaching hospitals and national institutes of expertise

wise, medical care norms were derived and implemented by the government. The special features of this system are discussed in the next section.

E. Functional and Structural Imbalances

The health sector in Hungary has inherited both strengths and weaknesses from the previous political regime. Free access to a comprehensive range of health services, including the expensive high-tech facilities, resulted in a delivery system oriented toward specialists and institutions. Most of the investments went to the hospitals, leaving primary care far behind. Although the quality of services can be criticized, the access to a wide range of services was a lot better than what one might expect, given the capacity of the Hungarian economy. Likewise, the quality of care was also superior to the quality of care rendered among other nations with similar levels of productivity (Kincses, 1993). Only the very special and expensive services were not available or available in limited quantity (with waiting lists).

Accessing higher levels of service provision was relatively easy, given the very loose referral system. Although there was an official referral system in place, patients and physicians did not consistently follow protocol. Patients found the "unofficial" and informal pathways of the system more beneficial and more effective to follow. There are many reasons contributing to this characteristic of the system.

One factor involves a well-recognized problem of the health care market: the moral hazard. Patients' perception of the health services being free of charge encouraged utilization of services at higher levels, a higher rate of utilization than would otherwise have been considered efficient. Asymmetry of information between patients and doctors (consumers and providers) also contributed to inefficiency. Since patients have only limited knowledge in deciding what kind of services they need or in judging what treatments are appropriate and those that are not, they simply demand the best and the best is considered to be found at higher levels in the system.

Other reasons can be identified on the provider side. Shortcomings related to providing adequate primary care (which will be discussed later) are chief among them. The gratitude payment system, a special feature of the Hungarian health care system, should also deserve further mention. This payment is not a kind of copayment, despite the fact that it is paid by the patient at the point of service utilization. This payment goes directly to the pocket of the doctor and it has a fee-for-service character. As a result, doctors receiving this extra money are motivated to provide more services than would otherwise be necessary.

Generally, there are two basic forms in which this additional physician payment occurs:

1. The first type involves providing the physician with a gratuity after care has been provided.

2. The second type involves giving the gratuity prior to receiving services to insure seeking closer attention or better or extra services and to acquire services that are available in limited quantity (shortages).

Even if the above purposes are not present, there is still a willingness on the part of patients to pay this extra money since it is historically a sort of cultural expectation in Hungary to reward doctors for their services this way.

All of the aforementioned factors orient patients toward medical specialists and higher levels of services. As a result, today there is a widespread cultural reliance in Hungary on specialized and institutional care. The high professional quality of specialists and good access to services on one hand and adverse financial incentives and inefficiency on the other constituted the main features of the socialist reality of a national health care system.

The historical shortcomings involved in the delivery of primary care services deserve further discussion. During the past decades primary care did not receive appropriate attention in the specialist care–centered Hungarian health system. Patients habitually proceeded directly to specialists practicing in polyclinics or hospitals whenever possible. Resources of primary care settings were chronically inadequate. Furthermore, it was more prestigious and financially rewarding for physicians to work in hospitals and specialized clinics than to work in primary care settings where basic equipment, supplies, and drugs were often inadequate. Access to diagnostic facilities was often difficult and general practitioners found their work isolated from that of their hospital-based colleagues.

Twenty-nine percent of all physicians work in primary care. Figure 4 shows the increase in the number of primary care physicians and specialists (hospital or

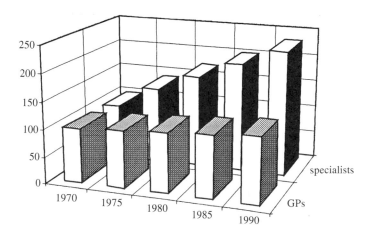

Figure 4 Increase in the number of GPs and specialists (in percent). (From: Kincses, 1993.)

polyclinic based) between 1970 and 1990. The increase in the number of specialists working in a hospital or polyclinic is far greater than that of the primary care doctors. The international comparison of the number of physicians per 1000 population shows that the total number of physicians in Hungary is high. In fact, this rate is the highest among the formerly socialist countries and one of the highest among all European countries (Table 8). According to the database of the Ministry of Welfare, the ratio of physicians to population in 1990 was 3.68 doctors per 1000 population, which is more than double the British proportion and higher than most of the Western European countries. At the same time, the nurse/doctor ratio is very low by Western standards. The mix of medical personnel is characterized by the predominance of specialists, even at the primary care level. Over 76% of Hungarian physicians are specialists, and more than 50% of these have a subspecialty.

Figure 5 shows the consequences of easy access to the secondary (specialist) care that has been created by the absence of a controlled referral system. The number of specialist consultations has risen dramatically by virtue of patient use of the cost-intensive facilities of polyclinics and hospitals. In a large number of instances, such use is clinically unjustifiable as the first point of contact with the health service. Likewise, as a consequence of patients having proceeded directly to specialists for the bulk of their primary care, the number of GP consultations has decreased between 1970 and 1990. Outpatient consultations per person and the total number of hospital cases are both higher than in many other European countries and the average rates for OECD nations. In Hungary there are more consultations by specialists than by GPs as compared to the typical European pattern.

Table 8 Number of Physicians and Hospital Bed Capacity in Selected Countries

Country	Number of physicians per 1000 population (1995)	Number of hospital beds per 1000 population (1990)	Changes in bed capacity (1990) (1980 = 100%)
Austria	3.04	10.04	92.7
France	2.63	9.82	105.9
Netherlands	2.43	8.07	90.0
Sweden	2.83	11.9	84.0
United Kingdom	1.41	6.38	78.5
United States	2.38	4.91	82.0
Czechoslovakia	3.23	7.9	n/a
Poland	2.06	6.6	n/a
Hungary	3.68	10.1	111.5

Source: Ministry of Welfare, Hungary, 1995.

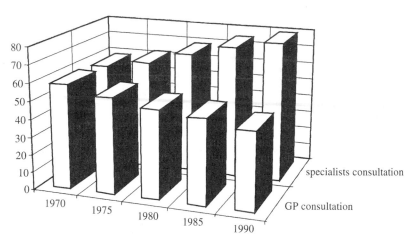

Figure 5   Number of consultations by GPs and specialists (in millions). (From: Kincses, 1993.)

Clearly, one of the most important issues facing the Hungarian health sector is this skewed allocation of resources between primary and secondary (or even tertiary) care services. Extensive, but poorly targeted investments during the 1970s led to a massive buildup of acute care hospitals and training of medical specialists at the expense of adequate primary care, long-term care, and rehabilitation services. International comparisons show that the number of hospital beds per 1000 population is higher than the average OECD figure. Table 8 provides information on hospital bed capacity in selected countries. In 1990, this figure was 10.1 beds per 1000 population, while it was 6.38 in Britain and 4.91 in the United States. More important is the trend of changes in the number of hospital beds. In Hungary, unlike most European countries, where continuous decrease has been observed since 1980, the number of hospital beds increased through 1990 (Ministry of Welfare, 1995). The lack of hospices and the shortage of nursing homes partly explain these excessive hospitalizations. However, these high bed rates also suggest that social problems and the care of the elderly have been inappropriately addressed by medicalizing these problems. The occupancy rates of hospitals were also in excess of 80% (around the same as the Western European average figure) giving a good reason, but not epidemiological justification, for continuous expansion. The medicalization of social problems and the lack of an adequate referral system led to overutilization of expensive hospital services, clearly an inefficient use of the scarce resources.

A skewed allocation of resources can also be observed in relation to preventive versus curative services. Health care is not only about finance and delivery of curative services, although many medical professionals prefer this narrow definition. According to the World Health Organization, the quality of curative services is not a major determinant of the health status of the population (WHO, 1994). More important factors include life-style, health behavior, environmental factors, and disease prevention. In Hungary, the capacity of curative health services has increased with substantial quality improvements in both professional and technical terms.

The health status of the population, however, has worsened. Life expectancy has decreased, and both mortality and morbidity measures are unacceptably poor. During the years of socialism, health-damaging environmental policy, unhealthy life-styles, and negative behavioral attitudes resulted in the continuous decline in national health status. The political response to this decline, i.e., the further provision of curative services rather than developing public health interventions, has proved to be clearly inappropriate. The argument that more financial resources need to be allocated to the health care delivery system to improve the health status of the population is simply false unless this entails improving allocations for preventive and public health services. Health policymakers need to respond to the underlying conflict between policies that are health-centered and those that are health service provision–centered.

Although the general belief that disease prevention is cheaper than curative efforts is not substantiated as far as the overall costs of health services are concerned, it is nevertheless preventive care that should be developed as a function of reformed health policy (Kincses, 1994). Preventive screening programs unavoidably result in more patients utilizing health services, thereby directly increasing the cost of health care. Since effective prevention extends life and elderly people are frequent users of health services, prevention directly and indirectly increases the cost of health care. So it is not appropriate to justify investments in preventive services on the grounds of such investments being less costly than the costs of curing the diseases. Priority, therefore, should go to prevention because it has significant impact upon improving the health status of the population and it improves the avoidable mortality figures. Prevention is not a general tool for policymakers to contain costs but a way to a healthier population.

In the years of socialism, the Hungarian population did not attach great value to health. However, it is probably not the population who was responsible for this oversight as much as it was the dominant social and health policy. How much is health worth? To attach value to something it has to have a price or value. In Hungary, health did not have either for decades. There was no price consideration in the free health care system. Patients simply did not know how much health services cost (Kincses, 1994). Health had only limited worth of use or value. Where everybody is employed and where there are artificially equalized income level conditions, there is no difference between good health and bad health in terms of income, social welfare, and social security. In some (extreme) cases, bad health was worth more than good health. For some people it was more beneficial to qualify for a disability pension than to work at a workplace where there are no incentives or clearly stated goals and opportunity for promotion.

Since there was no price indication in the historical Hungarian health care delivery system, the nation's patients consumed more health services than the average European patient. Health economics theory suggests that this normally happens where there is no market (Normand, 1994). In Hungary a person visits a physician 14–16 times per year (including dentists) compared with a range of 2.0–12.8 physician visits per person reported in the OECD countries (Ministry of Welfare, 1995).

The very high utilization of services leads to high consumption of drugs. Patients want the doctor to prescribe medication and it is also easier for the doctor to prescribe than to make use of holistic medicine. The very low prices of drugs (payable by the patients) contributed to this situation. Patient fees for drugs were unrelated to the real costs of these products, since the production of drugs was controlled and subsidized by the government. Imported drugs were available in limited quantity. (This situation was addressed in 1990, as will be discussed later in the next section.)

The uncontrolled referral system made it possible for patients to use unjustifiably high levels of service. Medical professionals also wanted the patients to use the services because of the financial incentives of the gratitude payment system. Kincses (1993) gives a good example of the deformed system in action when he observes that patients could readily be transported by ambulance to a hospital and treated for a problem that could have been solved by a general practitioner whom the patient could reach on foot. Even richer countries than Hungary cannot afford this kind of waste of financial and human resources.

The case of hypertension in Table 9 illustrates the main problems facing the Hungarian health care system. Hypertension is a widespread disease (cardiovascular mortality is the highest among all causes). Approximately 20% of the population have hypertension. Fifty percent of these patients are aware of their diagnosis, but only half of them visit the doctor regularly to treat the disease. Moreover, only half of those visiting the physicians receive correct treatment.

Table 9 Hypertension in Hungary

1000	Out of every 1000 adults,
200	200 have hypertension,
100	of whom 100 know about it;
50	Only 50 patients visit the doctor regularly, and
25	there are only 25 patients whose hypertension is controlled correctly.

Source: Szollar, 1989.

The case gives a good illustration of the health status and health behavior of the population and the effectiveness of both the preventive and curative (especially primary care) services. The poor control of hypertension in Hungary clearly needs urgent intervention, yet this is but only one example.

III. A HEALTH CARE SYSTEM TO BE REFORMED

In summing up the discussion so far we can define several major features of the system to be reformed. The Hungarian health system is specialist-centered and institutional care–dominated. Primary care has become weakened in terms of both human and technical resources. As a result, the care provided is disease-centered instead of being patient-centered. A historical lack of investment in health facilities within the nation, coupled with the technical shortcomings of the health system, have been, in part, compensated for by increasing the number of doctors. There are imbalances between the number of physicians compared to the number of nurses and other health care workers, as well as between the number of specialists and general practitioners. The low salaries of physicians, the lack of output (performance) financing, and inadequate resource allocation (shortages) have fueled the growth of the gratitude payment system to an uncontrollable level. Prevention has not received appropriate attention, pressures to invest in high-technology curative services, which carry little benefit to health status, have dominated, and investment in effective disease prevention, health promotion, and primary care has eroded.

As political changes proceeded in 1990, health policymakers and politicians, seeing the state of the health care system, concluded that only a major restructuring of the whole health sector could avert its collapse and stop the worsening trends in health status. The ultimate goal of the reforms was to increase efficiency in a way that preserves achievements of the previous system and avoids new anomalies.

Because health status worsens when barriers to access to care exist (Starfield, 1992), good accessibility of health services should still be a priority in Hungary. However, it is very important to clarify what access means in a system that is efficient. Ideally, access should involve full admission of citizens to services that are simultaneously appropriate, adequate, and cost-effective.

The proposed reforms were comprehensive, aimed at changing the whole system. The political decision about a shift to social health insurance financing involved the withdrawal of the central government from the direct management of health care.

It is worth reminding the reader that social health insurance has historical roots in Hungary. Before World War II, Hungary had a social health insurance system that was transformed under Soviet influence into an enterprise that was wholly financed and operated by the central government. By setting up an independent administration of the Health Insurance Fund and collecting the revenues as social health insurance contributions, funds available for health care became more visible and accountability increased.

Today eligibility for services depends upon the status of being insured by virtue of having made contribution to the system, as opposed to the previously existing situation in which insurance was linked to right of citizenship within the socialist system. Social health insurance was introduced as a compulsory national health insurance scheme based upon the principle of solidarity to ensure financial security for the population in caring for their health.

Direct government control of the pharmaceutical industry ceased in 1990 and drug imports were liberalized, and hundreds of new, mostly imported, medicines became available. This transition involved serious cost consequences. Total pharmaceutical spending and patient copayments for drugs increased exponentially to the point where presently approximately 30% of the total health budget is dedicated to pharmaceuticals compared to the Western European average of 15% (Pharma FELAX, 1995).

As a consequence of the decentralization process, ownership of health care institutions was affected by two significant changes after 1990. Health care facilities previously owned by the state, but operated by the local councils, became property of the—now so-called—local governments and private health enterprises and businesses were allowed and encouraged.

The bureaucratic distribution of resources in the socialist system did not promote efficiency. There was no clear link between the performance of health care institutions and the budget they received. The annual budget was regularly based upon the budget of the previous year and was further influenced by informal negotiations between politicians and influential interest groups. The institutions therefore had no interest in saving, or, for that matter, in achieving efficiency. The introduction of new methods of performance-based financing was yet another goal of the reforms. As the National Health Insurance Fund took over the administration of health care services from the government, a new contractual relation evolved between purchasers and providers of services.

Diagnosis-related groups (DRGs) were introduced as the new method for performance-based remuneration for hospital services. Although the DRG system is still in the implementation phase and adjustments are made on an annual basis, it is clear that this system has exerted a tremendous impact upon the hospital sector, especially in terms of service utilization patterns. Average lengths of stay (ALOS) in hospitals have declined significantly, while the number of cases has substantially increased and the case-mix index has increased dramatically since the advent of DRGs.

These changes were fundamental and important. However, the main principle underlying these reforms was to prioritize prevention and primary care. Indeed, the principal goals of the Action Plan of the Ministry of Welfare (1992) were:

1. To strengthen primary care so as to be able to provide patients an appropriate first contact with the health service, possibly with definitive (complete) treatment in a more personalized setting with choice of provider.
2. To shift the center point of the service provision from expensive institutional care to less costly primary and outpatient care.
3. To implement cost-containing strategies and give priority to those cost-effective services where the highest health gains can be observed.
4. To introduce preventive programs and encourage general practitioners to provide more preventive services to the population so as to improve health status.
5. To reduce geographical imbalances in terms of health status and access to health services.

To assess the impact of these goals upon the Hungarian health care system, it will be necessary to evaluate the effects of all the changes in the whole system. However, because of its great importance, the following sections focus on examining the reforms of primary care and on highlighting important issues in the light of the reform's objectives.

IV. THE PRIMARY CARE REFORMS IN THEORY

Significant reform of Hungary's primary care service is an essential prerequisite to improving the bleak health status of the population and to reducing the health and mortality gap between Hungary and its Western neighbors. Moreover, a well-functioning primary care system is an essential feature in increasing efficiency, since such a system not only provides needed tertiary services, but is also a key link in disease prevention. Ideally, such a system also promotes preventive measures, provides patients with appropriate first contact with the health care system, and serves to manage the flow of patients into specialized secondary and tertiary care services.

To achieve the objectives set by the Ministry of Welfare, the first involves forging a new relationship between the citizens and the primary health care delivery system. What is required is a kind of relationship that will increase patient satisfaction with the primary care and trust in the primary care physician (Ministry of Welfare, 1992). In this new setting, every citizen can freely choose a general practitioner and have the opportunity to change him/her every year in case of dissatisfaction.

This approach differs significantly from the previous system that mandated the physician a patient would use. Such provider-mandated approaches motivated patients to bypass the primary care physician and go directly to specialists for care, thereby creating a deleterious impact upon the general practitioner's income. Hopefully, the new model that allows for choice and change in a person's physician will once and for all make the GP primarily responsible and accountable for the overall health of his/her patients. In the end, it is anticipated that the possibility for patients to choose their own physician will also result in increased patient satisfaction.

However, choice alone is not enough. The quality of primary care needs to improve at the same time. Now, local governments are responsible for providing primary care services to the community by ensuring adequate allocation of financial, technical, and human resources. Local governments own the facilities and contract with physicians to provide services. Today, physicians have a choice regarding the way they want to operate their practice, and physicians can either be employed by local governments or become private entrepreneurs and contract with local governments to use their premises. In the Hungarian context, this is called functional privatization of the primary care practice.

As a third option, it is also possible and encouraged for physicians to operate a fully private office. Operating costs are covered by the National Health Insurance Fund. All general practitioners have a contract with the National Health Insurance Fund according to the type of the GP practice. Physicians can open a practice anywhere, provided they have a certain number of patients on their lists. This regulation introduces competition for patients in areas where the size of the population allows. Competition, in turn, improves the quality of services, patient satisfaction, and results in cost-conscious and more efficient services.

Policymakers wished to encourage GPs to provide definitive services, to reduce the rate of referrals to specialists, and to do more preventive care. Providing definitive services means complete care at the primary level that avoids overtreatment, unnecessary referrals to specialist, and unjustifiable utilization of higher levels of care. The financing system should contain incentives that yield results in this direction. The primary tools in the hands of policymakers include the new reimbursement method of capitation for primary care physicians and the possibility of functional privatization of primary care services, allowing GPs to have their own budgets. Such GPs can employ nurses and health workers and are responsible for all operational costs. Cost-consciousness, improved performance, and quality improvements are the major outcomes expected by policymakers given the changes that have been implemented in the health system.

The system of paying providers has a major influence upon the cost of services and also upon the attitudes of providers toward users (Abel-Smith, 1994). Under a capitation system physicians are paid a fixed amount per month for each person who chooses to register with them for primary care, whether that person uses the service or not. Capitation, as compared to salary, performs better in containing costs and provides better quality of services and higher patient satisfaction (Normand and Weber, 1990; Abel-Smith, 1994).

The applied capitation system is adjusted to the age structure of the population, as well as in regard to other factors, including:

1. The qualifications and experience of the physician,
2. The rate of definitive treatment provided,
3. The rate of referrals to specialists, and
4. The location (rural vs. urban) of the area served.

The latter factor is intended to encourage physicians to practice in remote, underserved areas of the nation. In addition to these weighting factors, GPs can expect further increases in income if improvements in the health status of the population they are responsible for can be detected.

Primary care physicians can play a very important role in reducing the high utilization of specialist services in Hungary. The administrative sanction that patients can go to a specialist only if they are referred by their GP is meaningful, but not sufficient. Although there was an official referral system in place in the socialist health care system, it did not work. Primary care was bypassed causing an imbalance of the care level structure. Only by providing high-quality services and adequate first contact for patients with the health services can GPs be the effective gatekeepers in the system. The payment method to physicians—capitation—appears to be working more effectively than the previous salary system in reducing the flow of patients into specialized secondary care services. The weighting factor for the referral pattern of the doctor in the capitation formula is of great importance since it is to be an incentive for the GP to provide all necessary services to the patient within his/her competency.

Another issue concerning capitation is the limitation in the size of the patient list. The government argued that it is not possible for doctors to provide good-quality curative and preventive services if the list size exceeds an "ideal" level. Empirical evidence backs up this argument. Groenewegen et al. (1992) looked at the relationship between workload of GPs and the quality of services they provide and found that the higher the patient list size and the workload, the lower the quality of services provided. This is especially true with respect to preventive services by primary care physicians. The introduction of the concept of "degression" was intended to discourage GPs from increasing the size of their patient lists for primarily financial reasons. Degression means that doctors get less payment for each patient over a certain limit.

To improve the professional standards of and respect for general practitioners, the government aims to strengthen continuing education and establish postgraduate institutes to train general practitioners so as to meet the anticipated increased demand for their services. Primary care should be provided by physicians trained for primary care in a primary care setting rather than by those trained in tertiary medical centers (Starfield, 1992). Specialists may overtreat patients. Data from an international collaborative study of medical care utilization demonstrated that areas with higher specialist-to-generalist ratios have higher rates of physician visits, which cannot be accounted for by greater health needs (Kohn and White, 1976). The government puts great emphasis upon training general practitioners; however, in the current situation with almost 80% of physicians trained as specialists, they also want to encourage specialists working in hospitals and outpatient clinics to retool and become GPs.

V. THE PRIMARY CARE REFORMS IN PRACTICE

General practitioners initially received the reform package with ambivalent feelings. However, as the initial glut of administrative workload eased, the reform was welcomed by many of them. Patients, having been given the right to choose their own general practitioners, seized the opportunity, and physicians immediately began to experience the positive financial consequences of the new system as they were chosen by patients (Balogh, 1993).

During the first year, only a few GPs chose to run their practice in the privatized setting and have their own budgets. In such cases, the GP decides how to spend the overall budget available for a practice. A lack of managerial experience is one of the reasons that the reformed program got off to a cautious start. However, by the second year of reform, an exponential increase was observed in the number of privatized practices. Less than 10% of all practices were privatized in the beginning of 1993. In 1994—the second year—there were already 2951 privatized GP practices out of a total of 6772 such practices. This constitutes 44% of the total, and, according to the National Health Insurance Fund Administration (1994), they provide services for 50% of the population. This means that these practices have slightly larger list sizes, which can be explained by motivation factors; for example, GPs tried to increase the list size to have a bigger budget to cover all expenses.

In a recent study, the Social Research Informatics Center (1997) found physicians operating private practices to be more competitive. These GPs try to attract more patients by establishing a different type of patient-doctor relationship. They spend more time with the patients and give more attention to the needs of the patients and to the quality of services. Figure 6 illustrates that the number of privatized practices continued to increase in 1995 and 1996. Today, almost three-quarters of the total number of practices are privatized.

The data from the National Health Insurance Fund Administration (1994) also shows that the overutilization of special outpatient clinics has decreased. Before the reforms, the total cases of medical treatment in outpatient clinics had stagnated at the same level for years, but after the reforms in primary care there was some decrease in this respect. At the same time the number of GP practices increased by 10%. Table 10 provides very interesting data from the outpatient clinics. The number of cases of medical treatment per 100 population before 1992 was almost the same (around 750), but after the changes it has decreased to 539 cases per 100 population.

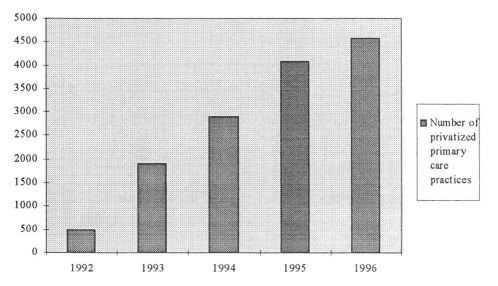

Figure 6 Changes in the number of privatized primary care practices (1992–1996). (From: National Health Insurance Fund Administration, 1993–1996.)

Table 10 Utilization of Outpatient Services (1990–1995)

Year	Number of outpatient cases per 100 population
1990	754
1991	n.a.
1992[a]	748
1993	695
1994	539
1995	583

[a] Year of the introduction of the primary care reforms.
Source: National Health Insurance Fund Administration, 1993–1995, and Ministry of Welfare, 1995.

Behind these nationally averaged figures one finds significant variation at the regional level. The lowest rate to be found is 293 cases per 100 population in the least-developed county at the Ukrainian border of the country. The highest figures are in Budapest (1054 cases per 100 population!) and in the more developed western counties (around 800). These regional differences call for major interventions that should be based upon epidemiological and health services research findings.

Regional differences can also be observed in the number of patients per practice. The average patient list sizes in the different counties range from 1350 patients per practice to 1768 patients in 1994 (Ministry of Welfare, 1995). The data on individual practices show even greater ranges. There are 300 practices with less than 1000 patients on the list and 2430 practices with more than 1800 patients on the list. The government, observing the regional differences, changed the adjustment figure in the capitation calculation according to the regional characteristics of the area served to attract more GPs to underserved, underdeveloped areas of the country.

The change in the average number of inhabitants per practice is, however, in the direction of smaller list sizes, which was a chief goal of policymakers. This figure has dropped from more than 1700 patients per practice before the reforms were introduced to 1510 patients per practice in 1994. There is evidence that very large patient list sizes have had a negative effect on consultation time and competition among GPs (Bosanquet, 1991; Heaney et al., 1990). Policymakers also welcome decreases in the size of patient lists because they tend to equalize the geographical distribution of GPs. Urban-rural differences tend to decrease if list sizes are limited (Shimmura, 1988).

General practitioners were complaining about two main features of the reimbursement method. The first one was the adjustment for the age structure of the patients. The argument was that the weighting points given for children on the list were too small compared to the time GPs spend with them. In the second year of the reform this was corrected. Table 11 shows the new figures.

The other complaint was about the method of degression, i.e., the payment per capita decreases over 2800 points, which equals about 1800 "average" patients. It is a false belief among GPs that they are penalized for each patient over 1800 on the list. Because there are fixed and variable costs of the practice, the income generated by patients is proportionately more than the expenditure for each additional patient on the list. It is true that policymakers would like to discourage high list size, but the application of this degression method aims to make income proportionate with the workload. GPs with list sizes of more than 1800 patients would like to see the degression abolished but their argument is not justified by either health economics theory or health policy research.

Despite the fact that the overutilization of special outpatient clinics has decreased (which can be attributable to the reforms—see Table 10), patients and

Table 11 Adjustments for the
Age of Patients in Calculation
of Capitation Payment

Age	Points per capita
Under 1	4.5
1 to 3	3.5
3 to 14	2.0
14 to 35	1.0
35 to 60	1.5
Over 60	2.5

Source: Ministry of Welfare, 1995.

doctors complained about the administrative rigor of the referral system. Patients could use specialist services only if they were referred by their GP. As discussed in previous sections, there is a cultural reliance on specialized secondary care inherited from the socialist system. Although today more than 85% of the patients contact their primary care physician when they need to see a doctor, they still prefer to have the opportunity to visit a specialist without any restriction (Social Research Informatics Center, 1997).

The government, responding to this growing pressure, eased the strictness of the referral system. Now, there are certain specialist services, for example gynecology, dermatology, and psychiatry, which can be used without a referral from the GP. The findings of a representative survey by the Social Research Informatics Center (1997) suggest that even for specialist services where referral is required (such as internal medicine, rheumatology, and neurology), about 20% of patient visits occur without referrals. This figure for gynecology and dermatology, where referral is not required, is more than 50%. The study looked at the effectiveness of the gatekeeper function of the GPs and found that the only significant factor that influences patient behavior, in respect to visits to internal medicine specialists without obtaining a referral from the GP, is the level of satisfaction with the general practitioner. Those who are less satisfied with their GPs are the ones who visit specialists without referral.

This finding suggests that the only nonadministrative way to control the flow of patients into specialized secondary care is to improve the quality of primary care services and, as a result, the satisfaction of the patients. According to the opinion of the specialists, almost 30% of the patient visits are unjustified and GPs could manage the treatment of these patients effectively (Social Research Informatics Center, 1997). Specialists find the lack of adequate resources in the GP's office, the insufficiency of professional knowledge of the GP, and patient behavior to be the most important factors causing unnecessary utilization of specialist services.

General patient satisfaction survey results (Social Research Informatics Center, 1997) seem to be in contradiction with some of the previously cited findings. Most of the population is satisfied or very satisfied with the GP they have chosen, while satisfaction with the whole system is much lower. People are informed about the reforms and they welcome the possibility to choose their own primary care physician. More than 80% of the representative sample said that they had real opportunity to choose their GP. However, less than 20% of the population used this opportunity and changed their GP after the introduction of the reforms. People feel that doctors, especially those who operate privatized practices, are competing for patients and that they try to do their best to improve the quality of their services. The time doctors spend with each patient increased significantly, but waiting times are still too high. Overall, the majority of the population claims that primary care services in general are better now than before the reforms.

One of the main objectives of the reforms, i.e., to encourage GPs to do more preventive work, did not receive sufficient attention. The idea of incorporating adjustment into the calculation of the capitation payment for health status improvement seems to be illusory. It is not possible to measure the change in health status of the population served by a GP in the short run. Also, other factors such as patient fluctuation make it difficult to measure any real change in health status attributable to the doctors' performance. In practice, the calculus of the payment does not include any adjustment for providing preventive services as was envisioned in theory.

It is a great dilemma, however, whether to use a special reimbursement method to encourage GPs to do more preventive work. There is no consensus on this issue in the literature. Some authors stress the responsibility of the government for preventive care provision, admitting that fee payments to the physician for some determined cost-effective services can increase the access to preventive care (Davis et al., 1990). The OXCHECK study in England by the Imperial Cancer Research Fund (1994) concluded that the appropriateness of promoting certain preventive measures in a general practice setting is questionable. While researchers have observed improvements in life-style modification, the public health importance of these changes depends on whether these life-style changes are sustained.

Other authors suggest that it is the short consultation period utilized by physicians that primarily contributes to the ineffectiveness of health promotion (Wilson et al., 1992). These authors argue that if the length of consultations were longer, the effects of life-style counseling and preventive health checks would be significantly better. The previously mentioned study by the Social Research Informatics Center (1997) reports that length of consultation time increased in Hungary after the reforms. There is also evidence that general practitioners working in teams can do effective preventive work in the area of cardiovascular diseases (Lau et al., 1992) and assist patients with behavior changes (Rollnick et al., 1993).

Recent governmental proposals stress the need for applicable incentives for GPs to provide effective preventive services. It seems that the method of using financial incentives—if they are to be used—needs clarification. It is difficult to calculate preventive services into the existing capitation method. Likewise, it is difficult to include such considerations into the fee-for-service type of reimbursement, since physicians tend to focus more on the administration of the work done and less on the effectiveness. Whatever method will be used should be based on negotiation with general practitioners, public health professionals, and health policymakers if it is to be successful. Sufficient epidemiological research is a prerequisite to the introduction of any new preventive services in the primary care provision.

It seems that 5 years after the introduction of the reforms many of the objectives are still to be achieved. Nevertheless, significant improvements can be attributed to the reforms. General practitioners report that they are in a better financial situation, with their incomes having increased significantly. However, there are no significant improvements regarding technical resources for primary care services. The smaller list sizes can also be attributed to the reforms, as well as the increase in the average length of time doctors spend with each patient. Physicians also pay more attention to the health needs of the patients and to the quality of their services.

There is a promising start in shifting the specialist-centered service provision to a primary care–centered one, and this has exerted a great effect upon the cost of providing health care for the population. Data from 1994 demonstrate that the decrease in outpatient consultations resulted in savings (National Health Insurance Fund Administration, 1994). However, further research is to be conducted to examine the referral pattern of GPs and changes in referral rates and patient behavior. This seems to be a crucial feature of the Hungarian health care system and needs to be explored in more depth.

Reviewing the Hungarian literature, it is surprising that there is little research done to evaluate the effects of the reforms. Patient satisfaction surveys are rare. It is also very difficult to draw reliable conclusions from crude "before and after" analyses and using aggregate data. Although there are often practical constraints on the choice of a study design, prospective evaluations using consultation-based data should be favored (Scott and Hall, 1995).

VI. SUMMARY

The health status of the Hungarian population is one of the poorest in Europe. Among the reasons for this is the ineffectiveness of health care services in promoting health and preventing diseases. The level of spending on health care is a topic of great debate in the literature; however, the structure of expenditure and the allocation of resources seem to be more important for understanding the problems of the Hungarian health sector. Priority should go to services where the most health gain can be expected at the least cost.

The health sector in Hungary inherited both strengths and weaknesses from the previous political regime. High professional quality of specialists and good access to services on one hand and adverse financial incentives and inefficiency on the other were main features of the socialist reality of the national health care system. The delivery system was specialist-centered, institutional care dominated, and, as a result, unjustified overutilization of higher levels of services was significant.

The proposed reforms were comprehensive and designed to change the whole system. The shift to social health insurance financing involved the withdrawal of the central government from the direct management of health care. Ownership was passed on to the local governments and privatization was encouraged, especially in primary care. The introduction of new methods of remuneration of providers represents a serious effort to improve efficiency by linking payment to performance.

A significant reform of the Hungarian primary care services is a critical prerequisite to improving the poor health status of the population and alleviating the functional and structural imbalances of the inherited health care system. Changes in the finance and provision of primary care aim to strengthen those services so as to be able to provide an appropriate first contact with health services to the patients, possibly with definitive treatment in a more personalized setting. As a result the center point of the service provision shifts from expensive institutional care to the less costly primary care.

The freedom to choose primary care physicians brought competition among doctors for patients. Competition improves the quality of services and patient satisfaction. Only by providing high-quality services and adequate first contact for patients with health care needs can GPs be effective gatekeepers in the system.

The possibility of functional privatization of the GP practices and the applied capitation method of payment seem to work well in many respects. The length of time doctors spend with each patient increased significantly and patients are very satisfied with their GPs. General practitioners are in a much better financial condition. However, there are also weaknesses of the implementation in light of the reform's objectives. Resources in the primary care setting are still insufficient. The question of how to encourage general practitioners to do more preventive services remains unsolved. Efforts to reduce the referral rates are not successful enough. Factors influencing the referral patterns need to be explored in more depth.

The primary health care reforms in Hungary provide a promising track to achieve more efficient use of scarce resources. Continuous monitoring of the implementation and evaluation of the effects of the changes are essential if these reforms are to be successful.

REFERENCES

Abel-Smith, B. An Introduction to Health: Policy, Planning and Financing. New York: Longman, 1994.

Balogh, S. Néhány adat a háziorvosi vállalkozásokról. Lege Artis Medicinae 3(11):1071, 1993.

Bondár, A. Egészségügyi kiadásaink és a nemzetközi tendenciák. Lege Artis Medicinae 3(4):364–371, 1993.

Bosanquet, N. Family doctors and payment system: the local option. Br Med J 303:233–234, 1991.

Davis, K., Bialek, R., Parkinson, M., Smith, J., Velozzi, C. Reimbursement for preventive services: can we construct an equitable system? J Gen Intern Med 5:S93–98, 1990.

Groenewegen, P., Hutten, J., Van der Velden, K. List size, composition of practice and general practitioners' workload in the Netherlands. Soc Sci Med 34(3):263–270, 1992.

Heaney, D.J., Howie J., Porter, A. Factors influencing waiting times and consultation times in general practice. Br Med J 300:1698–1701, 1990.

Imperial Cancer Research Fund OXCHECK Study Group. Effectiveness of health checks conducted by nurses in primary care: results of the OXCHECK study after one year. Br Med J 308:308–312, 1994.

Jávor, A. A magyar egészségügy szervezeti és működési kérdései, Proceedings of Issues in the Hungarian Health Care. Budapest: Semmelweis University of Medicine, 1994.

Kincses, G. Macroenvironment and target system of the reform of Hungarian health care and steps toward its realization. Egészségügyi Gazdasági Szemle 31(3):215–238, 1993.

Kincses, G. Drága egészségünk. Budapest: Praxis Server, 1994.

Kohn, R., White, K. Health Care: An International Study. London: Oxford University Press, 1976.

Lau, J., Antman, E.M., Jimenez Silva, J., Kupilecz, B., Mosteller, F., Chalmes, T.C. Cumulative meta-analysis of therapeutic trials for secondary prevention of myocardial infarction. N Engl J Med 327:248–254, 1992.

Ministry of Welfare. Cselekvési program egészségügyi rendszerünk megújítására. Orvosi Hetilap, melléklet. Budapest: Springer Hungarica, 1992.

Ministry of Welfare. Program of the Modernization of the Hungarian Health Care System. Budapest: Ministry of Welfare, 1995.

National Health Insurance Fund Administration. Statistical Yearbooks. Budapest: National Health Insurance Fund Administration, 1993, 1994, 1995, 1996.

Normand, C. Lecture Notes on Demand and Supply. London: London School of Hygiene and Tropical Medicine, 1994.

Normand, C., Weber, A. Social Health Insurance: A Development Guidebook (unpublished). 1990.

Pharma FELAX. A gyógyszefelhasználás átalakulási tendenciái. Gyógyszerpiac 8:32–43, 1995.

Rollnick, S., Kinnersley, P., Stott, N. Methods of helping patients with behaviour change. Br Med J 307:188–190, 1993.

Scott, A., Hall, J. Evaluating the effects of GP remuneration: problems and prospects. Health Policy, 31(3):183–195, 1995.

Shimmura, K. Effects of different remuneration methods on general practice: a comparison of capitation and fee-for-service payment. Int J Health Planning Management 3: 245–258, 1988.

Social Research Informatics Center. Az egészségügyi alapellátási reform értékelése: egy kérdőíves vizsgálatsorozat tanulságai. Budapest: TARKI, 1997.

Starfield, B. Primary Care: Concept, Evaluation and Policy. New York: Oxford University Press, 1992.

Statistical Yearbook of Hungary. Komáromi Nyomda és Kiadó kft. Budapest: Central Statistical Office, 1992.

Szollar, J. Atherosclerosis. Budapest: Medicina, 1989.

Wilson, A., McDonald, P., Hayes, L., Cooney, J. Health promotion in general practice consultation: a minute makes a difference. Br Med J 304:227–230, 1992.

World Bank. World Development Report 1993. New York: Oxford University Press, 1993.

World Health Organization. The Lalonde-model. Lege Artis Med 4(11):1075, 1994.

3

Russia's Health Care System
Caring in a Turbulent Environment

Elena A. Bourhanskaia, Aren Kubataev, and Mary A. Paterson
University of Nevada, Las Vegas, Nevada

> My most pressing problem is that half of our pediatric beds have been
> destroyed during the civil war, and we don't have enough bread for the
> children.
> —Participant in a management seminar, Former Soviet Union, 1995

I. OVERVIEW OF THE HEALTH CARE SYSTEM

The Russian health care system exists in a turbulent social and economic environment. Consideration of this environment is important since health is determined by more than the delivery of health care. The following sections offer a brief overview of geography and government, demographic characteristics, the environment, and education. All of these factors shape the mission and goals of a system that provides health care and improves the nation's heath.

A. Geography and Regional Government

Russia has a land area of 17 million km^2, approximately 1.8 times the size of the United States. The Russian Federation consists of 89 ''subjects of the Russian Federation,'' which are legally constituted equal units of the Russian Federation. Depending on their size, these administrative territories may have the title of autonomous republics, krays, autonomous okrugs, or autonomous oblasts. Each of these territories has equal rights and is equally represented in the upper house of the Russian Parliament, the Council of the Federation. Each territory has its

59

own constitution or charter and legislation, but all are subject to the Constitution of the Russian Federation and federal laws.

These territories are further subdivided into districts (rayons), smaller administrative units that are in direct subordination to their regional authorities. The structure of health care authority in the Russian Federation follows this administrative hierarchy. Table 1 summarizes the 12 regions of Russia and provides information on the number of federative units, districts, and population of these regions.

As shown in Table 1, large urban centers such as Moscow and St. Petersburg are considered main cities and are themselves autonomous federative units. The autonomous role of large urban centers has historical roots in the concept of the oblast. *Oblast* is a term used to describe administrative units such as large metropolitan areas. Moscow, St. Petersburg, and other major cities are also oblasts. During Soviet times the oblast committee (obkom) of party members supervised the administrative and political matters of the province or city. The obkom bureaus provided administrative services and were responsible for mobilizing resources to carry out the economic target defined by the central committee. (U.S. Library of Congress, 1989, p. 133). Since independence in 1991, greater regional and local autonomy has been granted, and the oblast has assumed greater responsibility for both financing and delivery of many services including health care.

Table 1   Regions of the Russian Federation

Region	No. of federative units	No. of districts	Population
Central	12	302	21,287,200
Central Chernozamic	5	122	7,878,628
Far East	10	148	7,659,200
Main cities[a]	3	13	14,481,800
North	5	62	4,461,800
North Caucasus	10	179	17,750,100
Northwest	4	82	4,789,600
Siberia East	10	172	9,456,000
Siberia West	9	219	13,604,800
Urals	8	235	16,673,800
Volga	8	214	16,885,900
Volga Vatka	5	143	8,472,600

[a] Moscow, St. Petersburg, Kaliningrad.

Source: Raw data reported by Norsk Utenrikspolitisk Institutt (NUPI), Senter for Russlands-Studii, Database, 1997.

B. Demographics

According to 1994 estimates, the Russian population is 149.6 million people (NATO-Environmental Clearinghouse, 1996, p. 2). The areas of greatest population density are the large cities of Moscow and St. Petersburg in the European region of Russia. The areas of lowest density are in the north and include territories in Siberia and the Far East. Population growth trends in Russia prior to 1991 were largely the result of natural events since immigration and emigration were tightly controlled. Revolution, wars, and the resulting famines and political instability also profoundly influenced the growth of the Russian population. Experts note that the single most devastating event was World War II, which caused an estimated loss of 20–25 million people throughout the former Soviet Union (U.S. Library of Congress, 1989, p. 176). In addition, the gradual stagnation and deterioration of societal infrastructure, which began in the mid-seventies, resulted in a profound decrease in average life expectancy. Analysts project that Russian males born in 1993 have an average life expectancy of 58.9 years, a decrease of 5.3 years from the 1989 average life expectancy of 64.2 years (World Bank Group, 1997, p. 2).

The World Health Organization (WHO) groups the Russian Federation in a cohort of lower-middle-income countries of the former Soviet Union. Figure 1 compares life expectancy in the Russian Federation (the lower-middle-income cohort) with countries representative of the lower-income cohort and the upper-middle-income cohort in the newly independent states of the former Soviet Union.

C. Economy

Since Russia's independence and the dissolution of the former Soviet Union in August 1991, the government has moved rapidly toward a market economy. Changes included removing most price controls, controlling currency exchange rates, and beginning an ambitious privatization program. The resulting inflation and rapidly rising unemployment created a situation in which private entrepreneurs were able to make large gains while those on government salaries or fixed incomes suffered large losses in real income. Chaotic economic conditions in 1989–1991 caused a dramatic drop in the GDP, disruption of international trade, and resulting shortages of imported goods. As the distribution problems stabilized, Russian citizens often could not afford to purchase newly available goods because wages lagged behind the rapid inflation. While progress has been made in stabilizing the economy since independence, those who depend solely on fixed incomes or government salaries remain economically worse off now than they were under the controlled economy of the former Soviet Union. These economic changes were accompanied by internal unrest and political instability in many

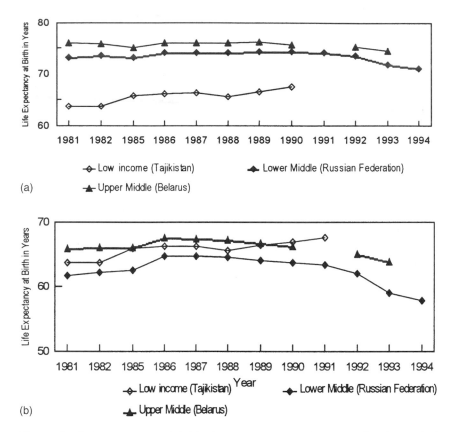

Figure 1   Life expectancy at birth by income groups and by sex: (a) female population, (b) male population. Breaks in line denote data not available. (Based on data from: WHO Statistics Annual, 1995.)

regions; particularly serious was the armed conflict between Russian and rebel forces in Chechnya.

D.   Environment

Prior to dissolution, the Soviet Union was a highly industrialized country that produced large quantities of such raw materials as coal, oil and gas, and iron ore, and had secondary manufacturing industries that depended on these raw materials. Soviet emphasis on increasing production of raw materials and secondary manufacturing was exemplified by the quota system that required steadily increasing production in the industrial sector. As Russia developed industrial capacity, air and water pollution, the problems common to all industrialized nations, also developed. Rapid expansion and development also caused overuse of agricultural fertilizers since additional productivity from arable land was needed. This practice led to serious pollution of inland lakes and rivers as a result of agricultural runoff and depletion of natural wetlands. Additionally, scattered areas of intense radiation have been created, primarily as a result of the nuclear reactor accident at Chernobyl and the production and testing of nuclear arms. The economic instability after 1991 placed additional pressures on Russia's farms, factories, and nuclear facilities. Those that were able to remain in production were not able to retain experienced workers and simultaneously had difficulty obtaining high-quality raw materials and spare parts. This situation increased the possibility of excess air and water pollution as well as the risk of dangerous industrial ecological accidents (Martynov et al., 1995, pp. 2–11). The availability of clean potable water for household consumption was also at risk since, in many areas, the households had to compete with agriculture and industry for this scarce resource. Thus economic transition interacted with the environmental threats common to all industrialized countries to produce threats to the ecology as well as to the health of the population.

E. Education

Soviet educational strategy focused on quantity rather than quality. This is understandable if you consider that tsarist Russia's literacy rate before the Bolshevik Revolution was barely 25%, as compared to a current rate of almost 100%. This achievement, accomplished in less than 100 years, is impressive. However, the familiar tradeoff between quantity and quality was a problem in Soviet-era education. By the mid-1980s, both Soviet and Western experts agreed that schools in the Soviet Union were not developing the technically skilled workforce needed in a modern industrialized society (US Library of Congress, 1989, p. 166).

The training of health care providers was no exception. The general lack of modern pharmaceuticals, medical technology, and access to modern medical educational resources seriously impeded the training of Russian doctors, nurses, and other midlevel health professionals. Health care administrators in clinical facilities were typically physicians lacking any specific training in health care administration, and were assisted by accountants trained in general budgeting and accounting procedures.

II. DESCRIPTION OF THE HEALTH CARE SYSTEM

A. Historical Development

To understand the Russian health care system, it is important to realize that 80 years ago, before the Bolshevik Revolution, medical care was unavailable to the majority of the Russian population. Tsarist Russia was a society in which only the elite minority, the aristocrats and upper-level civil servants, were able to get medical care. A national system of health care were introduced to Russia in the 1920s, based on the mandate in the Russian Constitution that entitles Russian citizens to free health care financed by the state. By the mid-eighties basic medical and hospital care were available to most Soviet citizens. Placed in historical perspective, the development of basic access to health care services in this large and diverse country was achieved quickly. This massive effort to disseminate health care to Russian citizens required a cadre of administrators, clinicians, and supporting ancillary health care workers called feldschers. Feldschers are midlevel practitioners with responsibility for immunizations, primary care, normal childbirth, and minor surgery. The feldscher is similar to the American nurse practitioner but performs many services that are restricted to physicians in the United States (Rowland and Telyukov, 1991, p. 80).

B. Health Care Infrastructure

Highly centralized planning and production quotas were the methods by which Soviet planners fostered development and industrialization. The development of health care services was no exception to this approach. Hospital size, the number of hospital beds, and the number of physicians and other health workers were important to planners as measures of the "production capacity" of the health care system. Figure 2 shows the supply of physicians, nurses, and hospital beds in the Russian Federation from 1985 to 1994. It is difficult to compare the Russian supply of hospitals and health workforce to that in Western industrialized countries. Such comparisons are rendered difficult due to differences in the social structure of the society, geography, and role expectations. On average, the Russian system has about three times as many hospital beds and twice as many physicians per capita as the United States (Rowland and Telyukov, 1991, p. 72).

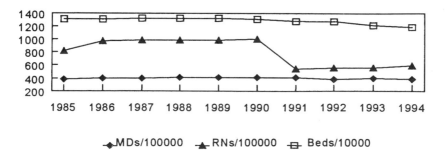

Figure 2 Hospital and health workforce supply. (From: WHO Health for All Database, 1997.)

In the Russian health care system there was little analysis of health outcomes. The focus of providers was on delivering a certain volume of services rather than on the quality of the service delivered. A strictly hierarchical and strongly centralized bureaucracy administered the system and ensured the fulfillment of production quotas. This system was effective in moving Russia from a feudal economy to an industrialized nation in less than 100 years. In fact, analysts estimate that on average the Soviet economy was growing twice as fast as that of the United States during the years 1968–1974 (Smith, 1976, p. 219). Health indicators during this same period were comparable with those of Western Europe, despite the fact that, by Western standards, health care was delivered inefficiently and was of lower technical quality (World Bank Group, 1997, p. 1).

Before reform the Russian system was a centrally planned, regionalized system that was divided between general and specialized hospitals. Russian citizens access hospital care through a system of ambulatory care centers called policlinics. In urban areas every urban resident was assigned to and was required to register at a local policlinic that provided both adult and pediatric care. In rural areas feldschers provided basic primary care services (Rowland and Telyukov, 1991, p. 80).

The period of stagnation and social unrest that preceded independence in 1991 was a difficult time for the Russian health care system. Information about the health status of the population was increasingly unavailable as the bureaucratic system began to fail. Rising costs and currency instability coupled with unstable political and social conditions made access to Western medicine and technology difficult, both for treatment of maladies and for training of the health workforce. Predictably, doctors and nurses were increasingly unprepared to provide quality health care to the Russian citizens. At the same time, incomes of physicians, nurses, and other health providers were grossly inadequate in the face of rapid inflation and reduced government budgets. The highly centralized bureaucratic planning model of health administration was not flexible enough to deal with these turbulent times and system reform focused on decentralization of both health financing and delivery of care.

C. Health Service Financing and Expenditures

Health care delivery institutions in Russia are still owned predominantly by the government and publicly financed. The government exercises control over health services through a hierarchy of agencies, as shown in Figure 3. Financing for health care in Russia was traditionally done through a centralized federal budget. All health care facilities were owned by the state, and providers were state employees. As the Russian fiscal crisis deepened, overall spending on health services decreased. This financing system is now changing. Two important laws were passed that empower decentralization:

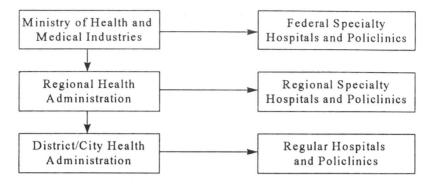

Figure 3 Chart of administration control in the Russian health care system.

1. The law "On Local Self-Management," which allows health care financing decisions to be made at the regional level without consultation with the Russian Ministry of Finance; and
2. The establishment of Territorial Health Insurance Funds, which manage the 3.6% payroll tax deduction for health care (Semenov et al., 1996).

The compulsory insurance system was designed to be a backbone of financing Russian health care. Territorial Compulsory Health Insurance Funds collect money from enterprises through payroll taxes to cover health services for the working population, and from territorial state budgets for the nonworking population (children, elderly, and unemployed). However, the compulsory insurance system does not cover all health care services. Some specialized services that are considered to be critical for the health of the population by the government such as tuberculosis hospitals, cancer centers, and federal specialty hospitals, which provide specialized tertiary services for populations from all of Russia, are fully financed from the federal budget. However, the compulsory insurance system is the predominant scheme of health care financing. The main health care actors in the territories are health care providers, territorial health administrations, and territorial compulsory insurance funds and insurance companies. Four general models can be used to examine the distribution of health care funds from insurers to providers.

1.   Model 1: Compulsory Insurance Model (Fig. 4)

In the first model, collected funds are distributed to the providers through participating health care insurance companies. In this model, insurance companies serve

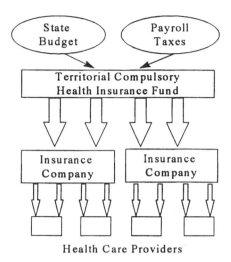

Health Care Providers

Figure 4   Compulsory insurance model.

as intermediaries between the funds and the providers. Competitive pressures among the insurance companies and between providers should increase efficiency in the system and improve the quality of health services. This effect of insurance companies has not been realized and insurance companies are seen as only another unnecessary bureaucratic layer in the system. It is widely perceived that the insurance companies consume scarce resources devoted to health care with no positive contribution to the system's effectiveness. This organizational model currently covers 30% of the Russian population (data for 1995, source: newspaper *Economika I Zhizn*, issue #26, July 1996).

2.   Model 2: State Insurance Model (Fig. 5)

The second model does not include insurance companies, since the providers are financed directly from the compulsory insurance funds. This organizational model is used to cover health care services for 14% of the Russian population.

3.   Model 3: Mixed State Insurance-Compulsory Model

The third model is a mix of the first two, so some health services providers work directly with compulsory health insurance funds, and some through insurance companies. This scheme is used in 36 regions, and accounts for 45% of the Russian population.

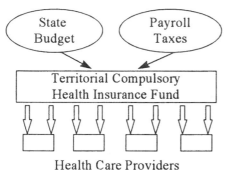

Figure 5   State insurance model.

4. Model 4: Payroll Tax Collection and Disbursement

The least common model does not include either insurance companies or compulsory insurance funds. Eighteen regions (12% of the Russian population) have not yet established compulsory insurance funds. In these regions, payroll taxes are collected in the regional state budget and then distributed among providers in the traditional Soviet fashion, through regional health administrations.

Regardless of the model selected, overall financing for health care consumes a very small share of the GDP. Table 2 compares the share of the GDP allocated to health care in Russia, the United Kingdom, and the United States.

D. Health Status

Given the turbulent conditions in Russia and the comparatively small resource base for health care, health status in Russia has deteriorated. Statistics for the 1970s and 1980s from United Nations, Russian, and U.S. sources all showed rising infant mortality rates and increases in infectious disease. Infant mortality is a sensitive indicator of the health status of a population. Overall, the infant mortality

Table 2   Health Care Expenditures as a Percentage of GDP

Year	1989	1990	1991	1992
Russia	2.18	2.26	3.00	2.30
United Kingdom	5.80	6.00	6.60	7.00
United States	11.5	12.2	13.2	13.6

Source: WHO Health for All Database, 1997.

in Russia is estimated by most experts at approximately 18.56 deaths/1000 live births in 1994. However, there is wide variation in this rate; as shown in Table 3, the Volga Vatka and Central Regions have lower rates than Siberia and the Far East. It is important to note that the Russians have been working to improve infant mortality rates. It has been a priority of the National Ministry of Health to reduce neonatal morbidity and mortality through establishing neonatal resuscitation training programs for physicians, nurses, and midwives and through introducing internationally recognized principles of newborn care in the Russian hospitals.

During periods of social unrest and economic stability, increases in the diseases of poverty such as typhoid, diphtheria, and tuberculosis, are expected. Controlling these diseases will be as much a result of improving social conditions as improving health care. There is, however, an important trend that has been obscured by the crisis in Russian health status of the last few years. During the Soviet era, analysts observed that the region's health indicators compared favorably with those of similar countries, but that strategies to control the increase in chronic, noncommunicable diseases had not been well developed (World Bank, 1997, p. 1).

Western industrialized societies are in the midst of developing strategies and health systems to support the increase in chronic disease that accompanies

Table 3 1994 Infant Mortality Rate
Selected Countries and Regions

Country/region	Infant mortality rate/1000
West Germany	5.08
Norway	6.47
Hungary	11.55
Russia	18.56
Volga Vatka	15.88
Urals	16.36
Central	17.37
North	17.47
Central Chernozamic	17.63
Main City	17.87
Volga	18.71
North Caucasas	18.79
Siberia West	20.36
Far East	21.11
Siberia East	22.35

Source: Norsk Utenrikspolitisk Institutt (NUPI), Senter for Russlands-Studii, Database, 1997.

the aging of society. It is likely that European Russia will need to develop strategies soon to respond to this trend while Siberia and the Far Eastern regions will continue to prioritize strategies to control the spread of communicable disease and maternal and infant deaths. The wide geographical variation and the difference in the burden of disease from region to region present challenges in both the delivery and financing of health care for the Russian people, and provide a demographic rationale for the decentralization of health financing and delivery.

III. CURRENT HEALTH SYSTEM ISSUES

The Russian health care system is still in transition. The territories are trying different health financing models to solve the problem of financing health care to a geographically and culturally diverse population. The final system will have to remain flexible and able to provide health care under quite different social and economic conditions. To achieve this flexibility, much depends on the development of a trained and knowledgeable health workforce. Thus, reconfiguration of the health care workforce is an important objective of the reform activities. To appreciate recent changes in the health care workforce in Russia, it is important to understand the traditional roles of medicine, nursing, and other health care–related professions in the former Soviet Union.

A. Physicians

Traditionally, physicians dominated health care systems in the countries of the former Soviet Union. Physicians not only make most of the decisions related to patient care, they often perform tasks that in many developed countries of the world are undertaken by other health care workers, such as nurses, midwives, laboratory technicians, etc. Also, physicians have long played a key role in managing health care facilities and in policymaking at the levels of the local, regional, and national health authorities. It is not by chance that the position of a hospital chief executive officer in Russia is called Chief Physician. Typically, this position is occupied by an experienced physician who assumed management responsibilities after years of clinical practice without necessarily any formal training in health administration. Often, Chief Physicians continue to spend a limited part of their time practicing medicine. There are some positive and negative features to this situation. On the positive side, the Russian CEOs of health care institutions command respect from clinicians. However, they often lack sufficient knowledge and skills to manage their institutions effectively and to lead them to financial stability. As more physicians in the United States are involved in management activities, it is interesting to see how the American and the Russian systems, in a way, are moving together in search of an optimal solution.

Statements about the oversupply of physicians in Russia as well as in other NIS countries are very common in the current literature (Cassileth et al., 1995, p. 1571). However, when comparing numbers of physicians in the NIS versus other countries, it is often forgotten that in the NIS, laboratory technicians, ultrasound specialists, public health professionals, physical and vocational therapists, occupational health specialists, etc. hold a medical doctor degree. Ways to achieve higher efficiency in the use of health care personnel will be found not only in cutting down the number of admissions to medical schools but, more importantly, in redefining roles of different health care professionals and in developing a team approach to providing patient care. This approach should involve reshaping the relationships between physicians/nurses and physicians/other health care workers as well as specialists/general practitioners' interactions. More than ever before, health care policymakers in Russia are struggling with how to institute better financial incentives for health care providers and to improve productivity of health care institutions while ensuring quality of care. For example, the insurance reforms described above are an effort to replace the physician's salary with payment for actual care delivered. In such a system, earnings depend on productivity. It is also hoped that decentralization of health care financing to the territories will make the providers more accountable, since the payment for care is closer to the actual delivery of care and territorial health agencies can more closely monitor quality.

B.   Nurses, Feldschers, and Other Clinicians

Although nurses, midwives, and feldschers compose a significant proportion of the NIS health care workforce, they have had few opportunities to participate in policymaking or health care administration. These professionals are classified as "middle-level personnel" and typically, they report to and are taught by physicians. Recently, some major changes in nursing have occurred. With assistance from the United States and other international organizations, the Russian nurses have formed strong professional associations, developed new undergraduate and graduate-level educational programs, and assumed increasingly more responsibilities for immediate patient care. As a more market-oriented approach to health care develops in Russia; nurses will play a crucial role in improving efficiency of their institutions and in ensuring patient satisfaction.

While the future of nursing in Russia is a source of great hope and excitement for anyone who is involved with the Russian health care system, feldschers have yet to clarify directions for the development of their profession. A cadre of feldschers was originally created to fill in for the lack of physicians in rural and remote areas. Feldschers generally receive better training than nurses and are qualified to practice independently to provide basic primary care and first aid to the local community. In the reformed system, feldschers still play an important role as primary health care providers in the rural and remote areas. At the same time, they function as emergency medical service technicians in urban areas. These are clearly different roles and they should be articulated in the near future. Currently, it seems as if feldschers are splitting into two distinct professional groups, emergency medical service technicians and primary health care providers. For the Russian health care workforce reform to be successful, it is very important to define a role for each of these groups (feldschers–EMS technicians and feldschers–primary health care providers) and to provide appropriate training for each.

C. Epidemiologists and Public Health Professionals

Traditionally, public health functions in Russia have been the responsibility of the Ministry of Health and the State Sanitary-Epidemiological Surveillance Committee. Public health in Russia means primarily communicable disease control and social hygiene. Additionally, epidemiologists in the Russian system have different roles than do the U.S. epidemiologists. This is particularly true when talking about hospital epidemiologists. In the United States, the hospital epidemiologist is a clinician who typically practices as an infectious disease doctor. In Russia, the position of the hospital epidemiologist did not officially exist until a few years ago. Traditionally, the Russian epidemiologist has been functioning as an outside public health official and has never had strong collegial relationships with hospital clinicians. As the Russian health care system becomes more and more decentralized and health care facilities gain higher authority and assume increasing responsibilities for their own budgets, hospital infection control programs become absolutely necessary for improving the quality of medical care as well as for cost savings. The hospital epidemiologist should be a key player in establishing an effective infection control program in the hospital. One of the challenges of the current reform efforts in Russia is to establish new training programs for hospital epidemiologists so that they can contribute to reducing hospital morbidity and mortality while eliminating unnecessary costs through effective infection control programs.

D. Health Administrators

As previously discussed, most health administrators who work in the Russian health care system were originally trained as physicians. Only a small fraction of administrators who deal with financial matters have specialized training in this area. This training usually consists of general accounting and bookkeeping although a few financial managers are trained in economics. The financial manager's role is predominantly technical and externally oriented to assure compliance with accounting laws and government regulations in health care. Regardless of their training, financial personnel work under the supervision of administrators with medical backgrounds who have the responsibility for allocating and controlling resources in the health care industry.

It should be understood that health care providers employ only a portion of the health management workforce. A large number of health administrators work in regulatory agencies at the territorial and district level that do not provide health care services. This system has been characterized as a giant pyramid with the Ministry of Health and Medical Industries on the top and health care providers at the bottom. All intermediate agencies are structured by Federative Units with health administrations at the Federative Unit level, and district (*rayon*) health administrations representing an area equivalent to a county level. Each level is in strict subordination to the next upper one. This huge bureaucratic apparatus used to be the basis for central planning and decision making and strict government control over the whole health care industry.

Health care reforms initiated in the early 1990s aimed at restructuring health care into a decentralized system responsive to specific needs in the regions and financed from several sources such as payroll taxes, regional and local budgets, and a limited central state budget. As with any reform process, the transformation could be implemented only through a reallocation of resources to make the system operate more efficiently. No matter how a particular health system operates—by laws of free market or through strict central planning—it is the health administrators who monitor the system's resources and who make decisions about allocation and reallocation of resources. Surprisingly, it turned out that among various actors in the field of health care, administrators happened to be least prepared for this transformation in the Russian health system.

Two factors might explain this phenomenon. The first is the general attitude of health administrators to any change in a system. Administrators constituted an "interest group" during the process of health care reform. Any effort to decentralize the inert and overregulated Soviet system obviously implies cutting down on this huge bureaucracy, a direction that was certainly opposed by health administrators in controlling agencies of the Russian health system. The second factor that is equally important in impeding the course of reforms is the low level of professional competence in the specialized field of health management. There is a strong leadership potential in the existing Russian health management cadre with many talented, experienced, and enthusiastic leaders open to new ideas, but for this potential to be realized it is essential to have an effective system of health management education that is responsive to industry needs.

E. Health Management Education

In Russia the education of health managers was and still is part of the general medical education system. To get a valid certificate to work as a health administrator, one must first be a graduate of a medical school. The United States approaches such education differently, and health management education is provided mostly outside of medical schools and does not require a medical background from applicants. In the Russian system, there is no specialty training in health management at the graduate level. All medical students have to take a course in social hygiene and health organization. This course, as with all courses in medical school programs, is required for all students, but it is not designed for professional training in health management. The curriculum is mostly descriptive and does not provide any tools or focus on skills that could be used in decision-making processes of management practice. For example, the course gives only general descriptions of the Russian health care system and a basic overview of regulations in the health care and health insurance system. It also includes some basic biomedical statistics and epidemiological analysis. It is obvious that this relatively short survey course was not designed to provide skill and knowledge sufficient to prepare professionals in health management. All students, including those who want to become health care administrators, cannot specialize in health management. They have to receive training in some clinical subspecialty and start practicing medicine in a hospital or policlinic after graduation. If, in the course of work, a physician shows more interest and abilities in administrative work, he or she can be promoted to a position of management responsibility; first to department head, then to deputy head physician and eventually to head physician of a hospital or a policlinic. The most capable from this pool of provider-level health managers, although often just more loyal to the authorities, could then be promoted to management positions in local regulatory health agencies and government structures through governmental appointments.

When appointed to management positions, physicians have to take short postgraduate courses at departments of continuous education for health managers at medical schools or at the Institutes for Continuous Medical Education. These courses usually take from 2 weeks to 4 months and provide graduates with certification in the specialty of social hygiene and administration in health care. The curricula of these courses have to be approved by the educational department of the Ministry of Health and Medical Industries, but certification standards lag far behind the current demand in management skills and knowledge. The educational approach taken in these courses reflects the old system of compliance with the policies of government control, and for the most part the curriculum is designed only to inform students of recent changes in the regulatory environment. The content does not provide tools necessary for independent decision making in a decentralized environment and does not encourage leadership or problem-solving skills. The lack of these management skills in current health managers certainly translates into an inability to support new trends in management practice. These new practices are needed especially now when there is a dramatic transformation and decentralization in Russian health care financing and delivery. To summarize, we could say that the existing system of health management education offers limited content to support the urgent demands of the rapidly changing decentralized Russian health care environment.

In this critical situation, some medical schools and higher educational institutions took steps toward establishing a more responsive system of health management training that keeps pace with current needs. Such transformations are happening now mainly in schools in big cities such as Moscow and St. Petersburg, but the trend is toward dissemination of these new programs into other geographical regions. Most of the effort is being put in postgraduate training targeted to practicing administrators. At this beginning stage of program development, the feedback from experienced administrators who go through these courses certainly helps in fine-tuning the curriculum to the needs and realities of management practice. The courses are relatively short and their curricula more closely reflect the growing demand for up-to-date health care management training. Topics are not limited to general information content on the health care system, but are oriented toward more practical content and skills. At present, the content of these courses is focused in the areas of strategic planning, management and leadership, quality management and management information systems, decision making, communications and human resources management, and financial management in health institutions.

The most recent development in health management education involved the establishment of a new school of public health that is designed to provide more fundamental training at the graduate level. This is a 2-year program named after Sechenov that was launched by the Moscow Medical Academy, the leading medical school in Russia. The new school is a joint effort of the Moscow Medical Academy and the School of Public Health of the University of Minnesota. The program is structured in the same way as most programs in health management in the United States. It is mainly targeted to regular students with bachelor-level diplomas, and it provides graduate-degree certification in health management. The program's alumni will be the first Russian professionals specially trained in the area of health management. It should also be noted that all these new programs utilize new approaches in teaching management with less focus on the traditional didactic presentation of materials and a higher level of student participation. There is more interaction among participants and faculty, greater use of interactive training techniques such as case studies, small-group work, business games, and role-playing. Some class sessions take place in real-world practice settings.

The initial steps in the restructuring of the training and role of the Russian health care administrators are fundamental to the future of Russian health care reform. Redesign of the system to decentralize financing and administration has created a need for a manager who can respond in a flexible and innovative way to system incentives. Russian educators, assisted by international consultants and advisors, are responding to this need through simultaneous efforts to retrain the current management cadre and educate the future generation of health care administrators differently. This reeducation has been one of the significant challenges in Russian health care reform, and will certainly shape the future of Russian health care.

F. Learning from Russian Health Care Reform

It has been suggested that comparative health policy is a field that engenders optimism in the researcher and pessimism in the consumer. One of the causes of this pessimism is that very few studies make the leap from description and analysis to suggestions for health policymakers (Stone, 1980/81). The previous discussion of Russian health care reform, in addition to describing the system and its changes, placed particular emphasis on the role and training requirements of physician, midlevel providers, nurses, and health administrators as they continue to provide health care in this chaotic changing environment. It is from their adaptive behavior that the suggestions for health system management and policy can be drawn.

Russia's health care reform is taking place in a turbulent environment of political instability and change, economic unrest, and social instability. Despite these chaotic conditions, Russian health care administrators and providers are changing their systems and delivering better and more efficient care. Peters' (1987) discussion of strategies for managing within chaotic systems can be used as a framework for learning from Russian health care reform. Peters suggests three strategies for building systems in a chaotic environment: reconstitute the system tools of control and empowerment, measure what is important, and establish trust via systems.

Russian health care reform started with a reconsideration of the system tools of control and empowerment. The earliest changes to the system involved movement away from the centralized mode of financing and management and toward decentralized systems at the regional and local level. As decentralization became a reality, it was clear that the management approaches that worked well in the centralized system were no longer appropriate. The current focus on redesigning health management training and retraining Russian's health care management cadre is the next step in the redesign of the system control structure. Thus, Russian health care reform began with system reconfiguration and is evolving through management retraining. This change process contains important information for all in health care adapting to new systems. Managers cannot respond to new incentives if they lack the knowledge necessary to respond. As systems change, it is important to provide concurrent training for practicing managers and rapidly restructure generic management training programs to provide new managers with the necessary skills to survive in the reformed system. Recognition of the central role of training and education to support health care reform is a vital lesson to be learned from the Russian experience and applied to every health care system in the process of reform. As the Russian experience so clearly illustrates, retraining cannot be limited to a small group of influential leaders nor can it be narrowly applied to the current managers. If reforms are to be effective, current and future managers as well as those who train them must be involved.

Redesigning the system of measurement and measuring what is important has also been identified as a part of Russian health care reform. Peters (1987) suggests that practicing managers need simple measures that are useful and important to them rather than stacks of computerized reports with too much irrelevant information. The recent emphasis on quality management in Russian health care facilities is an excellent example of adaptive measurement strategy within the Russian reform. The centralized system of the past produced information that measured the production of health care, but contained less useful information on the process of care, and none on the satisfaction of the consumer with care in an individual hospital or clinic. Russian health care managers are now focusing on institution-specific measures of the process and outcomes of care, and creating measurement systems that provide simpler and more relevant information to the practicing manager. In the Russian case, centralized bureaucratic health information systems failed as the centralized bureaucracy collapsed. These huge systems are being replaced by smaller, more accessible systems better suited to supporting delivery of quality health care despite the turbulent situation. The lesson to be learned is that of measuring close to the source, keeping information pertinent to the mission of the organization, and resisting the urge to overcomplicate systems to the point where little useful information is produced.

One of the most important challenges of the Russian reform is to replace the suspect systems of the past with trustworthy systems. For example, the production targets and goals set in Russian 5-year plans were often unrealistic. The production targets demanded an infrastructure that did not exist. Thus, managers could not meet them and had to create exaggerated production reports to satisfy central planning committees. This process resulted in a loss of credibility at all levels of the system. As turbulence increased in the society, managers could not believe in the system nor could they believe in themselves. As the bureaucracy collapsed it became clear that system performance had been seriously overstated. One of the most important consequences of this lack of system credibility was the damage done to the managers and practitioners within it. Peters (1987) points out that in turbulent times employees must be able to trust their ability to define a production target and actually deliver. Exaggerated requirements that are unachievable damage the employees' trust in themselves and result in failure. Thus the absence of ambitious production promises is a hopeful sign in the reformed Russian system. As more conservative goals are defined at territorial and district levels, managers will be held accountable for goals that can be met. Evaluation of the manager's performance will increasingly depend less on political acumen and more on objective results. This will reestablish trust in the system and refocus the health care manager and practitioner on achievable outcomes. The damage done to the Russian health care system by unrealistic production targets contains another important lesson for health care reform in any country. Efforts to justify reforms should not sacrifice the integrity of health care managers and practitioners. Unrealistic expectations result in exaggerated claims of performance and outcomes produced to satisfy authorities. This process erodes rather than promotes quality health care in any health care system.

The final lesson to be learned from Russian health care reform is that health care systems must grow and change with society. As the Russian social and economic system evolves, the health care system must also change. Thus, the real lesson of health reform is that it is a continuous process of learning and improvement. Health care in Russia, as in any country, supports and is a part of the human endeavor, failure, and achievement within the society. The lesson of Russian health care reform is that there is no final solution; there is only an effort to continuously improve the system in an environment of constant change.

REFERENCES

Cassileth, B., Vlassov, V., Chapman, C. Health care, medical practice, and medical ethics in Russia today. JAMA 273(20):1569–1575, 1995.

Economika I Zhizn July 1996:26.

Martynov, A.S., Vinogradoz, V.G., Denisov, A.V., Yelokhin, A.N., Sorogin, A.A. The current economic situation. In: Feshbach M., ed. Environmental and Health Atlas of Russia. Moscow: PAIMS Publishing House, 1995.

NATO Environmental Clearinghouse (ECHS) Web Site. Country Data Base. Russia. http://echs.ida.org/ccms/general/countrydb/: NATO, 1996.

Norsk Utenrikspolitisk Institutt (NUPI), Senter for Russlands-Studii. Database, 1997.

Peters, T. Thriving on Chaos. New York: Knopf, 1987.

Rowland, D., Telyukov, A. Soviet health care from two perspectives. Health Affairs 10(3): 71–86, 1991.

Semenov, V., Sheiman, I., Rice, J.A. The context of provider payment reforms in the Russian Federation: a challenging area for managerial development for twenty-first century Russia. J Health Admin Educ 14(2):115–132, 1996.

Smith, H. The Russians. New York: Quadrangle, 1976, p 219.

Stone, D.A. Obstacles to learning from comparative health research. Policy Stud J 9:278–285, 1980/81.

United States Library of Congress. Country Studies: Soviet Union. Washington, DC: US Government Printing Office, 1989.

World Bank Group, Europe and Central Asia Health Sector. Improving Health and Reforming Health Systems in Central and Eastern Europe and the Former Soviet Union. Washington, DC: World Bank Group, 1997.

World Health Organization. Health for All Database. www.who.dk/www.who.dk/mainframe.htm, World Health Organization, 1997.

World Health Organization. Statistics Annual. Geneva: World Health Organization, 1995.

4

The Canadian Health Care System

Kant Patel and Mark E. Rushefsky
Southwest Missouri State University, Springfield, Missouri

> Canada's system of universal public insurance for health care . . . expresses
> the fundamental equality of Canadian citizens in the face of disease and death
> and a commitment that the rest of the community, through the public system,
> will help each individual with these problems as far as it can.
> —Evans, 1992, p. 740

The Canadian health care system, known as Medicare, developed incrementally
over a period of time. As with the United States, there was considerable opposition to this development, especially from the medical profession. But unlike the
U.S. system, the opposition was overcome. Medicare has been shaped by the
federalist nature of the Canadian political system and the values that underlie
the political and health care systems.

I. EVOLUTION OF THE HEALTH CARE SYSTEM

Graig (1999) traces the origins or roots of the health care system to the British
North American Act of 1867. This act gave the provinces responsibility for oversight of hospitals. The federal government was limited to caring for the health
of special groups (i.e., Eskimos, military). But financing remained in private
hands. Initial legislation for public financing of health care was introduced in
1919 but delayed by the onset of the Great Depression and then World War II
(Graig, 1999).

Support for a public plan was strong in the period during and after the war.
With that support, and that of the medical profession, the federal government
proposed a plan of public financing whereby the federal government would help

79

the provinces pay for health care in return for which the provinces would turn over all income tax revenues. The provinces rejected the offer (Graig, 1999).

This then led to the development of private insurance, commercial insurance, Blue Cross/Blue Shield, and doctor-controlled. The support for publicly financed health care by the medical profession turned to strong opposition. As Graig points out, "medical, hospital and insurance groups developed their own power bases" (Graig, 1999, p. 125). It was action by the provinces that would lead to the current system.

The story begins in the province of Saskatchewan. Under the leadership of the New Democratic Party, the province began a system of hospital insurance, which was later adopted by the other provinces (Tuohy, 1994). During his 1960 campaign for reelection, Saskatchewan premier Tommy Douglas pledged to establish a public health program that focused on physician services. The medical profession, in conjunction with the opposition party, sought to defeat Douglas' party. They lost and Douglas proposed legislation in 1961. Physicians and their backers began an intensive campaign against the proposal, echoing the opposition to President Truman's national health insurance proposals in the late 1940s (see Starr, 1982, pp. 280–286; see also Marmor, 1973). Woodrow Lloyd, Douglas' successor, was as strong a supporter of the proposal as Douglas, and on July 1, 1962 the legislation, the Saskatchewan Medical Care Insurance Act, took effect. That same day, doctors went on strike to force repeal of the law. The strike was broken when a planned rally against the new law fizzled. The provincial medical association asked for some concessions, which the government was prepared to make, and the opposition ended (Finn, 1992; see also Maioni, 1997). By 1971, all 10 provinces and the two territories covered physician and hospital services (Graig, 1999; Maioni, 1997; Rakich, 1991). Virtually all Canadians were covered by what came to be called Medicare.

The federal government's efforts followed that of the provinces, and generally took the form of financial support coupled with standards of coverage. A 1940 report suggested a financial role for the federal government (Maioni, 1997). Maioni (1997) argues that it was the presence of a third political party, the Cooperative Commonwealth Federation (CCF), which arose in the 1930s, coupled with strong public support, that helped pressure the federal government to act. By 1957, the federal government began to take action.

As was true in the provinces, federal government action first covered hospital and then physician services. The Hospital Insurance and Diagnostic Services Act (1957) provided for coverage of 25% of national and provincial inpatient hospital care. In 1966, the Medical Care Act was passed, covering physician services. The federal responsibility was 50%. In 1977 the Federal-Provincial Fiscal Arrangements and Federal Post-Secondary Education and Health Contributions Act of 1977 was passed. It changed the financial responsibility arrangements and importantly tied the federal contribution to growth of the economy [as measured by gross domestic product (GDP)]. Rather than paying 50% of expenses, a fixed per capita rate was established (Chernomas and Sepehri 1995). All of these features were consolidated in the 1984 Canada Health Act, which remains the fundamental federal legislation regarding health care (Rakich, 1991). By 1971, the private insurance companies had been purchased by the provincial governments (though often run the same as before) and the Canadian health care system could be "characterized as a single-payer government health insurance run by the provinces with general federal rules and financial contributions" (Chernomas and Sepehri, 1995, p. 183).

Tuohy makes the important point that Canadian Medicare essentially "froze" the delivery system in place. In essence, there was an accommodation between the provinces/federal government and health care providers to maintain the system as it was in the 1960s (U.S. policies in the 1960s made the same bargain; see Krause, 1977, and Starr, 1982). The result is that while there has been considerable organizational change in the United States (see Patel and Rushefsky, 1999; Robinson, 1999), there has been much less in Canada (Crichton, 1994; Tuohy, 1994). The Canadian system is still very much controlled by providers (especially physicians) and remains very individualistic, i.e., fewer group practices and managed care–type organizations (Crichton, 1994).

II. FEATURES OF THE SYSTEM

A. Coverage

Medicare covers "medically necessary" hospital and physician services. Each provincial resident receives an insurance card entitling him or her to services, not only in the home province but anywhere in Canada. All provincial plans must meet five criteria set forth in the 1984 Canada Health Act.

The first criterion is that the plans must be *publicly administered*, that is, by a public body on a nonprofit basis. Second, the plans must be *comprehensive*. Third, the plans must be *universal*, covering all residents. Fourth, the plans must be *portable*, so that residents can obtain needed services in all territories and provinces. The act contains provisions for paying for out-of-province services (including out-of-country services). Finally, the plan must be *accessible*. This means that services are to be available to all and not impeded by charges (though some provinces do impose charges on recipients); that there be reasonable compensation for providers; and that hospitals be paid based on their costs (Health Canada, 1998).

The covered services vary somewhat from province to province. In general, all medically necessary hospital and physician services are covered. To take one example, the province of Saskatchewan, the birthplace of the system, covers the following hospital services:

public ward accommodation; necessary nursing services; operating room and case room facilities; surgical dressings and cast, as well as other required surgical materials and appliances; x-ray, laboratory and other diagnostic services; radiotherapy; anaesthetic agents and the use of anaesthetic equipment; physiotherapeutic procedures; all other services rendered by individuals who receive any remuneration from the hospital; and all drugs, biologicals and related preparations administered in hospitals and approved by the Minister (Health Canada 1998, p. 40).

For physician services, under the provincial medical care plans, insured services are those deemed as required by physicians. It should also be pointed out that patients have freedom of choice of which providers to go to.

Note the medical ''necessary'' or ''required'' phrases. This phrase is ill-defined in the federal as well as provincial/territorial legislation. According to Charles et al. (1997), the definition of the phrase has evolved through four phases: starting with ''what doctors and hospitals do'' to ''the maximum we can afford'' to ''what is scientifically justified'' and finally to ''what is consistently funded across all provinces.''

What is not covered by the plans also varies by province and territory. This may include long-term care, dental care, and prescription drug coverage (Graig, 1999). Depending on the province or territory, some of these services may be covered on a cost-sharing basis (see Health Canada, 1998).

B. Delivery of Services

The delivery of medical services in Canada is in the hands of the nonpublic sector. Hospitals are run on a nonprofit basis (they are essentially community hospitals) and physicians generally work as solo practitioners, though increasingly moving toward group or managed care practices. In other words, health care delivery is *not socialized* in Canada; it is the insurance or payment system that is socialized (Evans, 1992). Primary care physicians predominate as caregivers.

C. Funding of Services

Here we note several features of the Canadian system (see Fig. 1). First, how are providers paid? Physicians are generally paid on a fee-for-service basis, with payments based on fee schedules negotiated between each provincial government and provincial medical associations. The fee schedules, based on ones originally used by Blue Shield, are updated to account for new procedures and established through relative value scales (i.e., how much each procedure is worth compared to other procedures), similar to Medicare in the United States. The fee schedules have been a constraining device on cost control. Physicians in Canada are paid

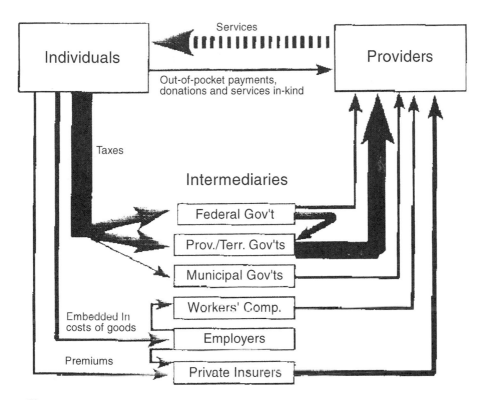

Figure 1 The financial structure of the Canadian health care system.

fees per service that are less than half of charges for private insurance in the United States, and about 59% of the fee the U.S. Medicare program allows (White, 1995). Provinces have gained control over the fee schedules, and as a result, fee increases have been less than 1% a year for much of the 1990s (Graig, 1999). This reimbursement problem has kept Canadian physicians disaffected from the system, leading at one point to a physicians' strike in Ontario in 1986. This can also be seen in articles in the *Canadian Medical Association Journal* (see, for example, O'Reilly, 1995, and Gordon et al., 1998; for research suggesting that physicians have become more accepting of Medicare, at least those who have grown up with the system, see Williams et al., 1995).

To prevent physicians from increasing the number of services offered to increase income, the provinces have established caps (limits) on physician expenditures. In some cases, provinces have put limits on physician incomes (Graig, 1999).

Hospitals, which, as in the United States, account for the largest portion of health expenditures, are paid on the basis of global caps (White, 1995; Graig,

1999). That is, each province fixes a budget for hospitals and then the hospital decides how to allocate its funds. This means that each hospital has to decide how many of each procedure it is willing to undertake (Graig, 1999). The provinces do allow the separation of operating and capital budgets (expansion, purchase of new equipment) with strict controls on the capital budgets.

D. Financing of Services

The financing of health care is primarily through taxes, individual and corporate, at the federal and provincial level. The federal government, as mentioned, pays provinces on a per capita rate tied to changes in the GDP. In 1996, federal transfer of funds to the provinces was merged into a block grant, the Canada Health and Social Transfer, which combined health and social program funding. The recession that hit Canada in 1990 caused a relative decline in the size of the transfers and some fiscal distress for the provinces. Additionally, Alberta and British Columbia charge premiums for services, though they are not risk-rated (i.e., charging more for recipients more likely to use services, such as those with preexisting conditions), nor do the provinces allow ability to pay the premiums to act as a barrier to obtaining services.

As Figure 1 shows, individuals may also pay premiums to employers and insurers for noncovered services; individuals may also pay providers directly for such services. Indeed, private-sector spending for health care has been increasing over the years. In 1960, private health expenditures were almost half of total expenditures, falling to about 22.6% by 1976. By 1997, private health expenditures as a proportion of total expenditures exceeded 30% (see Graig, 1999; Canadian Institute for Health Information, 1999; O'Reilly, 1995). O'Reilly makes the point most strongly in arguing that the private sector is increasingly gaining on the public sector and that the public sector is no longer capable of providing the health care services Canadians have come to expect; hence, privatization, already underway, should be the subject of debate and action.

Some interesting trends are seen if we look at health care spending (both total and public) as a percent of gross domestic product and compare the United States and Canada. Table 1 presents the data and shows that total health care spending in 1960 was about the same as in the United States, though public health expenditures were, relatively speaking, twice as large in Canada compared to the United States. By 1970, total health expenditures were about the same in the two countries, with public health expenditures still relatively much larger in Canada than in the United States. It is after 1970 that the United States and Canada go off in different directions. Both total spending and public health spending in the United States consistently increase; health spending in Canada is restrained. Total health spending in Canada in 1997 was at the same level as in 1990; public health spending, as a percent of GDP, actually declined. In the United States,

Table 1 Comparing Canadian and United States Health
Expenditures (percent of gross domestic product)

Year	Type of expenditure	Canada	United States
1960	Total health	5.4%	5.2%
	Public health	2.3%	1.3%
1970	Total health	7.1%	7.3%
	Public health	5.0%	2.7%
1980	Total health	7.1%	9.1%
	Public health	5.4%	3.9%
1990	Total health	9.0%	12.6%
	Public health	6.7%	5.1%
1997	Total health	9.0%	13.6%
	Public health	6.3%	6.3%

Source: Canadian Institute for Health Information. *The Evolution of
Public and Private Care Spending in Canada, 1960–1997.* Ottowa,
Ontario: Canadian Institute for Health Information, 1999.

both increased during the same period. Clearly the legal changes in the federal
contributions to the provinces, especially bundling health and social spending,
and tying the federal contribution to changes in GDP had an impact. When the
recession hit Canada in 1990, federal contributions stagnated or fell. What follows is that private sector spending on health care has increased or at least did
not decrease in the middle and late 1990s (see Health System and Policy Division,
1997).

   Where does the money for health care go. Table 2 presents the data. The
largest portion goes to hospital spending, with physician and pharmaceutical
spending next. The sectors differ in where the money is spent, as might be
expected given the nature of Medicare. The public sector spends the bulk of
the money for institutional (hospital and other institutions), physician, and capital expenses. The private sector spends the bulk of the money on drugs, with
other significant contributions for capital, other professionals, and other institutions.

E. Cost Control

We mentioned earlier that though Canada spends relatively less than the United
States (as measured by health expenditures as a percent of GDP), the health care
system has faced the need to control costs. In this section, we look at how Canada
has attempted to restrain costs.

Table 2 Percent Distribution, by Sector, of Health Expenditures by Category (1996)

Sector	Hospitals	Other institutions	Physicians	Other professionals	Drugs	Capital	Public health	Other
Total	34.9%	10.0%	14.9%	8.2%	13.9%	2.5%	5.2%	10.5%
Public	42.9	9.7	20.5	1.8	7.3	2.5	7.2	8.0
Private	13.9	10.6	0.5	25.0	31.0	2.2	0.0	16.8
Ratio of public to private	87.7:12.3	68.1:31.9	99.0:1.0	14.3:85.7	35.2:64.8	72.4:27.6	100.0:0.0	52.6:47.4

Source: Health System and Policy Division. *National Health Expenditures in Canada*. Ottawa, Ontario: Health Canada, 1997, pp. 9–12.

Some of the features already discussed work toward limiting expenditures. From the standpoint of the central government, limiting increases in contributions to the provinces to changes in GDP provides a ready check on its share of costs. Global budgets for hospitals and fee schedules for physicians (including, in some provinces, a global budget for physician expenditures) are important ways in which costs are controlled.

An important way that Canada controls costs is through controlling the spread of technology, an important factor in health care cost increases (see Patel and Rushefsky, 1999, Chapter 8). Purchase of new equipment, especially the more expensive and larger items, requires provincial consent. High-technology medical equipment, such as magnetic resonance imaging (MRI) machines, is located largely in the academic medical centers. This means the equipment is used more efficiently than in the United States (White, 1995). White writes (p. 71) that "less capacity for more expensive treatments means that those treatments are not as likely to be overused and that each use costs less."

The Canadian system also seeks to control costs by limiting the number of providers, a supply-side action to restrict the capacity of the system. This seems to have been accomplished largely without hurting the quality of care (see Roos et al., 1998).

There is another important way (as well as a significant comparison with the U.S. system) that the Canadian system controls costs: administration of the system. The Canadian system is a single-payer system. By contrast, providers in the United States face a multitude of payers: Medicare, Medicaid, private insurance companies, managed care organizations, and so forth. Marmor (1993) notes the simplicity of the Canadian versus the U.S. billing system. The Canadian system does not require the marketing found in the United States, nor does the Canadian system figure premium charges based on risk. Claims payments are simpler. Billing is much simpler and less detailed records need be kept (Armstrong et al., 1998). Much of the difference in costs between Canada and the United States lies in the difference in administrative costs (see Tuohy, 1994, and the citations within; and Armstrong et al., 1998). One estimate is that if the United States adopted a single-payer system, getting rid of much of the private bureaucracy (i.e., insurance companies), some $100 billion per year might be saved, sufficient to cover those lacking health insurance (Chernomas and Sepehri, 1995).

III. VALUES AND THE SOCIAL WELFARE STATE

What particularly distinguishes the Canadian system from its southern neighbor are the values that underlie the health care system. Jecker and Meslin (1994) argue that it is the Canadian's conception of justice that underlies first the adoption and then the retention of Medicare. They compare the U.S. and Canadian conceptions.

The U.S. conception is largely based on the concept of self-interest. Canadian conceptions (and Jecker and Meslin are clear here that work on bioethics and justice is much better developed in the United States) are based on two principles. The first principle, they write, is

> the idea that government had a social and ethical responsibility to promote the general social welfare. This responsibility was itself buttressed by considerations of the welfare of the most vulnerable members of society (Jecker and Meslin, 1994, p. 188).

The second principle, they continue, is the "ethical principle of humanitarianism, or care and concern for fellow citizens" (Jecker and Meslin, 1994, p. 189). Health care is viewed as a social good, and the five principles of the Canada Health Act of 1984, discussed above, contain that vision.

Tuohy (1994) has a somewhat different way of looking at the values underlying the Canadian health care system. She first describes four models of a welfare state. The social democratic welfare state assumes that anybody who is a citizen of the country is entitled to benefits and there is little or no private market. The corporatist welfare model gives different set and levels of benefits to clearly defined groups, who make contributions to the system. The residualist welfare model relies largely on private markets, with public benefits for needy groups on a means-tested basis. The final model is the Beveridge model, which consists of elements of the other three: contributions, universal benefits, and limited in generosity. Tuohy labels the Canadian health care system as a "social democratic health insurance system" (Tuohy, 1994, p. 205).

IV. PROBLEMS AND CURRENT CONTROVERSIES

During the early 1990s, there was a major push in the United States to reform its health care system. Reform proposals varied from moderate plans designed to tinker with the existing system to more dramatic and comprehensive reforms designed to overhaul the system and provide universal coverage to all citizens. One of the more dramatic reform proposals was the American Health Security Act proposed by Senator Paul Wellstone (D-Miss.) and Representative Jim Mc-Dermott (D-Wash.), called the single-payer system (Rushefsky and Patel, 1998). This proposal was modeled after the Canadian health care system. It would have provided universal coverage under a single-payer system to be administered by the state governments. As we know, all of these reform proposals failed. However, it is ironic that while a Canadian-style health care system was being advocated in the United States, at about the same time, the Canadian health care system was beginning to show some signs of strain and problems (Rachlis and Kushner, 1989). In the following discussion we explore some of the major problems and controversies confronted by the Canadian health care system in the 1990s.

A. Budget Cuts

Canada experienced several recessions during the 1980s and the 1990s (Deber and Swan, 1999). During this time, the federal government in Canada engaged in deficit spending and its share of the aggregate debt grew from 40% of the gross domestic product in 1982–1983 to more than 65% in 1992–1993 (Tholl, 1994). At the same time, spending on health care increased dramatically. By 1989, Canada ranked second with respect to per capita expenditure on health, second only to the United States (Francis, 1991). By 1992, health care spending had reached 10.2% of the total economic output. This was second only to the United States ("The High Cost of Healing," 1998). In 1993, Canada spent $72 billion on health care, 10.1% of its GDP compared to 7.3% of GDP in 1980 (Janigan et al., 1995, p. 10). Many observers were beginning to wonder aloud how long the country could maintain a health care system that was taking up an ever-larger share of resources ("The High Cost of Healing," 1998). Some observers described Canada's health care system as a "sick puppy" in need of a cure (Francis, 1991). However, during 1994, 1995, and into 1996, health care spending amounted to 9.8, 9.6, and 9.5% of the GDP, respectively (Policy and Consultation Branch, Health Canada, 1997).

As explained earlier, transfer payments from the federal government to the provinces constitute a major financing mechanism for the Canadian health care system. Federal revenue sharing plays a critical role in the Canadian health care system because of significant disparities that exist across Canadian regions and provinces. Federal cost sharing ensures the provisions of a uniform level of services nationwide (Deber, 1993). An increased budget deficit and health care spending led to intense pressure to reduce the federal budget deficit and to reduce federal public sector health care expenditures (Iglehart, 1990). In 1990, the federal government announced that it was freezing some transfer payments to the provinces for 2 years. Later, the federal budget freeze was extended until 1995 (Underwood, 1991). Beginning in 1995, drastic cuts in federal transfer payments to the provinces were made in health, education, and income support programs as part of a concerted effort to reduce the federal budget deficit (Schrecker, 1998). In fact, in 1996 the federal government changed the way it financed health care by combining contributions for health, welfare, and postsecondary education into a single block grant fund, the Canadian Health and Social Transfer. The cash flowing from this new program was expected to fall from $14.9 billion in 1996–1997 to $12.5 billion in 1998–1999. In 1998, the federal government covered 21.5% of the provincial government's health expenditures. This was considerably lower compared to 24.1% in 1990 and 30.6% in 1980. Nationally, funding for hospitals as a percentage of total health care spending dropped from 40.6% in 1987 to about 33.6% in 1997 ("The High Cost of Healing," 1998).

As the federal government reduced its share, the provinces were left to pick up the slack, particularly for new programs. Provincial and territorial government spending increased from $42.1 billion in 1990 to $48.6 billion in 1997 ("The High Cost of Healing," 1998). However, the provinces also were wrestling with their own budget deficits. This created a bandwagon for balanced budgets, which in turn led to a widespread consensus that the Canadian health care system was in urgent need of reform.

B. Hospital Closings, Manpower Reductions, and Physician Migration

Attempts to reduce budget deficits and control rising health care costs have led to various cost containment measures making health care services more cost-effective. This has led to revamping and reorganization of the health care delivery system. As each province began to feel the budget pinch, it was forced to take dramatic action. Attempts at cost containment have led to a significant increase in the number of hospital closings, reduction in hospital beds, and reduction in health services manpower. This has also increased stress and tension among health care workers and produced dissatisfaction with what is happening in the Canadian health care system. However, others argue that such reforms were un-necessary.

In November 1991, the B.C. Royal Commission on Health Care and Costs released a report containing more than 350 recommendations, many of which emphasized the need to realign health care funds to provide more effective ser-vices. In fact, earlier in the month the Ontario Hospital Association announced that the 224 hospitals in the provinces were facing massive job cuts and bed closures because the provincial government could not provide the funds needed to maintain current service levels (Underwood, 1991). In May 1998, the CEO of St. Joseph's Hospital announced that the 101-bed chronic-care rehabilitation facility would close in April 2000 ("Shock to the System," 1998). In October 1998, the Calgary General Hospital was demolished in a few seconds by a series of explosions. The 960-bed hospital was simply no longer needed. In Ontario, 11,000 hospital beds were closed, about 25% of the total. By 1998, more than 100 Canadian hospitals had closed their doors (Decter, 1998).

Across Canada, the number of hospital beds, nurses, and, to a limited ex-tent, doctors is decreasing ("The Health Report," 1998). Nova Scotia, which in the early 1990s enjoyed one of the highest hospital-bed-to-population ratio in the country, had dropped to ninth place by 1995–1996 ("Shock to the System," 1998). Aside from hospital closings, there has also been a dramatic increase in hospital consolidation. At the beginning of the 1990s Canada had about 900 hospitals. Each hospital had its own governing board, management, and clinical staff, and often its own laboratory. However, it is estimated that the rapid consolidation of stand-alone hospitals will result in 150–200 integrated health systems by the end of the century (Decter, 1998).

Health care providers and patients are feeling the pinch of Canadian health care reform and cost containment measures. Almost every province has slapped ceilings on its overall budget for physicians. Hospitals have set strict limits on the number of individual procedures such as cataract operations they will perform each year (Janigan et al., 1995). The result is anxious patients waiting a long time for surgical procedures. Health care providers are also feeling the impact of various cost containment measures. Nurses are struggling under the burden of staff cuts, and hospital policies are demanding longer work hours. A study in 1998 revealed that about 40% of nurses in Quebec suffered from severe stress and were thinking of quitting their jobs. Doctors are also frustrated by their heavy workloads, lower financial rewards compared to their counterparts in the United States, and decreased access to diagnostic equipment. A survey of Canadian physicians indicated that 55% were "somewhat unhappy with their lifestyle" because of the considerable demand on their time. Specialists, on the average, work about 65 hr a week, while generalists work about 57 hr a week (Charters, 1999).

Some doctors are migrating to the United States. In 1996, 513 active physicians left Canada. This is less than 1% of the total physician base in Canada; however, it is up 130% from 1991. According to Robert McKendry, Professor of Medicine at the University of Ottawa, who has studied the number of Canadian doctors migrating to other countries to practice, 2500 of the country's 52,000–55,000 doctors have left Canada in the last 4 years (Possehl, 1997). Some have argued that Canadian physicians, at least in the early 1990s, showed satisfaction with the health care system (see Marmor, 1993; Hayes et al., 1993; Mizrahi and Fasano, 1993). In terms of per capita doctors, Canada overall ranks 20th among 28 members of the Organization for Economic Co-Operation and Development ("A Staffing Crunch Looms," 1998).

C. Delays and Waiting Lists

One of the consequences of budget cuts, hospital closings, and other cost containment measures is huge backups in emergency rooms and the fact that patients often have to wait a long time for certain surgeries. Anxious patients often wait for months for surgery, often unaware of their choices and their chances. According to a study by the Fraser Institute in Vancouver, the waiting time to see a gynecologist after being referred by a family physician is 3.9 weeks. The lag time between seeing a specialist and getting treatment is about 6.2 weeks. To see an ophthalmologist takes about 7.6 weeks and another 10.2 weeks to receive treatment (Possehl, 1997). The waiting line for certain types of elective surgery such as knee replacement is considerably longer in Canada than in the United States (Fegan, 1998). The Canadian system responds to excess demand, particularly for nonemergency services, by making people get in line for medical treatment. There is also considerable variation in waiting time from one province to the next. For example, the average waiting time to see a specialist after being referred by a general practitioner for treatment ranges from 11.5 weeks in Ontario to 21 weeks on Prince Edward Island (Boaz, 1993).

Some research argues that American commentators overstate the problem of waiting lists and that much of the waiting list problem is attributed to a lack of coordination among providers rather than a lack of resources. In addition, it is argued that the waiting list problem is partly due to the fact that Canadian institutions are sometimes slow to respond to changes in practice patterns. Furthermore, the defenders of the Canadian system argue that studies that contrast the number of units available for certain procedures miss the point that what is more important to look at is the actual number of procedures performed. Deliberate government policy in Canada restricts the number of available units; however, the Canadian units operate at far higher volumes compared to the United States (Deber, 1993; see also Armstrong et al., 1998; Marmor, 1993).

One means by which Canadian doctors and patients deal with long waiting lists and inability to get prompt, high-quality medical care is to get treatment in the United States. Almost a third of Canada's doctors have sent patients outside the country for treatment. For example, about 10% of all British Columbia residents requiring cancer therapy have been sent to the United States (Boaz, 1993). Private entrepreneurs are also getting in on the action. Furthermore, some U.S. companies are tapping into this market. For example, the International Medical Referral Service, based in Kirkland, Washington, has brought several Canadians to hospitals and clinics in the United States for orthopedic surgery, organ transplants, and cardiovascular surgery (Possehl, 1997). Douglas Hitchlock, in 1996, set up a Canadian health care venture called the Free Trade Medical Network to get a piece of the growing trade that helps Canadians jump long waiting lines and receive faster medical care in the United States. He also advocates that Canada needs more for-profit health care (Possehl, 1997).

V. RISE IN PRIVATIZATION AND FOR-PROFIT HEALTH CARE

One of the major trends in the Canadian health care system is the increased privatization of certain medical services and for-profit health care facilities. Hospital closings and consolidations brought about by reductions in the federal government's contribution to Medicare have encouraged the growth of for-profit medical service provider organizations in the private sector. In 1997 in Calgary, a private organization, the Health Resource Group, invested $2.5 million to build what it labeled as Canada's first private medical center. The medical clinic would offer medically necessary services covered by Medicare on a user pay basis only (Eisler, 1997). Toronto and Calgary have seen the growth of health centers that employ many doctors charging heavily for diagnostic services and some orthopedic and dental surgery ("Edging to Market," 1999). Alberta's conservative government, in fact, favors a two-tier health care setup: fast, deluxe service for those who pay and tax-supported basics for those who do not. The province allows 15 private specialist clinics to charge the public system for some services and to charge patients extra fees ("Canada's Medicare on the Risk List," 1995).

As mentioned above, individual provincial health care plans do leave some health care costs uncovered, so many Canadians purchase supplemental health policies (Henderson, 1992). Private spending within Canada on those items not covered by provincial plans amounted to $22.7 billion out of total expenditures of $75.2 billion in 1996, and the relative importance of privately financed expenditures is increasing. Over two-thirds of Canadians have supplemental insurance coverage, usually employer-purchased, which covers part of the cost of prescription drugs, dental care, and other services not covered by provincial insurance plans (Schrecker, 1998).

The privatization of the Canadian health care system has gained momentum in the 1990s. As noted earlier, the percentage of private sector health care expenditures of the total health care expenditure in Canada increased from 25.4% in 1990 to 30.1% in 1996 (Policy and Consultation Branch, 1997). Some of the country's largest corporations have argued that they can save the system money by performing certain tasks more efficiently than the public sector. Privatization has also taken roots in many hospitals. For example, to cut costs the Toronto Hospital, Canada's largest with a budget of about $470 million and over 1200 beds and 6000 employees, asked the private sector to take over many of its functions. Since 1993, the hospital has been able to shave almost 25% off its operating budget (Fennell, 1996).

Many Canadians are worried that the increased privatization of the Canadian health care system will create a two-tier system like the one in the United States and undermine the values inherent in the system. This issue has been all the more troublesome for Canadians because the principle of public financing has been a well-accepted cornerstone of the Canadian health care system for over a generation. Unfortunately, the emergence of a parallel private system of health care services and financing is likely to be irreversible because of the commitments written into the North America Free Trade Agreement (NAFTA). The absence of legislation forbidding for-profit care under NAFTA is problematic for the Canadian health care system. Although the NAFTA agreement does provide some protection for the Canadian public health system, it also makes it difficult to reverse the privatization process already underway (Armstrong, 1999).

VI. DECLINE IN PUBLIC CONFIDENCE

On the whole, Canadians appear to be satisfied with their health care system, especially as compared to Americans. Polls taken in the early 1990s show that large majorities (exceeding 60%) of Americans preferred the Canadian system (this was among those who had health insurance) and only about one-third of Americans were very satisfied with their system. By contrast, about two-thirds of Canadians were very satisfied with their system and only about 3% said they preferred the American system (Mizrahi and Fasano, 1993; Rakich, 1991).

Since the early 1990s the problems discussed above have taken their toll on the level of public confidence in the Canadian health care system. *Maclean's, Medical Post*, and Angus Reid surveys of the general public as well as doctors provide some insight into this declining public confidence. Overall, more than 80% rated the Canadian health care system as good, very good, or excellent. However, 58% also felt that the system was likely to get worse in the future (''A Special Bond,'' 1995). A majority of the respondents also expressed unhappiness about access to doctors, with a majority of 56% expressing displeasure with long waits to see a doctor and 60% feeling that doctors require too frequent visits. In fact, nearly two-thirds of respondents felt that doctors were maintaining their own income levels by encouraging patients to come for more visits than are strictly necessary. What is more interesting is the fact that almost seven out of 10 doctors agree that some of their colleagues are maintaining their income by seeing patients when it is not strictly necessary. However, almost four out of 10 doctors defend the practice as a reasonable response to an ever-decreasing payment schedule (Posner, 1995).

On a number of other issues, a significant gap is developing between the general public's views and views of the doctors. Only 42% of the public at large support development of a second-tier health care system—compared with 59% of the country's doctors. Many doctors feel that a two-tier system is inevitable. Similarly, 56% of doctors agree that Canada should not have adopted a publicly financed Medicare system, and that the quality of care would have been better under a private insurance system. In sharp contrast, only 37% of Canadians believe that the quality of care would be better today if Canada had opted for private insurance or copayment (Posner and Nemeth, 1995). A 1996 Gallup Poll survey found that support for the two-tier system among Canadians had increased slightly from 42% in 1995 to 44% in 1996. Forty-nine percent of Canadians were opposed to the establishment of a two-tiered system of health care (Edwards and Hughes, 1996).

In a Maclean's/NBC year-end poll conducted in 1998, 22% of Canadians said that the most important problem facing Canada was the need for better health care and other social services. Three years prior to this survey, this concern hardly registered in polling. However, since 1996 the number of people who cite the need for better health care has climbed. Eleven percent of the respondents in

1996 and 15% in 1997 cited the need for better health care as a problem facing the country. In fact, by 1998, the need for better health care had become the number two worry of the Canadians, topped only by 28% citing concern over unemployment and the economy ("A Cry for Better Services," 1998). According to pollster Frank Graves, satisfaction levels with the Canadian health care system have fallen to 30% compared with 60% 2 years ago (Gray, 1998).

It appears that the public dissatisfaction, combined with hospital over-crowding, is beginning to have some effect on politicians. During the 1997 federal elections, the liberals made a lot of promises about health care in recognition of Canadians' concern about the deteriorating health care system. During the election season, nothing is closer to a politician's heart than the sanctity of Canada's health care system (Gray, 1998). Provincial governments have increased some of their funding in recent years. In February 1999, the Quebec health minister increased a previously announced $15 million health care plan by $5 million to allow 900 temporary nurses and health care workers to be hired, and 830 short-term beds in hospitals and nursing wards to be opened. Thirteen Quebec hospitals that have managed their emergency wards judiciously were rewarded with a $3.2 million bonus. Similarly, in British Columbia hospitals were given an additional $10 million to reopen empty wards to deal with the backlog of patients seeking emergency services. Meanwhile, the federal government's strategy appears to be to force the provincial governments to make some fundamental changes before funding will be increased. The federal government has promised to restore some of the cuts in federal health transfers to provinces (Kondro, 1999, p. 653). The centerpiece of the preelection budget in 2001 will without a doubt be the sanctity of Medicare (Gray, 1998).

VII. CONCLUSION

The Canadian health care system is going through a pattern of evolution common to other countries, including (to some extent) the United States system. The first stage of this pattern is the establishment of a public funding mechanism for covering health care expenses that, as we have seen in the Canadian case and is also true in the United States, can take decades. This is followed by a reexamination of the system, which might focus on reorganization and obtaining better value (Livingston 1998). In England, this led to the development of the national health service; in Canada, it appears the very basis of the system in being questioned.

As we discussed earlier, the Canadian system faces a number of problems. These include budget restraints on fund transfers from the national government to the provinces; dissatisfaction among providers, especially physicians; continued long waiting times for elective procedures; concerns about the efficiency of the system; and some growing dissatisfaction with the system among the public.

One of the major pressures, one facing Canadian citizens if not the system, is the increasing costs of pharmaceuticals. Despite the fact that Canadians spend considerably less on health care than Americans, as measured by percent of gross domestic product, it remains the case that the Canadian system is the second most expensive system in the world (using the same measure). Perhaps most significant is that the public sector is paying for relatively less and the private sector is paying for relatively more.

While the public still sees the system as a source of pride and important values (Jecker and Meslin 1994), the pressure for change is apparent. The budget pressures, originating from an economic slowdown, remain. Medical providers continue their assault on the system, calling for increased privatization. In some respects, the Canadian system is a version of the American Medicare program, applied to the entire population. The same criticisms of the one are made of the other. For example, neither system covers outpatient pharmaceutical costs. Some of the same solutions are suggested, such as managed care and privatization. Graig (1999) suggests that there is convergence between the two systems. While it is highly unlikely that the Canadian system will be abandoned, significant changes in the twenty-first century are likely.

REFERENCES

Armstrong, H. Decentralized health care in canada. Br Med J 318(7192):1201, May 1, 1999.

Armstrong, P., Armstrong, H., Fegan, C. The best solution: questions and answers on the Canadian health care system. Washington Monthly 30(6):8–11, June 1998.

Boaz, D. Canada offers faulty model. Insight on the News 9(37):30–31, Sept 13, 1993.

Canadian Institute for Health Information. The Evolution of Public and Private Health Care Spending in Canada, 1960 to 1997. Ottawa, Ontario: Canadian Institute for Health Information, 1999.

Canada's Medicare on the sick-list. Economist 336(7933):33, Sept 23, 1995.

Charles, C., Lomas, J., Giacomini, M. Medical necessity in Canadian health policy: four meanings and . . . a funeral? Milbank Q 75(3):365–394, 1997.

Charters, L. Canada's health care system based on Canadian values. Ophthalmol Times 24(11):27, June 1, 1999.

Chernomas, R., Sepehri, A. The Canadian health care system as a managed care model for the United States. Health Care Management 2(1):183–190, 1995.

Crichton, A. Health insurance and medical practice organization in Canada: findings from a literature review. Med Care Res Rev 51(2):149–158, 1994.

A cry for better services. Maclean's 111:22, Dec 28, 1998.

Decter, M. The road to better health: a revolution in Canadian care. Maclean's 111:52, Dec 7, 1998.

Deber, R. Canadian Medicare: can it work in the United States? Will it survive in Canada? Am J Law Med 19(3):75–93, 1993.

Deber, R., Swan, B. Canadian health expenditures: where do we really stand internationally? Can Med Assoc J 160(12):1730–1735, June 15, 1999.

Edging to Market. Economist 351(8118):1, May 8, 1999.

Edwards, G.R., Hughes, J. Public remains divided on two-tiered health care. Gallup Poll 56(67):1–2, Sept 19, 1996.

Eisler, D. Opening doors: a tangled feud over health-care services. Maclean's 110(24): 58, June 16, 1997.

Evans, R.G. Canada: the real issues. J Health Politics Policy Law 17(4):739–762, 1992.

Fegan, C. The best solution: questions and answers on the Canadian health care system. Washington Monthly 30(6):8–11, 1998.

Fennell, T. The privates' progress: the role of business in health care is growing. Maclean's 109(49):54–55, Dec 2, 1996.

Finn, E. The summer of '62. Can Forum 71(811):13–15, July–Aug 1992.

Francis, D. Expensive and dangerous myths. Maclean's 104(35):13, Sept 2, 1991.

Gordon, M., Mintz J., et al. Funding Canada's health care system: a tax-based alternative to privatization. Can Med Assoc J 159(5):493–497, Sept 8, 1998.

Graig, L.A. Health of Nations: An International Perspective on U.S. Health Care Reform, 3rd ed. Washington, DC: CQ Press, 1999.

Gray, C. The brutal politics of health care. Can Med Assoc J 158(7):922–923, Apr 7, 1998.

Hayes, G.J., Hayes, S.C., Dykstra, T. Physicians who have practiced in both the United States and Canada compare the systems. Am J Public Health 83(11):1544–1548, Nov 1993.

Health Canada. Canada Health Act Annual Report 1997–1998. Ottawa, Ontario: Minister of Public Works and Government, 1998.

The health report: the statistics reveal uneven levels of care. Maclean's 111(24):14, June 15, 1998.

Health System and Policy Division. National Health Expenditures in Canada. Ottawa, Ontario: Health Canada, 1997.

Henderson, N. Budget blues in Canada's health care system. Kiplinger's Personal Finance Mag 46(3):102–103, March 1992.

The high cost of healing: it's not how much, but where it's spent that counts most. Maclean's 111(24):16, June 15, 1998.

Iglehart, J.K. Canada's health care system faces its problems. N Engl J Med 322(8):562–568, Feb 22, 1990.

Janigan, M., Welbourne, K., Cardwell, M., Nemeth, M. A prescription for Medicare: ten ways to heal the health-care system. Maclean's 108(31):10–16, July 31, 1995.

Jecker, N.S., Meslin E.M. United States and Canadian approaches to justice in health care: a comparative analysis of health care systems and value. Theor Med 15(2):181–200, June 1, 1994.

Kondro, W. Hospital overcrowding forces Canada to boost healthcare spending. Lancet 353(9153):653, Feb 20, 1999.

Krause, E.A. Power and Illness: The Political Sociology of Health and Medical Care. New York: Elsevier, 1977.

Maioni, A. Parting at the crossroads: the development of health insurance in Canada and United States, 1940–1965. Compar Politics 29(4):411–431, July 1997.

Marmor, T.R. The Politics of Medicare. Chicago: Aldine, 1973.

Marmor, T.R. Commentary on Canadian health insurance: lessons for the United States. Int J Health Serv 23(1):45–62, 1993.

Mizrahi, T., Fasano, R. Canadian and American health care: myths and realities. Health Soc Work 18(1):7–13, Feb 1993.

National Forum on Health. The Public and Private Financing of Canada's Health System. http://wwwnfh.hc_sc.gc.ca/publicat/public/idxpuble.htm.

O'Reilly, M. The privatization of Canadian health care is moving into high gear. Can Med Assoc J 152(11):1877–1878, June 1995.

Patel, K., Rushefsky, M.E. Health Care Politics and Policy in America, 2nd ed. Armonk, NY: ME Sharpe, 1999.

Policy and Consultation Branch, Canada. National Health Expenditures in Canada, 1975–1996. Ottawa, Ontario: Minister of Public Works and Government Services, 1997.

Posner, M. Feverish relations. Maclean's 108(46):52–54, Nov 13, 1995.

Posner, M., Nemeth, M. Condition critical. Maclean's 108(46):46–50, Nov 13, 1995.

Possehl, S.R. Northern plights. Hosp Health Netw 71(17):56–58, Sept 5, 1997.

Rachlis, M., Kushner, C. Second Opinion: What's Wrong with Canada's Health-Care System and How to Fix It. Toronto: Collins Publishers, 1989.

Rakich, J.S. Canada's universal-comprehensive healthcare system. Hosp Top 69(2):14–19, 1991.

Robinson, J.C. The future of managed care organization. Health Affairs 18(2):7–24, March–April, 1999.

Roos, N.P., Brownell, M., Shapiro, E., Roos, L.L. International update: good news about difficult decisions: the Canadian approach to hospital cost control. Health Affairs 17(5):239–246, Sept-Oct 1998.

Rushefsky, M., Patel, K. Politics, Power and Policy Making: The Case of Health Care Reform in the 1990s. Armonk, NY: ME Sharpe, 1998.

Schrecker, T. Private health care for Canada: north of the border, an idea whose time shouldn't come? J Law Med Ethics 26(2):138–148, 1998.

Shock to the system: the scapel of health care reform has left painful wounds. Maclean's 111(24):33, June 15, 1998.

A special bond. Maclean's 108(46):58–59, Nov 13, 1995.

A staffing crunch looms. Maclean's 111(24):20, June 15 1998.

Starr, P. The Social Transformation of American Medicine: The Rise of a Sovereign Profession and the Making of a Vast Industry. Basic Books: New York, 1982.

Tholl, W.G. Health care spending in Canada: skating faster on thinner ice. In: Blomqvist A. Brown D. eds. Limits to Care: Reforming Conada's Health System in an Age of Restraint. Toronto: CD Howe Institute, 1994.

Tuohy, C. Hughes. Principles and power in the health care arena: reflections on the Canadian experience. Health Matrix J Law Med 4(2):205–242, 1994.

Underwood, N. Cross-border checkup: two countries re-evaluate their health care. Maclean's 104(47):58, Nov 25, 1991.

White, J. Competing Solutions: American Health Care Proposals and International Experience. Washington, DC: The Brookings Institution, 1995.

Williams, A.P., Vayda, E., Cohen, M.L., Woodword, C.A., Ferrier, B.M. Medicine and the Canadian state: from the politics of conflict to the politics of accommodation? J Health Soc Behav 36(4):303–321, Dec 1995.

5

The United States Health Care System

Carole M. Pohl
Florida Atlantic University, Boca Raton, Florida

The U.S. health care system has undergone much transformation since the late 1970s. Because of this, consumers of health services as well as the health professionals delivering those services are confronted daily by new technologies, complex ethical issues brought about by advanced technology, reimbursement changes, and ever-changing delivery models. For consumers and health professionals alike, interacting with a health care system that grows more unfamiliar, and thus, more difficult to maneuver, has resulted in widespread doubt about the system's ability to meet the demands of its stakeholders. And yet, this health system thrives.

In this chapter, an examination of the complex and controversial U.S. health care system will be conducted to gain insights on the many factors affecting delivery of services that might benefit other countries embroiled in similar reform of their health care systems. This analysis will focus on an overview of the U.S. health care system's development as well as a description of its various components. A synopsis of the changing reimbursement mechanisms will be presented. Outcomes of the system, in terms of health status of the U.S. population, will be reviewed and emerging issues discussed.

I. DESCRIPTION OF THE HEALTH CARE SYSTEM

A. Historical Development of the Health Care System

According to Torrens (1993), the U.S. health care system has completed three stages of development and entered a fourth stage that began around 1980 (pp. 3–

4). Health problems of the general population also changed during these stages, as did the availability of medical technology and the structure of the system. Table 1 provides an overview of the stages of development of the health care system in the United States.

The first stage commenced during the mid-1800s with the institutionalization of health care in the United States, through the introduction of hospital services and professional health departments. Massachusetts General Hospital, in 1846, served as the first facility where ether was used to eliminate pain during operations on the inner cavities of the body; still, most patients died from subsequent infections (Raffel and Raffel, 1989, p. 144).

Adoption of the scientific method into medical education and practice initiated the second stage of development around 1900. During this time the American Medical Association began major reform efforts to improve the practice of physicians. In 1910 Abraham Flexner published an important study that revolutionized medical education by eliminating substandard medical schools and vastly improving the overall quality of the medical curriculum. Gradually, physicians were trained as scientists as well as practitioners and some began to specialize in a particular area of medicine (Torrens, 1993, p. 9).

Workers' compensation was introduced in 1914 by New York state (and continued state by state until 1950); this program provided a portion of income for wages lost due to injury as well as payment for all or part of necessary medical services to over 80% of the U.S. workforce. This was a mandatory social health insurance program instituted to reduce the costs and pain of suffering job-related accidents (Koch, 1999, p. 123). Also notable in this time period was the broader role that local and state public health departments assumed. Major federal funding was allocated in 1935 and resulted in the implementation of maternal and child health services as well as more general public health activities (Raffel and Raffel, 1989, p. 263).

Prior to the 1930s family members provided nursing care for older people at home or sought assistance from religious or governmental homes for poor elderly people. Private, proprietary nursing homes took hold after passage of the Social Security Act of 1935 when welfare payments for patients in nongovernmental facilities became available. The Joint Commission on Accreditation of Hospitals (JCAH) was formed in 1951 as a private organization that established quality standards and evaluated hospitals that voluntarily sought accreditation. JCAH was renamed in the 1980s, becoming the Joint Commission on Accreditation of Healthcare Organizations (JCAHO). The new JCAHO additionally evaluated and monitored home health agencies, hospices, and nursing homes. As the commission's purview expanded, its emphasis changed from measuring process to focusing on patient outcomes (Evashwick, 1993, p. 212).

The third stage emerged during the 1940s and was a time of expansion for the health care system and a greater concentration of power in the federal

Table 1 Major Trends in the Development of Health Care in the United States, 1850 to Present

Trends	1850–1900	1900 to World War II	World War II to present	Future
Predominant health problems of the American people	Epidemics of acute infections	Acute events, trauma, or infections affecting individuals, not groups	Chronic diseases such as heart disease, cancer, stroke	Chronic diseases, particularly emotional and behaviorally related conditions
Technology available to handle predominant health problems	Virtually none	Beginning and rapid growth of basic medical sciences and technology	Explosive growth of medical science; technology captures the health care system	Continued growth and expansion of technology, with attempts to depersonalize the technology
Social organization for the use of technology	None: individuals left to their own resources or charity	Beginning societal and governmental efforts to care for those who could not care for themselves	Health care as a right; governmental responsibility to organize and monitor health care for everyone	Greater centralization of responsibility and control in federal government; greater use of organized systems of health insurance and financing to shape and control developments within the health care system

Source: Torrens, P.R. *The American Health Care System: Issues and Problems.* St. Louis: CV Mosby, 1978.

government. The national focus in health care from the late 1940s into 1970 was on emerging growth, initiated by the passage of the Hill-Burton Act in 1946 (McManus and Pohl, 1994, p. 333). This Act funded the tremendous growth of hospitals that continued until the mid-1980s, which unfortunately led to questionable duplication of services and rising health care costs. Other reasons for rising health care costs during this growth period were the increasing numbers of physicians, the expansion and availability of health insurance coverage, and the growth of medical technology (Torrens and Williams, 1994, p. 60). During the same period, the National Institutes of Health grew from a small federal research agency in the 1930s to become the most significant biomedical research organization in the world by 1970 (Lee and Benjamin, 1993, p. 410).

Because of the rapid growth of scientific research, physicians found it necessary to specialize to have a focused concentration of knowledge. By the mid-1960s approximately 80% of the U.S. physicians had become specialists (Torrens, 1993, p. 9). As physician specialization increased, so did the demand for advanced technology. Physicians and hospital administrators, who wanted to be perceived as innovators, and thus gain a competitive edge, drove some of that demand. However, the American public also believed that more technology was important and should be used to eradicate deadly diseases (McManus and Pohl, 1994, p. 334). As a result, enormous sums of money were appropriated for the development of technology. This significant infusion of money contributed to rising health care costs while simultaneously stimulating major advancements throughout the health care field. For example, the discovery of tranquilizers resulted in the deinstitutionalization of psychiatric patients through the introduction of community mental health centers in the 1950s.

Medicare and Medicaid, two large federal programs that provide funding for health care services (to people aged 65 and older as well as the permanently disabled, those with end-stage renal disease, and the poor), were passed in 1965 (Raffel and Raffel, 1989). The inception of both Medicare and Medicaid increased the federal government's share of the costs of medical care, but also increased access to hospital care for the poor through Medicaid funding (Aday and Anderson, 1981) and eased Medicare recipients' worries about obtaining health care.

All the above conditions ushered in the next (fourth) stage, which has been characterized as a time of cost containment, restricted resources, and restructuring of delivery systems through incremental efforts by both the public and private sectors. Other countries have had similar patterns of rising health care spending, but took different approaches to correct the problem. For example, the German and Dutch health care systems experienced similar high increases in health care spending in the early 1970s but "through government intervention imposed a series of tight sector-specific expenditure controls," which proved effective (Altman and Wallack, 1996, p. 2).

The passage of federal legislation to reverse the spiral of health care spending in the United States was not as successful. One particular example, the National Health Planning and Resources Development Act of 1974, was introduced to contain community health care costs through a two-tier regulatory structure. It was thought that by requiring hospital administration to use a review mechanism, known as Certificate of Need (CON), unnecessary duplication of health services and costly technology could be avoided (McManus and Pohl, 1994). This rational approach, instituted at the federal level but conducted at the community level by health providers, consumers, and public officials, failed because of inadequate funding and political controversy.

The federal government was more successful with the passage of the Health Maintenance Organization (HMO) Act in 1973. HMOs were established to provide comprehensive health services to voluntarily enrolled populations in exchange for a prepaid, usually capitated, fee. Government's costs could be controlled by shifting the risk arising from increased costs (due to heavy utilization of services) from the government to the providers of health services. The growth of HMOs was gradual until employers realized that employee enrollment in HMOs would be a benefit by limiting what employers would have to pay (Raffel and Raffel, 1989, pp. 75–76).

B. A Description of the Hospital Subsystem

The hospital domain of the U.S. health care system is complex, diverse, and still evolving. Hospitals currently are classified as community hospitals or noncommunity hospitals. Community hospitals are all short term (less than 30 days' stay), including nonfederal hospitals, investor-owned, or not-for-profit, and offer general and other special services (such as orthopedics or obstetrics). Noncommunity hospitals are long term and include the following: psychiatric hospitals; tuberculosis and other respiratory disease hospitals; chronic disease hospitals; and hospitals that care for persons who are mentally retarded, or are alcohol or chemically dependent.

Table 2 details the number of hospitals in the United States by ownership, the number of beds, the number of admissions, average lengths of stay (ALOS), and the number of outpatient visits for the years 1985 and 1995. The hospital data in Table 2 summarize the dramatic changes that have occurred throughout the hospital sector in the United States during the past decade.

There were 6291 hospitals in the United States in 1995, which included community and noncommunity hospitals. Of the total number, most hospitals are community hospitals (5194), providing a wide range of medical, surgical, obstetrics, or pediatric services. These facilities are identified in Table 2 as investor-owned, nongovernmental, not-for-profit, and state/local government hospitals. These hospitals have experienced a decline of 9.4% since 1985 with 12.8% fewer beds. The

Table 2 U.S. Hospital Data for 1985 and 1995

		Number of hospitals	Number of beds (in thousands)	Admissions (in thousands)	Average lengths of stay (in days)	Outpatient visits (in thousands)
Total beds	1985	6872	1318	36,304	—	282,140
	1995	6291	1081	33,282	—	483,195
Investor-owned hospitals	1985	805	104	3,242	6.1	12,378
	1995	752	106	3,428	5.8	31,940
Nongovernment, nonprofit community hospitals	1985	3349	707	24,179	7.2	158,953
	1995	3092	610	22,557	6.4	303,851
State/local, government community hospitals	1985	1578	189	6,028	7.2	47,386
	1995	1350	157	4,961	7.4	78,554

Source: American Hospital Association. *Hospital Statistics, 1996–1997 Edition*. Chicago: AHA, 1996.

number of patients admitted to community hospitals dropped 7.5% between 1985 and 1995. However, a positive change occurred in the number of community hospital outpatient visits; an 89.4% increase between 1985 and 1995 reflected the move toward more cost-effective delivery of health services [AHA, Hospital Statistics (1996–1997), p. xxvii]. In the past decade, the number of hospitals, beds, and admissions all declined, while outpatient visits increased dramatically.

Investor-owned hospitals represent approximately 12% of all U.S. hospitals and 14.5% of the community hospitals. The presence of investor-owned hospitals has influenced the overall delivery of health care services in the United States because of their strong business management emphasis. Other countries, such as Japan, where law prohibits investor-owned, for-profit hospitals (Graig, 1993), or the Netherlands, where all hospitals are not-for-profit institutions, have not experienced this business management trend. What has been most significant about the investor-owned hospitals' management is their aggressive acquisition of other hospitals to form larger multihospital corporations (Haglund and Dowling, 1993).

The nonfederal, but government-owned hospitals are the state and local government hospitals. State hospitals usually include three types: the state medical school hospitals, those hospitals that are part of the criminal justice system, and in some states, hospitals that serve the poor. Local government hospitals are either large urban facilities (now serving both poor and private patients) or hospitals serving a defined government district, such as a county (Raffel and Raffel, 1989, pp. 156–157).

There were 299 federal government hospitals in 1995 (included in the total number of U.S. hospitals in Table 2). Federal hospitals, which provide services to military personnel, Native Americans, and veterans, complement the private sector of the U.S. hospital industry. For example, the Veterans Administration (VA) hospitals are part of the Veterans Healthcare System, one of the largest integrated health care systems in the United States with 173 hospitals (Kizer, 1997). The VA recently reorganized its system to cope with declining funds and an older, sicker patient population; this reorganization was achieved by establishing 22 networks (known as Veterans Integrated Services Networks), which function as integrated delivery systems (Halverson et al., 1997, p. 404).

Average lengths of stay in the United States reflect what has occurred worldwide. Table 3 provides a comparison between 1980 and 1992 of the average length of stay (ALOS) in acute-care hospitals of 10 countries. The trend has been toward lower lengths of stay in acute-care hospitals. Australia and the United States had the lowest ALOS of the identified countries in 1980. However, it is notable that even though the ALOS of all countries declined from 1980 to 1992, ALOS for Australia, Denmark, and Sweden dropped to lower rates than that of the United States.

During the past 150 years the delivery of health care services within the United States has come full circle. Health care moved from the community into

Table 3 Average Length of Stay in
Acute-Care Hospitals, 1980 and 1992

	Days	
	1980	1992
Australia	7.6	5.2[a]
Austria	14.5	9.6
Canada		
Denmark	9.1	6.3
Finland		
Greece	10.3	7.4[a]
Iceland		
Italy		
Luxembourg	13.	10.3
Japan		
New Zealand		
Norway	10.9	7.8[a]
Portugal	13.6[b]	9.3[a]
Sweden	8.6	6.0
Switzerland	15.5	12.1
Turkey		
United States	7.6	7.2[a]

[a] 1991.
[b] 1982.
Source: *OECD Health Data* (1993) and
chapters 6 et seq. in *The Reform of Health
Care Systems: A Review of Seventeen OECD
Countries*, 1994.

hospitals during the mid-1800s and became more technical, impersonal, and costly with each decade. It is apparent now that health care is moving away from hospitals toward lower-cost alternatives in the community (Gillies et al., 1997, p. 320). The U.S. health care system has always been loosely structured, but recent organizational restructuring has facilitated the reduction of hospital utilization. As noted by Longest (1998), "the healthcare industry is changing from a past in which almost all healthcare organizations were organized independently to a future in which many, perhaps most, healthcare organizations will be structurally integrated with others" (p. 116).

The uncertainty of today's environment is pressuring hospital administrators to consider alliances and integration into a continuum of care model whereby economies of scale and more effective outcomes can be achieved. This current model of service delivery is known as an integrated delivery system (IDS). As of 1995, 27.7% of community hospitals became part of health care networks. This was an increase of 6% from 1994. The greatest network participation has been in the Mid-Atlantic and East-South-Central part of the United States, the lowest in the Pacific states and New England area (AHA, 1997, p. xxiv). The American Hospital Association (AHA) defined network as ''a group of hospitals, physicians, other providers, insurers and/or community agencies that work together to deliver a broad spectrum of services to their community'' (p. xxiv).

Networks can be considered integrated delivery systems when vertical integration and an insurance product are present in the ''system,'' since both components are essential in a definition of an IDS (Shortell et al., 1993; Stahl, 1995; Young and Barrett, 1997). Furthermore, the truly integrated delivery system, according to Anderson (1998), is one that has a unifying concept and culture; defined organizational and administrative structures; assets and finances that are integrated; synergism; and a continued responsiveness to the marketplace (p. 31). Young and Barrett (1997) indicated that for hospitals to be considered successful as part of an IDS, a refocus from acute to primary care must occur; this might prove difficult because of hospitals' entrenched interests to deliver mainly acute-care services.

C. A Description of Long-Term Care Services

There is no single structure for long-term care (LTC) in the United States. In fact, a variety of health facilities attempt to deliver long-term health care services, including some hospitals. LTC has become an important component of the U.S. health system, owing to the dramatic increase in life expectancy and modern technology that has allowed persons with life-threatening disabilities (who might have died in earlier decades) to live longer and better. LTC services are those health and social services provided over an extended period to people with chronic or functional disabilities (Evashwick, 1996, p. 4). These individuals might receive services while living in institutions or in their homes. It has been said that friends and families supplemented by different health care organizations provide much of the informal LTC in the United States (Doty et al., 1996, p. 130). However, since fewer than 15% of older persons live with or near their children, unlike Asian countries where multigeneration family households have been more common (Martin, 1988), the need for optional long-term health services has led to utilization of formal LTC alternatives. These formal types of support include nursing homes and community-based care such as home health agencies, adult day care, and assisted living facilities (ALFs).

1. Nursing Homes

Nursing homes include two types: those that provide some personal care, but not licensed nursing services (e.g., residential care facilities), and those that offer skilled nursing services 24 hr a day (e.g., skilled nursing facilities) (Wallace et al., 1996, p. 181). Data pertaining to skilled nursing facilities bear further discussion.

There are 16,995 skilled nursing facilities in the United States, which have an 83% occupancy rate (HCFA's Online Survey, March 1997). Of these facilities, 52% are owned or leased by multifacility organizations; the remainder are individually owned and operated. The growth of for-profit skilled nursing facilities has been significant since the introduction of the government reimbursement programs of Medicare and Medicaid in 1965. Currently it is estimated that 66% of skilled nursing facilities are for-profit, with most profits coming from the private-pay residents and some from those who are approved for Medicare services. Of the remaining skilled nursing facilities, 27% are nonprofit and 7% are government facilities (HCFA's Online Survey, March 1997). Residents of skilled nursing facilities currently number about 1.5 million persons, but the demand for services is predicted to grow by almost 30% in the next decade, representing an increase of 7–9 million older people (Yeh, 1996). More than 70% of the residents in nursing homes (and residential care facilities) are women, two-thirds of whom are divorced or widowed (Lair and Lefkowitz, 1990).

To qualify for skilled nursing facility services that would be reimbursed by Medicare, residents must have been hospitalized for at least 3 days, have entered a Medicare-approved facility usually within 30 days after hospital discharge, and require skilled nursing or skilled rehabilitation services (Burwell et al., 1996, p. 200). Sure restrictive Medicare criteria have limited the number of short-term admissions to nursing homes.

Long-term services, however, often become a necessity and increase as individuals age, to the point that one of every two individuals will be admitted to a nursing home during his or her lifetime (Kemper and Murtaugh, 1991). When funding for nursing home services is available from other sources (such as private insurance, Medicaid, or out-of-pocket funds), older persons will seek admission to nursing homes usually because the level of support they require can no longer be provided in their home setting. Typical nursing home services include basic services (such as nursing care, supervision of medications, assistance with activities of daily living, or recreation and social services); special services (such as infusion nutrition or ventilator care); and special programs such as adult day care (Evashwick and Langdon, 1996, p. 48).

Federal, state, and private regulations have improved how nursing homes are operated and evaluated. State requirements must be met for nursing homes to be licensed; federal government requirements for Medicare and Medicaid must be met for certification and, thus, eligibility to receive either Medicare or Medicaid reimbursements. The 1987 Nursing Home Reform Act, incorporated into the Omnibus Budget Reconciliation Act of 1987, brought about significant improvement. It did so by changing evaluation of nursing home services from a focus on physical and task criteria to criteria that focused on care outcomes, residents' feelings, and the caring process (Evashwick, 1999, p. 316).

In summary, nursing homes are recognized as a necessary and important link in the integrated health care system of the United States, for without them, a continuum of care would not be feasible. Yet it is further evident that at least 15% of nursing home residents could be cared for at lower levels of care by other organizations, such as home health agencies (Spector et al., 1996).

2. Home Health Services

Home health services have become an encouraging option for many older Americans, younger people with physical or developmental disabilities, and those individuals with chronic diseases that require long-term care. Home health services have helped individuals who lack private health insurance, who would not qualify for Medicare or Medicaid coverage for nursing home services, or who prefer not to depend on family or friends. The advantages of home health services, therefore, are twofold: individuals remain in their familiar home setting while receiving essential services but at lower cost for those services.

Home care services are of four types in the United States: personal care, such as homemaking services; high-tech services, such as parenteral nutrition and intravenous therapies; palliative care, such as hospice services; and skilled nursing services (Hughes, 1996). All care is provided under the direction of the client's physician because home health personnel must work under a physician's order. Home health personnel include registered nurses, licensed practical nurses, home health aides, certified nursing assistants, homemakers, social workers, and licensed therapists such as those in occupational, physical, or respiratory therapy. Nearly 6 million persons used home health services in 1987 (Altman and Walden, 1993), and 75% were clients aged 65 years or older, with an average age of 70 years (Sultz and Young, 1997, p. 219).

The major organization providing home health services is the home health agency, which can be for-profit or private nonprofit. Other organizations providing home health services are public health departments, some hospitals, and visiting nurse associations. An additional classification is the Medicare-certified home health agency; this agency has eligibility requirements, just as a Medicare skilled nursing facility does. Medicare-certified home health agencies increased from about 2900 in the 1980s to 9120 agencies in 1995 (Evashwick, 1998, p. 320). Specifically, patients of a Medicare-certified home health agency must be homebound; require short-term, intermittent nursing care or rehabilitative therapies prescribed by a physician; but be capable of improvement (Evashwick, 1999, p. 320).

The majority of these patients are older and referred directly from hospitals. Home health agencies that deliver primarily homemaker or nonclinical support services, and are not certified to receive Medicare reimbursement, are known as private home health agencies. However, these agencies do provide high-tech and palliative services (just as Medicare-certified agencies do), but only the private agencies provide 24-hr nursing care (Evashwick, 1998). Private home health patients tend to be of a wider age range with more varied health problems than those served by the Medicare-certified agencies. Both Medicare-certified and private home health agencies have increased rapidly in number from a total of 1100 in 1963 to more than 12,000 agencies in 1993 (Hughes, 1996, p. 63). Most of the growth can be attributed to the entry of private for-profit agencies after Medicare reimbursement became available to the for-profit sector; their numbers increased from zero in 1967, to more than 400 in mid-1980s, to 2000 by mid-1990s (Sultz and Young, 1997, p. 220).

3. Adult Day Care

Adult day care evolved out of social concern for the general welfare of older people during the 1960s, but grew slowly due to the absence of a funding base or supportive national policies (Sultz and Young, 1997, pp. 216–217). Adult day care programs are provided during the daytime in a local community facility. The services consist of medical supervision, socialization, personal care assistance, some rehabilitation services, nutritious meals, and transportation. These programs promote the independence of their older clients through the participation in the day program as they continue to live at home; the family caregivers benefit, also, by having the freedom to continue their work or to have respite time. It is estimated that by the mid-1990s approximately 3000 day care centers had been established throughout the United States (Cox and Reifler, 1994).

Some of the centers serve only clients with special needs such as those individuals diagnosed with Alzheimer's disease, mental retardation, blindness, or developmental disorders. Other centers, known as medical model adult day care centers, will serve clients who are physically dependent, free of mental impairments, elderly, and white (Cefalu and Heuser, 1993). Adult day care centers that are based on the social model will serve mostly women who are physically independent, but might have some mental impairment. In general, the majority of the adult day care center clients use the facilities for an indefinite period of time, while others will attend during recovery from an acute illness or injury.

Licensure and certification ensure that minimal standards are followed to safeguard the clients' welfare. State laws regulate most adult day care centers, but licensing is not required in all states. There is no federal certification or national accreditation (National Institute on Adult Daycare, 1994–1995). The cost of day care will vary, depending on the geographical location and the services provided; the range is between $25 and $65 per day (Cefalu and Heuser, 1993, p. 723).

Medicare does not pay for adult day care, but Medicaid is the major payer, followed by fees paid by clients and family (Evashwick, 1999, p. 327).

4. Assisted Living Facilities

A more recent development in LTC services is the assisted living facility (ALF). These facilities provide residents with a small apartment, "meals, housekeeping, social services, limited transportation, and personal assistance" (Evashwick, 1998, p. 328). These facilities are of a lower cost with fewer health personnel than a nursing home and offer a more home-like environment. Neither Medicare nor Medicaid regulates the ALF, but some are licensed by states. It is estimated that there are approximately 30,000 facilities, serving at least 1.5 million residents (Assisted Living Federation of America, 1996).

The ALF evolved as part of the concept of the continuing care retirement community (CCRC), which requires a lifetime commitment. Specifically, health services are prepaid and guaranteed for life by the CCRCs through the use of an insurance-based model. The clients pay a substantial initial entrance fee and a continuing monthly fee; in addition, they must sign over their Medicare benefits (Sultz and Young, 1997, pp. 223–224).

D. Health Care Personnel

Health administrators, physicians, and nurses, in addition to many other health care personnel, have had a significant impact on the US health care system. Since this system is a service-oriented industry, the values, skills, and education of its personnel greatly affect the quality and cost of the health services they provide. As demand for more specialized and high-tech health services grew along with an aging population, so, too, did the number and types of health personnel. Approximately 9.5 million people are employed in health care throughout the United States in about 400 job titles (Mick, 1999, p. 404).

1. Health Services Administrators

Traditionally, physicians dominated most of the managerial as well as clinical decisions affecting patient care in this country. But as hospitals became larger and more complex, the health care administration profession evolved in the United States to improve the management of these organizations. The necessity for well-trained individuals to direct and oversee the hospitals culminated in the implementation in 1934 of the first formal education program, the University of Chicago's Graduate Program in Hospital Administration (Davis, 1984). Although this first program was placed within the School of Business, the program's founders stated that the essential objective of hospital administration was "quality medical care for the public as opposed to the business of institutional management'' (Filerman, 1984). This emphasis on individuals who were health-oriented and not just business administration-oriented, underscored ''the complex nature of the health sector and the historical context within which the agencies and health professions operate'' (Raffel and Raffel, 1989, p. 121).

The dual emphasis of a health *and* business orientation remains as an important characteristic of most health administration programs today. Students received their academic preparation in Hospital Administration Graduate Programs, until the early 1970s; then the name of the programs changed in recognition of the diversity of organizations and agencies employing health administrators. Graduate programs can seek accreditation by the Accrediting Commission on Education for Health Services Administration (ACEHSA), which ensures that accredited programs have met numerous criteria, including the provision of a common core of knowledge, typically taught during 2 years of academic courses and internships. There were 66 master-degreed programs accredited in 1998 (ACEHSA, 1999, http://www.aupha.org). Graduates of master-degreed programs are employed in key positions in both public and private organizations that are involved in policymaking, financing, evaluating, and delivering health services. Many graduate programs offer a doctoral-degree program to prepare graduates as health researchers, policymakers, university faculty, and, recently, administrators of large networks or corporations; however, low enrollments in these programs have resulted in a higher demand than can be supplied (*Health Professions Education for the Future*, 1993, p. 60).

Health administration baccalaureate programs were established in the late 1960s and early 1970s to meet the demand for ''middle-level managers.'' These programs grew rapidly, matching the expansion of managerial positions in health care facilities. There are no reliable data pertaining to the current number of baccalaureate programs offering health administration programs, since many are located in small colleges as well as universities. Baccalaureate programs are not accredited, but can seek ''affiliation'' with the Association of University Programs in Health Administration.

Graduates of either master or baccalaureate degree programs can be identified by different titles, such as health care managers, hospital administrators, nursing home administrators, or health administrators. Administrators and managers who are employed in hospitals are not licensed; however, many seek membership with the American College of Healthcare Executives (ACHE). Through its efforts ACHE promotes the profession's values and standards of practice and ''works toward its goal of improving the health status of society by advancing healthcare management excellence'' (http://www.ache.org). On the other hand, nursing home administrators have been licensed since the 1960s, with the states having the primary responsibility for specifying minimum qualifications for licensure. Since 1987, the bachelor's degree is the minimum national standard for licensure, as established by the Omnibus Budget Reconciliation Act (Singh et al., 1997).

2. Physicians

From the time this country's first physicians graduated in 1768 at the College of Philadelphia (later, University of Pennsylvania), until the publication of the Flexner Report in 1912, physician education and practice were variable. During the 1800s, some physicians in the United States were educated in small, ill-equipped schools while others went abroad to train in well-established schools in Scotland, England, France, or Germany. The length of training as well as the selection of courses that were taught differed from school to school. Apprenticeship practices varied, and even licensure was rare (Raffel and Raffel, 1989).

The Flexner Report improved the curriculum and how the content was to be taught. A 4-year scientific program of university study along with clinical training became the widely accepted model for contemporary medical education. The Flexner Report caused the closure of many inadequate schools and the establishment of state laws that required ''graduation from a medical school accredited by the American Medical Association as a basis for a license to practice medicine'' (Dowling, 1998, p. 265).

Enormous expansion of medical education occurred after World War II owing to perceptions of a serious shortage, public demands for more services, and continuing technological innovations. Medical schools increased from 88 (in 1965) to 125 schools (in 1995) with a concurrent increase in the number of physician graduates, from 7574 to 16,029 (Mick, 1999, p. 408). The percentage of women and minority applicants had increased as well. For women, the percentage increase was from 9.6% of total students in 1970 to 41.8% in 1995, and for minorities, from 8.8% to 34.1% (Mick, 1999, pp. 416–417). Three factors contributed to these increases:

1. The passage of antidiscriminatory legislation (the 1964 Civil Rights Act and Title IX of the Education Amendments of 1972),
2. An equal opportunity resolution passed by the Association of American Medical Colleges in 1970, and
3. Changing public attitudes toward women and minorities and their roles in society (Braslow and Heins, 1981).

Financial support for medical education was derived from public funds through federal and state student loans, state-supported medical schools, federal health education programs, and Medicare payments for graduate medical school education in teaching hospitals, referred to as medical residency programs (*The Reform of Health Care Systems*, 1994). Until recently, federal funding to medical residency programs amounted to approximately $9 billion a year (Terhune, 1998), but beginning in 1999, federal funds for medical residents will amount to 30% less, or a decrease of $12.2 billion to hospitals.

The typical premedical educational program is broad-based at the undergraduate level, consisting of basic sciences and a variety of other courses terminating with a baccalaureate degree. Upon successful completion of the premedical program, students apply to a medical school program that is approximately 4 years in duration, and then spend 3–8 years of residency training in a given specialty.

There were approximately 738,000 physicians in 1996, or one physician per 360 persons (American Medical Association, 1998, p. 34). Even though there has been growth in primary care specialties (general practice, family practice, general internal medicine, and general pediatrics), other specialty groups continue to expand. In 1995 only 27% of physicians, or about 205,000 physicians, were in primary care specialties. Mick (1999) further estimated that between 1986 and the year 2000 "whereas primary care will increase by 22%, other specialties will enjoy greater growth—the specialties of internal medicine, 50%; general surgery and surgical subspecialties, 27%; and all other specialties, 39%" (p. 412). In addition to the growth of specialists in medicine is the continued influx of foreign-trained physicians. Twenty-three percent (139,086) of the total active physicians in 1992 were foreign-trained; many of these physicians continue to practice in geographical locations, in employment settings, and in specialties avoided by physicians trained in the United States (Mick, 1999).

In theory, consumers have free choice in selecting their general practitioner or specialist; however, with the advent of managed care, some restrictions now limit the number of encounters as well as the preference of physician, owing to the "gatekeeper" concept of the HMOs. At the same time, all physicians who practice in managed care arrangements have lost some of their autonomy (e.g., discounted fee schedules and less utilization review control) (Raffel and Raffel, 1989, p. 78).

3. Registered Nurses

Nurses represent the largest occupational group working in the health care system. As of 1995, it was estimated that there were 2.1 million active registered nurses (Bureau of the Census, 1997, p. 123). Fewer than 7% of nurses were men and less than 17% were of different minorities (*Health Professions Education for the Future*, 1993, p. 84). As of 1993, there were more than 1400 nursing education programs preparing students to become nurses (*Health Professions Education for the Future*, 1993, p. 84). Nurses are educated primarily in two types of educational programs: university programs and, since the mid-1950s, community college (2-year programs). A third type of program, the hospital diploma school of nursing, is being phased out; only 9% of new nursing students in 1991 were in diploma programs (Mick, 1999, p. 427). All three programs require a clinical component in health care facilities plus academic course work.

Following completion of the basic nursing program, graduates of the three programs must successfully pass the same state-licensing examination to attain registered nurse status. All program graduates initially have the same roles and responsibilities along with similar salary, but opportunities for advancement to leadership positions occur more often and sooner for those with baccalaureate degrees. Baccalaureate-degree nurses may enter one of the 200 graduate programs to work toward a master's degree that would prepare them for supervision or nurse practitioner roles, or continue on into doctoral programs to pursue careers in research and/or teaching. The National League of Nursing is the accrediting body for the nursing programs.

Nurses' skills and knowledge have kept pace with the technological and organizational changes in the health sector; more autonomy in clinical decision making is happening, especially with the emergence of the nurse practitioner role. But physicians as well as the general public lag in their perceptions of nurses as independent practitioners. Although registered nurses have strength in numbers (the largest group of health professionals), one-third work part-time and many have traditional family responsibilities as spouses and/or parents that divert their energies away from promoting a unified profession. These conditions have resulted in nurses still having a secondary role behind physicians with much lower salaries. However, opportunities for the individual nurse are encouraging, as employment positions continue to evolve in ambulatory care settings, in community/ public health, and in regulatory or policymaking facilities (Mick, 1999).

4. Pharmacists

The traditional role of the pharmacist was that of preparing drug products and filling prescriptions. As of the 1980s, their role expanded to include managerial and financial aspects of working in a retail business, serving as an expert about drug interaction, advising clients and patients about generic drug substitution, and advising physicians and clients about drug dosage and side effects (Sultz and Young, 1997, p. 147).

Pharmacists are licensed health care professionals who have graduated from an accredited college of pharmacy, completed an internship with a licensed pharmacist, and passed a state exam (U.S. Department of Labor, April 1994). The pharmacy curriculum requires at least 5 years of university study to earn a Bachelor of Science degree in pharmacy or at least 6 years to earn a Doctor of Pharmacy degree (Sultz and Young, 1997, p. 147). The Doctor of Pharmacy degree allows the pharmacist to pursue research, administrative, and teaching positions beyond the traditional clinical role. Currently, there are 75 colleges of pharmacy in the United States (Sultz and Young, 1997). Female enrollment in pharmacy schools was about 30% in the 1970s, but increased dramatically to 63% of enrollees in the 1990s. A somewhat lower trend was noted with minorities' enrollment, which increased from 12% in the 1980s to 21% in the early 1990s (Mick, 1999, p. 428).

Community pharmacies, most of which are owned by large drugstore chains, employ about 60% of all pharmacists. Twenty-five percent are employed in hospitals and the balance work in a variety of settings such as nursing homes, health maintenance organizations, or governmental facilities (U.S. Department of Labor, 1994, p. 169). There are twice as many pharmacists per capita in the United States as there are in Great Britain, where the typical pharmacist dispenses only medications (Jonas, 1998, p. 42).

5. Physician Assistants and Nurse Practitioners

Two health professions that emerged during the 1960s were physician assistants (PAs) and nurse practitioners (NPs). The reason for their development was to augment the inadequate supply of physicians in mostly rural communities through utilization of specially prepared nurses and former military corpsmen. Although PAs and NPs appear interchangeable in their practice capabilities, each is distinct from the other because of their different professional focus and educational preparation.

The PA is a licensed health professional who works *with* physician supervision to perform medical diagnosis and therapeutic functions. PAs may evaluate, monitor, diagnose acute and chronic illnesses, perform routine therapeutic procedures, develop treatment plans, and refer patients when necessary. Many states grant prescription-writing privileges to PAs (Jones and Cawley, 1994, p. 1271). To become licensed, PAs must graduate from an accredited PA bachelor or master degree program and pass the national certifying examination that is administered by the National Commission on Certification of Physician Assistants (Rodican, 1998). Certification is required before licensure.

Most PA programs were established by schools of medicine and offer a 4-year baccalaureate degree. The typical curriculum of study includes the basic sciences, introduction to clinical studies, and supervised clinical instruction. Programs differ in the amount of time devoted to each segment and the design of the clinical component (Oliver, 1993, p. 87). Innovations in PA curricula include specific content on the health and medical problems of disadvantaged populations and linkages with community/migrant health centers, rural health clinics, and other primary health care facilities (Jones and Cawley, 1994, p. 1267). As of 1997, there were 98 accredited and provisionally accredited PA programs in the United States (Rodican, 1998, p. xi).

PAs were mostly employed in primary care settings for about a decade, but the number of PAs in primary care specialties has fallen steadily over the past 15 years (Cawley, 1993, pp. 24–25). PAs now practice in a variety of areas including emergency medicine, occupational medicine, psychiatry, surgery, and obstetrics and gynecology. Most PAs are salaried employees, but many also are self-employed. Women now number more than half of all newly graduated PAs. Approximately 91% of all PAs are white, non-Hispanic (Mick, 1999, p. 430).

NPs are registered nurses who have completed a master's degree in nursing and who are certified in a specialty area (Sultz and Young, 1997, p. 144). They are certified by states for advanced or expanded practice and upon successful completion of an examination, will attain national certification. There were some 48,200 NPs in the United States as of 1992 (Mick, 1999, p. 432). NPs provide health promotion activities, order laboratory tests, prescribe limited medications in more than 40 states, obtain health histories, manage therapeutic plans of care for acute and chronically ill patients, counsel, and assess health status (Abdellah, 1982). NPs are employed mainly in the areas of adult medicine, pediatrics, women's health, student health, and geriatrics.

NP master's programs of study range from 10 to 21 months (Sultz and Young, 1997, p. 144). There were 212 NP educational programs in the early 1990s. The curricula of the NP programs allow students to concentrate on certain specialty areas such as medical surgical practice, maternal and child specialties, or other specialties in mental health, community health, and gerontological specialties. Ryan (1993) reported that "the direct costs of education for NPs are approximately one-fifth of those for physicians. . . . Thus, several NPs could be trained for the cost of educating one physician" (p. 42).

Despite an apparent need for their services, both PAs and NPs initially encountered physician opposition and legal restrictions, although these conditions were more typical of NPs. NPs resisted physician supervision of their clinical practice because NPs are separately licensed practitioners who do not require physician involvement in their clinical practice. Nurse practice acts were challenged state by state, which led to gradual acceptance of a national certification by 1975 (Sultz and Young, 1997, p. 143), but physician acceptance of NPs remains limited.

Another issue related to NP practice pertains to uncertain third-party reimbursement for NP services. Federal law requires direct Medicaid reimbursement of certain NP categories, whether or not the NP is under direct supervision. Private health insurers have been reluctant to reimburse NP services, so coverage is optional (Mick, 1999, p. 431).

Studies were conducted in the late 1980s and early 1990s to measure patient satisfaction with PA and NP clinical practice. The 1986 study concluded that the services provided by PAs and NPs were of equivalent quality to physician services (U.S. Congress, 1986). Feldman et al. (1987) reported similar findings with the technical quality of services provided by NPs, in addition to better interpersonal skills of NPs and equivalent or better patient outcomes than those attained by physicians. Jones and Cawley (1994) indicated that PAs, too, managed "patient problems at physician-equivalent levels of patient satisfaction and quality of care" (p. 1269). In summary, the demand for PAs and NPs is increasing because the general public has indicated a willingness to receive more health care from PAs and NPs, and managed care plans want practitioners who emphasize primary care, prevention, and cost-effective services.

6. Conclusion Regarding Health Personnel

Overall, the demand for health services will be significantly affected in the next decade by changes associated with demographic trends of the United States, different disease patterns evolving, technology requirements, managed care influences, and possible health care reform. Because health care is labor intensive, the pool of eight million health care personnel is bound to increase in response to the growing demands for health services but with some shift in the level or type of services provided and a concurrent shift in the health professionals delivering those services. Health policies regarding the education, employment, and reimbursement of health care professionals have been challenged, as economic concerns about the delivery of health care became paramount. Many of the decisions regarding the structure of a future health care workforce in the United States may be left to the unpredictable influences of supply and demand, and not to influences that promote access and quality of care.

E. Financing the U.S. Health Care System

Health care costs have risen dramatically in all industrialized countries, but have been of particular concern in the United States since the 1980s, and were a major issue in recent national elections. This country has invested significantly in its health care, about $989 billion, or 13.6% of its gross domestic product (GDP) in 1995 (Levit et al., 1996, pp. 178–214), and $1 trillion by the end of 1998. These figures indicate that the United States consistently spent more on health care as a share of GDP than any other country (*The Reform of Health Care Systems*, 1994, p. 39).

Financing the health care services occurs through a private-public system of reimbursement. Since implementation of the Medicare and Medicaid programs in 1966, total health care spending by the public sector increased to 42% in 1990 (*The Reform of Health Care Systems*, 1994, p. 321) and continued upward to 46% in 1995. Specifically, Medicare finances 19% of the nation's health dollar, followed by Medicaid (14%) and other governmental (state and local) programs (13%) (Levit et al., 1996, p. 200). Payroll taxes and retiree supplemental insurance premiums cover two-thirds of Medicare expenditures with the balance from federal monies, while the states pay for less than half of their Medicaid programs after receiving federal matching grants.

1. Funding Hospitals

Hospital reimbursement is funded predominantly (60%) by Medicare, other government programs, and Medicaid (Koch, 1999, p. 117). In an attempt to limit the growth in what the federal government had to pay for inpatient hospital services, the Tax Equity and Fiscal Responsibility Act (TEFRA) was passed in 1982. It successfully converted Medicare reimbursement for hospital services from a retrospective system to a prospective payment system (PPS) based on diagnosis-related groups (DRGs). Hospitals now are reimbursed a flat fee for all the hospital services provided for a particular diagnosis, regardless of the actual costs incurred. Conversion to PPS has resulted in major reorganization in the delivery of hospital services and initiated the movement toward integrated delivery systems described earlier (Newscomer et al., 1985).

2. Private Financing

Private financing covers 54% of all health care expenditures, with private health insurance providing 31% of the financing, direct (out-of-pocket) payment 19%, and other private funds (mostly philanthropy) 4% (Levit et al., 1996, p. 200). About 70% of the U.S. population were covered by private health insurance in 1995, and most of these individuals (about 85%) were insured through work-related insurance plans as benefits (U.S. Bureau of the Census, 1996). The pattern of private health insurance enrollments in the United States steadily changed from 1975 to 1994, as more employers offered insurer options to their employees. Enrollments declined in the commercial insurers (from 50 to 30%) and in the Blue Cross/Blue Shield Plans (from 43 to 26%), but increased in health maintenance organizations (HMOs) or managed care plans (7–44%) (*Source Book of Health Insurance Data, 1996* (1997, p. 41)).

Numerous problems that developed since the introduction of the HMOs, such as interference with physicians' treatment decisions, quality concerns, restricted provider choice, etc., have resulted in mixed reviews of HMO effectiveness and the subsequent development of other reimbursement models, namely preferred provider organizations (PPOs) and point-of-service (POS) networks. Many managed care health plans have diversified to provide a combination of HMO, PPO, and POS options. PPOs, an offspring of HMOs, selectively contract with physicians and hospitals to provide services at a discounted price schedule, in exchange for securing a share of the patient market, but with no emphasis on coordination of care. In return, PPO enrollees have guaranteed lower coinsurance rates but more provider choice when enrollees select physicians who have agreed to the discounted price. If a nonpreferred provider were selected, the PPO would reimburse the patient only at 80–90% of the charge, and the patient would pay the balance (Raffel and Raffel, 1989, p. 78). The PPOs are not insurers and, generally, do not assume any financial risk for arranging health care services;

such risk is assumed by self-insured employers or by another underwriter. In contrast, the POS networks combine HMO features and the selection of nonpreferred providers, with economic incentives for using the POS providers (for example, a fixed copayment instead of a coinsurance rate of 10–30%) (Dial, Hatch, Newman, and Sullivan, 1997, p. 98)

3. Overall Health Care Expenditures

Total health care spending in the United States in 1995 was allocated to five categories. Hospital services had the largest share of the U.S. health care budget (36%), followed by 25% for other personal health care (for home health care, dental services, drugs, etc.). Physician services accounted for 20%, other spending costs (for public health services, construction, and research) were 11%, and finally, 8% for nursing home services (Levit et al., 1996, p. 200).

The average cost of nursing home services ranged from $2000 to $4000 per month in 1990 (Evashwick, 1993, p. 191), exceeding the income of many older people. Only 23% of nursing home reimbursements are derived from private payment (HCFA's Online Survey, March 1997), even though 40% of the people who are admitted to nursing homes pay privately. Many residents soon deplete their own resources and must obtain financial assistance from the Medicaid program (Wallace et al., 1996). Currently Medicaid reimburses $85.05 per diem and accounts for 68% of all nursing home reimbursement (HCFA's Online Survey, March 1997). This heavy dependence on state Medicaid payments has resulted in a financial burden for state budgets, causing many states to consider health care reform to reduce nursing home costs (Paul-Shaheen, 1998; Neubauer, 1993; Kane et al., 1998).

Until recently, Medicare-certified nursing homes were paid using a cost-reimbursement method, but passage of the Balanced Budget Act of 1997 brought about a dramatic change. The Balanced Budget Act of 1997 instituted a prospective payment system, using "resource utilization groups" (RUGs) rather than the "diagnostic-related groups" (DRGs), which the Health Care Financing Administration introduced in the early eighties for hospitals (O'Sullivan et al., 1997). The prospective payment system (PPS) per diem rate pays a daily charge based on the patient's condition and health care needs classified into 44 categories. Such a dramatic change in reimbursement requires implementation in stages. So, during 1998 (the first year) a facility would receive 75% of the facility-based reimbursement rate of 1995 along with 25% of the federal rate, followed by an even split in 1999 of the facility-based rate and federal rate. During the third year facilities would receive some (25%) of the facility-specific rate and mostly (75%) federal rate.

Unfortunately there were delays in implementing the PPS for skilled nursing facilities (SNFs). Consequently implementation was delayed while the specifics of the new RUG system were hammered out among stakeholders, and the entire PPS system was automated. Once implemented, SNF administrators quickly discovered that the new "rehabilitation" orientation of the PPS was going to cost them significantly if they continued to care for large numbers of residents needing palliative and chronic care. Consequently, there has been a significant shakeout of SNFs following the introduction of the new PPS system. Likewise, industry leaders are actively lobbying Congress to revise the PPS model to provide a more reasonable reimbursement schedule for the wide array of patients served in skilled nursing care (Stoil, 1999).

By the year 2001, facilities would be reimbursed only the federal PPS rate (Stone, 1998). In 1996 approximately $36 billion was spent on home health services. Of that amount, Medicare paid about 60%, Medicaid 14.4%, private insurance 8.4%, with the remaining 3.1% paid out-of-pocket (National Association for Home Care, 1996). Private home health agencies, which are neither funded nor regulated by Medicare, are reimbursed by private pay patients or other payers such as private insurance or government contracts (e.g., Workers' Compensation) on an hourly or per visit basis (Evashwick, 1999, p. 323).

4. Physician Reimbursement

Physicians can be reimbursed by one of these three methods: fee for service (FFS), salary, or prepayment. *FFS* incorporates the adoption of a schedule of charges used for both individual payers and third-party payers. Insurance companies using an indemnity payment reimburse physicians by applying a "resource-based relative value scale" to indicate the relative technical difficulty (and time cost) of the procedure; each point is then matched by so many dollars. Insurance companies using a service benefit payment reimburse physicians using a "usual, customary, and reasonable" (UCR) fee (usually 80%) with the balance covered by the patient. A final FFS method (often used by Medicaid, some private plans, and many HMO plans) is a fixed fee set by the third-party payer. It usually has minimal or no cost sharing by the patient. *Salaried* physicians are usually employed in urban public hospitals, paid by a unit of time, rather than by the services they deliver or the number of patients served. Physicians reimbursed on a *prepayment* basis are paid a fixed fee per patient for a given unit of time no matter what physician services are used or not used (Koch, 1999, pp. 132–133).

5. Pharmaceutical Reimbursement

Of the total expenditures allocated to health care in 1995, pharmaceuticals constituted almost 9% (U.S. Department of Health and Human Services, 1995). Consumers pay directly for a portion (copayment) or for all of the drug cost, since many third-party payer plans exclude drug cost coverage and those that do reimburse will usually cover less than 100% of drug charges. For example, both governmental and private health insurers covered 96% of hospital services in 1992 and 82% of physician services, but they covered only 72% of the cost of pharmaceuticals (Health Insurance Association of America, 1994). This gap of coverage is a major burden for the elderly, who require a significant number of prescriptions as they succumb to increasing chronic health problems. Congress has attempted to address the problems associated with Medicaid reimbursement for drugs by passing the Omnibus Budget Reconciliation Act (OBRA). This Act "guaranteed a state's Medicaid recipients access to all drugs manufactured by any company that agreed to grant to that state's Medicaid program the greatest price discount it offered to any other purchaser" (Schweitzer and Comanor, 1999, p. 399).

6. Summary of Health Financing in the United States

The United States continues to spend more on health care services than any other country in the world, yet inequities continue. Universal health coverage has not been realized, and thus, a growing percentage of the population remains uninsured (Koch, 1999, p. 149). The "system" of financing and reimbursing for health services is complex and uncoordinated, as noted by the plethora of players in the system and the overall bureaucracy at all levels. Corporate profit-making goals of managed care organizations (MCOs) and corporate-owned hospital chains have become a major driver of health policy (Jonas, 1998, p. 101). It is likely that managed care principles and the marketplace will continue to reshape all components of the U.S. health care financing system. What will emerge is unpredictable at this time owing to the volatile nature of the health care system.

II. HEALTH STATUS OF THE UNITED STATES POPULATION

A. Infant Mortality

The health status of the U.S. population, overall, is improving when measured by conventional indicators of infant mortality, life expectancy, and mortality and morbidity rates. Infant mortality, for example, declined dramatically since the 1970s. The infant mortality rate per 1000 live births was 20 in 1970 (Bureau of the Census, 1996, p. 92), but had been reduced to 7.3 per 1000 live births in 1996 (National Center for Health Statistics, Sept. 11, 1997, p. 28). Factors relevant to the recent improved rate include greater accessibility to prenatal care in some states through expansion of the Medicaid program to cover pregnant women with incomes up to 185% of poverty (Ray, 1997) and a drop in the birth rate for unmarried women. Yet, the infant mortality rate of the United States has remained behind that of many industrialized countries as indicated in 1993: Japan (4.35

per 1000), Sweden (4.84), England and Wales (6.24), Canada (6.3), and France (6.5) (National Center for Health Statistics, 1997). Possible explanations for the lag are the heterogeneity of the U.S. population and the high proportion without health insurance or with inadequate insurance (*The Reform of Health Care Systems*, 1994, p. 43).

B. Life Expectancy

Overall life expectancy at birth for the U.S. population in 1996 was 76.1 years and, as true in other countries, was higher for women (79 years) than men (73 years) (National Center for Health Statistics, Sept. 11, 1997, p. 31). Encouragingly, the difference in life expectancy also lessened between black and white Americans, with blacks now at 70.2 years and whites at 76.8 years (*The Nation's Health*, September 1998, p. 36). Life expectancy varies not only by race and sex, but also by family income levels, with longevity increasing as income increases, regardless of sex or race. Again, when comparing the United States to other countries, this health indicator (life expectancy rate) is lower for the United States. Using 1993 data as a basis for comparison, the United States ranked behind most industrialized countries, such as Japan, Sweden, Canada, England and Wales, and France (National Center for Health Statistics, 1997). The heterogeneity of the U.S. population along with its complex social problems (violence, accidents, and infectious disease) might be reasons for the lower life expectancy rate of the United States (Williams and Torrens, 1999, p. 66).

C. Mortality Rates

Current health care problems and diseases prevalent in the U.S. population are primarily chronic and disabling with genetic, environmental, and life-style etiological factors (McManus and Pohl, 1994, p. 345). In fact, the most prevalent chronic diseases, namely heart disease, cancer, and stroke, are also the major causes of death in the United States. In 1995 nearly 75% of all deaths in the United States for persons 25–64 years of age were due to chronic disease, followed by intentional and unintentional injuries (15%) and communicable diseases (11%) (National Center for Health Statistics, 1998, p. 90).

Two major factors contributing to these death rates were education and income; each increase in either education or income increased the likelihood of an individual being in good health. Adults with less education died younger for all major causes of death than more educated adults. Persons with lower education or income also had a higher prevalence of health risk factors, were less likely to receive preventive care, and were more likely to report unmet health care needs (National Center for Health Statistics, 1998). Another significant factor affecting death rates was sex; specifically, men had a higher injury death rate (three times higher) than women and also a higher mortality from communicable diseases (3.5 times higher) than women (National Center for Health Statistics, 1998, p. 90).

Heart disease death rates dropped since 1970, but heart disease still remains the leading cause of death in the United States, accounting for an estimated $79 billion in direct medical costs (Hodgson, 1997). Cancer is the second leading cause of death, with lung cancer accounted for about 28% of all cancer deaths in 1996 (Ventura et al., 1997). Between 1980 and 1992, death rates attributed to strokes declined at an average rate of 3.6% per year, but the rates were stable between 1992 and 1996. However, in 1996 the stroke death rate was 80% higher for the black population than the white population (National Center for Health Statistics, 1998, p. 11).

One positive change was the fewer deaths attributed to the HIV infection in 1996 in persons 25–44 years of age; their death rate for HIV infection declined 30%. This change resulted in HIV infection dropping from first to third in the causes of death among persons 25–44 years of age (National Center for Health Statistics, 1998, p. 11).

Smoking is the leading cause of preventable death and disease in the United States. More than $50 billion in direct medical costs and approximately 400,000 deaths are due to smoking each year (Centers for Disease Control and Prevention, 1993). Between 1990 and 1995, the rate of decline in smoking prevalence was much less than what had occurred during 1974 to 1990, but one finding was still evident, namely, greater declines in smoking occurred among educated adults.

In summary, certain chronic diseases continue to prevail, thus lowering the quality of a longer lifespan while raising the health care costs of the health system. On the other hand, women and men in the United States are living longer; more infants are living beyond their first year; and as income and education levels improve, so, it seems, does the health of the nation.

III. CURRENT HEALTH CARE SYSTEM ISSUES

A. Limited Access

The United States is the only major industrialized country that has neither planned nor provided universal access to health care services for its people (Davis, 1993, p. 320). The lack of universal coverage has become a political issue as the number of people without health insurance coverage continues to increase. There were 39.7 million persons, or 15.3% of the U.S. population, who were without health insurance coverage in 1993 (U.S. Census Bureau, 1997). This number increased to 40.3 million people in 1995, or 17.4% (American Hospital Association, 1997, p. xxii). The same pattern prevails from year to year, in that young and middle-aged adults are those most likely to have no access to public or private insurance.

Those individuals, aged 18–64, who were among the highest rate of uninsured workers in 1995, were those working in agriculture (36%), personal services (33%), and construction (32%) (American Hospital Association, 1997, p. xxii). Even though a third of these people had incomes below the official poverty line, they were not considered poor enough to qualify for the government's Medicaid program or had failed to meet other entry criteria.

The refusal to embrace a bureaucratic approach to health care, such as universal health care coverage, has been influenced by fierce individualism and the pursuit of free enterprise. Therefore, most of the health insurance coverage for the U.S. population is attained through voluntary employer programs for their employees and dependents, while government programs are limited to the poor, aged, or disabled. The debate continues on how to join together the private and public sectors. According to Morone (1997): "Proponents greet each new government program with cries of tyranny, illegitimacy, and bureaucracy run amok. The rhetorical storms provoked by national health insurance proposals offer a century-long catalogue of examples" (p. 995). Lee and Benjamin (1994) supported this perception by saying government's role remains restrained because of persistent beliefs about free enterprise as the most appropriate environment for the delivery of health services. Some governmental programs, such as Medicare, Medicaid, and the Veterans Administration Health program, had been implemented in spite of controversy. These programs escaped defeat because they were designed for specific populations who were viewed as needy (e.g., the elderly, the poor, and wounded veterans), and therefore, it was believed that these programs would not interfere with the marketplace.

B. Geographical and Population Factors

The size and population of a country can have a significant impact on its health care system. This is especially true of the United States, which is one of the largest industrialized countries, in terms of the area of its 50 states, estimated to be 3,615,211 mi^2 (9,363,396 km^2). Another indication of its size is that the United States has one of the world's longest geometrical borders separating the states from its northern neighbor, Canada (de Blij, 1995). Table 4 details the size and population data of the United States. As a point of comparison, five other countries are also presented in Table 4. Two of these countries border the United States and the other three are our trade partners. The size of the United States and the number of states it encompasses have resulted in many differences relative to a number of health-related factors. These differences include: regional pay scales, inconsistent availability of personnel, seasonal demands for services, differences in bureaucratic decision making and nursing home expenditures, variation in tackling health care costs, and controversy on accepted standards of care (Kane et al., 1998; Paul-Shaheen, 1998; Raffel and Raffel, 1989).

Table 4 Comparison of Land Size and Population Data

Country	Area in mi²/1000	Population in millions 1994	Population in millions 2000	Population in millions 2010	Percent urban population	1994 Population density persons/mi²
Canada	3831	27.8	29.1	32.1	78	7
Germany	137.8	80.5	80.2	78.2	90	584
Japan	145.7	125.2	127.6	129.4	77	859
Mexico	761.6	91.8	105.4	119.5	71	121
United Kingdom	94.2	58.1	59.0	59.9	90	617
United States	3678.9	259.6	272	295.5	75	71

Source: de Blij, H. *Harm de Blij's Geography Book*. New York: John Wiley & Sons, 1995, pp. 302–306.

Overall, the population density of the United States is 71 persons/mi², which is a greater density than Canada's (seven/mi²). However, three of the countries depicted in Table 4 have a much greater population density than the United States, namely Japan (859/mi²), Germany (584), and the United Kingdom (617). These three countries already have encountered problems commonly associated with highly populated areas, such as a strained health care system.

One of the United States' most populated areas is the Los Angeles Area in southern California. It had 10 million people in 1990, but increased to 10.4 million by 1995. The Los Angeles population growth was due not only to a natural increase but to another kind of growth: immigration. Millions of people have entered the United States in recent years from Mexico, Central America, and the Caribbean; many are legal immigrants, as was typical of immigration to the United States by the Irish, Italians, and other Europeans between the late 1800s and 1930. However, many more people now enter as illegal immigrants, which has led to debate in the southern and western regions of the United States about who shall receive health care from an already strained health care system and who shall pay for those services? When many people with ethnic and cultural differences are thrown together, the challenge to effectively and efficiently provide health services can be undermined by the broader societal issues of environmental degradation, decaying inner cities with inadequate tax bases, and political disharmony as to who to serve (de Blij, 1995).

As of 1995, there were 261,638,000 persons in the United States; it is estimated that this number will continue to grow, increasing to 392 million by 2050 (U.S. Census Bureau, 1997). In addition to population size, the composition of the U.S. population is unique because of its significant diversity, and this diversity is steadily increasing. The non-Hispanic white population will decrease from

75.7% of the total U.S. population in 1990 to less than 72% in the year 2000. Meanwhile, the African-American population, the Hispanic-origin population; the Asian and Pacific Islander populations; and the American Indian, Eskimo, and Aleut populations will all increase.

A major change is occurring with regard to the proportional size of the nation's Hispanic population. This population is expected to increase from an estimated 31 million people in the year 2000 to more than 60 million by the year 2015 (U.S. Census Bureau, 1997). This growth rate is indicative of a number of other U.S. ethnic groups. Currently, more than 200 ethnic groups have been identified in the United States, as well as more than 1200 religious sects (Thernstrom, 1980; Melton, 1979). It is this wide range of "associated groups" that sets the United States apart from most other countries and enriches its existence.

C. Technology-Driven System

The United States allocates significant funding to research and to the health care system, which has resulted in state-of-the-art medical technology that is widely distributed throughout the nation. Advances in diagnostic equipment, such as magnetic resonance imaging machines (MRIs), and laboratory tests have improved accuracy and reduced the waiting time before treatment. Other technology has emerged, such as laser surgery, which allows patients to be treated in outpatient settings with less pain, faster recovery time, and at a lower cost. Developments in health information systems are improving the processing of health data. Artificial limbs and cardiac pacemakers enhance individual lives. Biotechnology, a growing segment of the U.S. health care system, is expanding our knowledge about diseases and helping to develop new drugs and vaccines (Goodman and Gelijns, 1996, p. 274). All of this technology has benefited the U.S. population, but at a price, which underscores its importance as an issue.

Technology has caused problems within the health care system. Specifically, there is an inbred overreliance on technology to diagnose and treat, culminating in too much competition among hospital administrators to have the most current equipment to appease physicians. Although widely distributed, some of the high-tech equipment is often not available in certain geographical areas nor accessible by certain segments of the population who lack insurance or financial resources. This lack of access is in part responsible for the continuing discrepancy in morbidity and mortality rates between black and white Americans.

Another concern about technology is the cost of new drug development. Essentially, the development of new and improved products is highly profitable for the pharmaceutical companies producing them, since development costs become part of the price to the consumer. Schweitzer and Comanor (1999) estimated that after-tax research and development costs range between $140 million and $194 million for each new drug product (p. 387), which is then "absorbed" into the price by all those who pay for the drug. Since consumers pay a high share of pharmaceutical costs directly, those high prices are very visible.

In summary, the overall technology issue pertains to how much longer the United States can afford to allocate millions of dollars to a health policy that is technology-based. Public funds generously support acute episodic illnesses, while token dollars filter down to early detection, health promotion, and disease prevention programs. "Since many health programs require significant outlays of public funds, hard choices must be made regarding priority" (McManus and Pohl, 1994). Thus far, the issue remains of how to resolve technology-related concerns.

D. Other Issues

A system as large as the U.S. health care system will have many issues to be resolved affecting the optimal delivery and outcome of services. Even though all these issues cannot be discussed, some warrant acknowledgment, to stimulate fresh ideas and creative strategies that can shape a better, more effective health care system. One immediate issue is how to improve the health status of black Americans and poor children; insufficient attention has been paid to the special needs of these two groups and how best to serve them. Second, how can we achieve a more coordinated, less complicated health care system—one that links together both public and private sectors in a rational delivery system? A third issue concerns our older population: how to think differently about growing old in order to redesign a health and social services framework that supports and encourages independent, dignified living. A fourth issue addresses quality: how can we more accurately measure the quality of health services and then better inform our stakeholders? A fifth issue is how to streamline the financing and reimbursement processes of the health care system, thus achieving better cash flow? Resolution of these five issues and the others mentioned earlier might help us to achieve the goals of the system, namely, better quality, lower costs, and improved access.

IV. SUMMARY

The United States has resisted rapid change to have a unified health care system as evidenced in the failure of the Clinton Plan in 1994. Universal health policies and planning efforts at the federal level remain sporadic and at the whim of the political party currently in power. Thus, the U.S. Congress has addressed reform, but does so incrementally. This piecemeal approach, however, has not relieved any of the pressures on the health care system (Graig, 1993, p. 26). Public dissatisfaction and provider frustration about the increasing numbers of uninsured, the complexities of delivering health services equitably to diverse populations throughout the country, and the escalating health care costs, ensure that health reform will continue to occupy a more prominent place on the U.S. public policy agenda. Perhaps then, legislators will reach consensus on passing reform that will result in a more unified health care system for the United States.

REFERENCES

Abdellah, E. The nurse practitioner 17 years later: present and emerging issues. Inquiry 5:470–497, 1982.

Accrediting Commission on Education for Health Services Administration (ACEHSA), 1999. Web Site, http://www.aupha.org.

Aday, L., Anderson, R.M. Equity of access to medical care: a conceptual and empirical overview. Med Care 19(12):4–27, 1981.

Altman, B., Walden, D. Home Health Care: Use, Expenditures and Sources of Payment. National Medical Expenditure Survey, Research Findings 15. AHCPR Pub. No. 93-0040. Rockville, MD: Agency for Health Care Policy and Research, 1993.

Altman, S.H., Wallack, S.S. Health care spending: can the United States control it? In: Altman, S.H., Reinhardt, U.E., eds. Strategic Choices for a Changing Health Care System. Chicago: Health Administration Press, 1996, pp 1–32.

American College of Healthcare Executives (ACHE), 1999. Web Site, http://www.ache.org.

American Hospital Association. Chicago: AHA Publishers, 1997.

American Hospital Association. Hospital statistics (1996–1997). Chicago: AHA Publishers, 1997.

American Medical Association. Physician characteristics and distribution in the U.S. 1997–1998 edition. Chicago: AMA, 1998.

Anderson, S.T. How healthcare organizations can achieve true integration. Health Care Financial Management 31–34, Feb 1998.

Assisted Living Federation of America. Overview of the Assisted Living Industry. Fairfax, VA: Author, 1996.

Braslow, J.B., Heins, M. Women in medical education: a decade of change. N Engl J Med 304(19):1129–1135, 1981.

Bureau of the Census. Statistical Abstract of the United States. 116th edition. Washington, DC: Bureau of the Census, 1996.

Bureau of the Census. Statistical Abstract of the United States. 117th edition. Washington, DC: Bureau of the Census, 1997.

Burwell, B., Crown, W.H., O'Shaugnessy, C., Price, R. Financing long-term care. In: Evashwick, C.J. The Continuum of Long-Term Care: An Integrated Systems Approach. Albany, NY: Delmar Publishers, 1996, pp 193–221.

Cawley, J.F. Physician assistants in the healthcare workforce. In: Clawson, D.K., Osterweis, M. The Roles of Physician Assistants and Nurse Practitioners in Primary Care. Washington, DC: Association of Academic Centers, 1993, pp 21–39.

Cefalu, C.A., Heuser, M. Adult day care for the demented elderly. Am Fam Physician 47(4):723–724, 1993.

Centers for Disease Control and Prevention. Cigarette smoking-attributable mortality and years of potential life lost. U. S. 1990. Morbid Mortal Weekly Rep 42:654–659, 1993.

Clawson, D.K., Osterweis, M. The Roles of Physician Assistants and Nurse Practitioners in Primary Care. Washington, DC: Association of Academic Health Centers, 1993.

Cox, N., Reifler, B. Adult day care: the state of the art. LTC News & Comment, Oct 1994, p 5.

Davis, K. Equity and health care policy: the American experience. In: Doorslaer, E.V., Wagstaff, A., Rutten, F., eds. Equity in the Finance and Delivery of Health Care: An International Perspective. New York: Oxford University Press, 1993, pp 320–347.

Davis, M. Development of the first graduate program in hospital administration. J Health Admin Educ 2(2):121–134, 1984.

de Blij, H. Harm de Blij's Geography Book. New York: John Wiley & Sons, 1995.

Dial, T.H., Hatch, H., Newman, M.G., Sullivan, J. 1997–1998 Edition: Profile of Health Plans and Utilization Review Organizations. Washington, DC: American Association of Health Plans, 1998.

Doty, P., Stone, R., Jackson, M.E., Adler, M. Informal caregiving. In: Evashwick, C. ed. The Continuum of Long-Term Care: An Integrated Systems Approach. Albany, NY: Delmar Publishers, 1996, pp 125–141.

Dowling, W.L. Hospitals and health systems. In: Williams, S.J., Torrens, P.R., eds. Introduction to Health Services. Albany, NY: Delmar Publishers, 1998, pp 257–295.

Evashwick, C.J. The continuum of long-term care. In: Williams, S.J., Torrens, P.R., eds. Introduction to Health Services. Albany, NY: Delmar Publishers, 1993, pp 177–218.

Evashwick, C. The continuum of long-term care. In: Williams, S.J., Torrens, P.R., eds. Introduction to Health Services. Albany, NY: Delmar Publishers, 1999, pp 295–348.

Evashwick, C. The Continuum of Long-Term Care: An Integrated Systems Approach. Albany, NY: Delmar Publishers, 1996.

Feldman, M.J., Ventura, M.R., Crosby, F. Studies of nurse practitioners effectiveness. Nurs Res 36:303–308, 1987.

Filerman, G. Professional maturity and the University of Chicago. J Health Admin Educ 2(2):117–119, 1984.

Gillies, R.R., Shortell, S.M., Young, G.J. Best practices in managing organized delivery systems. Hosp Health Serv Admin 42(3):299–321, 1997.

Goodman, C.S., Gelijns, A.C. The changing environment for technological innovation in health care. In: Altman, S.H., Reinhardt, U.E., eds. Strategic Choices for a Changing Health Care System. Chicago: Health Administration Press, 1996, pp 269–315.

Graig, L. Health of Nations: An International Perspective on U.S. Health Care Reform. Washington, DC: Congressional Quarterly, 1993.

Haglund, C.L., Dowling, W.L. The hospital. In: Williams, S.J., Torrens, P.R., eds. Introduction to Health Services. Albany, NY: Delmar Publishers, 1993, pp 135–176.

Halverson, P.K., Kaluzny, A.D., Young, G.J. Strategic alliances in healthcare: opportunities for the Veterans Affairs healthcare system. Hosp Health Serv Admin 42(3): 383–410, 1997.

HCFA's Online Survey, Certification and Reporting Data, March 1997.

Health Insurance Association of America. Source Book of Health Insurance Data. Washington, DC: Author, 1994.

Health Professions Education for the Future: Schools in Service to the Nation. Report of the Pew Health Professions Commission. San Francisco, CA: Pew Health Professions Commission, Feb 1993.

Hodgson, T.A. Unpublished estimates. In: Health, United States, 1998. National Center for Health Statistics, Centers for Disease Control and Prevention, 1997, p 92.

Hughes, S. Home health. In: Evashwick, C. The Continuum of Long-Term Care: An Integrated Systems Approach. Albany, NY: Delmar Publishers, 1996, pp 61–81.

Jonas, S. An introduction to the U.S. Health Care System. 4th ed. New York: Springer Publishing Company, 1998.

Jones, P.E., Cawley, J.F. Physician assistants and health system reform. JAMA 271(16): 1266–1272, 1994.

Kane, R.L., Kane, R.A., Ladd, R.C., Veazle, W.N. Variation in state spending for long-term care: factors associated with more balanced systems. J Health Politics Policy Law 23(2):363–389, 1998.

Kemper, P., Murtaugh, C. Lifetime use of nursing home care. N Engl J Med 324:595–600, 1991.

Kizer, K.W. The veterans healthcare system: preparing for the twenty-first century. Hosp Health Serv Admin 42(3):283–298, 1997.

Koch, A.L. Financing health services. In: Williams, S.J., Torrens, P.R., eds. Introduction to Health Services. Albany, NY: Delmar Publishers, 1999, pp 113–150.

Lair, T., Lefkowitz, D. Mental Health and Functional Status of Residents of Nursing and Personal Care Homes. National Medical Expenditure Survey, Research Findings 7. DHHS Pub. No. 90-3470. Rockville, MD: Agency for Health Care Policy and Research, 1990.

Lee, P.R., Benjamin, A.E. Health policy and the politics of health care. In: Williams, S.J., Torrens, P.R., eds. Introduction to Health Services. Albany, NY: Delmar Publishers, 1993, pp 399–420.

Lee, P.R. Benjamin, A.E. In: Lee, P.R., Estes, C.L., eds. The Nation's Health. 4th ed. Boston: Jones and Bartlett Publishers, 1994, pp 121–137.

Levit, K.R., Lazenby, H.C., Braden, B.R., Cowan, C.A., McDonnell, P.A., Sivarajan, L., Stiller, J.M., Won, D.K., Donham, C.S., Long, A.M., Stewart, M.W. National health expenditures, 1995. Health Care Financing Rev 18(1):175–214, 1996.

Longest, B.B. Managerial competence at senior levels of integrated delivery systems. J Healthcare Management 43(2):115–133, 1998.

Martin, L.G. The aging of Asia. J Gerontol Soc Sci 43(4):599–611, 1988.

McManus, S.M., Pohl, C.M. Ethics and financing: overview of the U.S. health care system. J Health Hum Resources Admin 16(3):332–349, 1994.

Melton, J.G. The Encyclopedia of American Religions. Wilmington, NC: Consortum Books, 1979.

Mick, S. Health care professionals. In: Williams, S.J., Torrens, P.R., eds. Introduction to Health Services. Albany, NY: Delmar Publishers, 1999, pp 403–435.

Morone, J.A. Enemies of the people: the moral dimension to public health. J Health Politics Policy Law 22(4):992–1020, 1997.

National Association for Home Care. *Basic Statistics about Home Care 1996.* Washington, DC: Author, 1996.

National Center for Health Statistics Births and Deaths: United States, 1996. 46(1), Supplement 2, Monthly Vital Statistics Report: Centers for Disease Control and Prevention, Sept 11, 1997.

National Center for Health Statistics. July 30, 1998. Health in America tied to income and education [On-line], Available: http://www.cdc.gov/nchswww/releases/98news/98news/huspr98.htm.

National Center for Health Statistics. Health, United States, 1998. Hyattsville, MD: Public Health Service, 1998.

National Institute on Adult Daycare. Responses from State Adult Day Care Association survey. Washington, DC: National Council on Aging, 1994–1995.

The Nation's Health. Washington, DC: American Public Health Association, 1998.

Neubauer, D. Hawaii: a pioneer in health system reform. Health Affairs 12:31–39, 1993.

Newscomer, R., Wood, J., Sankar. Medicare prospective payment: anticipated effect on hospitals, other community agencies and families. J Health Politics Policy Law 10: 275–282, 1985.

Oliver, D. Physician assistant education: a review of program characteristics by sponsoring institution. In: Clawson, D.K., Osterweis, M. The Roles of Physician Assistants and Nurse Practitioners in Primary Care. Washington, DC: Association of Academic Health Centers, 1993.

O'Sullivan, J., Franco, C., Fuchs, B., Lyke, B., Price, R., Swendiman, K. CRS Report to Congress: Medicare Provisions of the Balanced Budget Act of 1997 (BBA 97, P.L. 105-33). Washington, DC: Congressional Research Service, 1997.

Paul-Shaheen, P.A. The states and health care reform: the road traveled and lessons learned from seven that took the lead. J Health Politics Policy Law 23(2):320–361, 1998.

Raffel, M.W., Raffel, N.K. The U.S. Health System: Origins and Functions. 3rd ed. New York: John Wiley & Sons, 1989.

Ray, W.A. Effect of Medicaid expansion on preterm birth. Am J Prevent Med 13(4):292–297, 1997.

The Reform of Health Care Systems: A Review of Seventeen OECD Countries. Health Policy Studies No. 5. Paris: Organisation for Economic Co-Operation and Development, 1994.

Rodican, A.J. Getting into the PA School of Your Choice. Stamford, CT: Appleton & Lange, 1998.

Ryan, S. Nurse practitioners: educational issues, practice styles, and service barriers. In: Clawson, D.K., Osterweis, M., eds. The Roles of Physician Assistants and Nurse Practitioners in Primary Care. Washington, DC: Association of Academic Health Centers, 1993, pp 41–49.

Schweitzer, S.O., Comanor, W.S. The role of pharmaceuticals in the health care system. In: Williams, S.J., Torrens, P.R. Introduction to Health Services. Albany, NY: Delmar Publishers, 1999, pp 383–401.

Shortell, S.M., Anderson, D.A., Gillies, R.R., Mitchell, J.B., Morgan, K.L. Building integrated systems: the holographic organization. Healthcare Forum J 36(2):20–26, 1993.

Singh, D.A., Shi, L., Samuels, M.E., Amidon, R.L. How well trained are nursing home administrators? Hosp Health Serv Admin 42(1):101–115, 1997.

Source Book of Health Insurance Data, 1996. Washington, DC: Health Insurance Association of America, 1997.

Spector, W.D., Reschovsky, J., Cohen, J.D. Appropriate placement of nursing home residents in lower levels of care. Milbank Q 74(1):139–160, 1996.

Stahl, D.A. Integrated delivery system: an opportunity or a dilemma. Nurs Management 26(7):20–23, 1995.

Stoil, M.J. Remember Vencor. Nurs Homes Long Term Care Management 11(48):20–24, 1999.

Stone, D. Rethinking reimbursement. Subacute Care: An Annual Supplement to Contemporary Long Term Care, 1998, pp 6–8.

Sultz, H.A., Young, K.M. Health Care USA: Understanding Its Organization and Delivery. Gaithersburg, MD: Aspen Publishers, 1997.

Terhune, C. Drop in residency funds will hit hospitals hard. Wall Street J, Jan 14, 1998, pp F1, F4.

Thernstrom, S., ed. Harvard Encyclopedia of American Ethnic Groups. Cambridge, MA: Harvard University Press, 1980.

Torrens, P.R. Historical evolution and overview of health services in the United States. In: Williams, S.J., Torrens, P.R., eds. Introduction to Health Services. Albany, NY: Delmar Publishers, 1993, pp 1–28.

Torrens, P.R., Williams, S.J. Understanding the present, planning for the future: the dynamics of health care in the United States in the 1990s. In: Lee, P.R., Estes, C.L., eds. The Nation's Health. 4th ed. Boston: Jones and Bartlett Publishers, 1994, pp 60–66.

U.S. Bureau of the Census, 1996.

U.S. Census Bureau, 1997.

U.S. Congress, Office of Technology. Nurse Practitioners, Physician Assistants, and Certified Nurse-Midwives: A Policy Analysis. Health technology case study 37, OTA-HCS-37. Washington, DC: U.S. Government Printing Office, 1986.

U.S. Department of Health and Human Services. Health, United States. Washington, DC: Author, 1995.

U.S. Department of Labor, Bureau of Labor Statistics. Occupational Outlook Handbook, April 1994, pp 169–171.

Ventura, S.J., Peters, K.D., Martin, J.A., Maurer, J.D. Births and Deaths: United States, 1996. Monthly Vital Statistics Report, vol. 46, no. 1, supp. 2. Hyattsville, MD: National Center for Health Statistics, 1997.

Wallace, S.P., Abel, E.K., Stefanowicz, P. Long-term care and the elderly. In: Andersen, R.M., Rice, T.H., Kominski, G.F., eds. Changing the U.S. Health Care System: Key Issues in Health Services, Policy, and Management. San Francisco: Jossey-Bass Publishers, 1996, pp 180–201.

Williams, S.J., Torrens, P.R. Introduction to Health Services. 5th ed. Albany, NY: Delmar Publishers, 1999.

Yeh, E. How to Achieve Quality of Life and Care in a Nursing Home. Houston, TX: Rosenwasser Publishing Company, 1996.

Young, D.W., Barrett, D. Managing clinical integration in integrated delivery systems: a framework for action. Hosp Health Serv Admin 42(2):255–279, 1997.

[On-Line] Available: http://www.aupha.org.

6

Like Plugging the Holes in a Colander
Health Policy and Provision in the United States Circa the Millennium

Edward T. Wimberley and Arthur J. Rubens
Florida Gulf Coast University, Fort Myers, Florida

I. OVERVIEW: PLUGGING THE COLANDER

So why describe the current state of American health care as a leaky vessel that is being plugged one hole at a time? Understanding the question requires recognizing that the current "system" (or "nonsystem") of U.S. health care with its primary link to employee-based coverage, and secondary link to age-related entitlements or demonstrable indicators of poverty or disability, still leaves many gaps in basic access to health care services that need to be filled. Moreover, even among the insured, or among those receiving Medicare or some version of Medicaid, there are still gaps in coverage that leave recipients and policyholders vulnerable to significant costs and limitations in care. Comparing the current system to a colander also reflects the significant hemorrhages in efficiency, effectiveness, and costs associated with a system seeking to rationalize itself via the rubric of managed care. While the growth in the rate of health care inflation has been significantly reduced from an annual growth rate of 11.6% in 1985 to a comparably modest 5.5% in 1995, health care costs remain a significant portion of the nation's gross domestic product (GDP), consuming 13.5% of the GDP and earmarking approximately $328 billion in federal revenue in 1995, or approximately 33% of the nation's (1995) health care expenditures ($988.5 billion) (Minor, 1998, pp. 102–103).

The imagery of a colander also reflects the reality within the American political system that all policy changes are incremental in nature. Despite efforts during the enactment of the Social Security Act in the thirties to introduce "national health insurance" and subsequent support for one form or another of comprehensive health insurance coverage by virtually every U.S. President since Franklin D. Roosevelt, the policy process has tended to build upon the status quo of an ingrained third-party insurance system supplemented by categorical aid to significant need groups (i.e., the aged, disabled, and impoverished women and children) (Wimberley, 1980a, 1980b). Incremental policymaking is inherent to a multi-interest political system that seeks balanced action among a wide range of constituent interests. This approach to policymaking tends to assume an "if it ain't broke don't fix it" approach to policy deliberation and only engages in substantive (broadly incremental) policy shifts during periods of national crisis (Wimberley and Morrow, 1981).

Since the early seventies, Congress has regularly visited and revisited the idea of comprehensive health care coverage for all of its citizens under a variety of labels: national health insurance, comprehensive care, universal coverage, and single-payer models. Congressional legislation to implement such plans has consistently met with failure as resistance emerged from the hospital industry, pharmaceutical firms, professional medical organizations, and other interest groups who have long associated comprehensive care plans funded with federal dollars with socialistic or communistic policies (Wimberley and Morrow, 1981). While comprehensive coverage has never been fully achieved, proponents of such coverage have been successful in implementing categorical legislation that has incrementally served to "plug the holes" in the health care coverage colander. While the net effect of these legislative efforts has been to improve health care access (Berk and Schur, 1998) these same programs, lacking cost control mechanisms, have also served to escalate the costs of health care to the point where they have threatened the stability of the federal budget.

II. SO JUST HOW DID WE GET OURSELVES INTO THIS MESS? DOWNSHIFTING AND SLOWING SPENDING

A. Overrelying on Hospital Care

Health care has always been a contentious issue in the United States since the early portion of the twentieth century, if for no other reason than because Americans have a difficult time determining exactly what health-related activities and costs are the responsibility of individuals and families and what costs should be assumed by the public. As the "science" and "practice" of medicine improved and as hospitals were transformed from places where people went to die to places where healing occurred, Americans increasingly looked to their physicians and to hospitals as essential community resources. While public health initiatives, such as the polio vaccine, also made significant contributions to the improvement of the health status of America's citizens, it was the tertiary approach of modern medicine that received the most enthusiastic financial, popular, and ultimately political support. With significant improvements in tertiary care resulting from U.S. involvement in World Wars I and II, the Korean War, and the Vietnam War, hospitals increasingly became sites for state-of-the-art surgical and nonsurgical care, occasioned at least in part by the rapid development of medical technologies that emerged during each war and conflict, and that were later stimulated by a combination of public and private investments in research and technology. Similar gains were made in the area of pharmaceuticals and rehabilitation (Stevens, 1989).

As a consequence of improved public health and the emergence of hospitals as technologically sophisticated workshops utilized by largely independently practicing physicians, by the 1970s and 1980s the hospital had become the center of the U.S. health care system. Physicians were primarily trained within such inpatient settings, and patients came to expect the liberal utilization of hospital resources as a part of their health care benefits.

Unfortunately, (1) an increased reliance upon medical technology, (2) unchecked utilization of ancillary products and services such as pharmaceutical and allied health care services, along with (3) an ever-inflating rate of reimbursement for physician services, combined with (4) an "open-ended," employer-based, third-party reimbursement mechanism continued to reinforce the two historical problems confronted by the U.S. system of health care: growing health costs and shrinking access to needed health care services (White, 1995, p. 1).

B. Health Care Costs and the Prospective Payment System

Predictably, as hospital costs and investments in technological, physical, and human capital increased so did the cost of health care. In fact, U.S. health care costs literally exploded from 1962 to 1982. During this 20-year interval, total health care expenditures grew from approximately 5.5% of GDP to 10% (White, 1995, p. 18). Alternatively stated, per capita health expenditures in the United States (expressed in 1995 dollars) increased from approximately $180 to approximately $1200 (White, 1995, p. 19). Given this rate of increase, the significant contribution of federal dollars to the health economy (approximately 40% in 1982), and the emergence of a growing federal budget deficit, by the early eighties the time had finally arrived to do something serious and definitive about health care costs.

The "something definitive" that emerged during this period was the prospective payment system (PPS), more commonly referred to as "DRGs": the diagnosis-related groups that the prospective payment system was developed around.

The Medicare PPS was introduced by the Health Care Financing Agency in 1983, after being authorized by Congress in 1982 as a part of the Tax Equity and Fiscal Responsibility Act of 1982 (TEFRA, 1982). At the point of implementation of the legislation, federal health care expenditures had risen from $6.9 billion in 1960 to $247.2 billion in 1980 (Fig. 1) and were steadily increasing (Minor, 1998, p. 103). With such runaway costs, Congress felt compelled to act quickly and effectively to curb these costs. After developing demonstration projects designed to reduce health care costs that were piloted in several states, Congressional leadership and the Health Care Financing Association (HCFA) agreed to adopt the PPS as a means for managing health care costs effectively.

Under PPS all inpatient procedures and treatments were categorized as falling within an initial set of 65 DRGs (groupings of similar disorders, treatments, etc.) that were believed to reflect the entirety of all possible hospital treatments and care. By 1999, these 65 DRGs had mushroomed into 490 DRG categories as defined by HCFA. After establishing a set of inclusive DRGs, HCFA did national cost comparisons to determine average costs for treating each DRG. With this information in hand, HCFA designed the remainder of the system in

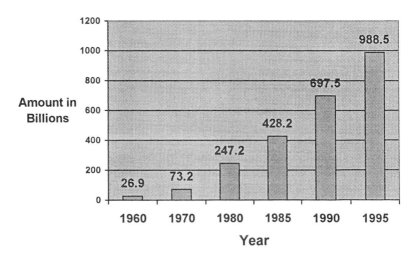

Figure 1 National health expenditures 1960–1995. (From Health Care Financing Administration, Health Care Financing Administration Review, Fall 1996.)

which hospitals were to be paid "prospectively" (up front) rather than "retrospectively" (after the fact and on a cost-based model). When patients were admitted to the hospital, and upon determination of which DRG patients fell within, hospitals could seek prospective reimbursement. In so doing they agreed to care for the patients at the prospective rate. If hospital costs were less than the DRG rate, then hospitals could pocket the difference. However, if costs exceeded the rate of reimbursement, then the hospitals were liable for the cost difference.

During the first year of the PPS implementation U.S. hospitals averaged a 14.5% operating margin, followed by a 14% operating margin in year 2. These high margins reflected a phase-in period for PPS spanning 3 years. This approach was intended to provide a "weaning" process during which hospitals could make a transition to the new system, implement cost-saving measures, and adapt to less than "full cost" reimbursement. However, by year 3 of the PPS, hospital operating margins fell to 9.5%, and dramatically fell to 1.4% during the sixth year of the system. Years 7–9 were particularly dismal for the industry, as operating margins turned negative (−.5, −1.4, −1.0, respectively). Responding to this growing financial crisis in the hospital industry, Congress adjusted DRG reimbursement rates during years 9 and 10, and operating margins increased from 1.2% in year 9 to 9.1% in year 13 (ProPac, 1996).

Since the introduction of the PPS, per enrollee expenditures increased from $2127 in 1984 to $4484 in 1994 (ProPAC, 1996) while the annual average growth rate in such expenditures fell from 14.5% during the period 1979–1984 to 9.8% during the period 1993–1994 (Minor, 1998, p. 82). Comparatively, the number of community hospital beds per 1000 population fell from 4.5 beds in 1982 to 2.9 beds in 1995. Similarly the average length of hospital stay (LOS) dropped from 7.6 days in 1982 to 6.5 days in 1995, and the average number of hospitalized patients decreased from 3.4 patients in 1982 to 2.1 patients in 1995 (see Fig. 2) (AHA Statistics, 1996–1997; Minor, 1998, p. 128).

With such dramatic changes occurring in hospitals, patients found themselves increasingly discharged more rapidly to their homes than ever before, and in many cases in greater need of home-based and institutional nursing and rehabilitation care. This concern was readily voiced by patients and was soon to be recognized and addressed by state and federal health authorities. However, the most important aspect of this change in health care delivery and finance was that the acuity of care needed by patients began to be shifted away from the hospital toward long-term care, home care, ambulatory care, and other community health settings. In effect, costs and acuity were being squeezed down and patients were being squeezed out. By 1994, long-term care costs had grown to 33% of all national health expenditures (Feder et al., 1997), with significant and continued growth, especially in the area of home care and assisted care, anticipated in the future.

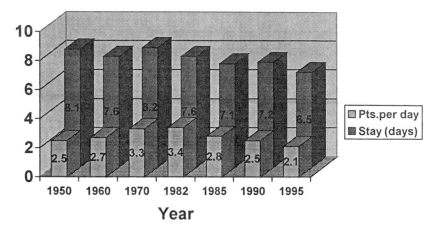

Figure 2   Average number of hospitalized patients per day and length of stay, selected years. (From American Hospital Association, Hospital Statistics, 1996–1997.)

C. Squeezed Down, Squeezed Out

Cost escalations, following the introduction of the Medicare PPS, have been reduced as the health care system's capacity shifted from high-cost inpatient care to lower-cost ambulatory, community, subacute, and long-term care. Hospital utilization rates have dropped significantly from their elevated levels in the 1980s (dropping from 160.2 admissions per 1000 population and an average LOS of 7.62 in 1982 to 119.5 admissions per 1000 and a LOS of 6.5 in 1995) (Minor, 1998, p. 128). Hospital bed capacity has also been significantly reduced from an average of 1012 beds in 1982 to an average of 873 in 1995 (Minor, 1998, p. 129). Meanwhile, health care costs have been shifted to outpatient surgical centers, group practices, and other community-based providers, especially home health agencies (Minor, 1998, p. 114). The effort to squeeze "excess costs" from the system initiated in the early eighties has resulted in a situation where the fat continues to be squeezed to different sites in the health care continuum, points more distant from the inpatient setting. In so doing, the very definition of health care has been redefined at every level below the inpatient tier, with definitions increasingly being imposed by technological capacity and cost constraints.

   From the patient or consumer perspective, the processes that have "squeezed down" costs, have also served to "squeeze out" patients from inpatient settings and into ever-lower levels in the delivery system (i.e., the physician's practice, outpatient surgical centers, home settings, the assisted living facility, and the skilled nursing facility) (Minor, 1998, p. 117). In some instances, such as in the case of cataract care and mastectomies, the shifting of surgery from the hospital to the ambulatory surgery suite has resulted in lower costs and improved care (Warren et al., 1998; Meddings et al., 1997). Indeed, as of 1994, the annual number of ambulatory surgeries performed on the eyes averaged 4.6 million (NCHS, 1998). However, in the instance of chronic illnesses and diseases, reduced hospital stays and limitations on any form of care beyond tertiary or rehabilitation care in outpatient and community settings have sometimes imposed significant hardships and challenges for elderly Americans (Rubenstein, 1995; Holloway et al., 1988; Gooding and Jette, 1985).

D. Toying with Comprehensive Health Care Reform: The Medicare Catastrophic Coverage Act of 1988

In 1988 Congress took its first serious step toward reversing some of the untoward trends associated with the Medicare hospital PPS by providing broader and more comprehensive care via the enactment of the Medicare Catastrophic Coverage Act. This act (P.L. 100-360) constituted the single largest expansion of the Medicare program since its inception. Among the benefit changes included in the act were the following:

1. The elimination of patient cost sharing for inpatient care beyond payment of the deductible,
2. An annual cap on physician service costs of $1370,
3. A phased-in pharmaceutical benefit,
4. An expanded level of coverage for skilled nursing care (Minor, 1998, p. 194).

The provisions of this legislation essentially increased citizen access to "catastrophic care": i.e., those health care costs primarily occurring during the latter stages of the disease process when hospital and long-term-care costs are most intense, as compared to the early stages, where health care costs for basic ambulatory and preventive care are much less costly. Realizing that such catastrophic costs were the leading cause of medical insolvency and indigence, support for such coverage (so-called "rear end" coverage as opposed to "front end" ambulatory costs") was viewed by legislative sponsors as the most prudent and cost-effective way to utilize federal funds to improve coverage and protect the resources of most Americans.

The legislation's provisions were drafted in an era of significant Congressional concern regarding the reduction of the federal budget deficit. Consequently, the bill needed to be "revenue neutral" to pass Congress and be endorsed by the President (i.e., all expenses had to be offset by either reductions in spending for other federal programs or through a mix of tax increases, user fees, and copayments). To that end, the act was to be in part funded by a "user fee" or tax assessed upon Medicare recipients. In so doing Congress hoped to expand needed benefits by enlisting more affluent recipients of this federally funded health care benefit in providing support to those recipients who were less affluent. This concept was rationalized by proponents of the Catastrophic Coverage Act as consistent with the concept of redistributive justice (see Rawls, 1971) and was also consistent with the emerging concept of utilizing user fees to assist in providing needed services (commonly referred to in Congress as requiring beneficiaries to help ''carry the freight''). Likewise, it was anticipated by many that the new catastrophic coverage provision under Medicare would reduce the need for citizens to purchase so-called Medigap insurance, resulting in a net savings to most Medicare recipients.

E. No Good Deed Goes Unpunished

Unfortunately, the logic of this legislation was not effectively communicated to the American public, nor were the entire set of provisions contained within the legislation, nor their implications. Unfortunately, what Medicare recipients saw (and were encouraged to see by interest groups opposed to the bill) was the imposition of taxes on the elderly to help pay for extended benefits. While Rawls' theory of distributive justice enjoyed much support among proponents of the legislation on both sides of the aisle, those affected by the new tax were vocal in their unwillingness to pay any additional taxes, especially in the service of ''redistributive funding'' that many conservatives associated with incipient socialism.

As a consequence, Congress returned (noticeably annoyed with those interest groups that had alleged that most elderly citizens would welcome the legislation) and promptly vowed to repeal the legislation in 1989. Many, such as then-Chair of the Senate Finance Committee, Sen. Lloyd Bentsen (D-TX), who had ardently supported the Catastrophic Coverage Act, vowed not to be ''set up'' again by those in support of expanded coverage, and speculated that it would be ''a while'' before Congress would be willing to risk such humiliation again (Wimberley, 1990).

III. A LOST OPPORTUNITY FOR COMPREHENSIVE HEALTH CARE REFORM

A. "Full of Sound and Fury; Signifying Nothing": The Health Reform Debate 1993–1994

Feeling ''burned'' by the 1988 Medicare Catastrophic Care fiasco, Congress remained reluctant to substantively deal with comprehensive health care reform during the Bush presidency, and waited until a Democratic governor from Arkansas, Bill Clinton, was elected President. Vowing to address the issue of national health insurance while on the campaign trail, Clinton initiated the process of developing a comprehensive national health insurance program which he initially envisioned as resembling the model utilized in Canada. Riding on the coattails of an impressive election victory, many proponents of comprehensive and universal health care coverage were encouraged for the first time in decades that sweeping legislation on the scale of the Social Security Act could be passed by Congress and signed into law by the President early in his administration.

What followed was perhaps the most spirited, far-reaching national debate ever held on the nation's health care system. Unfortunately, as William Shakespeare's line in *The Tempest* reads, it was a debate "full of sound and fury," but one that in the end "signif(ied) nothing." The President made a series of "zigs and zags" through a variety of health policy options (Johnson and Broder, 1996, pp. 1–48), until finally adopting a version of a "managed care" approach that included global budgeting (i.e., overall budget limits) rather than more narrowly relying upon the actions of competitive market forces to control costs (White, 1995, p. 224). In adopting this approach (which in many respects reflected the administration's interest in introjecting market efficiencies into health care provision while remaining skeptical as to whether generally unregulated market forces would successfully reduce costs without reducing access) (Gradison, 1997b), the Clinton administration embarked upon one of the most complicated political and policy courses available.

In choosing to graft a competitive approach such as "managed care" to a federal cost-regulatory model, Clinton was forced to develop an extremely complicated health reform package that would prove to be very difficult for even the most seasoned health policy experts to understand. Comparatively, it would have been much less complicated, more straightforward, and more comprehensible to the America public had the President embraced an entirely new approach [such as the managed care proposal developed by Alain Enthoven and the Jackson Hole Group (White, 1995, p. 224)] than it was for the administration to "fix" an already complicated and inefficient system. We will return to this observation later.

Ultimately, Clinton's choice of a global budget approach to managed care, coupled with (1) the complexity of the legislation, (2) the protracted period of time it took to develop the plan, and (3) the extent to which key players in the health care debate were excluded from discussions [such as the medical profession, hospital representatives, the pharmaceutical industry and the Health Insurance Association of America (HIAA), which later ran a series of *Thelma and Louise* commercials that helped bury the legislation], conspired to completely undo support for health care reform, and the Health Security Act of 1994 (HSA '94) died without even being debated on the floor of Congress (Wilson, 1995, p. 119). As Paul Starr, a noted sociologist and historian who was an "insider" in the development of the Clinton plan, observed after its demise,

The collapse of health care reform in the first two years of the Clinton administration will go down as one of the greatest lost political opportunities in
American history. It is a story of compromises that never happened, of deals
that were never closed, of Republicans, moderate Democrats, and key interest
groups that backpedaled from proposals they themselves had earlier co-spon-
sored or endorsed. It is also a story of strategic miscalculations on the part
of the President and those of us who advised him (Johnson and Broder, 1996,
p. 602).

In the interest of not becoming further entrapped in the complexity and
nuance of this landmark piece of legislation, suffice it to say that HSA '94 was
eventually defeated partly under the weight of its size and complexity (which
was difficult to impossible to explain to the American public), as well as by a
political system that is not accustomed to making sweeping changes in public
policy. Sadly, in the end the health care debate of 1993–1994, despite its "sound
and fury," "signified nothing."

B. The Health Security Act in Historical Perspective

The Health Security Act represented one of those rare moments when Congress
considers truly "broadly incremental" policy options. The last such substantive
legislative efforts included the 1935 Social Security Act and the implementation
of Medicare in the early sixties. Social Security was implemented during the era
of the Great Depression, a period of significant economic and social turmoil
within the United States. Similarly, Medicare was passed during the Great Society
period of the Johnson administration, when the nation was recovering from the
unfulfilled promise of a lost "Camelot," was embroiled in racial strife and a
costly war in Indochina, and was confronting out-of-control inflation (Starr, 1982,
pp. 355–419). It was during this paradoxical period of "paradise lost," "paradise
sought," and "reality saturation" that the Congress was willing to consider shor-
ing up the health care needs of the nation's elderly.

The Health Security Act represented only the third time in the century that
the Congress and administration sought to do something really "paradigm shifting," and the bill died. It died not only under its own weight, complexity, inconsistency, and isolation from principal interest groups, but also died in a time when
there was really no unified public/political understanding or consensus on what
the health problem really involved and how to solve it. What resulted was an
embarrassing debacle for the newly elected president, and a remedial lesson for
Congress that substantive legislation cannot be created out of such broad cloth,
but must be quilted together from smaller, categorical, targeted legislation aimed
at incrementally improving upon the current system by plugging one cost or access hole at a time until the colander becomes a bucket that, at worst, only drips.
Furthermore, the timing for reform was not right. As this author has observed

(Wimberley, 1980) and as Victor Fuchs recently observed: "The enactment of comprehensive reform could only occur in the wake of some major political upheaval, such as a war, depression, or large-scale civil unrest" (Iglehart, 1998, p. 92).

IV. THE AFTERMATH OF THE HEALTH SECURITY ACT

A. Managed Care

Managed care emerged as the theme for health care reform since 1994 even though what the term means and how it is applied is somewhat controversial. For instance, White (1997) describes how managed care works by referring to it as "an effort to control health care costs by focusing on incidents of treatment, including the appropriateness of caregiver's decisions," and continues to observe that: "This management of treatments might be asserted to provide a more effective and rational source of cost control than [can] be achieved by other methods such as price regulation or a squeeze on capacity that might create waiting lists" (White, 1997, p. 73).

Comparatively, Ginsburg and Pickreign (1997, pp. 151–155) attribute the effectiveness of managed care to a "focus more on limitations in choice of provider than use of management techniques." In making this distinction between plans that "selectively contract" with providers as compared to those that "manage treatments," Ginsburg and Pickreign observe that "non-selective indemnity plans" apply management techniques such as utilization review and continuous quality improvement (CQI) and sometimes enroll many to all physicians in a community as "gatekeepers" to health care resources (i.e., engage in management treatments *and* seek a limit on provider choice) to hold down health costs. Comparatively, plans that selectively contract with providers can achieve costs savings without ever having to resort to managing treatment. In such situations, management of treatments is not mandated by the plan but becomes an internal incentive of group practices and other providers who seek to contain costs within the limits of their contractual agreements. Consequently, in such situations, it is legitimate to ask what is the "management" that occurs in such managed care arrangements.

In short, the managed-care term may already have become hackneyed in the health care arena of the late nineties, and may accurately refer to the industry's embracement of "market-oriented" approaches to product/service development, delivery, reimbursement, and evaluation.

Indeed, this is where the 1994 health care debate concluded. What began as a discussion between those who advocated for a single-payer model either funded or coordinated by the federal government and those who advocated a more market-oriented approach eventually became a belief (albeit a divided belief) that the most politically acceptable and effective direction for health care reform to proceed in was in the direction of ever-increasing market-oriented management and reform in the health care industry. With promarket interests having prevailed in the health care debate of 1993–1994, the Congress and administration focused upon efforts to assist patients in making more informed health care decisions based on price, care options, out-of-pocket costs, and quality, developing a patient bill of rights on behalf of patients, expanding access of to third-party health insurance, and other efforts designed to reduce waste and duplication and contain costs. In addressing these key ingredients to the operation of a "market" in health care it was anticipated that market forces under the aegis of a managed care delivery model would largely deal with problems of access, cost, and quality in health care and should significantly reduce the need for federal regulation of the industry.

In embracing a managed care philosophy, Congress considered its next obligation to be the revitalization of the economy via tax relief and budget deficit reduction, tax revision to encourage additional entrepreneurial activities (which would create capital and increase employment), and expansion of health coverage through making employer-based plans portable for employees who switch jobs. The Congress and administration also sought to improve the access of citizens to health care resources by encouraging states and employers to purchase plans (via a variety of incentive models) and by increasing workforce participation. In short, the best solution to the health care access problem was to increase employment and employee benefits thereby leaving the issue of health care where it has historically resided: in the marketplace between employers and providers. By introducing efficiency and quality into the health care system via managed care, allowing consumers in the marketplace to freely play their roles without undue government interference (i.e., beyond necessary regulation), and increasing levels of employment to jobs with benefits, it was optimistically anticipated that the health care cost, quality, and access issues would sort themselves out without excessive government intervention.

B. Guarded Optimism

However, this optimism has been tempered to the extent that some have expressed concern regarding the long-term viability of managed care plans if they fail to make long-term contributions to the community, particularly in the areas of indigent care and so-called "safety net" services (Schlesinger and Gray, 1998, pp. 152–166). This concern may be surprising to some, since one of the rationale's supporting managed care (particularly HMOs) is an emphasis upon prevention and health promotion. Even so, there have long been incentives for plans to "skim" paying customers from the market, leaving high-cost patients (such as many of the indigent and elderly) to be cared for through public hospitals, clinics, and programs. In the current era of cost containment at the local, state, and federal level (relative to health care costs), all providers are increasingly expected by local communities to "carry their share" of the burden.

This growing emphasis on "community benefit" emerged in the 1960s and reemerged in the 1980s when nonprofit hospitals were increasingly being queried relative to what is was about their services that justified their tax-exempt status. In response the IRS issued a standard in 1969 that ruled that hospitals must render some services to the community benefitting all residents, and must operate under the aegis of a board of directors that was representative of the community (Schlesinger and Gray, 1998, p. 154). In more recent years state certificate-of-need requirements have also been utilized to encourage not just hospitals, but providers who operate inpatient, outpatient, and community resources, to include indigent care and other community services in the mix of their health care benefits and programs.

Currently, these incentives for managed care providers to participate in "community benefit" activities are being weakened by the following factors (Schlesinger and Gray, 1998, pp. 159–162):

1. Comoditication of American medicine (i.e., the transformation of medicine from a "service" to a product or "commodity"),
2. Individual consumer orientation of managed care (versus a "community" product orientation),
3. Multistate managed care plans (regionalization of care replaces a more local, community emphasis),
4. Increasingly narrow definitions of community benefit (community benefit concepts developed by the IRS for hospitals can only be applied loosely to the realities of the managed care industry).

Despite these reservations regarding the community benefit of managed care plans, their growth has continued to accelerate with as many as 73% of all the nation's insured covered by one form or another of managed care in 1995, as compared to 51% in 1993 (Jensen et al., 1997, pp. 126–127). By 1998 the rate of insured covered by managed care plans had reached 81%, a level well above the 29% of the nation's insured that were enrolled in managed care plans in 1988. This represents an 8% increase in enrollment in managed care since the failed health care debate of 1993–1994.

Ironically, while the percentage of enrollees in managed care plans has steadily risen since the late eighties, actual enrollment in employer-based health plans has fallen over the same period, primarily in response to increasing premium costs (Ginsburg et al., 1998). In 1987, 76.2% of workers had acquired employer-based health care coverage while 81.8% of employed workers had been offered benefits, resulting in an insurance "takeup" rate of 93.2%. Comparatively, in 1996, 73.2% of employees had chosen to accept employer-based coverage out of 82.2% who had access to such coverage, for a takeup rate of 89.1% (Cooper and Schone, 1997).

C. Responding to a Backlash: Regulating Managed Care

In developing the Health Security Act, President Clinton chose to support a version of managed care with a heavy federal regulatory component, despite the advice of advisors associated with the Jackson Hole Group, who favored a more market-driven approach. Adopting a global budgeting approach to managed care was considered prudent policy in the short term until market forces could demonstrate that less strenuous regulation was required. In the aftermath of the failure of Clinton's health plan, it would be expected that the managed care industry would actively seek to elude federal regulation in the interest of stimulating market forces. Consequently it is an irony to learn from Donald Moran (1997) that "from the managed care industry side, a growing (if until now highly private) consensus is emerging that at the end of the day, federal regulation may not be all that bad—provided that it conveys the benefits of federal preemption of diverse state efforts to regulate the same matters" (p. 8).

Clearly, being regulated by one entity is superior to being regulated by 50, but why the demand to regulate period? The answer is manifold. With the spread of managed care plans in the employer-based market and with the number of Medicare beneficiaries in managed care plans having doubled since 1991 (projected to reach 30 million beneficiaries by 2007), an increasing number of citizens had either transitioned or were in the midst of transitioning from traditional fee-for-service health care reimbursement plans. This transition was rendered particularly difficult because beneficiaries had previously enjoyed significant choice relative to physicians, treatments, etc., as compared to their more immediate predicament of dealing with a "gatekeeper," managed approach in which choices of physician, treatments, hospitals, and even pharmaceuticals are increasingly constrained (Brodie et al., 1998).

In making these transitions, some have become frustrated relative to problems of access to care, provision of inadequate or incomplete care, barriers to accessing favored physicians, changing benefit packages, changing providers and provider networks, and restrictions in coverage. Throughout the nation state legislatures are being encouraged by citizens to increase their regulatory oversight of managed care plans. For instance, communities have expressed concern regarding managed care pressures that result in the closing or sale of nonprofit or community hospitals to proprietary providers. While instances abound where inefficient local hospitals have closed, forcing residents to travel farther to obtain access to care, recent research indicates that "the acquisition of nonprofit hospitals by investor-owned corporations does not uniformly lead to less uncompensated care" (Young et al., 1997, p. 140).

Other groups have criticized the capacity of managed care models to provide effective care to the aged, the disabled, to children [especially chronically ill children (Kuhlthau et al., 1998)], and to mentally ill populations. Criticisms in this vein have been particularly targeted toward HMOs, whose historical development in the seventies revolved around enrolling essentially healthy working persons and avoiding health costs by promoting health and implementing prevention efforts. Early HMOs, which were primarily group and staff models as compared to today's IPA models (Luft and Greenlick, 1996), contained costs by avoiding chronically ill populations (leaving these patients to public and community hospitals). Currently, complaints relative to the provision of a variety of types of care to include primary, specialty, and geriatric care, as well as (Jensen et al., 1998; Hegner, 1996) children's health care (Glied et al., 1997) and long-term care (Cogswell et al., 1997), are becoming increasingly frequent. For instance, a 1997 CNN survey indicated that overall most HMOs deserve no better than a "B" rating. More specifically, 59% of respondents complained that managed care makes it "tougher to see a specialist," while another 51% of respondents "worry that the quality of treatment has gotten worse." Finally, another 55% of respondents expressed the opinion that "HMOs care more about money than about providing the best treatment" (Levine, 1997). This concern may be well illustrated in the current trend for HMOs and managed care corporations to merge in the interest of exerting more market control locally, regionally, and nationally (Christianson et al., 1997).

A more recent poll conducted by the Employee Benefits Research Institute (EBRI, 1998), the *1998 Health Confidence Survey*, rendered a similar picture of the U.S. public's view of health care coverage in general and managed care in particular. Some of the salient findings from this survey include the following:

> Satisfaction with health care and insurance is high, but managed care participants feel differently. Overall 52% of respondents rate health care in America highly, 32% rate health care as fair, and 14% rate it as poor. Comparatively, managed care participants rate their health care less positively, with 45% rating their care highly, as compared to 77% for fee-for-service participants.
>
> The managed care conundrum: most do not see their health insurance as "managed care." Even though 80% of U.S. workers are enrolled in some form of managed care plan, the majority of all respondents indicated that they are currently not in a managed care plan and have never been enrolled in one.
>
> Managed care is generally alright with few having negative opinions. Managed care receives high ratings (52% excellent rating) regarding quality, and rates lowest (22%) in terms of access to experimental treatments and costs.

Respondents have grave concerns about the future of health care. Only 21% of respondents expressed confidence in having access to affordable health care (i.e., anticipating medical hardships) over the next decade. Managed care enrollees are the most concerned about the future of health care, with approximately 20% indicating that they are not confident in having future access to affordable health care (as compared to only 12% of fee-for-service respondents who responded similarly).

Respondents say that health care issues need policymakers' attention. Eighty-one percent of respondents believe that health care costs have gotten worse over the last 5 years, and another 57% believe that the state of their health insurance coverage has declined.

Concerns from the *1998 Health Confidence Survey* are also reflected in more recent research conducted by Robert Blendon (1998) and his colleagues. Blendon evaluated two sources of consumer information relating to satisfaction with health plans. One source involves a study conducted by the Henry J. Kaiser Family Foundation and Harvard University of a randomly selected number of consumers nationwide (1204) and 500 respondents from California. The other pooled source of data utilized by Blendon et al. involves results from 21 other surveys conducted between 1995 and 1997.

In essence what this evaluative research concluded was that Americans are generally satisfied with their health care plan (a finding consistent with the *1998 Health Confidence Survey*) but are vocal about their belief that government should more closely regulate the managed care industry. These results, while at face seemingly contradictory, become more clear when specific items among the surveys are more closely analyzed. For instance, while 76% of respondents rated their fee-for-service plan as deserving a grade of "B or better," only 66% of managed care enrollees rated their plans similarly. Clearly respondents from managed care plans were less enthusiastic in their support than were their traditional third-party-insured colleagues.

This variation in enthusiastic support for plans becomes more understandable when responses are separated into three groups based on the number of "managed care characteristics" reported by respondents. These three groups are defined as enrolled in "heavy" managed care (intensely managed), "light" managed care (moderate intensity of management), and "traditional" third-party plans (i.e., plans lacking the managed care characteristics). Respondents falling within these categories were asked to rate their plan in terms of how confident they were that their plan would:

1. Pay for emergency room visits,
2. Pay for the bulk of costs resulting from a serious injury,

3. Consistently "do the right thing" relative to care,
4. Be more concerned about saving money than about delivering the best treatment.

The responses to these questions were consistently related to the extent of managed care intensity. For instance, while the average response of all groups was that 64% believed that their plans would pay for an emergency room visit, only 56% of respondents enrolled in "heavy" plans shared this optimism, as compared to 63% among enrollees in "light" managed care plans and 78% enrolled in traditional plans. This same pattern applied to respondents' belief that plans would pay for the costs of a serious injury (55% overall, 44% for heavy managed, 54% for light managed, and 69% for traditional plans). Obviously the extent of respondent optimism was reduced at the point of querying about a potentially catastrophic health event. Respondents were even less enthusiastic when asked about their belief that their plan would "do the right thing" (41% overall, 30% for heavy managed, 31% for light managed, and 55% for traditional) or when asked if they believed the plan would value costs savings over quality of care (47% overall, 61% heavy managed, 51% light managed, and 34% for traditional).

Essentially, while respondents were generally comfortable with their health plans *now*, they were much less confident in what the *future* would hold as they remained in managed care plans. Consequently, respondents tended to favor more regulation of the managed care industry (52%) with respondents in fair to poor health asserting an even stronger desire for more regulation (65%) (Blendon et al., 1998, p. 83). Blendon's research also noted that Americans seem to believe that managed care has served to reduce the quality of care (45% plurality) and has made it harder for enrollees to gain access to specialists (59%). On a more optimistic note, 51% of respondents believe that the trend of managed care will be to contain costs and 56% believe that managed care allows them to pay less for their health insurance. Nevertheless, 72% of respondents believe that the primary function of managed care for health providers is to maximize corporate profits. Only 49% indicated that they believe that cost savings ultimately make health care more affordable for "people like them" (Blendon et al., 1998, p. 88).

D. Physician Backlash

Depending upon whether practices are located in regions experiencing a high or low penetration rate by managed care plans (Donelan et al., 1997), it goes without saying that one of the most prominent players in the health care industry, physicians, are increasingly backlashing against managed care. In so doing they are demanding that they be returned to their central and pivotal role as caregivers, replacing managers who increasingly control not only the scope, but the very nature of the health care services delivered (Ginsburg, 1998, p. 166f.). The clearest indicator of the extent to which physicians have become "fed up" with restrictions imposed by managed care providers can be found by looking at the recent support from the American Medical Association, the nation's largest professional medical association, for H.R. 4277 (currently before Congress), known as the Quality Health-Care Coalition Act of 1998. This proposed legislation would allow individual physicians to collectively bargain with health plans, in the interest of restoring more physician control and a stronger patient orientation in the delivery of care. Speaking for the AMA, trustee Donald J. Palmisano recently addressed the AMA house of Delegates and observed that "physicians have seen their negotiating ability whittled away to the detriment of patients, and efficient and effective health care delivery" The AMA has long believed an antitrust exemption for self-employed physicians is needed to level the playing field. Too often the individual physician and the individual patient stand alone against the enormous health plan bureaucracies" (Palmisano, 1998).

In so declaring, the AMA continues to move in the direction of endorsing activities (unionization) on the part of physicians that would have been unthinkable not so many years ago. Palmisano continues, saying, "Most physicians don't want to be part of a trade union, but they do want to be able to engage in joint negotiations with big health plans. The [Quality Health-Care Coalition Act] would improve patient care and redirect the medical decision making back toward the physicians and patients—where it belongs" (Palmisano, 1998).

Those familiar with the evolution of health policy in the United States cannot help but be impressed with the gravity of this current AMA position. While their reluctant embrace of physician unions is new to this organization, its sentiments on the dangers of managed care to the physician role as coordinator and primary deliverer of care are not new. Consider, for instance, the comments of Dr. Stephen Harlin quoted in the *New York Times* (Harlin, 1996): "Managed care innovations" are encroaching upon the doctor patient relationship. Insurers are demonstrating and expanding repertoire of practices designed to reduce the provision of medical care. Medical decision-making is no longer a privileged domain for those involved in direct patient care. The market has been brought to bear in health care."

The values expressed by Dr. Palmisano of the AMA and by Dr. Harlin can perhaps be best summarized by a veteran health policy analyst and industry observer: Victor Fuchs. Fuchs was recently asked to comment on some of the forces that he found disturbing in the current managed care environment. Fuchs cited three major concerns: (1) excessive commercialization of the product, (2) the erosion of professional norms, and (3) the stampede to mergers and acquisitions (Iglehart, 1998, p. 90). When asked to expound upon his concerns relative to the erosion of professional norms, Fuchs stated:

> Professional power is eroding in two ways, at least. One is through intense competition. Another is through the transfer of power and control from the physician to managers. To some extent, that was inevitable because physicians (with some exceptions) were not willing to step up to the plate and try to deal with the problems of exploding costs and managing the delivery of reasonably good quality care. It was almost inevitable that power would shift away from the physician. But that doesn't mean that I'm happy about the shift. Nor am I happy about intense competition between physicians or between physician groups. Medical care can suffer from too much competition, just as in the past, it suffered from too little. The conditions that make textbook competition so appealing are often lacking in medical care. Physicians and patients possess very different information; honesty and trust on both sides are extremely important; and patients often benefit from cooperation among physicians (p. 91).

In making this statement, Fuchs asserts what an increasingly vocal number of physicians are now claiming, that state and federal regulation are increasingly needed to insure that managed care plans make decisions that are first and foremost in the interest of the patient rather than narrowly serving the interests of the plan, practice, or corporation providing care (Colby, 1997; Hadley and Mitchell, 1997).

E. Managed Care Backlash: Blame It on the Media!

Despite the critique of critics emanating from a number of fronts, the managed care industry tends to discount the extent of the so-called backlash to managed care as essentially a creation of the media (Ignagni, 1998). Brodie et al. (1998) recently evaluated this claim by evaluating stories about managed care that appeared in general newspapers, business presses, special series articles, and on broadcasts. Upon evaluating stories throughout these sources, the researchers concluded that "the vast majority of media coverage is neutral, but the most visible media sources (broadcast and special series) are more negative and focus on more graphic examples of problems people have had" (p. 22). These researchers go on to observe that the public typically considers the media coverage of managed care and HMOs to be fair to the point that the coverage includes a mix of favorable and unfavorable stories. Consequently they tend to report that the personal feelings of consumers relative to managed care are influenced to a greater extent by their own personal experiences and on the basis of opinions expressed by family and friends, rather than upon media coverage. Thus Brodie et al. (1998) conclude that "based on our findings, it would be difficult to argue that media coverage is by itself creating whatever backlash currently exists" (p. 23). Given this conclusion, one must conclude that there must be legitimate reasons from a consumer perspective to seek regulatory relief from some of the more egregious aspects of managed care.

V. FILLING THE GAPS IN EMPLOYER-BASED INSURANCE COVERAGE: THEN AND NOW

A. Extending Health Coverage Across and Between Employers: COBRA, 1985

While the debate rages on regarding the utility and wisdom of continuing to pursue managed care approaches to health care delivery, there are still gaps in coverage that deny access to health care benefits for U.S. citizens. Since the 1993–1994 period of intense debate over the shape and future of U.S. health care, Congress has revisited the problem of closing gaps in health care coverage that result when workers change and or lose jobs and, in so doing, lose their health insurance coverage. In addressing these problems, Congress first acted in 1985 to pass the Consolidated Omnibus Budget Reconciliation Act (COBRA) and, more recently, further reduced gaps in the employer-based system with the passage of the Health Insurance Portability and Accountability Act of 1996 (HIPAA). Let's begin with a review of the basic provisions of COBRA and determine how it has been received by employers. Thereafter, we will address the more recent HIPAA statute.

In a nutshell, COBRA requires employers of 20 or more employees to extend health care coverage for 18–36 months, depending on whether the so-called "qualifying event" is related to discontinuation of employment (other than release for cause), which covers employees for 18 months, or family-related events, which can lead to up to 36 months' coverage. By statute, COBRA coverage must include the same set of benefits as those provided to others under the employer plan, and overall premiums cannot exceed 102% of the employer's plan cost. The only exception to this cap on premium regards disabled former employees, whose rate cannot exceed 150% of the employer's plan cost.

The COBRA plan has met with resistance from employers seeking to rid themselves of its regulatory burden. Items that employers find particularly burdensome include the following:

> Provision of written notice to employees of the availability of health coverage extension under COBRA at the point of inception of health benefits.
> Employer requirements to notify their plan's administration within 30 days of the death or termination of an employee, or whenever an employee becomes eligible for Medicare.
> Employers must make employees aware of their rights under COBRA within 2 weeks of notification of a "qualifying event" (Nichols et al., 1997, pp. 26–27).

Other employer criticisms center around concerns that unhealthy employees will choose COBRA options, thereby driving treatment costs above premium costs. This concern was recently documented by Charles A. Spence and Associates (1995), who reported cases in which costs have exceeded premium rates by as much as 150%.

Finally, employers claim that it is extremely difficult to keep track of past employees. This is particularly true in large industries, but is also a problem for smaller businesses, which possess fewer resources to engage in ongoing employee tracking. Worrisome to many observers are the regulatory burdens of COBRA, which may discourage small businesses with fewer than 20 employees from participating in the program (Nichols et al., 1997).

B. Kassebaum-Kennedy: The Health Insurance Portability and Accountability Act of 1996

A landmark piece of legislation, designed to introduce more regulatory mettle into the managed care environment, was passed by Congress 2 years after the 1993–1994 health care reform debacle. This legislation was fueled by citizen and professional concerns regarding the untoward effects of managed care. Sponsored by Sen. Nancy Kassebaum and Sen. Edward Kennedy, this bill was passed by Congress and is popularly known as the Health Insurance Portability and Accountability Act of 1996 (PL 104-191).

HIPAA marked the beginning of a new era in federal regulation to ensure health insurance coverage for countless Americans, preventing those switching jobs from having to sacrifice access to their health care benefits. HIPAA guaranteed coverage to employees of small businesses (businesses employing two to 50 employees) and to other "eligible individuals," as well as "renewal of health insurance in all markets" to include (Meier, 1997, pp. 3–4):

> Small-group insurers must offer at least one standard policy available to every small employer with two to 50 employees. Large-group insurers may issue insurance on an "accept-reject" basis to employers with 51 or more employees. If the insurer accepts a group, it may not exclude high-risk employees or those with preexisting conditions, and if it rejects a group, it must reject the whole group and not only the high-risk members.
>
> No group insurer is allowed to make insurance eligibility contingent upon individual health status, medical condition (physical and mental condition), claims experience, receipt of health care, medical history, genetic information, evidence of insurability (including hazardous activities and conditions arising out of domestic violence), or disability of any member of the group.

"Eligible individuals" must be guaranteed access to coverage. To qualify as an "eligible individual," a person must have had 18 months of prior coverage under a group plan, have elected and exhausted continued benefits coverage under COBRA (typically 18 months), and not be eligible for any other group coverage.

All group and individual insurance must be collectively renewable. This means than an insurer who elects to cancel a policy because of high claim costs is forbidden from offering any insurance in that market in that state for 5 years.

Beyond provisions to guarantee portability and access to plans, HIPAA also establishes what are known as "medical savings accounts" (MSAs), which allows employees to purchase less expensive, high-deductible insurance and invest the premium savings in a tax-sheltered account to be later depleted against future medical expenses. These MSAs are limited to self-employed persons and employees in small-group plans (those enrolling between two and 50 persons). HIPAA imposes an enrollment cap of 750,000 individuals who had been previously insured, but imposes no cap on enrollment for those without health insurance coverage during a 6-month period.

In a follow-up study of the implementation of HIPAA, GAO observed that some HIPAA-covered individuals were charged as much as 400–600% of standard premiums in four states. Fortunately, 22 other states that had adopted high-risk pools were able to implement the HIPAA requirements with premiums ranging to around 150% of standard premiums. In the interest of promoting the use of state risk pools, and to avoid situations where premiums skyrocket, Senator Kennedy and Representative Pallone have introduced the Affordable Health Insurance Act of 1998 (S. 1804/HR 3538), which would cap individual rates at 150% of standard market value (Gradison, 1998a, 1998b). Finally, HIPAA mandated the development of "qualified" long-term-care insurance contracts, in an effort to curb federal and state obligations for carrying the bulk of long-term-care costs.

VI.   HEALTH POLICY INNOVATION AND ACTIVITY IN 1997

A.   Addressing the Thorny Issues Currently Confronting U.S. Health Care: Introduction

When the Clinton-led health care debate of 1993–1994 finally collapsed, it was assumed that it would be quite a while before health policy debate would rage on Capitol hill. Then in 1997, the health policy discussion unpredictably heated up. The impetus behind this renewed interest was fueled by some of the very issues that we have been discussing so far (Ginsburg, 1998, pp. 165–169):

1. Consumer desire for a greater choice among health options,
2. A backlash directed toward managed care,
3. Consolidation of providers,
4. The ongoing problems of the uninsured (especially children and the disabled),
5. Concerns over quality of care,
6. Medicaid managed care,
7. Overall health care costs.

Each of these issues will be addressed in some detail in the following sections. However, owing to the complex and comprehensive changes to Medicare enacted into by the Balanced Budget Act of 1997 (Moon et al., 1997), discussions of Medicare, Medicaid, and managed care (as it applies to these two programs) will be separately discussed later in this chapter.

B. Consumer Choice

Consumers have been increasingly compelled to join managed care plans, as the sheer number of plans nationwide has increased. Predictably, many consumers miss the ease of access to the family physician and relatively unfettered ability to choose among providers and treatments. Consequently, it should come as no surprise that the spread of managed care plans has been accompanied by an increasing demand from enrollees for extended choices in the scope and substance of their care. Managed care plans have responded to this demand by largely abandoning earlier efforts to narrowly enroll selected physicians in a community, now choosing to broadly enroll physicians, sometimes all physicians in a community.

Given this consumer-driven emergence of managed care plans, a number of untoward outcomes have occurred. First, with physician practices dealing with a variety of health plans, no single plan has the kind of leverage on a practice that it would have under more selective provider enrollment strategies. Second, given the overlapping nature of health plans, there is a decreased capacity for any one plan to develop efficiencies in billing and patient information systems, etc. that would contribute to reduced operational costs. Similarly (third), physician practices are saddled with a plethora of reporting forms, schedules, policies, etc. that must be completed for each patient insured by each plan. The net result, of course, are increased transaction costs, treatment and billing inefficiencies, and patient frustration. Finally (fourth), the "paper jungle" confronted by many physician practices and groups contributed to the decisions of many practices to merge. Similarly, the option of organizing into provider service organizations (PSOs) and directly assuming responsibility for not only the patient's care, but also the risks associated with underwriting care became an increasingly attractive alternative. However, perhaps the greatest reason that consumer choice influenced extended health policy deliberation in 1997 has to do with the "backlash" issue previously discussed. Seventeen states enacted consumer protection legislation in 1997 (Stauffer, 1998), which, according to Ginsburg (1998), constitutes the first time that "so many states addressed a single legislative issue at the same time."

C. Managed Care Backlash

Having thoroughly addressed this issue earlier, suffice it to say that much of the backlash emanates from the fact that an increasing number of Americans were given no choice other than managed care. This generated significant anger and frustration. Indeed, the combination of limited choices and high out-of-pocket expenses had a particularly severe impact on small employers, who saw coverage for single individuals increase from $12 monthly in 1988 to $56 a month in 1996. Similarly, monthly premiums for family coverage increased from $34 monthly in 1988 to a high of $154 monthly in 1996. Such increases are likely responsible for much of the current managed care backlash (Gabel et al., 1997).

As for physicians, beyond facing even greater regulation from managed care plans and seeing their ability to exercise their judgment and skills simultaneously slipping away, there has arisen a sense that the "profession" and "craft" are being increasingly transformed into a commodity that can be readily replaced or substituted. This has led to a sense of alienation from their professional roles and has left some feeling superfluous or incidental to the field they have chosen. As noted above, this sense of alienation and exclusion from the caregiving decision process has prompted state legislatures to enact patient bills of rights, as has President Clinton through the President's Advisory Commission on Consumer Protection and Quality in the Health Care Industry (Ginsburg, 1998, p. 166).

D. Quality of Care

1. Quality of Care Initiatives

Quality of care has proved to be an ongoing issue particularly since the 1970s when John Wennberg's (1999) research identified significant variation in patterns of care in which medical decision making was often more influenced by local practice tradition and profit considerations than by the demands of the patient's condition. Quality-of-care concerns were also attenuated following the introduction of the 1983 Medicare PPS, which, upon introduction, resulted in more patients being discharged earlier from the hospital. Since then, one of the primary indicators of quality care during and following hospitalizations is the reduction in factors contributing to unnecessary hospital readmissions (Holloway and Thomas, 1989).

In response to both historical and recent concerns regarding the "quality" of today's health care system, the following steps have been taken by government, industry, and accreditation bodies to bolster the quality of care (Darby, 1992, p. 10):

> HCFA initiated clinical outcome studies to determine which treatments and practices were most effective in treating diseases and disorders.
>
> The Joint Commission for the Accreditation of Health Care Organizations (JCAHO) adopted total quality management (TQM) and continuous quality improvement (CQI) standards as a part of their accreditation process.
>
> The President created the Advisory Commission on Consumer Protection and Quality in the Health Care Industry.

Despite these efforts, and the realization that quality must be infused into every aspect of the delivery system, there remains a concern among some as to whether the broadspread interest in quality is more rhetoric than action. Indeed, given the regulatory and "paperwork" load under which the health care industry is already drowning, it is questionable as to how much "quality" (in terms of documentation activities at least) the industry can actually afford.

2. American Health Quality Association

Illustrative of this concern is the following statement of the American Health Quality Association:

> As managed care increasingly dominates the health care system, policy makers, health care experts, and consumers all are concerned that quality does not take a back seat to cost control. More and more purchasers of care—employers and government—are demanding meaningful quality measurement and assurance efforts as they choose among competing plans for their employees and beneficiaries. Adding to the importance of a national discussion about quality is this year's significant congressional debate about the future of Medicare and Medicaid, as millions of elderly, poor, and disabled beneficiaries of these programs are rapidly enrolling in managed care (AHQA, 1997, p. 1).

Having made this assertion AHQA's Josef Renum asserts that "the litmus test for any meaningful debate on the future cost of Medicare will be whether or not quality is afforded the same stature as an 'equal partner' with cost." Renum also goes on to observe that "it is a given that in the coming years Medicare must become a more prudent buyer of health services if cost inflation is to be controlled. However, in the rush to control costs we cannot in good conscience cut corners on quality" (AHQA, 1997, p. 7).

AHQA's comments bring the quality and effectiveness of Wennberg's work (Wennberg, 1999) full circle into the era of managed care. Unfortunately, measuring quality of care also requires further developments in medical informatics and other information technologies that, as was noted earlier, are being undercut by local market forces as the relationship among physician practices, hospitals, and other health care providers and plans unfold on a community-by-community basis. Broad overlap of providers utilized by plans is just one of many factors that mitigates against some of the coordination efforts that could contribute to better assessment of care quality. Of course, the other factors undercutting such developments are competitive market pressures that reinforce the tendency of providers and plans to differentiate between one another in terms of quality, or, in the case of Columbia HCA, create incentives for corporate managers to hide information that would link cost with quality.

3. Defining and Applying Quality Care Principles

Admittedly, there are major forces in the industry that contribute to quality improvement. Some are related to agreed-upon accreditation standards that embrace TQM and CQI, among other quality improvement tools. However, these approaches, when implemented independently in each provider setting, frequently yield outcomes that may demonstrate quality improvement at the particular site, but that are difficult to compare to similar efforts at other facilities, hospitals, or clinics. With the encouragement of Congress, HCFA is engaging in an ongoing process of clinical outcome assessments to identify "best practices." While these efforts are valuable, they are also costly, time consuming, and subject to constant changes in technology, making it difficult to immediately point to a large number of practices that should be immediately utilized. Furthermore, when such practices are identified, and are communicated via the medical literature, they are not easily understandable to the consumer public, or even readily usable by administrators who constantly sell their organization's "quality" to the public.

Despite these difficulties in communicating to the public what "quality" entails, HCFA and Congress have remained committed to pursuing quality on an ongoing basis through the Medicare and Medicaid programs. For instance, OBRA (1989) required HCFA to develop and utilize a minimum clinical data set (MDS) in the assessment and care of long-term-care patients. This comprehensive assessment tool has evolved into its second version and has become a universally used instrument (utilizing state-of-the-art assessment instruments) for the physical, functional, psychosocial, and demographic assessment of patients in skilled nursing facilities (SNFs). So effective has the assessment tool become that it has become the clinical information base upon which a prospective payment system for SNF is currently operating (BBA, 1997). Similar efforts have been forthcoming in the area of home health care, as HCFA moves to introduce a prospective payment system in 1999 built around what HCFA calls its Outcome and Assessment Information Set (OASIS). Finally, HCFA, in conjunction with state survey agencies, has developed a collaborative project known as Sharing Innovations in Quality (SIQ). The goal of this organization is to become a clearinghouse and repository for innovative ideas and practices that improve quality of care and life for residents of nursing homes.

4. Does Managed Care Render Quality Care?

As noted throughout this chapter, a major concern for quality of care involves the extent to which managed care contributes or detracts from quality care. A number of studies have been conducted, looking for the "truth" behind managed care's alleged association with quality care. Taken in sum, proponents and critics of managed care have found data to serve as ammunition for their particular perspective (Miller and Luft, 1997). In fact, "quality of care" is at the center of the battle raging between the proponents and opponents of managed care. In comparing selected research papers investigating the issue of quality of care in HMO plans, Miller and Luft (1997) created three points of quality comparison.

1. Quality-of-care results favorable to HMOs as compared to non-HMO providers: Areas in which quality of care in HMOs was ranked above the quality of care provided in non-HMO settings included: treatment of appendicitis (reduced risk of rupture), ICU care for both elderly and nonelderly (reduced mortality rate), care for chronically ill elderly and nonelderly (maintenance or improvement in physical/mental functioning), care for Medicaid-enrolled diabetics (stabilizing glycosylated hemoglobin levels), care for persons with cancer/breast cancer [reduced mortality (breast cancer) and more favorable outcomes given stage of diagnosis], and care for the mentally ill (symptomatic and functional stabilization and improvement) (Miller and Luft, 1998, pp. 15–17).

2. Quality-of-care results with similar or mixed outcomes as compared to non-HMO providers (not statistically significant)

Same or better results: Medicaid-enrolled elderly hypertensives (stabilized systolic/diastolic blood pressure), coronary surgery (reduced morbidity), rheumatoid arthritis (reduced pain and swelling), acute low back pain (functional recovery and pain relief), hypertensives (blood pressure control, function, and energy), and non-insulin-dependent diabetics (glycosylated hemoglobin levels, functional status, and energy).

Better and worse results (statistically significant): Chronically ill elderly (better and worse regarding both physical and mental health status).

3. Unfavorable quality-of-care results for HMOs compared to non-HMO providers: Areas in which quality of care for HMOs was ranked lower than for

non-HMO providers include: chronically ill and most severely ill low-income patients (physical and mental health), breast cancer (mortality risk), Medicare-enrolled elderly receiving home care (condition improvement, stabilization, discharge to independent living, and mortality risk), newborns (neonatal mortality risk).

Interestingly, Miller and Luft's (1997) research suggests that in many regards, HMO performance in the area of quality assurance is mixed. Consequently, on the basis of these results it is difficult to draw really definitive conclusions, beyond observing that HMOs seem to have the greatest difficulty dealing with chronically ill indigent patients, neonatal care, and home care. Clearly, more research into the quality of care under managed care approaches will be needed.

As demonstrated by the mixed results presented by Miller and Luft, current data and discussions still fail to move the quality-of-care debate to a more "quantifiable" level, if for no other reason than because there are so many indicators that could be associated with quality that it is difficult to prioritize from among them.

E. Health, Mortality, and Morbidity: Other Indicators of Quality Care

Currently, a source of critical data that can be loosely related to the quality of health care provision are selected mortality and morbidity figures. Connection between these data sets and the quality of provision of care can only be loosely associated, given the myriad underlying factors that contribute to death and disease. The availability and quality of care is only one factor among many, and is frequently not the definitive factor.

Available mortality data suggest that Americans have witnessed a steep decline in total mortality, with the total death rate for Americans having fallen from 803.6 per 100,000 in 1970 to 594.6 in 1995, and projected to fall to 506.7 by the year 2020 (see Fig. 3). When looking at disease-specific mortality rates, however, a somewhat different picture emerges. For instance, mortality associated with heart disease dropped from a rate per 100,000 persons of 308.4 in 1970 to 186.5 in 1995 and is projected to fall to 126.5 by the year 2020. Similarly, death related to vascular disease has plummeted from 144.9 per 100,000 in 1970 to 48.6 in 1995 and is expected to drop to 24.5 by 2020. Infant mortality also dropped from 24.7 in 1970 to 8.3 in 1995, as has diabetes [21.2 (1970), 12.2 (1995)] and violent death [45.6 (1970), 27.1 (1995)]. Unfortunately, cancer-related deaths are on the rise, increasing from 141.0 in 1970 to 156.4 in 1995 and may rise to 158 in 2020, as are respiratory diseases [38.5 (1970), 55.4 (1995),

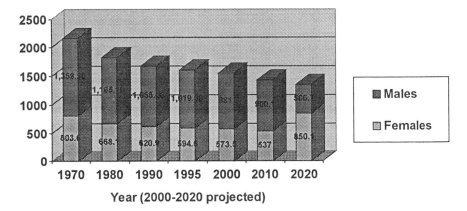

Figure 3 Age-adjusted death rates, selected years (per 100,000). Available mortality data suggest that Americans have seen a decline in total mortality. Overall death rate for all Americans fell from 2163.1 per 100,000 population in 1970 to 1613.9 per 100,000 population in 1995 (74.61% decline). This decrease is expected to decline into the next millennium. The projected death rate for Americans in 2020 is 1356.8 per 100,000 population. Although we are seeing overall declines in the death rates for all Americans, the death rate among women is projected to increase in the next century from 594.6 per 100,000 in population in 1995 to 850.1 per 100,000 in 2020. However, when one looks at mortality rates with specific causes of death we find a mixed picture. Heart disease, stroke or cerebrovascular accidents, and cancer have long been the three leading causes of death in the United States. In 1950, heart disease, cerebrovascular accidents, and cancer had death rates of 307.2, 88.6, and 125.3, respectively, per 100,000 deaths in the population. Although we find decreases in both heart disease and cerebrovascular accidents in 1995 (138.3 and 26.7, respectively, per 100,000 deaths in the population), cancer death rates have increased to 129.9 per 100,000 deaths in the population. Similarly, mortality rates for respiratory disease, AIDS, and homicide/suicides have increased. Mortality due to respiratory disease was 4.4 per 100,000 deaths in the population in 1950 and 20.8 per 100,000 deaths in the population in 1995. AIDS-related deaths increased from 9.8 to 15.6 per 100,000 deaths in the population from 1990 to 1995, and deaths due to homicide and suicide were 16.4 per 100,000 deaths in the population in 1950 and 20.6 per 100,000 deaths in the population in 1995. However, mortality due to accidents or external causes (unintentional injuries and motor vehicle crashes) decreased from 73.9 per 100,000 deaths in the population in 1950 to 52.2 per 100,000 deaths in the population in 1995. (From Social Security Administration, Office of the Actuary.)

60.5 (2020)] (see Fig. 4). Mortality rates also vary by age, gender, race, and economic status, with low-income black and Hispanic men and women demonstrating the highest mortality rates (Minor, 1998, p. 157).

The rise in mortality rates for some diseases and disorders raises questions regarding what underlying factors are contributing to these deaths. Some of the answers to those questions may involve improvements in the quality of care. However, each disease cited herein and others that could have been cited require a case-by-case, diagnosis-by-diagnosis assessment and evaluation to discover what is best for the care of the American public.

Nevertheless, as Cutler and Richardson report (1998), "people are healthier than they used to be" (p. 265). These researchers site decreases in infant mortality and better care and treatment for debilitating diseases as significant factors in this improvement. However, they do note some trends that are of significant concern to the organization, delivery, and financing of the nation's health care system. For instance, they observe that much of the improvement in the health of the nation has been the result of innovations in the diagnosis and treatment of cardiovascular diseases. While this improvement has been of great benefit to the elderly, it has been of less value to the young. This factor, among others, is one of the reasons Congress has made a concerted effort via the 1997 State Child Health Insurance Program (S-CHIP) to focus on children's health care, if for no other reason than because it seems to be "their turn" in the health policy cycle. Cutler and Richardson also observe that since the 1980s African-Americans have improved in health status relative to whites, and interestingly, they also note that "people's health has improved by more than per capita spending on medical care has increased" (p. 265).

1. Report Cards, Impediments to Quality Care, and Proposed Solutions

In the interest of improving the quality of the continuum of health care services, some members of Congress and individuals and groups purporting to represent the consumer public want to mandate that *all* health care providers be subjected to a performance "report card," upon which they can be evaluated (Zimmerman, 1994). While appealing in a bureaucratic sense, the reality is that the public is unlikely to utilize such an evaluation instrument in their choice of a health care plan or option. Typically people rely upon the advice of family or friends to make these important decisions (Brodie et al., 1998). Nevertheless, it remains necessary for the industry to identify lapses in quality in the interest of improving performance.

Rather than relying on accountability tools such as report cards to improve upon the quality of health care, David Eddy (1998, p. 11f) identifies a set of

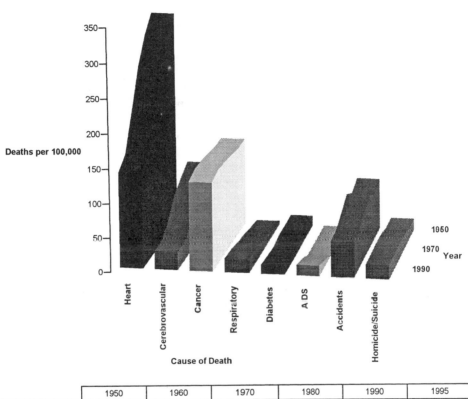

	1950	1960	1970	1980	1990	1995
■ Heart	307.2	286.2	253.6	202	152	138.3
▥ Cerebrovascular	88.6	79.7	66.3	40.8	27.7	26.7
▧ Cancer	125.3	125.8	129.8	132.8	135	129.9
■ Respiratory	4.4	8.2	13.2	15.9	19.7	20.8
▢ Diabetes	14.3	13.6	14.1	10.1	11.7	13.3
▦ AIDS					9.8	15.6
■ Accidents	73.9	65.7	77.4	66.1	55.1	52.2
▦ Homicide/Suicide	16.4	15.8	20.9	22.2	21.7	20.6

Figure 4   Age-adjusted death rates for selected causes, selected years. (From Health, United States, 1996–1997, National Center for Health Statistics.)

systemic problems that will need to be overcome to more effectively address the quality performance issue. These include:

Natural Factors: Probabilistic health outcomes, infrequent outcomes of interest, long delays in documenting survival rates, the ability of plans to control outcomes, level of clinical detail utilized in assessments (high detail = high assessment costs), comprehensibility of problems being evaluated by the public.

Manmade Problems: Inadequate information systems, excessive numbers of "measures" and "measures," health plan complexity, funding/cost restrictions in conducting performance assessments. Eddy's suggestion relative to mitigating these problems in quality assessment and performance measurement entails the following:

Process Measures: Health outcome measures are simply not adequate to comprehensively address issues of quality. Consequently, Eddy recommends that attention be shifted to using more "process measures" that can reorient plans in the direction of activities that have proven effective in improving health (i.e., such activities as cancer screenings, etc.).

Formal Workup: Prior to initiating any performance assessment, plans should conduct a formal analysis to determine the significance of the issue or issues to be investigated, including "statistical characteristics, relevance, feasibility and cost-effectiveness" (Eddy, 1998, p. 18).

Rotation: Utilize cost-effective and efficient measurement tools; rather than attempting to measure every conceivable aspect of performance, identify selected items to measure on a rotational basis.

Information Systems: Create systems that include an automated medical record (a controversial issue before the current Congress) linked to standards, dictionaries, and other necessary linkages.

Case-Based Measures: Problems of "bluntness, distortion, incompleteness and cost" require supplementing population based measures with case-specific measures (i.e., develop qualitative data resources to complement quantitative data).

Standardize Core Measurement Set: Promote efficiency by committing to a core set of measures (much like HCFA with their MDS in SNFs).

Funding: (1) Expect plans to collect performance data as a function of their normal operation expenses. (2) Relieve plans from having to comply with a multiplicity of measures. (3) Acknowledge that costs associated with collecting, analyzing, and applying data serve the greater public interest and should be publicly funded.

Certainly, Eddy's recommendations will not be universally received, but given the pressures and uncertainty that consumers and participants in health care face relative to the quality and cost-effectiveness of what is produced, such recommendations at least have the attribute of being commonsensical.

F. Provider Consolidation

In 1997 the rate of hospital consolidation declined, attributable at least in part
to the legal difficulties of Columbia/HCA. Hospitals and provider organizations
across the country had been planning for and initiating mergers, at least in part
to protect themselves from possible acquisition by the nation's largest health care
corporation. However, as Columbia/HCA's financial and legal woes forced them
to divest many of their resources, the rate of hospital consolidation probably fell
(Ginsburg, 1998, p. 166).

Comparatively, physician practice consolidation expanded, as a growing
number of physicians and practices sought to achieve savings, an economy of
scale, and improved bargaining power with plans, hospitals, and other providers.
As noted, fueled by consumer demands for choice, health plans have increasingly
moved to near-total community enrollment of physicians, which (given administrative duplication and costs resulting from servicing numerous insurers) may
further explain why smaller practices and solo practitioners are joining larger
group practices. PSOs, which are becoming an established fixture in the health
care environment, are now holding increasing promise to large practices considering the possibility of assuming not only responsibility for their patient's health,
but responsibility for the risks associated with covering them. In this regard,
possibilities for additional development of staff HMOs from among the consolidation of large-group practices may also be possible.

G. The Uninsured

One of the major efforts of Congress in 1997 involved dealing with the problem
of the uninsured. Unfortunately, it is difficult to definitively specify the exact
number of uninsured persons in the nation. This is a result of limitations in identifying all uninsured, variations in the length of time in a particular year in which
an individual or family are uninsured, the extent of coverage under insurance
plans, and who in the family carries coverage and for whom (Lewis et al., 1998).
In 1996 Blumberg and Liska projected that the number of uninsured nonelderly
citizens could be expected to increase from somewhere between 31.7 and 33.7
million persons in 1988 to between 39 to 42.1 million in 1996. The typical uninsured person was characterized as indigent or employed without health benefits.
Eighteen percent are adults (particularly young adults) and 11% children, nonwhite, and in families with one or no persons employed. HIAA (Minor, 1998)
estimates that in 1995 alone there were approximately 40 million uninsured persons, of whom at least 12 million were children.

Congressional leaders have been particularly interested in the plight of
these uninsured children. Data for 1995 reported by Douglas and Flores (1998)

indicate that combined state and federal spending ($126 billion) on children's programs breaks down as follows:

Medicaid	19%
AFDC	18%
Earned Income Tax Credit (EITC)	17%
Food stamps	15%
Other	8%
Nutrition	8%
Child welfare	6%
Child care and child development	5%
SSI	4%

Unfortunately, this "average" picture varies greatly from state to state. When Douglas and Flores compare the 10 states with the highest ability to contribute to the welfare of children to the 10 states with the lowest ability, a very different picture emerges:

High-ability states		Low-ability states	
Medicaid	22%	Medicaid	19%
AFDC	21%	AFDC	10%
EITC	14%	EITC	23%
Food stamps	13%	Food stamps	19%
All other	30%	All other	29%

Since these data were gathered and reported, states have totally revamped their welfare programs consistent with congressional welfare reform legislation in 1997. Nevertheless, there is a significant difference between the top 10 and lowest 10 states cited here not just in terms of how much they categorically spent on children, but also in terms of their total state-federal funds available. The 10 states with the highest ability to aid children had a total per capita spending base (federal, federal matching, and state and local) of $12,003 per child to work with. Comparatively, the 10 states with the fewest resources averaged $5588 per child (Douglas and Flores, 1998, p. 27). It was this kind of imbalance in state capacity to care for the needy that created the national welfare programs of the sixties and seventies. However, in the eighties, the move for such programs is back to the states, despite statistics such as those just presented.

Although funds are now being devolved from the national to the state level, concern over the plight of children (based on data such as those just presented) have culminated in the largest expansion of the Medicaid program since 1965: the State Children's Health Insurance Program (S-CHIP). This act provides for matching funds for states that choose to offer health insurance to children of low-income families, which, according to Congressional estimates, could result in S-CHIP serving some 2.3 million children. Unfortunately, the U.S. Census Bureau (Weil, 1998, p. 1) estimates that in 1995 approximately 10 million children under the age of 18 (14% of the nation's children) were uninsured. Clearly, even with the passage and implementation of S-CHIP and its adoption in 20 states, meeting the needs of the nation's uninsured children remains a high priority for Congress.

S-CHIP was enacted as a part of the Balanced Budget Act (BBA) of 1997, which will be discussed in greater detail later. S-CHIP was established as Title XXI of the Social Security Act and earmarked $20.3 billion in block grants to states to be distributed over 5 years for the expansion of health insurance and health care programs for children. States provide matching funds (70% of the state's Medicaid rate) to receive a 30% federal match. To become eligible for S-CHIP matching funds, states must make application through the Department of Health and Human Services (DHHS). Upon receipt of federal funds, state have the option of either directly providing care to children, purchasing health insurance on behalf of children, using the funds to further expand Medicaid, or utilizing a combination of approaches (Johnson and McDonough, 1998). If states so choose, they may impose out-of-pocket expenses upon beneficiaries, as well as cost sharing, provided that recipient premiums for families at the federal poverty level do not exceed the "maximum monthly premium for medically needy beneficiaries allowed under Medicaid" (Ullman et al., 1998, p. 5).

One major concern surrounding S-CHIP was that it would provide incentives for families to utilize S-CHIP benefits rather than their existing private coverage (Cutler and Gruber, 1997; Holahan, 1997). Such "crowding out" of private coverage could make the program's function redundant and inefficient. California has responded to this problem by refusing to enroll children in the S-CHIP program if the child was covered over the previous 3 months by an employer-based health plan. In 1998 the average S-CHIP cost per enrolled child was $1030 (Ullman et al., 1998, p. 21).

Unfortunately, children are only a portion of the nation's uninsured. Marsteller et al. (1998, p. 72; Liska et al., 1998, p. 22) report that the current rate of uninsured nonelderly persons (15.7% of the population) is only 0.5% greater than the uninsured rate in 1989. Comparatively, over the same time period the percentage of the population covered by private insurance fell from 74.3% in 1989 to 70.4% in 1995, while Medicaid recipients grew from 8.7% in 1989 to

12.2% in 1995 (Marsteller et al., 1998, p. 70). Comparatively, data from the Health Insurance Association of America (HIAA) indicate that the percentage of uninsured citizens rose from 12.9% in 1989 to approximately 15.7% in 1998, and is expected to reach a level of 16.2% by the year 2002 (Minor, 1998, p. 22) (see Fig. 5).

Several issues are associated with estimating the number of uninsured, including the methodologies by which they were counted (a common criticism directed toward the Census Bureau), how the term "uninsured" was defined, and with regard to problems in consistently defining the time period over which people were uninsured. All these factors contribute to disagreement by policymakers over the extent of the problem (Berk and Schur, 1998). However, projections by the prestigious Lewin Group of an average number of monthly uninsured for children under the age of 18 (17.2%) stands in sharp contrast to the 14% figure reported by the U.S. Census Bureau. Such disparities reinforce how difficult it is to define the scope of the problem being addressed and then design appropriate interventions. Consequently, even the best efforts of Congress (or at least one of its better efforts), such as the passage of S-CHIP, may still miss the mark of addressing the extent of the uninsured issue.

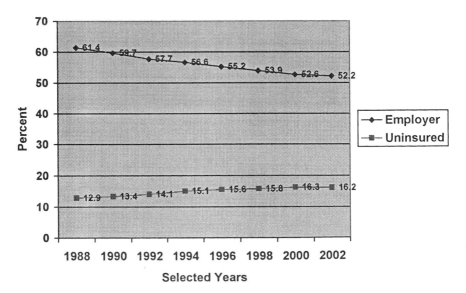

Figure 5 Employer-sponsored health insurance and uninsured, 1988–2002. [From Lewin Group estimates: current population survey for 1988–1994 (projections based on trends reported from 1988 to 1994.]

H. Health Care Costs

Some would argue that despite all of the talk, legislation, and regulation associated with issues of access and quality, what the whole health care reform issue boils down to is cost. Health care expenditures rose from $26.9 billion in 1960 to $247.3 billion in 1980 to $1035.1 billion in 1996 (HCFA, 1997; Minor, 1998, p. 103) (see Fig. 6). Alternatively stated, health care costs as a percentage of GDP increased from 5.1% in 1960 to 8.9% in 1980 and 13.6% in 1996. While the bad news is that health care costs continue to escalate, the rate of growth has slowed dramatically, with only a 4.4% average increase in health care's share of the GDP since 1990, and average annual growth rate of approximately 5% over the period of 1993–1996. Although, overall health care spending has fallen significantly, costs have actually been shifted from the hospital to other outpatient and community-based sites and services (Minor, 1998, p. 103).

Hospital inpatient care experienced an annual growth rate of 11.7% in 1970, and peaked at 13.9% in 1980 before falling to 9.6% in 1990 and tumbling to an average annual growth rate of 3.5% between 1994 and 1996. The annual growth rate of physician services also fell from a high of 12.8% in 1980 to 2.9% in 1996, but surprisingly, growth rates in virtually every other area of health care provision has also fallen including 1980 to 1996 comparative decreases in annual growth rate for home care (from 26.9% to 6.2%), nursing home care (from 15.4% to 4.3%), and nondurable medical supplies (down from 9.4% in 1989 to 7.7% in 1996). The only real exception to this pattern is the annual growth rate for pre-

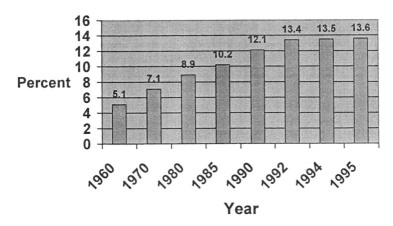

Figure 6 National health expenditures percentage of gross domestic product, selected years. (From Health Care Financing Administration, Health Care Financing Review, Fall 1996.)

scription drugs, which was at 8.2% in 1980 and in 1996 exhibited a 9.2% annual growth rate (Levit et al., 1998).

Meanwhile the percentage of national health spending emanating from consumer out-of-pocket expenses declined for the eleventh consecutive year, dropping to 16.5% in 1996. Out-of-pocket expenses include costs of coinsurance, deductibles, and direct payments for services not covered by insurance plans. Comparatively, employee premiums have increased as employers pay an ever-shrinking share of the cost of health care coverage, requiring employees to pay a larger proportion of the premium, particularly for dependent coverage. This cost shifting accounts for a total of $3.6 billion shifted to employees between 1990 and 1996. Fortunately, between 1993 and 1996 individual premium costs fell at an annual average of 4.7%. This decrease was at least in part due to a temporary decrease in elderly Medicare beneficiaries between 1993 and 1995, as well as due to costs savings achieved under managed care. Even so, the pattern of individual health care consumption between 1995 and 1996 indicates that benefit costs are still rising more rapidly than premiums, suggesting higher premium costs in the future (Levit et al., 1998, pp. 45–57).

Beyond an ongoing increase (albeit a less accelerated rise) in the cost of benefits, there are other factors that many believe will contribute to an ongoing escalation in health care costs and premium prices. These include:

1. Increases in pharmaceutical development and delivery costs,
2. Increasing technology costs,
3. Demographic trends relative to aging and employment (especially since welfare reform),
4. Limitations on behalf of health care providers in continuing to "cut fat" out of the system without curtailing services,
5. A growing public acceptance for the realistic need to "ration" care.

Such factors suggest that the debate over health care reform is far from over. Indeed, as minimum-wage jobs continue to flourish that lack health benefits, as the range of covered services is further reduced, and as costs continue to grow relative to premiums and tax revenue, it is very likely that the issues of access and equity may one day challenge the issue of cost as the most salient feature in the health care debate.

VII. MEDICARE AND MANAGED CARE

A. Introduction

Concerns regarding Medicaid, Medicare, and managed care approaches to delivering both programs continue to loom as significant problems confronting Congress and the public. Medicaid, of course, continues to be a major expenditure item for state governments, while Medicare coverage remains controversial not just because of the increasing utilization of managed care approaches (approaches also applied to Medicaid), but because of the overall costs and cost-effectiveness of the program, which continue to threaten the program's solvency.

B. Medicare: Demographic Profile

It is anticipated that the percentage of the aged population in the United States will increase from 12.3% of the nation's population in 1990 to 19.9% by the year 2030. These prospects have motivated Congress to streamline the program as much as possible in the interest of being prepared for the deluge of new beneficiaries that is to come. In 1997 there were a total of 38.6 million Medicare beneficiaries in the United States of whom 33.7 million were the nation's elderly (HCFA, 1998).

Currently the majority of Medicare beneficiaries are white (86% with 9% African-American and 1% Hispanic), but this is expected to change as of 2030 when minority populations are expected to constitute 25% of the elderly population. Alternatively stated, between 1990 and 2030, the non-Hispanic, white proportion of the elderly population is expected to grow by 91%, while the entire nonwhite, minority population is expected to grow by 328%, to include Hispanics (570% growth), non-Hispanic blacks (159%), Native Americans (294%), and Asian and Pacific Islanders (643%) (Jones, 1998; AARP & AoA, 1997).

Overall Medicare enrollment is expected to increase to a total of 44.0 million in 2007 (of whom 36.8 million will be elderly), and rise again to 56.3 million in 2017 (47.5 million elderly) (HCFA, 1998a, p. 10). Clearly, one of the major factors in the growth of this aging cohort is the increased life expectancy that has accompanied better public health and a remarkably extensive health care system. Life expectancy at birth has increased from 65.6 years (men) and 71.1 years (women) in 1950 to 72.5 and 78.9 years (1995), respectively. Similarly, life expectancy for men and women at age 65 has increased from 1950 figures of 12.8 and 15 years (men and women) to 15.6 and 18.9 years (1995), respectively. Furthermore, the rate of poverty among those 65 years and older has decreased from approximately 30% of the elderly in poverty in 1966 to approximately less than 10% in 1995 (HCFA, 1998, p. 12) (see Fig. 7).

In 1995 only 6% of the elderly receiving Medicare benefits reported incomes in excess of $50,000. Another 21% had incomes between $25,001 and $50,000, and 26% reported incomes in excess of $15,000 and up to $25,000 (see Fig. 8). Finally, 18% of all beneficiaries reported incomes from $10,001 to $15,000 and the remaining 28% were at income levels at or below $10,000. Clearly, these beneficiaries do not reflect great income affluence. However, their capital and investment resources are much higher given their age, years of savings and investment, and the relatively favorable position many find themselves in of

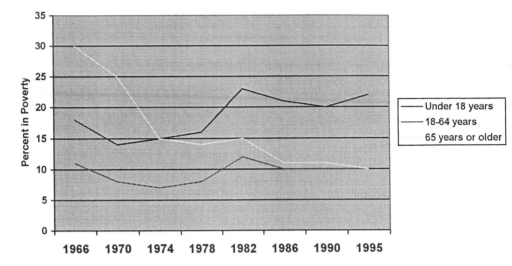

Figure 7 Poverty rates by age, 1966–1995. (From U.S. Department of Commerce, Bureau of Census, 1996.)

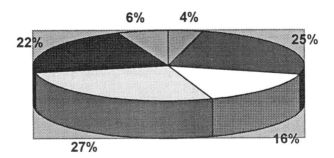

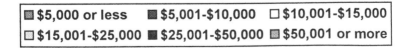

Figure 8 Income distribution of elderly Medicare beneficiaries, 1995. (From Health Care Financing Administration, Office of Strategic Planning; Medicare Current Beneficiary Survey.)

being in receipt of more benefits from Social Security and Medicare than they made in contributions (HCFA, 1998a, p. 16).

Disabled Medicare recipients have a much bleaker income profile than do the elderly beneficiaries. Fully 55% of these disabled persons report incomes at or below $10,000, while another 16% have incomes of $25,001–$50,001 and above, leaving another 29% at the $10,001–$25,001 level. For these individuals one can expect not just income but capital and investment resources to be much more limited (HCFA, 1998a, p. 17). These are truly vulnerable recipients (see Fig. 9).

C. Medicare Expenditures

Not surprisingly, given these income figures, 80% of Medicare program expenditures are on behalf of disabled beneficiaries with annual incomes of $25,000 or less, of whom the majority are women (HCFA, 1998a, pp. 14, 16). Comparatively, among total Medicare beneficiaries (those disabled and elderly) 45% of Medicare expenditures are on behalf of the 5% of the beneficiaries reporting incomes of $25,000 or less (HCFA, 1998a, p. 30). Fully 30% of Medicare beneficiaries live alone, and among these, 72% are women. In regard to functional status, 54% of recipients demonstrate no disabilities, rising to 58% for elderly beneficiaries (HCFA, 1998a, p. 20). So, one might summarize the bulk of the Medicare-served population to be low income, female, and minimally disabled.

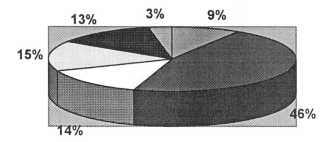

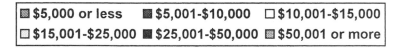

Figure 9 Income distribution of disabled elderly Medicare beneficiaries, 1995. (From Health Care Financing Administration, Office of Strategic Planning, Medicare Current Beneficiary Survey.)

These figures are encouraging in terms of cost considerations until one realizes that per beneficiary expenditures rise sharply as the number of functional disabilities increases [$3073 per beneficiary with no limitations in activities of daily living (ADL) to $12,102 per beneficiary exhibiting five to six ADL limitations] (HCFA, 1998a, p. 29). For many Medicare beneficiaries, particularly those most functionally impaired, Medicaid is utilized as coinsurance. In 1996, 16.5% of the Medicare population were dually enrolled in Medicare and Medicaid (HCFA, 1998a, p. 22).

As of 1994 the average per beneficiary spending was at $4484, or approximately 9.8% annual growth rate, down from an annual rate of 14.5% during the 1979–1984 period (Minor, 1998, p. 82). Comparatively, while the average overall growth rate in Medicare payments per enrollee between 1990 and 1996 ran around 8.5%, the most elevated growth rates occurred in the areas of hospice (33.1%), home health (27.9%), skilled nursing facilities (23.2%), and managed care (22.1%) (see Fig. 10) (HCFA, 1998a, p. 41).

Hospital spending dropped from 67.6% of all Medicare dollars in 1980 to 49.6% in 1996. In 1997, the hospital share of the Medicare dollar dropped to 43% (HCFA, 1998a, p. 35). These savings have been garnished by home health, hospice, and SNFs prompting (as we shall soon see) Congress to impose prospective payment systems upon these programs. It is anticipated that while Medicare

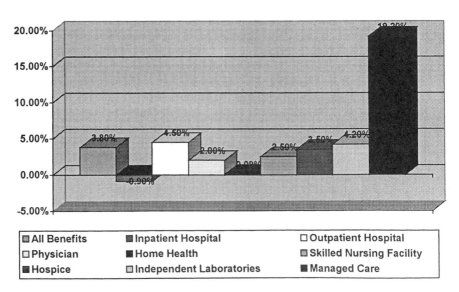

Figure 10 Projected annual average rate of growth in Medicare benefit payments per enrollee by type of service, FY 1997–2002. (From Health Care Financing Administration, Office of the Actuary, May 1998.)

administrative costs decreased from approximately 11% of the program funding
to approximately 1% (between 1970 and 1996), the annual average rate of growth
in Medicare benefit payments devoted to managed care will increase to 19.2%
by the year 2002 (HCFA, 1998a, p. 41). Obviously, managed care is considered
to be the most useful answer to the question: How do we contain program costs?
However, the "costs of managed care" are not so cheap.

Another method of cost reduction involves increasing beneficiary contributions to care. In 1994 20% of payment for medical outpatient services came out
of the pockets of beneficiaries (HCFA, 1998a, p. 47). To defray these out-of-
pocket costs, a growing number of beneficiaries purchased Medigap policies.
Such policies paid for 30% of Medicare costs for fee-for-service patients in 1996,
compared to 15% for beneficiaries enrolled in risk HMOs (HCFA, 1998a, p. 48).
Medicare risk HMOs are defined as an "HMO that is paid a predetermined per-
member payment from Medicare to provide all necessary covered services to its
Medicare enrollees" (HCFA, 1998a, p. 79). This same concept is also applied
to a newly recognized option under Medicare, the provider service organization
(PSO). PSOs are also allowed to enter into risk contracts, despite the fact that
to participate in such contracts they must be licensed in their states as HMOs.
There is concern among some that these PSOs may not have the financial solvency to assume responsibility for risk contracts (Polzer, 1997).

The emergence of ever-new ways to provide managed care creates incentives for Congress to mandate such programs, and for beneficiaries to utilize
them. Medigap premium increases are also fueling the move of beneficiaries to
managed care Medicare options. Depending on the type of plan one chooses, the
average rate of premium increase has escalated from 4.1 to 2.9% in the period
1992–1994 to 12.4% to 20.6% during the 1995–1996 period.

D. Managed Care and Medicare

As of 1996, 43% of persons enrolled in HMOs were commercially insured, as
compared to 13% for Medicare and 22% for Medicaid (HCFA, 1998a, p. 63).
In fact, enrollment in managed care plans has increased significantly since 1985
when only 441,000 beneficiaries were enrolled in risk HMOs. By 1997 this number had risen to 5,211,000 beneficiaries. Annual growth rates in managed care
increased from 5% in 1988 to 10% in 1991, and to approximately 25% in 1993.
By 1995 this annual average growth rate had reached 36% before falling to 33%
in 1996 (see Fig. 11). These growth figures compare to a much more modest
increase among the non-Medicare population, with annual growth rates beginning
at 12% in 1988, falling to 5% in 1990, and then increasing to 11% in 1994, 15%
in 1995, and falling to 13% in 1996 (HCFA, 1998a, pp. 63–65). Obviously the
move to embrace managed care has been much more volatile and progressive
within Medicare than for plans falling outside the program.

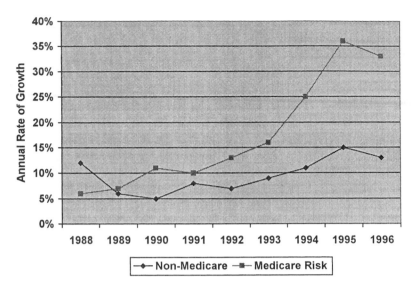

Figure 11   Relative growth in HMO enrollment, 1988–1996. (From Health Care Financing Administration, Center for Health Plans and Providers Monthly Managed Care Reports, American Association of Health Plans Data.)

Concomitant to this growth in Medicare's use of risk contracts in providing care has been an increase between 1985 and 1989 of contract terminations (reaching a peak of 38 terminations in 1989) followed by a steady decrease in terminations through 1997 (no terminations in 1995 followed by two in 1996 and three in 1997). During the period 1996–1997, the largest percentage of beneficiaries enrolled in risk contracts occurred in California (with a statewide enrollment percentage of 9.9% of the total Medicare population compared to 27.2% for the state's percentage of total risk enrollment). Predictably, Florida is second with 7.1% of Medicare beneficiaries enrolled in risk contracts as compared to 13.2% for the state's percent of total risk enrollment (HCFA, 1998a, pp. 66–67, 69).

E.   The Balanced Budget Act of 1997

Based upon trends in Medicare utilization, the spread of managed care arrangements, the diversion of funds historically dedicated to inpatient care to a variety of long-term and community care arrangements, and other emerging issues, Congress, in 1997, implemented a number of significant changes in the Social Security Act to address a number of concerns relating to both programs. Because of the extensive number of provisions relating to health care in the act, it will not be possible to fully discuss all of the health issues addressed therein. This important legislation is known as the Balanced Budget Act of 1997 (BBA 1997). Highlights of the changes instituted from this act include the following (to cite but a few) (HCFA, 1998a, p. 3; BBA, 1997):

Medicare + Choice: Established a part C of Medicare permitting an array of managed care options and choices for enrollees, developed an improved payment system to increase accuracy and reduce the growth of health care spending, and planned pilot studies regarding innovation in payment and service; expanded available preventive benefits. Major concerns regarding this legislation involve how HCFA will effectively communicate to beneficiaries the significant statutorial changes that were made to Medicare by BBA 1997 (Christensen, 1998; Jones, 1998, p. 3f.).

Establishment of a Skilled Nursing Facility (SNF) Prospective Payment System: In the interest of reducing the costs of long-term care, Congress directed HCFA to impose a prospective payment system somewhat similar to the hospital PPS, but based on a set of "resource utilization groups" (RUGs) (developed upon the resource intensity of caring for SNF residents) as compared to the 1983 utilization of "diagnosis-related groups" (DRGs) developed for hospitals.

Establishment of a Prospective Payment System for Hospital Outpatient Facilities: Directed HCFA to develop a PPS for hospital outpatient facilities as well as to develop conversion factors to translate regional outpatient costs to a national average. Finally, directed HCFA to establish a set of copayments to accompany the new PPS system.

Directed HCFA to Develop a Prospective System for Outpatient Rehabilitation Services: Congress similarly directed HCFA to develop a PPS to include the characteristics of conversion factors, copayments, and deductibles.

Directed HCFA to Develop a Case-Mix Index upon Which a Home Care PPS Will Be Developed and Implemented: Mandated the development of a case-mix system to drive an anticipated home health PPS. The proposed system may be driven by the newly developed OASIS database.

Established Medical Savings Accounts that Could be Used to Defer Future Health Costs: MSAs were to be piloted among 390,000 seniors and combined with a high-deductible insurance policy to provide for protection against catastrophic illnesses and injuries.

Established New Antifraud Provisions: Introduces a mandatory "Three Strikes, You're Out" clause as well as a "One Strike, You're Out" clause that can be used at the discretion of the secretary of DHHS.

Established the National Bipartisan Commission on the Future of Medicare: Designed to address Medicare's long-term solvency crisis that will shortly become critical with the retirement of baby-boomers.

It is worth noting that while these changes in Medicare and Medicaid brought about by BBA 1997 are not expected to deleteriously affect hospital profit margins (Gutterman, 1998), it is expected to have a negative impact upon the operating margins among home health and skilled nursing home providers. It is for this reason (and in the interest of brevity) that this chapter will not engage in an in-depth discussion of all of the health-related issues cited within BBA 1997. Rather, this chapter will focus on the development of PPSs for SNFs and home health care agencies, since these two areas are becoming increasingly responsible for some of the most accelerating health care costs.

F. Home Care and PPS

According to a 1993 report entitled "Medicare: Home Health Utilization Expands While Program Controls Deteriorate," controls over Medicare home health benefits "remain essentially nonexistent" (GAO, 1993, p. 3). Reinforcing this conclusion is John Newhouse, chair of the Prospective Payment Review Commission (ProPAC), who said, "While many of the [home health] services provided are presumably reasonable, necessary, and medically appropriate, it is nearly impossible to identify those which are or which are not" (Hegner, 1996). Newhouse continued in his remarks, indicting that the contributing factors to this situation included limited statutory authority, litigation, and budget cutbacks on the part of HCFA.

These observations are confirmed by utilization data. Home health costs were growing at an average of 8.6% in the Medicare program in 1988. However, by 1995 the annual average growth rate for home care in the Medicare program had reached 35.8%. Comparatively, in 1988, Medicaid was averaging an 18.3% average annual growth rate, which increased to 21.1% in 1991 before dropping to 15.6% in 1995. Consequently, while the Medicaid portion of home care costs has been arrested since the early nineties, Medicare home care costs are exploding (Kenney et al., 1998, p. 202).

Based on the pace of home care spending to date, the Congressional Budget Office CBO (1998) projected that during the 1995–2002 period Medicare home health spending will virtually double, from $16 billion to $31.3 billion, with significant variations in home health costs from state to state (Schore, 1996). Cost increases, coupled with charges of poor management of the program, motivated Congress to mandate that a PPS system be introduced for Medicare. While the system was not expected to be operational until 1999, if it follows suit with how PPS was approached in hospitals (DRGs) and has been introduced into SNFs (discussion to follow). Medicare home health prospective payments rely upon the new OASIS clinical database. Such an approach has met with stiff resistance from many interests representing the home health industry. For instance, consider a letter from Phyllis Wang, president of the Health Care Providers Inc. of New York State (HCP):

> At this time, there is not enough information on OASIS to definitively say that outcomes generated from this data set accurately reflect the quality of an agency. The OASIS demonstration projects need to progress further before it can be determined whether OASIS data is a good indicator of quality. In light of this, HCP recommends that HCFA postpone any efforts to use outcome measures to assess and survey an agency until some determination is made on whether the data collected by agencies is appropriate to use to assess quality (Wang, 1997, p. 2).

What HCP prefers and has recommended to Congress is a PPS model that has been developed by a coalition of home health industry representatives know as the Prospective Payment System Work Group (1997). The PPS Work Group has developed a plan that they say is ready for immediate adoption and is structured as follows (PPS Work Group, 1997):

> *Reimbursement on a per-visit basis until a per-episode model can be developed.* This would probably involve a 2–3-year period of transition, planning, and preparation for the industry.
> *Reimbursement on a per-episode basis, based on a case-mix adjustment for 0–120 days of care.* This concept has been borrowed form the Phase II Per Episode Demonstration Project approved by HCFA, which to date has been operating for approximately 2 years.
> *As an interim measure, utilize a reimbursement model based on a blend of agency-specific and regional database,* in the interest of assisting the industry in making a smooth transition from cost-based to rate-based reimbursement.
> *Develop a sharing savings plan between HCFA and the agencies* as an incentive to agencies to keep aggregate reimbursement limits at a minimum.

While these recommendations are expected to reduce the spiraling costs of home care, there is yet another reason for placing more restrictions on access to home care. This has to do with the so-called ''out of the woodwork'' phenomenon in which there is recognition by policymakers that the bulk of home care is provided by an informal provider network of friends and family, who may choose to reduce their caregiving efforts if reimbursable and more affordable and accessible home care services are made available to them. Even so, with the aging of the population, and with a significant increase in the oldest old (those 85 +), who are primarily women living alone, policymakers must recognize the reality that informal caregivers may become increasingly difficult to come by, thereby necessitating increased reliance on paid assistance. This factor is also exacerbated by the continued increase in two-income families.

As cutbacks and savings are planned for in terms of Medicare's revamping of home care services and reimbursement, it is worth noting that Congress is requiring HCFA to treat home care as a primarily rehabilitative service. This emphasis on rehabilitation flies in the face of the existence of a significant number of chronically ill homebound patients who are only sustained because of the informal care network. As managed care–oriented changes designed to reduce costs and emphasize rehabilitation and restoration have developed since 1994, some have been vocal in their criticism that the "elderly lifeline is under attack" (Bandonw, 1994). More recently, after Congress trimmed $17 billion from Medicare as a part of BBA 1997, concern emerged regarding the "interim payment system" (IPS) that is to be utilized prior to the introduction of the home care PPS. In particular, this IPS has imposed new and reduced limits on reimbursements to individual home care agencies, regardless of the amount of care ordered by a patient's physician (BBA, 1997).

While the new IPS was designed to curb costs, it has effectively resulted in penalizing patients by sometimes providing less care than patients legitimately need. In response, Sen. Chip Bond (D-MO) introduced the Medicare Home Health Beneficiary Act of 1998, following the closure of more than 1000 home health agencies since January 1997. This legislation is intended to guarantee that Medicare beneficiaries in need of extended home care services receive such services.

Clearly, Congress and HCFA are attempting to "bump" the care of chronically ill patients (i.e., those who cannot effectively be rehabilitated) down to the informal caregiver level of responsibility and thereafter down to the state level as an assisted-living expense. However, many in the home care and long-term-care industry advocate for home care services to recognize both rehabilitation and chronic care needs of the homebound. Long-term-care providers have long recognized, and the literature supports the fact, that patients and their caregivers fare better when supported in their functioning at the home level. Furthermore, a home and community orientation to care is consistent with the anti-institutional bent of health care policy since the 1982 era of the PPS. At issue is who should primarily carry the burden of the costs of care, and the answer in a nutshell is that families will bear the brunt of the costs of care until they either deplete their resources or the health of caregivers and those receiving care deteriorates to the point where they *must* seek an institutional solution.

Even so, HCFA continues to develop its PPS plan for home health care, and, beyond the problem of restricting access and options for care to homebound patients, it is anticipated that this effort will further reduce Medicare expenditures in this area and additionally result in consolidation within the industry, and a further reduction in the total number of home health agencies.

The National Association for Home Care (NAHC) identified 20,215 Medicare-certified "home care agencies" (home health care agencies and hospices are included in this grouping) in the United States (1996), up from 11,097 in 1989. Among these agencies the number of home health care agencies has almost doubled from 5676 in 1989 to 10,027 in 1996. Comparatively, hospice providers have virtually quadrupled over the same time period, increasing from a mere 597 nationwide in 1989 to 2154 in 1996 (NAHC, 1997). With hospice care having been identified as one of the other rapidly growing areas in the health care industry, it seems reasonable to expect that some form of more intensive managed care is somewhere in the not-too-distant future for hospices also.

G. Long-Term-Care PPS

1. Introduction

The new PPS that is now in effect for SNFs is built around the MDS (AHCA, 1998), which, as was observed earlier, is a highly sophisticated measurement and assessment tool. It is the database upon which a set of resource utilization groups (RUGs) are developed. The MDS itself and its RUG grouper (software designed to assign RUG groupings to patients and calculated reimbursement rates) are, in turn, both automated so that HCFA remains current with the case mix (mix of patients by functional and diagnostic level), resource utilization, and reimbursement levels of participating nursing homes.

Introduction of the PPS for SNFs was designed to reduce Medicare SNF growth by $9.5 billion over 5 years. HCFA asserts that the new reimbursement model will not create a substantial negative impact upon beneficiaries, particularly because there is a widespread belief among policymakers that there are many medically unnecessary services being provided in SNFs. Proponents of the PPS plan also point to the considerable consumer support for cost savings. Likewise, as is the case with the PPS being designed for the home care industry, PPS is seen as a necessary step in the direction of preserving Medicare from eventual financial ruin (Florida Health Care Association, 1998).

The PPS for skilled nursing facilities began in July 1998, and will be fully phased in by 2002. During that period facilities will be reimbursed on a blended facility-specific and federal rate during the first 3 years (75% facility-specific and 25% federal in year 1, followed by declining ratios of 50%–50% in year 2, 25%–75% in year 3, and 100% federal rate in year 4). The PPS began with mandatory cost-reporting periods in July 1998, utilizing an automated version of the MDS (MDS version 2.0). All rates were based upon 1995 HCFA cost report data, with mandatory ratings of patients into RUGs (using the RUG III case-mix grouper system). New SNFs that opened on or after October 1, 1995 automatically came under the full federal reimbursement rate and experienced no transition period. The RUGs utilized by HCFA entail 44 categories or groups, which are classified according to ADL functioning, clinical indicators, and on the basis of the presence of cognition, limitation, and depression. These factors essentially determine the case mix of residents within SNFs. The RUG III classification and payment scheme is as follows (HCFA, 1998c; Florida Health Care Association, 1998):

Clinical hierarchies	7	(hierarchical categories)
Classification groups	44	(total groupings and subgroupings)
Rehabilitation	14	(reimbursed at a special rehabilitation rate)
Presumptive Medicare	26	(skilled nursing facility reimbursable rate groupings)
Data collection	MDS	(minimum data set version 2.0)
Data collection time frames	Serial	7, 14, 30, 60, 90 Days
ADL index	Targeted	Eating, toileting, transfer, bed mobility
CMI (case-mix index based on NY demonstrations):		
Routine services range		0.62–2.56
Routine and rehabilitation range		1.18–5.69 (rehabilitation reimbursement rate)

In developing the case-mix index (CMI) for a facility, each resident is classified via the RUG grouper into one of seven major groupings (clinical hierarchies). In order of the intensity of resources utilized in caring for SNF residents and in order of the magnitude of the CMI assigned (the higher the CMI, the higher the reimbursement), the seven groups are (Fries et al., 1994; Florida Health Care Association, 1998, pp. 1–89):

1. Rehabilitation,
2. Extensive services,
3. Special care,
4. Complex care,
5. Cognitively impaired,
6. Behavioral problems,
7. Reduced physical functions.

2. Rehabilitation Reimbursement Level Rate for Nursing Home PPS

Rehabilitation is the most lucrative of the seven groupings. CMI is determined for this grouping based on the number of ADLs that the resident needs assistance with. There are five ADL ranges under this grouping with the intensity of resource utilization required to care for the resident ranging from a rating of low, through medium and high, to very and ultrahigh. The greater the resource utilization demanded, the higher the CMI and the resulting reimbursement. To qualify for the rehabilitation grouping the patient care needs of the patient as they relate to attending to ADLs must involve a level of resource activity that, at minimum, requires at least two (daily) nursing rehabilitation treatment activities for a minimum of 6 days, with 3 days weekly devoted to treatments at least 45 min in duration. The highest reimbursable subgroup within rehabilitation entails rehabilitation treatment by at least two disciplines, one of which must provide 1–5 days of treatment, and the second of which must provide at least 3 days of treatment.

3. Skilled Nursing Reimbursement Rate (Extensive, Special, and Complex)

Extensive services is the second most resource-intense grouping and is based upon whether the patient exhibits seven or more ADLs and requires any three of the following treatments: intravenous (IV) feeding, IV medication, suctioning, tracheotomy, and ventilator/respirator care.

Special care is one step lower in its resource utilization intensity than extensive services and entails three groupings based on the number of ADLs. To fall within this grouping requires that one either fully qualify for extensive services (except for demonstrating less than seven ADLs) or exhibit any of the following:

1. Ulcer stages 3 or 5 and two or more skin care treatment sites;
2. Exhibit more than 10 ADLs associated with multiple sclerosis, cerebral palsy, or quadriplegia;
3. Be treated with radiation therapy;
4. Exhibit fever accompanied by vomiting, weight loss, pneumonia, and/ or dehydration;
5. Require tube feeding with high enteral or parenteral intake;
6. Require tube feeding associated with aphasia and requiring a high intake;
7. Require respiratory therapy for at least 7 days.

Clinically complex assignment involves six groups sorted on the basis of the number of ADLs and on the documented presence of depression. Conditions falling within this grouping include: second- or third-degree burns, coma, septicemia, chemotherapy, pneumonia, foot wounds and infection, diabetes (requiring two or more 7-day injections or doses), dialysis, tube feeding, hemiplegia or hemiparesis (ADL of 10 or above), required physician visits of one or more, ESRD, dehydration, oxygen, and/or any person qualifying for special care but who has a full or nearly full functional capacity.

4. Subskilled Reimbursement Rate: Cognitively Impaired, Severe Behavioral Problems, and Reduced Physical Function

These final three categories fall below Medicare SNF reimbursement levels and are therefore reimbursed at a lower rate.

Cognitive impairment and behavioral problem categories both involve four groups sorted on the basis of ADLs and related nursing rehabilitation resource requirements. To fall within the impaired cognition group, one must exhibit one of the following symptom patterns: impaired decision making, impaired short-term memory, and/or impaired orientation. To be classified under the severe behavioral problem category a resident must exhibit one of the following behavioral problems: daily problems with inappropriate behavior, physical abuse, verbally abusive or wandering, resistance to care, and/or hallucinations.

Reduced physical function involves 10 grouping sorted by ADL and nursing rehabilitation requirements. All residents not included in any other category fall within this, the lowest RUG of the seven hierarchical categories. This last RUG is anticipated to eventually be divested from the Medicare program and assigned as a service under state Medicaid plans.

5. Untoward Consequences

Just as the imposition of cost restraints on the home care industry has resulted in the closing of 2000 home care agencies in the period following BBA 1997, it is anticipated that the restructuring of skilled nursing care around a predominantly rehabilitation-oriented reimbursement model, along with the mandated computer automation of both the diagnostic, grouper, and billing systems, will tend to drive many independent agencies out of business. Indeed, there is concern in the home health care industry that once their PPS model is fully implemented (probably based on the OASIS data set), issues associated with experience of agencies with automated clinical and billing systems may also conspire with lower reimbursement rates and caps on service to drive even more agencies out of business. It is also anticipated that in the absence of tort reform rising liability insurance premiums will continue to drive even more agencies into bankruptcy.

There is a significant disparity in the financial resources and management acumen among the nation's long-term-care facilities. There is considerable concern in states with a large number of elderly (states like Florida, California, and

Texas), as to whether there is a level of sophistication across the range of nursing homes requisite to quickly acquire skill not only in utilizing the automated resources required by HCFA, but also in terms of the rapidity with which SNF administrators and staff can and will adapt to accurately completing and utilizing the MDS in determining their facility's current and optimal case mix. Finally, there is the inevitable concern of those who witnessed the introduction of PPS into hospitals in the early eighties that the rehabilitation focus of the new PPS coupled with the financial incentives associated with the program will entice facilities to develop their MDS database in the interest of improving their reimbursement level (RUG creep) and/or change the orientation of the facility to primarily attract the best-reimbursing RUGs and avoiding admitting lower-paying RUG categories of patients. This approach, known as "skimming," may force many who need chronic care either back into their homes or into assisted living facilities where access to informal care and support services are lacking, or into situations where caregivers are utilizing out-of-pocket resources to provide institutional care (probably at the assisted living level) in the absence of adequate financial support from Medicare, Medicaid, or other insurance plans.

With BBA 1997 mandating PPS programs in SNFs, home care, and outpatient settings, the phenomenon of "squeezing out" those in need of services becomes even more of an issue. However, it may be that in the future, funding of all of these health care services may no longer be addressed independent of one another. As Rosalie Kane suggests (1995), future reimbursement programs may more fully recognize the continuum of long-term-care services and programs, and expand the concept of "home care" to include a broad array of institutional and other community-based long-term-care services.

VIII. MEDICAID AND DISPROPORTIONATE SHARE HOSPITAL PAYMENTS (DSH)

A. Introduction

Medicaid benefit payments increased from $24 billion in 1980 to $176.1 in 1998, as the number of recipients increased from 21.6 million to 37.7 million. Over this same period, the average cost per recipient increased from $1200 (1980) to $4700 (1998) (Minor, 1998, p. 81). In response, state Medicaid programs increasingly adopted managed care approaches to improve access while lowering costs. In 1993, 166 participating plans served 2.6 million enrollees. Three years later (1996) the number of participating plans almost doubled to 355 and the number of Medicaid patients served by Medicaid managed care plans increased to approximately 7.7 million (Felt-Lisk and Yang, 1997).

Comparatively, the rate of participation in Medicaid managed care plans among all available managed care plans has not increased as rapidly. The 166 participating plans in 1993 constituted 21% of all plans, while the 355 participating plans in 1996 represented only 36% of plans. Furthermore, 62 participating plans terminated their participating plan status during the same period. Consequently, while the number of persons served in Medicaid plans dramatically increased in 3 years, the willingness of the larger population of plans to participate in Medicaid managed care arrangements has not grown so quickly, and there has been a sizable turnover in participating plans. These trends pose serious concerns for policymakers in terms of ongoing access, continuity of care, and service quality (Felt-Lisk and Yang, 1997). Such concerns fuel some members of Congress to make additional changes in the Medicaid program, changes that may take this program into a new phase of program organization, funding, and growth.

B. Entitlement Growth Phases and Fluctuating Medicaid Costs

Generally speaking, Medicaid, along with major federal entitlement programs, including Social Security and Medicare, have gone through three phases of growth since the 1960s. These phases include (Gist, 1996):

> Phase 1: Rapid growth in entitlements from the early 1960s through 1975,
> Phase 2: Growth stabilization from 1975 to 1991,
> Phase 3: Growth resumption from 1991 onward.

Early growth rates in these programs reflected cyclical economic responses to expanding and contracting market forces. During phase 1, entitlement growth outstripped GDP (8.4% growth compared to GDP growth of 3.3%). Phase 2 reflects years of recession and economic downturn. Entitlements grew at only 2.7% while the GDP expanded at 2.3%. This restraint in growth is also attributable to actions in Congress designed to slash entitlement benefits and contain costs. Chief among these efforts is the passage of welfare reform in 1996. The Personal Responsibility and Work Opportunity Reconciliation Act of 1996 placed the burden of finding a job upon welfare recipients (DHHS, 1996). Benefits are limited over a lifetime to 5 years. Consequently, while the act maintains access to Medicaid for indigent children, the disabled, pregnant women, the elderly (i.e., for those on some form of welfare), it severely curtailed the length of such benefits, thereby reducing Medicaid cost as the welfare roles declined in length.

Such legislation signaled the beginning of a new era in which a ''New Federalism'' began to take hold. Revenue sharing ceased, limits to entitlement expansion, entitlement indexing, and a more fiscally conservative electorate worked together to reduce the expansion of entitlement growth. During this same period federal deficits grew steadily while other nonentitlement spending (particularly in defense) expanded (Gist, 1996; Bishop and Walleck, 1996).

Medicaid's annual growth rate fell from 29.51% during the 1962–1975 period to 7.23% from 1975 to 1991 during the first two phases. However, during the period 1991–1995, annual growth rate exhibited a marginal increase, averaging 8.67% (Gist, 1996, p. 384). The Congressional Budget Office (CBO, 1995) projected, however, that with the advent of risk contracting, Medicaid managed care arrangements, etc., annual Medicaid growth would fall to 6.74% between 1995 and 2000.

This slowing in growth is of the highest significance to policymakers since Medicaid and Medicare represent the two most important sources for short-term budget containment. While growth is slowing, what is of most concern is that, taken together, Medicare and Medicaid are expected to increase from 3.9% of GDP in 1996 to 5.5% of GDP in the year 2005 (CBO, 1998). Comparatively, nonhealth entitlements are expected to display a much more modest growth rate over the same period, rising only 0.3% (Gist, 1996, p. 357).

Public expenditures on Medicare and Medicaid, while decelerating in their rate of growth, are still growing at a much faster pace than the private health insurance sector, which has actually witnessed a decline in employee participation. Since the period 1989–1991, annual growth rates in private health care expenditures fell from 11.3% in 1990 to 7.4% in 1992 and 3.0% in 1996. Meanwhile Medicare's average annual growth rate increased from 10.5% in 1990 to 13.8% in 1992, before falling to 6.7% in 1996 (see Fig. 12) (HCFA, 1998b, Table 9).

Unfortunately, when policymakers and other interest groups meet to deliberate the future of the nation's health care system, the disparity between public and private per capita annual average health care growth rates tends to remind

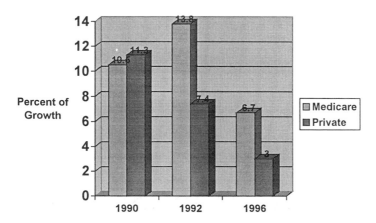

Figure 12 Medicare versus private health care expenditures, selected years. (From Health Care Financing Administration, A Profile of Medicare, 1998.)

them that the rate of annual growth in private health care is still much smaller than for Medicare or for Medicaid (down to a per capita annual average growth rate of 4.5% in 1996) (HCFA, 1998b, Table 9). Consequently, regardless of differences in some of the characteristics of public and private health insurance beneficiaries, the ongoing disparity in efficiency (as demonstrated by comparatively elevated Medicare and Medicaid growth rates) will lead many in Congress to call for even more stringent managed care controls. Based on this perception among many members of Congress, it can be anticipated that the response of Congress to future requests from HCFA and the states for additional federal funding for health care will be that they should better utilize the funds that are currently available to them.

This philosophical orientation has resulted in state legislatures and Congress increasingly looking to managed care solutions to hold down costs while maintaining quality (GAO, 1992). In the interest of encouraging innovation within various state approaches to applying managed care to the Medicaid problem, Congress made a number of ''waiver'' options available to states for demonstration projects and pilot testing (Matherlee, 1993).

C. Trouble Brewing

While federal and state governments continue to embrace managed care as the solution to the nation's cost and access problems, there are clear signs of trouble emerging. On August 12, 1998, the Consumers Union (an organization that views the rhetoric of the managed care industry as being ''disingenuous'') released a year-long report it had been conducting on issues facing the elderly relative to managed care plans and Medicare. Data compiled by the Consumers Union from 19 cities were analyzed and the investigators concluded (Consumers Union, Aug. 12, 1998): ''Consumer Reports has found that seniors are facing higher out-of-pocket health expenses, cutbacks in HMO benefits such as prescription drugs and vision care, and a burdensome array of Medicare choices, some of which could jeopardize the future of the [Medicare] program.''

Other key study findings include the following (Consumers Union, Aug. 12, 1998):

Wide variations in costs and coverage of Medicare supplemental plans across regions,
Premium increases of 35% since 1994 for Medicare supplemental insurance,
Anticipated doubling of Medicare Part B premiums between 1998 and 2006 (increases from $526 per annum in 1998 to $1172 in 2006),
Increases in Plan C of the Medicare supplemental plans of 41% since 1994,
Increased limitations in the formularies utilized by HMOs.

The Consumers Union report additionally cites provisions in BBA 1997 that are designed to siphon off relatively healthy Medicare recipients to contracted health plans, leaving only the sickest and most seriously ill in the program. This outcome is considered to be particularly unsettling because historically Medicare has spread the risk of these most seriously ill and disabled individuals across the broader risk pool. Consequently, by isolating these beneficiaries in the Medicare program and by siphoning off so much money to managed care contractors, Congress may have created a situation where the program cannot sustain the actual costs of care. According to Trudy Lieberman, principal investigator of the study, "The Medicare system as we know it is being dismantled" (Consumers Union, July 12, 1998). These are sobering assertions that will be discussed later. Even so, in the interim Congress continues to encourage states to more frequently utilize risk HMOs as sites for care, as well as modify its approach to funding indigent care for "disproportionate share hospitals" (DSHs).

D. Disproportionate Share Hospitals Payments

The DSH issue became a prominent part of Congress's Balanced Budget Act of 1997. However, to understand what action Congress took and why, one must have a basic understanding of how DSH payments came to be (Coughlin and Liska, 1998a). DSH payments were initially created by the so-called Boren Amendment to the Omnibus Budget Reconciliation Act of 1980 (OBRA, 1980) and were designed to maintain access for poor and disabled persons to the services of hospitals that serve a "disproportionately" large portion of this population. At the time it was believed that without such support, many public and nonprofit hospitals serving the indigent would be forced to curtail services or close altogether. States only slowly began using the DSH funds, so Congress made additional changes to the program, via the Omnibus Budget Reconciliation Act of 1986 (OBRA, 1986), to stimulate more interest and state participation. This key provision allowing states to pay DSH providers a rate above the current Medicare rate, as well as exceeding the "Medicare upper payment limit," effectively primed the pump and increased DSH payment utilization by states during in the early 1990s (Coughlin and Liska, 1998b).

Between 1990 and 1996 DSH payments to states increased from $1.4 billion to $15 billion, accounting for one of every 11 dollars spent by state and federal governments combined. The popularity of this program is exemplified by an illustration provided by Coughlin and Liska (1998b, p. 3):

> Consider for a moment that a state receives revenue from a provider. In this example, the state receives $10 million. The state then makes a DSH payment back to the provider as a lump sum payment or an increase in the Medicaid inpatient reimbursement rate. Here the state makes a $12 million DSH pay-

ment to the same provider that made the [initial] donation. At this point in the transaction, the provider has received $2 million in DSH payments while the state is "out" $2 million. Since DSH payments are matchable Medicaid expenses, the federal government reimburses the state anywhere from 50 to 80 percent of the DSH payment, depending upon the state's federal Medicaid matching rate. In this example the state matching rate is 50 percent, and the federal government reimburses the state half of the $12 million, or $6 million. At the end of the transaction, the provider has received $2 million in DSH payments while the state has received $4 million in federal money without spending any of its own funds. The federal government has paid $6 million in DSH payments. However, only $2 million was channeled to the DSH provider; the balance was retained by the state.

The inefficiency of this program was not lost on Congress, which acted again in 1991 to pass the Medicaid Voluntary Contribution and Provider-Specific Tax Amendments of 1991 (PL 101-234), the key provisions of which are as follows (Coughlin and Liska, 1998b, p. 4):

Private donations from providers were essentially banned.

Provider taxes were capped so that tax revenues would not exceed 25% of the state's share of Medicaid expenditures.

Provider taxes were defined around "broad criteria" to widen the tax base, and providers were no longer "held harmless" under the law.

With DSH payments capped at 1992 levels, national DSH payments were restricted to a maximum of 12% of total Medicaid payments.

P.L. 101-234 effectively checked the growth in DSH payments to states; however, it failed to satisfy members of Congress that the DSH payments were really reaching those whom it was designed to serve. So, Congress approached the issue again via the Omnibus Budget Reconciliation Act of 1993, adding two more key provisions (Coughlin and Liska, 1998b, p. 5):

Receipt of DSH payments depended upon the demonstration by a provider that their hospital had a Medicaid utilization rate of at least 1%. This provision was designed to deal with the problem that DSH dollars were being funneled to hospitals doing very little Medicaid business.

Total DSH payments must be less than the "unreimbursed costs" associated with providing inpatient care to Medicaid and uninsured patients.

Having been forbidden from asking for provider donations, and having had provider taxes defined so broadly that it was difficult to implement them, many states went the route of using intergovernmental transfers funds (IGTs) to develop matching revenue to attract DSH payments. In so doing, DSH payments were largely redirected toward public hospitals. Concurrently, however, states were increasingly adopting managed care approaches that, by necessity, moved patients from expensive inpatient sites to less costly outpatient and community settings. Consequently, while DSH funds moved toward public hospitals, state indigent and Medicaid efforts were moving patients and financial resources out of public hospitals in particular and from all hospitals in general. Given these cross trends, states were finding it difficult to actually spend the DSH payments they had received, and in many cases sought waivers from HCFA to find creative ways of spending their funds (Coughlin and Liska, 1998b, p. 6).

Then came the 105th Congress, which, in the interest of identifying ways to reduce costs to balance the federal budget by 2002, chose to again consider DSH payments, which many still thought were ill conceived, untargeted, and poorly utilized. As a result, changes were made in BBA 1997 to further rein the DSH program (Coughlin and Liska, 1998b, p. 7). Specifically, the BBA 1997 provisions involved:

> Establishing state-specific DSH allotments yearly from 1998 to 2002. This effectively reversed the allotment provisions of the Medicare Voluntary Contributor and Provider-Specific Tax Amendments of 1991, and permitted DSH expenditures post 2002 to increase at a rate consistent with the Consumer Price Index (CPI).
> Limiting the proportion of federal DSH funds allocated to states that can be designated for care in institutions for mental disease.
> Requiring that payments on behalf of Medicaid patients who participate in managed care plans be directed toward hospitals rather than to managed care organizations and providers.

Based on simulations developed by Coughlin and Liska (1998b, p. 8), it would appear that over the period 1998–2002, DSH savings will amount to approximately $5.8 billion, or an 11% decrease in spending. Thus, DSH payments will impact states disproportionately. States that used very little of the DSH payments will experience no appreciable reduction in funding, while those that have heavily relied upon DSH payments to support their state Medicaid programs will experience cuts of as much as 58%. States like Rhode Island, which uses DSH payments to cover 38.7% of its Medicaid expenditures, along with Louisiana (30%), Missouri (26%), New Jersey (23.9%), Colorado (23.3%), and Alabama (21.4%), will be those most affected by BBA 1997 changes in DSH payments (Liska et al., 1998, p. 151).

IX. CONCLUSION: THE NEW FEDERALISM AND THE FUTURE OF U.S. HEALTH CARE

A. Devolution to the States and the New Federalism

The current trend to devolve responsibility for a host of formally federal programs (welfare, child care, health care, long-term care, etc.) to the states is often referred to as the ''new federalism.'' An historical perspective on this trend underscores that prior to the 1960s, the states were the level of government where health, education, and welfare programs had historically resided. Only after the civil rights struggle of the 1960s, during the Kennedy "Camelot" era and in the 'Great Society' era of Lyndon Johnson, did the federal government begin to assume an ever-growing role in managing welfare, social service, education, and health programs (Sparer, 1998).

In many instances, the rationale for assuming more central control over health care issues was the great disparity in resources available to states in addressing health care issues. Certainly states like Mississippi, West Virginia, and New Mexico were comparatively resource-poor in their ability to provide for their state's medically needy, especially when compared to states such as New York, California, and Massachusetts. Increased federal management over state health care via the introduction of Medicaid served to redistribute resources in the interest of serving all citizens more equitably.

Cries for increased state autonomy which were asserted in the sixties from a "states rights" perspective, primarily among governors of southern states, never really died away in that region over the next 30 years. However, current demand for increased state autonomy is now a national agenda, supported by virtually all states: i.e., return government control to states and localities. Politicians in the nineties, motivated by concerns of costs, inefficiency, and lack of input from local constituents, have increasingly demanded that states be empowered to assume more local control in the interest of providing truly cost-effective services to local residents.

Consequently, by the early nineties, Congress found itself not only enacting legislation to devolve such things as state welfare related initiatives, "economic development," "workforce development," and "school-to-work" down to the states, they also acted, with increasing frequency, to move health entitlement programs into state hands.

A reasonable observer might ask, if states like West Virginia, Mississippi, and other states had difficulty managing historically "health and welfare" programs in the sixties (given political and funding constraints), what makes one believe that they will fare so much better in the late nineties? Of course, the answer to be proffered is "managed care," which utilizes market forces to reduce costs and provide better access.

Currently, the Congress and HCFA are utilizing managed care approaches in the implementation of four key priorities to control health care program costs and to improve program efficiency (Sparer, 1998, p. 15):

Encourage Medicaid clients to enroll in managed care,
Expand insurance coverage for children,
Make insurance more affordable for small businesses,
Contain long-term-care costs.

Despite the optimism expressed by many in the industry, members of Congress, governors, state legislators, and others, the "managed care" models being implemented during this period of "new federalism" have met with:

1. Patient and provider backlashes against "managed care,"
2. Incentives for many persons to divest themselves of health insurance in the face of increasing managed care costs,
3. Metastatic growth of bureaucratic paper jungles,
4. Limits in coverage, and
5. Projections of more complexity at ever-growing prices for the delivery of fewer services to those in medical need.

In the end, managed care has not yet proven to be a cure for the nation's health care system woes. In fact, increasing evidence suggests that it may actually prove to be an expensive proposition and a model of care that is complex and difficult to manage. Furthermore, in at least some cases, managed care has proven to be a model that may not effectively deliver some essential services (mental health, long-term care, and care for the elderly and disabled). While some might observe that it is naive to expect managed care in and of itself (given its promarket orientation) to really solve all problems facing the health care system, others, such as Sparer (1998), have concluded that "we need an intergovernmental partnership that both respects the diversity among the states and provides a federal management framework" (Sparer, 1998, p. 15). It seems that despite all efforts to turn this problem over to the market to solve, governmental officials and industry leaders reluctantly return to some measure of federal regulatory control.

As noted earlier, the decision by the Clinton administration to stop short of fully releasing health care to market forces (i.e., Clinton's insistence on utilizing global budgeting) reflected the administration's caution and concern that unfettered managed care at the state level could lead to chaos, a position that historically reflects problems with state health care provision prior to the sixties. Paradoxically, at a period in which the "new federalism" is widely and optimistically discussed, the administration and many in Congress might be considering a policy shift that may ultimately devolve some state authority back to the federal government. At issue is not whether such reverse devolution will occur, but rather what form it will assume.

B. Still Plugging Holes in the Colander: A.K.A. Maybe We Need a Bucket, or Better Yet, a New Boat

Which brings us back to where this chapter began, "plugging holes in a colander." Finding ourselves unwilling or perhaps just unable to develop more comprehensive approaches to solving the U.S. health care conundrum of increasing access to health care while reducing costs, we return to our historical practice of plugging holes in the colander. In some eras, plugging the holes entails filling the holes with state-oriented approaches, or filling holes with market-oriented approaches, or a combination of both. However, at other times filling holes may entail more federal regulatory solutions and fewer market-oriented ones. After more than 60 years of modern debate on the health policy issue, we continue to stick to an incremental hole-filling approach.

Suppose, though, that the real problem confronting the nation is that we are trying to keep the health care "boat" afloat by trying to bail it with a colander. At issue is whether the colander is the tool we should be using. It could be that it is filling in for a bucket. If so, maybe what we really need to do is create a bucket to bail the boat. Certainly a decision to scrap the colander and design a bucket is a more broadly incremental approach than our current practice of bailing with a colander (which we constantly plug). Perhaps an even greater departure for Congress is to consider the boat itself, and decide whether "remodeling" really makes any sense any more. Perhaps the time has come to commission a "ship." Now that would be a very large incremental change from what we are doing now.

If we followed along with this analogy a little further, then we would have to recognize that building a ship takes a great deal of time and would require significant planning, consensus building, and resource acquisition. In other words, we could not do it quickly. It would take years to develop, perhaps over several congressional and legislative sessions. Indeed presidents may come and go over the period, but building a ship would necessitate a commitment to ensuring an appropriate period of time for cooperation and focus.

For those familiar with the workings of Congress and the Executive Branch, Washington politics simply does not work that way. Despite numerous presidential commissions to study Social Security, Medicare, national health care, etc., the political process "gums the health issue to death" and at best only incrementally changes things, often in an uncoordinated and piecemeal fashion that makes a complicated matter even worse.

C. Incrementalism and Mixed Scanning: Old Theories Reapplied

Many policymakers have had to make an uncomfortable peace with the reality that all public policy is incremental policy (of which the corollary is that all budgeting is incremental). This truth means that we just don't "spin on a dime" and take off in a new policy direction, nor should we. But it does mean that directing a course toward a better policy future is a lot like sailing; the political winds have to be just right and match the policy opportunities available at any given time to make a significant change in an issue. Typically what we call "broadly incremental" changes (i.e., significant changes from the status quo) only occur during times of national calamity, upheaval, and social unrest. When policy opportunities and political realities fit just right, the nation sees really momentous legislation, such as Social Security and Medicare. However, during most times, even when market and political forces are ripe for change, unless there is a sense of immediate risk to the public, broadly incremental change just does not happen, even when it may need to.

So we tend to make incremental changes from our current policy status quo in the face of relatively routine issues for which incremental changes are appropriate, as well as making small incremental changes in areas where we often ought to be looking for a broom and a dustpan. Amati Etzioni (1968) developed a theoretical position on this very problem some years ago when he developed the concept of mixed scanning. At the risk of oversimplifying his theory, to a great extent it involved recognizing that all decisions are incremental in nature (Wimberley and Morrow, 1981), and that while some routine decisions require very little thought and consideration of options beyond those in place, really important decisions deserve really broad exploration, i.e., very broadly incremental examinations of alternatives prior to actually making a decision.

In a nutshell, Etzioni's (1968) admonition is to use simple strategies to solve simple problems, but to also be willing to invest considerable time and resources in searching for options to current policy on really important problems. In regard to the health care issue, we tend to persist using fix-it kits to build a great ship. So we should not be surprised that the "great ship of health" leaks and is rapidly becoming Titanic-like in its size and complexity. Like the Titanic, many will say "it can't sink," but in fact it can, and in regard to those being squeezed out of the system via health, access, provisions, or costs factors, for them the ship already rests on the bottom.

D. A Test of Will, Capacity, and Wisdom to Lead

The health care problem is in reality only one of a number of truly intractable policy issues that the nation and its governments find particularly difficult to address and solve. To a great extent, the underlying political and social tension surrounding the entire issue of health care provision is one of trust. In essence, the public and policymakers are not sure whether they can trust their physicians, provider plans, or public and elected officials to prioritize their health over the profit margins of health care corporations (Gray, 1997). Likewise, there is an ethical dimension to the debate, which is entirely related to the issue of trust, and that is whether we can count on the "profession" of medicine to remain a profession or become transformed into "purveyors" of health care (Kassier, 1998).

Other issues, such as the environment, education, economic development, racism etc., also buffalo our leaders from the local to the national and international level. In a global community, it seems that all the easy problems are solved. What remains are the really difficult ones, the kinds of problems that do not fit within quarterly investment reports, terms of Congress, or presidential administrations. These problems involve mechanisms that persist across longer periods of time and require a distinct departure from politics as usual.

This realization of the need for multipartisanship, cooperation, and collaboration is most effectively seen at the international level, and is often the product of the U.S. foreign policy, the United Nations, other foreign governments, and other committed nongovernmental organizations. While the capacity of these processes and organizations is even more compromised than is the health care debate that rages among and within states and in Congress, the philosophical perspective for problem solving is more sophisticated. In these settings participants clearly understand that the complexity of the issues they confront necessitates very different tools and approaches for problem solving.

E. Shipbuilding Tools

Whatever changes take place to move the current health care system beyond its current situation, it seems clear (to this author) that the nation will not be building any really effective and new "health care ships" until it designs the appropriate tools with which to construct the vessel. The review of the most recent debate on health care, as well as the more recent debate surrounding BBA 1997, is persuasive in that it illustrates how flawed processes create flawed programs. Recognizing that what is being made is still "sausage," the American public and their representatives should become concerned that on the really big issues, administrations and Congress just cannot seem to grasp and resolve them. Certainly, it is the recognition of this fact that has led many to try to take the issues to the local level and solve them there. However, as is the case with the environmental issue, health care problems are not easily confined geographically. This becomes even more obvious in the light of a growing economy.

So if taking a big issue and treating it like a cluster of small issues fails to move the process along, and if large complex issues such as health care just leave the Congress flatulent and with indigestion, then perhaps the time has come to consider the metatask of building tools that can later be used to build ships.

One very effective tool, utilized by politicians when on the time constraints of a campaign agenda, is the community or town hall meeting. These were widely utilized by the Clinton administration throughout the defunct health care debate of 1993–1994, and they were well received by the public. Town meetings hold the promise of engaging the public in a discussion, as does the media (as demonstrated by many efforts on the part of CNN). However, these are the relatively simple tools to build in revamping health care to better serve the nation. The really tough work is to pound the swords brandished by industry interests, politicians, and interest groups into productive plowshares. In theory, presidential commissions or similar organizations emanating from among government and industry interests ought to be able to fashion useful tools for change. In reality, local politics and self-interests have ultimately reduced the recommendations of some of the most impressive planning groups to rubble.

What this author proposes is for the nation to consider developing a free-standing, semiautonomous, quasi-governmental organization serving the health care sector in a way similar to that provided by the Federal Reserve Board in the banking industry. While this analogy is proposed in only the loosest terms, it is seriously presented *not* as a "solution" to the health care issues of the nation but as a "tool" with sufficient "authority" and "longevity" to address a set of problems that, by their very complexity and endurance over time, simply baffle the best efforts of a legislative body to "manage."

"Manage" is probably the right word here, at least in the loosest sense of the word, because Congress, in discharging its oversight responsibility, is much more interested in and adroit at making legislation than ensuring that legislation, once past, involves effective management. Health care, is simply too involved to be managed by Congress. Consequently, this author suggests that the next most productive step that the nation could make toward long-term (not short-term) solutions of health care is to recognize qualities associated with the issue that make it similar to banking, nuclear energy, environmental issues, and others, and design a "policy tool" or apparatus that is truly appropriate to the task at hand.

F. Final Thoughts

After having struggled with the issues involved with improving the nation's health care system for many years, it seems that not just around the health care issue, but around many substantive policy issues, the very organization of the congressional and "federalist" system of government needs to be seriously re-thought, not in terms of its historical values, philosophy, and tradition, but in terms of the new realities of global markets, global corporations, and global gov-ernment. In daring to suggest just one approach that might be worth considering at this point in the nation's history relative to the health care issue, what these authors are really suggesting is that the legislative, administrative, economic, and regulatory systems that in combination define government in the United States need to be rethought and reworked in terms of creating effective policy, and in terms of developing a legislative and regulatory infrastructure capable of effec-tively responding to and proactively dealing with the growing list of momentous policy issues.

At this writing, the Congress is preoccupied with the outcome of the Presi-dent's testimony relative to whether he actually engaged in sexual contact with a young White House aide. The author is at once impressed and disheartened at the extent to which government and the American people seem to concern themselves with trivia while truly important issues are ignored. In fact, in this media generation, it is the simple story that gets the play and the relatively ''simple'' political stances that are so frequently parlayed in public discourse.

These dalliances cumulatively distract the public and public officials from the truly important issues and make sustained deliberation, study, and response to complex policy issues virtually impossible. I suppose that Congress has long realized its penchant for trivialization, and in its wisdom placed the day-to-day management of its economy (i.e., its money) in a safe place where sober professionals watched it, obsessed about it, and ultimately managed it from day to day. While, upon reflection, it is frightening to realize just how much power the chairman of the Federal Reserve Board has, most people sleep well at night feeling that the nation's economy is being both conservatively and fairly managed.

The nation's health should be at least as important as the nation's money. Certainly nobody would want an Alan Greenspan clone dictating what an individual's treatment would involve. However, when one realizes the size, scope, and complexity of the health care industry and its myriad markets, and also recognizes the necessary regulatory role of insuring quality, equity, and cost-effectiveness, it is not so difficult to conceptualize an entity that regulates for quality outcomes, while also applying global budgeting and market controls. Though loosely conceptualized, this kind of thinking is what is required if the nation is to insure that serious problems get serious attention, and that the appropriated regulatory and market tools are developed to effectively manage this important service and industrial sector.

REFERENCES

AARP & AoA. A Profile of Older Americans in 1997. Washington, DC: Joint Report by the American Association of Retired Persons and the Administration on Aging, An AARP Publication, 1998.

AHA. AHA Statistics. Chicago: American Hospital Association, 1996–1997.

AHCA. Automation of MDS. Washington, DC: American Health Care Association, 1998.

AHQA. Beyond the Anecdotes: Advancing the Health Quality Debate. Washington, DC: American Health Quality Association Report, 1997.

Balanced Budget Act of 1997, P.L. 105-33.

Bandonw, P. Medicare: elderly lifeline under attack. Consumer's Res, August 1994, pp 30–34.

Berk, M.L., Schur, C.L. Measuring access to care: improving information for policymakers. Health Affairs 17(1):180–188, 1998.

Bishop, C.E., Walleck, S.S. National health expenditure limits: the case for a global budget process. Milbank Q 74(3):361–376, 1996.

Blendon, R.J., Brodie, M., Benson, J.M., Altman, D.E., Levitt, L., Hoff, T., Hugick L. Understanding the managed care backlash. Health Affairs 17(4):80–94, 1998.

Blumberg, L.J., Liska, D. Uninsured in the United States: A Status Report. Washington, DC: The Urban Institute, 1996.

Brodie, M., Brady, L.A., Altman, D.E. Media coverage of managed care: is there a negative bias? Health Affairs 17(1):9–25, 1998.

CBO. An Analysis of the President's Budgetary Proposals for 1999. Washington, DC: Congressional Budget Office Report, 1998.

CBO. The Economics and Budget Outlook: Fiscal Years 1996–2000. Washington, DC: Congressional Budget Office Report, 1995.

Christensen, S. Medicare + choice provisions in the balanced budget act of 1997. Health Affairs 17(4):224–231, 1998.

Christianson, J.B., Feldman, R.D., Wholey, D.R. HMO mergers: estimating impact on premiums and costs. Health Affairs 16(6):133–141, 1997.

Cogswell, M.E., Nelson, D., Koplan, J.P. Surveying managed care members on chronic disease. Health Affairs 16(6):219–227, 1997.

Colby, D.C. Doctors and their discontents. Health Affairs 16(6):112–114, 1997.

Consolidated Omnibus Budget Reconciliation Act of 1985 (COBRA), P.L. 99–272.

Consumers Union Press Release. Comments of Consumer Reports principal investigator, Trudy Lieberman, analyzing data relating to managed care and Medicare, July 12, 1998.

Consumers Union Press Release. Consumers Union asserts that managed care industry's concern about health care affordability is disingenuous. Washington, DC, April 27, 1998.

Consumers Union Press Release. Seniors face rising costs and vanishing benefits, 19 city Medicare study by consumer reports finds. Washington, DC, Aug 12, 1998.

Cooper, P.F., Schone, B.S. More offers, fewer takers for employment based health insurance: 1987 and 1996. Health Affairs 16(6):142–149, 1997.

Coughlin, T.A., Liska, D. Changing state and federal payment policies for Medicaid Disproportionate-Share hospitals. Health Affairs 17(3):118–136, 1998a.

Coughlin, T.A., Liksa, D. The Medicaid Disproportionate Share Hospital payment program: background and issue. In: New Federalism: Issues and Options for States, no. A-14. Washington, DC: Urban Institute, 1998b.

Cutler, D.M., Gruber, J. Medicaid and private insurance: evidence and implications. Health Affairs 16(1):194–200, 1997.

Cutler, D.M., Richardson, E. Measuring the Health of the U.S. Population. Washington, DC: Urban Institute, 1998.

Darby, M. Robert Brook: appropriateness research should inform health care. Report on Medical Guidelines and Outcomes Research, December 23, 1992.

DHHS, The Personal Responsibility and Work Opportunity Act (1996), Fact Sheet: Administration for Children & Families, Press Office, U.S. Department of Health & Human Services, September, 1996.

Donelan, K., Blendon, R.J., Lundberg, G.D., Calkins, D.R., Newhouse, J.P., Leape, L.L., Remler, D.K., Taylor, H. The new medical marketplace: physician's views. Health Affairs 16(5):139–148, 1997.

Douglas, T., Flores K. Federal and State Funding of Children's Programs. Washington, DC: Urban Institute, 1998.

EBRI. The 1998 Health Confidence Survey. Washington, DC: Employment Benefit Research Institute, 1998.

Eddy, D.M. Performance measurement: problems and solutions. Health Affairs 17(4):7–25, 1998.

Etzioni, A. Active Society. New York: Free Press, 1968.

Feder, J., Lambrow, J., Huckaby, M. Medicaid and long-term care for the elderly: implications of restructuring. Milbank Q 75(4):425–460, 1997.

Felt-Lisk, S., Yang, S. Changes in health plans serving Medicaid, 1993–1996. Health Affairs 16(5):125–133, 1997.

Florida Health Care Association. Medicare Prospective Payment System. Tallahassee: Florida Health Care Association, 1998.

Fries, B.E., Schneider, D.P., Foley, W.J., Gavazzi, M., Burke, R., Cornelius, E. Refining a case-mix measure for nursing homes: resource utilization groups (RUG-III). Med Care 32(7):668–665, 1994.

Gabel, J.R., Binsburg, P.B., Hung, K.A. Small employers and the health care benefits, 1988–1966: an awkward adolescence. Health Affairs 16(5):103–110, 1997.

GAO. Medicare Home Health Utilization Expands Choice, Program Controls Deteriorate. Washington, DC: U.S. General Accounting Office Report, 1993.

GAO. Medicaid States Turn to Managed Care to Improve Access and Control Costs. Washington, DC: U.S. General Accounting Office Report, 1992.

Ginsburg, P.B. Health system change in 1997. Health Affairs 17(4):165–169, 1998.

Ginsburg, P.B., Gable, J.R., Hunt, K.A. Tracking small-firm coverage, 1989–1996. Health Affairs 17(1):167–171, 1998.

Ginsburg, P.B., Pickreign, J.D. Tracking health care costs: an update. Health Affairs 16(4):151–155, 1997.

Gist, J.R. Entitlements and the federal budget: facts, folklore, and future. Milbank Q 74(3):327–360, 1996.

Glied, S., Hoven, C.W., Moore, R.E., Garrett, A.B., Reigier, D.A. Children's access to mental health care: does insurance matter? Health Affairs 16(1):167–174, 1997.

Gooding, J., Jette, A.M. Hospital readmissions among the elderly. J Am Geriatr Soc 33(9):595–601, 1985.

Gradison, B. Federal perspectives. President, Health Insurance Association of America (HIAA), News Release, July 31, 1997a.

Gradison, B. The threat of regulation of the health care industry. The Hill, Oct 22, 1997b (editorial).

Gradison, B. Position statement: S.1804/H.R. 3538. Washington, DC: Health Insurance Association of America, 1998a.

Gradison, B. HIAA statement on implementation of the Health Insurance Portability and Accountability Act P.L. 104-191. President, Health Insurance Association of America (HIAA), testimony before the U.S. House of Representatives Committee on Ways and Means, March 18, 1998b.

Gray, B.H. Trust and trustworthy care in the managed care era. Health Affairs 16(1):34–49, 1997.

Gutterman, S. The Balanced Budget Act of 1997: will hospitals take a hit on their PPS margins? Health Affairs 17(1):159–165, 1998.

Hadley, J., Mitchell, J.M. Effects of HMO market penetration of physician's work effort and satisfaction. Health Affairs 16(6):99–111, 1997.

Harlin, S. Physician protest and the Hippocratic oath. New York Times, June 15, 1996.

HCFA. National Health Expenditures. Washington, DC: U.S. Department of Health and Human Services, Health Care Financing Administration, 1997.

HCFA. A Profile of Medicare Chart Book. Washington, DC: U.S. Department of Health and Human Services, Health Care Financing Administration, 1998a.

HCFA. National Health Expenditures Aggregate and per Capita Amounts, Percent Distribution, and Average Annual Percent Growth, by Source of Funds: Selected Calendar Years 1960–96. Washington, DC: U.S. Department of Health and Human Services, Health Care Financing Administration, National Health Expenditure Data, 1998b, Table 9.

HCFA. Multistate Case-Mix and Quality Demonstration: RUG-III. Washington, DC: U.S. Department of Health and Human Services, Health Care Financing Administration, 1998c.

HCP. Letter to Health Care Financing Administration: Re: Comments on Proposed Rule Medicare and Medicaid Programs: Use of the OASIS as part of the conditions of participation for home health agencies. Albany, NY: Health Care Providers Inc., New York State, June 3, 1997a.

HCP. Proposed Revisions to Federal Medicare Regulations (Conditions of Participation). Albany, NY: Health Care Providers Inc., New York State, March 7, 1997c.

HCP. Prospective Payment System: An Alternative to Medicare Home Health Copayments and "Bundling." Albany, NY: Health Care Providers Inc., New York State, February 21, 1997c.

HCS. Summary of Findings: 1998 Health Confidence Survey. Washington, DC: Employee Benefit Research Institute, 1998.

Health Insurance Portability and Accountability Act of 1997, P.L. 104 191.

Health Security Act of 1997, H.R. 1200, 105th Congress.

Hegner, R.E. Medicare coverage for home health care: reining in a benefit out of control. National Health Policy Forum, Issue Brief no. 694, 1996.

Hegner, R.E. Mental health parity: unresolved issues affecting employers, consumers, and insurance coverage. National Health Policy Forum, Issue Brief no. 709, 1997.

Holahan, J. Crowding out: how big a problem? Health Affairs 16(1):204–206, 1997.

Holloway, J.J., Thomas, J.W. Factors influencing readmission risk: implications for quality monitoring. Health Care Financ Rev 11(2):19–32, 1989.

Holloway, J.J., Thomas, J.W., Shapiro, L. Clinical and sociodemographic risk factors for readmission of Medicare beneficiaries. Health Care Financ Rev 10(1):34, 1988.

Iglehart, J.K. Physicians as agents of social control: thoughts of Victor Fuchs. Health Affairs 17(1):90–96, 1998.

Ignagni, K. Covering a breaking revolution: the media and managed care. Health Affairs 17(1):26–34, 1998.

Jensen, G.A., Morrisey, M.A., Gaffney, S., Liston, D.K. The new dominance of managed care: insurance trends in the 1990s. Health Affairs 16(1):125–136, 1997.

Jensen, G.A., Rost, K., Burton, R.P.D., Bulycheva, M. Mental health insurance in the 1990s: are employers offering less to more? Health Affairs 17(3):201–208, 1998.

Johnson, H., Broder, D.S. The System: The American Way of Politics at the Breaking Point. Boston: Little Brown, 1996.

Johnson, K.A., McDonough, J.E. Expanding Health Coverage for Children: Matching Federal Policies and State Strategies. New York: Milbank Memorial Fund, 1998.

Jones, N.S. Communicating to beneficiaries about Medicare + Choice: opportunities and pitfalls. National Health Policy Forum, Issue Brief no. 723, 1998.

Kane, R. Expanding the home care concept: blurring distinctions among home care, institutional care and other long-term care services. Milbank Q 73(2):161–186, 1995.

Kassier, J.P. Managing care—should we adopt a new ethic? N Engl J Med 339(6):397–398, 1998 (editorial).

Kenney, G., Rajan, S., Soscia, S. State spending for Medicare and Medicaid home care programs. Health Affairs 17(1):201–212, 1998.

Kuhlthau, K., Walker, D.K., Perrin, J.M., Bauman, L., Gortmaker, S.L., Newacheck, P.W., Stein, E.K. Assessing managed care for children with chronic conditions. Health Affairs 17(4):42–52, 1998.

Levine, J. The HMO backlash. CNN Interactive: Health Story Page, Nov 5, 1997.

Levit, K.R., Lazenby, H.C., Braden, B.R., and the National Health Accounts Team. National health spending trends in 1996. Health Affairs 17(1):35–51, 1998.

Lewis, K., Ellwood, M., Czaika, J.L., and Mathematica Policy Research Inc. Counting the Uninsured: A Review of the Literature. Washington, DC: Urban Institute, 1998.

Liska, D.W., Brennan, N.J., Bruen, B.K. State-Level Databook on Health Care Access and Financing, 3rd ed. Washington, DC: Brookings Press, 1998.

Luft, H.S., Greenlick, M.R. The contributions of group- and staff-model HMOs to American medicine. Milbank Q 74(4):445–468, 1996.

Marsteller, J.A., Nichols, L.M., Badawi, A., Kessler, B., Zuckerman, S., Rajan, S. Why health insurance coverage varies across the country and within a state: full report. Washington, DC: Urban Institute White Paper, June 1998.

Matherlee, K.R. Walking a tightrope between research and policy: the Medicaid and Medicare waiver process. National Health Policy Forum, Issue Brief no. 632, 1993.

Meddings, D.R., McGrail, K.M., Barer, M.L., Hertzman, C. The eyes have it: cataract surgery and changing patterns of outpatient surgery. Med Care Res Rev 54(13):1, 1997.

Medicaid Voluntary Contribution and Provider Specific Tax Amendments of 1991, P.L. 101-224.

Medicare Catastrophic Coverage Act of 1988, P.L. 100-360.

Medicare Home Health Beneficiary Act, 1998, S2354, 105th Congress, Second Session.

Meier, C.F. How to implement Kassebaum Kennedy. Washington, DC: Heartland Institute White Paper, 1997.

Miller, R.H., Luft, H.S. Does managed care lead to better or worse quality of care? Health Affairs 16(5):7–25, 1997.

Minor, A., ed. Source Book of Health Insurance Data: 1997–1998. Washington, DC: Health Insurance Association of America, 1998.

Moon, M., Gage, B., Evans, A. An examination of key Medicare provisions in the Balanced Budget Act of 1997. Washington, DC: Urban Institute White Paper, September 1997.

Moran, D.W. Federal regulation of managed care: an impulse in search of a theory? Health Affairs 16(6):7–21, 1997.

NAHC. Basic Statistics About Home Care 1997. Washington, DC: National Association for Home Care, 1997.

NCHS. NCHS FastStats. Washington, DC: National Center for Health Statistics, 1998.

Nichols, L.M., Blumberg, L.J., Acs, G.P., Uccello, C.E., Marsteller, J.A. Small employers: their diversity and health insurance. Washington, DC: Urban Institute White Paper, 1997.

Omnibus Budget Reconciliation Act of 1980, P.L. 96-499.

Omnibus Budget Reconciliation Act of 1986, P.L. 99-509.

Omnibus Budget Reconciliation Act of 1993, P.L. 103-66.

Palmisano, D.J. Testimony on behalf of the American Medical Association, in support of the Quality Health-Care Coalition Act. Testimony before the U.S. House of Representatives, Judiciary Committee, July 29, 1998.

P.L. 104-191, The Health Insurance Portability and Accountability Act of 1997.

P.L. 100-360, The Medicare Catastrophic Coverage Act of 1988.

Polzer, K. The Medicare risk contract game: what rules should PSOs play by? National Health Policy Forum, Issue Brief no. 702, 1997.

PPS Work Group. Rationale for Revised Unified Prospective Payment Plan. Health Care Providers, Inc., New York State, 1997.

ProPAC. Analysis of Medicare Cost Reports: 1983–1995. Washington, DC: Prospective Payment Assessment Commission, 1996.

Rawls, J. A Theory of Justice. Cambridge, MA: Belknap Press of Harvard University Press, 1971.

Rubenstein, E. How not to cut. National Rev 47(14):15, 1995.

Schlesinger, M., Gray, B. A broader vision for managed care. Part 1. Measuring the benefit to communities. Health Affairs 17(3):152–168, 1998.

Schore, J. Regional Variation in Medicare Home Health: Taking a Closer Look. Washington, DC: Mathematica Policy Research, Inc., 1996.

Shakespeare, W. The Tempest. New York: Moonbeam Publications, 1979.

Sparer, M.S. Devolution of power: an interim report card. Health Affairs 17(3):7–16, 1998.

Spence, C.A. 1995 COBRA Survey, Spencer Research Reports. Charles A. Spence and Associates, 329.04, 1995, pp 1–7.

Starr, P. The Social Transformation of American Medicine: The Rise of a Sovereign Profession and the Making of a Vast Industry. New York: Basic Books, 1982.

Stauffer, M. Comprehensive consumer bill of rights. Health Policy Tracking Service, Issue Brief no. 1, 1998.

Stevens, R. In Sickness and in Wealth: American Hospitals in the Twentieth Century. New York: Basic Books, 1989.

Tax Equity and Fiscal Responsibility Act (TEFRA) of 1982, 97-248.

Thompson, J.W., Bost, J., Ahmed F., Ingalis, C.E., Sennett, C. The NCQA's quality compass: evaluating managed care in the United States. Health Affairs 17(1):152–158, 1998.

Ullman, F., Bruen, B., Holahan, J. The State Children's Health Insurance Program: A Look at the Numbers. Washington, DC: Urban Institute, March 1998.

Victor, C.R., Vetter, N.J. The early readmission of the elderly to hospital. Age Aging 14(11):37–42, 1985.

Wang, P. Letter relating to OASIS demonstration. President of Health Care Providers, Inc., of New York State, June 3, 1997.

Warren, J.L., Riley, G.F., Potosky, A.L., Klabunde, C.N. Trends and outcomes of outpatient mastectomy in elderly women. J Natl Cancer Inst 90(11):1, 1998.

Weil, A. The New Children's Health Insurance Program: Should States Expand Medicaid? Series no. A-13. Washington, DC: Urban Institute, 1998.

Wennberg, J.E. Understanding Geographic Variations in Health Care Delivery. N Engl J Med 40(1):32–39, 1999.

White, J. Competing Solutions: American Health Care Proposals and International Experience. Washington, DC: Brookings Institution Press, 1995.

White, J. Which "managed care" for Medicare? Health Affairs 16(5):73–82, 1997.

Wilson, G.K. Interest groups in the health care debate. In: Aaron, H.J., ed. The Problem that Won't Go Away: Reforming U.S. Health Care Financing. Washington, DC: Brookings Press, 1995, pp 110–129.

Wimberley, E. The non-movement toward national health insurance. J Public Int Affairs 1:135–157, 1980a.

Wimberley, E. Toward national health insurance in the United States. Soc Sci Med 14c: 13–25, 1980b.

Wimberley, E. Personal communication with Senator Bentsen while serving as a Robert Wood Johnson Health Policy Fellow, 1989–1990, 1990.

Wimberley, E., Morrow, A. Mulling over muddling through again. Int J Public Admin 3: 483, 1981.

Young, G.J., Desai, K.R., Lukas, C.V. Does the sale of nonprofit hospitals threaten health care for the poor? Health Affairs 16(1):137–141, 1997.

Zimmerman, D.L. Grading the graders: using "report cards" to enhance the quality of care under health care reform. National Health Policy Forum, Issue Brief no. 642, 1994.

7

The Health Services System in Mexico

Program of Organization and Management of Health Systems and Services
Division of Health Systems and Services Development
Pan American Health Organization
World Health Organization, Washington, D.C.

I. INTRODUCTION

Some of the most important actions undertaken as part of Pan American Health Care (PAHO) and World Health Organization (WHO) technical cooperation are those aimed at strengthening national capacity to design, implement, and make effective use of methodologies and information systems that are geared to:

1. Identify and assess changes in the living and health conditions of the population
2. Develop capacity for the analysis, planning, and formulation of policy
3. Strengthen the capacity for leadership and management in the ministries of health and other institutions of the sector both for normal operating conditions and for the Health Sector Reform (HSR) processes

Even though a number of initiatives have been undertaken since the middle of the past decade in support of such efforts, it was not until 1998 that a report on the health system was available for each country. Each report provides a systematic synthetic and analytical description of the respective health systems and the development and impact of HSR initiatives.

A Health System Profile is a document that systematically describes and analyzes the context, structure, and dynamics of the health system of a given country, including any experience it has had with HSR. The Profile does not intend to offer an exhaustive analysis of all possible topics, or even of all the topics that it mentions. It only addresses relevant aspects of a set of selected topics that are considered to be indispensable. Detailed analyses of the topics that have been included (or of others that have not been included) are possible and, in many cases, necessary. Other methodological instruments are being developed by PAHO for this purpose.

Although the Profile may be useful for a variety of purposes and users, two main types of users are kept in mind:

1. In the countries, the health authorities and personnel involved in directing and managing institutions in or related to the health sector (national and subnational levels)
2. At the international level, managers and professionals in the cooperation agencies, and health authorities in the other countries of the region

For preparation of the first version a Guideline was designed to be used by a team of professionals in the area of health systems and services in the PAHO/WHO Representative Offices and by the corresponding professionals in the ministries of health, and other health sector institutions in the countries. This profile contains both quantitative and qualitative information. With regard to the quantitative information, an effort has been made to limit the requests for information to that which is known to be available and has been previously reported by most of the countries. Whenever possible, quantitative information should be presented in the form of a table or graph, followed by comments on the evolution of the data over time, if that information is available, the expected trends, and the causes or factors that contribute to the picture.

For the qualitative information, the Guideline tries to be fully explanatory (for example, clarifying the scope of the information requested and/or clarifying the terms) and suggest the approximate space that should be devoted to the topic in the Profile (for example, one line, a few lines, or a paragraph). It differentiates between "qualitative information," "expert opinion," and "value judgment" and recommends avoiding the latter.

The Profile's synthetic and objective nature must be emphasized. This means that long, detailed descriptions have been avoided and that the topics should be dealt with on the basis of the information available, avoiding value judgments and unfounded conclusions.

The work of preparing the Profile does not end with the writing of the first version; this is an ongoing process that will involve repeated approximations. As experience has shown, a country's Profile will not be considered fully satisfactory until the second or third version.

Subsequent global reviews will be undertaken on a regular schedule, normally every 2 years, but partial updates in specific chapters or sections may be provided at any time, as long as they are justified. We have 25 Health System

Country Profiles currently available in the LAC Health Sector Reform Initiative web page, six of them partly or totally revised since the beginning of this work. The following profile of the health services system in Mexico is one of the profiles that we maintain and update on a regular basis (for further information, see http://www.paho.org/english/country.htm). A second edition of this profile is expected to be available by the end of 2001.

II. OVERVIEW

Mexico is a representative democratic republic, comprised of 31 free and sovereign states and a Federal District that are united in a federation. In 1997, the total population of the country was 94.2 million, with 26.5% residing in rural areas and 73.5% in cities. This population is distributed across 2418 municipios. According to UNDP data, in 1997 the Human Development Index (HDI) for Mexico was 0.853, putting the country in 50th place. In 1995, 24 million people were living in extreme poverty, with the total number of poor approaching 40 million. The monthly income of 19.4% of the employed population is less than the minimum wage (below US$ 90), while the income of 9.6% is more than five times the minimum wage (above US$ 500). In 1997 the national illiteracy rate was 9.7%, and the average schooling 6.6 years.

The health services system consists of three major subsectors:

1. The Social Security institutions, which include the Mexican Social Security Institute (IMSS), the Social Security Institute for Government Employees (ISSSTE), and the medical services of Petróleos Mexicanos (PEMEX) under the Secretariat of National Defense (SEDENA) and the Secretariat of the Navy (SEMAR)
2. The public health services provided basically by the Secretariat of Health (SSA), the IMSS-Solidarity Program (IMSS-Sol), and the National Indigenous Institute (INI)
3. The private sector

Under the General Health Act, the SSA exercises the steering role in the sector. Its basic functions include reviewing the norms governing health in general, evaluating service delivery, operating the national epidemiological surveillance system, and strengthening sanitary control. In 1992 national per capita health expenditure was MN$ 360.4; in 1996 it fell to MN$ 324.8. In the 1990s the figure varied. Similarly, health expenditure as a proportion of public expenditures has grown from 1.6% in 1990 to 2.5% in 1996. During the period 1990–1996, the year with highest figure was 1994, with 2.7%. In a related vein, the rate of physicians per 10,000 population in 1992 was 9.3, increasing to 11.2 in 1996. The rate of nurses per 10,000 population rose from 16.8 to 18.3 in the same period. In 1996 there were 0.81 countable beds per 1000 population. Coverage of screening for cervical cancer in 1997 was 20%. That same year, vaccination coverage included: Sabin (polio), 98.4%; measles, 98.1%; DPT, 98.2%; BCG (tuberculosis), 99.7%.

In 1996 the rate of outpatient consultations per 1000 population was 1414.6; for consultations with dentists, 124.3; emergency consultations, 235.5; and laboratory tests, 1577.9. That same year, the total hospital occupancy rate was 68.6% and the average length of stay was 4.1 days.

In 1996 the Health Sector Reform Program 1995–2000 was announced. Its objectives are:

> To develop instruments to promote quality and efficiency in service delivery
> To expand the coverage of care in Social Security establishments, facilitating affiliation by the nonsalaried population and workers in the informal sector
> To conclude the decentralization of the health services for the uninsured population
> To expand service coverage to the marginalized population in rural and urban areas that currently have little or no access

In late 1997 the transfer of human resources (103,000 workers), infrastructure (7,400 pieces of real estate), and financial resources (*MN*$ 6,132 million) to all the states of the Republic was concluded. This transfer was intended to foster a clearer definition of goals, responsibilities, and evaluation systems in the states to ensure better health policies, while the SSA was designed to prioritize regulatory and coordination functions. Also in development is the Program for Expanded Coverage, consisting of a basic package of health services for the more marginalized areas.

The Health Sector Reform Program includes specific activities through two lines of action:

> 1. Promoting and facilitating voluntary affiliation with the social security system and providing health insurance for families
> 2. Making essential health services available to marginalized population groups through a basic package of services

In mid-1998, the head of the SSA stated publicly that, thanks to the PAC, care had been provided to seven million Mexicans who prior to 1995 had had no access to any type of health service. According to this same source, it remained to bring services to three million inhabitants located mainly in the states of Chiapas, Guerrero, Hidalgo, and Oaxaca.

III. CONTEXT

A. Political Context

Mexico is a representative and democratic republic, comprised of 31 free and sovereign states and a Federal District, united in a federation. The federal and state governments are of equal rank and espouse the principles of autonomy and association. The third order of government is the municipal level, with 2428 municipios across the country. The Political Constitution establishes a separation of powers, creating the executive, legislative, and judicial branches. Planning and federal government activities are guided by a 6-year National Development Plan (NDP). Drawn up by the Federal Executive, this Plan contains the objectives, goals, and strategies for all sectors. The Plan for 1995–2000 contains two broad goals in health:

> To improve quality by restructuring health institutions
> To expand service coverage, strengthening coordination and promoting the federalization of the services (1)

The federated entities and municipios have Committees for Development Planning (COPLADE and COPLADEM, respectively). Government social policy is defined around the Education, Health, and Nutrition Program (PROGRESA), designed to substantially improve the education, health, and nutritional situation of poor families, particularly boys, girls, and their mothers, offering schooling and health services of adequate quality, as well as nutritional assistance (2). The Secretariat of Social Development (SEDESO) is responsible for social policy, which it carries out in close collaboration with the Secretariats of Education (SEP), Health (SSA), and the National Program for Integral Development of the Family (DIF). Some of the major political and social problems affecting the health of citizens are:

> High levels of marginalization, particularly among the rural population (seven out of every 10 localities are rural) and indigenous groups (95% of localities in which 40% of the inhabitants or more speak indigenous languages exhibit some degree of marginality).
> The presence of armed groups in several states of the Republic (Chiapas and Guerrero).
> Malnutrition among young children (according to official data, 16.9% of the under-5 population suffered from this problem in 1996, while other studies put the figure at 43% in rural areas).

B. Economic Context

As shown in Table 1, after several years of steady economic growth, an economic crisis in late 1994 led to the devaluation of the national currency, a drop in the

Table 1   Economic and Social Indicators, 1991–1996

Indicator	Year					
	1991	1992	1993	1994	1995	1996
Per capita GDP, constant prices in US$	2970	3390	3610	4010	3320[a]	3456.3[a]
Annual percentage variation in GDP	4.2	3.6	2.0	4.4	—	—
Total public expenditure, as a percentage of GDP	28.5	26.9	27.2	28.1	26.6	23.0
Social public expenditure as a percentage of GDP	6.6	6.4	6.6	6.3	6.9	8.0[b]
Total health expenditure, as a percentage of GDP	3.8	4.5	4.6	4.7	4.1	3.9
Proportion of total public expenditure devoted to social expenditure	41.1	45.6	50.8	52.9	55.0	53.3

[a] Taken from: *Basic Indicators* 1997 and 1998, published by PAHO/WHO.
[b] Estimate.
Sources: INEGI, *Anuario estadístico de la República Mexicana*, 1997. Banco de México, Annual reports from 1992 to 1997. *Estudios económicos de la OCDE, 1997–1998*: México, France, OECD, 1998.

gross domestic product (GDP), and a contraction in domestic demand. Between 1996 and 1997 the macroeconomic foundations were laid for recovery, but in 1998 the crisis in Asia and the drop in oil prices forced the government to cut public spending by some US$ 3 billion. The 1997 distribution of GDP by economic activity was: 6.1% in the primary sector; 28.3% in the secondary sector; 65.6% in the tertiary sector. External economic cooperation did not have a significant effect on GDP.

C. Social Context

In 1997 the total population of Mexico was 94.2 million: 26.5% in rural areas and 73.5% in the cities. That year, the Human Development Index (HDI) was 0.853, placing the country in 50th place; Mexico also ranked 50th on the Gender Development Index (GDI) (3). The rate of open unemployment was 6.2% in 1995, 5.5% in 1996, and 3.7% in 1997; a slight decline was forecast for 1998 and 1999, without considering the impact that crises in other countries and the drop in oil prices will have on the national economy. Between 1989 and 1992 poverty increased annually by 6.3%, impacting on 13.6 million people. In 1995, nearly 40 million people were poor; 24 million of them were living in extreme poverty, with rural localities accounting for 64.1% of the total. Localities with a high concentration of indigenous population tend to exhibit higher frequencies of poverty and marginality (4–6). The ratio between the 20% of population with the highest income and the 20% with the lowest income was 8 in 1994. Between 1984 and 1994 the gap between these groups widened (Gini coefficient 0.4562 and 0.513, respectively). Some 19.4% of the employed population report a monthly income of less than one minimum wage (below US$ 90), while 9.6% have a monthly income of over five times the minimum wage (above US$ 500) (7). In 1995, the national illiteracy rate was 9.7% and the average years of schooling 6.6, with large variations between states (Nuevo León reported 3.8% and 8.1 years of schooling, while Oaxaca reported 13.9% and 4.7 years) (8).

IV. HEALTH SERVICES SYSTEM

A. General Organization

The health care system in Mexico is organized by segments, each of which covers different population groups (Tables 2 and 3). These groups include:

> Public services for uninsured people (also known as the "open population," this group is estimated at 48% of the population), provided chiefly by the SSA, IMSS-Sol, and the INI.
> Several Social Security institutions, which workers in the formal economy must subscribe to; the most important of these institutions are: IMSS, ISSSTE, health and social security services for the employees of PEMEX, the Armed Forces (SEDENA), and the state governments.
> The private sector, with and without insurance plans, which operates in an unsupervised context.

The segments of the health services system generally operate independently of one another. Each institution has developed its own forms of financing and service delivery. There is little coordination among providers, and each has its

Table 2 Organization of Health Services for the Uninsured Population, 1998

Characteristics	SSA	IMSS-Solidarity	INI
Legal nature	Secretariat	Program within the regulatory structure of the IMSS	Structurally under the Federal Executive, with legal status and its own resources
Decentralization	Well underway	Projected	Projected
Sources of financing	Federal	Federal and supported by the IMSS administration	Federal

Table 3 Organization of the Social Security Health Services, 1998

Characteristics	IMSS	ISSSTE	PEMEX	SEDEN A	State
Legal nature	Tripartite: government, business, and workers	Public institution with legal status and its own resources	Public enterprise with legal status and its own resources	Secretariat	Public institutions in several states
Decentralization	Partial	Nil	Nil	Nil	Projected
Sources of financing	Tripartite: federal, workers, and employers	Federal	Own	Federal	Federal/state

own network of primary care units and second- and third-level hospitals. The SSA has 11 institutes for specialized care, located in the federal capital. Mechanisms for referral and back-referral have not been established. In practice, some patients from the Social Security institutes are transferred to specialized facilities of the SSA or to private facilities when the capabilities of the center in which the initial contact takes place are inadequate, and increasingly, owing to cost-benefit considerations. The staffs of all public health institutions are salaried, and the units operate within global annual budgets.

The SSA has made the greatest progress in decentralization. It transferred functions and resources to 14 states in 1988 and, after several years of inaction, resumed decentralization within the framework of health sector reform. The IMSS has decentralized some of its functions and resources toward the regions (an intermediate level distinct from the political-administrative division). ISSSTE, INI, SEDENA, and PEMEX have more centralized systems for budget management and decision making.

B. Private Health Facilities

Private health facilities operate independently of one another and provide care at the primary and secondary level. The majority of these facilities are corporations. Their users come from every economic level, from the most affluent (some 3.6 million have private insurance) down to the middle class and the poor, who tend to pay for services out of pocket. Managed care organizations are in their infancy, while NGOs do not play a significant role in the delivery of services.

The organizational model of the services is based upon primary care, with a health team consisting of a general practitioner or family physician and nurses (the SSA includes a community health worker in the team and calls it the "basic group"). This team attends to the demand of the population assigned to it and engages in health promotion and disease prevention activities under priority programs. Admission to the secondary and tertiary level of care is by referral from the primary level; this care is provided in hospitals.

C. System Resources

1. Human Resources

Human resources in the sector have grown steadily in recent decades, and no significant changes are forecast in the number and proportion of students completing undergraduate and graduate health programs in the coming years (Tables 4 and 5).

The largest public employer is the IMSS, followed by the SSA. In 1997 the SSA listed 18,587 physicians and 22,750 nurses in private practice, which raises the rate per 10,000 population to 15.58 and 20.58, respectively. In all institutions concentration of technical staff is greater in urban than in rural areas.

Table 4 Human Resources for Health (Public Sector), 1990–1997

Type of resource	1990	1991	1992	1993	1994	1995	1996	1997
Total physicians	89,842	97,971	103,356	107,495	114,329	119,433	123,114	129,031
Total nurses[a]	130,620	141,404	148,957	154,852	166,644	168,170	171,144	172,294
Staff of diagnostic and treatment services[b]	22,135	22,921	24,780	25,244	26,612	27,836	31,360	33,602
No. of graduate students completing programs in the health sciences	3,807	4,211	4,036	3,110	3,024	4,109	4,451	NA
Physicians per 10,000 pop.	NA	8.9	9.3	10.1	10.7	11.1	11.2	13.6
Nurses per 10,000 pop.	NA	15.8	16.8	17.5	18.4	18.3	18.3	18.1

[a] Includes nursing auxiliaries, general and specialized nurses, and other nursing categories.
[b] Refers to professionals, technicians, and auxiliaries working in the diagnostic and treatment services.
Sources: INEGI, *Anuario estadístico de 1996*, Mexico, 1997; ANUIES, *Anuario estadístico. Posgrado* (1989–1997), Mexico; SSA, *Boletín de información estadística*, vol. I, 1991–1996 and 1997 (in preparation).

Table 5 Distribution of Human Resources among Public Institutions, 1996

Institution	Physicians	General and specialized nurses	Nursing auxiliaries[a]	Administrative staff	Other staff
SSA	37,620	21,898	29,158	27,955	35,398
IMSS-Sol	5,434	855	8,183	2,187	2,617
IMSS	47,813	43,355	27,964	22,126	65,579
ISSSTE	15,945	10,703	7,500	10,858	17,571
PEMEX	2,393	1,521	1,128	1,549	4,244
Others	13,909	9,981	8,898	7,708	15,294
Total	123,114	88,313	82,831	72,383	140,703

[a] Includes undergraduate nursing interns and nursing interns fulfilling their social service requirement.
Source: SSA, *Boletín de información estadística*, No. 16, 1996; vol. I, Mexico, September 1997.

2. Drugs and Other Health Products

In 1997, 6905 pharmaceutical products and 13,540 registered drugs were marketed. Separate registration of drugs by generic and brand name began in 1998 after the amendment of the General Health Act of 1997 to increase the presence of generic drugs in the national market (formerly, several forms of every registered product were permitted). In July 1998, there were 180 generic forms registered and in August the first list of 174 interchangeable generic drugs was published. No reliable information is available for drug expenditures in either the public institutions or the national accounts system of the Mexican Health Foundation (FUNSALUD). The five groups of drugs with the highest sales in the country in 1997 included antibiotics, antacids, antihypertensives, analgesics and anti-inflammatories, and cancer drugs. There is a Basic Drug Table for the primary level and a Catalog of Drugs for the secondary and tertiary level of care, which together list 776 key compounds (January 1998). These tools are updated biennially by the General Health Council, an autonomous agency with a budget from the SSA, and their use is compulsory in the public sector. Private pharmacies must have a pharmacist on staff, but not hospitals. Public institutions make consolidated purchases of generic drugs, and the SSA authorizes the states to make purchases, if they so desire. Five pharmaceuticals distributors with over 1000 warehouses throughout the country operate in the private sector. To guarantee a safe blood supply, the National Center for Blood Transfusion (CNTS) and the State Centers were created. No figures are available on the number of donated units of blood.

Table 6   Availability of Equipment in the Health Sector per 1000 Population, 1996

Institution	Countable beds[a]	Clinical laboratories	Blood banks	Radiodiagnostic equipment
SSA	0.87	0.023	0.003	0.026
IMSS-Sol	0.16	0.006	0.0	0.006
Subtotal uninsured population	0.75	0.019	0.003	0.023
IMSS	0.71	0.012	0.001	ND
ISSSTE	0.72	0.014	0.007	0.043
PEMEX	1.79	0.040	0.035	0.116
Others	2.69	—	—	—
Subtotal insured population	0.8	0.005	0.003	NA
National average (public sector)	0.8	0.016	0.003	0.017[b]
National average (private)	1.09	0.024	ND	0.032[b]

[a] Data for 1997. Obtained through direct consultation with the Bureau of Statistics. SSA.
[b] Not including the equipment of the IMSS and the Secretariat of the Navy.
Source: SSA, *Boletín de información estadística*, No. 16, vol. I, Mexico, September 1997.

3.   Equipment and Technology

The SSA and the IMSS absorb more than 50% of the material resources of the sector. No information is available on their distribution by level of care, nor on equipment that is either defective or out of order. Both the public and private sectors have improved their equipment and technology in recent years, especially state-of-the-art radiodiagnostic equipment (9) (Tables 6 and 7).

D.   Functions of the Health Services System

1.   Steering Role

The SSA is responsible for managing the sector and prepares the Official Mexican Health Standards (NOM), which determine the specific procedures and contents of the national sanitary regulations. The legal framework for the sector consists of two general laws that are periodically updated at the initiative of the government:

1. The General Health Act and the Social Security Act, which are implemented through the NOM
2. The Regulations and Agreements of the public institutions, published in the official journal of the Federation

Table 7 Other Material Resources of the Health
Sector, 1996

Institution	Delivery rooms	Operating rooms
SSA	4955	776
IMSS Solidarity	68	68
Subtotal uninsured population	5153	1156
IMSS	482	939
ISSSTE	147	278
PEMEX	25	66
Other	104	129
Subtotal insured population	758	1412
National total (public sector)	5911	2568
National total (private)	8401	NA

Source: SSA, *Boletín de información estadística*, No. 16, vol. I,
Mexico, September 1997.

Supervision and control of public health financing is the province of the chief administrator of each institutional service provider. Supervision and control occurs under the direction of and in close coordination with the Secretariat of the Treasury and Public Credit (SHCP), which allocates the budget, and the Secretariat of the Office of the Comptroller and Administrative Development (SECODAM), which monitors expenditures. Following the decentralization of the SSA in 1997, the Federation retained the authority to regulate the health services; exercise sanitary control of products, facilities, and services; oversee the certification of professionals; accredit health facilities; generate national statistics; and represent the sector internationally. The state and district health bureaus share responsibilities in the organization, operation, and monitoring of public and private health services, sanitary control of the environment and population, and the implementation of health promotion activities. Coordination between the Federation and the states in the areas of technical cooperation, logistics, and the evaluation of health programs (10) takes place through the National Health Council (CNS). Currently, the coordination between the SSA and the Social Security institutes is inadequate. Each employs its own model without sharing technical and administrative procedures—except in the information systems, where common criteria do exist, and the data from public providers are consolidated at the national and state level. These data are also used for national health days and emergencies, where all institutions work in close collaboration.

The links between public and private service providers are limited, except for the roughly 4% of IMSS subscribers whose quotas are forwarded to private services. Such transfers, which transfer responsibility for subscriber and related family care, involve a procedure whose official regulations are currently being drafted by the IMSS. Health information is readily available, and the SSA publishes the consolidated data on services, mortality, morbidity in consultations, and epidemiological surveillance of all public providers (1996 is the last available year).

Every 4 or 5 years the SSA conducts surveys of the population on topics such as chronic diseases, addictions, and nutrition. The National Population Council conducts another survey pertaining to family planning. The institutions of higher education determine the policies for human resources education in health, and the Mexican Association of Medical Schools and Colleges (AMFEM) is responsible for the accreditation process. More recently, the National Federation of Nursing Schools (FENAFE) initiated a similar process. Each health institution drafts its own policies for training and upgrading its staff, linked to priority programs and salary increases. The SSA is responsible for accrediting public and private health services through the General Bureau for Health Services Regulation, which is responsible for application of the NOM. In the National Institutes Coordination Office under the SSA, there is a technical unit in charge of health technology assessment.

2.   Financing and Expenditure

The information on financing and health expenditure in the public sector is reliable and the responsibility of the SHCPs and the SSA. National per capita health expenditure in 1992 was US$ 86; in 1994 it was US$ 264; and in 1996 it fell to US$ 115 (preliminary figure). Total health expenditure with respect to GDP rose from 3.8% in 1990 to 6.5% in 1994, falling to 3.3% in 1996 (preliminary figure). Both indicators of expenditure rose between 1990 and 1994, fell in 1995 as a result of the economic crisis, and then gradually recovered (11) (Table 8).

Historically, the IMSS executes more than half of the public health budget. This situation is not expected to change in the short term, even after the implementation of health sector reform. Financial cooperation in health has become important in recent years. In 1996 the World Bank (IBRD) provided US$ 330 million (over a 5-year period) for the PAC (12), and in 1998 it granted a loan in the amount of US$ 700 million to modernize the IMSS.

The information sources for private health expenditure are the national household income and expenditure surveys conducted by the National Institute of Statistics, Geography, and Informatics (INEGI) and the national health accounts system of FUNSALUD. In 1994 estimates put the distribution of private expendi-

Table 8 National Health Expenditure, 1992–1994 (%)

Agents	1992	1993	1994
Sources			
Households	49	50	49
Employers	30	29	28
Federal government	21	19	20
State governments	0	1	3
Total	100	100	100
Funds			
Social security	45	42	43
For the uninsured	12	13	13
Private	2	2	3
Private insurance	40	42	42
Total	100	100	100

Source: Frenk, J. (ed.), *Observatorio de la Salud*, FUNSALUD, Mexico, 1997.

ture as follows: 36.5% fees; 26.7% drugs; 20.2% hospitalizations; 9.4% laboratory and other tests; and 7.0% orthopedic appliances. Out-of-pocket health expenditure in rural households fell between 1992 and 1994 but held steady in urban households (13) (Table 9).

3. Insurance

The insured population rose in 1996 to 52% of the total population. Some 49% (48 million people) are affiliated with the Social Security institutions. The IMSS is the largest of these entities, with 39.5 million insured. Private insurance covers

Table 9 Budget Execution in the Public Sector by Program (in millions of US$)

Year	Total	Preventive care	Curative care	Social services	Other programs
1992	9,624.0	435.8	5448.2	495.9	2624.8
1993	9,835.8	623.6	5965.7	467.1	2551.7
1994	7,248.9	455.9	4283.4	358.4	1970.8
1995	5,908.2	342.0	3695.4	273.6	1422.4
1996	7,397.0	493.1	4878.5	230.4	1795.1

Source: SSA, *Boletín de información estadística*, No. 16, vol. I, 1996, Mexico, September 1997.

3% of the nation's population. The uninsured population constitutes 48% of the total population (47 million people), with the SSA responsible for the majority (approximately 80%) and the rest served mainly by IMSS-Sol. In 1995 some 10 million Mexicans were without regular access to health services; it is for this group that the PAC was implemented (14). The Social Security institutions do not have the same benefits (e.g., retirement and disability funds). In 1996 the SSA established a basic package of health services, which is a series of 13 high-impact, low-cost benefits to which all Mexicans have access. The IMSS is instituting a quota reversion system for insured workers that will enable them to use private health care providers that will be remunerated through their contributions.

E. Service Delivery

1. Public Health Services

The health services provided by public institutions are universal and range from outpatient care to hospital care at the highest level of complexity. The SSA supports their efforts with community health workers, grouped into local health councils in primary care units; in 1997 there were 20,111 of these councils. A quota recovery system is used in SSA units. Fees are commensurate with the income level of the household, and 85% of them go directly to the programs for which they are charged, and the rest to the state and federal governments. The SSA is responsible for public health services (for example, the struggle against vector-borne diseases). The Social Security institutions also have community health programs with activities for health promotion and disease prevention in the home, school, and workplace. Ongoing mass communication campaigns are waged by the health services to reduce smoking and sedentary lifestyles and promote healthy eating habits and self-care of health. All the public services take part in the National Health Days, which are held three times a year and include vaccination activities and the administration of parasiticides and vitamin A supplements. Public institutions conduct programs to prevent hypertension and diabetes. A program for AIDS prevention is underway, with the SSA reporting distribution of over 20,000 care guidelines and 600,000 educational materials in 1997. Numerous NGOs are making a significant contribution in this area, but their activities are not well quantified. In 1997 coverage of the screening program for cervical cancer was 20% of women; this gave rise to a new program whose goal was to cover 70% of women by the year 2000. Vaccination coverage in 1996 for children under 1 year of age included vaccines for polio (95%), DPT (95%), measles (93%), and BCG (99%). Coverage of prenatal care with trained personnel was 93% of pregnancies in 1995, and the cover-

Table 10 Health Services, Number and Rate per 1,000
Population, 1996

Type of service	Number	Rate per 1000 population
Outpatient medical consultations	197,554,137	1,414.6
Dental consultations	11,585,839	124.3
Emergency consultations	21,943,196	235.5
Laboratory examinations	1,577.9	1,577.9

Source: SSA, *Boletín de información estadística*, No. 16, vol. I, 1996, Mexico, September 1997.

age of births with trained personnel was 84.1% in 1997 (includes private services) (15).

2. Personal Health Care Services

There is a single information system supporting these services for all public facilities, sustained by software that processes and consolidates the information at all administrative levels of the subsystem (Tables 10, 11, and 12).

Primary Care. No reliable information is available on the coverage provided by the various networks of public and private health care providers. Likewise, no information is available on primary care units with computerized information systems for administrative and personnel management. Fee-for-service arrangements have been growing in public institutions, with the IMSS providing the greatest volume of outpatient consultations of all types. The five most frequent causes of consultations in primary care facilities in 1996 include respiratory infections, intestinal infections, intestinal amebiasis, ascariasis, and hypertension (16). Some programs provide for house calls by nursing personnel and/or social workers. A more recent creation is the Directly Observed Treatment Short-course (DOTS) for the monitoring and control of cases of pulmonary tuberculosis.

Secondary Care. No reliable information is available on coverage by the different networks of public and private health care providers, nor is there information on hospital units with computerized information systems for administrative and personnel management. The states of Oaxaca, Tabasco, Durango, Aguascalientes, and San Luis Potosí have made an effort to use systems, such as the Management Information System (SIG) developed by PAHO/WHO, to improve management in SSA and Social Security units.

Table 11 Outpatient Consultations by Institutions, 1996 (in thousands)

Institution	Total	General	Specialty	Emergency	Dental
SSA	44,854	33,398	5,277	2,892	3,287
IMSS-Solidarity	10,880	9,583	335	865	416
IMSS	99,744	65,602	14,645	18,930	4,742
ISSSTE	22,090	14,784	5,202	1,993	1,382
PEMEX	5,482	2,490	1,937	896	351
SEDENA	3,700	1,541	1,308	531	727
Others	10,804	4,413	3,509	2,200	682
Total	197,554	131,811	32,213	21,943	11,587

Source: SSA, Boletín de información estadística, No. 16, vol. I, 1996, Mexico, September 1997.

At the secondary level of care, service output has risen. The IMSS is responsible for half of all hospital discharges in the country. The five most frequent causes of hospital discharge in 1996 included:

Direct obstetric causes (16.8%)
Normal delivery (13%)
Injuries and poisonings (7.1%)
Perinatal disorders (4.2%)
Nephritis, nephrotic syndrome, and nephrosis (3%) (17)

For some pathologies, Social Security facilities provide for house calls by physicians and nursing staff, as well as home management.

3. Quality

Technical Quality. Quality is an emerging issue in all institutions in the public and private sector. In 1997 the SSA launched a program for continuous improvement of quality in six states, with advisory services provided by a private

Table 12 Some Indicators of the Hospital System at the Secondary and Tertiary Level, 1996

Total discharges	3,632,352
Percentage of occupancy	68.6
Average length of stay in days	4.1

Source: SSA, Boletín de información estadística, No. 16, vol. I, 1996, Mexico. September 1997.

consulting group to 517 medical units, 36 of them at the secondary level. In addition, the IMSS and the ISSSTE promote programs to improve technical quality, with a strong supervision and evaluation component administered by the upper levels of the hierarchy and the self-evaluation committees created in the health facilities.

The percentage of deaths with medical certification is 95.8% (1995). According to SSA data, the percentage of cesarean sections in total deliveries was 29.2% in the public sector; in the private sector the figure was 44% (1996) (18). All deaths from acute respiratory infections (ARI) and acute diarrheal diseases (ADD) in children under 5 are audited through a procedure called "verbal autopsy." Maternal deaths are audited by so-called interinstitutional committees (state and local) created to this end.

Perceived Quality. UNICEF, having created a certification for hospitals as being "Mother-and Baby-Friendly Hospitals," has certified some 84% of SNS hospitals. Moreover, one of the programs promoted to meet the NOM for maternal and child health care is the promotion of breast feeding. One of the guidelines issued by the commission for the continuous improvement of the quality of the services of the CNS is the creation of modules to provide information and investigate complaints in primary care units, at least in urban areas. At the start of the present administration, the General Bureau for Quality Health Care conducted a series of surveys for internal and external users throughout the country, but the results are not available. In 1996 the National Medical Arbitration Commission (CONAMED) was created to act as a mediator and investigate complaints of negligence and/or malpractice by public and private medical services. The Commission has the authority to conduct investigations, issue findings, and resolve disputes over presumed irregularities in the delivery of services. The authorities, professional organizations, and users find it a useful mechanism, although in the beginning it stirred controversy and was resisted by the professional organizations.

V. MONITORING AND EVALUATION OF SECTORAL REFORM

A. Monitoring of the Process

1. Monitoring of the Dynamics

The PND 1995–2000 issued the general guidelines for health sector reform, later detailed in the Health Sector Reform Program 1995–2000, whose preparation entailed some 70 meetings to consult with the public on health and another 200 consultations with the commissions created by the CNS. The SSA assumed leadership of the discussions and negotiations with the various sectors (medical schools, academies, universities, unions, chambers of commerce and industry, health institutions, and state governments) on the contents and dynamics of the sectoral reform. Four basic objectives were established for health sector reform:

1. To promote quality and efficiency in service delivery
2. To finish decentralizing the services for the uninsured population
3. To expand coverage of the care provided by the Social Security institutions, facilitating voluntary affiliation
4. To expand coverage to marginalized populations in rural and urban areas who currently have little or no access (19)

The sectoral reform agenda follows six guidelines:

1. The freedom of users to choose their physicians at the primary care level of the Social Security institutions
2. Greater municipal participation through the Healthy Municipios movement
3. The creation of voluntary family insurance in the IMSS for people with the ability to pay
4. Expansion of coverage through a basic package of services for people without regular access to health services
5. Decentralization to the states of health services for the uninsured population
6. Strengthening of the steering and regulatory role of the SSA and the separation of functions in social security to achieve more comprehensive and coordinated health care

The decentralization undertaken by the SSA is occurring within the framework of a broader political process known as the "New Federalism," and the changes in the IMSS model of health care are part of the overall modernization of that institution. Health sector reform is viewed as a long-term effort that will be carried out in successive phases through a variety of methods. Basic action has already been taken to expand coverage, implement decentralization, and create family insurance; for the strategies to permit the selection of physicians at the primary level and for the separation of social security functions, the basic regulations have yet to be published and the changes implemented. In the longer term, the SNS will operate with a new model in which the SSA will concentrate on regulation and the development of standards, sectoral financing will expand its contribution base, and public and private health care providers will compete to provide services. Social security and private insurers are expected to cover a larger segment of the population than they currently do; services for the uninsured will become the responsibility of the states; and the entire population will have access to medical care (20).

B. Monitoring of the Contents

1. Legal Framework

The health sector reform strategies are grounded in the General Health Act and the IMSS Law, which were amended in 1997 to permit achievement of the objectives laid out. These instruments are complemented with the presidential decrees establishing the New Federalism and Decentralized Public Agencies and the agreements on decentralization of the health services and sectoral coordination. The amendments to the IMSS Law revamp the pension and health systems, reduce employer contributions, and increase government contributions; they create voluntary family health insurance and strengthen the quota reversion option for groups that prefer other service providers, with the IMSS continuing to collect the contributions. Fifty-two changes were made in the General Health Act to institute deregulation in matters related to health, including:

A new drug classification

The promotion of generic medications in the private market

Improved monitoring of biotechnology products

Granting the SSA the authority to regulate package labeling for alcoholic beverages and cigarettes. In 1996 CONAMED was created by presidential decree

2. Right to Health Care and Insurance

The right to health care is guaranteed in Article 4 (amended in 1983) of the Political Constitution, which states that every person has the right to health protection and that the law will define the conditions for access to the services. This concept was widely disseminated in 1995 during the preparation of the Health Sector Reform Program 1995–2000. Two methods for expanding the coverage of public health services are envisioned:

1. Facilitating voluntary social security affiliation for people able to prepay family health insurance
2. Bringing essential health services to marginalized populations through the basic package of health services

In June 1997 the IMSS regulations governing family health insurance were published. These regulations give all members of a subscriber's family access to virtually the same benefits as other beneficiaries, through the payment of a quota equal to 22.4% of the annual minimum wage, paid in advance. In 1996 the SSA implemented the Program for Expanded Coverage, directed to the 10 million Mexicans without regular access to health services. The Program consisted of 12 controlled interventions:

1. Basic sanitation.
2. Parasiticide treatments for families.
3. Family planning.
4. Management of acute respiratory infections.
5. Prenatal care and care in childbirth and the puerperium.
6. Prevention and control of pulmonary tuberculosis.
7. Monitoring of nutrition and growth in children.
8. Prevention and control of hypertension and diabetes mellitus.
9. Immunization.
10. Accident prevention and initial management of injuries.
11. Standard case management of diarrhea in the home.
12. Community training for self-care of health. In 1998 screening for cervical cancer was added (21).

3. Steering Role

Health sector reform reaffirmed the steering and regulatory role of the SSA, and decentralization delimited federal and state responsibilities in health. In 1997, the National Agreement on Decentralization of the Health Services was signed between the Federal Executive Branch and the state governments, creating decentralized public agencies, new administrative entities with legal status and their own resources, in every state. These new agencies are responsible for

> Directing, administering, operating, and supervising the health facilities transferred by the SSA to the state governments
> Administering the resources assigned to them, as well as recovered quotas or quotas received from any other entity
> Compiling information and documentation that will enable the authorities and competent research institutions to study and analyze health (22)

The IMSS has decentralized functions and responsibilities to its seven administrative regions and has strengthened management and decision-making capabilities in the operational areas. Sectoral reform involves integration of the IMSS-Sol program into the decentralized public agencies, although little progress has been made to date.

4. Separation of Functions

The regulation of the services and the surveillance and control of health facilities and health products are the responsibility of the SSA. Service delivery to the uninsured population has been decentralized to each decentralized public agency. It is envisaged that the Social Security institutions will separate the collection of contributions from the financing function in health service delivery.

5. Decentralization Modalities

Decentralization of the health services for the uninsured population was concluded during this administration, with the administration and management of human and financial resources transferred to the decentralized public agencies. The health services contributions fund in the Expenditures Budget of the Federation for 1998 expanded state functions for the execution and auditing of their respective budgets.

6. Participation and Social Control

Health sector reform encouraged social participation in health through promotion of the Healthy Municipios movement, with the health initiatives of the mayoralties receiving significant technical support from the SSA. Health Committees have been organized in the health care units that the SSA promotes throughout the country.

7. Financing and Expenditure

Sectoral reform is expected to modify health expenditure patterns by increasing the number of subscribers to the IMSS family health insurance plan and encouraging the development of private service providers, the latter linked to fostering competition among service providers. However, the regulations for implementing some of the basic changes in the IMSS have not yet been drafted.

8. Service Delivery

Health sector reform transformed the model of care by incorporating the basic package of health services. The basic package of health services is a strategy to expand coverage without altering the supply of benefits in the established health units. Delivering services through the Program for Expanded Coverage of populations has created a model that allows the health services system to define a population's level of marginality and/or lack of effective coverage, and, through the Education, Health, and Nutrition Program (PROGRESA), make a nutritional assessment based on a family's defined level of poverty. Mobile units that include a physician serve a high percentage of the population covered by the Program for Expanded Coverage.

9. Management Model

To date, changes in the health care management model for the uninsured population have been grounded in the creation of the decentralized public agencies and geared toward more comprehensive management that provides efficient solutions for gaps or duplications in coverage, faster responses to local problems, and greater community participation. For Social Security, changing the management model depends on making more flexible regulations for quota reversion and the subrogation of services, and also on adopting business criteria for managing health regions and tertiary-level hospitals.

10. Human Resources

The sectoral reform does not include actions in human resources education. The protocol creating the decentralized public agencies empowers them to promote and support all activities geared toward educating, training, and updating the human resources necessary for health services delivery. To date it has been difficult to verify the progress made in this regard. This may be due to the fact that institutions of higher education are autonomous, and there is little coordination with health institutions.

Workers and their representatives have played an important part in the reform process, given their influence and negotiating power. To make decentralization a reality, the SSA acknowledged the status of the National Union of Workers of the Secretariat of Health (SNTSSA) and agreed on the general working conditions for its union members. The sectoral reform does not envisage changes in the functions of personnel, contracts, schedules, or workloads.

11. Quality and Health Technology Assessment

There is no precise information on activities to improve technical and perceived quality in the sectoral reform, except with regard to strategies for selecting the family physician in the Social Security institutions, which have not yet been implemented. Some of the SSA's principal lines of work for 1998 are the development of regional centers and services affiliated with the National Institutes of Health (Oncology, Cardiology, Women's Health, and Care Pediatric) for health care, teaching, and research in the effort to improve quality. In addition, an incentive program to upgrade professionals has been launched, targeting more than 26,000 professionals, including some 6800 working in remote rural areas. The sectoral reform seeks to include elements in the health care system that will ensure higher quality services and promote other services that focus attention on health, the true goal, rather than the treatment of disease. However, the strategies to be adopted have not yet been defined (23).

One of the objectives for 1998 is to consolidate the results of the program for the continuous improvement of quality, disseminating it to all primary care units and hospitals. One of the indicators for monitoring and evaluating the basic package of services is the average percentage of supplies in the health centers, taken from the list found in the basic table of the basic package of services, calculated on a quarterly basis.

C. Evaluation of Results

1. Equity in Coverage

A little more than 2 years after the Health Sector Reform Program 1995–2000 was announced, the SSA extended coverage of the Program through delivery of the basic package of services under the Program for Expanded Coverage and PROGRESA. The Program for Expanded Coverage serves 6.5 million people in 600 municipios in 18 states, and operated with a budget of *MN*$ 689.1 million in 1998. PROGRESA covers 1.9 million families in 1423 municipios in 28 states, and operates on an annual budget of *MN*$ 923.1 million (24). In 1997 the SSA and PAHO/WHO signed an agreement to evaluate universal coverage with the basic package of services in the states; to date, Nuevo León has been certified, and Aguascalientes and Tlaxcala are currently being evaluated. Other increases in the coverage of specific programs in recent years can be associated with the delivery of the basic package of services. Between 1994 and 1996, vaccination coverage for children under 1 year of age increased for DPT (from 91% to 95%), polio (from 92% to 95%), BCG (from 98% to 99%), and measles (from 90% to 93%). Births attended by trained personnel increased from 74% in 1995 to 84.1% in 1996 (25). Moreover, the IMSS extended its coverage through its family health insurance plan, providing services to 350,497 people in 1997 who without the sectoral reform would not have had the right to coverage.

2. In Distribution of Resources

In recent years the budget of the SSA has grown at an annual rate of 7.2% in 1996, 23.2% in 1997, and 24.4% in 1998; and the programmable expenditure of the sector rose by 9.5% in real terms between 1997 and 1998. There is no evidence that sectoral reform has had an impact on the distribution of resources.

Following changes in the IMSS Law and after the publication of the Health Sector Reform Program, there is evidence of a change in the composition of financing. These changes include

> Growth of the government's contribution to the IMSS for 1997, increasing the federal government's contribution from 4.5% to 28.5% of the total income of that institution and reducing workers' and employers' contributions by a similar proportion
>
> Efforts on the part of the SSA to increase the participation of state governments in the health budget

3. In Access

There is no evidence to attribute the decrease in the percentage of deaths without medical care to sectoral reform. However, the Program for Expanded Coverage has reduced geographical barriers thanks to its mobile units (serving 600 municipios in 18 federative entities), and its commitment to establish a primary care unit by the end of 1998 in 2827 localities around the country with more than 2500 inhabitants.

4. In Resource Utilization

Although no precise information is available at this time, an increase in the number of consultations and discharges per 1000 population can be attributed to the sectoral reform. Likewise Mexico has witnessed an increase in the percentage of births attended by trained personnel due to the extension of service coverage through the PAC, PROGRESA, and PAZI programs.

D. Effectiveness and Quality

1. Effectiveness

Infant mortality has declined in recent years, a phenomenon that is difficult to link with health sector reform (rate adjusted for underreporting: 26.5 for 1994, 25.9 for 1995, and 24.9 for 1996). Maternal mortality exhibited little change in the period (4.9 for 1994, 5.3 for 1995, and 4.8 for 1996), and deaths from cervical cancer increased from 4392 in 1995 to 4530 in 1997. Mexican health authorities expect to see a greater impact on these indicators in the coming years, thanks to the Program for Expanded Coverage, mentioned above, and other measures introduced in 1998, such as the national health card for women to facilitate perinatal monitoring and control, and the NOM for the prevention, diagnosis, and control of cervical cancer (26,27).

2. Technical Quality

There is no evidence to suggest that health sector reform has contributed to a reduction in the incidence of nosocomial infections or in the percentage of patients who receive a report on discharge or care.

3. Perceived Quality

In its first year CONAMED investigated 4025 complaints from patients about health care, 2071 of which were resolved through orientation and assistance. Another 1831 were classified as complaints, with 123 cases being submitted to expert opinion. In addition, the Mother-and-Baby-Friendly-Hospitals Program has grown steadily, expanding from 49.4% to 83.2% of all hospitals in the national health system between 1995 and 1997.

4. Efficiency in Resource Allocation

The transfer of services for the uninsured population to the states, concluded in 1998, was intended to increase the efficiency of the services. It is too soon to evaluate the degree to which this was accomplished (28). As part of the sectoral reform and to overcome inertia and promote equity among the states with respect to resources, a budget allocation process that takes variables such as the prevalence of health impairments and indexes of marginalization into account has been incorporated into the Fiscal Coordination Act of 1998.

5. In Resource Management

During 1997, 48 sectoral procedures were eliminated (a 42% reduction); 90 types of services were exempted from health inspections (a 30% reduction) and 94 business categories requiring a license to operate were exempted from this requirement (an 89% reduction). The changes mentioned, as well as the new regulation on the control of health inputs and the new Catalog of Commercial Categories introduced that same year are expected to improve management efficiency (29).

6. Sustainability

There is no evidence that health sector reform has contributed to an increase in the legitimacy or acceptance of institutional service providers. The quality and timeliness of the information on the public and private health expenditure is not linked to the sectoral reform. Decentralizing service delivery to the states and establishing health impact criteria for programming and budgeting are intended to guarantee success in priority programs such as the EPI or family planning.

7. Social Participation and Control

Health sector reform facilitated an increase in the number of municipios participating in the healthy municipios from 110 in 1995 to 884 in 1997 (36.5% of the total). In addition, the number of health committees in primary care units rose from 8817 in 1995 to 20,111 in 1997. SNS authorities believe that social participation in local decision making and in the execution of health activities has increased in the past 3 years (30).

REFERENCES

1. Ejecutivo Federal. Plan Nacional de Desarrollo, 1995–2000. México DF, 1996.
2. Ejecutivo Federal. Programa de Educación, Salud y Alimentación. México DF.
3. UNDP. Human Development Report, 1997. Washington, D.C., 1998.

4.   INEGI. Indicadores de empleo y desempleo. México DF, INEGI, 1998.
5.   INEGI, OEA-CEPAL. Magnitud y evolución de la pobreza en México, 1984–1992. México DF, INEGI, 1993.
6.   Secretaría de Desarrollo Social. Programa para Superar la Pobreza, 1995–2000. México DF, 1996.
7.   Secretaría de Salud. Programa de Ampliación de Cobertura; Evolución y Perspectivas. México DF, 1996, pp 53–54.
8.   INEGI. Conteo de población y vivienda 1995. INEGI, México DF, 1996.
9.   Secretaría de Salud. Boletin de información estadistica. No. 16, vol. I, 1996, México DF, September 1997.
10. INEGI. Op. Cit. México, 1996.
11. PAHO/WHO. Basic Indicators. Washington, D.C., 1995, 1997, and 1998.
12. PAHO/WHO. Division of Health Systems and Services Development. La descentralización, los sistemas de salud, y los procesos de reforma del sector. Informe final. Valdivia, Chile, 1997. Washington, D.C., 1997.
13. FUNSALUD. El sistema de cuentas nacionales de salud en México. Documentos de análisis y convergencia 15, México, D.F., 1997, p 50.
14. OCDE. Estudios económicos. Capítulo especial sobre Reforma del sistema de salud. México, D.F., 1998, pp 99–100.
15. PAHO/WHO. Basic Indicators. Washington, D.C., 1997, 1998.
16. Secretaría de Salud. Op. cit., September 1997.
17. Secretaría de Salud. Op. cit., September 1997.
18. Secretaría de Salud. Op. cit., September 1997.
19. OCDE. Op. cit., 1998, p. 109.
20. OCDE. Op. cit., 1998, p. 110.
21. Secretaría de Salud. Modelo de Atención a la Salud para Población Abierta. México, D.F., 1995.
22. Gobierno del Estado de Morelos. Decreto que crea el organismo público descentralizado denominado Servicios de Salud de Morelos. México, D.F., 1996.
23. Secretaría de Salud. Op. cit., 1995.
24. Secretaría de Salud. Principales líneas de trabajo de la SSA. Síntesis Ejecutiva. México, D.F. January 1998.
25. PAHO/WHO. Op. cit., 1996, 1997, and 1998.
26. UNICEF. Programa Nacional de Acción a Favor de la Infancia Evaluación de 1997. México, D.F., February 1998.
27. Secretaría de Salud. Principales líneas de trabajo de la SSA. Síntesis Ejecutiva. México, D.F., January 1998.
28. Secretaría de Salud. Principales líneas de trabajo de la SSA. Síntesis Ejecutiva. México, D.F. 1997.
29. Secretaría de Salud. Op. cit., 1997.
30. Secretaría de Salud. Op. cit., January 1998.

8
France's Health Care System

Peter L. Cruise
California State University, Chico, California

I. INTRODUCTION

As the United States and other industrialized countries continue their struggles with health care reform, perhaps policymakers should look to France for new approaches. In France, almost universal coverage exists with a uniform benefit plan that follows consumers from job to job, even during periods of unemployment. In this age when many consumers are faced with medical care restrictions and gatekeeping imposed through managed care, the French are able to readily access services such as pharmaceuticals, physical therapy, and even medically prescribed spa treatments, and are also able to have a free choice of office-based physicians and other ancillary services. Even out-of-pocket costs to individuals are capped to reduce potential financial problems. Can the health care system in France provide insights for those interested in health care system reform? This chapter will examine this question by providing an overview of France's health care system, including important historical and political developments associated with its health care system's evolution. To assist in this analysis, France's health care system will be compared and contrasted with those of four similar Organization for Economic Cooperation and Development (OECD) member countries.

Formed in 1960, the OECD originally comprised 20 mostly European countries (the United States being the notable exception in this founding group) whose primary goal was to foster joint economic cooperation among member and non-member countries (Poullier, 1993). In this chapter expenditure sources, reimbursement mechanisms, and consumption patterns will be analyzed for France and four other similar OECD countries. The health status of the population will be profiled in an attempt to gauge the results of expenditure and consumption patterns. Finally, current issues in France's health care system will be discussed, especially those related to quality, access, and cost.

II. OVERVIEW OF THE FRENCH HEALTH CARE SYSTEM

Unlike the United States and other OECD countries, explicit principles undergird the French health insurance system (Fielding and Lancry, 1993). One is the shared perception that government has the prime responsibility to protect all citizens and permanent residents against having to pay large out-of-pocket fees for health care. In contrast, from the founding of the United States in the seventeenth century through the formation of the first employer-sponsored indemnity insurance plans early in the twentieth century, American health care has been primarily an individual responsibility not collectively shared beyond one's family (e.g., Starr, 1985). Only comparatively recently has this mindset changed in the United States with the introduction of employer-sponsored insurance plans and, later, government involvement through Medicare and Medicaid.

A second principle in France is intergenerational solidarity. This principle acknowledges that younger working generations will subsidize the health and support the basic needs of older cohorts within the society. Although this concept has also been articulated in the United States for many years, it is now a point of controversy as the number of younger workers is declining rapidly in proportion to the growing number of retirees.

A third principle in the French health care system is intergroup cross-subsidization. For example, in France, where the number of agricultural workers has declined while the number of agricultural retirees has increased, the agricultural health insurance fund has been increasingly subsidized from the general insurance fund to which most of the population contributes (Fielding and Lancry, 1993). In the United States, various governmental insurance funds are held in "trust" (i.e., the Social Security Trust Fund) and are therefore not commingled, regardless of potential fiscal or actuarial concerns (Kovner, 1995).

A fourth principle in France's health care system is mandatory participation by all citizens in one of the major Sickness Insurance Funds (SIFs). By 1978, all French citizens had to be covered in one of three major SIFs. The general fund [or *Caisse Nationale d'Assurance Maladie des Travailleurs Salaries* (CNAMTS)] is the largest SIF, comprising over 81% of the total population. Although SIF membership and the size of taxable contributions are based upon the type of employment and salary level of each member, since 1988 even the unemployed were assigned to the general fund, with local governments subsidizing the cost of membership (Le Faou and Jolly, 1995). By contrast, in the United States there is no universal system or compulsory health insurance coverage, only a limited range of voluntary, need-based plans subsidized by federal and state

Table 1 Percentage of Population Eligible for Medical Care Under Public Plans for France and Selected Countries, 1960–1990

	1960	1970	1980	1990
France	72	90	96	99
Germany	78	82	85	89
Austria	76	80	85	90
Switzerland	72	84	86	99
Italy	83	87	88	99

Source: Poullier, J. *OECD Health Systems, Facts and Trends 1960–1991.* Paris: OECD, 1993, p. 274.

governments, most notably Medicaid. Table 1 details the percentage of France's total population who are eligible for medical care benefits under the SIFs. As a point of comparison, four other OECD member countries are also detailed in Table 1. As the data in Table 1 indicate, by 1990, virtually all of France's population was covered under one of the major SIFs.

Additional key principles that form part of the complex pattern of France's health care system include the citizen's right to free choice of physician and the freedom for those physicians to treat patients as they so choose and to set up ambulatory (nonhospital based) practice wherever they wish. These principles were incorporated in the Medical Charter of 1927 and articulated again in the Code of Ethics in 1979 (Fielding and Lancry, 1993). In this complex and fragmented system, with many apparently conflicting concerns, a listing of the key players would include:

1. the patient,
2. the SIFs (specifically the CNAMTS),
3. private insurance funds,
4. physicians (both private and hospital-based),
5. hospitals (both private and public),
6. the pharmaceutical sector, and
7. the French government (particularly the Ministry of Health).

Figure 1 shows these key players in the French health care system and indicates the flow of funds and services in the system, as well as the key interrelationships.

In sum, with the guiding principles of central government responsibility, intergenerational solidarity, cross-subsidization, mandatory universal coverage, free choice of physician, and physician freedom of when and how to practice, France's health care system presents many opportunities for citizen access to (at least) basic primary care without many limitations. Although not an explicitly

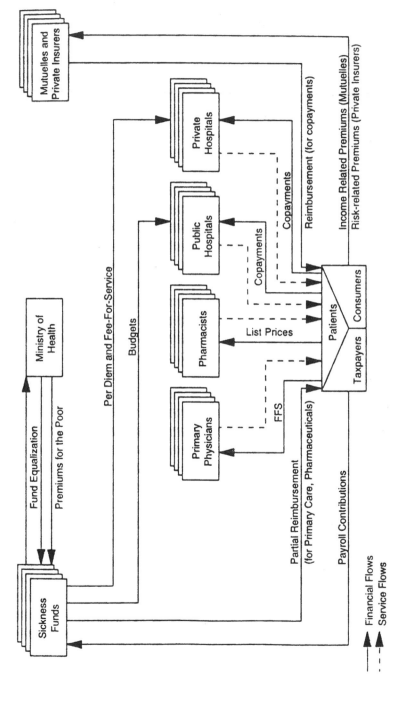

Figure 1   Key participants in the health care system in France. (Adapted from Burstall and Wallerstein, 1994, p. 357.)

stated health care system principle, perhaps the most important factor to consider when examining the French health care system is the deeply rooted political tradition in the country of never revoking a right previously granted. With such a tradition, the French health care system has a complexity developed from the many compromises required to achieve only the incremental change that is possible with such a tradition. In the next section, a more detailed description of France's health care system, including expenditure sources, consumption patterns, and provider reimbursement mechanisms, will be discussed.

III. DESCRIPTION OF THE HEALTH CARE SYSTEM

A. Historical Development

Since 1927, the national government in France has been involved with the financing and provision of health care. With the adoption of the Medical Charter of 1927, the French health care system has been characterized by three distinguishing features, a strong central state, a quasi-public national health insurance system, and a powerful medical profession (Kervasdoue et al., 1984a). The medical profession, through a world war and a series of national health care reforms, has consistently promoted four bedrock principles:

1. free choice of the physician by the patient,
2. freedom of prescription by the doctor,
3. mutual agreement by the physician and the patient on the price of services, and
4. fee-for-service payment.

Although in the intervening years these principles have been widely accepted in France, they are often not compatible with the interest of the other players in the system.

When the three distinguishing features of the French system noted above and the strong principles espoused by the medical profession interact, there can be conflict. According to Kervasdoue et al. (1984b), the conflicts grow out of two contradictory ideologies: solidarity and liberal-pluralism. In the name of solidarity, the French government (through the Ministry of Health) has actively intervened in the health care system and has assured its citizens the right of access to health services and pays most of the bills through the CNAMTS. In the name of liberalism (or *la médecine libérale*) the medical profession promotes its four principles noted above and, in the name of pluralism, has demanded the continued existence of institutional diversity, most notably in the form of large, mostly doctor-owned private proprietary hospitals (or *cliniques*). Since World War II, there is no other European country in which the private practice of medicine has become so well established.

Following World War II through the early 1970s, the French health care system grew rapidly and without many constraints. Health insurance coverage grew by stages, however. The first social insurance law, enacted in 1928, covered about 45% of the population. This percentage remained unchanged, despite the creation of a social security system and the CNAMTS in 1945, until 1950, when further growth began. Key events in this process included the creation of health insurance for agricultural workers in 1961, professionals and other self-employed individuals in 1966, and the balance of the population through individual insurance in 1978.

Coverage under the CNAMTS itself increased to 81% of the population by 1991 (Fielding and Lancry, 1993). In effect, the vast majority of the French population is covered by the CNAMTS, with seven much smaller SIFs covering the other industries listed above. Several hundred much smaller private insurers, or *mutuelles*, providing reimbursement for patient copayments and other services (described later), also exist in France.

To achieve virtually universal health insurance coverage, France has retained workplace-based insurance as a foundation and extended coverage to those not included at the workplace. Specifically, France passed laws with mandates requiring that:

1. workplace-based insurance cover most employees and their dependents, and one or more payers—public or nonprofit—cover most of the remainder of the population;
2. the minimum package of benefits cover a wide range of specified services; and
3. health insurance be financed predominantly by payroll contributions.

As a result of France's mandated approach to insurance, most people have little choice of insurer, as their occupation has predetermined their assignment to a particular sickness insurance fund. Once a worker accepts a job in a given industry, coverage through that industry's insurance fund is automatic. Correspondingly, most insurers have no opportunity to seek out individuals with low risk of illness, nor attract more customers by offering lower premiums or better packages. Also, employers are legally restricted from choosing the SIF that will cover their employees.

B. Current Structure and Reimbursement Mechanisms

The French hospital system is divided into public hospitals (with 65% of the beds), private not-for-profit hospitals (15% of the beds), and private, for-profit hospitals (20% of the beds). Since 1985, public and private not-for profit hospitals have received funds from the government, based upon an annual global budget.

Private, for-profit institutions, on the other hand, are paid according to the medical services provided (Fielding and Lancry, 1993).

Hospital care is mixed, with about three fifths of short-stay beds housed in public hospitals. The period 1960–1980 saw a transformation of hospitals with tremendous growth, particularly of centrally financed regional hospital centers, and rapid improvement in technological sophistication. During this period the hospital sector grew at an annual rate 4% greater than the ambulatory sector, producing a more hospital-centered health care system. Public hospitals, once known in France as the place where the poor went to die, became regional centers with the most technologically advanced services and with highly trained physicians often linked to universities.

One approach to studying the growth of the hospital sector in any health care system is to review the average length of stay over a period of years. Table 2 details, for inpatients for the period 1960–1990, the average length of stay (ALOS) for patients in France and four other similar OECD countries.

As the data in Table 2 indicate, the ALOS for French inpatients was one of the lowest in 1960 (22.8 days), and was still one of the lowest in 1990 (12.4 days) in the comparison group. A further analysis of the French hospital sector itself can be found in Table 3, which reveals the number of hospital beds by type of hospital (public versus private).

As Table 3 demonstrates, in the period 1975–1990, the total number of hospital beds (public and private) grew 1.8% while the ALOS dropped to 12.4 days. More specifically, public hospital beds grew 7.8% over the years analyzed, while private hospital beds actually declined 8.3%.

When considered in totality, all public hospitals and a significant number of private nonprofit hospitals account for over 71% of short-stay beds in France. These facilities receive annual global budgets (funded by tax revenues) from the government to cover all services, including those of salaried physicians. Private

Table 2 Average Length of Stay (in days) for Hospitalized Patients for France and Selected Countries, 1960–1990

	1960	1970	1980	1990
France	22.8	18.3	16.8	12.4
Germany	28.7	24.9	19.7	16.2
Austria	24.8	22.2	17.9	11.9
Switzerland	31.7	26.0	24.7	25.2
Italy	27.0	19.1	13.5	11.7

Source: Schieber, G., Poullier, P., Greenwald, L. U.S. health expenditure performance: an international comparison and data update. Health Care Financ Rev, Summer 1992, p. 33.

Table 3 Number of Beds and Average Length of Stay (ALOS) by Hospital Type for France, 1975–1990

	1975	1980	1985	1990
All hospitals				
Total no. of beds	548,543	594,084	588,377	558,693
ALOS (days)	19.8	16.7	15.5	12.4
Public hospitals				
Total no. of beds	336,628	377,499	378,002	363,115
ALOS (days)	20.1	16.5	16.1	13.7
Private hospitals				
Total no. of beds	211,915	216,585	203,616	195,578
ALOS (days)	19.4	17.1	14.6	11.6

Source: Hoffmeyer, U., McCarthy, T., eds. The health care system in France. Financing Health Care, 1994, p. 415.

hospitals not subject to global budgets receive per diem payments for their inpatient services. These payments emanate from the government and, in the form of copayments, from the *mutuelles*.

Ancillary services, including laboratory and radiological services, are billed on the basis of a fee schedule. There is no competition based on price. Physicians can recommend that patients go to a particular laboratory or radiological facility, but patients are free to choose any such service provider. According to law, physicians are not allowed to have a financial interest in these facilities. Part of the improvement in hospital care has been attributed to the establishment of 26,000 full-time, hospital-salaried positions for physician specialists. Of these, 8000 are university affiliated, carry academic titles, and provide income comparable to non-hospital-based practice (Kervasdoue et al., 1984a).

There were approximately 5.2 acute care beds per 1000 population in France in 1989. Current estimates are that France has about 60,000 excess acute care beds, out of a total of 558,693 total available beds. This is not surprising, based upon the data contained in Tables 2 and 3. Some of the reasons for the excess capacity probably lie in the global budget process, in place since 1983 for all public and some nonprofit hospitals. The global budgeting process, which uses historical costs as the basis for assigning future budgets, is an economically inefficient method.

In an attempt to address excess capacity in the system, the Hospital Law of 1991 permitted the introduction of a system similar to the U.S. Diagnosis Related Groups (DRGs). The French system is called *Programme de Médicalisation du Système d'Information* (PMSI). It was also created to promote a better understanding of the hospital production function and for planning for hospital services. However, efforts to fully implement PMSI in hospitals with global budgets have been opposed by hospitals and physicians due to (1) the lack of any incentives to switch from the current programs and, (2) a mistrust that the PMSI itself can accurately group cases (Burstall and Wallerstein, 1994).

In France, office-based physicians cannot care for their patients as inpatients in public hospitals. However, the estimated 20% of office-based physicians, who are *attaches*, can admit patients for outpatient procedures in these same hospitals. Inpatient care in public hospitals is supervised by salaried hospital-based physicians of the appropriate specialty. Patients cannot generally choose their physician in public hospitals, except by seeing the physician during his or her limited private practice time, usually at substantially increased out-of-pocket costs. Under French law, private patients cannot occupy more than 8% of beds in public hospitals (Fielding and Lancry, 1993).

Private hospital care now accounts for over 24% of total hospital expenses but over two-fifths of patient days in short-stay hospitals. These facilities, smaller on average than public hospitals, mostly evolved from *cliniques*, the for-profit doctor's hospitals. Many believe that these facilities provide the most attentive patient care, and they are often used for routine operations, for maternity care, and for particular types of health problems, such as cancer treatment. Physician arrangements with these private hospitals range from full-time salaried positions to agreements permitting office-based practitioners to admit and care for patients. In private hospitals, 7100 physicians are salaried and 36,000 are in private practice, of whom 10,000 are full time (Burstall and Wallerstein, 1994).

French physicians are fairly unique, as compared with their U.S. counterparts or those in other OECD counties. In a relatively hassle-free environment, office-based practitioners usually do not have to divide time between the office and the hospital; have their utilization monitored by only one agency (a directorate located in the Ministry of Health); are rarely subject to malpractice claims; and receive payment directly from their patients on a fee-for-service basis. Patients are reimbursed for these fees by the appropriate SIFs and/or their *mutuelles*. Hospital-based physicians, almost all specialists, are subject to minimal utilization review or systematic quality assurance and, like their office-based colleagues, rarely have to counterbalance patient advocacy with cost-containment goals (Fielding and Lancry, 1993).

From 1960 through 1991 the total number of physicians in France increased by 250%. In 1971 the government, realizing the connection between numbers of physicians and aggregate health care demand, began to limit the number of students enrolling in medical schools. This has led to a significant decrease in numbers of new graduates in the years since 1971. Although the numbers of new graduates have been reduced, the number of existing physicians was not affected by the government policy and those individuals will remain in the French health care system for many years to come.

All medical students study at university hospital centers, with specialty training being highly prized. Office-based specialists earn about twice as much as those in general medicine, and university hospital positions are available only to specialists (Poullier, 1993). Table 4 traces the growth in the number of physicians in France and four other OECD countries from 1960 to 1990.

As the data in Table 4 illustrate, in 1960 France had the second largest number of physicians in the comparison group, and held the same position again in 1990. Office-based physicians in France are traditionally paid on a fee-for-service basis by the patient and receive the same payment from all patients regardless of which SIF the patient belongs to. At the time of service, physicians receive full payment from patients eliminating the need for billing procedures. Patients are later reimbursed by the appropriate SIF and/or *mutuelle*. The payments are based upon a universal procedure coding scheme, somewhat related to the American Medical Association's Current Procedural Terminology (CPT) procedure coding system. Since 1971, the rates assigned to each procedure code are negotiated nationally by representatives of the major SIFs and the physicians unions.

Physician unions, such as the *Confédération des Syndicats Medicaux Français* (CSMF) and the *Fédération des Médecins de France* (FMF), have been present in one form or another in France since 1928. The oldest physician union, the CSMF, represents about 45% of private-practice physicians in France. Following a series of physician strikes relating to fee schedule levels that occurred in France during the late 1970s and early 1980s, a dissident group of physicians broke away from the CSMF and formed the FMS. This union now represents about 15% of private-practice physicians (Kervasdoue et al., Stephan, 1984b; Fielding and Lancry, 1993).

Fee schedules, which are renegotiated yearly, were mandatory for physicians in France. With restrictions similar to those imposed in the United States

Table 4 Growth in the Number of Physicians in France and Selected Countries, 1960–1990

	1960	1970	1980	1990
France	44,600	65,191	108,054	152,096
Germany	79,350	99,654	139,431	188,225
Austria	9,573	10,137	12,017	16,425
Switzerland	7,227	8,890	15,865	20,030
Italy	26,459	41,961	67,744	76,367

Source: Schieber, G., Poullier, P., Greenwald, L. U.S. health expenditure performance: an international comparison and data update. Health Care Financ Rev, Summer 1992, p. 44.

under the Medicare Participating Provider program, physicians in France could not "balance bill" under normal circumstances. However, before 1980 physicians could "opt out" of the participating system by being approved as a "superior" (*Droit Permanent*) by a local commission of their peers. In effect, this allowed physicians to receive the national fee schedule, but they could ask the patient to pay an additional amount out of pocket. This system was permitted by the French government. By 1980, under great pressure from physician unions, the government stepped in again and allowed physicians to enroll in a second tier. For physicians in this second tier, the SIFs pay the national fee schedule, but the physician and the patient can negotiate the total price for the procedure "with restraint and tact" under the code of medical ethics.

This ability for French physicians to "balance bill" has afforded them a reimbursement rate that is approximately 1.5 times greater than the rate available on the national fee schedule for the same procedure. Unfortunately, the exact cost of each procedure is not easily anticipated by the average French patient, since prices are rarely posted by physicians, and patients often learn the cost of a procedure only after having completed their visit (Fielding and Lancry, 1993). This can add to confusion if the amount reimbursed by the SIF and *mutuelle* is still short of the total amount billed to the patient by the physician. When this happens, patients must absorb the difference themselves.

By permitting physicians to opt out of the national fee schedule, the government was able to respond to physician complaints of being undercompensated without agreeing to increase the SIF fee schedules. The broadened availability for physicians to opt out of the fee schedule spurred a rapid increase in the number of tier two physicians and, in particular, medical specialists. Tier two physicians comprised more than 26% of the total physicians in France in 1991 (Poullier, 1993).

The strong French ethic of equality, including equal access for all, combined with a concern that physician expenditures would race out of control, compelled the government to suspend the ability of physicians to enter tier two in 1990. However, the equally strong French legal tenet of not revoking previously granted rights means that even with the closure of tier two, there will be a large number of physicians in this more costly realm for many years to come.

C. Total Amount of Expenditures

Expenditures for health care in France are high by OECD standards and are continuing to rise. However, this problem may not be as serious as it may appear. Rates of growth in expenditures are appreciably lower than in the 1970s. The proportion of spending financed by French taxpayers is also slowly falling. Within the total amount of expenditures for health care, it is apparent that the rate of growth of spending on hospitals (particularly public hospitals) has been greatly reduced in the past decade. However, the rates of growth in ambulatory care and spending on pharmaceuticals are now rising at a faster rate than before.

France shares some of the demographic and structural problems that have influenced health care costs and financing mechanisms in the United States and other OECD countries. The French population is aging with 13.5% now age 65 years or older. This situation increases overall expenditures while reducing the percentage of the total population contributing to the system. A compounding problem is a persistently high unemployment rate, 10.3% in 1993, which places pressure on the government's ability to generate needed revenue (Burstall and Wallerstein, 1994). Table 5 analyzes France's growth in terms of total health expenditures, as a percentage of GDP, in comparison with four other OECD countries from 1960 through 1990.

As the data in Table 5 illustrate, in 1960 France was the second highest country in the comparison group in terms of health care expenditure growth as a percent of GDP. By 1990, France was the highest in the comparison group. Moreover, aggregate health care spending as a percentage of GDP grew slightly from 8.5% to 9.1% from 1985 to 1992, more than for most OECD countries. France also had the highest rate of increase in real per capita spending relative to the real GDP (Burstall and Wallerstein, 1994).

By sector, the French health care system demonstrated a trend toward greater utilization of hospital services during the 1960s. Policies favoring the increased use of home care and ambulatory services were developed by the government during the 1980s. An analysis of the structure of expenditures on health by hospital, ambulatory care, and pharmaceutical services for France and four other OECD countries from 1960 through 1990 is included in Table 6. The table also illustrates that, in 1960, France spent less on hospital care than two of the

Table 5 Total Health Care Expenditure Growth as a Percentage of GDP for France and Selected Countries, 1960–1990

	1960	1970	1980	1990
France	4.3	5.9	7.5	8.8
Germany	4.9	6.0	8.4	8.8
Austria	4.4	5.6	7.7	8.4
Switzerland	3.3	5.1	7.0	7.9
Italy	3.6	5.2	6.6	8.1

Source: Poullier, J. OECD Health Systems, Facts and Trends 1960–1991. Paris: OECD, 1993, p. 18.

Table 6 Health Care Expenditures on Hospitals, Ambulatory Services, and Pharmaceuticals in France and Selected Countries (as a percentage of total health care expenditures), 1960–1990

	1960			1970			1980			1990		
	Hosp	Ambu	Phar	Hosp	Ambu	Phar	Hosp	Ambu	Phar	Hosp	Ambu	Phar
France	34.7	26.7	22.1	38.0	26.6	23.2	48.1	24.8	15.9	44.2	28.4	16.8
Germany	—	—	—	35.7	29.0	19.5	36.1	26.6	18.7	36.6	28.0	21.3
Austria	23.8	24.8	17.2	28.8	23.9	16.2	28.3	20.2	12.0	29.2	21.2	11.3
Switzerland	44.6	—	—	41.7	—	19.1	42.6	45.5	15.2	42.8	—	12.3
Italy	43.2	35.8	19.8	47.6	36.2	15.5	54.0	29.5	13.9	46.7	27.3	18.4

Source: Poullier, J. OECD Health Systems, Facts and Trends 1960–1991. Paris: OECD. 1993, p. 28.

three comparison countries. By 1990, France was ranked second highest among the comparison group.

D. Sources of Expenditures

The funding of national health care systems has been an increasingly important subject of debate in a number of countries, including those comprising the OECD. The share of public involvement in the financing of health care influences totals medical care consumption in most nations, including France. From 1960 to 1990, public spending on health care among many OECD counties increased, on average, beyond 50%. Table 7 details the increase for France and four other OECD countries. France's public share in total health care expenditures ranked it fourth among the comparison countries from 1960 through 1990 (Table 7).

In France, a system established to finance insurance against high individual health care costs has evolved to one that finances all costs, even those amenable to family or individual budgeting. Therefore, despite the good financial protection provided by the SIFs, supplemental insurance has a well-entrenched role as the reimburser of some or all of the copayments required by the basic system, particularly for ambulatory services. The main SIF, the CNAMTS, is self-supporting through payroll contributions by employers and employees. As a quasi-public entity, it is operated by a governing board composed of representatives from government, unions, and employee and employer groups. The other SIFs in France operate in a similar manner. The Ministry of Health also plays an oversight role over the CNAMTS and other SIFs, providing various mechanisms for interfund financial stability and funding for premiums for the poor. Even though each sickness fund is self-supporting, including cross-subsidies, there are deficits in some years that must be made up through increased sources of revenue or reduced expenditures.

Table 7 The Public Share in Total Health Care Expenditures, as a Percentage, for France, Germany, Sweden, Spain, and Italy, 1960–1990

	1960	1970	1980	1990
France	57	73	80	75
Germany	67	70	74	73
Sweden	74	85	90	90
Italy	85	88	86	76
Spain	54	66	78	79

Source: Poullier, J. OECD Health Systems, Facts and Trends 1960–1991. Paris: OECD, 1993, p. 246.

Contribution levels differ by fund. Employers contributing to the general fund pay 12.8% on gross salary while employees pay 6.8% as of 1993. Self-employed individuals are required to enroll for coverage and must pay the employer payroll tax rate of 12.8% (Fielding and Lancry, 1993).

In France, supplemental insurance has benefited from consistent support from the government. The government uses the supplemental insurance system to reduce pressure on it to increase employer and employee contributions to keep pace with health care cost increases. In 1991, 83% of the population was covered by supplemental health coverage. In general, those without supplemental coverage have limited resources, are 100% covered by their SIF, or are the young and others who believe their risk of serious illness or injury is too low to justify the expense (Le Faou and Jolly, 1995).

In principle, supplemental insurance in France is voluntary. However, many employers require their employees to obtain competitive rates for supplemental insurance from mutual insurance funds. Lack of employee deductibility from income for payroll and income taxes, together with deductibility of employer contributions, generates a strong incentive for the employer to pay most or all of the cost of supplemental insurance. Payments to the mutual funds (the providers of the supplemental insurance plans) are a fixed percentage of salary, with higher-paid employees subsidizing lower-paid employees for these voluntary insurance services.

E. What is Purchased with Those Expenditures

In France, as in a number of OECD countries, a mandated package of health insurance benefits is made available. Benefits generally include coverage for physician services, hospital care, laboratory tests, prescription drugs, and some dental and optical care. Patients in most OECD countries do not pay deductibles for health care services; however, copayments for physician and hospital services cover a wide range. In France, for outpatient services and inpatient hospital care, most treatment and diagnostic services are covered. Maternity care, including prenatal, maternity, and well-baby care services, is also available. Cash benefits are available for mothers—about US $150 per month—paid for 9 months. Additionally, a 16-week maternity leave is paid to the mother. The rate is based on the mother's previous income and is limited to a maximum of US $50 per day (Committee on Governmental Affairs, 1991; Poullier, 1993).

Preventive care is also covered under the basic benefit plan. Covered services in this area include one free preventive examination every 5 years and annual mammograms for women over age 45. Immunizations are also available, as are dental and vision services. Long-term care services are reimbursed, including home health care, day care, and some inpatient care for chronic conditions. Prescription drugs are also covered, subject to some restrictions. Finally, France offers an income maintenance program to workers who become ill. Generally, workers are entitled to 50% of their wages, up to about US $33 a day, for up to 360 days in any 3-year period. For certain diseases, such as cancer, these benefits may be granted for an unlimited number of days, up to a maximum of 3 years (Poullier, 1993).

In France in 1990, direct payments from individuals accounted for 18.8% of total health care expenditures. The principle of copayment has been retained in all reforms of health care financing since its introduction in France in 1930. However, the degree of application of copayments is limited by a shared perception that the health insurance system in France should prevent high out-of-pocket costs. The copayment rate varies by SIF and by type and place of service. For example, for ambulatory care, it is higher for common medicines such as aspirin (65%) than for laboratory tests (40%) or physician visits (30%), and higher for office consultations (30%) than for those in a public hospital (25%) (Burstall and Wallerstein, 1994).

All SIFs pay a higher percentage reimbursement (e.g., 100% for drugs and hospital and ambulatory care) for covered services for 30 "long, costly or otherwise defined sicknesses" including diabetes, cancer, AIDS, end-stage renal disease, and heart attacks. It is estimated that at any one time nearly 9% of the population is covered at these higher reimbursement rates (Fielding and Lancry, 1993).

Medical care in long-term-care beds is covered at 100 percent, but the lodging portion, usually about US $75 per day, or two-thirds of the total costs, is not covered and is paid by the individual or his family. Consequently, someone with a serious health problem will have little or no copayment while in a short-stay hospital but will have only about one-third of the costs covered when he is moved to a long-term-care facility (Fielding and Lancry, 1993).

This patchwork of reimbursement rules is the end product of many policies enacted over several decades in France. Yet, for all the incremental additions over the years, the rules are clearly defined, providing both specificity and predictability. For example, the exact amount of how much an individual must pay and how much reimbursement will be obtained can be calculated in advance for those who seek care from physicians who accept nationally negotiated fee schedules.

New technologies have played an increasing role in the French health care system. However, for the most part, the introduction of technology has not been followed by its rapid diffusion. Diffusion of some technologies, particularly biological tests, is supported by real expenditure growth for ancillary tests of 6.2% per annum (1985–1991). Many types of diagnostic tests, including all biological and biochemical tests, are performed only in independent laboratories and hospitals. Physicians are prohibited under law from charging for most biochemical tests performed in their offices (Burstall and Wallerstein, 1994).

Hospitals and clinics may purchase only products and services approved by the government. For all institutions, a process similar to the U.S. Certificate of Need process is required for the purchase of capital equipment. Implementing a new service also requires approval from the central government, and only after a quantitative analysis and demonstration of need for the particular service has been accomplished.

Private and hospital pharmacies have a monopoly on the distribution of medicines in France. Unlike many other OECD countries, no pharmaceuticals, even aspirin, can be purchased in a supermarket, department, or convenience store. There are about 23,000 private pharmacies, or about one for every 2500 inhabitants in France (Gross et al., 1994).

Prices for most pharmaceuticals that are reimbursable under the national basic benefit package are negotiated between the drug manufacturers and the several ministries involved. The percentage of reimbursement differs by the type of medication. For example, under some SIFs certain drugs for cancer treatment are considered ''indispensable'' and are reimbursed at 100%. Drugs such as antibiotics used to treat serious, but not life-threatening, conditions are reimbursed at 70%. These drugs constitute about 75% of the total drug market in France. Medications for conditions not considered a serious health threat (e.g., aspirin) are reimbursed at 40%. These drugs account for about 25% of the total drug market in France (Fielding and Lancry, 1993; Gross et al., 1994).

Pharmaceuticals account for about 18% of total health care costs in France. Compared with other OECD countries, this is not an exceptional figure. Table 8 illustrates France's 1990 pharmaceutical expenditures as a percentage of total national health care costs as compared with three other OECD countries. Also

Table 8 Pharmaceutical Expenditures as a Percentage of Total National Health Care Costs (1990) and Cumulative Pharmaceutical Growth (1985–1990) for France and Selected Countries

	1990	1985–1990
France	18.0	4.8
Sweden	7.5	4.5
Germany	23.5	4.0
United Kingdom	12.4	3.6

Source: Gross, D., Ratner, J., Perez, J., Glavin, S. International pharmaceutical spending controls: France, Germany, Sweden and the United Kingdom. Health Care Financ Rev, Spring 1994, pp. 129–132.

reflected in the table is the cumulative growth rate for pharmaceutical expenditures as compared to selected other nations (1985–1990). Although Germany's pharmaceutical expenditures rank the highest in this comparison, France ranks second, with 18% of its total national health care expenditures devoted to pharmaceuticals. Considering the nature of government control of drug prices in France's health care system, the demonstrated growth in pharmaceutical costs should not be considered excessive. However, as the data in Table 8 also illustrate, pharmaceutical expenditure growth from 1985 to 1990 in France and three other OECD countries demonstrates that France's cumulative pharmaceutical expenditure growth rate ranks first among the comparison counties.

F. Health Status of the Population

Although French health care policy does not officially refer to health outcomes or even to the concept of health promotion, adding years to life has long been an objective of most public health policy in OECD countries. In many OECD

Table 9 Trends in Added Years of Life for Females and Males (per 100,000 population, ages 0–64) for France and Selected Countries, 1960–1989

	Potential female life years gained			
	Total	Breast	Circulatory	External
France	3299	−30	371	−61
Austria	4928	−43	407	270
Germany	4519	−72	321	388
Switzerland	2785	− 3	320	171
Italy	6321	−52	640	101
	Potential male life years gained			
	Total	TB	Circulatory	Lung
France	3919	375	461	−146
Austria	6632	301	478	15
Germany	5931	254	352	−26
Switzerland	4045	152	545	26
Italy	7423	428	606	−112

The column totals for both females and males include gains in avoidable death for causes other than those listed.
Negative entries indicate a loss in potential years of life.
The breast and lung columns refer to cancer, TB to tuberculosis, circulatory to circulatory disorders, and external to causes such as accidents, homicides, and poisoning.
Source: Poullier, J. OECD Health Systems, Facts and Trends 1960–1991. Paris: OECD, 1993, p. 34.

Table 10 Female and Male Life Expectancy at Birth for France and Selected Countries, 1960–1990

	Life expectancy at birth										
	1960		1970		1980		1990	
	Female	Male	Female	Male	Female	Male	Female	Male
France	73.6	67.0	76.1	68.6	78.4	70.2	80.9	72.7
Austria	71.9	65.4	73.4	66.5	76.1	69.0	79.0	72.5
Germany	72.4	66.9	73.8	67.4	76.6	69.9	79.0	72.6
Switzerland	74.1	68.7	76.2	70.3	78.8	72.3	80.9	74.0
Italy	71.8	66.8	74.6	68.6	77.4	70.6	80.0	73.5

Source: Schieber, G., Poullier, P., Greenwald, L. U.S. health expenditure performance: An international comparison and data update. Health Care Financ Rev, Summer 1992, pp. 52–55.

Table 11   Infant and Perinatal Mortality (as percent of live births) for France
and Selected Countries, 1960–1990

| | 1960 | | 1970 | | 1980 | | 1990 | |
	Inf	Per	Inf	Per	Inf	Per	Inf	Per
France	2.74	3.13	1.82	2.33	1.01	1.29	0.72	0.89
Austria	3.75	3.50	2.59	2.70	1.43	1.41	0.78	0.69
Germany	3.38	3.58	2.34	2.64	1.27	1.16	0.75	0.64
Switzerland	2.11	2.56	1.51	1.82	0.91	0.95	0.73	0.77
Italy	4.39	4.19	2.96	3.12	1.43	1.75	0.82	1.10

Source: Schieber, G., Poullier, P., Greenwald, L. U.S. health expenditure performance: an international comparison and data update. Health Care Financ Rev, Summer 1992, pp. 64–67.

countries, including France, a number of public health policies do exist to prevent the onset of disease, to reduce premature mortality, to restore dysfunctions, to rehabilitate, or to relieve suffering. Premature death, defined as years lost before age 65, has been halved, notably in areas with substantial advances in medical technology, such as cardiovascular therapies (Poullier, 1993). Table 9 exhibits trends whereby years are added to life for both women and men for France and four other similar OECD countries. In general, many of the gains achieved in France (and among the other OECD comparison nations) have assumed the form of fewer disability periods for those whose life span was shortened, longer spells of healthy life for most elderly, and a reduction of pain and suffering for others.

Additional indicators commonly used to make longitudinal comparisons of the health status of populations include female and male life expectancy at birth and infant mortality and perinatal mortality. These indicators for France and four other OECD countries are detailed in Tables 10 and 11, respectively, for the period 1960–1990.

According to these two tables, France (1960–1990) ranks well among the comparison group countries in terms of the growth in female and male life expectancy at birth, the reduction of infant mortality, and the reduction of perinatal mortality.

In France, medical services directly linked to preventive care, although not officially called such, are present. These services represent 2.13% of the total expenditures for health services in 1992 alone (Le Faou and Jolly, 1995). This percentage refers to services that are free of charge for the patient, such as programs to protect mothers and infants and programs in schools, prisons, and workplaces. However, this percentage does not take into account all the preventive activities of medical professionals. In fact, physicians in hospitals, general practitioners, midwives, physical therapists, and others practice preventive medicine in the context of their normal office visits, while administering immunizations, prenatal and postnatal care, and rehabilitation services. The French government does not classify these acts as preventive measures, however, but rather as routine medical services. Nevertheless, the government is beginning to recognize the medical and financial advantages of such preventive programs. For example, it now promotes flu immunization programs for the elderly and breast cancer screening. These programs are provided without charge to the patient.

III. CURRENT HEALTH CARE SYSTEM ISSUES

A. Advantages and/or Disadvantages of the Current System

Unlike the United States, though similar to many OECD countries, the French health care system is very centralized, with most system-wide organizational, financing, and health care provision decisions made in Paris. The resulting fragmentation of powers and short-term orientation mitigate the potential for integration, coordination, and long-term planning.

Achieving consensus within the government is hampered by the dispersion of budgeting, financing, pricing, quality assurance, and education functions among six different ministries. The CNAMTS negotiates with physicians and private hospitals, but the Ministries of Finance and Social Security must approve any increase in payroll deduction rates. Coordination of long-term planning is hindered by the 18-month average tenure of a minister. A new minister is generally preoccupied with what must and can be accomplished within a 1–2-year period, and often concentrates on short-term programs (Burstall and Wallerstein, 1994).

The strengths of the French health care system are many: virtually universal coverage, a single comprehensive benefit plan, moderate per capita expenditures for health care, all within the context of having structures for financing and providing health care that have substantial private components. Those interested in health care reform efforts might look to France's uniform benefit package and unified financing and payment schemes. This combination provides almost universal comprehensive insurance with good financial protection. Uniform provider insurance payments, which in turn are predictable and not subject to multiple layers of utilization review, curtail cost shifting and permit simplified, less costly administrative procedures and structures. A unified payment system also better supports the achievement of general system objectives, such as limiting overall health care expenditures (Fielding and Lancry, 1993; Burstall and Wallerstein, 1994).

With all the attendant benefits in the French health care system, the single biggest problem acknowledged across the political spectrum is lack of control of costs in the out-of-hospital and private hospital sectors. Private spending is providing an increasing amount of growth in the health care bill, especially in those areas where there may be optional services available to patients. Expenditures are actually rising faster than the GDP. A survey carried out by for the CNAMTS revealed that 50% of the French people thought that health care spending had risen excessively in recent years and 90% felt that the entire French health care system faced great difficulties in the future. When asked what should be done to control expenditures, 93% of the respondents favored policies to promote cost awareness. Ironically, increases in individual health insurance contributions were opposed by survey respondents, as were reductions in the services offered under the national system (Burstall and Wallerstein, 1994).

B. Quality and Access Issues

Under France's universal coverage approach to health care, access to the system is generally not an issue. Almost the entire population is covered by the SIFs, which provide most kinds of medical care. The differences between the SIFs are marginal. The delivery of health care is also quite equitable. If any problem exists in delivery, it may be the distribution of physicians. Most tend to practice in urban areas, and fewer in rural areas. Some access and choice for patients can be reduced as a result, but not to any extent reported as a problem.

As regards quality of care delivered, there are no nongovernmental national health care organizations comparable to the U.S. Joint Commission on Accreditation of Healthcare Organizations (JCAHO) or the U.S. National Committee for Quality Assurance (NCQA) that independently rank quality of health care delivered in France. "Accreditation" of all hospitals by the Ministry of Health is required. However, the Ministry of Health accreditation, as well as many others conducted by other such government-sponsored entities, is primarily concerned with determining the range of reimbursable services to authorize at each location. Therefore, the best available assessments of quality are those provided by the French populace themselves. The behavior of the French patients shows that they have an unusually positive attitude toward the benefits of medicine. There is a greater emphasis upon maintaining the physical constitution than in some other OECD countries. For example, alternative therapies such as homeopathy and spa treatments are popular. This has an impact on the expectations of patients and therefore reinforces the behavior of physicians—a significant factor when health care system changes are under consideration.

On the whole, French patients are reasonably satisfied with the French system of health care. An international comparative study (Blendon et al., 1990) found that 41% of the population thought that the health care system works pretty well and that only a few changes were necessary to make it better. The comprehensive scope of French health care is clearly valued by the population and attempts to reduce its scope have been resisted. The principle that the patient should be free to choose the provider of health care is widely supported and none of the numerous projects for reform have tried to seriously limit this right.

C. Cost Containment/Control Efforts

As the rise in total health care expenditures has been the single most important item of concern to the French public, of particular concern was the rise in out-of-hospital and private hospital expenditures. Until 1984 all hospitals were funded on the basis of a standard daily rate, which was the same regardless of the treatment given or the length of stay. Many private hospitals in France are still reimbursed through this mechanism. The single most successful cost control plan introduced to date in France has been the system of global budgets for hospitals in the public sector and some private hospitals.

Between 1970 and 1982, real expenditures were rising at between 6.5 and 9% annually. Since that time they have been rising at no more than 3% annually. Although, as noted earlier, the introduction of the DRG-like system of PMSI was approved in 1991, opposition from the hospital and physician sectors has minimized the potential effect of this prospective reimbursement mechanism.

Elsewhere in the French health care system fee-for-service medicine still prevails. The only way to control costs has been through the fees themselves, which are negotiated each year. In 1991 a bill was introduced to limit the annual growth in all forms of primary care expenditure to a fixed percentage. Although this particular bill was not passed, a somewhat watered-down version was reintroduced in 1992 and eventually became law. Although strict limits on reimbursement are not included, medical guidelines were laid down that offer direction on diagnosis and treatment and specify how much consulting and prescribing each physician should generate each year. On the basis of these guidelines, annual forecasts of spending will be developed and will form part of the physicians' contracts with each SIF. Sanctions will be imposed on physicians who do not adhere to the guidelines (Burstall and Wallerstein, 1994).

Controls over pharmaceutical prices in France have been in place for many years, without much success. Medicine consumption has continued to rise rapidly. In 1991, a system of establishing a total drug sales budget for each manufacturer was proposed. Under this plan, drug manufacturers would have been able to set prices freely, as long as their total revenues from sales to the SIFs did not exceed the budget. This system was not enacted due to political opposition. However, in January 1991, representatives of the pharmaceutical industry and the French government reached an informal agreement that, when fully implemented, will include many aspects of the original 1991 proposal (Gross et al., 1994).

Governments can limit the drugs eligible for reimbursement through lists that explicitly identify specific drugs as ineligible for reimbursement. Drugs may be excluded from the payment system because they (1) offer questionable thera-peutic value or (2) have prices that are high relative to alternative medications of similar or equal therapeutic value. In January 1994, France established a list of 24 drugs and procedures that would not be reimbursed (Gross et al., 1994).

D. Current Reforms

In France current health care reforms center on restraining expenditures through cost containment. There are no indications that any radical departures from this approach in the present system are planned. The aims of the government appear to involve a pattern of ongoing incremental changes, in the hope that growth in health care spending will be brought down to an acceptable figure, which appears to be somewhere between the annual rate of inflation and the annual growth of the economy. The political constraints on other forms of more decisive action have been noted earlier. The government has always been forced to back down when faced with opposition from powerful interest groups.

As noted at the beginning of this chapter, the French health care system goes back to 1945—and certain elements of it date back to the turn of the twenti-eth century. This by itself limits the potential of radical change. The French con-sider that they should be free to choose who will deliver their health care with a minimum of restrictions. Moreover, the right of physicians to practice as they see fit and where they will is ingrained in the French culture. A mixture of private and public hospitals is seen as normal. As far as financing is concerned, the French prefer to pay for health care by means of earmarked contributions rather than from general taxation. This can be seen as insulating health care spending from other financial pressures.

The traditions of French administration emphasize central control. This seems normal, both to the administrators and to the administrated. Examples of this central control have been mentioned throughout the chapter, from global budgets, through the permitted reimbursement rates, to the number of medical students allowed to continue through school. However, even in the face of strong central control, the French health care system is quite fragmented, mainly as a result of the many compromises that had to be made over the years as the system moved from a predominantly private to a predominantly public basis.

Finally, there is a further constraint on reform. As mentioned earlier, the overwhelming majority of the French public appear to be satisfied with their health care system as it is. This may not be an unreasonable position as the French health care system is good even if it is expensive and economically inefficient in many ways. Therefore, in the eyes of the average French citizen, the present system reconciles a variety of important but diverse objectives at a price that is high by many standards but acceptable to those who must ultimately pay the bill.

REFERENCES

Blendon, R., Leitman, R., Morrison, I., Donelan, K. Satisfaction with health systems in ten nations. Health Affairs 185–192, Summer 1990.

Burstall, M., Wallerstein, K. The health care system in France. In: Hoffmeyer, U., McCarthy, T., eds. Financing Health Care. Dordrecht, GE: Kluwer Academic Publishers, 1994, pp 345–418.

Committee on Governmental Affairs. Cutting Health Care Costs: Experiences in France, Germany, and Japan (Serial No. 102-15). Washington, DC: U.S. Government Printing Office, 1991.

Fielding, J., Lancry, P. Lessons from France: the French health care system and US health system reform. JAMA 270(6):748–756, 1993.

Gross, D., Ratner, J., Perez, J., Glavin, S. International pharmaceutical spending controls: France, Germany, Sweden, and the United Kingdom. Health Care Financ Rev 15(3): 127–140, 1994.

Kervasdoue, J., Kimberley, J., Rodwin, V. Introduction: The end of an illusion. In: Kervasdoue, J., Kimberly, J., Rodwin, V., eds. The End of an Illusion: The Future of Health Policy in Western Industrialized Nations. Berkeley, CA: University of California Press, 1984a, pp xvii–xxii.

Kervasdoue, J., Rodwin, V., Stephan, J. France: Contemporary problems and future scenarios. In: Kervasdoue, J., Kimberly, J., Rodwin V., eds. The End of an Illusion: The Future of Health Policy in Western Industrialized Nations. Berkeley, CA: University of California Press, 1984b, pp 137–166.

Kovner, A. Health Care Delivery in the United States. New York: Springer Publishing Company, 1995.

Le Faou, A., Jolly, D. Health promotion in France: toward a new way of giving medical care. Hosp Topics 73(2):17–21, 1995.

Poullier, P. OECD Health Systems: Facts and Trends 1960–1991. Vol. I. Paris: OECD, 1993, pp 1–251.

Schieber, G., Poullier, J., Greenwald, L. US health expenditure performance: an international comparison and data update. Health Care Financ Rev 13(4):1–77, 1992.

Starr, P. The Social Transformation of American Medicine. New York: Basic Books, 1985.

9
Universal Coverage and Cost Control
The United Kingdom National Health Service

Karen Bloor and Alan Maynard
University of York, Heslington, York, England

I. OVERVIEW

The United Kingdom (UK) health care system is dominated by the National Health Service (NHS), which was established in 1948. It remains a publicly financed and largely publicly provided health care system, giving universal coverage for the population with a zero price at the point of consumption for the majority of treatment. The use of prospective global budgets and a single (tax) "pipe" of finance has facilitated cost containment and the control of provider-induced expenditure inflation.

During the 1980s, restrictions on public expenditure and perceptions of underfunding, manifested in particular by waiting times for non-acute surgery, created a great deal of media and public debate within the United Kingdom and formed the background to the "wide ranging and fundamental review" of the NHS announced by Prime Minister Thatcher in 1988. This review resulted in the publication of a White Paper, *Working for Patients*, in 1989 (Department of Health and Social Security, 1989), which together with proposals for reform of community care in the White Paper *Caring for People* (Department of Health, 1989), formed the basis of the National Health Service and Community Care Act in 1990 (House of Commons, 1990) and the implementation of radical reforms introduced cumulatively from 1991.

In 1997, the Conservative government was replaced by a Labour administration; since then further reforms have taken place, building on the 1991 system.

Both sets of reforms maintained the tax finance of the NHS and a non-market allocation system.

In principle, allocating on the basis of "need" requires the United Kingdom governments to identify cost-effective treatments, target resources to maximize health gain from the health care budget and decide how much they will pay from public expenditure to buy additional health gain. In reality, of course, the health care policy debate confuses objectives and ideologies, often hindering the pursuit of efficient and equitable delivery of health care and the maintenance of cost control (Maynard and Williams, 1985).

In practice, all health care systems are "mixed economies," to the extent that they consist of public and private provision and finance that includes both the willingness to pay and benefit principles. The United States' system, based on an insurance-financed, privately provided "free market," nonetheless has considerable government input (40 cents in the U.S. health care dollar are publicly financed). The U.K. health care system is dominated by the public sector. Its private sector is relatively small and specializes in non-emergency (elective) surgical procedures. This pattern of finance and provision has proved remarkably stable for over 50 years and has provided for all U.K. citizens a health care system with universal and relatively equitable coverage at moderate cost but with some scope to improve its efficiency.

II. THE UNITED KINGDOM HEALTH CARE SYSTEM

A. Historical Development

In 1942, the publication of the Beveridge Report recommended a postwar system of welfare services in the United Kingdom and a comprehensive national health insurance system with continued public and private provision of health care. In 1943, the wartime coalition government, led by Prime Minister Churchill, accepted the need for a comprehensive system. After the appointment of a Labour government in 1945, with Aneurin Bevan as Minister for Health, the National Health Service Bill (House of Commons, 1946) was published in March 1946. The Act was passed in November 1946 and the National Health Service came into existence on the "appointed day," July 5, 1948. The NHS was designed as a "comprehensive health service to secure improvement in the physical and mental health of the people and the prevention, diagnosis and treatment of illness (House of Commons, 1946).

The NHS is publicly financed, largely from general taxation, and most of its services are publicly provided. This "socialist" model of health care has been managed with provider (physician) dominance at the local level. Until recently, the government controlled aggregate NHS expenditure and left the provision of care to clinicians. Clinicians did not challenge the government's funding decisions and, in exchange, maintained discretion in the use of resources within the fixed global budget ("clinical freedom").

This provider-government agreement was challenged by Prime Minister Thatcher, who demanded an account of how efficiently resources were being used by the profession: what she called "value for money." Following a review of the NHS in 1988, "internal market" reforms were introduced cumulatively from 1991. These reforms separated purchasing from provision of care, and intended to achieve a radical improvement in supply (provider) efficiency. The Labour government has developed and regulated the internal market since 1997. The 1991 and 1997 reforms are described in Section IV, following a description of the financing of the NHS in the remainder of Section II and a discussion of the demand for health care in Section III. Section V considers the evidence base for the provision of health care in the United Kingdom, and Section VI concludes with a summary of the main characteristics of the NHS, with past objectives, present systems, and future possibilities.

B. Financing the U.K. National Health Service

The NHS is funded largely from general taxation, which covers approximately 86% of the total cost of the NHS. National Insurance contributions (proportional payroll taxes to individuals and employers) finance 12% of expenditure and user charges (for dental care and prescribed pharmaceuticals) finance the remaining 2% (Office of Health Economics, 2000).

Around 11.5% of the population have some form of private insurance coverage, with expenditure of £4.4 billion in 1999 (OHE, 2000). Expenditure is, however, focused on a relatively narrow range of elective procedures such as abortions, hip replacements, and hernia repairs (Monopolies and Mergers Commission, 1994). In addition, private funding of dental and ophthalmic care has increased greatly over the last two decades. In 1998, the proportion of expenditure on NHS dental care contributed by patients was 30% of overall costs, compared with 20% in 1973 (OHE, 1995), as a result of increased user charges. In addition, a substantial proportion of dentists now provide only private dental care. Ophthalmic care has been more overtly "privatized" over time: although real spending on ophthalmic services has grown in recent years, their share of NHS resources has fallen from 5.3% in 1949 (at the inception of the NHS) to 0.6% (£298 million) in 1998 (OHE, 2000). In 1989 free NHS sight testing and supply of eyeglasses to the general population was restricted to children under 16, those who needed complex lenses, diagnosed diabetics and glaucoma sufferers, registered blind or partially sighted, and people who received social security benefits.

In 1999, the United Kingdom spent £61 billion on health care, £52 billion (86%) on the NHS, £4.4 billion (7%) on private health care, and £4.4 billion (7%) on pharmaceuticals and other products without NHS prescriptions. Overall, this represents 6.9% of gross domestic product (GDP) compared with an average of 10% of GDP in the OECD as a whole in 1997 and 14% of GDP in the United States. Health care expenditure is dominated by the cost of the National Health Service; the private health sector in the U.K. is small. Over the period of 1979 to 2000, the gross cost of the NHS grew by around 98% in real terms (adjusted using the GDP deflator). The annual average real growth rate in expenditure over these two decades was over 3.4% but there were marked fluctuations in this rate. These variations tend to reflect the political cycle (e.g., elections in 1983 and 1987) and the cost of implementing the 1991 reforms. For the first two years of the Labour government (1997–1999), the expenditure commitments of the previous Conservative administration were kept, but since then planned expenditure on the NHS is increasing substantially, and a pledge of 6.5% real growth in expenditure has been made for the next three years.

C. What is Purchased with These Expenditures?

The majority of services provided by the NHS are free at the point of delivery. This includes access to all hospital and primary care services. Patients' access to the health care system tends to be through the general practitioner (GP), who fulfills a "gatekeeper" role, providing entrance to the secondary care sector by referring patients to hospital specialists, although patients can also enter the hospital sector through accident and emergency departments. GPs provide the majority of primary care services, increasingly in teams including practice nurses and sometimes other health professionals such as physiotherapists and counselors.

Individuals do pay for some NHS-provided services, such as dentistry and prescriptions. Prescription charges are currently £6.10 per item (around $9), but there are substantial exemptions to this charge. Children and the elderly are exempt, as are people with certain chronic diseases such as diabetes, and people with low incomes receiving state benefits. Finally, some prescribed items are exempt, for example, oral contraceptives. The exemptions mean that only 14% (OHE, 2000) of prescriptions are chargeable and so user charges cover only a small proportion of overall NHS costs.

D. How Do These Expenditures Reach the Providers?

The government decides the total size of the U.K. NHS budget for each of the four countries. The annual cycle of the Public Expenditure Scrutiny Committee requires the English Department of Health (and counterparts in Scotland, Wales, and Northern Ireland) to present a funding case to the Treasury. The case for increased funding generally focuses on demographic and technological change, which is asserted (on a very weak knowledge base) to increase demand for health care. Once the overall budget is decided, the Department of Health in England

(and its counterparts in Scotland, Wales, and Northern Ireland) then allocates the hospital and community health services (HCHS) budget between regions by a weighted capitation formula. Population is weighted by age and other determinants of the "need" for health care resources.

The Resource Allocation Working Party originally devised the English formula in 1976 (Department of Health and Social Security, 1976) and, more recently, this has been reviewed and refined by a team from the University of York (Carr-Hill et al., 1994; Smith et al., 1994). The refined formula uses comprehensive data and sophisticated statistical methods to identify population-based indicators of the need for health care using small area analysis of the determinants of hospital use. This formula is used to allocate resources between NHS regions. It applies only to HCHS budgets within the constituent parts of the United Kingdom (England, Scotland, Wales, and Northern Ireland) and not between them (Birch and Maynard, 1986). In addition, weighted capitation formulas are not fully applied to primary care budgets—the distribution of resource for the income of general practitioners is not yet determined in this way. Such an application would result in a considerable transfer of resources (and GPs) from the South of England, particularly the Southwest, to Northern Regions (Bloor and Maynard, 1995). The primary care budget has demand-determined and cash-limited components; it is a function of the number of general practitioners and their prescribing behavior. However, attempts are now being made to derive an appropriate weighted capitation formula for allocating both cash-limited and non-cash-limited primary care resources.

Local purchasers of secondary health care (Health Authorities and, increasingly, Primary Care Trusts) use their allocated budgets to contract with hospital and community health care trusts to provide secondary care services. The relatively low cost of the NHS in comparison to other health care systems is a result of tight control of expenditure by central government (i.e., there are global budgets within a "single pipe" of tax finance). Salary systems for remuneration of hospital doctors reduce the incentives for overtreatment and supplier-induced demand, which may exist in fee-for-service systems (Robinson and Luft, 1987). Finally, the "gatekeeper" system, where patients enter the health care system via their family GPs, who care for approximately 90% of all patient episodes in the community, may keep overall costs down. Remuneration of GPs combines a capitation element (weighted by the age of individuals on the GP's list and a measure of local deprivation), a basic practice allowance and some fee-for-service elements.

Table 1 illustrates the number of hospital doctors and general practitioners in the United Kingdom. There are considerable differences in the systems of remuneration of GPs and hospital doctors in the NHS. GPs are independent contractors to the NHS, required to provide comprehensive care 24 hours a day, 365 days a year, to the patients on their list. The average list size for a GP is around

Medical Staff (Absolute Numbers and per 100,000), 1998 (OHE 2000)

Consultant	19,379
Staff grade practitioner	2,873
Associate specialist	1,224
Registrar	11,065
Senior house officer	14,598
House officer	2,443
Total[a]	54,416
Hospital medical staff per 100,000 population[b]	115
All GPs[b]	36,653
GPs per 100,000 population[b]	62

[a] England
[b] United Kingdom

1800 people. The majority of a GP's salary (60%) is paid on a capitation basis and additional payments are also made for individual services. These additional payments include:

target payments for childhood immunizations (payments for 90% or 70% coverage of the children on a GP's list);

target payments for cervical cytology (payments for 50% or 80% coverage of women aged 25–64 on a GP's list);

additional payments for holding health promotion clinics;

fee-for-service elements such as payments for minor surgery and payments for provision of contraceptive services.

The system of payment for GPs is based on a contract initiated in 1990. It has been subject to some criticism, as the services that GPs are encouraged to provide are of unproven effectiveness and cost-effectiveness (Scott and Maynard, 1991). There was also a dispute during the summer of 1995 regarding the pay and responsibilities of GPs working out of hours. This dispute was resolved by providing additional funding and contractual arrangements for after-hours work. Since then, further attempts have been made to reduce the after-hours workload of GPs, including the progressive introduction in 1998 of NHS Direct—a 24-hour telephone and computer helpline staffed by nurses to provide health-related advice—and the introduction in some areas of NHS walk-in centers, also staffed by nurses, which complement general practice by providing treatment for minor ailments and injuries, health promotion, and self-care advice.

A dual-payment system of GP remuneration is emerging. In addition to the capitation system, complemented by fee-for-service payments, some younger practitioners are opting for payment by salary and a fixed work week, as the government has over recent years piloted different contracts and work plans for GPs, known as Personal Medical Service pilot schemes.

Hospital doctors in the U.K. NHS are paid on a salary basis, with fixed salary scales applying across all specialties, earning a basic salary of £48,905 to £63,640 for the year 2000/01. The majority of consultants also undertake some private practice, with varying levels of remuneration—minor levels in medical specialties, and potentially substantial levels of private income primarily for surgeons and anesthetists working in specialties where wait times are longer and there is more opportunity for private practice. There are payments for medical examinations or other requests from individuals, insurance companies, employers, or courts, which are thought to be outside normal duties. Finally, consultants may receive a distinction award, paid in addition to their basic NHS salary.

The system of distinction awards is one element of doctors' pay that may be influenced by trusts. Distinction awards are paid to consultants in the NHS to reward "excellence" and can double a consultant's NHS salary. At present, around one-third of consultants have an award and two-thirds will receive one at some time in their careers. However, the system for allocating awards is vague and secretive and there has not been adequate demonstration that it reflects any measure of "excellence" or efficiency in practice. The uneven distribution of awards cannot be explained by efficiency or equity indicators (Bloor and Maynard, 1992). Distinction awards are costly to the NHS and to individual trusts that have to fund them. They are one area where payment could perhaps more closely relate to performance, and are under review as part of a renegotiation of the consultant contract (Department of Health, 2001a, 2001b). It is, however, very difficult to link pay to performance in health care. Ideally, rewards should be related to outcomes, and data on the outcomes of health care are rarely available. In the United States, the Medicare fee schedule attempts to reimburse doctors on the basis of their inputs to health care, as defined initially by the resource-based relative value scale (Hsiao et al., 1988). Contract reform and performance measurement for consultants in the NHS is inevitable and would benefit from informed debate about the appropriate form of contract and well-designed evaluation (Maynard and Bloor, 2001).

E. Health Status of the Population

U.K. health outcomes appear to be similar to those achieved by higher-spending countries, despite relatively low health care expenditure. Table 2 illustrates life expectancy at birth and infant mortality in selected OECD countries. These data and others, such as perinatal and infant mortality, potential years of life lost, and life expectancy at birth and at age 80 suggest that United Kingdom health is close to G-7 and OECD averages. This suggests to observers that the NHS "was and is, a remarkably cost-effective institution" (OECD, 1994).

Table 2 Crude Health Outcomes in Selected OECD Countries (OHE, 2000)

	Life expectancy at birth, male, 2000–2005	Life expectancy at birth, female, 2000–2005	Infant mortality per 1000 births, 2000
OECD	74.1	80.3	
EU15	74.9	80.9	
Australia	76	81.6	6
Canada	76.6	82.3	6
France	75	82.5	6
Germany	74.7	80.7	5
Italy	75.8	81.7	7
Japan	77.2	83.3	4
Netherlands	75.5	81.2	6
UK	75.3	80.6	7
USA	74.2	80.6	7

Trends in some causes of death in England and Wales appear to have fallen over recent years (see Table 3). Nevertheless, deaths by various causes per 100,000 population compared to other OECD countries show that the United Kingdom has above OECD and EEC average death rates, particularly from circulatory and respiratory disease (Table 4).

III. THE DEMAND FOR HEALTH CARE: SCARCITY AND RATIONING

> Who shall live and who shall die, who shall fulfill his days and who shall die before his time? (Yom Kippur [Day of Atonement] Prayer Book)

The health care demands of individuals, groups, and society exceed the available resources to fund these services. Resources are limited and the problem of scarcity means that choices have to be made—resources must be allocated (rationed) between competing ends. This inevitable conclusion has been highlighted in recent years by great advances in medical technology: "the good news is that modern medicine can work miracles. The bad news is that it is very expensive and many health care expenditures do not seem to yield benefits worth their costs" (Aaron and Schwarz, 1984). Variations in medical care between and within countries illustrate the rationing process—individual clinicians ration care (even acute care) in many ways (Andersen and Mooney, 1990).

In general, it has been left to clinicians to make rationing decisions and to decide when not to "strive officiously" to keep people alive. Governments have

Table 3 Trends in Death Rates per 100,000 Population

ICD Causes		1980	1990	1992	1994	1996	1997	1998
I	Infectious and parasitic diseases	5	5	5	6	7	7	7
II	Neoplasms	262	286	284	278	274	270	265
III	Endocrine diseases 2	13	19	20	15	15	14	14
IV	Blood and blood-forming organs	3	5	5	4	4	4	4
V	Mental disorders	7	25	24	16	18	19	19
VI	Nervous system and sense organs	13	22	22	18	18	18	18
VII	Circulatory system	590	515	500	507	473	461	442
VIII	Respiratory system	164	124	120	176	173	169	175
IX	Digestive system	33	36	37	36	38	39	39
X	Genito-urinary system	16	15	11	13	14	13	13
XI	Pregnancy, childbirth etc. 2	0	0	0	0	0	0	0
XII	Skin and subcutaneous tissue	1	2	2	2	2	2	2
XIII	Musculo-skeletal system	6	10	10	7	7	6	7
XIV	Congenital abnormalities	7	3	3	3	3	3	3
XV	Conditions of the peri-natal period 2	6	1	1	1	1	1	1
XVI	Ill-defined conditions 2	5	9	10	12	17	19	22
XVII	Injury and poisoning	43	37	34	35	33	33	33
All accidents		30	26	21	21	20	21	21

Source: OHE, 2000.

been extremely reluctant to discuss explicit rationing criteria, owing to the political and emotional sensitivity of the subject. Even when rationing criteria have been explicitly tackled (for example, in Oregon, The Netherlands, and New Zealand) it has proved extremely difficult to draw up a list of "core services" that should be publicly funded to the exclusion of other services. This applies even using only clinical criteria. Economic criteria increase the complexity of the decisions.

The problem of scarcity and implied rationing decisions exist worldwide and are inevitable. In private health care systems, rationing takes place on the basis of ability to pay. The price of health care determines its allocation. In the publicly dominated United Kingdom health care system, rationing also exists.

Table 4 Age Standardized Death Rates per 100,000 Population in Selected OECD Countries (OHE 2000)

Country	Year	All causes	Neoplasms	Circulatory system	Respiratory system	Digestive system	External causes
OECD*	1997	727	184	274	61	33	52
EU15*	1997	703	192	274	56	33	42
Australia	1995	653	185	267	48	20	38
Canada	1995	657	193	239	56	24	44
France	1995	638	198	183	42	33	63
Germany	1997	724	194	324	40	37	38
Italy	1993	668	199	270	36	36	40
Japan	1997	530	146	160	61	22	43
Netherlands	1996	734	173	220	63	26	31
UK	1997	737	201	292	108	29	28
USA	1996	759	193	298	68	26	54

Source: OHE, 2000.
* weighted average.

One of the ways that care is rationed is on the basis of waiting time. At any time, around 1 million people are on a waiting list in the U.K., waiting for hospital therapy. Such lists are used to ration access to elective therapy on the basis of "need," as more urgent cases are treated first when possible. Even within a system of waiting lists, priority setting must take place. GPs and hospital doctors in the United Kingdom tend to group patients into "urgent," "soon," and "routine" to indicate priorities within the waiting list.

The elective procedures for which patients wait for care in the United Kingdom represent a small proportion of overall health care interventions. The majority (over 86%) of GP presentations are dealt with by GPs themselves. Only 7% result in an elective hospital procedure and 7% in emergency hospital admission (Pereira Gray, personal communication, August 1994). In 1991–92 there were 34,785 consultations with GPs per 10,000 person years at risk. This consisted of 5451 serious conditions, 14,370 intermediate conditions, and 14,963 minor conditions (Office of Population Censuses and Surveys, 1995).

The numbers of patients on waiting lists in the United Kingdom do, however, attract a great deal of political and media attention. The first of a series of "waiting list initiatives" was introduced in 1987, and has attempted to mitigate a problem by targeting expenditure at it. A waiting list fund was established, focusing on reducing the time patients wait for elective therapies. The Labour Party, during the 1997 election campaign, pledged to reduce the number of people waiting for NHS care, but in the 2001 election campaign switched their manifesto aims to addressing waiting times, rather than lists. The most recent pledge is to reduce waiting times so that by 2005 no patient will have to wait more than six months for hospital admission, and to reduce the average waiting time for an outpatient appointment to five weeks. Targeted expenditure by successive Conservative and Labour governments has reduced the time patients wait, but this focus on activity is not necessarily efficient. Targeting nonurgent cases waiting for long periods may be at the risk of not spending more on urgent cases with shorter waits (Yates, 1987). The cost-effectiveness of continued downward pressure on waiting time in improving patient outcome has not been demonstrated.

Individual decisions taken to ration health care can also attract considerable media and public attention. The editor of the British Medical Journal, however, suggests:

> Doctors are less shocked by rationing than is the public. They have been at it for years. Decisions have regularly been taken not to continue treatment of terminally ill people, not only because it would be kinder for the patient but also because it would be a waste of resources. Patients above a certain age have been denied admission to intensive care units; diabetic patients have been refused renal dialysis; and alcohol misusers have been turned down for liver transplants (Smith, 1991a, p. 1561).

In general, doctors feel happier making clinical rather than economic decisions. If there is a clinical rationale, this is thought acceptable, but as medical technology advances, the "gap between what you want and what you will pay for" (Sabin, 1992) becomes more apparent and health care decisions inevitably involve economics. For efficient allocation of limited budgets, rationing decisions must be based on cost-effectiveness, not solely on clinical effectiveness. Constraints on public funding in the NHS and the gap between demand for health care and supply of health care resources in the United Kingdom during the 1980s created a public perception of "underfunding" in the health service and were the precursors to the radical NHS reforms of 1991.

IV. RECENT U.K. HEALTH CARE SYSTEM ISSUES: THE 1991 REFORMS AND NEW LABOUR POLICIES SINCE 1997

A. Historical Background to the 1991 Reforms

During the 1980s, the Conservative government under Mrs. Thatcher constrained overall public expenditure to reduce public borrowing and inflation. The NHS, particularly the hospital sector, was not immune to this constraint. By the winter of 1987/88, public and media attention to the "underfunding" of the NHS, along with a pay dispute and strong criticism from the medical establishment, created an atmosphere of crisis in the NHS. The debate was highlighted by media attention to two young boys who had to wait for operations for congenital heart defects. During the "media storm" created, Mrs. Thatcher announced, unilaterally in a TV interview, a "wide ranging and fundamental review" of the health service.

Earlier in the 1980s, the Nuffield Provincial Hospitals Trust had invited Alain Enthoven, a professor at Stanford University, to visit Britain and examine the ways in which the NHS might be reformed. The resulting publication (Enthoven, 1985) was regarded by some as being the original blueprint for the internal market model of the NHS, although this is not supported by Mrs. Thatcher's own recollections (Thatcher, 1994). The document's criticism of the NHS included its resistance to change, the lack of economic incentives for efficiency, and the limited consumer power within the NHS. In combination, these factors were believed by Enthoven to have created an organizational "gridlock." The purchaser/provider divide within the NHS structure was suggested as a prescription for change.

Also, in the early 1980s, other academics had developed ideas and models for a primary-care-led NHS (Marinker, 1984; Maynard, 1986; Maynard et al., 1986), which led to the development of general practice fund holding, introduced in the 1989 White Paper (DHSS, 1989).

B. The 1991 Reforms

The White Paper *Working for Patients* (DHSS, 1989) retained the public funding of the NHS, focused on the reform of the supply side (i.e., health care provision) and sought to introduce competition in the form of an internal market to enhance efficiency in the provision of health care. The key elements of the changes, introduced initially in 1991, were:

> *The development of the purchasing function.* Existing District Health Authorities (DHAs) were re-established as purchasing agencies to increase flexibility and delegate decision making to the local level. The purchaser is required to assess the needs of its local population and to purchase the services that meet those needs most cost-effectively. Efficient purchasing requires information on the cost-effectiveness of competing procedures, to facilitate prioritization on the cost-effectiveness of competing procedures, and reflect efficiency and social values. Purchasers (DHAs and general practice fund holders) can purchase from public and private providers.
>
> *The establishment of NHS trusts.* Hospital and community health services before the reforms were managed as part of the DHAs. Increasingly,

they have become independent, "self-governing" NHS trusts, managed separately from the purchasing authority. The change has been introduced gradually since 1991, with hospitals and providers choosing to become self-governing. By 1995, all hospitals were trusts. Trusts continue to be owned by the state but have some greater autonomy in decision-making and resource allocation. They can vary local rates of pay and borrow capital within annual financing limits. Prices, however, are regulated by government and reflect the concern that local monopolies would use their power to make excess profits. The "rule" is that prices should equal average cost, so that trusts break even (with a 6% return on capital).

The introduction of GP fund holding. GP fund holders were allocated cash budgets to purchase certain hospital services (mostly elective referrals) and diagnostic tests for their patients, and for prescribing costs. They acted as purchasers of services on behalf of their practice populations, as well as providers of care. Fund holding, like trust status, was introduced cumulatively. GPs could choose to become fund holders or retain non–fund holder status. By 1996, fund holders cared for over half of patients in England and Wales, but the scheme was changed substantially by the incoming Labour government in 1997. Initially, a practice had to have at least 11,000 patients on its list before applying for fund holding status, but this was subsequently reduced.

C. Overview of the 1991 Reforms: Markets and the Need for Regulation

The NHS reforms were introduced as a response to intense political pressure and were designed and implemented with great haste. Competition is a process (or means) by which the health care market can be made more efficient (the end, or objective, of policy). This fundamental concept appears to have been almost lost in the design and implementation of the NHS reforms. The process of reform may have been too hasty to design adequate means of creating and sustaining competition. Indeed, the president of the Royal College of Physicians, Sir Raymond Hoffenberg, suggested that "instead of ready, take aim and fire, the Government chose to make ready, fire and take aim!"

The reforms, as a consequence, contain some policy contradictions and deficiencies. The contracts and prices set by purchasers and providers tend to have been large block contracts allowing expenditure for services to long-standing providers with little attention to the detail of quality and audit. More innovative purchasers are providing a fuller definition of contracts, but their behavior is constrained by lack of information, particularly regarding cost-effectiveness.

The creation and maintenance of an internal market requires improved information systems. It is paradoxical that the NHS market was established before the information upon which it depends was available (Petchey, 1993).

Pricing rules set by central government guidelines (National Health Service Management Executive, 1993) instructed provider units to estimate the short-run average total cost of every set of procedures that may be a transaction in the internal market, and set prices equal to this average cost. This generated an open set of unique prices for transactions and purchasers choose the quantity to purchase. These pricing guidelines have been subject to criticism. Dawson (1994) suggests that there has been a general misunderstanding of the role of prices in the internal market. The emerging internal market in the NHS is not a competitive market, with many suppliers with posted prices and many purchasers. Rather, it is characterized by contestability, small numbers, and high fixed costs, so contracts and prices tend to be negotiated and usually secret. In this type of market, pricing rules set by accountancy procedures are not meaningful. They do not reflect opportunity cost or marginal cost in the short or long run and are not market clearing prices (Dawson, 1994). The accountancy rules used to regulate the market and set pricing guidelines are inappropriate and do not take into consideration the nature of the market being regulated.

Only in late 1994 did government publish competition rules for providers (Department of Health, 1994b). The Department of Health is given the role of prosecutor, judge, and jury in investigating anticompetitive behavior, despite the inherent conflict of interest between the department's role in rationalizing capacity in the NHS and enforcement of competition policy.

The legacy of a "command economy" has largely remained in labor, capital, and product markets in the NHS. Doctors' contracts and remuneration remain centrally determined and very few trusts have sought to vary these terms, despite their freedom to do so. The centralization and rigidity in pay bargaining has meant that incentive structures are inefficient and factor substitution and changes in skill mix are limited. In the United States, managed care firms are making radical changes in skill mix, in particular by developing primary care. Research in the United States suggesting that 30 to 70% of the tasks performed by doctors could be carried out by nurses (saving considerable resources) is not, however, directly transferable to the United Kingdom, where there is already more emphasis on primary care (Richardson and Maynard, 1995). In the United Kingdom, the volume of clinical labor (particularly doctors) is controlled centrally, through a workforce policy determining the entry to medical schools. Following the Calman report (Department of Health, 1993), more hospital consultants have been employed in a move toward a "consultant based service." Attempts have been made to decentralize part of the labor market in health care. Trusts are free to set their own contract terms and pay levels and the Department of Health has strongly encouraged the use of performance related pay (Department of Health,

1994a). This is resisted by trade unions and professional organizations, particularly the British Medical Association.

The potential decentralization of contract and salary terms in the NHS, and the subsequent erosion of central control, creates the risk of cost inflation. Central control of salaries has been one of the most important elements of cost control in the U.K. NHS. The few trusts that have attempted to change contract terms for hospital doctors have found this to be costly, both in terms of offering incentives for changes in contract terms (such as higher pay for accepting short-term contracts rather than ''jobs-for-life'') and in administration costs of drawing up new contracts. In future, trusts may also compete for staff in shortage specialties and this could bid salaries up, increasing overall costs to the NHS. Considerable transaction costs will occur if individual hospitals introduce contracts differing from those previously recommended centrally. Trusts, with no experience in this form of negotiation, may grant considerable wage increases while learning negotiation skills, when confronted by powerful health care trade unions (such as Unison) and professional bodies (such as the British Medical Association). The potential loss of cost control implied by decentralization of contract terms cannot be neglected, and this may be one of the reasons why few trusts have taken the opportunity to change contract and salary terms.

In capital markets, current policies have a cash-limited block of central funds allocated to capital investment in the health service. Trusts and other health care purchasers and providers bid for this capital funding. They are required to submit an option appraisal for evaluation by the Department of Health and the Treasury, and from the bids, priorities are set according to the size of the total budget. To reduce public expenditure, the government is strongly encouraging the use of private capital, similar to the situation in New Zealand, where health service capital investment is financed through the private sector. In November 1992, the Private Finance Initiative was launched throughout the government, to promote and encourage the use of private-sector expertise and capital with the intention of transferring risk to the private sector. The implications of this policy in the United Kingdom depend critically on set ''market'' rules. If the overall amount of funds is cash limited, even when obtained from the private sector, there may be little change in the current situation. If, however, the overall amount is not cash limited, as seems more likely, there may be incentives for hospitals to compete on quality (as measured in terms of process or facilities) rather than on price, causing potential cost inflation. The cost inflation caused by quality competition has been very well illustrated by the experience of the United States (Culyer and Posnett, 1990).

The liberalization of both capital and labor markets, therefore, involves some risks of loss of cost control. In a situation where the overall NHS budget is cash limited, trusts are more likely to turn to the private sector. As health care costs rise, if public expenditure on the NHS is limited, the quantity of services that can be purchased falls. The implied reduction in NHS services may result in a progressive privatization, with individuals more likely to purchase private health care and insurance as rationing devices such as waiting lists increase.

D. Evaluation of the 1991 Internal Market Reforms

The United Kingdom government did not evaluate the 1991 health care reforms, so the ability to identify the strengths and weaknesses of the overall package has been restricted severely. The NHS reforms were an ideologically-based experiment, introduced without information on the impacts of markets or their costs. In 1989, the then-Secretary of State for Health, Kenneth Clarke, freely admitted that he had "no idea" how much the reforms would cost (House of Commons, 1989). It is also very difficult to disentangle the effects of the reforms themselves and the energy and innovation created by them, from simultaneous increases in funding of health care.

Observers have attempted to evaluate the reforms, the King's Fund (Robinson and Le Grand, 1994) as an instance, but this work is limited. Glennerster et al. (1994) reported on GP fund holders, with an optimistic view of the success of the fund holding initiative, concluding that "fund holding is probably one of the few parts of the reforms that is having the competitive efficiency effects on the hospital system that the reformers hoped for" (p. 105). However, this is based on anecdotal evidence from only 17 fund holding practices. It does not include non–fund holders in a comparative study and it neglects the issues of equity that may arise from fund holding. Fund holders cover 36% of the United Kingdom population, which still leaves 64% treated by non–fund holding practices. There is marked variation in the purchasing power of fund holders and allocations per patient. It is difficult to measure "quality" of care in general practice using outcome measures, so proxy measures tend to be used. These include the availability of GPs, quality of premises, range of services and use of ancillary staff. Using such measures, the "quality" of primary care in non–fund holding practices is very uneven, which raises problems of equity and public concerns over a "two tier service."

The lack of evaluation of the United Kingdom health care reforms has resulted in ignorance about costs, processes, and outcomes of the internal market. Other countries implementing health care reform should ensure that adequate evaluation mechanisms are in place (using, optimally, well-designed trials or, at least, other designs such as controlled before-and-after studies to identify whether or not reforms are increasing efficiency in the delivery of health care).

A market is a network of buyers and sellers and these parties may contract to exchange in the public or private domain. It is a means to an end (in the case of health care markets, the end or objective should be the efficient delivery of health care). Without regulation, markets in health care do not lead to efficiency; wherever they occur worldwide, they are regulated. There are numerous imperfections in health care markets that prevent them clearing efficiently and also prevent implementation of equitable health care policies. Regulation of markets is essential and this is recognized in health care systems that are based on a free market (e.g., Ellwood et al., 1992) and in those dominated by the public sector. The use of market reforms in an attempt to improve efficiency in health care is an ideological experiment. It is not based on any sound evidence indicating efficiency gains (Enthoven, 1991; Maynard, 1993).

E. Developments Since 1997: The "New NHS"

The Conservative government was defeated by Blair's Labour Party in the 1997 election and there was considerable public confidence in Labour's ability to improve the NHS. The new government, however, had ill-defined policies prior to its election, except for its "rejection" of Thatcher's market reforms.

The first structural reorganization by Labour was announced in November and December 1997 and was characterized by the rhetoric of rejection of Thatcher's reforms combined with the reality of their modification and extension. These new reforms replaced "competition" with "collaboration" when most agree that generally exchange relationships between purchasers and providers combine competition (in the selection of trading partners) and collaboration (in working with the trading partner to ensure cost control, quality, and timeliness).

Labour retained the purchaser-provider split and contracts, in principle for a three-year term, but in fact remaining the product of annual bargaining rounds. It has altered the purchaser structures by cumulatively replacing the Health Authorities with smaller Primary Care Trusts (PCTs), which will in future hold the whole cash limited budget (for primary and secondary care) for a population of 100,000–150,000 in different geographical locations.

The rhetoric of Labour included the abolition of the failed GP fund holders of Thatcher, which covered 50% of the population in England in 1997. However, the Primary Care Groups and trusts that replaced fund holding are a form of compulsory and comprehensive GP fund holding, although the incentive structures in terms of inducing economy are less evident.

In essence, Labour retained Thatcher's reforms, but elaborated them significantly, particularly in the area of "quality." The National Institute for Clinical Excellence (NICE) was created following governmental and academic discussion (Maynard and Bloor, 1997), its purpose to evaluate the clinical and cost effectiveness of new technologies, and "set standards" for NHS care. Its performance has been controversial, and it has tended to approve at least partial NHS use of most of the pharmaceutical and other technologies, and rejected or limited relatively few. Once approved by NICE, the combined effects of advice, provider advocacy, and patient group lobbying makes wide adoption of new technology inevitable, whatever its relative incremental cost-effectiveness. Thus, NICE's advocacy of marginally cost-effective products can distort the efficiency of resource allocation in the NHS toward newly introduced technology, at the expense of investment in superior and well-established technologies such as hip replacements and cataract removals.

The second substantial area of reform has focused on practitioner performance. A series of disastrous cases involving poor practice and the death of hospital surgical patients, together with the activities of a serial-killer general practitioner, who may have killed 200 patients by lethal injection, has created a debate similar to that concerning medical errors in the United States (IOM, 1999). This has led to the creation of the Commission for Health Improvement (CHI), which visits and reviews the performance of hospitals, and the National Patient Safety Agency, which aims to log and report all failures, mistakes, errors, and "near-misses" across the health service. In addition, the General Medical Council is developing systems of regular reaccreditation and retraining of medical professionals.

These developments, which Labour calls "clinical governance," are systems of better risk management and appraisal of clinical practice. It is essential that these efforts are informed by the evidence base on cost-effectiveness, but, as ever, "medical experts" rather than evidence tend to dominate.

The Labour reform targets set in 2000 (Department of Health, 2000) and its "modernization" agenda are very ambitious. For example, they aim to reduce all inpatient waiting times to less than six months, which will require considerable development of currently inadequate systems to manage patient and GP demand. After adhering to the previous government's parsimonious expenditure plans for two years, more recently Labour has pledged to increase public expenditure on the NHS by 6.5% per annum in real terms. The effects of this significant funding may be dissipated by "shortages" of doctors and nurses and an inadequate bed stock reduced by over-optimistic planners during the last decade.

Labour was re-elected in 2001 with onerous obligations to reform the public services. One of its most difficult challenges is to improve efficiency in the NHS. Mere restructuring of the service is unlikely to be the core of any reforms, as such "redisorganization" has produced little in the past. Increased efficiency in the NHS can only come with better measurement, particularly of outcomes, and evidence-based incentive systems, which alter the behavior of key decision-makers, especially physicians.

V. THE EVIDENCE BASE FOR HEALTH CARE PROVISION IN THE UNITED KINGDOM

Certain central characteristics of health care are often ignored. The majority of interventions in use today have no scientific base. In 1991, the editor of the BMJ noted that a health care conference in the United Kingdom had been told that "only about 15% of medical interventions are supported by solid scientific evidence" (Smith, 1991b). A more recent study (Ellis et al., 1995) suggests that this pessimism is misplaced, after analyzing the evidence of effectiveness of patients treated in one general medical team. The authors studied the treatments given to 109 patients managed during one month, looking for evidence that the treatments were effective, and found that 82% were evidence based (i.e., there was support from randomized controlled trials [53%] or unanimity on the team about the existence of convincing non-experimental evidence [29%]) (Ellis et al., 1995). This study has, however, been widely criticized owing to problems of generalizability and the broad definition of "scientific evidence" it used. The aura of science as an attribute of medicine is well established but unsubstantiated. The costs and effects of most interventions are unknown. Decision-makers (clinical and managerial) do not know which interventions "work." Cochrane (1972) highlighted this problem and apparently little has changed:

> Allocation of funds and facilities are nearly always based on the opinions of senior consultants, but, more and more, requests for additional facilities will have to be based on detailed arguments with "hard evidence" as to the gain to be expected from the patient's angle and the cost. Few can possibly object to this.

Clinical choices are often ill informed, made under great uncertainty and, as a consequence, there are large variations in clinical practice. Clinicians tend to confuse experience with evidence.

What evidence there is about effectiveness and cost-effectiveness tends to be ignored. Behavior of clinical decision-makers is difficult to change, even when evidence exists. Thus, incentives are of central importance. Unproven regulation may create worse incentives.

These characteristics of health care are by no means unique to the United Kingdom health care system. Variations exist in all health care markets and are generally ignored by both policymakers and health care managers. For example, Wennburg et al. (1984) illustrated systematic variation for a number of causes of admission among 30 hospital market areas in Maine. This showed variations in admission rates of over eight and a half times in certain medical and surgical interventions. Some of the medical conditions with the highest variation included chest pain, chronic obstructive lung disease, and hypertension. Surgical conditions with the highest variation included knee, transurethral and extraocular operations, breast biopsy, dilatation and curettage, and tonsillectomy. Similar variations have been identified in Britain and mainland Europe (McPherson, 1989).

Clinicians, wherever they are located in these distributions of practice, assert that their practices are appropriate and this is difficult to counter because of the general ignorance about "what works" in clinical practice. There is an urgent need for good-quality data about the effectiveness and cost-effectiveness of health care interventions. There are relatively few well-designed randomized controlled trials (RCTs) in any therapeutic area. One example in the United Kingdom is rehabilitation services, for which effectiveness is very poor. It may be difficult to establish RCTs in the rehabilitation field because such trials require that certain individuals be assigned to a no-treatment option, but this assumes that rehabilitation is currently available, which is not always the case. Also, where treatment is provided there is often a presumption, rather than any strong evidence, that it is having a positive effect. For example, stroke and severely brain-injured patients will usually make some sort of recovery, and it is important to separate this "standard" recovery from subsequent gains that may be due to rehabilitation (McKenna et al., 1992). In addition, RCTs may apply only to the specific sub-group of a population that is in the trial, and there are frequent problems of generalizing the results of such trials to normal clinical practice.

As a result of this lack of RCTs, there tends to be an over-reliance in many therapeutic areas on the results of consensus conferences and the opinions of expert panels. Former Israeli foreign minister Abba Eban remarked, "Consensus means that lots of people say collectively what nobody believes individually!" Attempts to use these "expert panels" to define appropriateness guidelines to evaluate clinical practice are fraught with difficulty, as much of the material on clinical guidelines is process- rather than outcome-oriented. Clinical guidelines are generally insufficiently based on good evidence and there is also a severe lack of economic input into the development of clinical guidelines (Effective Health Care, 1994). As the American physician Feinstein (1988) remarked: "The agreement of experts has been the traditional source of all the errors through medical history."

There is also a need for information about cost-effective ways of changing provider behavior. For example, the use of expert panels to determine appropriateness in angiography and coronary bypass practices in the Trent region of England resulted in the following conclusions: "inappropriate care, even in the face of waiting lists, is a significant problem in Trent. In particular, by the standards of the UK panel, one half of coronary angiographs were performed for equivocal or inappropriate reasons and two fifths of CABGs were performed for similar reasons. Even by the more liberal United States criteria, the ratings were 29% equivocal or inappropriate for clinical angiography and 33% equivocal or inappropriate for CABG" (Bernstein et al., 1993, p. 8). However, can such strong conclusions be supported when cost-effectiveness is poor and much of the appropriateness definitions are based on expert judgements and consensus?

The problem of inadequate evidence upon which to base health care choices is twofold. In many therapeutic areas, the volume of research is inadequate. In this case, decisions tend to be made on a basis of judgement that is not informed by adequate research. Decision-makers are likely to be influenced by enthusiasts and blinded to the inadequacies of the evidence base.

Even when the volume of research is sufficient, the quality of evidence must be carefully monitored. Altman (1994) stated "huge sums of money are spent annually on research that is seriously flawed through the use of inappropriate designs, unrepresentative samples, small samples, incorrect methods of analysis and faulty interpretation" (p. 283). The reasons for this include pressure upon doctors in the United Kingdom and elsewhere to publish research to advance their careers, inadequate review of proposed studies, and the insufficient use of statistical referees by medical journals (Altman, 1994). This can result in inadequate and biased results being published in peer reviewed journals. "Data torture" is not new. Bailar (1976) argued "there may be a greater danger to public welfare from statistical dishonesty than from almost any other form of dishonesty" (p. 120). The practice of clinical trials has developed in recent years and many sets of criteria to measure the quality of trials have also been developed. Guidelines have been developed to encourage good practice in economic evaluations. In Australia, new pharmaceutical products must be demonstrated to be cost-effective before they are reimbursed. The United Kingdom government has also published guidelines for the economic evaluation of pharmaceuticals, and requires evidence of cost-effectiveness to be provided to the National Institute for Clinical Excellence. However, the inadequacy of much published research, despite the long-standing availability of good practice guidelines, suggests that "both clinical and economist researchers do not always practice what they preach" (Freemantle and Maynard, 1944, p. 66).

To increase efficiency in health care, it is necessary not only to fund and publish good quality research, but also to implement the results of research, thus changing the behavior of professionals. Currently, even when effectiveness and cost-effectiveness information is available, it is frequently ignored. In England, the rate of dilatation and curettage in young women is around six times that in the United States, and available evidence indicates that this excess brings no clinical benefits at high cost and with risks to patients (Coulter et al., 1993). Children with "glue ear" often undergo surgical interventions unnecessarily, as "watchful waiting" often ensures the children recover from their deafness autonomously in time which avoids the risks of anesthesia and saves resources (Freemantle et al., 1992). High-profile marketing by pharmaceutical companies has meant that to treat depression, doctors prescribe drugs that are without superior efficacy and patient compliance characteristics, but cost up to 30 times as much as existing products (Song et al., 1994).

Changing the behavior of professionals and decision-makers is complex. Attempts to induce knowledge-based behavior from practitioners in all health care specialties encounter resistance to change. Training arrangements for doctors in the United Kingdom tend to be unsystematic and not knowledge based, and remuneration systems can reward inefficient practices rather than cost-effective behavior. While remuneration systems clearly influence behavior, non-financial factors may be more important. Professional activity that is governed by duty, particularly if executed in a knowledge-based manner, may be more cost-effective than the creation of bureaucratic regulation. However, the cost-effectiveness of alternative ways of changing clinical behavior is not well researched.

In summary, the policy background for health care reform in the United Kingdom and elsewhere can be summarized by two points: we do not know which interventions are cost-effective, and we know little about the cost-effectiveness of alternative ways of changing professionals' behavior. Decision making in a world of limited health care resources is determined by opinion and judgement, with all clinicians facing great uncertainties in diagnosis and treatment. Such behavior, implemented with reference to finance activity (e.g., DRGs) and in ignorance of outcomes, is inefficient and unethical: inefficiency in health care deprives patients elsewhere in the system of care from which they could benefit. The major deficiencies in knowledge need to be addressed by research and evaluation if health care policies are to become more efficient and practitioners are to become more accountable.

VI. SUMMARY AND CONCLUSIONS

The United Kingdom NHS has a number of important strengths. It gives universal access to care and its costs are relatively low compared to the health care systems of other developed countries, owing in part to cash-limited central budgeting. It is generally popular with the electorate, and surveys show overall satisfaction with the NHS, despite some dissatisfaction with waiting lists and a public perception of underfunding.

The role of the United Kingdom GP combines providing primary care and acting as a gatekeeper to secondary care. This provides reasonably equitable access to health care for the population and assists in cost containment. As a model, it has been emulated in other countries, including Sweden and U.S. managed care organizations, but as in these countries, the United Kingdom primary care model has been evaluated poorly.

There are, of course, continuing weaknesses in the United Kingdom health care system. There is insufficient knowledge upon which to base health care services and increase efficiency. In the future, if a knowledge based health service is to be created, a considerable amount of research and evaluation is required to identify "what works" in health care (i.e., what is effective) and also the cost-effective ways of altering provider behavior to maximize the amount of health gain achievable using a limited budget.

In addition, an efficient NHS requires further attention to pay and incentive structures, which have been neglected for decades. Pay structures in primary and hospital care remain largely unchanged since 1948, and management of the activity of clinicians has tended to be minimal. The new consultant contract, currently under negotiation, is a challenge to policymakers (to design) and NHS managers (to implement). Similar issues exist in reforming the contract for general practitioners. Without careful design and evaluation, and rigorous management, there is a risk that the new contracts will increase doctors' incomes and NHS costs without any change in NHS activity. Variation in consultant and GP activity is well-established and has been ignored for decades. NHS management is characterized by caution (in particular a reluctance to work well with clinicians, challenging them as necessary) and lack of quantitative analysis. Reform of the contracts must be simple, explicit, and based on expectation of modest initial change. They must also be accompanied by rigorous monitoring and management, using and supplementing available data sources.

The 1991 and subsequent NHS reforms created a lot of enthusiasm and energy, but its effects are difficult to disentangle from the simultaneous increases in funding and preceding changes in management structure (Griffiths, 1983). There is little evidence from the United Kingdom or elsewhere that competition in health care produces improvements in resource allocation. Evaluation is required to identify which of the reforms are increasing efficiency. Competition needs to be used with caution and recognized as a means and not an end in itself. Developments of the NHS since 1997 have focused on regulating the "internal market," leaving a separation of purchasing and provision, but encouraging "quality" in health care by standard setting (by the National Institute for Clinical Excellence and National Service Frameworks), delivering standards, particularly by clinical governance, and monitoring standards, by the Commission for Health Improvement.

It is remarkable how both clinical practice and health policy reform, in the United Kingdom and worldwide, is poorly evaluated. Medical practice varies substantially locally, regionally, and internationally (e.g., patients with similar age and stage of cancer get very different levels of radiotherapy across Europe). For most interventions, the appropriate level of treatment is asserted but not based on cost-effectiveness knowledge.

Health policy analysts, like clinicians, make assertions about competition and other health care reforms that are value rather than knowledge based. Both groups of decision-makers should be more cautious, informing their choices with research rather than relying on unsubstantiated optimism. Better analysis is dependent on the production of improved data and investment, and that is a decision which politicians are reluctant to make. As Campbell argued, when discussing social reform as experimentation meriting evaluation over thirty years ago, there is political vulnerability from knowing the outcome of a reform, and "safety under the cloak of ignorance" (Campbell, 1969).

REFERENCES

Aaron, H. and Schwartz, W. The Painful Prescription: Rationing Hospital Care. Washington, DC: Brookings Institution, 1984.

Altman, D. The scandal of poor medical research. BMJ 308:283–284, 1994.

Andersen, T.F. and Mooney, G., eds. The Challenges of Medical Practice Variations. London: Macmillan, 1990.

Atkin, K. et al. Nurses Count: A National Census of Practice Nurses. University of York: Social Policy Research Unit, 1993.

Bailar, J.C. Bailar's laws of data analysis. Clin Pharmacol Ther 20:113–120, 1976.

Bernstein, S. et al. The appropriateness of the use of cardiovascular procedures: British versus U.S. perspectives. Int J Technol Assess Health Care 9(1):3–10, 1993.

Beveridge, W. Social Insurance and Allied Services. Cmnd 6404. London: HMSO, 1942.

Birch, S. and Maynard, A. The RAWP Review: RAWPing Primary Care; RAWPing the United Kingdom. York: Centre for Health Economics Discussion Paper 19, 1986.

Bloor, K. and Maynard, A. Rewarding Excellence? Consultants' Distinction Awards and the Need for Reform. York: Centre for Health Economics Discussion Paper 100, 1992.

Bloor, K. and Maynard, A. Expenditure During and After the Thatcher Years: Its Growth and Utilisation. York: Centre for Health Economics Discussion Paper 113, 1993.

Bloor, K. and Maynard, A. Equity in Primary Care. York: Centre for Health Economics Discussion Paper 141, 1995.

Campbell, D.T. Reforms as experiments. American Psychologist 24:409–429, 1969.

Carr-Hill, R. et al. Allocating resources to health authorities: a small area analysis of inpatient utilisation. I. Background and methods. BMJ 309:1046–1049, 1994.

Cochrane, A. Effectiveness and Efficiency. London: Nuffield Provincial Hospitals Trust, 1972.

Coulter, A. et al. Diagnostic dilatation and curettage: is it used appropriately? BMJ 306(6872):236–239, 1993.

Culyer, A.J. and Posnett, J.W. Hospital behaviour and competition. In: Culyer, A.J., Maynard, A.K. and Posnett, J.W. Competition in Health Care: Reforming the NHS. London: Macmillan Press, 1990, pp 12–47.

Dawson, D. Costs and Prices in the Internal Market. York: Centre for Health Economics Discussion Paper 115, 1994.

Dawson, D. Regulating Competition in the NHS. York: Centre for Health Economics Discussion Paper 131, 1995.

Department of Health. Caring for People: Community Care in the Next Decade and Beyond. London: HMSO, 1989.

Department of Health. Press Release, 29 June 1994a, 94/301.

Department of Health. Health and Personal Social Services Statistics for England. London: HMSO, 1994c.

Department of Health. The NHS Plan: a plan for investment, a plan for reform. London: HMSO, 2000.

Department of Health. The NHS Plan—proposal for a new approach to the consultant contract. London: HMSO, 2001a.

Department of Health. Rewarding commitment and excellence in the NHS—consultation document—proposals for a new consultant reward scheme. London: HMSO, 2001b.

Department of Health and Social Security. Report of the Resource Allocation Working Party (RAWP). London: HMSO, 1976.

Department of Health and Social Security. Working for Patients. London: HMSO, 1989.

Effective Health Care Bulletin No 8. Implementing Clinical Practice Guidelines: Can Guidelines be Used to Improve Clinical Practice? Leeds: University of Leeds, 1994.

Ellis, J., Mulligan, I., Rowe, J. and Sackett, D.L. Inpatient general medicine is evidence based. Lancet 346:407–410, 1995.

Ellwood, P., Enthoven, A. and Etheridge, L. The Jackson Hole initiatives: a twenty-first century American health care system. Health Econ 1(3):149–68, 1992.

Enthoven, A. Reflections on the Management of the National Health Service. London: Nuffield Provincial Hospitals Trust, 1985.

Feinstein, A. Fraud, distortion, delusion and consensus: the problems of human and natural deception in epidemiology studies. Am J Med 84(3):465–478, 1988.

Freemantle, N. and Maynard, A. Something rotten in the state of clinical and economic evaluations. Health Econ 3(2):63–67, 1994.

Freemantle, N., Long, A., Mason, J., Sheldon, T., Song, F., Watson, P. and Wilson, C. The treatment of persistent glue ear. Effective Health Care 4. Leeds: School of Public Health, 1992.

General Medical Services Committee. General Practice: A British Success. London: GMSC, 1983.

Glennerster, H., Matsaganis, M., Owens, P., and Hancock, S. GP fundholding: wild card or winning hand? In: Robinson, R. and LeGrand, J., eds. Evaluation of the NHS Reforms. London: King's Fund Institute, 1994, pp 74–107.

Griffiths, R. Report of the NHS Management Enquiry. London, HMSO, 1983.

Healthcare 2000. UK Health and Healthcare Services: Challenges and Policy Options. London: Healthcare 2000, 1995.

Hoffmeyer, U. The Economics of Health Reform: A Prototype. London: National Economic Research Associates, 1994.

House of Commons. The NHS Act. London: HMSO, 1946.

House of Commons. Paper 214. London: HMSO, 1989.

House of Commons. National Health Service and Community Care Act. London: HMSO, 1990.

Hsiao, W., Braun, P., Dunn, D. and Becker, E. Resource based relative values. JAMA 260(16):2429–2438, 1988.

Jones, L. In: Core Services Committee. The Core Debater 3. Wellington, NZ: October 1994.

Klein, R. Health care reform: the global search for utopia. BMJ 307(6907):752, 1993.

Marinker, M. Developments in primary care. In: Teeling-Smith, G., ed. A New NHS Act for 1996? London: Office of Health Economics, 1984, pp 17–23.

Maynard, A.K. Performance incentives in general practice. In: Teeling-Smith, G., ed. Health Education and General Practice. London: Office of Health Economics, 1986.

Maynard, A.K. Competition in the UK NHS: mission impossible? Health Policy 23(2): 193–205, 1993.

Maynard, A. and Bloor, K. Reforming the contract of UK consultants. BMJ 3;322(7285): 541–564, 2001.

Maynard, A., Marinker, M. and Pereira Gray, D. The doctor, the patient and their contract. III. Alternative contracts are viable? BMJ 292(6533):1438–1440, 1986.

Maynard, A.K. and Williams, A. Privatisation and the National Health Service. In: Le Grand, J. and Robinson, J., eds. Privatisation and the Welfare State. London: Allen and Unwin, 1984.

McKenna, M., Maynard, A. and Wright, K. Is Rehabilitation Cost Effective? York: Centre for Health Economics Discussion Paper 101, 1992.

McPherson, K. Why do variations occur? In: Andersen, T. and Mooney, G., eds. The Challenge of Medical Practice Variations. London: Macmillan, 1989, pp 16–35.

Monopolies and Mergers Commission. Private Medical Services. Cm 2452, London: HMSO, 1994.

National Health Services Management Executive. Costing for contracting: acute services. FDL (93):51, 1993.

Office of Health Economics. OHE Compendium 2000. London: OHE, 2000.

Office of Population Censuses and Surveys. Morbidity Statistics from General Practice: Fourth National Study, 1991–92. London: HMSO, 1995.

Organisation for Economic Co-operation and Development. OECD Economic Surveys: United Kingdom. Paris: OECD, 1994.

Pereira Gray, D. Personal communication, 1994.

Petchey, R. NHS internal market 1991–2: towards a balance sheet. BMJ 306:699–701, 1993.

Richardson, G. and Maynard, A. Fewer Doctors, More Nurses? A Review of the Knowledge Base of Doctor-Nurse Substitution. York: Centre for Health Economics Discussion Paper 135, 1995.

Robinson, J. and Luft, H. Competition and the cost of hospital care. JAMA 257:3241–3245, 1987.

Robinson, R. and Le Grand, J. Evaluating the NHS Reforms. London: King's Fund Institute, 1994.

Sabin, J. Mind the gap: reflections of an American HMO doctor on the new NHS. BMJ 305(6852):514–516, 1992.

Scott, A. and Maynard, A. Will the New GP Contract Lead to Cost Effective Medical Practice? York: Centre for Health Economics Discussion Paper 82, 1991.

Smith, P., Sheldon, T.A., Carr Hill, R., Hardman, G., Martin, S. and Peacock, S. Allocating resources to health authorities: a small area analysis of inpatient utilisation. II. Results and policy implications. BMJ 309:1050–1054, 1994.

Smith, R. Rationing: the search for sunlight. BMJ 303(6817):1561–1562, 1991a.

Smith, R. Where is the wisdom? The poverty of medical evidence. BMJ 303:798–799, 1991b.

Song, F., Freemantle, N., Sheldon, T.A. et al. Selective serotonin reuptake inhibitors: meta-analysis of efficacy and acceptability. BMJ 306(6889):1367–1373, 1994.

Tengs, T.O. Dying too soon: how cost effectiveness analysis can save lives. In: Jones, L. (ed.). Safe Enough: Managing Risk and Regulation. Vancouver: Fraser Institute, 2000.

Thatcher, M. Speech to the Conservative Party Conference, 1983.

Thatcher, M. The Downing Street Years. London: Harper Collins, 1994.

Treasury. Public Expenditure Analyses to 1995–1996. Cm 2219, London: HMSO, 1993.

Wennburg, J., McPherson, K. and Caper, P. Will payment based on DRGs contain hospital costs? N Eng J Med 311(5):295–300, 1984.

Yates, J. Why Are We Waiting? Oxford: Oxford University Press, 1987.

10
Sweden's Health Care System

Paul Gunnar Kaati
University of Umea, Umea, Sweden

I. INTRODUCTION

The health care organization in the county of Vasterbotten provides health care for 256,000 inhabitants and consists of a total workforce of 20,000 employees including 1100 physicians. There are 35 health care centers, two rehabilitation centers, and three hospitals with a total of 1300 beds. The facilities are modern; most of the health centers were built within the last 20 years.

This northern Swedish county stretches 250 km from south to north and 500 km in the east-west direction. The majority of the population live in the county's coastal region while the large and mountainous western inland, bordering Norway, is sparsely populated. The health status of the population does not differ significantly from that of the Swedish population in general (Fig. 1).

A. Guiding Principles

Why begin with a sketch of a county's health care organization? The main reason is that a unified Swedish health care system does not really exist; what exist are a number of health care organizations organized along county lines. This is made clear by the fundamental principles guiding the health care provision in Sweden as laid down in the Health and Medical Care Act (Westerhäll, 1997). The most important of these principles are the following:

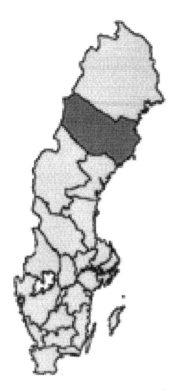

Figure 1   Sweden and county of Västerbotten.

1. Every citizen is entitled to good health care.*
2. The goal of health care is to equitably secure good health and provide good health care to all citizens.†
3. The delivery of health care shall meet the requirements for good care.‡
4. Health care shall be based on the population's need for care.§
5. Every county is responsible for the provision of good health care to its inhabitants. (This obligation also applies to one municipality at present outside the county system.)¶

The fifth postulate is of fundamental importance since it determines the structure of the current Swedish health care system and defines the lines of contention about health care policy. The Health and Medical Care Act assigns, then, the

---

* This is the wording in The Health and Medical Care Act (1982:763), §3.
† §2; it is not the intention of the lawmakers that the goal should be reached by a certain date.
‡ §2a; also a number of specific requirements are enumerated here.
§ §7.
¶ §3; hereafter no mention is made of the municipality but what is said about counties also applies to this municipality.

responsibility for providing health care to 21 regional county governments each of which has set up its own health care organization based on its own interpretation of what health care is and what it should achieve.

B. Implementation of the Guiding Principles

The Swedish health system consists therefore not of one national system, like the English National Health Services, but, at present, of 21 separate, independent health care organizations. In the Swedish constitutional order the counties and municipalities are local-government units (Gustafsson, 1996). As such they are self-governing political subsystems, with their governing bodies being elected in local elections held at the same time as general elections. Counties and municipalities are granted liberal powers of freedom to manage their own affairs within the law, the cornerstone of this freedom being the right to levy taxes.*

The counties and municipalities operate on different levels and have different spheres of responsibility. Municipalities, of which there are 289, operate at the most local level providing a very wide range of services. In comparison, the 20 counties operate across much wider geographical areas and may be considered primarily as special regional government bodies for the provision of health care; 85% of the counties' expenditure is devoted to health care and 88% of county employees work in health care settings (Landstingsförbundet, 1999). Counties vary considerably in size from the smallest county of only 150,000 inhabitants to the largest of 1.8 million (Stockholm County).

In addition to assigning counties responsibility for the provision of health care, the Health and Medical Care Act also delineates goals and guiding principles for the delivery of services. These goals and guidelines are, however, very general and in reality the only restriction on the counties' authority in the health sector is that they must operate within the framework of the existing legislation (Westerhäll, 1997). While the Health and Medical Care Act does proscribe some specific, binding requirements upon the counties, it nevertheless grants them virtually complete freedom in designing their health care systems and adapting them to local conditions and requirements (Sahlin, 2000).

It is not then surprising that the 21 county health care systems differ from one another in several aspects, a "typical" county health care system being perhaps difficult to identify. Recent developments might even suggest that the differences are increasing—for example, in one county the governing political majority has sold one hospital and intends to privatize more or less all health care. However, the majority of the counties exhibit certain similarities in their basic structure as is required by the statutes.

Having established the counties' responsibility for providing health care we can ask: How have the counties met their obligation to secure good health,

---

* Instrument of Government [Regeringsformen (RF), §7].

to provide good health care, and to promote the health of the population in other ways? This question will be answered by focusing on the current functioning and design of the health care system in the county of Vasterbotten and how an intricate set of actors and processes have contributed to the evolution of this system and continue to exert their influence upon it. The description and analysis that follows is structured according to a systems perspective. The systems perspective is used here mainly as a structuring device. Special attention is paid to the goals and objectives, resources, and management of the system. However, the central feature of the descriptive part of this chapter is presentation of the amount and combination of resources and their organization; the goals and objectives are considered as secondary phenomena. Why this is the case will be made clear later.

II. OVERVIEW

Before describing the actual delivery of health care in Sweden it is necessary to discuss basic facts: first, that the historical trajectory leading to the current system has a great bearing on the current functioning and developments, and, second, that the counties are the building blocks of the health care organization; it is at the county level that the health care organization is set up, organized, and put in operation. The actual delivery of health care in the counties is performed on three levels, and for some highly specialized care, at one or two more levels beyond the county.

A. The Historical Dimension

The Swedish Health Care System, in the twentieth century, developed a rather affluent and hospital-based system with a high degree of specialization. Interestingly, the hospital in Umea (the featured city here) was built in 1752. From about 1960 onward doctors inside hospitals outnumbered physicians working outside hospitals. This development has continued despite the national policy prioritizing primary health care.

Since 1970 all hospital-based doctors and the majority of those working outside hospitals are employees and salaried.

Since about two decades ago, however, private practice, private nursing homes, and the contracting out of hospital and nursing homes have all slowly increased. Hospital services are nevertheless nearly all public, as are the majority of the nursing homes and primary care services outside the big cities. Private practices, although privately operated, are in fact included in the counties' planning efforts and funding; private physicians receive insurance-based remuneration with a ceiling imposed upon the number of insurance-reimbursed visits per year.

The private and cooperative sickness funds merged in 1956 into a compulsory National Health Insurance, which is financed by a portion of the wage bill that employers must pay for social security.

Since about 1982 the health services share of GNP has decreased from 9.9% to about 7.4% in 1998. This decrease is mainly attributable to a steady decrease in the number of hospital beds. In political decision making the tendency during the last decade has been to divide the role of government into two parts: the politicians purchase and the management delivers. The most troublesome result of this, according to some observers, has been a shift of power away from political organs. Another tendency has been to use the DRG formula for budgeting. The practical consequence of this has been to increase productivity, measured as the number of visits, while total costs remain unchanged and outcomes are hardly affected.

B. Provision of Health Care in the County

A very basic fact can be stated immediately: in terms of resources, processes, programs, utilization, and outcomes the Vasterbotten system does not differ in any significant way from the other 20 health care systems. The differences that do exist actually put the county in a slightly better-than-average position in a number of respects. However, the ongoing and heated debate concerning the "health care crisis" in both the local and national news media would suggest that the health care delivery systems are in disarray and underfunded. To a certain extent this health care crisis debate can be evaluated by our analysis of the situation in this particular county.

1. The Nature of Health Problems

Since the health care system exists to resolve, or at least control, health problems it is reasonable to ask what the health problems are in the county and how they have been tackled, and to what extent this picture differs from the health problems in Sweden at large and how they in turn have been tackled

Vasterbotten county's (population 256,000) most populated areas are the municipalities of Umea, Skelleftea, and Lycksele, with populations of 90,000, 70,000, and 15,000, respectively. There are an additional 12 smaller municipalities* (Fig. 2).

The Municipality of Umea has been one of the most dynamic parts of the country during the 1990s. Skelleftea, by comparison, is an older industrial region with large rural areas and the Lycksele district is largely rural and mountainous. Both Skelleftea and Lycksele have declining populations.

---

* The municipalities are not "members" of the county; they are only geographically within the county. The county also usually occupies the same physical space as the central government Regional Administrative Region (Län), also with no relation to the counties.

Figure 2 County of Västerbotten.

Rural areas are more common in Vasterbotten than in most of Sweden's other counties.

The demographic profile of the county is favorable for a positive health profile because the proportion of young people aged 0–15 is higher (20.7%) and the proportion of older people lower (16.8%) than national averages. The proportion of elderly in the county's rural areas has been decreasing, lately at an accelerating pace, since the 1960s while the population decline in the municipalities of Skelleftea and Lycksele is a relatively new development.

The health of the county population is comparable to the average health status for the whole country. The average life expectancy in the county is 76.5 years for men and 81.6 years for women and both figures are within tenths of a percent of the national average (EpC, 1999). The rate of infant mortality is at present 0.4/1000, which is the national rate. The number of deaths per 100,000, however, has two significant differences: the rates for injuries and for infectious diseases were higher than the national averages. In terms of disease-specific mortality and disease prevalence and incidence, the average for the county was also significantly higher in respect to hypertension and diseases of the muscular-skeletal organs. All in all, the health status of the population, as measured by the usual measures, does not differ from the national average in any significant way. This should not, however, conceal the fact that there are differences that seem to be slightly increasing in health status between the different parts of the county.

It is remarkable that although all the "objective" measures of health status have continuously improved over the years, the "subjective" health measures point in the opposite direction and the pressures on the health and medical care system have increased. This is made clear from existing data about objective and experienced health (Hur mår Sverige?, 1999).*

2. Goals and Objectives of the County Health System

The county is charged by the Health and Medical Care Act with the task of providing health care that will lead to the accomplishment of "good health," a concept that is not developed or defined in the act. How, then, are the act's goal and the accompanying requirements for good care translated into goals and objectives at the county level? What one would expect to see is the objective of "generating health" operationally defined and acted upon by the county. This is approached in the county's health care plans adopted by the governing assembly. In the plan for 1997–1999 the following objectives are formulated for the planning period:

> Prevention of alcohol and drug abuse
> Prevention of ill health in general as well as in particular high-risk groups
> Improvement of patient access to health services and improvement of health status through the dissemination of knowledge and information
> Access to primary care physicians on the same day as the need arises (Landstingplaner, 1997)

In the revised plan for the period 2000–2002 these goals are not mentioned and appear to have been supplanted by the following goals: to provide care according to need, to equalize health status between social groups, to improve the

---

* Hur mår Sverige? Version 4.3, 1999 (How are you Sweden?) is a statistical database published by the National Board of Health and Welfare and contains more than 1000 variables describing the social and health conditions of the population of Sweden. All data reported in this chapter about health conditions as well as medical care utilization are based on this database.

patients' position in medical encounters, to improve the accessibility of health care, and to provide good care for older people, children, and youths (Plan, 1999).

The goals and objectives in the plan, then, do not make it entirely obvious what the country health care system is expected to accomplish. The operational characteristics of the system, as well as other developments outlined below, make it increasingly evident that the primary goal of the system is to provide *medical care*.* Although this is not a particularly revealing insight, it does underscore the fact that the real focus of the county's efforts appears to be to concentrate on *medical care* as opposed to goals that put emphasis on *good health* (Evans et al., 1994). The county's policy may, in fact, be described as a *medical care policy* and only to a minor extent a *health policy* in the sense this concept is normally used (Evans et al., 1994). This has a number of consequences that will be discussed later.

At this point an "iron law" of Swedish health care organizations can be introduced: The existing pattern of the institutional structure is extremely difficult to change. As will be made clear later, this pattern is to a large extent the product of decisions and actions taken over many decades in other circumstances than those prevailing today, political and administrative decisions that, in principle, consisted simply in reacting to the proposals of the medical professions. Nevertheless, the existing setup with a geographical structure of institutions is found to be very difficult to change, thus practically ruling out radical system changes or changes in the geographical distribution of structures.

The current planning process and the problems of planning are discussed later.

3.   County Health Care Resources

With the nature and size of the "problems" and the goals and objectives related to the problems defined, the resources available to tackle the problems or reach the goals can be assessed.

The resources of the county health care system are shown in Table 1.

The net cost for operating the county health care system in 1999 was 3.3 billion SEK (Budget, 2000; Landstingsplaner, 1997–1999).

The actual number of health centers gives a disproportionate picture of the share of resources devoted to primary care, which is in fact less than 20 percent of the county's total net budget, while the personnel share is only about 10 percent. This pattern of resource allocation has changed little over the last 10 years (Landstingplaner, 1992–96). The transfer of patients from hospitals to health care centers that has been occurring over the last few years has not yet resulted in a

---

* By medical care is meant here basically the services provided in hospitals, and other units in what is called here health care, by physicians and physician-answerable professionals, to those seeking care. See also Ewans et al., 1994.

Table 1 Health Care Resources in the County

Facilities		
Health care centers	37	
District hospital	3	
County general hospital	1	
Spa	1	
Neurological rehabilitation center	1	
Personnel		
Total employees	10,500	
Physicans	1,000	
Finances 1999		
Operating budget (net), allocated to	3,310	MSEK[a]
Umeå health district	1,460	MSEK
Skellefteå health district	952	MSEK
Lycksele health district	646	MSEK
Revenues 1999		
Taxes	2,500	MSEK
Government grant	800	MSEK

[a] Million SEK.
Source: Landstingsplan, 2000.

reallocation of resources and the gap between rhetoric and reality has therefore widened during this period. There are, however, plans currently underway regarding additional allocations to the primary care sector.*

The number of physicians per 1000 is comparatively high by international standards, as is also the case with nurses and other health care personnel. The material resources, facilities, and equipment are at the same level as in other county systems. The same applies to personnel. Comparing this level of resources with the 29 OECD countries shows that the level of resources is above average for the OECD countries (OECD Health Data, 1999).

The resources are organized to provide a structured system with different levels of care: The entry, or primary care, level is supposed to provide undifferentiated access at the grassroots level to the system; at the next level, the secondary care level, specialized care at a general district hospital is provided; and at the third, or county, level highly specialized care is provided. The primary and district hospital levels of care are provided in each of the three district systems of Skelleftea, Lycksele, and Umea (Fig. 3).

---

* A new national plan for health care issued by the government in June 2000 put heavy emphasis on primary care (see Regeringens Prop. 1999/2000:149, the government's proposal).

Umeå Health Care		Skellefteå Health Care		Lycksele Health Care	
Population	137,000	Population	80,000	Population	42,000
Health Care Center	16	Health Care Center	13	Health Care Center	7
Hospital	1	Hospital	1	Hospital	1
Personnel	6,000	Personnel	1,700	Personnel	900
of which Physicians	750	of which Physicians	200	of which Physicians	100
Operating expenses		Operating expenses		Operating expenses	
Net operating budget	1,460 MSEK	Net operating budget	952 MSEK	Net operating budget	646 MSEK

Figure 3   The health care districts, 1999.

Each district hospital may refer patients who require more specialized care to the most specialized level at the county general hospital. The county hospital basically serves as a referral center for patients requiring more specialized care than can be provided at district levels but it is also possible to be referred to the county hospital directly from a health care center.

4. Political Government of Health Care

As a public system, financed mainly through taxes, it is the elected political representatives in the county's governing body who have the ultimate responsibility for the provision of health care to the inhabitants of the county. It is the task of the political governing body to formulates goals and policies, to acquire the resources necessary to accomplish the goals, and to monitor the implementation of its policies and decisions. As political systems the counties and municipalities are rather unique organizations, which calls for a brief review of their most important characteristics as they bear on the provision of health care (Holmberg and Stjernquist, 1998). The basic premises that govern the constitutional standing of municipalities (*kommuner*) and counties (*landsting*) in general and their self-governing status in particular are outlined in the law of municipalities (Holmberg and Stjernqusti, 1998). As mentioned earlier, the difference between municipalities and counties relates basically to the scope of their tasks and to their geographical coverage. They operate on different levels and have responsibility for different public policy areas.

In the division of public responsibilities the municipalities or primary local governments, of which there are 289, are assigned a wide range of services, including schooling up to secondary level, social services, public health, and the social and health care of the elderly. The counties, or secondary local governments, on the other hand, have a more narrow focus in that their basic responsibilities revolve around the provision of health and medical care. Currently, around 85% of their budgets are devoted to health care.

The counties serve a wider geographical area than the municipalities and in most cases territorially correspond to the central government's administrative regions (*län*) although the counties have no connection either to the central government's regional administrative regions or to the municipalities.

The fundamental pillar upon which the power of counties and municipalities rests is their constitutional right to levy the county and municipal tax on those living in the county and municipality. This fundamental entitlement gives the local governments their freedom of action. Historically it has meant that the expenditure for health care has not had to compete for attention at the national level with other expenditure areas and could therefore grow rather unrestrictedly up until the early 1990s at which time the central government imposed some penalty measures, which in reality meant a cap on tax levels (Fig. 4).

The power of the people (the electorate) is lodged in the elected county council, known as the county council or parliament (*landsting*). The county governing board (*landstingsstyrelsen*) wields the executive power.

Ultimately it is the county's elected assembly that is responsible for seeing that those living in the county are provided with necessary health care, to secure the resources needed to finance the system, to allocate those resources, to adopt policy, to accomplish the goals and objectives adopted, and to assess what is accomplished. The delivery organization is the manifest expression of the political will to provide that care.

The majority political party, or the parties that can form a majority, in elected county general assembly forms the county government, that is, takes charge of the system. At present the governing coalitions are almost always either

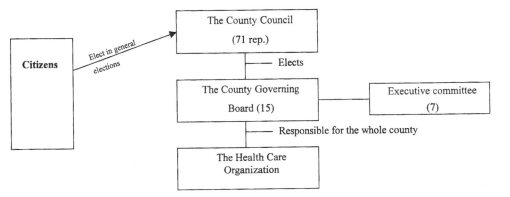

Figure 4   The political organization of the county.

a social-democratic-left or a conservative-liberal coalition. The most characteristic point of contention between these two blocks is their position in regard to privatization of health care. The conservative-led coalitions strongly argue for and, at present in two of the largest counties, actively press for privatization of health care.* Since the conservative-led majority coalitions strongly opposed tax increases, the only alternative route for them to financing health care is downsizing and privatization. Interestingly, the private providers will be paid from the county treasury, so this form of Swedish private health care is a safe haven for the private providers in that they are more or less guaranteed a profit independent of how the system will work.

5. Management of the County Health Care Organization

In charge of the delivery organization is the county general manager, who serves as the chief executive officer of the county and reports to the county governing board.† The district organizations are headed by district general managers, who, in turn, report to the county general manager. The managers are public servants and are ultimately responsible to the democratically elected decision-making bodies.

This partial picture of how the system is managed gives at least a formal picture of how the county system is steered (Morgan, 1997).

6. Total Expenditures and Revenues

Calculating the total amount of health care expenditure is a complicated process. For instance, it is, not always obvious what is and what should be include in health care. The health care expenditures for the counties are calculated in two different ways: as total costs and as the net costs for counties (Table 2).

The total health care costs in 1998 amounted to 139 billion SEK, or 17,700 SEK per person, 7.4% of the GNP. Of this, 20.6 billion SEK involved private consumption (payment of drugs, other medical articles, eyeglasses, patient charges), 112 billion SEK went to public consumption (minus patient charges), 4.6 billion SEK was directed toward investments, while subventions for pharmaceutics amounted to 12.5 billion SEK and reimbursement to private physicians and dentists totaled 9.7 billion SEK (Hälso och sjukvårdsstatiskt årsbok, 1999).

---

* Both the conservative party's and the liberal party's dominating value premises are distinctly neoliberal in that privatization as well as tax cuts are ends in themselves. In fairness it must be mentioned that even the social democrats in several counties actively pursue privatization of certain programs but not generally; even here the value premises seem to be neoliberal ideas.
† The executive committee or government of the county.

Table 2 Health Care Costs

		Consumption and investment in health care		Total cost of health care		
	GNP at market price	Total SEK	% of BNP	Total SEK	Cost per person, SEK	% of BNP
1985	866,601	70,416	8.13	76,708	9,180	89
1994	1,531,102	96,864	6.33	112,983	12,920	7.4
1998	1,873,000	112,000	6.33	13,000	15,700	

Source: Hälso- och sjukvårdsstatistisk årsbok, 2000.

The counties report their net costs for health care for 1998 at 93.5 billion SEK (Statistisk Årsbok för Landsting, 1998) of which 64% was for the provision of acute somatic hospital care, 12% for psychiatric care, and 17% for primary care. To this total net cost should be added 4 billion SEK that the counties invested in health care facilities and equipment.

Other costs of health care are the cost that municipalities bear for the burden of providing long-term care to the frail and elderly. At present the municipalities operate 500 nursing homes with 38,000 beds. Municipal expenditure on nursing home health care for the elderly can only be expected to steadily increase as the population continues to age.

The Swedish Health Care system is primarily funded through a combination of county income taxes, central government transfers, and patient fees and premiums. Approximately 72% of the counties' incomes are generated from taxes collected, 13% from grants awarded via the central government, 3.4% from patient fees, 1.7% from Social Security, and the remainder from fees and transfers and from services rendered to other counties.

7. What Is Purchased and How Expenditures Reach Providers

The planning process starts after the county council has presented its planning directives for the coming years. These directives present the economic conditions from a short-term perspective and are generated according to historical records of income and expenditure streams. Such historical documentation serves to outline the various budget options to be considered, as well as suggesting the implications of expenditure and taxation decisions over both the short and long term. The planning processes at the district level and at the clinic/departmental levels is similarly based upon historical and projected spending trends. (See Table 3.)

Table 3 Health Care Resources 1998

	1985	1998
Primary care sector		
Health care center 906		
No. of employees 35,000		
General Practitioners 3,100		
Visits per 1,000	1,079	1,377
Hospital care		
Hospitals:		
district hospitals, county general hospitals, regional hospital 79		
No. of beds	79,130	32,978
Beds per/1000 individuals	9.5	3.8
Inpatient admissions		1,603,104
No. of inpatient days/year		11,398,200
No. of patient days/1,000 inhabitants		1,289
Activities (total)		
Visits to physician (in 1,000s)	19,505	21,050
Primary care	46%	56%
Visits to physician/1,000 inhabitants	2,334	2,469[a]
Visits to private physician		6,068
Health situation in Sweden		
Infant mortality rate	6.8	3.8
Average length of life, men, years	74.0	76.5
Average length of life, women, years	80.0	81.6

[a] Including visits to private general practitioners.

Source: Basårsstatistik 2000 (Statistical Yearbook for Countries 2000).

Ultimately, the council formally decides how it will allocate its budget, moves to implement this budget, and almost immediately begins planning for the next budget cycle. While it is beyond the scope of this chapter to comment broadly upon the eventual outcome of this budget process in terms of overall national health status, let it suffice to say that, based upon a number of key indicators, the health status of the general population is very good (OECD, 1999).*

---

* This data set contains data from all OECD countries; the number of variables included is large. Among health status variables included are: life expectancy, potential life years lost, premature mortality, morbidity, and perceived health status. In terms of these variables the health status in Sweden is very good.

III. THE DELIVERY OF HEALTH CARE

A. Provision of Health Care at the Local or District Level

What probably matters most to the ordinary citizen at the grassroots level when in need of health care services is prompt access to a physician or another health care worker most capable of diagnosing and treating his or her particular ailment. How well does primary health care meet the challenge of this problem? One approach to answering this question is to consider the workings of primary care in Umea through the eyes of a typical patient, Sven Andersson, a secondary school teacher, who one morning feels that he ought to consult a physician. Mr. Andersson lives in the Alidhem community in the Eastern part of the city of Umea. Alidhem is a mixed community in terms of population and housing (Umea kommun, 1999). It is close to the university campus and the hospital, which is reflected in the demography and mix of nationalities living in the community. Today (1999) the population of the Alidhem community is 15,000. A health care center, a primary school, and a mall occupy the most prominent places in the heart of the community.

When Mr. Andersson decides that he has to consult a doctor for his persistent flu, he would probably not even consider turning to a private practitioner. The natural thing for him is to approach the nearby health care center. Should he consider a private practitioner he would soon realize that there are no private practitioners in his community and very few in the whole city. Mr. Andersson either phones the center to book an appointment or comes in during the center's open surgery hours.*

If he needed immediate attention as in case of emergency, the hospital's emergency department is just a few minutes away. (See Fig. 5).

Mr. Andersson has easy access to all basic health care at the health center in his community and to almost all imaginable secondary and tertiary care at the hospital just a short distance away, paying only a nominal charge at the point of delivery.†

Given the scenario described above, one might be tempted to assume that this community is exceptionally well endowed with health care resources but individuals in other parts of the county have the same access to basic, i.e., primary and secondary, health care resources as those persons living in Alidhem. They do not, of course, have a university hospital nearby, but the level and quality of the secondary care provided at the hospitals elsewhere in the county is on the whole on par with the level of care provided in Umea.

---

* He can of course approach another health care center if he prefers.

† At present (Jan. 1, 2000) he pays 100 SEK for a visit to health center, 200 SEK for a visit to an outpatient clinic at the hospital, never more than 1000 SEK per year. The exchange rate as of Jan. 1, 2000 was 100 SEK = $12.25.

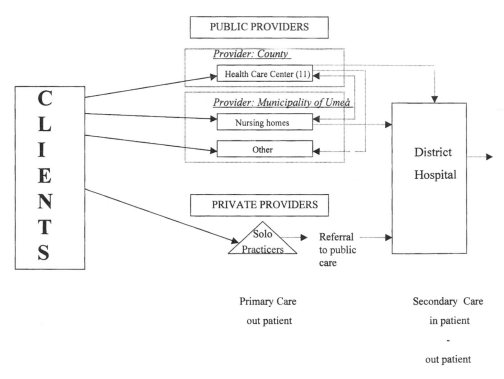

Figure 5 Health care in the city of Umeå.

The health care center in Mr. Andersson's community is, as in the other communities, the central component in a publicly financed and organized health care system. Such centers are thought to be easily accessible entry points to the health care system; only in emergency cases is an individual expected to turn directly to the hospital. This is, however, not how the system works, as will be discussed later.

In the above case the health and medical care in the city of Umea was described but the city of Umea is just one geographical component of the Umea Health Care District. (See Fig. 6).

Health care in Vasterbotten is delivered through three geographically bounded subsystems or delivery organizations called districts. These districts are also political subsystems within the county system although their political position has changed lately, as will be discussed later. They have therefore enjoyed a certain amount of freedom of action within the county system. The three areas of Umea, Lycksele, and Skelleftea exhibit social, economic, political, and cultural

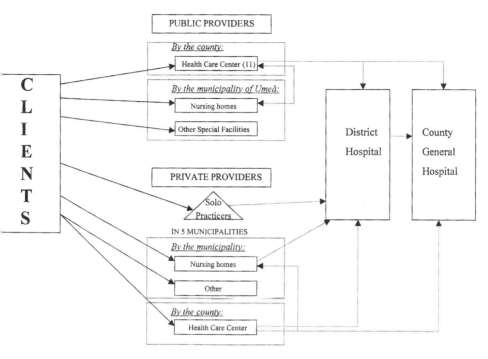

Figure 6 Health care in Umeå health care district.

differences of long standing, which even today impact on the structure and functioning of the county health care system. The early stated "iron" law is especially applicable here.

The structure and function as well as the policy and operating problems of a district are most visible in the Umea Health Care District; therefore, the focus here will be on that district. The Umea Health Care District consists of the municipality or city of Umea and five neighboring municipalities. Of the total population of 137,000, 103,000 live in the municipality of Umea. Geographically the district stretches 150 km from south to north and 70 km from east to west; 45% of the county's population live in this district.

The municipality of Umea is, of course, the major political entity in the Umea health care district. The smaller municipalities within the district have populations ranging from 2800 to 8600. These municipalities are historically old farming and lumbering communities although today these pursuits are of minor importance. Nevertheless, the municipalities in the district are on the whole rather prosperous.

1. Resources

The district of Umea's population of 137,000 is served by 16 health care centers and one district hospital although this hospital differs from the two other district hospitals in the county in terms of its threefold functions as district, county, and regional/university hospital.

Eleven of the 16 health care centers in the district are located in the municipality of Umea, with each of the remaining five municipalities hosting one health center each. The health centers are manned by more than 100 general practitioners and the hospital by more than 700 different specialists.

The amount of resources, both material and immaterial, available in the district is by any comparison very high. To a certain extent it reflects the special character of the district with a hospital performing the functions of county, regional, and university hospital (Table 4).

Comparing the number of physicians per 1000 population across systems suggests that the district is comparatively well staffed with physicians. In 1999 the number of physicians in the district per 1000 individuals was 13. This ratio compares to a county average of almost four physicians per 1000 population, or 240 residents per physician. Interestingly, even this figure is well above the national average of 3.2/1000 (Statistisk Årsbok för Landstinge, 2000), which, in turn, is by international standards very high (OECD, 1999).

The private health care in the area consists of a small number of practitioners, all of them reimbursed from public sources.

Table 4 Health Care Resources in Umeå Health Care District

Facilities	
Health care centers	16
Neurological rehabilitation center	1
Hospital	1
Hospital beds	850
Staff	
Doctors	750
In hospital	650
General practitioners	100
Nurses, assistant nurses	2,700
Private practitioners	
Physicians	18
Physical therapists	15
Total	7,000

Source: Accounting department, NUS.

However, despite these rosy statistics, since 1992 an ongoing downsizing of the hospital has decreased bed utilization from 1500 beds in 1992 to 832 in 1999, a reduction of more than 40%. This has been accompanied by considerable staff reductions, particularly reductions in the number of assistant nurses and nurse aides, while at the same time the numbers of physicians and nurses have continued to increase. (See Fig. 7).

2. Goals and Objectives

It is perhaps not to be expected that the goals and objectives formulated at county level should be directly translated—or even be translatable—into goals and objectives at the district level. As was observed earlier, the goals and objectives formulated at the county level can hardly provide realistic guidance for planning at the district level since they are rather ambiguous, to put it mildly, as providers of direction at the county level. Hence, it is not surprising that at the district level the prime goal adopted is "to provide a health care for the people in the district that is comparable to the highest international standards" (Umea Sjukvård, Plan 1997/2000, 1997). The other goals and objectives adopted in the district's plan deal mostly with internal efficiency issues.

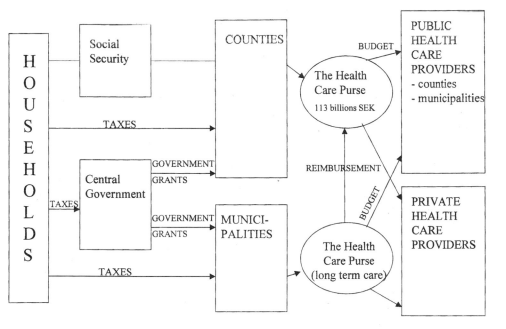

Figure 7 Flow of money in health care.

The structure of the goals and objectives formulated in the district plan is only vaguely related to the actual pattern of services delivered, activities performed, and allocation of resources within the district health care system. On the other hand, it is obvious from the services provided and the activities performed that the goal of the system is simply to provide *medical care services* and to achieve efficiency improvements. Again, this is not a remarkable insight, but it clearly demonstrates, at this level, as was also shown to be the case at the county level, that the relationship between planning documents and the actual operation of the system has been and remains weak or nonexistent.

3. The District System at Work

The district system provides primary health care services as well as some secondary care services; more specialized secondary and tertiary care is provided on the next level of care, that is, the county level at the county hospital, and eventually on the regional level, that is, the regional hospital level.

The Umea district health care organization is of course dominated by the hospital that provides several levels of care:

> as a *district* hospital it provides secondary care to the patients in the district
>
> as *county* hospital it provides specialized secondary care for the entire county
>
> as *regional* hospital it provides highly specialized tertiary care for the population of the four counties that constitute the Northern Health Care Region, with a population of 900,000
>
> as a *teaching/university* hospital it serves the medical school and other medical training programs.

The first two functions are normally performed in all county hospitals. What is special about the Umea hospital is, of course, that it has performed a central role in providing health care to the region for the last 30 years.

Together with its function as a teaching hospital, it has grown to a university hospital that provides comprehensive high-level care, that is, tertiary medical care, for a population of around 920,000. Approximately 20% of the workload of the hospitals can be classified as "regional medical care." However, increasing economic pressures on counties, coupled with changing assumptions of where high-level medical care can be performed, which in turn is a product of medical-technological developments, have for some time exerted significant pressure on the regional hospital. The counties in the health care region (the four northern-most counties) have reduced the number of referrals to the regional level and begun to a certain extent building up high-level resources at their own county hospitals.* The accelerating pace of medical technology innovation has created

---

* This is based on interviews with officials in each county and the county's program plans.

an environment in which district and county hospitals are increasingly undermining the dominance of large hospitals as the sole provider of certain services.

The primary health care sector in the Umea health care district consists of 16 health care centers located in the different communities in the district; seven of the health care centers are within a 10-km radius from the hospital, four more within 25 km. As is to be expected, the dominant position of the hospital affects health care centers in a variety of ways, not all of which are positive. The popular perception of the hospital as the ultimate place for healing and health tends to overshadow the health care centers as places of good care. Especially the centers adjacent to the hospital suffer from this public perception.

It can be concluded that the people living within the boundaries of the Umea health care district have access to almost all conceivable primary, secondary, and tertiary health care services. The exceptions are very few; for example, the care of heavy burn injuries is centralized to the university hospital of Uppsala. Pediatric heart surgery is concentrated at the university hospitals in Lund and Gothenburg, while certain types of transplantation surgery are referred to other university hospitals.

The combined resources of health care centers and the district hospitals are intended to meet most of the health care needs in the districts; needs that cannot be met at the first two district levels are transferred to the county general hospital. The only difference between the Umea health care district and the two other districts is that the district level of care is provided at the county general hospital in Umea.

4. Management of the District Health Care System

The district health care system is headed by a district general manager (DGM). The DGM, in turn, is responsible to the county general manager (CGM), who is in charge of the county health care system.

The hospital and the health care centers are grouped into five divisions* headed by divisional managers (mostly physicians) responsible to the DGM.

The cost of management in the district, and generally in the county and the nation as a whole, is rather moderate. No more than 6–8% of the health care budget is spent on management, although this percentage seems to be on the rise.†

---

* At present five divisions but in practice only three since three divisions are headed by the same manager.

† In this district the number of high-level managers has increased by 6% since 1997. It is notoriously difficult to extract exact figures about the cost of administration, but the figure mentioned seems to be realistic. There are, however, data that show that the cost of administration in primary care has increased by 18% during the last 3 years (Pockettidningen, 1997).

B. Delivery of Care: Primary Health Care

1. The Concept of Primary Care

In Swedish health policy discussions, the concept of primary health care conveys two rather distinct connotations: one, as a broad, comprehensive, health-oriented approach that concerns itself with the whole range of health problems of communities and populations; and, second, as a general practice dealing with routine complaints and illnesses. These two conceptions of primary health care can be seen as endpoints of a continuum (Kaati et al., 1982). Over time the emphasis has changed as the focus in health policy discussions has changed. In actual policy and particularly in the actual working of the system, the reality of primary health care can be described as more like the latter conception; that is, primary health care is basically a set of more or less independent programs the most visible among them the general practitioners' surgery mostly dealing with rather minor illnesses. The programmatic content of primary health care—responsibility for the health of a population within a designated area; delivery of comprehensive health care; work in multiprofessional teams; a broad, humanistic systems view; close links to social services, social security, job rehabilitation, voluntary organizations; and promotion of health*—is not realized in many localities.

The health center was conceived as the basic structure from which the work of primary health care would be conducted. And in the current primary health care organization the health center is indeed the central structure, though only in terms of its being a "container" of different activities.

2. The Health Care Center

Thus the Health Care Center is the basic institutional structure as well as the visible manifestation of primary health care.

In each of the city's 11 communities the health centers provide basic primary health care services. Quite a broad spectrum of services are provided within the centers, including physician surgery, district nurses surgery, mother and child-care surgery, and the visiting activities of the district nurses and midwives as well as by physical and occupational therapists. Of the original intentions, outlined above, that the health care center should be responsible for *the health of the population* within the community, the reality of the centers' role is more accurately described as providing basic medical care services. The health and medical care services provided at the typical health care center are, however, often not delivered in a coordinated manner.

Primary care is defined in the Health and Medical Care Act as "that part of out-patient care which, without restrictions regarding diseases, age, or groups

---

* These are statements published by counties, professional organizations, etc. (see Kaati et al., 1982).

of patients, shall meet the needs of the population of such basic medical treatment, nursing, preventive work and rehabilitation that neither require the medical and technical resources of the hospital nor any other form of special skills'' (Sahlin, 2000; HSL, §5). The act requires that primary care should be accessible to all citizens.

(a) The Resources. A typical health care center serving a community of 10,000–20,000 is staffed by 5–10 general practitioners and 25–30 nursing and allied health professions.* For example, the Alidhem health care population of 15,000 has a staff of 35 including seven general practitioners, nine district nurses, three midwifes, four physical therapists, one occupational therapist, one social worker, and a number of assistant nurses and clerical workers. From time to time there are also internists attached to the center. The physicians working in health care centers are certified specialists with a 5-year specialist training in general practice.

The annual net budget for the health care center is 17 million SEK.

(b) Goals of the Health Center. At the health center level more specific goals and objectives are seldom formulated. As mentioned earlier, the professional association of general practitioners put forward in a policy document that the mission of primary health care in general and of general practitioners in particular should be the promotion of health and the prevention of ill health, but these statements are hardly a reality anywhere. Very little, if any, health promotion or preventive activities are carried out in or from health centers by the general practitioners. So what the general practitioners in general do, though there are of course exceptions but they are few, is to conduct surgery. On the other hand, the district nurses have been very active in preventive work, that being part of their historical mission.

Health care centers provide basic medical services to the population living in the health center service area, which is either a local community or a subdivision of that community. The term ''basic medical services'' refers to medical services that do not require the technical resources of the hospital or the type of special competence that can only be found in hospitals (Socialstyrelsen, 1995).

In the original planning it was estimated that up to 90–95% of all patients should have their needs for care satisfied at the health care center. It is not clear whether the anticipated range of utilization is actually occurring.

---

* If the population of the service area is smaller, the size of the center is accordingly smaller; a center in a community of 3000 is staffed by two physicians. One general practitioner per 1500 population is the target in primary care, as stated in the plan that the government introduced to the Riksdag in June 2000, mentioned above.

(c) Programs in Primary Care. The dominating and the most visible program at the health care center is the general practitioner surgery. At some centers specialist physicians from hospitals schedule surgery and consultations.

Another distinct program in primary care is the so-called "district care" conducted by the district nurses.

The content of the general practitioner surgery is broad although the majority of the visits are for minor or rather trivial ailments (Tierp, 1999). In many health care centers, such as this one, the general practitioners as well as other health professionals work with patients with complex sociomedical problems in teams with members from outside authorities and professions.

The district nurses' "district care" program is of long standing and consists of a mix of activities including medical care in both surgery and patient homes, home nursing, and preventive activities directed toward different groups. District nurses are specially qualified nurses with the right to issue certain types of prescriptions. In fact, the district nurses can be described as the "barefoot doctors" in the Swedish system. The district nurses and midwives also schedule daily surgery hours.

Another program of long standing in primary care is the child-and-mother health care program, which consists of surgery and home visits both during and after pregnancy, followed up by medical care programs in day care centers and in schools. The remarkably low infant mortality rates in Sweden can partly be attributed to these activities (Hur mår Sverige? 1999).

The work at the Alidhem Health Care Center is conducted in teams consisting of a doctor, a district nurse, a midwife, a physical therapist, an occupational therapist, a social worker, and sometimes other allied health practitioners. The teams serve different subcommunities with populations of 2000–4000. However, how the work is organized at the health care centers may differ greatly even from center to center in the same district.

(d) Management. A unit manager leads the health care center. The unit manager is often, but not necessarily, a physician. In the health care center presented here the unit manager is a nurse. Early on, only physicians were allowed to assume the management of the centers. The unit manager reports to an area manager, who leads three to four health care centers, and in turn reports to the divisional manager in the district management team, a rather cumbersome administrative hierarchy that probably will not survive a commonsense evaluation.

C. The Delivery of Care: The District Hospital

Secondary care is delivered in the district by the district hospital. The district hospital's task is to provide most of the secondary care that the population needs; only a small fraction of the patients should be referred to the next level of care.

The district hospital in the health care district of Umea is, as has been outlined, not a very typical district hospital because of its size and various unique functions and roles. To describe a more typical district hospital we have to go to the neighboring district of Skelleftea, which lies 140 km (85 miles) north of Umea.

This district hospital serves a population of 80,000 of whom 75,000 live in the municipality of Skelleftea and 5000 in the nearby municipality of Norsjo. The primary care in the district is delivered from 13 health care centers.

The district hospital provides such health care that requires a degree of specialized knowledge, certification, and equipment not available within health care centers. In the case of a referral from a health care center, it is the responsibility of the referring physician to route the patient either to the district hospital or to the county hospital.

The 270-bed hospital in Skelleftea is a typical example of a district hospital in Sweden both in size and in the number of specialties. The number of employees is 1500 of whom 110 are physicians. As is the case with other hospitals in Sweden, Skelleftea has been through considerable downsizing in recent years and has reduced its bed capacity from 452 beds in 1972 to 270 in 1999. (See Table 5.)

Although small, the hospital is relatively complete, which is due in part to the distance to the regional hospital in Umea. It is a modern, well-equipped hospital with departments of internal medicine, surgery, gynecology, anesthesia, pediatrics, ophthalmology, ENT, psychiatry, rehabilitation, and radiological diagnosis. The radiology department, for example, is equipped with a modern CT scanner, MRI apparatus, a well-equipped angiography laboratory, and well-developed ultrasound facilities.

Owing to subspecialization in recent years, most subspecialties within surgery and medicine are represented. The hospital has video conference facilities and is linked to the pathology and cytology laboratories in Umea for ISDN-transferred microscopic image analysis.

As is the case in Swedish hospitals, the departments, or clinics, as the operative units are called, are headed by a departmental manager, usually a physician.

Table 5 Resources in a District Hospital (Skellefteå)

Number of employees	
Physicians	140
Nurses, assistant nurses, nurses' aides	1,000
Physiotherapists and occupational therapists, social workers	90

Source: Information from personnel department.

He or she heads a management team although the departmental manger is empowered with all decision-making powers.*

D. The Delivery of Care: The County General Hospital

The county general hospital serves the county, as the other county hospitals do, with specialized care that cannot be provided at primary health care or at district levels in the county.

The 26 county general hospitals in Sweden differ from the district hospitals primarily in terms of size and the number of specialties. Until the mid-1990s county hospitals included a number of 1000-plus-bed hospitals. Today, however, a typical county hospital operates 600 beds with a medical staff of 300–600 physicians (Statistisk Årsbok för Landsting, 1999).

The county hospital in Umea is rather unusual since it performs three roles; it is the district hospital for the Umea district, the county hospital for Vasterbotten county, and the regional/university hospital for the Northern Region serving a population of 960,000 inhabitants in the four Northern counties.

The county hospital in Umea operates 850 beds, covering a wide variety of specialities. The workforce consists of 5300 employees of which 750 are physicians. They work in 40 operative units such as departments or clinics, centers, and laboratories each headed by a unit manager with a management team.

E. The Delivery of Care: The Regional Medical Center

The counties are required by law (Sahlin, 2000) to cooperate in the provision of highly specialized care. This is done in regional health care systems, of which there are six. Each region has a regional hospital† providing such high-level care as neurosurgery, thoracic surgery, pediatric surgery, and plastic surgery. For certain types of diseases and injuries there exists an additional ''national level'' of care, in the sense that care is centralized to one or two hospitals. The regional level of health care is financed and governed through a special committee by the participating counties. The smallest region has fewer than one million inhabitants (the Umea region), the largest around two million. Approximately 20% of the activities at the hospital in Umea can be considered to be regional medical care activities.

County and district hospitals are finding themselves under increasing eco-

---

* The district management structure is similar to that in the other district with a district general manager with a management team in charge of all county health care activities in the district. The district manager reports to the county general manager and is a member of the management team for the county.
† At present nine hospitals are designated as regional hospitals and six as university hospitals.

nomic and policy pressure to increase their utilization rates as well as care capacity and to reduce their rate of referrals to the regional level. This pressure also coincides with ongoing medical-technological developments that may drastically change the role and function of hospitals. This phenomenon is most clearly observed in the hypermodern new Sunderby County Hospital in nearby Norrbotten County.

F. Other Health Care Providers at the Local Level

1. The Municipal Health Care System

Although most of the health care in Sweden is provided by the 20 counties,* home-based health care for the elderly, as well as service houses, old-age homes, group dwellings, nursing homes, and the like, are assigned in the Health and Medical Care Act to be the responsibility of the 289 municipalities. The municipalities are also responsible for school health care. (Occupational health care is the responsibility of the labor market organizations.)

Every municipality is obliged to provide health care to the elderly in nursing homes and other forms of accommodation as well as special accommodation for individuals with long-term psychiatric illnesses (Sahlin, 2000; Health and Medical Care Act, §18).

In the municipality of Umea the total number of elderly in special accommodations is 900, of whom 250 are in nursing homes. The operating budget of the municipality of Umea is 4000 million SEK, of which 1400 million is allocated to social services. The care of the elderly costs 525 million SEK, of which 282 million goes to nursing homes (Budget Umea Kommun, 1997). This corresponds to the average municipal cost for nursing home care.

The issue of who is and who should be responsible for the care of elderly has been debated for years and the current division of labor between the two local governments, dating from 1992, is not without problems. It was recently reported that the quality of the care of elderly has deteriorated since 1992. The medical content of the care has decreased, with serious consequences in some cases (Socialstyrelsen, 1997). Factors that seem to have contributed to this crisis are the downsizing of health care in general and of nursing staff in particular. The increasing privatization of nursing homes, where most of the examples of substandard care have been discovered, is also a factor.

G. The Private Health Care Sector

Since the health care system is basically a public funded system and a large sector, it is attractive to corporate interests. The private health care sector is today

---

* And one municipality that at present stands outside the county system.

fairly small and basically financed from the public purse. Today there are 340 private health care units, of which six are hospitals with several specialities. The private hospitals' share of the total acute care was 4.5% in 1998. Of the 340 private health care units most are nursing homes, but most of the private care is outpatient. The total number of privately practicing physicians is around 2500 (Sjukvården i Sverige, 1999). In 1996 1.2 million visits were made to private general practitioners (the total number of visits to primary care was 10.2 million). In addition, another five million visits were made to other forms of private care (Basårsstatistik, 1999).

In Vasterbotten county there are at present 56 private health care providers, all financed by the public purse, i.e., the county council, at a cost of 56 million SEK.

IV. POLITICS, POLICY, AND PLANNING

A. Politics and the Weight of History at the County Level

As is by now clear, each county has considerable freedom to design its care system and formulate its policies independently of other counties and the central government. This is so because the counties operate within the relatively open-ended legal framework of statutes governing health care and the structure and function of local and regional political self-government. The freedom of action given the counties by this loose framework is jealously guarded by the county politicians against any encroachment by the central government.

To change the system is often very difficult since policymaking at the county level is embedded in layers of more or less invisible, but nevertheless real, restrictions. These restrictions stem from the last 150 years of the county's history and have led to a situation where policymaking has as its premise the fact that the current pattern of resource allocation to the three health districts is more or less frozen. Such unwritten restrictions are often not uncommon in "old" institutions such as the county system. This was labeled as the iron law of policymaking in the county.

Another aspect of policymaking at the county level, very much related to the above situation, is the duality of the politicians' role. Policymaking at the county level can be conceived as a theater or stage where the participants often perform two simultaneous roles: that of representing a political party and that of representing an electoral district. In certain issues, such as those not directly concerning care resources in their districts, they act as members of their political parties, whereas on medical care issues, especially regarding allocation of resources, they act as members of a cross-cutting group representing their respective districts. This makes policymaking at this level a rather cumbersome process.

1. Health Care Policy Changes

The last 40 years of development of the county health system can broadly be divided into two stages: (1) the period of unlimited expansion (1960–1990) and (2) the period of retrenchment or downsizing (1990–present).

(a) The Period of Expansion.   During the first period the major thrust of policy was to construct a modern, well-equipped, hospital-based health care system and from about 1970 onward to structure the resources into levels of care:

Primary care, or entry-level care
Hospital care in well-equipped institutions
Specialized secondary care in the county hospital
Tertiary care at the regional hospital level

The economic situation of the counties during this period was extremely good and the annual rate of growth among health care organizations was around 5% per annum (Bygren, 1998). The main thrust of the development was to expand the hospital sector; the general practitioners' part of health care was very minor, though an increased interest in primary care began to emerge.

(b) The Period of Retrenchment and Refocus.   The next period, roughly beginning in the early 1990s, can best be described as a period of retrenchment and refocus involving efforts at

downsizing the hospital sector and upgrading the primary care sector
enacting measures to increase the productivity of health care
centralization of management to the county level
restricting the sphere of democratic influence by transferring power from the political sphere to the management and by shrinking the number of political representatives involved in policy- and decision making especially at the district levels
refocusing policy concerns, in particular shifting the focus away from health promotion and prevention to medical care system issues

2. The Changing Directions of Policy

This new thrust of policy was basically caused by an economic crisis that engulfed the counties in late 1980s. Downsizing the health care systems, especially the hospital system, now become goal number one on the health policy agenda. The targeted reduction of costs, for example, over the period 1995–2000 was around 5% of the allocated budget. Primary care was often perceived as a cheaper form of health care.

The three hospitals in the county have reduced considerably their number of beds and decreased the size of the staff, mostly assistant nurses. However, the numbers of qualified nurses and, even more so, of physicians have continued to grow at an accelerating rate. The growth rate of physicians in 1999 was almost 10%.

The number of physicians in the primary care sector has grown exceptionally but this growth has not occurred by reallocation of resources from the hospital sector.

The county's planning documents have been framed in health policy perspective but the county's actions, at least from mid-1990s onward, have no longer been in rapport with these policy formulations. The actions undertaken by administrative and political decision makers reveal clearly an intention to focus on medical care in a restricted sense and discard programs and institutions that focus on health promotion and preventative medicine. Currently almost all such activities are discarded and the transformation of the health care system into a medical care system has by and large been accomplished.

All in all, this period can be characterized as a continuing retreat from a policy that focused on health goals and concerns toward concentration on medical care in a narrow sense. These changes, which have deeply affected the districts, have exacerbated the historically based antagonisms between the districts.

These currents have to be understood against the history of the county and the political developments occurring over a long time period. Up to the early 1990s the districts were self-sufficient systems with their own local governing bodies for running the district health care systems. The county governing board, the executive board, at the center exercised relatively weak control over the districts. The allocation of resources to districts was largely based upon what can be called an equity principle, which in practice entailed that the Skelleftea and Lycksele districts should be provided with essentially the same resources as those afforded the Umea health district. Consequently, it can asked whether the resources were distributed on the basis of medical need.

It is the county council (the governing assembly or parlament) that formally allocates resources to the districts by adopting the district budget. Typically the council's budget has been somewhat open-ended; the situation, however, has changed during the last 7 years in that the central county politicians and administrators have made determined efforts to centralize policymaking powers to the county level and to introduce a system-wide planning perspective in which all county health care resources (especially the hospitals) are considered as parts of a single system. Currently, it is not at all clear whether this effort will be successful given the historical antagonism among the three communities. The changes accomplished so far are rather modest.

The districts' relatively free-standing status during the period 1950–1990 was not particularly problematic since there was neither a lack of resources nor a pressing need for frugal management. The yearly rate of the growth of resources during this period was in excess of 5% and the only limit on expansion was the lack of manpower, chiefly physicians (Bygren, 1998). From 1990 onward, when the economic situation for this county and other counties changed dramatically, the political and administrative leadership at the county level began downsizing the health care system and withdrawing the policymaking discretion of the districts. The latter is exemplified by the transformation of the district health boards from governing boards into what may be described as consumer contact organs.

The health care districts were up to 1992 governed by district health care boards consisting of politicians; then the health care boards were transformed into ''purchaser boards'' and assigned the responsibility for purchasing health care from the ''producers'' (i.e., those in the public, and private, sector who produce the full range of health care services). The role of the purchaser boards was defined as representing ''consumer'' interests in the procurement of health care services. In effect, the result was a centralization of power.

The local health care boards' political power to supervise district health care was then transferred to a certain extent to the county governing board and to a greater extent to the district manager. Together with the county general manager, the district managers absorbed a considerable amount of power previously held in the hands of politicians in district and county governing boards.

From a strictly democratic perspective, it is a rather remarkable period during which a significant retreat has occurred from democratic government. A centralization of political power into fewer hands has taken place and administrative officials have enjoyed a significant increase in power and authority (Elmbrant, 1997). There is no doubt that the image of management that pervaded this period (and still does among some managers and politicians) was based upon the concept of the ''corporation'' as the organizational model to imitate. Given this perspective, some politicians began to view themselves as managers rather than as elected officials.

Elmbrant (1997) enumerates the ''deficits of democracy'' in local governments during the 1990s. He notes in particular the drastic reduction of citizen representation and the increased concentration of political power among a political elite associated with the administrative class. Ordinary citizens appear to share Elmbrant's view.*

In summary, it can be said that the building blocks of the county's ''modern'' health care system were laid in the last century. The changes and developments that have occurred since then have built upon these foundations. In essence,

---

* Public poll presented in *Aftonbladet*, a national newspaper, Nov. 27, 1997.

what most clearly defines the current health care organization, at the county level, is the historical legacy, clearly discernible today in the relationships between the different parts of the system.

3. Planning at the County Level

The notion that there should be goals and objectives for health care is a rather modern development in Swedish health policy. Goals for health care were first introduced into the Health and Medical Care Act in 1982. Prior to this, legislation concerning health care did not contain any goal statements or formulations (Sahlin, 2000).

Various stakeholder groups, primarily physicians, established priorities by selecting certain areas for attention. Ultimately, the allocation of resources was based more upon the power of professional interest than on a rational goal structure. During the period 1950–1985 the driving force behind the considerable annual growth of hospital care (the primary care sector was not then included in the system) was on the whole the interests of the medical community. The expansion was not directly related to any consideration of general medical needs although it may have coincided with existing and emerging health needs.

Beginning slowly in the late 1960s and particularly with the introduction of the goal paragraph in the Health and Medical Care Act of 1982, attempts at the county level to formulate health care goals and objectives increased. The first countywide health care plan was produced in the early 1980s.

An analysis of these efforts as reflected in county health plans indicates, however, that they had only a marginal impact on the direction of the system (Landstingsplaner, 1985–1997).* It is obvious, as the earlier discussion of the goals and objectives in the county health plans has shown, that the role of goals and objectives in the health and medical care planning is muddled. The goals formulated in the last two county health plans are problematic in a number of respects including the following:

> The definition of the objectives to be accomplished is mostly unclear.
> The interrelationships among the objectives appear not to have been considered or clearly understood.
> Alternative actions or means to accomplish the objectives are not considered.
> Many goals are not particularly relevant to what health care organizations realistically do or may accomplish.
> Performance measures are also generally lacking (Churchman, 1979).

---

* An analysis of the county health plans during this period reveals that they were on the whole documents of good quality but that their role in the policymaking process was minor or nonexistent.

One may hypothesize that the muddled nature of the goal structure in planning is to a certain extent a function of the antagonism between the three health districts. In order to contain conflicts it is necessary to formulate goals so general that all of the political parties and the cross-cutting "district parties" (informal groupings of the elected representatives from different political parties into representatives from a particular district) can accept them. This allows the districts to formulate goals and objectives that are not at all or only marginally related to the goals and objectives of the county's health plan.

One must therefore question whether rational planning is possible in a context where planning has functions other than what we normally conceive of as planning, such as the solution of political conflicts. One question particularly worth asking is whether what is called rational planning and organization is possible at all in the absence of *clear* definitions regarding the objectives to be accomplished (Reeves et al., 1984).

At the county level the most pressing problem today involves achieving a balance between the costs of the health care system and the available financing. The mismatch of demand and financing is particularly frustrating at the county level since the politicians are reluctant to raise the county tax. Consequently, the only way to achieve a balance is to reduce costs (i.e., downsize the system) while improving efficiency. Downsizing has been going on since 1992 and will probably continue into the coming years. The Vasterbotten district system will be pruned by 5% over the next 3 years (Verksamhetsplan, 1997–2000) despite the fact that the county tax was hiked up for the year 2000.

4. Management

What has been badly lacking in the Swedish system for a long time is strong management, particularly at the department or clinic level.* It was only in early 1990 that a concerted effort began to introduce stronger formal management systems in health care. Managers of departments or clinics are now much more conscious of their roles than ever before, especially since their roles have undergone drastic change in the last 10 years or so. Managers at this level are with very few exceptions physicians, meaning that they have seldom received specific education or training in health care management.

B. Politics, Policy, and Planning at the National Level

The focus so far has been on politics, history, policy, and planning at the county level, and although it has been emphasized throughout that it is the counties

---

* One of the largest clinics or departments at the university hospital is internal medicine with a budget of 130 million SEK, 70 physicians, and 350 nurses and other types of health care workers. This clinic clearly demonstrates the need for management at the clinic level.

themselves that formulate and implement their own health policies with considerable independence from central government, there are nevertheless forces at the national level that exert influence on health care policymaking at the county level.

1. The Forces at the National Level

The central government, as ultimately responsible for the provision of health care, attempts, of course, to guide or steer the health care providers through a number of measures such as rules, the dissemination of knowledge, economic measures, research, and training.* Other actors use other measures.

The central national governmental organs—the parliament, the cabinet, and public administrative agencies—form a system for central health care policy development, control, and monitoring. Another policy development system at the national level consists of nongovernmental units. Thus the steering of health care and policy development proceeds on many different levels, each level with its own sets of actors, public as well as nonpublic:

> central government: the parliament and the cabinet
> central public administration
> central nongovernmental organizations
> counties
> municipalities
> local communities

These levels do not, however, stand in hierarchical relationship to one another. The relationships between the levels cannot be described in terms of one level formulating and sometimes deciding while other levels implement or make operational decisions that in one sense or another are derived from higher levels within the system. The relationships between the levels can in one sense be described as a continuing debate. In another sense the relationship can be conceived of as a scenario where the counties are adapting themselves to the loosely sketched design or framework created on the other levels. Alternatively, one may conceive of an even looser process where the different levels and actors join and leave the continuing health care process at different intervals in time. All of these concepts are true and have been true at different periods.

Health care policies and public policies encompassing health care concerns are of course formulated at the national level but their direct influence on health care is less obvious. They may or may not impact upon health care policies at the county level, or impact in certain areas or issues but not in others.

---

* The "SOUs" are a type of "white papers" that are produced by committees appointed by the government. In the health care field a number of such white papers has been published in recent years by the "HSU committee" on health care in the 2000s.

It was noted earlier that the goals for health care and some specific requirements of good health care are stated in the Health and Medical Care Act. The
act is in some ways a centrifugal force encouraging different solutions in different
counties and the differences between the counties' health care systems are in
some areas large and increasing. Even so, forces are clearly visible that encourage
developments leading to increased convergence between the counties.

The Swedish health care system is best viewed as a federation or conglomerate of 21 provincial health care systems. At the county level the health care
system does exist in the sense that systems are usually defined (Churchman,
1979). On the other hand, it is obvious that several actors behave and have be-
haved at the national level as if a unitary system existed that could be manipulated
in certain directions. Furthermore, the county systems sometimes respond or react
to initiatives from the national level as if they were parts of a national system.
There have been and still are attempts at the national level to steer the system,
sometimes successfully, sometimes with no effect at all. The government, of
course, often attempts to push the countries in a certain direction.

We will now identify the key actors at the national level of the health care
system and illustrate how they sometimes succeed in influencing the counties.

(a) Policymaking at the Central Governmental Level. At the central government level four discernible types of policies relate to health:

General health care policy
Economic policies in relation to levels of expenditure
Primarily economic incentive policies introducing incentives or disincen-
    tives in relation to specific health care issues or sectors
Regulatory policies that regulate the behavior of medical personnel and the
    training of health care personnel

Health and medical care or health policy development at this level must
of course acknowledge the premises that the individual counties are solely responsible for implementing policy at the county level. Health care policy development
at the national level therefore assumes a long-term perspective, focusing on
emerging developments and assessing the need for appropriate health care services. A typical example of governmental committees working at this level is
the Health and Medical Care Working Committee (HSU, 2000). Since 1992 this
committee has published 12 reports on topics ranging from the future of the health
care system to the rights of patients, from the need for appropriate quality care
to the resources available for this care. The government was also to present a
national plan for health some time during year 2000.

Economic regulatory policies are probably the measures that have most
impact on the counties and the provision of health care. This is illustrated by the
government's agreement with the Federation of County Councils on caps on the

counties tax levels, and regulations on how block grants to the counties are to be designed and implemented.

Primarily economic incentive policies are formulated to change the utilization of services and resources. The government provides special grants to the counties under certain conditions to reduce waiting lists for procedures such as hip replacements or cataract operations. At present (2000) talks are in progress between the government, the Federation of County Councils, and the Federation of Municipalities about, among other things, the expansion of primary care.

With regard to policies directed toward regulating the training of health care personnel, the practice of medicine, the physician-patient relationship, and disciplinary responsibilities, the system for exercising medical discipline is rather unique and differs radically from the American approach (Westerhäll, 1997). It is a system at the national level empowered to review and take action on complaints lodged by different actors against doctors and other types of health care personnel.

(b) The Role of Central Public Administrative Agencies.   In the Swedish governmental system public administrative authorities perform very important roles since they are empowered to independently implement the decisions of the government (Peterson, 1992). The central administrative agency in the field of health care is the National Board of Health and Social Welfare (SoS), which plays an interesting role in this context. SoS is charged with the responsibility for monitoring changes and developments in health and health care, advising the government about these developments, and supervising and monitoring health care personnel and health care organizations. In the latter capacity SoS has the authority to close down, with immediate effect, health care organizations or programs that do not perform according to quality standards (Sahlin, 2000).

There are also a number of other central administrative agencies influencing either directly or indirectly policy development and control functions in health care. Particularly relevant among these is the government agency that oversees universities and their training programs.

(c) The Role of Nongovernmental Organizations.   Two nongovernmental organizations are especially notable since they tend to pull in a common direction and have exerted considerable influence on long-term policy planning and the day-to-day functioning of the health care system. These are the Swedish Federation of County Councils (SFCC) and the Swedish Planning and Rationalization Institute (SPRI). The SFCC represents the governmental, professional, and employer-related interests of the counties. The Federation is the central employers' organization for the counties and is in other words an "employers" union and has no authority in the formal system of governance of the counties.

The SPRI was a planning and rationalization institute for health services that was jointly financed by the government and the counties and exerted its influence primarily through the generation, collection, and dissemination of information to the counties. In this respect SPRI served as a force of uniformity, at least in relation to the small and midsized counties that lacked operational research capacity of their own. The SPRI was, however, dismantled at the end of 1999.

(d) Private Interests. It ought to not come as a surprise that private interests ranging from the medical supply and pharmaceutical industry, and organizations representing different professions, to more general private-enterprise organizations play an active part in trying to shape both the direction and the content of medical care at all levels.

C. How Policy Is Formulated: A Case Study

As an example of how "policy" is formulated at the central level among some public organizations the following may be of interest. In 1968 the SoS and SPRI published a model (Socialstyrelsen, 1995) that has exerted an enduring influence upon the structure of Swedish health care. In this model, the health care system is structured into several levels of care, beginning with primary care as the single, undifferentiated entry point and secondary and tertiary care as referral levels. In this model primary care was elevated to a central position in the health care system, thus in practice necessitating a reallocation of resource from hospitals to the new primary care system. As has been discussed, this reallocation of resources from secondary to primary care did not materialize.

At this point it is important to remind the reader of the considerable independence that counties have enjoyed in relation to the central government. The counties and municipalities also wield considerable power and influence within the *riksdag* (the parliament). This influence is informally referred to as the "counties and municipalities party" and consists of parliamentarians from all political parties with close relations to their particular counties and municipalities. This picture of power brokering at the national level has to be extended if one is to fully appreciate who really decides what in health care, who really influences the development of health care policy, and where and by whom health care policy is ultimately formulated. Admittedly, it is rather difficult to pinpoint these decision-making processes, especially who decides what, when, and in what contexts. So far, very little research has been done about who actually influences Swedish health care policy processes and with what results. A complete picture should even include the corporate interests that work through different channels such as the media, as demonstrated in a recent manifesto published in the newspaper: "Let the Market Take Over Health Care" (Dagens Nyheter, 1997).

It can be asked whether the Swedish Health Care System exists as a system as defined within general systems theory. The answer is that it is a system only if one can imagine systems largely without management. The performance of particular system elements does not affect the performance of the other elements or, for that matter, the entire system. Obviously the Swedish Health Care System is not a unitary system such as the British National Health System. It is best described as a federation of 21 provincial health care systems.

Since it is the counties who are the "owners" of the health care sector, the policies formulated at the national level have had to take account of the fact that the policies cannot be forced upon reluctant counties. Nevertheless, it is obvious that this situation has began to change during the 1990s. Decisions reached in the parliament and the cabinet over the last 7 years have drastically affected the economic situation of the counties, forcing them to reconsider their policies and undertake dramatic downsizing of their health care systems. The number of employees was at its peak in 1990; in 1997 the number of employees had been reduced by 70,000 (13%) from 380,000 to 245,000 (Landstingsförbundet, 1999).*

The fact that health care policies formulated at the national level have earlier had little or no effect upon the health care practices of the counties is exemplified by the fact that despite the national health policy since the early 1970s to make primary care the central part of the health care system, the degree of actual restructuring of health care that has occurred within the counties has been nominal. It is obvious that counties, either due to professional barriers or on the basis of lack of support from decision makers, have not implemented critical portions of the national health policy. If national health policies and goals can be so consistently ignored, one must wonder about the purpose of having a Minister of Health.

V. CURRENT HEALTH CARE SYSTEMS ISSUES

As never before, the fundamental premises of the Swedish health care organization are under attack. At the most general level, at stake is the question of the "ownership" of the system; that is, should the system remain basically public or be transferred to private ownership. The next few years will be decisive as to which path will be taken. It is not at all certain that the current public system will be preserved.

A. Advantages and/or Disadvantages of the Current System

An analysis of the advantages and disadvantages of the current system would be instructive in many ways especially if compared with other existing systems around the world. Such an analysis cannot be performed here but one general statement may be made. According to available data covering the OECD countries relating to health status in general, but also in terms of maternal and infant

---

* From the figures are excluded 119,990 employees who were transferred to municipalities when they assumed the responsibility for nursing homes in 1992.

mortality, potential years lost, morbidity in terms of perceived health status, as well as health expectancy, infant death, dental health, communicable diseases, cancer, and injuries, Swedish is in the top rank; the same can be said about health care and expenditure on health resources (OECD, 2000). The issue whether it is health and medical care that sustains the health of individuals and population is not, for obvious reasons, considered here. An analysis of advantages and disadvantages of the Swedish system as such and in comparison to other systems would have to begin with the delineation of the values and the criteria for evaluation that such an analysis should be based on. No such analysis will be attempted here. What will be done here is to raise some issues that have figured in the debate and that directly or indirectly deal with assumed deficiencies of the system, more seldom with eventual advantages.

Some of these issues are general and concern the effectiveness of the system; others deal with the system's alleged lack of efficiency. Mostly the issues are of the latter type.

The most characteristic feature of the Swedish health care system is its complete coverage and its high accessibility. Barriers to access are few, if any. One particular barrier may be the copayment that patients pay when making contact with the health care system, but this appears to be an insignificant barrier. Children and youth under 20 years of age are excluded from paying the patient fee. This practice removes a considerable barrier that otherwise might deter young people from accessing the health care system when they need it. In the same sense, the system utilizes a high cost limit that allows individuals to readily utilize the primary care system without fear of bankrupting their own resources.

Other types of barriers to access, such as psychological, informational, social, organizational, spatial, or temporal, may or may not exist. Such barriers, apart from geographical, have not been widely observed or commented upon in public discussions and forums.

The geographical distribution of the care facilities is quite even, especially considering the uneven distribution of the population.

A policy of reducing barriers to care should probably be directed toward efforts at improving the turnover in hospitals, especially in some areas of surgery where waiting lists exist. Capacity expansions within health care centers may be yet another way of reducing barriers.

Another remarkable feature of the systems is, as will be discussed in the next section, that effective cost controls can be applied relatively easily. Again, whether or not this is an advantage depends on the perspective applied and the values used.

B. Cost Controls

Cost controls have been extremely successful in the Swedish health care system. A high annual growth rate has been transformed into a zero growth rate during the past few years. Similarly, health care costs as a percentage of GNP have fallen over the last 5 years from 10% to 7.4%. The other side of the coin is, of course, that the perception of a "crisis" in health care among large segments of the population has grown. Downsizing has negatively influenced the performance of the component systems that produce Swedish health care services but it is not yet possible to determine whether the effectiveness of treatment has been influenced.

In either case large groups within the nation perceive that something is seriously amiss with the nation's health care system. Although it is extremely difficult to interpret rates such as the number of doctors and nurses per 1000 of population, it is still a fact that the Swedish system is better provided for in these terms than almost any other system. The cost of the system is relatively moderate and in line with the average for Europe (OECD, 1999).

C. Management of the System

One obvious problem with the Swedish system is that it may not really function at all as a "system." It can be argued that to the extent that the system's parts move in slightly different directions, with the differences between these parts increasing, the system might not really be a system at all. This raises the question whether a unified system like the British National Health Service is a more effective and efficient mode of organization. It is not possible to answer such questions without outlining the value premises that should underlie the analysis. Perhaps the relative freedom of the 21 systems expands the portfolio of choices both for the system managers and for those seeking care. It is at least clear that these subsystems have been designed to flexibly tailor solutions to the health care needs of local constituencies.

There is no doubt, however, even to the most casual observer, that the "system" exhibits certain problems of design and management. For example, the roles of health care centers, hospitals, and outpatient clinics in the system are not clearly differentiated. From a strictly rational perspective (a value premise), an unequivocally clear point of entry into these systems would be preferable. But again, it would be necessary to offer criteria to be used to evaluate alternative modes of organization if the analysis were to be pursued further.

D. The Public/Private Division

At a more general level, the issue of who should "own" the health care organizations has emerged on the agenda. According to a recent manifesto signed, among others, by corporate representatives and leading members of the Medical and Nurses Associations, the Swedish system is said to be very inefficient (Dagens Nyheter, 1997). The apparent solution these signatories put forward is to dismantle the county systems and sell or lease the health care organizations and their human and capital resources to proprietary health care interests; as the title of the manifesto pronounces: "Let the Market Take Over Health Care!"

However, before recommending such a drastic solution to the problem of inefficiency (which is the main argument in the manifesto for privatization), it would be fruitful to ask the following questions: What are the presumed inefficiencies of the current system? And how do they compare with other systems, especially private systems? According to the manifesto, the chief problem in public medical care is that treatments and programs that do not produce positive results are allowed to linger on because there are no possibilities within the system for the continual follow-up and assessment of medical interventions and their results.

This assertion appears to be the core of the argument in favor of the privatization of the nation's health care system. But what are the authors of the manifest really stating? In short, they are stating that the feature they outline is inherent in publicly owned systems; that the possibilities of quality controls in a public system, owing to some inherent characteristics of public systems, neither exist nor will be utilized. Since the argument obviously cannot be true, one must suspect that the critics have ulterior motives for their calls to arms in the name of the free market. What is distinctly forgotten in the rhetoric is the fact that the Swedish system produces a health status outcome better than that of other nations that utilize far greater human, physical, and financial resources. One problematic case here is, of course, Japan, which exhibits a health status level that even exceeds that of Sweden, at least in terms of certain indicators.

The reality of Swedish health care performance ought to be a sufficient reason to take seriously the issue of developing criteria for evaluation of alternative modes of organization if the aim is to seriously analyze and discuss advantages and disadvantages of modes of organization.

While a case for system improvement clearly exists, the documented justification for the total overhaul of the current system at this point is simply not compelling, as has been indicated. Notwithstanding what was said earlier regarding the inefficiency of the Swedish health care system, the system is demonstrably effective by any conceivable end-point health measures. Information available about outcome, process, and structural indicators clearly shows that the system performs at least as well as, or in most cases better than, any other system (OECD, 1999, 2000). Yet the cry of "crisis" is louder than ever.

E. Health Problems

The health problems that the country health care organization has to face are disparate though not particularly large and different from what most other similar counties face. It was noted earlier that the health situation, although varying slightly between the different areas, is on the whole stable.

The health status of residents of the Umea district is slightly better than the average level for the country (Hur mår Sverige?, 1999). This is especially true of the Umea municipality where the population is much younger and have a higher educational level than the rest of county, as well as the national average; but even when taking account of the age composition and the educational level of the population, the level of health status in Umea is better than the average of the district as well as the average for the county and country, though the differences are minor.*

F. Issues in Primary Health Care

Health care centers in their current form began to emerge in the late 1960s. They were large organizations at the time because nursing homes were attached to the centers; in 1992 the nursing homes were transferred to the municipalities and the care of elderly and long-term sick became a municipal responsiblity.

One broadly discussed issue concerns the allegedly low productivity of general practitioners. Compared with German or English general practitioners, the productivity of the Swedish general practitioners is indeed very low, as was shown in a recent comparative study of general practice in Europe (Spri informerar, 1997). The study found that a Swedish general practitioner (GP) had on average 96 consultations per week, a German GP 393, and an English GP 273; they worked 38, 62, and 60 hr/week, respectively. These figures do not, of course, indicate the specific content of their work, which differs between countries.

There were also differences in the level of training and the equipment available, with the Swedish GPs exceeding their other European counterparts in terms of training, facilities, and equipment. These practice statistics pose a number of questions that cannot be discussed here.†

Another long-standing problem is the lack of coordination between the different programs and professionals at the health care centers. This problem is partly attributable to the antagonism that developed between physicians and district nurses when formerly independently functioning primary care services, delivered by district nurses since the early years of the twentieth century, were relocated to physician-managed health care centers. The district nurses and midwives resisted functioning within a physician-dominated primary care system because they considered themselves to be losing a degree of independence. Currently, they continue to resist interference from health center management. Be-

---

* This proposition as well as other propositions concerning the health status of the population are based on data in the Hur mår Sverige? (1999) statistical package.

† These broader issues include concerns over the quality of the work in different national and international settings, the role of general practitioners, and the division of labor between primary care and hospital care.

yond this particular area of tension, however, the various professionals at health care centers tend to work well together.

Another problem relates to the tendency among clients to bypass the health care centers and directly access the hospital emergency departments and outpatient clinics. Care becomes more expensive than necessary and, more importantly, the role of health care centers in general and of general practitioners in particular is undermined.

In a recent policy declaration, the Minister of Health stressed that health care centers are the central components in the Swedish health care system (Läkartidningen, 1998). This policy, however, was already formulated as early as 1968 by the National Board of Health and Social Welfare (Socialstyrelsen, 1968). However, changes in venue for delivery of care have not yet resulted in any reallocation of resources from the hospital system. What has become evident over the initial transition period is that the change of treatment venue has resulted in an increased pressure upon primary care physicians (Kaati, 1999).

A strengthening of the role of the health care center in the health care system has been on the policy agenda for a long time (Kaati et al., 1982). At the time of this writing the government has introduced a ''national plan'' for health care in which, among other things, the central role of primary care is stressed and grants promised to expand the primary health care sector. However, until the present time the role of primary care has changed little. The new tasks that the health care centers are supposed to take on, and to a certain extent already perform, have not yet in any discernible way influenced resource allocation to the health care centers. Thus, contrary to assumptions in coming national plans, at the county level there are no signs yet that the policy of strengthening health centers will be fully implemented.

It is obvious from what has been said here that the most fundamental issue concerning primary health care concerns the role the primary health care should have in the health and medical care system, what its mission as well as its mode of working should be. As it stands today, primary health care, or at least the work of general practitioners, consists of no more than normal general surgery of minor complexity. Expanding the number of general practitioners, as seems to be the direction of reform, does not tackle the problem inherent in the concept of primary health care, the role of primary health care in the health and medical care system at large as well as the larger issue of the role of the health and medical care system in society.

In planning the supply of general practitioners, according to a decision in the parliament (*riksdag*), the goal is to have one general practitioner per 1500–2000 population. This goal has not yet been reached (Socialstyrelsen, 1999). The health minister considered, in the new national plan, that a level of one general practitioner per 1500 individuals is reasonable in view of the expanded role that health care centers will play in providing medical care in communities (Regeringens Proposition, 1999/2000, p. 149).

VI. CONCLUSIONS

The problem overshadowing all other problems in Swedish health care policy today is the imbalance between revenues and costs. It is, however, basically a question that has to do with the role of the public sector and of taxation in today's so called liberal democracies, a topic that cannot be pursued although it can hardly be bypassed in discussing the future of health care in the Western world.

Despite heavy reductions during the last 8 years, this imbalance between resources in what the political systems is prepared to extract from the public and what the general public demands persists, though obviously not to the same degree as earlier. Until now the reductions have been spread more or less equally over the whole system. Realistically, however, these historically large cuts are probably insufficient to achieve balance. Up to the present the most obvious route to achieving balance between revenues and costs has, in practice, been closed, namely, raising taxes. This may change, although the countries are not generally likely to take this path. In Sweden, as well as in other countries, difficult questions about what health care should be about, what it can do, and what services should be prioritized are currently in need of direct attention.

The public sector's ability to raise the necessary taxes is in doubt since all political parties favor tax reductions. This is a difficult situation for Swedish health care at a time when the public has come to expect more from health care than before and come to expect to pay the same or even less in return for services.

It is in this troublesome setting that the issue of privatization of the health care is raised.

REFERENCES

Atonbladet, November 27, 1997.
Basårsstatistik. Stockholm: Landstingsförbundet, 1999.
Budget for the County of Vasterbotten. Umea: VLL, 1998, 1999, 2000.
Budget Verksamhetsplan. Umea: Umea Kommun, 1999.
Budget. Umea Kommun. Umea: Umea Kommun, 1997.
Bygren, L.O. The Health System of Sweden. Umea: Social Medicine, Umea University, 1987.
Churchman, C.W. The Systems Approach. New York: Dell Publishing, 1979.
Dagens Nyheter, November 25, 1997.
Elmbrant, B. Dom däruppe-dom därnere Om demokratin i Sverige. Stockholm: Atlas, 1997.
Epidemologiskt Centrum (EpC). Hur mår Sverige? Stockholm: Socialstyrelsen, 1999.
Evans, R.B., Barer, M.L., Marmor, T.R., eds. Why are some people healthy and others not? New York: Aldine De Gruyter, 1994.
Gustafsson, A. Kommunal självstyrelse. Stockholm: NNS, 1996.

Holmberg E, Stjernquist N. Vår författning. Stockholm Norstedts juridik 1998.

HSU 2000. Slutbetänkande av HSU 2000. God vård på lika villkor? -om statens styrning av Hälsa-och sjukvården. Stockholm: Hälsa och sjukvårdsutredningen, 1999.

Hälso-och sjukvårdsstatistik årsbok 1999. Stockholm: Socialstyrelsen, 1999.

Kaati, G. Some Critical Problems in Primary Health Care: A Revisit. Umea: Social Medicine, Umea Unversity, 1999.

Kaati, G., Måwe, U., Rudebeck, C.W. Some Critical Problems in Primary Health Care. Umeå: Social Medicine, Umea University, 1982.

Landstingsförbundet. Basårsstatistik. Stockholm: Landstingsförbundet, 1999.

Landstingsplaner 1985–2000. Umea: VLL, 1985–2000.

Morgan, G. Images of Organisations. Thousand Oaks, CA: Sage Publications, 1997.

OECD. OECD Health Data 1999. Paris: OECD, CREDES, 1999.

Petersson, O. Svensk politik Stockholm Norstedts juridik 1992.

Pockettidningen, R. 1997(2–3):37.

Reeves, P.N., Berwall, D.F., Woodside, N.B. Introduction to Health Planning. Arlington, VA: Information Resources Press, 1984.

Regeringens proposition 1999/2000:149. Stockholm: The Government Office, 2000.

Sahlin, J. Hälso-och sjukvårdslagen. Stockholm: Nordstedts, 2000.

Sjukvården i Sverige. SoS rapport 1995:25. Stockholm: Socialstyrelsen, 1995.

Socialstyrelsen. Socialstyrelsens redovisar 1968:1. Stockholm. Socialstyrelsen, 1968.

Socialstyrelsen. SoS rapport 1995: 25. Sjukvården i Sverige. Stockholm: Socialstyrelsen, 1995.

Socialstyrelsen. SoS rapport 1997: 13. Stockholm: Socialstyrelsen, 1997.

SPRI informerar. Stockholm: SPRI, 1997.

Statistisk årsbok för Landsting 2000. Stockholm: Landstingsförbundet, 1999.

Tierp. Diagnosredovisning for lakarbesök är 1998 vid vårdcentralen i Tierp. Uppsala: Social Medicine, Uppsala University, 1999.

Umea sjukvård. Plan 1997/2000. Umea: Umea sjukvårdsdistrikt, 1997.

Westerhäll, L. Medical Law An Introduction. Stockholm: Nordstedts, 1997.

Wilow, K. Författningshandbok 1997. Stockholm: Liber, 1997.

11

The German Health Care System

Balu Swami
AT&T Wireless Services, Inc., Bothell, Washington

I. INTRODUCTION

In 1997, Germany spent 10.7% of its gross domestic product (GDP) on health care, while the United States spent 13.9% of its GDP on health care (OECD, 2000). Yet, a comparison of the leading indicators of health status suggests that the health outcomes in Germany are more impressive than in the United States. Life expectancy at birth is 74.1 years for German males and 80.3 for German females. The comparative figures for American males and females are 73.6 and 79.4 years, respectively. Infant mortality rate is 4.8 per 1000 live births in Germany and 7.8 per 1000 live births in the United States (OECD, 2000). These facts have convinced many, including, reportedly, former President Clinton, that the German health care model is worth emulating in the United States (Prewo, 1994). However, there are many who are opposed to the idea of Germanizing the U.S. health care system. They point to the many problems the German system is facing (Chase, 1993; Marshall, 1993) and argue that recent attempts to introduce competition among the health plans suggest that the Germans, in fact, may be moving closer to a U.S. model (Koelbl, 1994).

Which side are we to believe? In attempting to answer this question, this chapter presents a broad description of the German health care system, identifies the strengths and weaknesses of the system, and discusses briefly some of the critical issues currently facing the system.

II. OVERVIEW OF THE SYSTEM

The German health care system is similar to the U.S. health care system in that the government does not run it. The German government neither finances nor pays for the provision of health care services. However, the government in Germany plays a much more prominent role in the health care sector than does the government in the United States. Among other things, the German government regulates drug prices, sets guidelines for private health insurance, and stipulates the rules by which employers are enjoined to provide health coverage to their employees. Nearly 90% of the German population is covered by "sickness funds," i.e., company-based, trade-based, or profession-based insurance plans, while the remaining 10% is covered through private insurance.

The system can be best understood by focusing on its institutional structure, consisting of five components: outpatient care, inpatient care, pharmaceuticals, public health, and occupational health.

A. Outpatient Care

Outpatient care is mostly provided by ambulatory medical practitioners who account for 41% of all physicians (Federal Statistical Office, 2000). These physicians, who operate from private offices, are reimbursed on a fee-for-service basis. Nearly 85% of these physicians' incomes comes from panel care, i.e., care provided to patients who are part of an approved sickness fund. Fees for panel services are paid according to a schedule agreed to by the managers of the fund and *kassenarztliche Vereinigungen* (the association of panel physicians.)

B. Inpatient Care

Inpatient care, namely, care within the hospitals, is provided by hospital-based physicians, who account for 59% of all physicians. These hospital-based physicians are salaried employees of the hospitals. While office-based physicians are restricted from treating patients in the hospitals, hospital-based physicians are restricted from treating patients outside the hospitals. In 1998, there were 7.0 beds per 1000 population in inpatient-care hospitals (9.3 beds per 1000 population including beds in preventive and rehabilitation facilities). The occupancy rate in inpatient care hospitals was 81.9% and there were 194 admissions per 1000 residents in inpatient care hospitals (Federal Statistical Office, 2000).

C. Pharmaceuticals

The distinguishing characteristic of the German pharmaceutical market is price controls. A 1989 law fixed prices of a number of prescription drugs in an effort at cost control. These fixed prices often amounted to less than a third of the market price. A 1993 law forced physicians to pay for the drugs they prescribe over and above the amount budgeted for pharmaceutical expenditures. The law also forced down some drug prices and froze the price of many others for 2 years.

In 1999, stricter restrictions were placed on drug expenditures and doctors who exceeded their pharmaceutical budget faced fines amounting to $7500 (Buck, 2000).

D. Public Health

Public health programs account for 16.8 percent of health care costs in Germany (OECD, 2000). The cost burden of public health programs falls upon local governments, which take care of the poor by either paying their contribution to the sickness funds or reimbursing hospitals and physicians for care provided to the poor.

E. Occupational Health

Industrial physicians provide occupational health services, i.e., health services at the workplace. They provide emergency first aid, periodic medical checkups, and other ancillary services. Many of them are salaried employees, but most work on a fee-for-service basis. Expenditure on occupational health care accounted for 4.3% of all health care expenditures in 1997 (Federal Statistical Office, 2000).

III. DESCRIPTION OF THE SYSTEM

This section describes the system by focusing on the historical developments, the various categories of health care expenditures, the financing mechanisms, and the health status of the population.

A. Historical Developments

The quintessential feature of the German health care system is the sickness fund. The origins of the sickness fund date back to the Middle Ages when guilds of working men—carpenters, blacksmiths, bakers, and other craftspeople—created funds to help members with the cost of health care, to pay for funeral expenses, and to aid families of disabled or deceased members. Journeymen who did not belong to guilds also formed associations for similar purposes. Members paid a flat rate or a share of their income for the health benefits they received from the fund (Zollner, 1982).

When the Industrial Revolution arrived, the need for community-based health insurance became more acute. As people flocked into the cities in the thousands in search of jobs, the existing charitable institutions, such as the Catholic Church, became overburdened. As a consequence, the state intervened to ensure the protection of workers' health. In 1854, a Prussian law obligated all mines and foundries to have sickness funds. The funds, the first compulsory, regulated health insurance system in Germany, provided for sick pay, medication, and rehabilitation (Knox, 1993). Soon, trade unions, political parties, churches, and employers began creating mutual aid societies inside and outside of workplaces.

In 1876, the Parliament enacted a number of regulations that set national standards for sickness funds. Although the law did not require workers to join the funds, it stipulated that workers pay two-thirds and employers one-third of the contributions to the funds. It also provided for governance of each fund by a board constituted by representatives of employees and employers (Zollner, 1982). In 1883, membership in a sickness fund was made compulsory for all laborers. In the following years, more and more people were brought under the statutory health insurance system. By 1900, 17% of the German population was part of that system (Stone, 1980).

Statutory health insurance expanded over the years to cover a large number of workers in various occupations, including transport and commercial workers, agriculture and forestry workers, civil service employees, and seamen. In 1918, the unemployed were made part of the sickness funds, and in 1930, benefits were extended to dependents of fund members (Stone, 1980). In 1951, the share of contribution by employees was reduced and that of employers was raised to one-half. The composition of the boards that managed the funds also was changed to give equal representation to employers and employees. In 1970, the income threshold for mandatory membership was indexed to increases in the national wage level. This ensured that the membership in the funds remained stable and the number of workers eligible to opt out of the system was small. In 1975, students and disabled persons were included in the statutory scheme (Zollner, 1982). More recently, the focus of the legislators has been on cost containment. A health reform law passed in 1989 set reference prices for drugs, while a more comprehensive law passed in 1993 placed strict controls on spending by physicians, pharmacists, hospitals, and pharmaceutical companies. In 1999, further restrictions were placed on health care providers.

B. Categories of Expenditures

In 1998, total health care expenditures in Germany amounted to $201 billion (purchasing-power parity terms). Public expenditures, including statutory sickness funds, accounted for $156 billion, or 77.6%, of the total. Both expenditures grew at an average annual rate of 7.5% between 1985 and 1995 (see Table 1).

In terms of the categories of expenditures, inpatient care accounts for the largest portion of the total health expenditures. In 1993, inpatient care accounted for 31.3% of the total, while ambulatory care accounted for the second largest share at 25.4% (see Figure 1).

Table 1 Health Care Expenditures in Germany, 1985–1995

Year	Total expenditures (millions, PPP $)	Change from the previous year (%)	Public expenditures (millions, PPP $)
1985	71,054		52,283
1986	73,861	3.95	54,726
1987	78,277	5.98	57,664
1988	86,177	10.09	63,674
1989	88,038	2.16	63,567
1990	96,067	9.12	68,962
1991	122,381	27.39	89,429
1992	140,441	14.76	104,167
1993	139,762	−0.48	102,000
1994	151,981	8.74	111,643
1995	158,278	4.14	116,316
Average annual growth rate		7.55%	

Source: Organization for Cooperation and Development (various years), *OECD Health Data*. Paris: OECD.

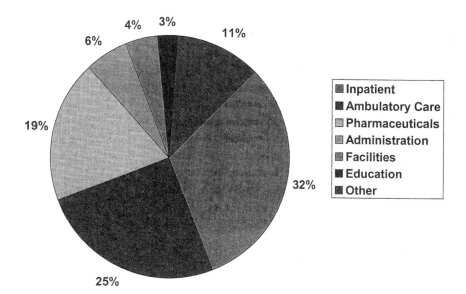

Figure 1 Categories of expenditures, percent share, 1993.

C. Inpatient Care

In 1997, inpatient care accounted for 40% of all treatment expenditures (Federal Statistical Office, 2000). Those covered under the statutory health plans pay a nominal charge a day for hospital stay. The patients thus have practically unlimited access to hospital care. Not surprisingly, therefore, hospital utilization is 1.5 times greater in Germany than in the United States (OECD, 1996). Additionally, the reimbursement method in effect until recently created an incentive for hospitals to lengthen patients' stay at the hospital. Until 1988, hospitals were reimbursed at a fixed per-day rate that took no account of the diagnosis. Since all cases were reimbursed at the same rate, hospitals tended to admit patients who did not require a hospital stay and prolonged the stay of some patients beyond the time they needed to stay in the hospital.

Until the 1993 reforms, hospitals were also able to recoup any cost overruns in a given year by simply charging the sickness funds a higher daily rate the following year. According to one estimate, annual payments by sickness funds to hospitals increased 100% between 1980 and 1992 (Koelbl, 1994). It is, therefore, no surprise that hospital expenditures top the list of all categories of expenditure. It should be noted, however, that hospital care in the United States is not only the leading expenditure category, but also accounts for a larger share (43% of total health expenditures) than in Germany. The difference is primarily due to higher hospital prices in the United States.

D. Ambulatory Care

Unlike inpatient care, there have been attempts to control the growth of ambulatory care costs since 1977. In that year, the federal government passed a law stipulating that ambulatory care expenditures could not grow faster than the average wage rate in Germany. In spite of these controls, ambulatory care expenditures grew faster than inpatient care expenditures between 1985 and 1993 (see Table 2). Since 1993, however, inpatient care expenditures have been growing faster than ambulatory care expenditures. Between 1993 and 1997, inpatient care expenditures grew at an average anuual rate of 7% compared to 3.5% for ambulatory care (Federal Statistical Office, 2000).

The mechanism through which ambulatory care physicians receive payment is rather unique. Each year, the association of ambulatory care physicians negotiates the annual budgets for ambulatory care with the sickness funds. The budget is determined on the basis of projected number of fund members and the expected cost per member. The association receives lump-sum quarterly payments from the funds that are disbursed to the ambulatory care physicians based on the total service points earned by them. Under this point system, each type

Table 2 Inpatient Care and Ambulatory Care Expenditures in Germany, 1985–1993

Year	Inpatient care (millions, PPP $)	Change from the previous year (%)	Ambulatory care (millions, PPP $)	Change from the previous year (%)
1985	26,055		18,965	
1986	27,454	5.37	19,875	4.80
1987	28,759	4.75	20,999	5.66
1988	30,729	6.85	22,536	7.32
1989	32,092	4.44	23,990	6.45
1990	34,708	8.15	26,066	8.65
1991	38,039	9.60	31,675	21.52
1992	42,932	12.86	36,910	16.53
1993	43,762	1.93	37,527	1.67
Average annual growth rate		5.93%		7.88%

Source: *OECD Health Data*. Paris: OECD.

of service is valued differently. Thus it is possible for a physician to receive a larger payment than another physician if she or he provided more high-value services, such as home visits, which carry more points than low-value services, such as office visits. The key to cost control in this system is the point value conversion factor, which determines the value of each point. If the total number of points earned is greater than the anticipated volume of service, the value of each point would drop and, thereby, the budget would be balanced. If, on the other hand, the actual number of points earned is less than the anticipated volume of service, the value of each point would increase and, again, the budget would be balanced. The conversion factor is, thus, intended to limit utilization of physician services.

According to a recent decision, starting in 2003, the complicated point system would be replaced by a flat-rate, fee-per-case reimbursement mechanism modeled on the Australian Refined Diagnosis Related Groups classification system (*Chemist and Druggist*, 2000b).

E. Pharmaceuticals

Pharmaceutical expenditures accounted for roughly 20% of total health care expenditures between 1985 and 1993. As can be seen from Table 3, the proportion fell to 19% in 1993 primarily owing to the 1993 health care reforms, which introduced several cost-cutting measures including a price freeze and increased copayments.

Table 3 Pharmaceutical Expenditures in Germany, 1985–1993

Year	Pharmaceutical expenditures (millions, PPP $)	Total expenditures (millions, PPP $)	Pharmaceutical expenditures as a percent of total
1985	14,017	71,054	19.73
1986	14,817	73,861	20.06
1987	16,010	78,277	20.45
1988	17,969	86,177	20.85
1989	17,979	88,038	20.42
1990	19,702	96,067	20.51
1991	24,731	122,381	20.21
1992	29,146	140,441	20.75
1993	26,462	139,762	18.93

Source: *OECD Health Data*. Paris: OECD.

The 1993 reforms were part of a series of attempts by the German government to control pharmaceutical expenditures. With each attempt, the government increased its role in the drug market. The most far-reaching of the reform efforts were made in 1989. The 1989 Health Reform Act introduced two changes that substantially affected the pharmaceuticals market. The Act made certain drugs ineligible for reimbursement on the grounds that they were ineffective. Second, the Act created a reference pricing system that limited the amount of reimbursement for a number of drugs. This forced patients to seek generic alternatives to brand-name products. This shift in demand caused pharmaceutical companies to bring down their prices to the level of the reference prices. In spite of the success of this measure, drug expenditures continued to rise due to a higher volume of prescriptions. The higher volume of prescriptions could be attributed to the increasing number of physicians. As can be seen from Table 4, the physician population was growing at a much faster rate than the general population between 1985 and 1994. Consequently, there were 3.4 physicians per 1000 population in 1997 as compared to 2.64 physicians per 1000 population in 1985 (OECD, 2000).

The 1989 reforms having failed to lower the escalation of expenditures on pharmaceuticals, the government introduced much more stringent reforms in 1993. The 1993 reform law established fixed budgets for prescription drugs and held physicians financially responsible for any prescription cost that exceeded the budgeted amount. It also froze the price of many drugs for 2 years and directed manufacturers to reduce the price of selected drugs. The copayment by patients was also increased from $1.43 to between $2.39 and $3.35 (Knox, 1993). It ap-

Table 4 Growth In the Number of Physicians in Germany, 1985–1993

Year	Number of physicians	Percent change in physicians	Population (000s)
1985	160,902		61,024
1986	165,015	2.56	61,066
1987	171,487	3.92	61,077
1988	177,001	3.22	61,449
1989	188,225	6.34	62,063
1990	195,254	3.73	63,253
1991[a]	244,238	25.09	79,753
1992	251,877	3.13	80,275
1993	259,981	3.22	80,975
1994	267,186	2.77	81,338
Average annual growth rate		5.20%	

[a] The large increase in the number of physicians and the population in 1991 is due to German reunification.
Source: Organization for Economic Cooperation and Development (various years), *OECD Health Data.* Paris: OECD.

pears, however, that the 1989 reforms did not have a lasting impact. In 1997, pharmaceutical expenditures accounted for over 25% of total health care expenditures (Federal Statistical Office, 2000).

F. Administration

According to Fitzgerald and Jaffe (1994), "American hospitals spend about 20 cents of every dollar on administration, Canada, nine cents; Germany, about eight cents." They argue that this is due to the fact that "despite the multiplicity of insurers, premiums are raised uniformly through payroll taxes, billing forms are similar if not identical, and payment procedures are standardized." They note how Schwabing Hospital, with 1372 beds, has only 18 members on its billing staff. Other commentators have also noted how a simplified claims process and limited quality assessment have helped to keep administrative costs low (Hofreuter and Mendoza, 1993). As can be seen from Table 5, administrative costs as a percentage of total health care costs declined from a high of 6.7% in 1985 to 5.4% in 1994. It appears that administrative costs have been on the rise in recent years. According to one report, administrative costs of health insurers rose by 4.6% between 1998 and 1999 (Tuffs, 1999).

Table 5 Administrative Costs in Germany, 1985–1994

Year	Administrative costs (millions, PPP $)	Total expenditures (millions, PPP $)	Administrative costs as a percent of total
1985	4,734	71,054	6.66
1986	4,768	73,861	6.46
1987	5,025	78,277	6.42
1988	5,270	86,177	6.12
1989	5,745	88,038	6.53
1990	6,180	96,067	6.43
1991	7,143	122,381	5.84
1992	7,992	140,441	5.69
1993	7,929	139,762	5.67
1994	8,146	151,981	5.36

Source: *OECD Health Data*. Paris: OECD.

G. Investment in Medical Facilities

German investment in medical facilities accounted for 4.1% of total expenditures in 1995. As can be seen from Table 6, the share of investment expenditures fluctuated between a low of 4% in 1990 and a high of 4.7% in the following year. The fluctuation may be a consequence of the fragmented system of hospital financing whereby capital expenditures are funded by the state governments, while operating expenditures are paid out of the hospitals' current revenue, the bulk of which is made up of payments received from the sickness funds. In the opinion of some observers, the fragmented system has made coordination of investment decisions a difficult task. The lack of coordination has, in turn, added to the difficulty of controlling overall spending increases (United States General Accounting Office, 1991; Knox, 1993).

Consistent data on German investment in equipment are difficult to find. For instance, according to Knox (1993), there were 207 magnetic resonance imaging (MRI) units in 1992. However, OECD data show that there were only 117 such units in 1993 (OECD, 1996). Regardless of this inconsistency, it appears that Germany has considerably increased the number of high-technology units in recent years. MRI units per capita increased from 0.7 in 1986 to 5.7 in 1996 and CT scanners per capita increased from 8.0 in 1986 to 16.4 in 1996 (Annell and Willis, 2000).

In the estimation of some observers, one of the problems facing the German medical system is maldistribution of resources, which has, reportedly, created undercapacity in some areas and overcapacity in others (Hofreuter and Mendoza,

Table 6 Investment in Medical Facilities in Germany, 1985–1994

Year	Investment in medical facilities (millions, PPP $)	Total expenditures (millions, PPP $)	Investment in medical facilities as a percent of total
1985	3,274	71,054	4.61
1986	3,287	73,861	4.45
1987	3,260	78,277	4.16
1988	3,480	86,177	4.04
1989	3,746	88,038	4.25
1990	3,837	96,067	3.99
1991	5,762	122,381	4.71
1992	6,471	140,441	4.61
1993	6,286	139,762	4.50
1994	6,522	151,981	4.29

Source: Organization for Economic Cooperation and Development (various years), *OECD Health Data*. Paris: OECD.

1993). According to one report, intensive care facilities have failed to keep pace with emergency services. Consequently, while modernization of emergency services has succeeded in reducing the average time for an ambulance to arrive at an accident site, it takes sometimes up to 3 hr to admit the accident victim to a hospital (Karcher, 1992).

Part of the problem stems from the "dual financing" mechanism referred to earlier, under which investments in hospital plant and equipment are financed by the federal and the state governments, while operating expenses are paid from revenues generated by the hospitals through charges to the sickness funds and the patient population. Originally intended as a mechanism for avoiding duplication and oversupply of high-technology equipment and other medical resources, the fragmented system of financing has made capital financing subject to bureaucratic battles and political decision making. There have been several attempts at reforming the investment financing mechanism. Since 1986, the role of the federal government has been limited to funding teaching hospitals. The 1993 Health Care Structural Reform Act has fundamentally altered the dual financing mechanism by allowing private funding of hospital capital investments.

H. Health Education and Training

Health education and training, on which $4.1 billion were spent in 1997, is an important component of the German health care system (Federal Statistical Of-

Table 7 Maternal and Child Health Expenditures in Germany, 1985–1993

Year	Maternal and child health expenditures (millions, PPP $)	Total expenditures (millions, PPP $)	Maternal and child health expenditures as a percent of total
1985	668	71,054	0.94
1986	696	73,861	0.94
1987	733	78,277	0.94
1988	866	86,177	1.00
1989	964	88,038	1.09
1990	1,121	96,067	1.17
1991	1,189	122,381	0.97
1992	1,352	140,441	0.96
1993	1,359	139,762	0.97

Source: *OECD Health Data*. Paris: OECD.

fice, 2000). In Germany, there are 340 doctors per 100,000 people compared to 270 per 100,000 in the United States. Each year, 12,000–14,000 students are admitted into medical schools. The estimated demand for additional doctors is between 4000 and 6000. Consequently, the number of residents per doctor has dropped from 700 to 300 in the last 30 years. The oversupply is partly caused by practically unrestricted access to medical school education. By law, anyone who fulfills the academic requirements is entitled to attend medical school. This situation has started to change with limits being placed on class size (Harper, 1992, 1993; Jones, 1993).

I. Other Category

The "other" category includes such items as research and development and maternal and child health. The bulk of research and development funds are invested in pharmaceuticals research. In 1993, Germany spent nearly $1.4 billion on maternal and child health. As can be seen from Table 7, maternal and child health expenditures accounted for roughly 1% of the total health care expenditures between 1985 and 1993.

IV. FINANCING MECHANISM

On the surface, health care financing in Germany appears to be a simple process. It appears simple because everyone belongs to either a statutory sickness fund or a private insurance plan. Nearly 90% of the population belongs to a statutory fund and the rest have private insurance. Since there are only two types of payers, one would expect the payment mechanism to be simple and straightforward. However, the system is quite complex and is complicated by several factors.

A. The Statutory Funds

There are nearly 1200 statutory funds and there are several types of these funds. The two major types of funds are primary and substitute. Primary funds, which account for two-thirds of all the funds, consist of geographically based local funds; craft funds that are dedicated to people belonging to a specific trade or craft; and company-based funds dedicated to workers belonging to a company. Substitute funds, on the other hand, are intended mainly for white-collar workers, although there are several blue-collar substitute funds. These funds account for the remaining third of the funds (Knox, 1993).

The geographically based local funds, which account for 23% of all funds, cover 37% of the German population. In general, these funds cover those not covered by the company-based and craft-based funds, such as workers in small-scale industries, the unemployed, and welfare recipients. The funds collect contributions from employers and employees; from local governments on behalf of the poor; from government pension funds on behalf of retirees; and from the unemployment insurance fund on behalf of the unemployed. Contributions by fund members are higher than contributions made on behalf of the retirees, the unemployed, and the poor. The higher contributions are intended to cover the additional cost of caring for the retirees, the unemployed, and the poor.

The company-based funds, which account for 60% of all funds, cover 11 percent of the German population. Individual companies that employ more than 450 people organize these funds. All employees whose income is less than the statutory ceiling are required to join their company-based fund. The craft-based funds are run by trade associations for the benefit of their members (Knox, 1993).

The substitute funds differ from the primary funds in that they are managed entirely by their members, who do not share authority with either the employers or the unions. The white-collar substitute funds are open to clerical workers as well as professionals and managers. The blue-collar substitute funds, on the other hand, are restricted to specific employment categories and certain geographical areas (Knox, 1993). The average contribution by a fund member is 13.5% of his/her wages (Menke-Gluckert, 2000). Half of this contribution comes from the employees and the other half from the employers.

The fund arranges for medical services for its members by entering into contracts with the providers. Each year, the fund negotiates with the regional Association of Sickness Fund Physicians, which represents ambulatory care physicians, an annual budget based on the projected volume of transactions and the cost per transaction. The Association then undertakes on behalf of its members to provide the needed services to the fund's members. As explained in the previous section, each quarter, the Association receives a lump sum payment from the sickness funds that are disbursed to the physicians according to the itemized services provided by them to the fund's members. A fee schedule determines the amount to be paid for each service. The schedule contains about 2500 items of service each of which is assigned a certain number of points. For instance, a phone consultation with a patient is worth 80 points; a home visit is worth 360 points, and so on. The number of points per service is determined nationally and does not vary across regions. Each point has a monetary value that differs from region to region and by the type of fund. The monetary value of services provided to members of substitute funds tends to be higher than that of services provided to members of the primary funds. A physician's income, therefore, depends on the number of services provided, their relative point value, and the monetary value of each point. Physicians are not allowed to balance-bill the patients who belong to a sickness fund. They can, however, balance-bill a private patient (OECD, 1992).

Since a physician's income is tied to the volume of services provided, and available funds are limited by the negotiated agreement between the Physicians' Association and the sickness funds, one would expect physicians to compete among themselves for a greater share of the total volume of services provided. To keep this competition in check, the Physicians' Association is empowered to conduct utilization review and monitor the volume of services provided by each physician (Knox, 1993).

The fund also negotiates with individual hospitals an annual budget that covers their operating costs (the capital costs of hospitals, including private hospitals, are covered mainly by state governments). The operating budget is based on the projected number of patient days and the per-diem rate that takes into account staffing ratios, staff compensation, and other factors. The per-diem rate paid to public and not-for-profit hospitals, which together account for 86% of bed capacity, includes physicians' remuneration, while the rate paid to proprietary, private hospitals excludes physicians' remuneration. The difference in rates reflects the different methods by which hospital physicians receive payment. While physicians in public and non-for-profit hospitals are salaried employees, physicians in private hospitals receive fee-for-service payments.

Prior to the 1993 reforms, hospitals could get reimbursed for patient days in excess of those budgeted at a marginal rate of 25% of the established per-diem rate. The 1993 reforms have discontinued this practice. Today, if the hospitals fail to stay within the budget, the doctors and the hospitals would have to pay the excess cost (Knox, 1993).

In the case of dentists, the reimbursement mechanism is the same as that for ambulatory physicians. However, no global budget is negotiated with the

Association of Dentists. Patients make a partial payment for dentures and crowns. Pharmacists receive payment for prescribed drugs from the sickness funds and the patients.

All members of statutory sickness funds receive a basic benefit package. Table 8 lists many of the benefits included in the package. In addition, members receive several cash benefits, including sickness benefits and maternity allowances. Employers are required to pay the wages of employees for the first 6 weeks of an illness. Beyond the 6-week period, the sickness fund pays 80% of the wages for a maximum length of 78 weeks (Hoffmeyer and McCarthy, 1994). Maternity benefits include 14 weeks of wages paid by the employer, lump-sum payments at the time of birth, and monthly cash allowances up to a year following a child's birth. Parents of sick children receive 5 days of full pay to care for children under the age of 8 (Knox, 1993). Some cash benefits, such as payment of taxi fares for doctors' appointments and payment of funeral expenses, have been severely curtailed since the 1989 reforms.

In 1996, a new law introduced competition among the funds. Since then, the local funds have been losing members to other, more prosperous, funds, leaving them with a disproportionately large number of older, sicker, and, therefore, more costly patients. According to one estimate, the local funds have lost more than 2.2 million members since 1996 (Buck, 2000).

Table 8   The Basic Benefits Package

Preventive care
Primary care, including home visits
Hospital care
Dental care
Maternity care
Rehabilitative services
Prescription drugs
Prescription eyeglasses
Medical supplies
Family planning services
Physiotherapy
Periodic stay at health resorts

Source: (1) Hoffmeyer, U. K. and McCarthy, T. R. (eds.). *Financing Health Care, Vol. 1*. Boston: Kluwer Academic Publishers, 1994, p. 436; and (2) Knox, Richard A. *Germany: One Nation with Health Care for All*. New York: Faulkner and Gray, 1993, p. 14.

B. Private Insurance

Those who earn more than a certain income (approximately $25,000 a year in purchasing-power parity terms) can opt out of the statutory funds and join a private insurance plan. There are 50 private insurers who provide coverage for over 6 million people. Private insurers pay the providers more than the statutory funds and often offer extra benefits. Unlike the fund members, who pay a flat premium, those who are privately insured pay a risk-adjusted premium. The privately insured pay a level premium that is the annualized cost of a person's estimated medical care expenses over a lifetime.

The reimbursement principle is the same as that which obtains in the United States for fee-for-service indemnity insurance. The patient pays the copay charge and the deductible, while the insurance company pays the balance.

V. HEALTH STATUS

As noted in the introduction, the health outcomes in Germany are better than the outcomes in the United States in some areas. In other areas, however, the outcomes are better in the United States than in Germany. Although the overall life expectancy is higher in Germany than in the United States, elderly men can expect to live longer in the United States than in Germany. The disability-adjusted life expectancy at age 60 for U.S. males is 15 compared to 14.3 in Germany (WHO, 2000).

Germans are much more likely to die from liver disease and cirrhosis than are Americans. The higher death rate due to liver disease and cirrhosis in Germany may be due to the higher level of alcohol consumption. Per-capita consumption of alcohol is 14.2 liters in Germany compared to 9.6 in the United States. In spite of the fact that "sausage and beer are regarded as benign if not salubrious" in Germany (Harper, 1992, p. 158), the death rate due to heart disease is higher in the United States than in Germany.

VI. STRENGTHS AND WEAKNESSES

In view of the dramatic changes the system is currently undergoing, it is difficult to identify the present strengths and weaknesses of the system. Conceivably, the 1993 reforms have succeeded in addressing the problem areas and added strength in other areas. To the extent current information is available, it has been incorporated in the following analysis.

A. The System's Strengths

The German health care system is admired mainly for its ability to provide comprehensive, uniform, and universal health coverage to all German residents, citizens and noncitizens alike. The coverage includes virtually free outpatient care, hospital care, and preventive care, dental and vision care, prescription drugs, and rehabilitative services. In addition, the system affords the population free choice of physicians. Any patient can see any physician within a geographical area without having to pay anything other than the stipulated copay amount.

Second, there is a strong national consensus in favor of preserving the present system. Surveys have found a very high degree of satisfaction among Germans concerning their health care system and the principle of "solidarity" that underlies it. The solidarity principle refers to the notion of each member of the society willing to support the health care needs of the others. According to a Louis Harris survey conducted in 1990, 92% of Germans were either very satisfied or somewhat satisfied with the health care services they received (Harvard Community Health Plan, 1990). According to another 1990 survey, more than 40% of Germans felt that only minor changes were needed to the German health care system, while 10% of Americans felt the same way about the system in the United States (Blendon et al., 1990). Health care providers, who were reportedly quite enthusiastic about the system until a few years ago (Harper, 1992), are reportedly growing disenchanted. In November 2000, doctors launched a week-long strike in Berlin to protest the Socialist-Green Party government's reform measures (Buck, 2000).

Third, the system's accomplishments in the area of maternal and child care are quite impressive compared to those of the United States. In terms of a number of indicators of maternal and child health—infant mortality rate, perinatal death, low-birth-weight babies, and pregnancy-related maternal mortality rate—Germany's performance outranks that of the United States. The results are due in large part to the wide range of benefits the health care system offers pregnant women. All expectant mothers get free maternity care that includes at least 10 prenatal visits, two ultrasound scans, and any necessary lab work. Maternity care also covers the cost of household help, family planning, and genetic counseling services. In addition, women get paid maternity leave before and after delivery and get time off from work to attend prenatal care appointments. As explained by Knox (1993, p. 283), "Every pregnant woman gets a Mutterpass (mother's pass), a checklist on which to record the results of each checkup." The Mutterpass is a 32-page booklet that was designed by physicians and the sickness funds in 1985 (Fitzgerald and Jaffe, 1994).

Fourth, as noted by Hofreuter and Mendoza (1993, p. 25), "A simplified claims process and limited quality assessment ensures lower administrative costs." Physicians do not have to contend with "preapproval" and "utilization reviews" (Fitzgerald and Jaffe, 1994). Although the Physicians' Association has the authority to conduct utilization reviews, it is seldom exercised.

Finally, the health care delivery system is very much patient-oriented. The primary care physician, who acts as a gatekeeper to the health care system, assumes the responsibility for providing all the needed care to the patient. In addition to seeing patients in their office, many physicians make house calls to attend to the frail and the elderly (Fitzgerald and Jaffe, 1994; Harper, 1992).

B. The System's Weaknesses

The primary weakness of the system is cost overruns. Curiously, this weakness stems from one of the primary strengths of the system, namely, a generous benefits package. Until 1989, the package included such benefits as coverage of taxi trips to doctors' appointments and funeral expenses. That year, payments for these two items were severely curtailed. However, the reforms did not affect other benefits, such as free meals at hospitals and rest and recuperation at health spas for up to 6 weeks. With the sickness funds' deficits reaching record highs in 1992, these benefits were also curtailed. In 1997, charges to patients for prescriptions, hospital hotel services, and transport increased by $2.50 to between $4.50 and $12.50. Charges for treatments were increased by 5% (Karcher, 1997). Evidently, the system is still in the process of resolving the inherent tension between comprehensive coverage and cost control.

The second weakness of the system is overconsumption. German patients see their doctors twice as often as patients in the United States. They also see a specialist more often than patients in the United States (Knox, 1993). German patients also utilize hospital care more often than do U.S. patients. Part of the problem lies in the fact that long-term care is provided in a hospital setting rather than in a less costly setting such as a nursing home (United States Government Accounting Office, 1991). Additionally, as explained in the section on categories of expenditures, the per-diem reimbursement mechanism encouraged overconsumption of hospital services. Recognizing the potential for moral hazard inherent in the global per-diem reimbursement mechanism, the government has replaced it with a system that is a combination of DRG-type payments, per-diem rates, and lump-sum payments. One of the consequences of the new system is patient dumping. Many hospitals have reportedly refused to admit even emergency cases because it would be too costly to perform the needed surgeries. Another consequence has been unequal treatment. Koelbl reports that "if a patient arrives at the beginning of the year, he will receive the highest quality of care. If he is admitted in December, when the budget has been used up, he possibly will get only absolutely necessary treatment" (Koelbl, 1994, p. 33).

The third weakness of the system is the division between ambulatory practice and hospital practice. An important consequence of the division is underutilization of outpatient care. The 1993 reforms attempted to break down the wall separating ambulatory care and hospital care by allowing hospitals to perform ambulatory surgery that did not require a hospital stay. In spite of the reforms, reports indicate that shift to outpatient treatment is still quite slow (*Clinica*, 1995). The second consequence of the division is inefficiency. As noted by Dale Rublee of the American Medical Association, "Because there is no communication between the two groups of doctors, a lot of tests get duplicated" (Stevens, 1992, p. 151). The third consequence is difficulty in ensuring continuity of care, as a result of which some patients suffer. Another possible consequence is that the division may have slowed the growth of group practice, which has proved to be more cost-efficient than solo practice because groups enable pooling of human and capital resources.

The fourth weakness is the dual financing system under which hospitals are responsible for operating costs while capital investments are financed by the state governments. This fragmented system of financing results in a number of consequences. The fragmented system distorts the true financial conditions of the hospitals; it creates a two-tier decision-making system, one at the hospital level and the other at the state level; and it creates conditions in which capital investment decisions become subject to political and bureaucratic considerations.

The fifth weakness is the unresolved tension between pluralism and central ization. Under the pluralist system in existence until the early 1990s, each sickness fund was free to charge whatever premium was needed to cover the risk mix of its members. Thus, members of some sickness funds paid as little as 8% of their income, while members of other funds paid as much as 16% of their income toward their health care premium. The 1993 Act attempted to minimize the variations among the various funds' risk structures, thus ensuring equalization of premiums. The equalization was intended to create conditions for vigorous competition among the various funds for members. According to some, however, the risk and premium equalization "opens up the prospect of a single national sickness fund in the near future" (Stillfried and Arnold, 1993). Should this happen, the German system, which is far more controlled by the federal government today than even 5 years ago, may be indistinguishable from other centralized systems such as the ones in Britain, Canada, Sweden, and many other countries.

The sixth and final weakness is cost shifting. In an attempt to hold down health care outlays, the government has been shifting the costs onto the employers and the employees. For instance, the cost of nursing home coverage, which until recently was paid for by the government and individuals, has now been made the responsibility of the sickness funds. Since employers pay half of the contributions to the sickness funds, the move is likely to increase production costs and thus affect Germany's ability to compete in the world market. The system, which already relies heavily on employers and employees for the financing of health care, may be failing to take into account the opportunity cost of its cost-shifting measures.

VII. CURRENT ISSUES

There are a number of issues that concern policymakers about the health care system in Germany. Notable among these are cost containment, physician supply, an aging population, and integration of the East German health care system.

A. Cost Containment

In December 1999, the Bundesrat (upper house) rejected the Socialist-Green government's "Reform 2000" bill that had been passed by the Bundestag (lower house) only a month earlier. The bill attempted to place severe limits on spending by physicians, dentists, and pharmacists and impose heavy penalties on doctors who exceeded their budgets. It also obliged the richer sickness funds to compensate funds that faced deficits (de Bousingen, 2000).

The Reform 2000 bill is the latest of many efforts to control costs in Germany. The 1993 Health Reform Act contained a number of provisions that took direct aim at the ballooning health insurance deficits:

Increased spending by hospitals and physicians were tied to increases in the revenues of the sickness funds, which, in turn, depended on wage increases.

A DRG-type system called patient management categories (PMC) was introduced, which supplanted the per-diem reimbursement system for 180 categories of services in hospitals.

Fixed budgets were set for pharmaceuticals. Physicians were made financially responsible for prescriptions that exceeded the budget for pharmaceutical spending.

Several drug prices were reduced and many other drugs were placed on the reference-pricing list, which essentially meant price control. In addition, many drug prices were frozen for a period of 2 years.

Some benefits were curtailed or eliminated, while copay for drugs and hospital stays was increased.

The reform measures resulted in a dramatic turnaround. A $6 billion deficit in the health insurance funds in 1992 turned into a $6.5 billion surplus in 1993 (Koelbl, 1994). However, the improvement in cost control proved to be temporary. Total public expenditures on health care, which fell by 2% between 1992 and 1993, rose by 9% between 1993 and 1994 and by another 4% between 1994 and 1995 (OECD, 1996). Between 1995 and 1998, public expenditures grew at an average annual rate of 8.6% (OECD, 2000). This development mirrors what happened after the 1989 reforms. In 1989, public expenditures on health fell by a very small amount over the previous year. However, in 1990 they rose by 8%, in 1991 by 30%, and in 1992 by another 16% (OECD, 1996).

As already noted, spending on drugs accounts for 19% of total health care expenditures. The 1993 reforms provided for tight monitoring of physician prescription practices. Physicians and the pharmaceutical industry were required to pay for drug expenditures in excess of the budgeted amount. Yet, deficits continue to plague the drug budget. In an effort to balance the budget, the Socialist-Green Party coalition negotiated an agreement with the health insurance schemes in August 1999. The agreement stipulated the following restrictions:

1. Costly innovations of doubtful therapeutic value should be avoided.
2. A second opinion should be obtained when new drugs are prescribed.
3. Patients should pay a larger share of the cost of medicines for minor illnesses.
4. Generic drugs should be used more widely.

In spite of these measures, the drug budget was expected to show a deficit in a majority of the regions (*Chemist and Druggist*, 2000a).

B. Physician Supply

As was shown in Table 4, the physician population has been growing almost twice as fast as the general population. Policymakers see the disproportionate growth rate as a cause for concern for several reasons. First, it exacerbates the unemployment situation among physicians. Given that less than 10% of ambulatory physicians are able to enter practice in the first year (Jones, 1993), between 6000 and 10,000 physicians are estimated to be unemployed (Hofreuter and Mendoza, 1993). Second, the unemployed physicians place an additional burden on an already strained social welfare system. Third, a surplus of doctors in a regulated market has led to overconsumption of medical services. In other words, more doctors have meant more prescriptions, more visits to the doctor's office, and more diagnostic and therapeutic procedures. According to one estimate, a 1% increase in the supply of physicians causes a 1.1% increase in health care expenditures (Abel-Smith, 1992).

To restrict the supply of doctors, a number of measures have been introduced. The 1993 reforms have placed limits on the number of practices that can be started in any one region. The government is also encouraging doctors to set up practice in rural areas. Starting in 1999, the government has placed limits on medical school admissions.

The reforms appear to have slowed the growth rate, but the number of doctors is still growing. Between 1992 and 1993, the growth rate was 3.2%.

Between 1993 and 1994, the rate fell to 2.7% and between 1994 and 1998, it fell further to 1.4% (Federal Statistics Office, 2000).

C. Aging Population

Nearly 16% of the German population is aged 65 and over (Federal Statistical Office, 2000). This proportion is expected to rise over the next several decades and reach 36% by 2035 (Menke-Gluckert, 2000). According to one estimate, people aged over 65 as a percentage of those aged 20–64 is expected to double from around 28% in 2000 to 56% in 2050 (*Economist*, 2000). At present, the cost of caring for the elderly is covered by contributions from three sources: the government's social security pension fund, the elderly person's pension income, and a 3% payroll tax. The contributions from the pension fund and the pensioners' income cover only half of the cost of caring for the elderly. The other half is covered by the payroll tax. This pay-as-you-go system of financing elderly care is expected to face a crisis as the dependent population increases relative to the working population. According to one estimate, if present trends continue, payroll contribution rates will increase to 23.6% of wages by 2030 (Jackson, 1997). To remain solvent, the sickness funds may be forced in the future to create large reserves to fund future liabilities (Stevens, 1992).

An additional problem caused by the aging population is that it tests the viability of the pension system. The German welfare system is under considerable strain with one-third of the country's GDP being devoted to social benefits, which includes old-age pensions (Wurzel, 1996). Should the fiscal strain affect pension benefits, it would also impact on the ability of the pension funds to pay for the elderly population's health care.

D. Integration of the East German System

The East German health care system at the time of reunification was a world apart from the West German system. It was a state-run system linking a network of ambulatories (primary care centers) and polyclinics (multispecialty outpatient care centers). Physicians were salaried employees of the state. The average physician worked 33 hr per week, of which 20 involved direct patient care. The average salary of an East German physician was $10,000 compared to an average physician's income of $100,000 in the West. The East German system placed a far greater emphasis on preventive care than did the system in West Germany (Jones, 1993; Knox, 1993).

In spite of the differences, however, the outcomes produced by the two systems were not markedly different. In 1985, there were 2.3 physicians per thousand population in East Germany compared to 2.6 in West Germany. Both countries also had similar numbers of dentists, pharmacists, and hospital beds per thousand population. In 1987, life expectancy at birth in East Germany was 69.9 years for men and 76 years for women. The comaparative figures for West Germany were 72.2 years for men and 78.9 years for women (OECD, 1992).

The East German system, however, suffered from a number of problems. Hospitals were significantly overstaffed. Many of the facilities were substandard and the infrastructure was old and decrepit. In 1990, the Kohl government decided to dismantle the East German system and began the process of making that system over in the image of the West German system. A number of sickness funds were established, which, within a year, covered nearly 70% of the population. Of the 177 funds that were in operation in 1991, nearly two-thirds were company-based funds. The predominance of company-based funds is explained by the fact that most East Germans were employees of state-run enterprises prior to reunification. The payroll contributions to the sickness funds were set at 12.8% of the wages and were shared equally by the employer and the employee (Hoffmeyer and Mc-Carthy, 1994).

While the sickness fund model appears to have established itself in the East, several problems remain. Chief among these problems is modernization. It is estimated that it would cost $20 billion to upgrade the East German infrastructure and bring it up to western standards (Jones, 1993). The federal government started a decade-long modernization program in 1995 that called for an annual investment of $1 billion in the planned rebuilding of the medical facilities in the East. Given the pace of progress, it is doubtful whether the East German system would reach parity with the system in the West by the year 2005. One of the difficulties is that modernization of the health care system is tied to the overall economic growth in the East. Since the income of the sickness funds depends on the wage rates, the real income of workers must grow at a faster rate in the East than in the West if benefits comparable to those offered in the West are to be provided.

Another impediment to the modernization efforts is the inadequate investment in research. In 1995, the East German share of the national research funding was 8.7%. Only 3 of 46 special research groups are located in East Germany. The problem stems from the fact that the state-owned biotechnology and pharmaceutical industry performed virtually no research prior to reunification. Since a private pharmaceutical industry is in its infancy in the East, there are very few industry-funded projects. Unless a private industry becomes established, research is likely to continue to lag behind in the East (Selbmann et al., 1996).

The second problem relates to the acculturation of physicians and other providers in a market-based system. Since most physicians have never owned and operated a practice, a market-based system is unlikely to take hold any time soon. Talking about her experience in establishing a private practice in which she would have to "see patients in terms of money," an East German doctor highlighted some of the problems involved in the transformation: "Nobody told us how complicated it was and how expensive it would be just to set up an office. And no one said we would have to work in a certain way in order to make sure we can make back the money to pay for loans and mortgages'' (Lewis, 1991). Apparently, the regulation of doctors' fees has made the transition to a market-based system more difficult. Doctors' fees in the East are set at 60% of the levels in the West. However, the prices doctors pay for medical equipment and supplies are rising to West German levels. Until private practice becomes fully established, it is difficult to avoid disparities in the quality of care provided in the East and the West.

The third problem is cost escalation in general. The West German system has been unable to control costs in spite of comprehensive controls on budgets and prices. Should costs start to escalate faster than productivity increases, the integration process could suffer setbacks. Integrating the East German system, therefore, remains a daunting task.

VIII. CONCLUSIONS

When one takes a close look at the German health care system, a couple of conclusions become inescapable. The first conclusion is that it is neither an unmitigated success nor an unmitigated disaster. Proponents of the system (Weil, 1992; Fitzgerald and Jaffe, 1994) overlook the system's weakness, which include an inability to control costs in spite of tight budget and price restrictions. Opponents of the system (Prewo, 1994; Koelbl, 1994) tend to focus on some of the excesses of the system such as paid trips to health spas and fail to recognize its real accomplishments in such areas as maternal and child health. As pointed out by a study by the McKinsey group (*Economist*, 1996), the German system fails in some areas, but does well in others.

The second conclusion is that the German system is neither moving in the direction of the managed care model a la the United States, nor in the direction of the centralized models in such countries as Sweden and Britain. It has adopted some of the features of the managed care model for the operation of the sickness funds and some of the features of a centralized system that allows governmental intervention whenever deemed necessary. It remains to be seen whether such a hybrid produces better results than other existing models.

REFERENCES

Abel-Smith B (1992). Cost containment and new priorities in the European community. Milbank Q 70(3):393–422.

Annell A, Willis M (2000). International comparison of healthcare systems using resource profiles. Bull WHO 78(6):770

Blendon RJ, et al. (1990). Satisfaction with health systems in 10 countries. Health Affairs 9(2):185–192.

Buck T (2000). Bad prognosis for German health reforms. Financial Times, London, November 6, p. 15.

Chase M (1993). German health care system hits snag. Wall Street J, July 30, p. A7A.

Chemist and Druggist (2000a). Germany's health reform plans in tatters (news item). Chemist and Druggist, January 1, p. 14.

——— (2000b). Germany opts for Aussie solution (news item). Chemist and Druggist, December 16, p. 19.

Clinica (1995). Shift to outpatient treatment still slow in Germany (news item). Clinica, August 7, n. 666, p. 3.

——— (1996). More doctors in Germany than last year (news item). Clinica, April 1, n. 699, p. 3.

de Bousingen, DD (2000). Health reform attempt fails to thrive in Germany. Lancet, 355(9197):52.

The Economist (1996). The economics of health care: heal yourselves (uncredited report). The Economist, November 9, 341(7991):91–92.

——— (2000). Germany and its chancellor grow ever stronger (uncredited report). The Economist, December 23.

Federal Statistical Office (2000). Germany. Figures and Facts, Wiesbaden, on-line.

Fitzgerald S, Jaffe M (1994). What Hillary could learn from Canada and Germany. Washington Monthly 26(3):26.

Harper T (1992). German medicine—through a doctor's eyes. Med Econ 69(1):156–159.

——— (1993). What we can learn from Europe. Med Econ 70(17):138–144.

Harvard Community Health Plan (1990). Annual Report 1990: An International Comparison of Health Care Systems. Brookline, MA.: Harvard Community Health Plan.

Hoffmeyer UK, McCarthy TR (1994). Financing Health Care. Vol. I. Boston: Kluwer Academic Publishers.

Hofreuter DH, Mendoza EM (1993). Study tour examines health care systems in Germany, Holland and the U.S. Physician Exec 19(4):25.

Jackson JL (1997). The German health system: lessons for reform in the United States. Arch Intern Med 157(2):155–160.

Jones F (1993). The German system. Physician Exec 19(5):58–62.

Karcher H (1992). Shortcomings in German emergency medicine. Br Med J 304(6827):595.

——— (1997). Germany's new health reforms. Br Med J 314:845.

Knox RA (1993). Germany: One Nation with Health Care for All. New York: Faulkner and Gray.

Koelbl S (1994). Access denied. National Rev 46(16):29–33.

Lewis C (1991). As Berlin wall crumbles and two Germanies unite, health care problems emerge. Can Med Associ J 144(11):1512.

Marshall T (1993). Anatomy of Germany's nationwide healthcare system. Los Angeles Times, August 24, p. H1.

Menke-Gluckert W (2000). Aging population creates critical situation. Europe, February, p. 43.

OECD (1992). The Reform of Health Care: A Comparative Analysis of Seven OECD Countries, Paris: Organization for Economic Cooperation and Development.

―――― (1996). OECD Health Data (computer file). Paris: OECD.

―――― (2000). OECD in Figures, 2000 (computer file). Paris: OECD.

Prewo W (1994). Germany is not a model. Wall Street Journal, February 1, p. A14.

Rublee DA (1989). Medical technology in Canada, Germany, and the United States. Health Affairs 8(3):178–181.

Selbmann HK, Flohl R, Volk H-D, Rainauer H, Konze-Thomas B, Troidl H, Lorenz W (1996). Germany. Lancet 348(9042):1631–1639.

Stevens C (1992). Does Germany hold the key to U.S. health care reform? Med Econ, 69(1):148–155.

Stillfried D von, Arnold M (1993). What's happening to health care in Germany? Br Med J 306(6884):1017–1018.

Stone, DA (1980). The Limits of Professional Power: National Health Care in the Federal Republic of Germany. Cambridge, MA: MIT Press.

Tuffs A (1999). German government breaks off talks with doctors. Br Med J 319:874.

United States General Accounting Office (1991). Health Care Spending Control: The Experience of France, Germany, and Japan. Washington, DC:USGAO.

Weil TP (1992). The German health care system: a model for hospital reform in the United States? Hosp Health Serv Admin 37(4):533–537.

WHO (2000). World Health Report, 2000. World Health Organization, on-line.

Wurzel E (1996). Germany: the welfare system. OECD Observer, October–November, 202:45–47.

Zollner D (1982). ''Germany.'' In Peter A. Kohler and Hans F. Zacher (eds.). The Evolution of Social Insurance 1881–1981: Studies of Germany, France, Great Britain, Austria, and Switzerland. New York, St. Martin's Press, 1–92.

12
Italy's Health Care System

Michelle A. Angeletti
Florida Gulf Coast University, Fort Myers, Florida

I. INTRODUCTION TO ITALY AND BASIC DEMOGRAPHICS

While the health care delivery system in the United States is characterized by its base in the free market, health care systems in European countries are often operated by the central government and have the objective of providing coverage to the entire population. Like other European countries, Italy has a national health care system that is responsible for the delivery of health care to its population. Generally, Italy has health care expenditures that are comparable to those of other European countries. For example, in 1996, 7.8% of Italy's GDP was spent on health expenditures. This is comparable to the United Kingdom at 6.9%, Germany at 10.5%, and France at 9.8%. The Figure was much higher in the United States, which spent 13.6% of its GDP on health care (OECD, 1998).

The standard of living in Italy has been improving over time and is comparable to that of other European countries. For example, the average life expectancy during the 1950s was 67.2 for females and 63.7 for males. This increased to 72.3 for females and 67.2 for males in the 1960s, to 74.9 for females and 69.0 for males in the 1970s, and to 77.8 for females and 71.0 for males in the early 1980s (SISTAN, 1996). By 1996, the life expectancy at birth had increased to 81.3 for females and 74.9 for males (OECD, 1998). These figures are comparable to those found in France, Germany, the United Kingdom, and the United States (Table 1). Additionally, since the early 1980s, the infant mortality rate has been steadily decreasing. Between 1983 and 1992, the infant mortality rate per 1000 live births decreased from 12.3 to 7.9 (SISTAN, 1996). However, there are significant regional variations in the infant mortality rate. The rates in the north (6.2) and central (6.4) regions are better than that of the south (8.9) (SISTAN,

Table 1 Health Care Expenditure and Health Status by Country (1996)

	Italy	France	Germany	United Kingdom	United States
Total health expenditure as % of GDP[a]	7.8	9.8	10.5	6.9	13.6
Life expectancy at birth: female	81.3	82	79.9	79.3	79.4
Life expectancy at birth: male	74.9	74.1	73.6	74.4	72.7
Infant mortality (% of 1000 live births)	0.6	0.5	0.5	0.6	0.8

[a] 1995.
Source: OECD, 1998.

1996). However, the overall infant mortality rate in Italy is comparable to that of other European countries. In 1996, the infant mortality rate, as a percentage of live births, was 0.6 in Italy, 0.6 in the United Kingdom, 0.5 in Germany, and 0.5 in France (OECD, 1998). On a measure of health status in terms of potential life years lost (PLYL), which represents the shortening of life expectancy due to avoidable diseases, Italy is comparable to most other OECD countries (OECD, 1997a).

However, the causes of death vary by age group. In 1992, for those in the age group 15–44, the primary causes of death were accidents (36%) and tumors (20%). For those in the 45–74-year age group, the primary causes of death were tumors (43%) and diseases of the circulatory system (32%). For those individuals aged 75 and above, the primary causes of death were diseases of the circulatory system (54%) and tumors (19%). Overall, the primary causes of death in the Italian population are diseases of the circulatory system (43%) and tumors (28%) (SISTAN, 1996).

Another important aspect of Italy's demographic structure is the combination of an exceptionally low birth rate with an increasing elderly population. In the decade between 1981 and 1991, the population growth was modest, increasing only 0.3% (SISTAN, 1996). This trend has continued through the 1990s, and the growth rate from 1996 to 1997 was only 0.2%, leading to a total 1997 population level of only 56,868,000 (OECD, 1999b). Currently, Italy has the lowest birth rate in the European Union. According to the OECD (1998), Italy has the lowest total fertility rate as measured by the average number of children for a woman aged 15–49. The fertility rate in Italy is 1.2, compared to 1.3 in Germany, 1.7 in France, 1.7 in the United Kingdom, and 2.1 in the United States. Additionally, within Italy there are regional differences in birth rates. In general, the birth rates in the north and central regions are lower than in the south (SISTAN, 1996).

The combination of the increase in life expectancy and the low birth rate

Table 2 Aging Index by Year and Region

	1982	1992	1996
North	81.2	134.2	152.3
Central	90.5	151.7	174.8
South	51.6	76.8	90.6
Italy	62.0	97.5	113.2

Source: Ministero della Sanita', 1997.

is resulting in an increase in the percentage of elderly in the population. This trend is demonstrated in the increase in the aging index (*l'indice di vecchiaia*), which expresses, in a percentage, the number of people over age 65 and younger than age 15 (Table 2). In 1971, the aging index was 45.8, which indicated that there were approximately 2.2 young people for each elderly person. In 1982, the index increased to 62.0, at which time, 21.3% of the population was under age 15 and 13.2% were over age 54. By 1992, it reached 97.5, which indicated an almost even ratio of 1 to 1 between youth and elderly populations. At that time, the population under 15 had decreased to 15.8% while the population over 65 had increased to 15.4%. In 1996, the trend continued as the elderly reached 16.8% of the population and exceeded the younger group, which had decreased to only 14.9% of the population. This resulted in an index of 113.2 (Ministero della Sanita', 1997). Again, there are large regional differences. As a result of the lower birth rates in the north and central regions, these regions are aging at a rate much higher rate than the south. In 1982, the aging index was 81.2 for the north and 90.5 for the central, but only 51.6 for the south. In 1996, although there was an increase in all regions, the north (152.3) and central (174.8) regions had much larger elderly populations than the south (90.6) (Ministero della Sanita', 1997).

In this regard, Italy is facing a similar situation to that of the United States as it plans for the health care burden that will be created by the aging of the baby boom generation. In Italy, there is concern because the ever-expanding population of elderly will consume a larger quantity of services and more expensive services. At the same time that the expenditure trend is increasing, the burden for these expenditures remains with a population of youth that is becoming increasingly smaller.

II. THE GOVERNMENT

Because the Italian health care system is operated by the government, many of the problems with the health care system are directly related to the structural problems of its government. Thus, it is important to have an understanding of the organizational structure of the government, its attempts for regionalization, and its primary problems, including the debt, bureaucratic complexity and rigidity, political involvement in the public administration, and general corruption.

A. The Government Organization

As a government, Italy is relatively young and was first unified as a state on February 18, 1861. At the time of unification, the form of government was a constitutional monarchy. However, on June 2, 1946, the Italian citizens voted to have their nation converted from a monarchy into a republic, and a new constitution became effective on January 1, 1948. The leadership of Italy consists of a president and a premier. The president is elected by the parliament and serves a 7-year term. The president represents the country on formal occasions such as the signing of treaties, and it is the responsibility of the president to appoint the premier. It is the premier who actually heads the government and decides its policies. However, this appointment must be approved by the parliament, and a vote of ''lack of confidence'' by either house of parliament requires the premier to resign. The parliament is composed of two houses: the Chamber of Deputies and the Senate. The Italian citizens elect the 630 members of the Chamber of Deputies, the 315 members of the Senate to 5-year terms, and the president may appoint five additional senators.

The public sector (*settore pubblico*) consists of two main categories: the general government (*amministrazioni pubbliche*) and the autonomous government agencies that provide market services, such as the state railroad, telephone company, and post office. The general government is composed of (a) part of the state sector (*settore statale*) (including the state and central administration, but excluding autonomous national companies, such as the state road department and forest department), (b) the local governments, which includes governments of the regions, provinces, and municipalities, and other local authorities such as universities, hospitals, chambers of commerce, housing administration, and local health units (*Unita' Sanitarie Locali*, USL), and (c) social security institutions, such as Social Security (INPS) and the Industrial Accidents Insurance Fund (INAIL) (OECD, 1999a).

B. Regionalization

Italy has had a relatively long history of regionalization (*regionalizzazione*). In 1934, a law was passed that provided the 8000 local governmental units, called *comuni*, with limited resources for basic services such as keeping birth and death certificates and providing for a local police force. In the 1948 Constitution, Italy provided for the development of regional governments, specifically, five special regions and 14 ordinary regions. Later, another ordinary region was added to the list. Although a part of the Constitution, four of the special regions were created at that time, but the ordinary regions were not created until several decades later. The failure to create these ordinary regions was seen as a tactic used by the Christian Democrats (*Partito della Democrazia Cristiana*), who were in control of the central government, to maintain power. From the late 1940s until the early 1960s, the Christian Democratic government was reluctant to transfer any power to the regional levels because it might have been used by the Left, especially the Communist Party (*Partito Comunista Italiano*) (Agnew, 1990). The decentralization of Italy became a power struggle between the Christian Democrats, who were opposed to it, and the Communists, who were its proponents. This political battle ensued until the 1960s when the Socialist Party (*Partito Socialista Italiano*), who also opposed the Christian Democrats, entered the political arena.

To maintain power, the Christian Democrats traded public jobs for votes, and in this transfer, little thought was given to government efficiency. However, later as the country was growing economically and more demands were being made on the government, it was clear that the inefficient government was unable to respond. In an attempt to resolve this problem, many Italians supported decentralization. They supported the idea of regional control and resolution of regional problems. For the next decade, support strengthened for the regionalization of Italy. Because support was stronger at the local level than the national level, a bottom-up approach was taken. At the local level, many communities developed their own local councils. Through increased pressure and the ever-constant need for public support, the Christian Democrats changed their position in support of regionalization. Finally, in 1970, this Constitutional objective was realized with the passage of a new law in which the ordinary regions were created. In 1976, when the parliament passed a law to regulate their activities, 60% of Italian cities already had local councils (Agnew, 1990).

Currently, Italy is divided into 20 regions, and these regions are subdivided into provinces. The provinces are then divided into local governmental units, or *comuni*. In the north are the regions of Valle d'Aosta, Piedmont, Lombardia, Veneto, Friuli-Venezia Giulia, Trentino-Alto Adige, Emilia-Romagna, and Liguria. Central Italy consists of Tuscana, Marche, Umbria, and Lazio. The regions of the South are Abruzzi, Molise, Campania, Puglia, Basilicata, and Calabria, and the islands of Sicilia and Sardegna. Often, statistics compare the standard of living in the north with that of the south. In this case, the regions of central Italy are combined with those of the north.

Although the standard of living for Italy is comparable to that of other countries, within Italy, there are great disparities. In general, the standard of living in the north is much higher than in the south. The northern region is highly industrialized, has direct access to the European marketplace, and is overall comparatively wealthier than the south. The south composes 40% of Italy's land area and 35% of its population, but only 24% of the GDP ("Italy," 1993). While unemployment rates in Italy averaged about 12% in the first half of 1998, the unemployment rate in the south continued to be far higher than in the north. In 1998, unemployment was 6.9% for north and central Italy, which is in sharp contrast to the unemployment rate of 22.5% in the south (OECD, 1999a). This 15.6% differential between the north and south represents a continuing divergence and compares to 11.6% in 1994 (OECD, 1999a). Additionally, the cumulative growth of GDP in 1995 and 1996 in the south was only 2.6, compared to 4.8 in the north and central regions (OECD, 1997a). In 1950, these economic disparities prompted the Italian government to establish the Fund for the South (*Cassa per il Mezzogiorno*). This was a generous package of financial aid that supported primarily public works projects, but also agriculture, industry, and tourism (Shinn, 1985). These public works projects were notorious for taking extended periods of time to build. This was seen as an informal conspiracy between unions, bosses, and the government and created an enormously swollen workforce on the public payroll ("Italy," 1990). In 1993, the Fund for the South project was discontinued.

The historical public support for regionalization and decentralization remains prevalent today. For example, there has been growing political support of regional political parties such as the Northern League (*Lega Nord*), which represents the interests of Northern Italy. Its leader, Umberto Bossi, has preached separation of the north and south into two states. He has also encouraged his followers to oppose state taxes because they feel that they are paying taxes to support the south.

The support for regionalization and decentralization is also evident in the current reforms of the health care system. Although not regions, the cities of Bolzano, Trento, and Valle d'Aosta were made into special health care regions with individual financing and organizational structures. Additionally, most of the current health care reforms are aimed at transferring responsibility for quality and delivery of services from the national level to the regions. It is believed that this move will decrease the bureaucracy related to the central government and allow the regions to respond to the needs of its citizens in a more efficient manner.

C. The Government Debt

Although Italy has been under pressure to stabilize the economy in order to join the European Monetary Union, and its government debt has been decreasing relative to its GDP since 1994, it remains huge at 121.6% (OECD, 1999a). It is believed that the root of the Italy's budgetary problems can be traced back to the early 1970s, when social reforms were implemented, but their costs were not matched by an increase in taxes. This unmatched spending quickly resulted in debt accumulation and rising debt service costs (OECD, 1997a). In 1970, Italy's public debt was 38% of the GDP. This level was relatively modest when compared to other nations, such as 45.5% for the United States, 53.2% for France, and 80% for the United Kingdom (Fazio, 1992). However, because of large social transfers and an inefficient bureaucracy, the gross public debt increased dramatically between 1970 and 1990. By 1997, Italy's gross public debt as a percent of GDP, 121.6%, was huge in contrast to that of other European nations, such as 58% for France, 53.4% for the United Kingdom, and 61.3% for Germany (OECD, 1999a).

More than three-quarters of the increase in spending in Italy over the past three decades can be attributed to social spending, including health, education, welfare, and pensions (OECD, 1997a). Although the growth of public expenditure over the last 30 years has been affected by most of Italy's spending categories, its spending on health care has had a significant affect on its debt. Among its functional categories, the increase in spending for health (3% of GDP) was second only behind pensions and welfare payments (7% of GDP) (OECD, 1997a). Thus, in an attempt to control spending and correct the fiscal disequilibrium, the government has made budgetary cuts in discretionary spending, with a large decline in spending for health-related services (OECD, 1997a).

D. Bureaucratic Complexity and Rigidity

Many of the problems with the Italian public administration have been created by its unstable political atmosphere. During the last 50 years, Italy has had more than 50 coalition governments, some of which were so unstable that they lasted only a few months. The OECD (1997a) states that because of the general instability of the government, Italy's public sector has also been characterized by complex bureaucratic structures and organizational rigidity. Significantly, these problems inhibit most attempts to reform the public sector and create organizational difficulties in the delivery of health care services.

A major effect of the unstable political environment is that it has increased bureaucratic complexity. As each administration has entered power, it has imposed new regulations. These new regulations, some of which even conflict with current regulations, serve to complicate an already difficult system. Thus, the numerous and uncoordinated laws make their interpretation extremely difficult. The OECD (1997a, p. 100) has also stated that the task of the public administration has been "exacerbated by a plethoric legal system." For example, in Italy, the number of laws in the early 1990s was estimated at between 100,000 and 150,000. This is excessive when compared to the 7000 laws in France and the 6000 in Germany. Additionally, this excessive amount of laws has compounded the rigidity of the public sector and increased costs to private citizens and institutions. The "hidden tax" derived from the complicated bureaucracy, in terms of days lost for contacts with the public administration, has been estimated at around 18–20 trillion lire annually (Roccella, 1996).

In Italy, another problem that results from the weak political structure is that bureaucrats are often fearful of making organizational changes. They are fearful of attempting to change the system because the current government may be replaced before all of the changes have been implemented. Thus, bureaucrats may be reluctant or unwilling to make changes implemented by a new administration and, instead, maintain a status quo mentality. This fear and reluctance leads systematic bureaucratic rigidity.

Other public administration problems include rigid employment rules, delays, cost overruns, waste, and gaps in infrastructure (OECD, 1997a). This is especially important in the health care sector because the expansion of public employment has been especially strong for hospitals. Additionally, rigid employment rules have led to inefficient deployment of workers across regions and administrations. In addition to problems with employment, there have also been problems with the inadequate distribution of resources. These gaps in infrastructure are especially critical in the south.

E.   Political Involvement in Public Administration

Unfortunately, Italy's public sector is notorious for its use of political appointees. Historically, the system of spoils began during the economic transformation at the end of World War II. At that time, Germany had been defeated and there were strong anticommunist sentiments. Importantly, the United States desired to defeat communist attempts to control any more nations. Through the Truman doctrine, the United States established military bases in Italy to protect the West against communism. Politically, the United States supported the Christian Democratic Party (*Partito della Democrazia Cristiana*) against the Communist Party (*Partito Comunista Italiano*), which was always the second largest party after the Christian Democrats. To maintain power, the Christian Democrats had to prevent other parties from forming a coalition government with the Communists. To maintain power, the politicians resorted to trading favors for political support. One tactic used by politicians to gain support was by providing jobs through political influence (*raccomandazioni*). These jobs were provided in return for political support.

In addition to trading jobs for votes through *raccomandazioni*, the Italian politicians also use another means to garner political support for their party. Once political parties gained strength and had been elected into government, jobs were portioned out between competing parties. For example, one public sector enterprise came under the control of the first party and another was controlled by the second party. After public enterprises had been portioned to parties, the parties then filled the job positions with their party supporters. The process of *lottizzazione* was another process of patronage that maintained party strength by trading jobs for votes. Historically, this system of patronage has been epidemic and was found at every level of government service.

Because Italy's civil servants were selected through the spoils system, their qualifications consisted predominantly of party loyalty. Appointments that are traded for votes use qualifications that are political and not job related. Indeed, individuals may have little understanding of the knowledge, skills, and abilities needed to perform their job. This lack of qualifications for public service added to the inefficiency. Another problem that results from patronage is that public sector employees do not view themselves as public servants. They are political appointees. They do not owe their allegiance to the government or to the public. Instead, they owe their allegiance to the politician who, through a *raccomandazione*, provided them with a lifetime position.

As a result of this patronage, public workers may not have the ability to work efficiently. Additionally, because of their political allegiance, they may not even feel the desire to work efficiently for the state or to provide efficient and courteous service to customers. In fact, one study found that over a third of respondents indicated that a source of discontent with the national health care system was the uncaring attitude of personnel (Bariletti et al., 1991). In another survey of the quality of public services by the OECD, the inefficiency of the Italian public sector was clearly demonstrated. For example, for postal services, the average delivery delay within 500 km for Italy was 3.5 days while Germany, the United Kingdom, and France had only 1 day delay. For telephone service, Italy had a success rate for urban calls of only 50.5%. This is in contrast with Germany at 99%, the United Kingdom at 86%, and France at 70.3% (OECD, 1994).

F. Corruption

In addition to political appointments, the Italian political and public administration have also faced outright corruption. Historically, Italian politicians formed direct connections with the mafia to garner political support. The politician would provide the mafia with government contracts and in exchange, the mafia provided the politicians with political support and votes. The Christian Democrats, who were in a constant struggle to maintain power, would provide public works and development assistance projects to the mafia in exchange for votes. Notoriously, this trade was successful at keeping the Christian Democrats in power in Rome and the mafia in power in the south ("Italy," 1993).

Corruption continues to be a problem in Italian politics. A parliamentary study released on October 29, 1992 stated that almost 60% of all government contracts for public works projects were awarded on a discretionary basis. In fact, the magistrates noted that this process encouraged corruption (OECD, 1992). The OECD (1997a) indicated that between 1989 and 1994, 4000 public employees were investigated, primarily for corruption, extortion, and abuse of power. For example, former leader of the Socialist Party Bettino Craxi was investigated for corruption involving bribes and kickbacks for public works projects, and Mario Chiesa, former Socialist Party official and nursing home administrator, was sentenced to 6 years in prison for accepting kickbacks (OECD, 1992). One estimate suggests that this corruption is responsible for 15% of Italy's budget deficit (OECD, 1992). As a means of reducing corruption, authorities are considering the use of stricter administrative sanctions and the creation of an independent authority for monitoring the assets of public employees (OECD, 1997a).

III. THE NATIONAL HEALTH CARE SYSTEM

Italy's health care system is controlled largely by the state. The organizational branch of government responsible for health care is the Ministry of Health (*Ministero della Sanita*). One of the most important responsibilities of the Ministry of Health is operation of the *Servizio Sanitario Nazionale* (SSN), the national health care system.

A. The *Servizio Sanitario Nazionale*

In 1978, through legislative act no. 833, the government established the SSN as its national health care system. This act was implemented in an attempt to reform and integrate Italy's fragmented health care system. Its goal was to substitute a fragmented system with a unified, national level system that would provide health services to all citizens. The 1978 legislation presented a new policy direction, outlined the organizational structure of the SSN, and defined methods of programming and financing the system. However, this piece of legislation had weaknesses. For example, it left many of the fundamental aspects for the implementation of the SSN to future legislative actions that were to occur at both the federal and regional levels. Indeed, some of the major problems that developed with the SSN resulted because intended legislation was never produced (Bruzzi, 1997).

Another problem that developed from the 1978 health care reform law was that it entrusted the implementation of the SSN to different levels of government, each having a certain level of autonomous power for decision making (Bruzzi, 1997). For example, the first level of government was the federal level, which was given the responsibility of financing the health care delivery system. It was also given policymaking responsibilities through the development of the national health plan (*Piano Sanitario Nazionale*, PSN). The second level of government given responsibilities in the national health care delivery system was the regional level. At this level, the regional governments were primarily responsible for programming and managing the supply. At the third level were local governments (*comuni*), which were given the responsibility of managing the health care services. At the local level, the law gave the local governments the responsibility of health care delivery through the *Unita' Sanitarie Locali* (USLs), which are local health units and the operative structure of the SSN. Additionally, hospitals are controlled at the local level because the 1978 reform placed them within the organizational structure of the USLs. This organizational structure based on different levels created an environment of fragmentation of the health care delivery system. Additionally, this fragmentation of responsibility often caused conflicts between the different levels regarding tasks and responsibility of service (Bruzzi, 1997).

IV. PROBLEMS WITH THE 1978 REFORM

Although Italy's expenditures on public health are no greater than those of other European countries, the organizational structure of its health care system was largely inefficient and in need of reform. The 1978 health reform established an organizational structure such that the delivery of services was decentralized to the regional level and provided by the local health units (USLs). At the same time, the payment of health services was attributed to the central government. The problems created by the separation of service provision and payment were compounded by limited accountability and a lack of competition among suppliers. Furthermore, this environment compromised spending controls and resulted in both the misallocation of resources and the inefficient production of services (OECD, 1997a).

A. Financing the SSN

The financing mechanism of the health care system was public, and formulated on a tax-based model. Although funds were derived primary from the central government, through health contributions (*contributi sanitari*) and general taxation (*imposte generali*), funds were also collected at the local level (Bruzzi, 1997). At the local level, revenues were raised through two primary means. The first was the use of the "ticket," a tax placed on the purchase of some pharmaceuticals and medical services. The second source of local revenue was through fees from services provided by public structures that were used to cover local health care costs. In 1995, public health expenditures were financed primarily through health contributions and budgetary transfers. For example, 53% of public health expenditures were financed through health contributions, 40% through budgetary transfers, 4% through local revenues, and the remainder through other sources (OECD, 1997a).

Since funding was transferred from the federal government to the local governments, revenues needed to go through a budget formulation process. First, at the federal level, revenues were collected through general taxation and health care contributions. Second, there was consideration of the federal budget (*bilancio dello stato*) and then the budget laws (*legge delle finanziaria*). From these considerations, a budget for the national health care fund (*fondo sanitario nazionale*, FSN) was developed. Funds were then transferred from the FSN to the regional health care funds (*fondo sanitario regionale*, FSR) that supplied the revenues to be spent by the regions. Funds were then transferred within the regions to the local health care units, USL, for the provision of health care services (Bruzzi, 1997). Previously, the only criteria to deliver funds from the central government to the regions and then from the regions to the USL was that of historical expenditure. Incremental budget increases were used, and the budget developed each year was proportional to the expenditures of the previous year. Beginning in 1993, legislation was introduced that changed the incremental budget process. The new method consisted of a quota based upon the incremental budget increase and an amount that was proportional to the population of each region (Bruzzi, 1997).

In addition to the local revenues produced, the amounts given to the USL from the regions were the maximum that they could spend. The established budget was an attempt to control expenditures in the health care system (Bruzzi, 1997). However, this system was not effective and failed to control health care expenditures. Part of the failure was due to the systematic underprovision of governmental transfers. As a result, the USL were authorized to incur debt with the local banking system. These debts were later incorporated into the state sector government debt. Between 1980 and 1992, this debt accumulation reached a level of 73 trillion lire (OECD, 1997a).

B. Health Care Spending

Between 1975 and 1990, Italy's health care spending steadily increased (Table 3). In 1975, Italy's total expenditure on health was 6.2% of GDP. This figure increased to 7.0% of GDP by 1985 and to 8.1% of GDP by 1990. It is believed that this increase was due to financial weaknesses in the 1978 health care reform law, which instituted the national health care system, the SSN. For example, the system was organized such that services were provided at the local level through the USLs and paid for by the central government. However, there were not sufficient mechanisms to control spending, and this led to increased expenditures (OECD, 1997a).

Table 3 Total Expenditure on Health by Country 1975–1995 as percentage of GDP

	1975	1980	1985	1990	1995
Italy	6.2	6.9	7.0	8.1	7.7
France	7.0	7.6	8.5	8.9	9.9
Germany	8.1	8.4	8.7	8.3	9.6
United Kingdom	5.5	5.6	5.9	6.0	6.9
United States	8.2	9.1	10.7	12.7	14.5

Source: OECD, 1997a.

Between 1985 and 1995, Italy saw an increase in total health care expenditure per capita as measured in $US purchasing power parities (PPPs) (Table 4). In 1985, Italy's total health care expenditures were $US 830 PPPs. This was comparable to other European countries, such as the United Kingdom at $US 670, France at $US 1088, and Germany at $US 1274. The United States was higher than the European countries and total health care expenditures were $US 1733 PPPs. By 1995, Italy's total health care expenditures increased to $US 1507 PPPs. This is comparable to the rates of the United Kingdom at $US 1246, France at $US 1956, and Germany at $US 2134. Again, the expenditures of the United States were considerably higher at $US 3701 PPPs.

Between 1975 and 1990, Italy's public expenditure for health care showed a constant increase (Table 5). In 1975, Italy spent 5.2% of GDP on health care. This was similar to other European countries. For example, spending was 5.0% in the United Kingdom, 5.4% in France, and 6.3% in Germany. However, public spending on health in the United States, which is characterized as a private payor system, was lower than in these European countries at 3.5% of GDP. According

Table 4 Total Health Care Expenditure Per Capita in $US Purchasing Power Parities

	1985	1995
Italy	830	1507
France	1088	1956
Germany	1274	2134
United Kingdom	670	1246
United States	1733	3701

Source: OECD, 1997b.

Table 5 Public Spending on Health by Country 1975–1995 as Percentage of GDP

	1975	1980	1985	1990	1995
Italy	5.2	5.6	5.4	6.3	5.4
France	5.4	6.0	6.5	6.6	7.8
Germany	6.3	6.3	6.4	5.9	7.0
United Kingdom	5.0	5.0	5.0	5.1	5.8
United States	3.5	3.9	4.3	5.2	7.0

Source: OECD, 1997b.

to the OECD (1997a), Italy's public health care expenditure remained relatively stable during the first half of the 1980s. However, between 1987 and 1991, spending increased by 1% of GDP. This increase in health care expenditure was attributed mainly to increasing health care prices. The rise in health care prices resulted from the higher costs of new medical technologies, organizational inefficiency, and fraud. However, other factors also played a role in the increase in public health care expenditure. For example, cost increases were also attributed to an increase in quantity of services utilized by the aging population. Other factors included rising per capita incomes and expanded insurance coverage (OECD, 1997a).

Two factors that affect government spending on health care are public investment in medical facilities and public expenditure on health administration (Table 6). Italy's public investment in medical facilities, as a percentage of public expenditure on health, is significantly lower than that of other European countries. For example, while Italy's investment in medical facilities was only 1.8% of

Table 6 Health Care Input Indicators by Country 1994

	Italy	France	Germany	United Kingdom	United States
Public investment in medical facilities (% of public expenditure on health)	1.8	3.9	6.1[a]	4.9	1.0[a]
Public expenditure on health administration (% of public expenditure on health)	6.3	0.2	5.5	3.6	2.7

[a] 1993.
Source: OECD, 1997b.

public expenditure on health, expenditure levels in France, the United Kingdom, and Germany were 3.9%, 4.9%, and 6.1%, respectively (OECD, 1997b). However, while public investment in medical facilities was lower than in other European countries, public expenditure on health administration was higher. In 1994, Italy's public expenditures on health administration as a percentage of public expenditure on health was 6.3%. This is comparable to the lower levels of other countries, such as Germany at 5.5%, the United Kingdom at 3.6%, and France at only 0.2% (OECD, 1997a).

C. Quality, Efficiency, and Consumer Satisfaction

As in most of Italy's public sector, its health care sector is deemed largely inefficient and unsatisfactory. This inefficiency includes factors such as waiting lists for treatment, shortage of nursing staff, poor quality of food and hygiene, the dilapidated state of many hospitals, and the general bureaucratic inefficiency of hospital administration (OECD, 1992). For example, a university hospital and one of the largest public institutions in Europe, Umberto Primo, in Rome was investigated after it was discovered that several of the patients in the ocular department obtained severe damages as a result of infections. As a result of this investigation, 411 specific violations were discovered. These violations included a fire system that was not connected to the central water supply and no established plan of evacuation. Additionally, surgical rooms were found to be below acceptable standards because of dirt and debris that was present. Although the hospital remained open, it was placed under judicial sequester and required to develop an action plan to address its inefficiencies (Micossi, 1998; Turno, 1998). As these investigations spurred further ones at other hospitals, surgical rooms in Florence, Naples, and Milan were closed as a result of substandard conditions (Micossi, 1998). In addition to quality issues, Italy's hospitals also have utilization problems. The OECD (1997b) indicates that turnover and occupancy rates suggest insufficient utilization of hospital resources (Table 7). This trend was also noted by the OECD in 1992 when it stated that the cost and productivity levels of medical laboratories and the utilization rates for hospital equipment suggest that the public sector is less efficient than the nonregulated private sector.

The low quality and efficiency in the public health care system is reflected in the opinions of Italy's health care consumers. Consumer surveys conducted in the early 1990s indicated comparatively low satisfaction with the quality of health care in Italy. For example, the level of satisfaction with health services in Italy was only 12%, while rates for the United Kingdom were 27%, and approximately 40% for France and Germany (OECD, 1997a). The most frequent sources of discontent were "long waiting lists for specialist consultations, lack of proper equipment, the dilapidated state of many hospitals and bureaucratic management" (OECD, 1997a, p.86).

Table 7   Utilization Rates of Health Care Structures (1994)

	Italy	France	Germany	United Kingdom	United States
Inpatient beds per 10,000 inhabitants	6.5	8.9[a]	9.7[a]	4.9	4.1[a]
Occupancy rates in all inpatient care institutions (% used beds)	72.5[b]	83.0	83.9[c]	NA	68.7[c]
Hospital turnover rate (number of cases per bed)	23.8[b]	25.0[b]	21.8[c]	49.5	34.0[d]
Average number of days in inpatient care institution	11.1[b]	11.7	13.9[c]	10.21	8.8[c]
Admission rate in all inpatient care institutions (% population)	16.0	22.8	19.9	21.6	13.0

[a] 1995.
[b] 1993.
[c] 1992.
[d] 1990.
Source: OECD, 1997b.

Almost half of all respondents indicated that long waiting lists was a source of dissatisfaction (Table 8). For example, a person may have to wait several months for an appointment. However, if someone wants immediate treatment, he usually has two options. First, if it is a medical emergency, the person can go the emergency room of the local hospital. However, if the person is not in an emergency, he can usually schedule a private appointment within a week with a physician. Often, physicians accept private pay patients in their offices prior to or after they see public patients. However, the individual seeing the physician on a private basis must pay out-of-pocket for the costs incurred because they are

Table 8   Sources of Dissatisfaction with SSN by Region (as Percentage of Population)

	Northwest	Northeast	Center	South	All Italy
Long waiting lists	51.3	54.8	51.4	36.2	46.6
Red tape	34.4	37.4	47.4	27.4	35.0
Lack of proper equipment	26.3	16.1	35.2	48.6	34.0
Uncaring attitude of personnel	32.3	29.0	27.7	40.6	33.7
Shortage of personnel	23.1	14.4	26.2	30.1	24.6

Source: Bariletti et al., 1991.

not covered by the SSN and are not reimbursable. In addition to long waiting lists, over a third of the respondents indicated dissatisfaction due to red tape, lack of proper equipment, and the uncaring attitude of personnel. Additionally, almost 25% of respondents were dissatisfied because of a shortage of personnel.

There also appears to be a large variation in level of satisfaction based on region (Table 8). For example, over 50% of respondents from the northern and central regions were dissatisfied with long waiting lists; the percentage dropped to 36% in the south. While 47% of respondents from the central regions were dissatisfied with the level of red tape, in the south only 27% were dissatisfied with this item. However, the respondents in the south indicated much higher levels of dissatisfaction with the lack of proper equipment and the uncaring attitude of personnel than respondents from the north and central regions. Also, in 1995, 45% of respondents from the northern regions were very satisfied with hospital medical assistance, compared to only 22% in the south (OECD, 1997a). While 49% of respondents from the northeast were highly satisfied with nurse assistance, that level dropped to 18% in the south. Finally, while 43% of respondents in the northeast indicated high satisfaction with hygienic services, this level decreased to 14% in the south (OECD, 1997a).

D. The North-South Division

Another major problem affecting the national health care system in Italy is the variation in quality of health care services between the regions. Specifically, services in the south are less favorable than those in the north and central regions. For example, while the infant mortality rate is 6.2 in the north and 6.4 in the central regions, it is 8.9 in the south (SISTAN, 1996). In fact, the OECD (1992) has noted that the south is characterized by a lack of provisions for health care infrastructure. This is exemplified in the variation in health care spending by region (Table 9). For example, the spending per inhabitant on health care for the north is 9% above the national average and spending in the central regions is 4% above the national average. However, spending on health care per inhabitant in the south is more than 7% below the national average. Additionally, these variations are exemplified in consumer satisfaction surveys of the early 1990s. For example, respondents in the south indicated greater dissatisfaction with the health care system because of a shortage of personnel and lack of proper equipment (Bariletti et al., 1991).

E. Political Involvement

Another aspect of the reform that is important is its attempt to make the health care system representative of the citizenry. The 1978 health care reform law that enacted the SSN established assemblies that had the responsibility to appoint

Table 9 Health Care Spending by Region (1996)

Region	Spending per inhabitant (Italian lire)	% Difference from national average
North		
Piemonte	1684000	−3
Valle d'Aosta	1898000	9
Lombardia	17775000	2
Bolzano	2174000	25
Trento	1867000	8
Veneto	1796000	4
Friuli-Venezia Giulia	1815000	5
Liguria	1879000	8
Emilia-Romagna	2049000	18
Central		
Toscana	1859000	7
Umbria	1766000	2
Marche	1877000	8
Lazio	1780000	3
South		
Abruzzo	1691000	−2
Molise	1644000	−5
Campania	1555000	−10
Puglia	1585000	−9
Basilicata	1581000	−9
Calabria	1560000	−10
Sicilia	1556000	−10
Sardegna	1679000	−3
All Italy	1734000	

Source: Ministero della Sanita', 1996.

members of a management committee for each of the USLs within its territory. The law expected that the USL would be administered by this committee, made up of five to seven members, of which one member would be the president of the USL. However, these assemblies were political organs representative of the local government (*consiglia comunali*) (Bruzzi, 1997). Importantly, because the assemblies were of a political nature and linked to the local government, it was possible that the committee representatives were selected because of their political connections and affiliations, rather than their management skills or knowledge of health care institutions. As a result of this organizational structure, the management of the USLs would often have scarce experience and competencies in administration. As in other public administration sectors, the management of the USLs often did not have the knowledge, skills, or abilities to operate a health care institution. In addition to the political selection of management, there was another factor that increased political involvement in the management of the USL. Once the assembly appointed the members of the management committee, it did not provide the committee with the independence to perform its functions. Instead the assembly had to approve the various acts of the committee, including the budget. Because of this complicated system of governance, with its relations to local government politics, the management of the USLs were often focused on political issues rather than management responsibilities.

V. THE 1992 REFORM OF THE SSN

As discussed, the SSN had numerous weaknesses that resulted in dissatisfaction with both the quality of the health service provided and the control of expenditures. The dissatisfaction with the SSN led to the 1992 Health Care Reform Law (*Decreto Legislativo* 502/92), which focused on regionalization, the implementation of management tools used in the private sector, and financial reforms. Additionally, the 1992 reform provided special attention to the structure and financing of the USL, hospitals, and pharmacies.

A. Regionalization

Two primary initiatives were involved in the structural reform of the Italian health care system (Bruzzi, 1997). The first aspect of the reform involved a change in the organizational structure of the health care system. The reform included a significant redefinition of tasks and responsibilities of the different government levels involved in health care delivery. The principal aim of this redefinition was the regionalization (*regionalizzazione*) of the health care system. Specifically, both legislative and administrative functions were transferred to the regions. Thus, the individual regions obtained more autonomy and control of decision making regarding the health care delivery system.

In exchange for this autonomy, the regions received increased responsibility in the budgetary process. Regionalization strengthened the financial responsibility of regions (OECD, 1997a). Funds continue to be transferred from the central government to the regions. Once funds are received at the regional level, the funds are used by the USLs and hospitals to provide health care services. However, because a primary goal of the 1992 health care reform law was to control health care expenditures, in 1996 Italy reduced its budget allocations to the SSN. It also required higher contributions for health spending from the autonomous regions (OECD, 1997a). Another important aspect of this reform is a change in the way deficits that are incurred by the regions are handled. Previously, when deficits were incurred by the regions, the central government would transfer more funds to the region or incorporate the deficit into the state government deficit. However, as a result of the new reform, if the regions develop a deficit, the central government will no longer provide additional funds to the regions. Instead, the regions must raise revenues to meet their health care expenditures.

The goal of this regionalization of the health care delivery system is to allow the regions to define the needs of its citizens and provide quality health care services in an efficient and cost-effective manner. However, since each region is responsible for the financing and delivery of health care services, this may result in regional health systems that are significantly different from one another (Bruzzi, 1997). Additionally, this system has been criticized because the regional variations limit the freedom of choice of the consumers (Micossi, 1998; Turno 1998). The choices given the consumer are provided by decisions made at the regional level. Because significant variation between regions may develop, consumers in one region may have fewer or less desirable choices than consumers in another region.

B. The Azienda

The second primary structural reform effort of the Italian health care system is the implementation of tools used in private enterprise. First, the reform includes the redefinition of responsibilities and roles of the management of the health care structures. This reform transforms the public health structure into a firm (*azienda*) through the introduction of new criteria used in the operation and management of private firms. An important aspect in the change in management procedures is the introduction of more commercial accounting arrangements (OECD, 1997a). Historically, the public sector has focused on compliance with regulations rather than on the production of results. The redefinition of the health care institution as an *azienda* attempts to change this. The *azienda* transformation is based on the principles that the health care structures need to maintain a certain level of autonomy and be responsible for the results they incur, whether positive or negative. The second aspect of the reform that implemented tools used in private enterprise is the method in which funds are calculated for transfer to the regions. Instead of an incremental budget process, there was the introduction of a new financing system based on a fixed rate for specific health service or treatment. It includes the introduction of specific accounting obligations that are used to contribute more accurate information to the system. This information can then be used to assist management in developing new strategic lines of behavior that will improve outcomes of the health care structure. A final aspect of this transformation includes the introduction of competition into the new health care market. For example, now hospitals may compete with one another. In addition, the law promotes greater competition between both public and private providers of health care services (OECD, 1997a). However, the implementation of true competition into the health care system has been questioned because of the use of reequilibrium or restructuring funds (*fondi di riequilibrio o di restrutturazione*) (Micossi, 1998). These are funds provided only to public sector institutions to restructure or become more competitive. The use of these funds is criticized because they provide an unfair advantage to public sector institutions, and they reduce the process of privatization of public sector agencies.

C. Financing Reform

In addition to the reforms to restructure the SSN, the government implemented reforms to address the expenditure problems associated with the separation of payment of services at the central government level and the provision of services at the local level. The reform of 1992 has reallocated financial responsibilities within the SSN. The central government allocates funding to the regions, which is made on a capitated basis set according to available resources. The regional governments then transfer funds to the local level where services are provided. This legislation increases the financial responsibilities of the regions. For example, the law prohibits the transfer of additional funds from the central government if the regions accrue deficits. These deficits remain with the regional government, which may raise local taxes or increase regional health care contribution rates to match expenditures. As a result of these reforms, spending control has improved and there has been a rapid deceleration of health care costs (OECD, 1997a).

The new reforms of 1992 gave specific attention to the financing and programming of the health care system at both the national and regional levels. At the national level, programming is developed through the national health plan (*Piano Sanitario Nazionale*, PSN) (Bruzzi, 1997). A new PSN is developed every 3 years, and the reform provides for a less bureaucratic process for the development of the PSN, which assists in speeding the implementation of the PSN. In addition to the national level health plan, each region must develop a regional health plan (*Piano Sanitario Regionale*, PSR). Within the PSR, each region must define its health care objectives and related strategy of implementation. Of course, the objectives of the PSR must be obtainable within the financial limitations available to the region.

Predominantly, regions are provided funding for health care services through the national health fund, FSN. If the transfers from the FSN are not sufficient to achieve the objectives as defined in the PSR, the regions may appropriate funds from local revenues to their health care budget. Regions have the authority to increase taxes, implement new tickets on new services, and increase mandatory health contributions. Under this plan, referred to as "regional auto-financing'' (*l'autofinanziamento regionale*), regions predominantly raise funds through citizen contributions as outlined in the finance laws, from revenues from fees charged by health care services at the USLs, and from revenues derived from financial and real estate investments of the USLs (SISTAN, 1996). Prior to the 1992 reform law, health care contribution made by employees, employers, and self-employed persons (*versamenti dei contributi per le prestazioni del SSN*) went to the FSN. As a result of the 1992 reform law, the funds derived from health care contributions now go directly to the region where the contributor resides. However, given these funding mechanisms, and the ability to raise health care revenues if the region does not have sufficient funds to meet the costs as outlined in their PSR, they must redefine their objectives. No additional funds will be provided by the federal government if the region develops a deficit. Thus, this strategy transfers the financial responsibility of local health care delivery from the federal government to the regions.

The law also developed a new method to distribute money to the regions from the national health fund, FSN, which is called *quota capitaria* (Bruzzi, 1997; Ministero della Sanita', 1997). Initially, a specified amount is deducted from the FSN, which is given to research. Then, the remaining funds in the FSN are divided by the size of the population in the country. This number is multiplied by the number of residents in each region, and the result is used to determine the amount of regional financing for health activities. Because patients from southern regions, who have the means, often travel to more northern regions for better services, funding rates take into account the additional needs of some regions because of interregional mobility of patients (OECD, 1997a). Once the funds are transferred to the regions, the regions distribute these funds to the local level based on criteria specified by the region in its health plan.

Generally, the regions follow two models to redistribute funds to the local level (Bruzzi, 1997). In the first model, both the USLs and hospitals are completely financed based on a system of payment for services. Funds are transferred from the regions to the institutions for payment for services that are provided to the residents. In this way, the region represents the only buyer of the services, and thus, the region assumes the responsibility of organizing the services. Additionally, individuals are guaranteed the freedom to choose the institution that will provide services. For example, based on reputation, location, or efficiency of service, an individual may choose to have services provided at one institution rather than another. Thus, the USLs and hospitals are in competition with other USLs, hospitals, and private service providers. However, even though this system guarantees that the patient has the choice of institution, the patient is not guaranteed access to the physician of his or her choice. The patient may enter the hospital and be assigned the physician who is on duty. If patients are not guaranteed access to the physician of his or her choice, this can undermine the patient/physician relationship and can compromise continuity of care. This is especially relevant when a patient has a long-term illness or is in need of continuous monitoring for conditions such as heart disease or pregnancy. However, if a patient desires the services of a particular physician, the patient can often pay out-of-pocket and see the physician on a private basis. In such cases, the patient pays for services twice. The initial payment is through health care contributions to support the public program and the second payment is made out-of-pocket to receive private services.

In the second model to distribute funds to the local level, the USLs are financed from the regions based on the population in the local area (*quota capitaria*), while the hospitals are financed from the regions based on the system of payment for service. With the funding provided to an USL, the USL may provide services to the public using its own institutions, or it may contract the services out to other institutions or professionals. In the case where the services are contracted out, the USL pays another services provider such as another USL, a hospital, private clinic, or professional for services provided to the citizens of that locale. Again, in this model, citizens are free to select the institution of their choice, but not the physician. The benefit of the second model is that it provides funds to the USL for services and projects that are difficult to use a payment-for-service system, such as public education and hygiene.

D. Local Health Units

In an attempt to reduce costs and improve efficiency, many local health units were closed. The number of health units was decreased from 659, one for every 86,000 residents, to 228, one for every 250,000 residents (OECD, 1997a). Additionally, the name and organizational structure of the remaining units was changed. The USL has been redefined as an *azienda*, or a public entity with organizational, administrative, accounting, managerial, and technical autonomy (Bruzzi, 1997). With this newly defined role, the USLs were converted into public firms (*azienda sanitaria locale*) or *azienda* USLs. The autonomy of the local health units was changed as they were transformed into "private-like" enterprises headed by managers. The organizational restructuring also included changes in the accounting practices. The local health units are provided a specified annual budget by the SSN. The *azienda* USL then has the responsibility to remain within budget, as additional funds are no longer provided for payment of local-level debts. This system has proven effective at reducing health care expenditures by the local health units. In 1995, the first year that the restructuring of public health care institutions was implemented, the USL deficit shrank dramatically (OECD, 1997a).

Another aspect of the reform of the USLs was the innovations that were aimed at reducing conflicts created by the lack of responsibility that had previously characterized the management of the health structure and institutions. As an *azienda* USL, the management and organizational structure are no longer part of the local government. As a result of the new reforms, the azienda USLs are detached from the local government, which can no longer preside over the policies and decision making of the *azienda* USL. Instead of being managed by a committee structure developed through local government politics, the *azienda* USLs are managed by a general director (Bruzzi, 1997). The general director has wide powers of decision making and is responsible for the economic and financial management of the *azienda* USL. In addition, the new reform law provides the general director, along with the administrative and health directors, who are appointed by the general director, 5-year renewable private contracts. These private contracts constitute an innovative and important change in the management structure of the public health system. The private contract enriches the structure of the *azienda* USLs because it guarantees greater flexibility compared to the public contracts that have been used in the past. For example, if the *azienda* USL violates the reform law by developing a deficit, the region has the power to terminate the contract and replace the general director.

E. Hospitals and DRGs

In addition to changes in the local health units, there was also reform in the financing and structure of hospitals. In Italy, there are three classes of hospitals: public, private, and psychiatric institutions. As of 1995, there were 990 public hospitals, 656 private hospitals, and 68 psychiatric institutions. At a national level, there are approximately 375,000 available hospital beds, 82% of which are in public hospitals and public psychiatric institutions (SISTAN, 1996).

As with other health care indicators, there are also regional differences within the hospital system. For example, the northern region of Liguria has the most public beds at 7.1 per 1000 residents, while the southern region of Campania has the least at 3.7 per 1000 residents. Overall, the northern regions have an average of six public hospital beds per 1000 residents, the central regions have 5.7, and the southern regions have 5.1 (SISTAN, 1996). These regional differences can also be found in the number of recoveries per 1000 residents. While the national average is 154 recoveries per 1000 residents, the three northern regions of Friuli-Venezia Giulia, Liguria, and Trento have more than 200 recoveries for every 1000 residents. This is in comparison to the southern region of Campania, which has only 106.5 recoveries per 1000 residents (SISTAN, 1996). Another important fact regarding regional differences in hospital function and financing is the interregional movement of patients from the region of residence to another region for treatment. For example, all of the southern regions, except for Molise, have a negative transfer of patients. The southern regions of Basilicata and Calabria have an exceptionally high rate of residents who seek treatment outside of their region. This is in comparison to the northern regions, which generally import more patients for treatment than they export (SISTAN, 1996).

In a move to make the hospitals more efficient through market mechanisms, those hospitals with national relevance or highly specialized practices were granted autonomy and transferred into hospital enterprises, or *aziende ospedaliere*. The 1978 reform, which created the SSN, transformed the public hospitals from institutions with legal and financial autonomy into a structural part of the USL. With the latest reform of 1992, this change has been reevaluated and reversed. If hospitals meet certain criteria, they can become a public hospital enterprise (*azienda ospedaliera*) (Bruzzi, 1997). In this way, public hospitals can be transformed into *azienda* hospitals and subsequently given the rights of a legal entity with economic and financing autonomy. As an *azienda* hospital, the public hospital is given the same autonomous characteristics and organizational structure of the *azienda* USL. Like the *azienda* USL, the *azienda* hospital is headed by a general director who is responsible for the efficient management of the hospital. However, not all hospitals have the means to become an *azienda* hospital. If the hospital does not meet the requirements to be independent, it will remain within the structure of the USL. In such cases, the hospital will be headed by a medical director, who is responsible for hygiene and organization, and an administrative director, who is responsible for the administrative coordination of the hospital.

The reform also included the decision to close hospital wards that have a utilization rate below a certain level (OECD, 1997a). The application of a national standard for the number of hospital beds per 1000 people was introduced. This contributed to an increase in hospital efficiency and a decrease in hospital spending through a rise in hospital utilization rates (OECD, 1997a). In addition to closing hospitals with low utilization rates, there was also a plan to close psychiatric institutions. Between 1992 and 1996, 18 psychiatric institutions were closed (Ministero della Sanita', 1997), and between 1991 and 1995, the number of available beds in psychiatric institutions decreased by 21% (SISTAN, 1996).

Another central component of the hospital reform was the implementation of a prospective payment system based on diagnostic-related groups (DRGs). Prior to the implementation of the DRG payment system, hospital were reimbursed for each hospital bed occupied. Under the previous payment method, hospitals would receive the same payment regardless of the diagnosis or amount of treatment needed. This system provided incentives to hospitals to withhold treatment because they were not provided addition funds for additional amounts of treatment. Additionally, this system provided incentives to lengthen patient length of stay, as the hospital was paid while the bed was being utilized.

The DRG system that has been implemented in Italy is the same type of payment method that has been used in the United States for the Medicare system. In this payment setting, illnesses are categorized into discrete groups. Payment levels are set according to diagnosed medical conditions and standardized treatment costs. The amount of payment made for each category is predetermined and fixed at a set level. The philosophy behind the DRG method of payment is that the "best" method of measuring hospital output is the diagnosis, rather than the type of services provided or the length of stay (Knickman and Thorpe, 1995). For this to hold true, two requirements must be met. First, the classification system used must be meaningful in a way that reflects cost of treatment. Second, the case mix within each group must be reasonably homogeneous (Knickman and Thorpe, 1995). If the cases are not homogeneous, some cases within the same category may be much more expensive to treat than others. If this is so, the hospitals would lose money on those more expensive cases. In the U.S.'s Medicare program, a major criticism has been that the DRG categories include patients with dissimilar resource needs because they do not account for differences in the complexity or severity of illnesses between cases (Knickman and Thorpe, 1995).

Additionally, several risks have been identified from hospitals' use of the DRG system (Bruzzi, 1997). Initially, hospital may discharge patients too early in hopes of reducing costs. In such a case, the patient may suffer from the early discharge and if the condition does not improve, the patient will need to be readmitted. In addition to the reduced quality of care for the patient, the cost of the two stays may exceed the cost that the hospital would have incurred if the patient had remained in-hospital longer during the first admission. Another risk involves patients who have conditions that are serious or expensive to treat. In these cases, hospitals may refuse to admit or admit and then transfer the patient to another institution to avoid the high costs of providing treatment. Hospitals may become involved in this type of behavior because patients with expensive-to-treat conditions may consume larger resources than the hospital receives for providing treatment. Another risk is the reduction in the level of quality of services because the hospital has implemented a diagnostic-therapeutic protocol that is less flexible. For example, a hospital may dictate a specific treatment protocol because it cost less. There is also the risk of falsification of codes and patients charts. In this case, falsification occurs in order to assign patients with DRGs that have larger remuneration. Other risks include the specialization of hospitals in those areas in which the DRG diagnosis is more profitable and cost shifting, or the transfer of costs to the private sector.

F. Pharmacies

In Italy, all pharmacies are private providers of health care products and are under contract with the USLs (OECD, 1997a). They are under contract with the USLs because as part of its national health care program, Italy subsidizes some pharmaceutical products. In general, individuals make a copayment to pharmaceutical purchases. However, exemptions to copayments are given to individuals with certain diseases, individuals with disabilities, those entitled to social pensions and pensions under a minimum level, children under the age of 6, elderly over 65 years, and individuals who are unemployed and qualify under a minimum income level (OECD, 1997a). However, in its attempt to control health care spending, Italy has made several measures to restrain expenditures on pharmaceutical services. In 1993, it placed a cap on pharmaceutical expenditures that were totally reimbursed by the state and transferred more costs to the consumer (OECD, 1997a). In 1994, the government introduced another reform measure to limit pharmaceutical expenditures. This reform introduced a new classification system for pharmaceuticals. Pharmaceutical products were divided into three classes and guidelines were established for state expenditures within each class (OECD, 1997a). In 1995, the government established decreases in the purchase of goods and services for the SSN and reduced the prices paid to producers and retailers of pharmaceuticals. It also established more stringent criteria for eligibility to exemption from pharmaceutical expenses (OECD, 1997a). As a result of these reforms, pharmaceutical expenditures declined from 0.9% of GDP in 1992 to 0.5% in 1995 (OECD, 1997a).

VI. ORGANIZATIONAL STRUCTURE OF THE HEALTH CARE SYSTEM

The health care system, the SSN, is comprised of several agencies that have divided responsibilities and structures into national, regional, and local levels. The Ministry of Health (*Ministero della Sanita'*) is the primary organ of the health care system. At the national level, the Ministry is responsible for health care policy, the accreditation and regulation of various health care services, and the allocation of financial resources to the regions. The Ministry of Health performs its functions through five departments and six services. The first department is that of Programming (*Dipartimento della Programmazione*), which is responsible for collection, development, and dispersion of the nation's health care information. It is also responsible for monitoring the newly incorporated repayment system used by hospitals, which is based on DRGs. The second department is the Department of Health Professions, of Human Resources and Health Care Technology, and State Competence (*Dipartimento delle Professioni Sanitarie, delle Resorse Umane e Technologiche in Sanita'e dell' Assistenza Sanitaria di Competenza Statale*), which controls and monitors public and private health care professionals, the manufacture and sales of medical devices, and accidents involving medical devices. The third department, the Department of Prevention (*Dipartimento della Prevenzione*), monitors communicable diseases and coordinates and implements policies to control and prevent infectious diseases. It also operates local offices that provide childhood and adult vaccinations. The final departments include the Department for the Assessment and Evaluation of Medicine and Pharmaceuticals (*Dipartimento per la Valutazione dei Medicinali e la Farmacovigilanza*) and the Department of Food, Nutrition, and Veterinary Public Health (*Dipartimento degli Alimenti e Nutrizione e della Sanita' Pubblica Veterinaria*). The services include the Service for the Organization, the Budget and Personnel (*Servizio per L'organizzazione, per il Bilancio e per il Personale*), the Service for International Affairs and European Union Policies (*Servizio per i Rapporti Internazionali e per le Politiche Comunitarie*), the Service for the Control of Institutions (*Servizio per la Vigilanza sugli Enti*), the Service for the Inspection and Crisis Management (*Servizio Ispettivo ed Unita'di Crisi*), the Service for Contracts and Agreements with the SSN (*Servizio per i Rapporti Convenzionali con il Servizio Sanitario Nazionale*), and the Service for Studies and Documentation (*Servizio Studie Documentazione*).

While the Ministry of Health performs most of its policymaking at the national level, the delivery of health care services is provided at the regional and local levels. Initially, funds are transferred from the central government to the regions. Once funds are received at the regional level, the funds are used by the *azienda* USLs and *azienda* hospitals to provide health care services. The *azienda* USLs have the responsibility to manage public hospitals that have not become autonomous *azienda* hospitals, and contract with private health care providers and pharmacies. As previously mentioned, all pharmacies are private and are under contract with the USLs because, as part of its national health care program, Italy subsidizes some pharmaceutical products.

Additionally, the azienda USLs are subdivided into local health districts, which they have the responsibility to manage. Within the local health districts, primary health care is provided by general physicians and pediatricians. Generally, services are provided to patients by these general physicians on demand. There is no cost per visit to the patient, no copayment, nor any limit to the number of visits a patient may have. When Italians receive their national health card, they are asked to select a general physician whom they visit for regular medical services. This physician provides general checkups, writes prescriptions, and acts as a gatekeeper by making referrals to specialist care.

In 1994, the average physician had a caseload of 1100 patients (SISTAN, 1996). This figure was consistent throughout the regions, except for Bolzano where physicians had caseloads over 1900 (SISTAN, 1996). Pediatricians care for children between birth and age 13, and they have similar responsibilities as general physicians. However, unlike the United States, routine vaccinations are not offered at the pediatrician's office. After a physical examination, the pediatrician signs a certificate stating the child is in good health. This certificate is then taken to the local Department of Prevention, where the child receives vaccinations.

In 1994, the average caseload for pediatricians was 661 (SISTAN, 1996). Because general physicians and pediatricians have relatively limited office hours, and are generally not available after hours, residents are provided afterhour medical services from the *guardia medica*. This is a physician who can make home visits when medical services are needed after regular business hours. Although the role of the *guardia medica* is to replace the general physicians and pediatricians after hours, the *guardia medica* may have no training in specialized medicine nor pediatric care. In such cases, the *guardia medica* may refer the patient to the local emergency room.

The SSN is also composed of other national level agencies, most of which are technical, scientific, or consultative. These include the National Health Council (*Consiglio Superiore di Sanita'*, CSS), which is a technical and consultative part of the Ministry of Health and performs research and develops policy regarding the health and well-being of the general population. The next agency, the National Institute for Prevention and Safety at Work (*Istituto Superiore per la Prevenzione E Sicurezza del Lavoro*, ISPESL), is a technical scientific body that performs research and manages the information and documentation to ensure the health and safety of workers. The Agency for Regional Health Services (*Agenzia per i Servizi Sanitari Regionali*, ASSR) is part of the Ministry of Health, and was designed to provide support to the regions to enhance delivery of health care services.

The final group of national level agencies are organizationally autonomous, but provide support for the national health system. Initially, the National Institute of Health (*Istituto Superiore di Sanita'*, ISS) is a technical and scientific agency that performs research and provides technical support and educational services to other institutions. Next, the Institute for Scientific Recovery and Cure (*Istituti di Ricovero e Cura a Carattere Scientifco*, IRCCS) pursues biomedical research, and the research and work of physicians regarding cure and recovery. The final autonomous agency is the Institute of Experimental Prophylactic Veterinary Medicine (*Gli Istituti Zooprofilattici Sperimentali*, II.ZZ.SS), which is the technical body of the SSN regarding the sanitation of animals and the safety and hygiene of meat food products.

VII. CURRENT FINANCIAL TRENDS

In contrast to the spending increases between 1975 and 1990, between 1990 and 1995, health care expenditures in Italy showed some decline. For example, total expenditure on health decreased from 8.1% to 7.7% of GDP, and public expenditure on health decreased from 6.3% of GDP to 5.4% of GDP (OECD, 1997a). This is in contrast to other European countries and the United States, which continued to see an increase in health care expenditures on both scales. Additionally,

Italy's total spending on health care was estimated to be 7.7% of GDP in 1995 (OECD, 1997a). This is largely in line with spending levels of other European countries. For example, spending levels in the United Kingdom were 6.9%, Germany spent 9.6%, and France spent 9.9% of GDP. These levels are considerably below the 14.5% of GDP that the United States spends on health care annually (OECD, 1997a). It is possible that this reduction in spending is a result of restructuring of the health care system and cost controls implemented in the 1992 health care reform law (*Decreto Legislativo* 502/92).

Briefly, the 1992 reform places more emphasis on regionalization and the implementation of management techniques from the private sector. Funds continue to be provided to the regions from the central government, but spending and deficits become the responsibility of the regions, not the central government. In this manner, the central government no longer incorporates regional government debts into the state sector debt. However, the OECD (1997a) notes that the savings found in public expenditure is partly attributed to a shift in expenditures to the private sector by 0.5% of GDP. There has also been an increase in private spending that can be directly attributed to higher copayments for pharmaceutical products, diagnostic treatment, and specialist care.

Comparing the financing per region between 1991 and 1995, it is possible to see the effects of some of the health care reforms and changes in budget policy (Table 10). In 1991, all regions received the same increase in funding, approximately 28%. At that time, budget increases were incremental and based on the spending rates from the previous year. However, in 1992 and after, there was a drastic change in budget allocations. In 1992, although most regions continued to receive more funding than the previous year, the percent increase was considerably smaller. The funding ranged from a decrease of 9.3% in Valle d'Aosta to an increase of 10.5% in Campania. However, in 1993, the first year when the 1992 reform law was implemented, all regions received considerably less funding than the previous year. Spending allocations from the FSN to the regions ranged from 50.3% less in Puglia to 253.0% less in the region of Friuli-Venezia Giulia. The national level decrease was 111.0%. In 1994, the budget transfers to the regions remained at a level lower than in the previous year. However, the decreases were not as dramatic and ranged from a decrease of 2.4% in Piemonte to a decrease of 30.0% in Sicilia, and the national decrease was 4.1%. In 1995, some regions receive small increases, ranging from 0.6% in Sicilia to 14.1% in Toscana, while many others continued to receive less funding than the previous year (Ministero della Sanita', 1997).

The trends observed in the regional analysis are also evident in the spending trends of the SSN between 1989 and 1995. As a percentage of GNP, the annual spending for the SSN was 5.8 in 1989. This increased to 6.1 in 1990, and reached a peak of 6.6 in 1991. However, after that year, there was a continuous decline as spending levels decreased to 6.4, 6.1, and 5.9 in 1992, 1993, and 1994, respec-

Table 10 FSN financing per Region 1991–1995 (% change from preceding year)

	1991	1992	1993	1994	1995
Piemonte	27.7	1.4	(170.1)	(2.4)	(23.1)
Valle d'Aosta	29.4	(9.3)			
Lombardia	27.8	6.4	(184.3)	(26.5)	(2.4)
Bolzano	27.9	(5.7)			
Trento	28.0	(4.7)			
Veneto	27.8	7.1	(143.5)	(7.0)	(12.2)
Friuli-Venezia Giulia	28.1	(6.5)	(253.0)	(19.3)	(39.4)
Liguria	27.7	1.5	(116.2)	(24.5)	0.0
Emilia-Romagna	27.7	6.1	(156.0)	(15.5)	(17.5)
Toscana	27.7	3.5	(130.9)	(22.3)	(0.7)
Umbria	27.6	3.1	(91.0)	(20.9)	14.1
Marche	27.6	10.4	(102.1)	(18.1)	(2.2)
Lazio	27.4	5.4	(140.0)	(17.8)	(7.3)
Abruzzo	27.5	3.7	(66.0)	(3.5)	3.5
Molise	27.3	0.5	(55.5)	(5.9)	2.6
Campania	27.5	10.5	(53.3)	(7.8)	6.3
Puglia	27.6	10.2	(50.3)	(4.1)	2.6
Basilicata	27.5	5.0	(58.0)	(4.2)	7.4
Calabria	27.6	6.9	(56.2)	(3.4)	6.9
Sicilia	27.8	2.4	(66.7)	(30.0)	0.6
Sardegna	27.7	6.8	(86.3)	(8.7)	(26.5)
Italy	23.2	5.1	(111.0)	(4.1)	(1.5)

Source: Ministero della Sanita', 1997.

tively. In 1995, the annual spending reached 5.6% of GNP, a level of spending lower than that found in 1989 (SISTAN, 1996).

Additionally, these trends can be observed when spending categories are separated by function and viewed using an index of variation (*indici di variazione*) (Table 11). The index of variation is calculated using constant 1995 lire and 1989 as a fixed base. Thus spending level of 1989 would be 100% and the levels represented in the following years are the percent variation from that amount. For example, the spending for the SSN increased 20% between 1989 and 1991. From 1991 through 1995, spending continually decreased and in 1995, it reached a level 1% below the 1989 level (SISTAN, 1996).

The first functional category of spending is for personnel (*spesa per il personale*) in the USLs. From 1989 to 1991, the index of spending for USL personnel increased 21%. Although it continued to remain higher than the 1989 level, after 1991 it showed a continuous decline. In 1995, spending decreased 6.2% from

Table 11   Index of Variation in Health Care Spending by Category and Year

	1989	1990	1991	1992	1993	1994	1995
SSN	100	109	120	116	110	108	99
Personnel	100	109	121	119	116	112	105
Goods and services	100	109	116	121	117	118	106
Pharmaceuticals	100	113	114	102	86	73	62
General medicine	100	101	107	99	95	94	87
Hospitals	100	106	114	119	118	117	106
Specialized medicine	100	97	97	78	63	56	48
Other assistance	100	133	166	176	178	185	177
Interest liability	100	151	251	410	407	297	59

Source: SISTAN, 1996.

the previous year and resulted in a level only 5% higher than that of 1989 (SIS-TAN, 1996). However, as a percentage of total SSN spending, the rate of spending on personnel has continued to increase slightly. For example, between 1989 and 1995, spending on personnel increased from 38.8% of total spending to 41.5% (SISTAN, 1996).

The second functional category of spending is for goods and services (*beni e servizi*). This includes such things as general goods and services needed in the operation of the health care institutions, laundry services, meals, and heating. Based on the index of variation, this category of spending has a different pattern than the others. Expenditures continued to increase between 1989 and 1994. However, in 1995, there was a slight decrease from the previous year (SISTAN, 1996). As a percentage of total SSN, spending has fluctuated only slightly, from its lowest level of 17.1% in 1991 to a high point of 19.2% in 1995 (SISTAN, 1996).

The third functional category of spending is for pharmaceuticals (*spesa per l'assistenza farmaceutica convenzionata*). Between 1989 and 1991, spending for pharmaceuticals increased 13.6%. However, after 1991 there was a sharp decrease in spending. By 1995, the index of variation reached 61.8% of its 1989 level. This pattern of decreased expenditures is also reflected in pharmaceutical spending as a percentage of total SSN spending. In 1990, spending on pharmaceuticals represented 17.5% of total spending. Between 1990 and 1995, there were sharp decreases, and in 1995, spending for pharmaceuticals accounted for only 10.6% of total SSN expenditures (SISTAN, 1996).

The fourth functional category is for general medicine (*spesa per la medicina generale convenzionata*). This category includes public sector general physicians, pediatricians, and *guardia medica*. Overall, spending for general medicine is similar to that of the other functional categories. In 1991, the index of variation reached a peak at 7.5% more than the 1989 rate. After that year, there was a steady decrease, and in 1995, spending had decreased to 86.8% of the 1989 level (SISTAN, 1996). As a percentage of total spending, expenditure on general medicine was at its highest point in 1989. Between 1989 and 1995, it averaged around 5–7% of total spending (SISTAN, 1996).

The fifth functional category of spending is for the hospitals (*spesa per l'assisstnza ospedaliera convenzionata*). Spending on hospitals increased 19% between 1989 and 1992. However, after that point, spending decreased. In 1995, spending levels for hospitals were only 6% higher than the 1989 rate (SISTAN,

Table 12 Italian Regions, Provinces, and Populations

Region	Province	Population
Abruzzo	L'Aquila, Chieti, Pescara, Teramo	1,270,591
Basilicata	Matera, Potenza	609,238
Bolzano[a]		451,563
Calabria	Catanzaro, Cosenza, Reggio Calabria	2,075,842
Campania	Avellino, Benevento, Caserta, Napoli, Salerno	5,762,518
Emilia-Romagna	Rologna, Ferrara, Forli, Modena, Parma, Piacenza, Ravenna, Reggio Emilia	3,924,456
Fruili-Venezia Giulia[a]	Gorizia, Pordenone, Triese, Udine	1,188,897
Lazio	Frosinone, Latina Rieti, Roma, Viterbo	5,202,098
Liguria	Genoa, Imperia, Savona, La Spezia	1,658,513
Lombardia	Bergamo, Brescia, Como, Cremona, Mantova, Milano, Pavia, Sondrio, Varese	8,924,870
Marche	Ancona, Ascoli Piceno, Macerata, Pesaro, Urbino	1,443,172
Molise	Campobasso, Isernia	331,446
Piemonte	Alessandria, Asti, Cuneo, Novara, Turino, Vercelli	4,288,866
Puglia	Bari, Brindisi, Foggia, Lecce, Taranto	4,082,953
Sardegna[a]	Cagliari, Nuoro, Oristano, Sassari	1,660,701
Sicilia[a]	Agrigento, Caltanisetta, Catania, Enna, Messina, Palermo, Ragusa, Siracusa, Trapani	5,094,735
Toscana	Arezzo, Firenze, Grosseto, Livorno, Lucca, Massa Carrara, Pisa, Pistoia, Siena	3,523,238
Trento[a]		461,606
Umbria	Perugia, Terni	825,910
Valle d'Aosta[a]		118,723
Veneto	Belluno, Padova, Rovigo, Treviso, Venezia, Verona, Vicenza	4,433,060

[a] Special regions.
Source: Ministero Della Sanita', 1996.

1996). In addition, between 1989 and 1995, spending for hospitals as a percentage of total SSN spending has remained relatively stable at approximately 10% (SIS-TAN, 1996).

The next functional category is for specialized medicine (*spesa per medicina specialistica convenzionata*), which includes such things as visits to public medical facilities and offices outside of the hospital, and to private health care institutions that provide contract services to the public sector. Since 1989, this category has had a constant decrease in spending. Specifically, the 1995 rate was 48% of that in 1989 (SISTAN, 1996). Additionally, this category has continued to consume a smaller portion of the total SSN expenditures. Spending levels declined from 4.9% of total spending in 1989 to 2.4% in 1995 (SISTAN, 1996).

The next functional category is for other assistance (*spesa per altra assistenza*). The primary components of this category are rehabilitation, thermal bath therapies, and assistance for elderly and disabled persons. Between 1989 and 1995, this category demonstrated a constant increase on the index of variation. The 1995 level was 77% higher than the base year of 1989 (SISTAN, 1996). Additionally, this category has consumed an increasing portion of the SSN's total expenditures. Between 1989 and 1995, this spending in this category as a percentage of total expenditures increased from 3.6% to 6.4% (SISTAN, 1996). The final functional spending category is interest liability (*spesa per interessi passivi*). This category showed a tremendous increase between 1989 and 1992. However, it leveled off in 1993 and showed sharp decreases in 1994 and 1995, at which time it was only 59% of the 1989 base level (SISTAN, 1996). This trend of dramatic increase and decline is also demonstrated in the spending for this category as a percentage of total SSN expenditures. For example, between 1989 and 1993, spending increased from 0.3% to 1.2% of total expenditures. It then sharply decreased to 0.2% in 1995 (SISTAN, 1996).

VIII. CONCLUSION

Italy has made numerous reform attempts within its health care structure. The reforms focusing on controlling expenditures have been generally successful, and the OECD (1997a) reports that in the 1997 budget, spending cuts to the health system include 0.6 trillion lire at the state sector level and another 0.6 trillion lire at the general government level. However, many weaknesses remain in the health care structure. For example, improvements need to be made in the access to and quality of services provided and in the area of improving customer satisfaction. The unsatisfactory performance indicators and consumer dissatisfaction with health care services in the public health sector emphasize the continued need for improvements in both efficiency and quality (OECD, 1997a, p. 12). The OECD (1997a) recommends that Italy strengthen the capacity of health care institutions responsible for health care policies at the national, regional, and local levels. It also suggests that it increase the financial responsibility of general physicians in their role as gatekeeper. For example, they should have budget constraints on pharmaceutical and specialist expenditures. The government should also relax its regulations on entry and pricing of pharmaceuticals. Additionally, it could decrease pharmaceutical costs by decreasing regulations controlling the use of generic medicine.

Another area for improvement in the Italian health care system is the decrease in quality variations between the regions. Currently, there are large variations in the funding allocations and quality of care provided regionally. Historically, the quality of services and the level of infrastructure of health care systems are poorer in the south than in the north and central regions. Current reform efforts aimed at regionalization may increase these regional variations. Although those southern residents with the means to travel obtain a higher quality of services by traveling to the northern regions for health care, those southern residents without the means must obtain a lower quality of care than is available in other regions. To protect the quality of service delivered to the poorer residents of the south, the government should implement national quality control measures and require minimal standards of care in all regions.

REFERENCES

Agnew, J.A. Political decentralization and urban policy in Italy: from "state-centered" to "state-society" explanation. Policy Stud J 18(3):768–785, 1990.

Bariletti et al. Aspetti distributivi del consumo di servizi sanitari in Italia. Econ Pubbl 1991.

Bruzzi, S. Finanziamento e gestione delle aziende ospedaliere. Milan: Giuffre' Editore, 1997.

Fazio, A. The public finance manoeuvre for the years 1993–1995. Rev Econ Conditions Italy (2):141–161, 1992.

Government debt. Economist 330(7849):113, Feb 5, 1994.

Italy: letting off steam. Economist 327(7817):3–22, June 26, 1993.

Italy: the odd country. Economist 315(7656):3–30, May 26, 1990.

Knickman, J.R., Thorpe, K.E. Financing for health care. In: Kovner, A.R., ed. Jonas's Health Care Delivery in the United States, 5th ed. New York: Springer, 1995, pp 267–293.

Micossi, P. Senza liberta' non c'e' efficienza. II Sole-24 Ore, p. 5, July 8, 1998.

Ministero della Sanita'. Ananlysi economica e funzionale della spesa sanitaria, Sistema Informativo Sanitario, Dipartimento Della Programmazione, 1996.

Ministero della Sanita'. L'allegato statistico della relazione sullo stato sanitario del paese 1996, 1997.

OECD. OECD Economic Surveys: Italy. Paris: OECD, 1985.

OECD. OECD Economic Surveys: Italy. Paris: OECD, 1992.

OECD. OECD Economic Surveys: Italy. Paris: OECD, 1994.

OECD. OECD Economic Surveys: Italy. Paris: OECD, 1997a.

OECD. OECD Health Data 97. Paris: OECD, 1997b.

OECD. OECD Health Data 98. Paris: OECD, 1998.

OECD. OECD Economic Surveys: Italy 1998–1999. Paris: OECD, 1999a.

OECD. OECD Labour Force Statistics: 1977–1997. Paris: OECD, 1999b.

Roccella, A. Senza avvenire con questa amministrazione. In: Bernardi, L., ed. La finanza pubblica italiana. 1996.

Shinn, R.S., ed. Italy: A Country Study, 2nd ed. Washington, DC: US Government Printing Office, 1985.

SISTAN. 1 Compendio del Servizio Sanitario Nazionale: Anni 1991–1995. Ministero della Sanita', 1996.

Turno, R. La malasanita' messa sottosequestro. Il Sole-24 Ore, pp 1,2, July 4, 1998.

13

The Political Economy of Health Care in Greece

Dimitris Niakas
Hellenic Open University, Patras, Greece

I. INTRODUCTION

Greece, a country of 10 million population, in the southeast corner of Europe has been following, with a short delay, the same developments in health care as elsewhere in continental Europe. More specifically, health care in Greece is closely related to the Bismarckian social insurance model that characterizes most of the countries of the European Union such as Germany, France, Belgium, Netherlands, etc. Although the social insurance system of Greece has its origin in the late nineteenth century, it had been fully established in legislation from the end of the 1950s, when pension and health insurance became obligatory for every working person and his/her family.

The main characteristics of the social health insurance system in Greece can be summarized as follows:

   a.   Health care is financed through compulsory contributions paid by both employers and employees. There is one exception to the above rule, which involves those persons working in agriculture (25% of the total) for whom no contributions have been established so far because of social and political reasons.* The public budget (state) contributes and

---

* Until the 1970s there was an objective situation (low economic and social status of the rural population) that may have justified the exception of farmers from contributions to health insurance. This is not the rule since all the economic and social indicators have been improved during the last two decades.

covers all the medical expenses for this segment of the Greek population.

b. Health contributions and funds are managed by public organizations and public agencies (called Sickness Funds) to which every population group belongs by statute. Managerial boards include both insured and lay persons and are appointed by the Secretary of Health and Social Security. Major decisions are made under governmental approval. Health contributions usually have a flat rate that is different in each Sickness Fund. There has been a permanent fiscal crisis (deficits) in social insurance for many years, in both Pension and Sickness Funds, because of economic and demographic factors (Skoutelis, 1989a). This crisis forced the Greek conservative government to pass a law in 1992 to bring into account the dangerous deficits. The purpose of this law was first, to save the collapsing system with the establishment of a state contribution and second, to equalize contributions for the insured in all the funds. Thus, some indirect contributions from special taxation, which had been criticized (Simitis, 1989) and proven unfair and unequal (Matsaganis, 1991), were replaced with an equal state flat rate. In other words, the Greek system of social insurance with two main sources of finance, because of its fiscal crisis, changed institutionally by adding a third source (state contribution), a development that was already in operation in many other European countries.

c. Sickness Funds may provide their own health services by appointing salaried health professionals or leave their members free to purchase services, in either the public or private sector. Of course, each Sickness Fund provides its own package of services. Nevertheless, a basic health entitlement includes hospital care, physician's services, other services (physiotherapy, eyeglasses, etc.), dental services, and pharmaceuticals. The range of such services, as well as the choices available among services, differ in each Sickness Fund. The copayment levels for services are defined by the Department of Health and Social Security. Nursing home and long-term care are rather limited in the case of Greece and these services for aged people do not involve social insurance.

d. There are a total of about 40 funds insuring all the categories of employees and their families. Table 1 depicts the main Sickness Funds and the number of the population insured in each. The unemployed in the rural and semiurban areas can use the health insurance of the farmers. The remainder in urban areas (4–6% of the population) can use the public hospitals free of charge, though they are not covered for services at the primary care level, such as consultations and pharmaceuticals and other services.

Table 1 Main Sickness Funds and Number of
Population Insured (in Thousands)

Sickness funds	Population	Percentage
IKA	4,510	42.8
OGA	2,460	23.4
TEBE	1,040	9.9
TAE	300	2.8
Public servants	1,100	10.4
Bank employers	220	2.1
Seamen	400	3.8
Other funds	500	4.8
Total	10,530	100.0

Source: Social Budget, annual editions.

    e. The Department of Health and Social Security regulates the market for health care and forces the Sickness Funds to follow regulations on both the methods of financing services and the prices. The method of reimbursement for services is retrospective. Hospitals are mainly reimbursed per diem, physician fee-for-service and other services per case. This method of reimbursement has its origin in the 1970s and the government defines the prices. In the beginning the imposed prices generally reflected the operational costs of the hospitals and the existing prices in the medical market. However, during the next decade inflationary forces forced the government to leave prices unchanged. This meant that the Sickness Funds were obliged to reimburse providers according to the official prices, which did not reflect the real costs to providers. In this respect, for many cases, the private providers (private hospitals, physicians) do not contract with the Sickness Funds. Consequently, many insured under the Sickness Fund that use services in the private sector are forced to pay significant out-of-pocket costs. In contrast, the public providers follow the imposed prices. This leads to high deficits for the public services (mainly hospitals), which result from the existing method of finance and the prices, which are not reflective of operational costs. Thus, the public budget is usually forced to cover operational costs to keep hospitals in business. In addition, the public budget finances investments (capital health expenditures) of the public hospitals or other public services.

    f. The provision of health is a public-private mix. Private hospital services (small clinics with from 10 to 60 beds) were mainly developed in the 1960s. Even now (after development of the National Health System,

Table 2 Number of Hospitals and Beds Before and After the NHS

	Hospitals		Beds	
	1980	1987	1980	1987
Public	112	136	25,905	35,290
Private for-profit	468	267	25,075	15,900
Private not-for-profit	28	5	8,347	243
Average number	648	408	59,359	51,443

Source: Social Welfare and Health Statistics, annual editions.

NHS), 31% of hospital beds are for-profit. Table 2 represents the number of beds before and after the NHS introduction, a major reform that was intended to create a public system of provision. Physicians working in the public sector are salaried (those working via public hospitals and reimbursed via Sickness Funds), as compared to their counterparts in private medical practice, who are mainly paid on a fee-for-service basis. Prices of this preferred method of reimbursement follow the "usual, customary, and reasonable" (UCR) fees, which are mainly defined by the profession (Feldstein, 1983).

In this framework of a public-private mix, a major reform was introduced in the 1980s to alter the Bismarckian tradition. In 1983, the Greek socialist government, which was in power from 1981 to 1989, proposed a radical reform intended to transfer health care from the Bismarck to the Beveridge or Semashko model.* The major changes of the reform concerned the establishment of the NHS with the following six principles:

1. Comprehensive health care for all, regardless of working status or Sickness Fund coverage
2. Free access for all at the point of use
3. Facilities owned by the state
4. Centralized planning and controlling operational policies
5. Salaried medical profession
6. Restriction of the private sector and replacement by the public

---

* The Semasko model refers to the ex-socialist countries of Central and East Europe. The Beveridge model refers mainly to the British NHS (Rathwell, 1995). They have common characteristics such as public financing and public provision, though some differences exist.

Unfortunately, as will be explained later, some crucial aspects of the new system, such as demographic changes, the size of the necessary health expenditures, and the sources of finance of the above transformation, were not well considered. As a result, many deficiencies and problems developed. All these problems surrounding the Greek transition of health care (which in a broad sense is called "the political economy of health care") are analyzed here, among other proposals that have been offered. The proposals attempt to combine the existing tradition of Greece and some of the new developments of managed competition in health care. Of course, these recommendations need to be consistent and fulfill, as far as possible, health policy criteria acceptable worldwide, such as efficiency, effectiveness, equity, quality, and choice.

II. THE GREEK HEALTH SYSTEM IN TRANSITION

Between the late 1970s and 1980s, Italy, Portugal, Greece, and Spain introduced radical reforms in health care, in an attempt to satisfy basic social criteria such as comprehensive health care and equality in access. The radical reforms seem to be the outcome of two factors: economic and political.

First, social protection and free and equal access to health care for all (some of the basic principles of what was called the European welfare state in the 1960s) were delayed in the south. This delay was primarily due to a lower level of economic development in this region. Consequently, when the economic situation improved, the aforementioned countries attempted to follow their counterparts integrating social systems of health care and social protection.

Second, the political environment may have precipitated the attempts to introduce national health systems in these southern countries. Interestingly, all efforts at health care reform were initiated by socialist parties after they had assumed power. Additionally, in most countries, such as Spain, Portugal, and Greece, liberal ideas and social rights were lessened in the 1960s and the mid-1970s because of a period of totalitarianism. This period of historical restraint in citizen autonomy introduced a period in the 1980s when numerous reforms were introduced in regard to political and social rights, as well as in regard to health service reforms. Thus, political factors played a significant role in reforming the existing health care systems, regardless of their tradition and success.

In this respect, the Greek socialist government declared its faith in the welfare state and wanted to provide universal health care for all. Especially during the first years of its administration, targets for equality in every aspect of daily life seemed to determine both economic and social policy (KEPE, 1983). Of course, except for the new ideological wave of the new socialist party, which wanted a national health system such as the British one, there were two official committees of experts during the conservative administration (1974–1981), which suggested some interesting alternatives (KEPE, 1976, 1979). Their findings referred to the fragmentation of social insurance, the lack of appropriate resources and management, social and geographical inequalities in health care provision, and lack of infrastructure, especially in the rural areas.

During the same period there emerged a strong radical movement of junior hospital physicians, who fought for drastic reform in health care, and who held strikes fighting for a NHS. These physicians called for direct intervention and involvement of the state in all health issues (prevention, treatment, and rehabilitation), and health for all, through the expansion of public services and public financing, with salaried doctors working full-time for the public sector.

The aforementioned factors (i.e., political reasons, the existing need for changes, and the radical movement of hospital physicians who pushed for reform in health care) may well explain the introduction of what is called the Greek National Health System. Three main principles defined Greek health reform during 1980s:

    a.   the provision of health should not be for-profit (this was done with the intent to minimize the troublesome private health sector existing at that time);

    b.   all citizens should enjoy equal rights to high-quality care; and

    c.   the protection of the nation's health is the responsibility of the state, which should be exercised through the NHS.

On the basis of these principles, major regulations on the supply side were arranged with the introduction of the NHS beginning in 1984. The most significant are concerned with the following:

Physicians who wanted to be employed by the NHS could only do so on a full-time basis. This was a costly regulation since the number of physicians paid by the public sector almost doubled and the salaries tripled. These developments took place because of the strong negotiation power of the junior hospital doctors, who managed to create more medical posts in public hospitals in connection with high levels of remuneration. They wanted to practice medicine as public servants, having a permanent assignment with a good level of reimbursement and keeping themselves away from economic uncertainties and market financial exchanges with the patients.

Nonprofit hospitals, financed by the public budget in the past, were taken into the public sector under direct control of the state.

Law prohibited any increase in beds in the private sector. At the same time, public hospitals were encouraged to buy some private clinics that went out of business.

There was construction of health centers in semiurban and rural areas, in favor of the rural population, to cover existing needs in health care infrastructure in these areas.

Health centers in urban areas were also arranged to address the primary health needs of the population. At the same time a network of family doctors, practising for the same purpose, was proposed, although the specialty of general practice was lacking in Greece.

Finally, a unified referral system for all levels of care was designed with the establishment of regional health councils for each of nine regions. The patient, except for emergency cases, had to follow a hierarchical structure from the family physician to other levels of referrals (health center, district hospital, and regional hospital).

The last three regulations, for family doctors, health centers in urban areas, and the regionalization of health services through the hierarchical structure, were never implemented. Some analysts involved in the foundation of the new system argue that these three regulations were not implemented because of the reactions from the medical profession and administrators of the Sickness Fund. Implementation was also thwarted by an absence of political will within the leadership of the socialist government during the second period of its administration 1985–1989 (Filalithis, 1993, 1995). The leadership therefore seemed to have little interest in some major issues of transition and especially in the financing crisis of the system. On the contrary, the present analysis argues that the partial implementation of the regulations of the new system was a result of the political economy of health care in Greece. More specifically, the main reasons relating to this are:

a. the scarcity of funds necessary for the full implementation;
b. the lack of any plan to find alternative sources of finance, except from the problematic public budget;
c. the absence of any adjustment for an effective method of financing services; and
d. the ignorance of the private sector, which traditionally operates and closes the gaps of the public sector in Greece. All these reasons contributed to what is called the "transition crisis," which lasted almost a decade and has created many problems and deficiencies.

In other words, the present Greek health system presents itself as an unmanaged ship without fuel (sources of funds) and compass (financing method). In addition, the captain (government), waiting for some external rescue, does not seem able to decide upon any action and the crew (patients) is looking for a way to save themselves. External help was requested a year ago, by an international committee of foreign experts, which presented a package of interesting proposals concerning some crucial aspects of the NHS. Unfortunately, no action has been taken to date by the government.

III. THE DEVELOPMENT OF THE CRISIS

The idea of the NHS was based upon the provision of comprehensive health care for all, regardless of Sickness Fund coverage. What was envisioned was a unified network of services owned by the public sector designed to fulfill citizen expectations and attractive for health professionals. Physicians with good work conditions and high salaries would be dedicated to their patients and operate as rationalizers on behalf of the patient's demand. This seemed to be the vision of the NHS founders. They considered a system of public provision with equity, effectiveness, and quality. It was believed, to a great extent, that such a system would be able to replace the piecemeal delivery of services by the Sickness Funds and to organize public hospitals, health centers, and family physicians, efficiently providing integrated health care for all.

Of course, to be attractive for all, the new NHS had to be expanded covering unmet health care demands of the population from any Sickness Fund. It was expected that a whole integrated system through the expansion of the public hospitals and health centers, with the appropriate medical professionals, would convince the insured and the managerial boards of the Sickness Funds to abandon their own provision and incorporate their services and personnel into the NHS. This was mainly concerned with IKA, a major Sickness Fund with a network of services in primary care in all urban areas of Greece. The expansion of public provision under the NHS required additional resources. Table 3 shows health

Table 3   Trends in Public Health Care Infrastructure

	1980	1990	Percent increase
Hospitals			
Beds	25,905	35,290	36.2
Physicians	8,635	14,810	71.5
Nurses	18,462	28,425	53.9
Other personnel	18,725	28,835	54.0
Health centers	—	168	
Physicians	—	1,913	
Other personnel	—	4,136	

Source: Social Welfare and Health Statistics, annual editions.

manpower and bed increases during the NHS introduction. It is clear that public beds increased about 36% and health personnel in hospitals expanded over 50%. Additionally, approximately 6049 health professionals were employed by the newly created health centers.

Although these resources provided better coverage of the population that was insured by the Sickness Funds, they were mainly raised by the public budget, which was not a regular source of financing for services and had never executed such a duty previously. At the same time, Sickness Funds, which were the main sources of finance, were not called upon to contribute any additional funds for this development, which favored the insured populations. This meant that major changes in the provision side were accommodated by the public sector and financed by the public budget, a source of finance that had been used mainly to cover the uninsured and the farmers and not the other insured populations for which Sickness Funds were responsible. The NHS introduction required more health care resources that came mainly from one source of finance, the public budget, which not only was planned to operate as an alternative source of financing for services, but also was problematic because of a general increased deficit. At the same time, the increased delivery of services through the NHS demanded a new effective method of financing other than the existing retrospective reimbursement. Thus, in a new system of health care provision there were no incentives or mechanisms to hold down accelerated costs.

Table 4 shows the annual increases in health care expenditures and the contribution of each source of finance. Health expenditures rose from 6.6% of

Table 4 Time Trends and Composition of Health Expenditures as a GDP Percentage

Year	Social insurance	Public budget	Private	Total
1980	2.2	1.6	2.8	6.6
1981	2.2	1.6	2.8	6.6
1982	2.2	2.2	2.6	7.0
1983	2.1	2.2	2.7	7.0
1984	2.1	2.2	2.6	6.9
1985	2.1	2.2	2.7	7.0
1986	2.2	2.4	2.8	7.6
1987	2.2	2.4	2.8	7.6
1988	2.3	2.7	2.8	7.8
1989	2.3	2.7	2.8	7.8
1990	2.3	2.7	2.8	7.8

Source: Adapted from Kyriopoulos and Niakas (1991).

GDP in 1980 (2.2 social insurance, 1.6 public budget, and 2.8 private) to 7.8% in 1990 (2.3 social insurance, 2.7 public budget, and 2.8 private). It seems that the NHS absorbed an additional 1.2% of GDP* that came mainly through the public budget. At the same time, the public budget was not able to finance such an increase because of the poor economic conditions in Greece (low level of growth, unemployment, and huge public deficits) during the same period. Given this economic situation and the nonexistence of any other source of financing health care, an impending crisis appeared in 1986. The government was faced with a dilemma: to provide more funding and appoint family physicians and other health personnel in urban health centers, or to postpone the expensive regulations containing public deficits. For any rational policy, the second option was the choice. This was followed by the government and some analysts criticized the alternative as the abandonment of the NHS. At the same time, some of them argued that this caused the NHS crisis (Sissouras, 1989). This argument systematically overlooks the main root of the problem, which was the lack of attention to finding the necessary funds to finance the new system.

The limited sources of financing for such a comprehensive system, in conjunction with the existing traditions in health care in Greece (lack of an effective method of financing services, Sickness Funds, private sector, and health attitudes), brought about, except for the nonunification of the NHS, an expansion in private practice. This happened because of the following reasons:

There was a great increase in the number of physicians in this period: In 1981, the total number was 24,724 and in 1990, 34,336. Although the NHS absorbed the doubled number of physicians who practiced only as public servants (in the NHS, there were 8759 physicians in public hospitals in 1981 and 16,723 in 1990), there was also a massive number of private practitioners. The remaining physicians numbered 17,613 in 1990 and almost 21,386 in 1994, which meant that one physician per 467 population was now practicing privately! It is worth noting that some of the above physicians also have an appointment with the Sickness Funds. Unfortunately, no measures for limiting entry into the profession have been taken to date. This large number of physicians (one physician per 280 population) in Greece, which is the second highest among the developed countries (OECD, 1993), seems to be related to the size of medical expenditures (Niakas, 1996).

It is also well known that medical technology is one of the most important factors in increasing health expenditures. Taking into account both the lack of resources in the NHS, which finally led to a delayed introduction of diagnostic

---

* According to OECD data health expenditures in Greece are only 5.3% of GDP. This is an incorrect estimation, which has its origin in the system of Greek National Accounts (Niakas and Kyriopoulos, 1994).

equipment, such as ultrasound, computerized tomography (CT) scanners, and nuclear magnetic resonance (NMR) equipment in the public hospitals, and the low productivity of the public sector, a number of private diagnostic health centers with such equipment appeared parallel to the NHS. Table 5 shows the development of biomedical technology in Greece where the diagnostic technology (CT scanners, NMRs) of the private sector overcame any optimistic expectation. It is worth mentioning that in 1991 there were 12 CT scanners per one million population in Greece and only five in the rest of Europe (Figueras et al., 1992). This particular development in diagnostic equipment has its origin in many factors:

    a.   in the Sickness Funds operations, which are institutionally obliged to cover health expenditures of their insured;

    b.   in the method of financing services (retrospective per examination);

    c.   in the prices charged for these services, which give rise to the private for-profit sector, and finally to the lack of any control and peer review, since any demands of physicians were met without any restriction from the funds or hospitals (Kyriopoulos and Niakas, 1993).

Another important reason for private practice relates to existing traditions. For many years, the Greek health care system had been a public-private mix. Medical professionals used to provide consultations in their offices practising solo medicine. At the same time, some major Sickness Funds (IKA, TEBE, etc.) never provided full and satisfying coverage giving the insured their right of choice among medical professionals. Thus, the population, especially in urban areas, used to ask for care, looking for the best care available and exercising its choice paying out-of-pocket. This may explain why the size of private health expendi-

Table 5   Time Trends in Biomedical Technology in Greece

	1980	1985	1990	1992
CT scanners	6 (4)	15 (10)	66 (22)	121 (22)
NMRs	—	1	4 (2)	9 (2)
Heart transplant centers		1 (1)	3 (2)	
Liver transplant centers			1 (1)	
Kidney transplant centers	2 (2)	4 (4)	4 (4)	
Lithotripters	2 (2)	3 (2)	5 (3)	

Figures in parentheses = the capacity of the public sector.
Source: Adapted from Kyriopoulos and Niakas (1993).

tures has remained steady for almost two decades, regardless of the rise in public spending.

Yet another noteworthy tradition of Greece is what is called the informal or hidden economy. It concerns every aspect of economic life and empirical studies estimate its size between 30 and 40% of the official GDP (Pavlopoulos, 1987; KEPE, 1992). In health care, the hidden economy has been estimated to be 20% of the total health expenditures, or 1.2% of the official GDP (Pavlopoulos, 1987; Niakas et al., 1990). This evidence of the hidden economy in health care is based upon household surveys where private expenses for health care involve payments to public or private sector doctors, for which no receipts have been received for services rendered.

What has happened to Greek health care during the NHS establishment seems to be the following. In a Bismarkian model of public-private mix health care, a Beveridgean model of public provision was introduced to unify services and create a comprehensive system, with free access for all at the point of use. This model of public provision relies mainly on a tax-financed system and includes mechanisms for an effective and equitable allocation of resources. These basic principles of the Beveridgean model seemed to be partial in the case of the Greek NHS since the financing side of the system almost remained the same and the operation of the Sickness Funds was left intact. However, the system was becoming more complex and less managed, because many protagonists, such as public officers of the Department of Health, hospital administrators, and local interests, were never recognized as key factors of the new system. For example, public health officers, without any appropriate training, took responsibility for financing hospitals using unknown criteria; hospital management was left in the hands of laypersons and not professionals; and local interests pushed the politicians for more services (beds and health centers) in their area. Thus, problems such as finding the necessary funds, escalating costs, effective resource allocation, and financial management emerged, which finally directed the Greek system not to a Beveridgean model, but to managerial chaos without any hierarchical accountability.

The problems of implementation that are analyzed in the next sections have produced a vicious circle of transition. This circle may be halted when some major interventions on both sides of the demand for and the supply of the system occur. In this framework, some proposals are put forward to help the policymakers in taking corrective decisions and integrating the Greek health care system. This integration may direct the system to a Bismarckian (more pluralistic and less unified) or a Beveridgean model (less pluralistic and more unified). While this is a major issue, it is nevertheless secondary in importance since it primarily concerns political agendas and politicians. The first issue, which is mainly related to the scientific evidence and is of professional interest, is how to formulate proposals and find alternatives, where criteria such as efficiency, effectiveness, equity, quality, and choice have the maximum potential to be satisfied in every component of the health system.

Nevertheless, in considering the existing problems and deficiencies of health care relating to the transformation of the system, it is necessary to mention that the health status of the Greek population is extremely high in comparison with other European countries (Lopez, 1990). Table 6 presents some vital health indicators in 12 European countries, such as life expectancy, mortality/100,000 population, and infant mortality, which reached 9.1 per 1000 in 1992 in Greece and is comparable to other European nations.

Greece enjoys a remarkable level of health in comparison with other more developed countries with more organized and comprehensive health systems. This statistic supports the existing evidence that the health status of a population is a very complex issue. Indeed, health status is not entirely reflected by health expenditures and the level of sophistication of health care provision, but rather reflects prevailing life-style and socioeconomic factors (OECD, 1987). What is critical in Greece is that factors favorable to good health, factors such as those associated with smoking, diet, stressful working conditions, sedentary styles, etc., are changing. As a result of these gradual changes in life-styles, accidents and heart and cancer diseases are increasing. Thus, Greece has been forced to focus on areas of health promotion and disease prevention and utilize the European Unification's cooperation in public health to improve the health status of the population and prevent avoidable mortality (Kalapothaki et al., 1992).

Table 6 Selected Health Indices in 12 Countries of the European Union 1986–1988

Country	Life expectancy		Mortality/100,000		Infant mortality/ 1000
	Males	Females	Males	Females	
Belgium	71.4	78.2	1157	677	8.3
Denmark	71.9	78.0	1103	689	8.3
France	72.6	81.1	732	524	7.8
Germany	72.3	79.1	1095	640	8.3
Greece	74.1	78.9	784	656	11.7
Ireland	71.6	77.3	1212	760	7.4
Italy	72.7	79.2	1066	629	9.6
Luxembourg	70.5	78.7	1253	659	9.4
Netherlands	73.6	80.3	754	568	7.6
Portugal	70.5	77.7	1155	703	14.2
Spain	73.1	79.7	999	604	8.8
United Kingdom	72.5	78.2	1088	656	7.1

Source: Adapted from Eurostat (1989) and Lopez (1990).

IV. MANAGERIAL AND FINANCIAL PROBLEMS IN INPATIENT CARE

It has already been noted that inpatient care is provided by public and private for-profit hospitals. Hospital reimbursement is based on a retrospective per diem method. Fees are determined annually by the government, and no negotiations between the purchasers (Sickness Funds) and the providers (public and private hospitals) exist. The determined rate of reimbursement does not cover the average operational cost of the hospitals such that the greater the difference between fees and operational costs, the greater the contribution is of the public budget in the financing of the public hospitals.

The insured have the right to ask for treatment in any public hospital regardless of medical condition and area of residence. In other words, there is no referral system in operation and patients can move freely inside the system. They may also choose to utilize private hospitals, of which there are two categories.

Some of the hospitals, about 50% of the total, are actually small clinics with 10–60 beds and are owned by a physician. They provide low technology and quality of care and usually admit aged or mental patients for drug therapy and nursing care. These hospitals are not competitive but rather complementary. They remain in operation because in Greece no alternative forms of care such as nursing homes and home care, which would be expected to cover some health or social needs, have been developed (Niakas and Beazoglou, 1994). In real terms, the small private clinics substitute for these forms and they survive accepting the official remuneration but providing low quality of care. Thus, a part of the insured with the above-mentioned conditions can utilize this type of private clinic without charge.

On the other hand, the remaining private hospitals that do not accept determined fees have their own rates following marketing strategies. Their strategy is based on the selection of the physicians on staff and high levels of technology, in combination with the provision of hotel-quality facilities. These private hospitals are very attractive for patients who do not accept waiting times in public hospitals and have the ability to pay out-of-pocket or use private health insurance. Patients with private health insurance,* which has a complementary but developing role in Greece, can use private services and are a potential pool for private hospitals. To complete the picture, it is worth noting that some of the Sickness Funds (e.g., bank employers) reimburse the patients for using private services.

---

* Private health insurance is mainly combined with life insurance. Its late introduction in Greece in the 1980s and the attempt of the companies to attract a big share of the market increased competition in health care programs. This led to full coverage and free use of any private hospital by the insured. This last development brought about a fiscal crisis in many private companies recently. Thus, discussions and dialogue have opened between private insurance and private hospitals concerning prices, or the method of financing.

The amount is usually equal to the costs of treatment in a public hospital (days ×
rate of daily reimbursement) and covers 20% of the total costs.

It has been mentioned that the method of financing hospitals has remained
unchanged and that fees (reimbursement rates) have been held at very low levels
not covering the actual cost of the hospitals (public or private). For example, the
daily reimbursement rate for the year 1981 was 1200 drs ($6.00) and in 1989 it
reached only 2400 drs ($12.00). During the same period, the actual average hospi-
tal cost per day was 4500 drs ($22.50) and 45,000 drs ($225.00), respectively.
Regardless of its planning (or lack thereof), this policy of low prices is of significance, and has resulted in both positive and negative results on the grounds of
efficiency and equity.

On the positive side, as a measure of efficiency, there has been a decrease
in hospital beds, which many European countries tried to implement, following
cost containment policies in the 1980s. The closure of beds and the development
of outpatient hospital day care was an appropriate measure for cost containment
(Abel Smith, 1984; OECD, 1987). In Greece the low rate of reimbursement by
the Sickness Funds forced many small private clinics out of business. In the
period 1980–1988, there was a steady decrease in private hospitals with a final
count of 7886 beds. Given Roemer's law that "a built bed is a filled bed,"
this was a welcome result of cost containment and efficiency. It is worth
mentioning that the elimination of these private beds did not create any access
problem for the population: first, because the total occupancy rate of Greek hospitals has never surpassed 72% and second, because existing waiting lists concern
medical services that use high technology and could not be provided by these
hospitals.

On the negative side, three problems have arisen because of the aforementioned financing policy that continues the same today. First, a major problem of
equity has appeared relating to the sources of financing. In Greece, because of
the hidden economy and the large percentage of the population who practice tax
evasion (mainly the majority who are self-employed), there is an uneven usage
of tax money, which makes direct taxation nonprogressive (OECD, 1990). Subsequently, the increased share of the public budget in financing health services
does not satisfy the equity criterion (according to the ability to pay), since public
revenues are not collected under a progressive method (Kyriopoulos and Niakas,
1991). It seems clear that salaried people, who do not avoid taxes and health
contributions, are financing health services twice, once for themselves and once
on behalf of the tax avoiders and other groups with low or no contribution, such
as farmers.

This major problem in the Greek health system seems to be exacerbated
due to the NHS, since the public budget share has increased, related to the inatten-
tion to the financing side by the NHS founders. This paradox, which is related
to the special aspects of the domestic economy, seems to confirm a broad view

that argues that health care financing is not a health policy issue, but mainly a public policy issue (Klein, 1988). In other words, financing health care is a major public policy issue and is related to many aspects of economic and social policy.

In this framework, the entire analysis and the full knowledge of the domestic economic environment of each country may lead to proposed solutions that are contrary to existing theory and that support financing of health care through insurance contributions. For instance, it is well established on a theoretical basis, using the British NHS as an example, that health systems financed through the public budget meet the criteria of social justice and equity in financing health more effectively than do systems financed through other sources (Barr, 1987). There is also evidence in a recent multinational study on various health systems, where financing via public budget is more equitable than other sources, such as compulsory or private insurance (Van Doorslaer et al., 1993). Of course, this occurs because in these countries direct taxation is rather progressive and not regressive, as are the contributions to social insurance. However, in the case of Greece, direct taxation, because of the large hidden economy and the extensive degree of tax evasion, does not seem progressive. Thus, financing health care through the public budget generates important equity problems in the country.

The second problem concerns the outdated method of financing hospitals, which seems to create essential inefficiencies. It is widely asserted that any method of financing, whether retrospective or prospective, and regardless of the evidence on efficiency, needs appropriate financial management to contain costs. This seems to be lacking in the case of Greece, since a third-party payer system (third-tier system) was created without any planning and coordination. Simultaneously, an open market, with prices that may drive the hospital market into some type of balance, does not exist. Thus, an expected inefficiency in Greek hospital care is mainly related to the following three ways of financing hospitals for which methods of regulation do not exist.

First, private hospitals (small clinics), which accept low remuneration rates by the Sickness Funds, provide low-quality care that could be delivered in other forms of outpatient or social care. A large number of these clinics have an average length of stay per patient of over 30 days, in comparison with the Greek mean length of stay for acute hospital care, which is only 8 days.

Second, private hospitals that do not accept determined remuneration fees have the ability to define their services according to their own strategy. Given that: (a) there is a small number of these hospitals; (b) their physicians are paid on a fee-for-service basis by the patient and have only a contract with each private hospital; and (c) there is an absence of any contract or negotiation with the demand side, monopolistic behavior that causes inefficiency is likely to emerge.

Third, public hospitals expect the public budget to cover their expenses. Since revenue from the Sickness Funds does not surpass 10% of the total hospital budget and hospital management is exercised mainly by lay persons (usually political friends of governments), there is little interest in cost-containment and hospital efficiency. At the same time, salaried physicians have no economic incentive to improve their personal clinical effectiveness, or to increase the number of hospitalized patients. Hospital management and producers usually consider the public budget as the only source of finance and attempt to influence governmental decisions. On the other hand, public allocations of resources to hospitals are not based upon a formula (e.g., health needs of the region, performance, etc.), but primarily take into account expenses for working personnel. Thus, the main objective of hospital management is to secure reimbursement, using social and political criteria.

Figure 1, following the classical distinction between purchasers and providers, attempts to show both the official and unofficial economic flows of the hospital market in Greece. This division between purchasers (Sickness Funds) and providers (public and private hospitals) is merely artificial in the case of Greece, because the government intervenes on both sides, rendering demand-and-supply factors difficult to discern. The government defines the remuneration method and the rate of reimbursement and thereby acts as a regulator. The government also intervenes on the demand side, since the public budget finances some Sickness Funds such as OGA (farmers). At the same time, the government plays an important role as purchaser since it directly finances over 90% of the total expenses of public hospitals. On the other hand, the government intervenes on the supply side by direct involvement in issues concerning hospital management and provision of health care (public hospitals, health centers). This triple intervention as regulator, purchaser, and provider in conjunction with the inherent bureaucracy and inertia of the public sector has brought the Greek health care system to a nonplanned condition, which creates some additional deficiencies, presented by the depicted economic flows.

Financial flows 1 and 2 come from the population, via insurance contributions and taxation, and end at providers without any appropriate and efficient method of finance or an allocation using some explicit criteria. Financial flow 3 is related to private health insurance. Even though its role is developing, total expenditures do not surpass 0.3% of GDP. More significant are flows 4, 5, and 6, which are related to the private expenditures of the population. The high percentage of private expenditures (out-of-pocket) seems to be another anomaly of the Greek health system. If one takes into account the compulsory role of social insurance and the lack of established copayments in health care and in hospital care in particular, it is difficult to explain all of these private expenses. Such private expenses represent the Greek paradox, which appears to cancel the institutional right of health care entitlement with no payments at the point of use. This also means that the NHS principle for free health care for all at the point of use

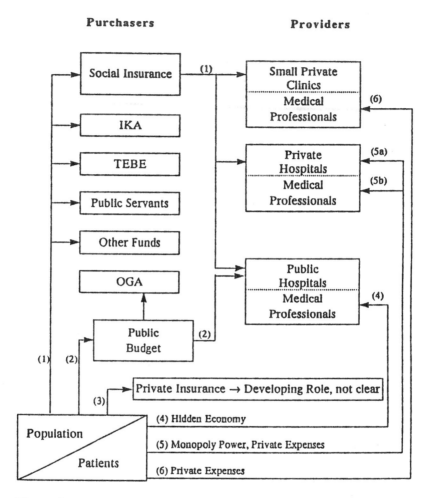

Figure 1 The market for hospital care.

has not been achieved. Thus, the need for changes and reforms in the Greek health system seems to be apparent. Delays add new problems that render the Greek health care system more inefficient and less equitable.

Setting aside the high percentage of private expenditures, and taking into account another dimension, the choice of the patients, flows 5a, 5b, and 6 may be explained. In many public health systems, patients exercising their choice may choose the private sector. It is expected in any public system that a part of the population that has the ability to pay for consuming medical care will purchase services in the private sector. This is related to the ability and willingness to pay, waiting times, and so on. What is critical and rather unique in the case of Greece is financial flow 4, which depicts not only the hidden economy (payments out-of-pocket by users), but illegal transitions (bribes and kickbacks) from the patients to salaried doctors who are employed by the public hospitals. This is illegal in terms of evading taxes (the additional income is never declared by the doctor) and in terms of breaking the working contract that the physician has with the hospital. This is a phenomenon in the doctor-patient relationship that has existed in Greece for many years and perhaps can be extended to other provider-client relationships in which a "tip" is thought to improve the services provided.

Of course, this situation does not apply to all services. It mainly concerns surgical interventions or high-technology therapeutic procedures, where there is uncertainty by the patient about the health outcome. It less concerns internal medicine and usual therapeutic procedures without operations. At the same time, neither all the public doctors nor the population accepts and practices this illegal exchange. Aside from patient uncertainty, there seem to be many factors (social, economic, and cultural) that may contribute to and explain this type of doctor-patient interaction, which the creation of the NHS intended to eradicate by tripling doctors' salaries. There is a tradition in Greece where the physician is paid directly by the hospitalized patient, as in the case of private practice. In some instances, in the public hospitals this takes the form of a gift for the doctor's interest. On the other hand, for some medical procedures there are waiting lists in some central public hospitals with distinguished doctors. Patients unwilling to put their name on a waiting list for a required medical service find ways to bypass this by paying a doctor privately, who in turn will find a bed in the hospital and provide the service. This is illegal, but common.

Another explanation is the operational rigidity of the NHS in an era where societies turn increasingly to privatization and choice. Salaried physicians who have received the same payments for years do not have any incentive to improve their productivity and/or the quality of services provided. At the same time, the notion of physician as public servant is not so developed in Greece and especially in the medical profession, whose members seem to prefer practicing privately by having a contract with a hospital.* On the other hand, a system of public provision with waiting times may operate well when the medical profession maintains high medical ethics and subsequently rations demand for medical care, according to medical needs and social priorities (Williams, 1988). This is not the case in Greece, since waiting lists are not kept objectively and both physicians and patients accept illegal transactions for their own benefit.

---

* It is characteristic that the Greek Medical Association is against full-time employment of the physicians by the NHS. The same is supported by the medical schools for their members, who kept the right to practice medicine both public and privately.

This illegal source of earning additional income for many public physicians in Greece is the well-known *fakelaki*, which means envelope. Many patients believe that only an envelope with money under the table could provide access to and quality of needed services. This interaction seems to have increased in recent years and reports of it have recently flooded the media. It should be noted that in 1992, the Committee of Social Affairs of the Greek Parliament took interest in this issue but unfortunately did not propose any action. This memorandum of the committee has recognized it as a legitimate problem of the NHS coming from two main causes: (a) the low salaries of the NHS physicians, which in the last 6 years have not increased, and (b) the general passive role of patients in receiving care and surpassing waiting lists. This year, the issue of *fakelaki* was revived with many accused physicians being referred to the courts.

Except for other dimensions, which are briefly mentioned above and may explain the *fakelaki* in Greece, analysis of demand for and supply of hospital services during the NHS may give reasonable explanations for the Greek policymakers. Demand for hospital care seems to be unsatisfied since there are waiting lists for some needed medical interventions, such as hip replacements, bypass grafting, etc. At the same time, waiting times are not acceptable to the majority of Greek patients though in other countries, e.g., Britain, which is an example for many Greeks, waiting times reach almost 2 years in some regions. In confronting this issue, an effective health policy has to follow two choices, intervening either on the demand for or the supply of services.

Interventions on the demand side may include either a price system with copayments to ration the increased demand, or a change in the method of financing to increase hospital caseloads, which reduces waiting time. The first option is not only politically difficult in a public system of provision, but it has been strongly criticized by many health economists because of the agency relationship in health care and especially for hospital admissions, which are mainly decided by the physicians. In addition, it is out of conformance with the basic principles of the NHS establishment. The second option of changing the method of financing seems to be appropriate in the case of the Greek hospitals.

On the other hand, intervention with the supply may also include two choices. Either expansion of hospital services, which is a very costly alternative, or exploitation of the existing services means increasing hospital productivity. Given that the economic environment prevents the first costly choice, the second one seems to be the only remaining alternative.

However, hospital productivity seems to be rather minimal because of the low salaries and the whole working relationship with the public sector that does not provide any incentives for the NHS physicians. In addition, hospital personnel do not face any danger of losing their employment and at the same time, unprofessional hospital management intensifies the problems of hospital effectiveness, efficiency, and quality.

An example may make the picture clearer. In areas of increased demand for health care, e.g, cardiac interventions, a steady monthly salary independent of the number of interventions pays surgeons working for the public hospitals. At the same time, in the private sector, a surgeon earns the same money for only one intervention. This large difference in the level of remuneration among physicians creates what is called the hidden economy. Such hidden economies are based upon health-related practices that tend to ignore the medical condition of the client, the number of required services (demand side), as well as the ability and the value of the production function of these services, i.e., supply side.

In other words, parallel to the existing NHS and the private sector, there is a hidden market in operation. This second market seems to be accepted by all (government, providers, public), since no measures have been taken against it to date. The hidden market is setting its own prices for any service needed. It is predictable that these prices are lower than the official prices in the private sector, where the prices include also hospital costs. Of course, the price of each service depends, again, on the demand for and the supply of the service, in any sector. As the demand for certain treatments and medical interventions increases and the supply of these services remains the same, hidden prices in the public hospital rise. This happens only when patients do not tolerate waiting times and the physicians are responsive to individuals who have the ability to pay out-of-pocket, and cooperate to surpass the waiting list. In this case, an equity-in-access problem arises for patients who do not have the ability to pay: they wait longer. This situation seems to be clarified within public opinion surveys in which citizens stated: "In nonemergency cases it is difficult for someone to get a serious medical intervention in public hospital without any private payment" (Abel Smith et al., 1994).

In further highlighting this critical problem in health care delivery, it must be mentioned that there is no official administration source of information regarding the number of patients on waiting lists and the length of wait in each hospital. Since there is no official logging system for patients on waiting lists, entrance of patients into hospitals can be exploited by users who can afford to pay and by health care providers with shabby medical ethics. At the same time, hospital outcome efficiency and effectiveness have not yet made the agenda. Thus, many surgical theaters of public hospitals are usually open and available during public servant working hours. This makes waiting times longer and favors the hidden economy that finally generates high incomes, free of taxes for some speculator physicians.

V. THE NHS DURING THE CONSERVATIVE ADMINISTRATION

During the conservative administration of the period 1990–1993, the NHS did not introduce any noteworthy changes in the financing or provision of health care. The conservative government was more supportive of the private sector, which it viewed as playing a more important role in health care provision, as compared to the previous socialist policy, which perceived the private sector as filling in the gaps of the NHS.

The specific changes that took place during this period in terms of hospital care included the following:

1. The creation of new private hospitals or increases in beds was again allowed. Any person or firm who wanted to invest in health care and create private clinics and hospitals was free to do so and had some financial incentives (low rates of interest) for some underserved areas.
2. The working relationship of the public doctors and hospitals was changed giving doctors the freedom to choose between full-time and part-time affiliation. Those working part-time could have their own private practice. Of course, the part-time physicians had their salaries reduced drastically and only about 2% of the doctors chose to go part-time.
3. Hospital reimbursement rates were increased in 1991 and 1993. Thus, the daily rate of 2400 drs ($12.00) in 1989 reached 15,000 drs ($75.00) in 1993. This measure, even though having the objective of reducing the public budget deficit and placing the financial burden directly on the Sickness Funds, had a positive effect on equity and the distribution of financing. Of course, these increases were not enough since the average daily costs in most public hospitals has surpassed 60,000 drs ($300). Given that Sickness Funds pay about 25% for the total hospital costs, the public budget covers the rest, which is 75% of the total operational costs of public hospitals.
4. Finally, during this same period, there was an ideological difference in attitudes toward the NHS. Although tremendous problems existed in the health system, there were no efforts for action to be taken. There was also support for and an obvious climate favoring the private sector. More specifically, the conservative government decided to change the method of financing hospitals for some major high-technology interventions, such as bypass surgery, with the intent of reducing waiting lists and averting patients from going abroad for care. To succeed, it gave special fees for these interventions, but only to the private hospitals and not to the public sector. Whether the action of the conservative government was reasonable, it was special treatment for the private providers and it brought about a major weakness in the public sector. The aim of the government to reduce waiting times and keep money for domestic providers would be more convincing if the same special fees also applied to public hospitals.

Moreover, in terms of primary care, the conservative government opposed the family physicians and health centers in urban areas. It favored the autonomy of the Sickness Funds and supported the free choice of the population to ask for services through either public or private providers. It also accepted fee-for-service remuneration of the physicians at the primary care level, utilizing the usual, customary, and reasonable fee. Unfortunately, this regulation was never executed because the Sickness Funds' budgets were not sufficiently prosperous to follow such an expensive regulation. Thus, no substantial change occurred in primary health care delivery.

In closing this section concerning the conservative administration, it is worth mentioning that the NHS had been in existence for almost a decade. Thus, some positive and negative achievements will be summarized. On one side are the problems that have been discussed. The most serious of them are:

1. Existent inequalities in the sources of financing health services and the lack of an effective method of financing services.
2. Unequal access to some special treatments and surgical interventions where waiting lists exist.
3. The escalating costs of services both in the private and the public sectors.
4. The critical problem of the hidden economy, which intensifies inequalities in access to services.
5. The low level of care (technology and quality) provided in the small private clinics, which accept the low reimbursement rates to keep them operable but with extended lengths of stay.

On the other hand, a series of positive developments helped to improve the accessibility to health services for some social classes living in less developed areas. These include:

1. Full medical coverage, including pharmaceutical consumption for the farmers, which together with the health care centers in the semiurban areas provided the coverage for this population. This created a positive climate for the improvement of primary health care concerned with the recommendations of the World Health Organization.
2. The creation of three modern high-technology public hospitals in disadvantaged regions, far from the two cities of Greece (Athens and Thessaloniki), aiming to improve access and finally reduce the flow of rural client referrals to city-based facilities.
3. The improvement of the geographical distribution of resources of the public sector in relation to the past, even though a specific formula of distribution was still not established (Niakas, 1993).
4. The modernization and improvement of the outpatient departments of

the public hospitals, with improved accessibility for residents of the urban areas.

VI. RECOMMENDED REFORMS IN INPATIENT CARE

Given the problems of escalating health care costs, equity in the financing of health care, and the inefficiencies of the system, the question arises as to what is the future of the health care system in Greece? Are there any prospects for creating efficiency, equity, and cost containment? Or, is the Greek public-private mix a new labyrinth without exit? This question seems to concern the Ministry of Health of the new socialist government, which came into power in power in October 1993, and an advisory committee of foreign experts was formed 6 months later to make proposals for reforming the NHS.

The foreign committee (a multinational group of experts) some months later delivered an interesting package of recommendations (Abel Smith et al., 1994). Some of the recommendations seem to be consistent with the results of the Greek studies and research that suggest the creation of a common-unified fund to take responsibility and finance health services (Skoutelis, 1989b; Kyriopoulos and Niakas, 1991; Niakas, 1992). Other suggestions, as in the case of primary health care, are mainly based on the British model of general practitioners becoming fund holders and purchasing services on behalf of their patients (Department of Health and Social Services, 1989). This model of GP fund holders, for which full evidence is not yet available since it is under investigation and being monitored by many research terms in Britain (Robinson and Le Grand, 1994), is suggested for Greece, where no appropriate conditions seem to exist (e.g., tradition of the country, number of GPs, acceptable operation of GPs at the primary health care level). This committee's proposals for primary health care raised a lively discussion and important criticisms (both positive and negative) have emerged (Merkouris, 1994; Niakas, 1995; Filalithis, 1995; Matsaganis, 1995). Unfortunately, the government did not present any plan or proposal until recently. In this section of the chapter, some key proposals are presented to promote dialogue for incorporation of the basic principles of today's health care systems into Greek health policy. These principles include efficiency, effectiveness, equity, quality, and choice.

Figure 2 presents the recommendations for an effective health care system, based upon quasi-market principles, which seem to characterize the representative systems of the Bismarkian model of health care (Schulenburg, 1994). At the same time, taking into account the existent problems of transition, the tradition of the country, and existing health attitudes of both the providers and the population, as well as the principle of "money following the patient," two primary regulations are proposed. First, there must be a real separation between the de-

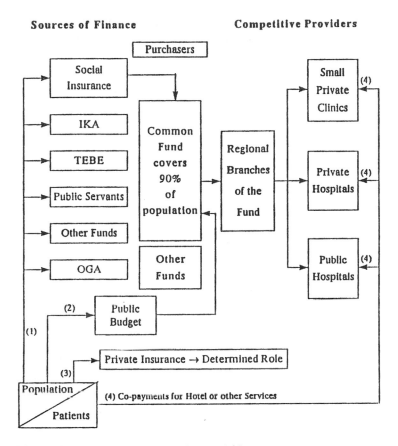

Figure 2   The proposed market for hospital care.

mand for and supply of the services, and second, managed competition needs to be introduced among the various providers of hospital services. With regard to the demand for health services, given the variety of Sickness Funds and the financing of hospital care through the public budget, the establishment of an agency (Common Fund) is recommended. The Common Fund would enact the role of purchaser of hospital services with the financial power to impose its priorities and establish accountability of the hospitals.

Separation of the financing from the delivery side and introduction of managed competition into the system exclude government intervention. The government would play a more supportive role during the first stages of the new system, monitoring and solving conflicts and imbalances. At the same time, the government may take full responsibility for the needed capital expenses of hospitals and control activities such as medical education and research, and the introduction of new technologies. Its main involvement would be oriented toward policy formation supporting and promoting public health and taking intersectoral measures to improve the nation's health. For example, public health issues such as smoking habits, vaccinations, road accidents reduction, and so on are governmental responsibility.

More specifically, the following are proposed for secondary care. One proposal calls for four major funds, which cover over 90% of the population, to join, creating an agency operating as an alliance on behalf of the insured interests. This alliance (Common Fund) would continue to have the contributions from the existent Sickness Funds in addition to the contribution of the public budget, which now goes to the public hospitals with no criteria for allocation. The Common Fund, serving as a new foundation or an artificial conglomerate, would have strong buying power for services and would operate as an oligopsony or monopsony, since the supply side depends merely upon the insured demand. The rest of the Sickness Funds, if so desired, can join this conglomerate (Common Fund) to increase their buying power. If not, remaining independent groups would lose any privilege to obtain resources, directly or not, from the public budget. This conglomeration of funds, because of its monopsonistic power, concentrates many possibilities to fulfill successfully the criteria of health policy such as effectiveness, efficiency, equity, quality, and choice as pointed out in the literature (OECD, 1992).

The alliance (Common Fund) would develop a universal package of services for the insured trying to achieve equity in accordance with its available resources. This package has to be determined annually depending on the basic health needs of the majority of the insured. Also important is the ability for the Common Fund to balance health insurance contributions of the Sickness Funds in a gradual fashion applying equity criteria, such as contributions according to the ability to pay. It would also have the ability to charge patients and impose copayments for services for which there is no high priority (e.g., cosmetic plastic surgery), or there would be a systematic overutilization of services. At the same time, it would choose which medical services would be funded, forcing physicians and hospitals to assure the efficacy and effectiveness of services provided, based on socioeconomic evaluations.

On the other hand, the provision side is separated from the public budget and the financing side. The public hospitals would be autonomous organizations managed not by laypersons, but by professionals or trained managers, who would have full responsibility for their efficient operation. This means that the operation of every hospital is not yet secured by the public budget, which covers 75% of their total costs. Given the full separation of the hospitals from the financing side, they have to fulfill their role and prove efficient in a competitive environment. Thus, they have to reduce costs and waiting times and improve quality. In other words, they have to introduce modern methods of health care management, are which now absent in the Greek public sector. Hospitals contracting with the Common Fund would be reimbursed by a prospective financing method, such as global budget, diagnostic-related groups, and so on. Of course, hospital managers would change methods of reimbursing medical and other personnel by replacing salaries with an effective payment system, taking into account case mix, workload, and performance criteria.

Moreover, another crucial problem, distribution of the available resources between the different geographical regions to achieve equality in access, seems to be addressed with the above proposals. This problem of the regionalization of health services is significant for the Greek health system, since Athens and Thessaloniki, the two major cities, receive patients from other regions. In terms of regionalization of hospital services and equal access, a branch of the alliance would be established in each region. Every year the Common Fund would allocate resources to each regional branch, which in turn would negotiate with the hospitals in that region. The equal distribution of resources in each region could be achieved by a formula, taking into account appropriate criteria, such as the size of the population, age structure, sex, health needs, and so on. Patients would be free inside the region to choose from which hospital to get the necessary service. Whether economies of scale exist, the Common Fund could include or exclude some services from the region. For example, since the population of each region does not permit the establishment of transplantation centers, it is expected that these centers would be limited to either Athens or Thessaloniki. At the same time, the principle of money following the patient has some positive results in the regionalization of hospital services. In this way hospitals with a high patient burden must be fully compensated, either by the regional branch to which the patient belongs or by the patients themselves when they choose to ask for treatment out of their region.

VII. MANAGERIAL AND FINANCIAL PROBLEMS IN OUTPATIENT CARE

Introduction of the Greek NHS was mainly intended to create homogeneity and to provide comprehensive health care for all, free at the point of use. For primary health care, there were two main regulations: first, the introduction of the family physician and second, the creation of health centers in urban and nonurban areas, where medical and other professionals could be provided with full outpatient care covering the health needs of the population. As in the case of hospital care, these regulations were not well planned. This is because the sources of financing and effective methods for reimbursement of these services were not considered. It has already been mentioned that only health centers in rural and semiurban areas and outpatient departments of public hospitals were implemented, owing to the lack of funds. As a result, the delivery and the financing of outpatient health care more or less remained the same as before the introduction of the NHS. Nevertheless, in 1992, there were 190 health centers in operation and regardless of their problems in financing and staffing, they seemed to provide remarkable services to the rural population (Economou, 1994).

Looking at the financing and delivery of outpatient care there is no split between demand for and supply of these services. It has been already noted that each Sickness Fund has its own organizational activities, providing alternative systems of delivering outpatient services. However, the following three options describe the majority of the existing patterns of financing and delivery.

First, there is the IKA, the largest of the Sickness Funds, where demand and supply of ambulatory care is fully organized and provided by it. This means that IKA is both the insurer and producer of health services. It is worth mentioning that IKA has many similarities with health maintenance organizations (HMOs), which operate in United States. In most cases, the health personnel (salaried physicians and dentists) provide their services in small centers (polyclinics) of IKA ownership, having a specific daily work timetable. There is at least one health center in every city with 15,000 insured. The insured have to get medical services in these centers where they live. In a few cases, when the number of the insured is less, some salaried physicians of IKA provide services in their medical offices operating as family doctors. In other words, financing and delivery of services in outpatient care is performed by IKA, which keeps for itself the double role of insurer and provider. The insured have the right to ask for treatment from different specialities in the health centers, but their choice is restricted because there are no more than two physicians for every basic medical specialty.

While theoretically those insured by IKA have full coverage and access to basic outpatient services (7200 physicians and dentists are available for them), there seem to be important problems with the quality of services, since the insured are not satisfied (Georgoussi et al., 1991; Theodorou, 1993). Low quality of care seems to be mainly connected with medical professionals, because their salaries are low in relation to other professionals or their NHS counterparts. It is worth mentioning that the monthly average salary of the professionals employed by IKA is 200,000 drs ($1000) in comparison to 600,000 drs ($3000) of the NHS physicians. However, the IKA physicians work short hours, work only 5 days a week, and keep the right to practice privately. Patients dissatisfied with the IKA provision who have the ability to pay turn to the private sector. This is another reason for the rise in private health spending. In general, this type of IKA provision with physicians earning low salaries provides no choice to the insured and seems to contribute to inefficient care with low quality of care rendered.

The second pattern of outpatient care concerns the rural population. It has already been noted that OGA, which is the Sickness Fund of farmers, does not play any role in the financing and delivery side of primary care, since this is of the state (public budget) interest. The government, through the public budget, finances health centers and rural dispensaries, where salaried physicians provide outpatient care to the rural population. At the same time, the government controls the management of these services, exercised through public administration. From this point of view, the state is the purchaser and the provider of outpatient services.

Although the introduction of health centers provided access to the rural population, no available information exists on the level of efficiency, effectiveness, or quality of these services. This absence of evaluation and evidence on performance is another attribute of the Greek health system, where major interventions in health care are not usually monitored or studied by independent or governmental bodies. Thus, it is difficult to comment on the effectiveness, efficiency, and quality of service provided by health centers, though this pattern also lacks any choice and is more or less similar to the first pattern of primary care used by IKA.

The majority of the Sickness Funds follow the third main pattern for outpatient care where they exercise no provision side. They are only involved in the financing side. The insured have the right to seek care in the marketplace (public and private sector), paying out-of-pocket and then being reimbursed from the Sickness Fund. When they use approved services (usually outpatient departments of public hospitals or some physicians who directly contract with some of the funds), the reimbursement is full (100%), because they are charged according to the official prices defined by the Department of Health. When they use unapproved services (shopping around in the marketplace), their reimbursement is only partial (about 30%), because real medical prices are higher than the defined ones. For example, a medical consultation in 1995 in the area of Athens ranged from 7000 drs ($35) to 15,000 drs ($75), depending on the specialty and the doctor's reputation. The official price, which the fund reimburses the insured, was only 2400 drs ($12) and the rest is paid out-of-pocket. This method of financing and intervention on the medical market leads to substantially high copayments to the insured and as a result private expenditures remain high.

The last pattern of outpatient care has some advantages and disadvantages. On the one hand, it separates the functions of demand for and supply of services, which seem to be necessary in every health market (open or planned). In addition, it enforces the right of patients to have a choice of providers. On the other hand, it encourages private spending and cancels the right of the insured to full and complete coverage. Moreover, since demand does not have any control on the provision side, overutilization with a high number of consultations may occur.*

---

* A recent unpublished study by the Department of Health Economics National School of Public Health found 6.5 consultations per person per year for a Sickness Fund utilizing this pattern of care in comparison with 4.2 for the insured through IKA.

The absence of a regulatory and performance system on the financing side may allow or offer incentives to the medical professionals to manipulate the patients, by inducing some kind of demand (for consultations, laboratory tests, etc.).

It has been explained that the NHS introduction was never fully implemented at the primary health care level. Apart from health centers, there was no important intervention to unify the different patterns of health care financing and delivery. The preceding analysis shows that outpatient care in Greece is not only fragmented and uncoordinated, but even some essential criteria such as cost containment, efficiency, quality, and choice are not fulfilled. In addition, complete coverage in a part of the population is not provided, though institutionally no charges exist except for a 25% payment for pharmaceuticals and other medical products such as eyeglasses.

In this way, the Greek NHS cannot be compared in real terms to either a Bismarkian or a Beveridgean health care system. This, of course, is not a problem itself. The problem is that the Greek NHS does not provide equity in accessibility or in the distribution of the cost. Neither is the system free for all at the point of use, as it was envisaged. It seems to be rather a market-oriented system without rules and regulations. It is difficult for someone insured to have easy access, if he/she is not prepared to pay a price at the point of use. The system mainly seems to favor the providers and not the patients, for whom it should exist. Otherwise, there is no conventional way to explain how such a large number of medical professionals (one physician: 180 inhabitants in Athens and 1 : 170 in Thessaloniki) managed to satisfy their income and professional expectations.

VIII. PROPOSALS FOR OUTPATIENT CARE

The problems described above concerning the demand for and supply of outpatient services need an appropriate and effective solution. This is not of course the introduction of a general family practitioner with a budget, as the proposal of foreign experts seems to suggest. Nor is the number of general practitioners sufficient with only 500 and a needed total of 5000, according to foreign experts. In addition, Greek attitudes (the existing tradition to ask treatment from specialized physicians without any referral or waiting time) are not similar to the British to accept such a restricted proposal. For example, it is impossible for the majority of Greek pregnant women to welcome medical consultation and followup from a general practitioner and not from a selected obstetrician. On the contrary, given the Sickness Funds tradition and the need of the insured for choice, a pluralistic delivery system of outpatient care based on quasi-market principles may be introduced to meet patient needs. This means that a real split of purchasers from the providers must be introduced to achieve some of the fundamental criteria of effectiveness, quality, equity, and efficiency.

Providers of outpatient care must be autonomous from the financing side, exercising their own structure of practicing medicine (solo or group, salaried or fee-for-service). Purchasers (Sickness Funds), as in the case of hospital care, may be artificially unified in a Common Fund that will also be responsible for outpatient care. The Common Fund on the demand side having financial power can operate efficiently, shopping around for services provided by the existing suppliers. The Common Fund could operate at the lower administrational level of Greece (prefectures), where the most important levels of outpatient provision and a local branch of the medical association exists.

Figure 3 shows how a complete separation of the purchasers and providers in conjunction with the Common Fund could operate. On the provision side are all the existing types of outpatient care provision (GPs, solo private practice, group practice, health specialists, health centers), which are fully autonomous from the demand side. All these types, or others, are going to compete with one another, negotiating with the local division of the Common Fund for contracts. The Common Fund may choose to have annual contracts attempting to promote efficiency. Every year the insured of the Common Fund may exercise their choice

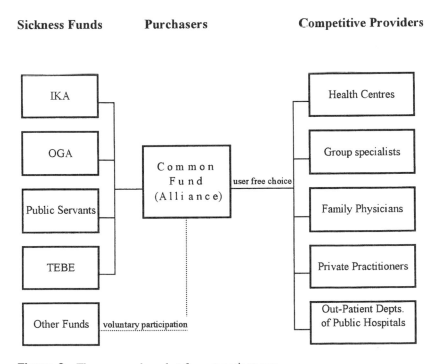

Figure 3   The proposed market for out-patient care.

and enroll themselves and their families in one type of provision (solo practitioners, group practitioners, health centers, or other new forms). A prospective
reimbursement method seems to be appropriate for any of these types of provision. Information to the patients is also the provider's responsibility and quality
of services is necessary if the providers want to survive. Efficient providers with
high quality would expect to have more patients, since the Common Fund could
establish special incentives for them (e.g., excluding charges and copayments).
Of course, the range of the competition between the providers depends on the
ability of the Common Fund to lead people to choose efficient types of care, in
conjunction with the number of competitive providers in each prefecture.

Operation of the Common Fund, at both the primary and secondary levels
of care and the split between purchasers and providers, offers some significant
advantages:

1. It introduces a managed competitive market on the supply side, mainly
   forcing the providers to negotiate contracts and become more accountable to patient demands and ensure quality.
2. It brings about efficient use of resources, since any side of the contract
   is directly involved at any stage of health care.
3. It ensures equity in financing and in access to appropriate care, since
   the package of care provided is the same for the insured belonging to
   the Common Fund, and at the same time, the range of services provided
   is determined annually.
4. It forces the providers (hospitals, physicians, specialists, health centers,
   and other organizations) to provide information on the quality of services rendered.
5. It provides consumers a free choice of providers.
6. It can easily place high copayments upon or exclude from coverage
   interventions and services for which there is no available evidence of
   efficacy and effectiveness.

IX. CONCLUSIONS

There is no doubt that every health care system faces many problems and deficiencies. What is more critical, in the case of Greece, is that although deficiencies
seem to be larger, no action has been undertaken to bring a balance between
consumers, insurers, and providers. Despite the fact that the current system has
been planned to be fully regulated by the government, in real terms a completely
unregulated open market is in operation, which increases the problems in effectiveness, efficiency, equity, and quality and restricts the choice of the patients.
Major issues of the political economy of health care, such as sources of finance,

financing methods, reimbursement of the providers, and access to the appropriate services, have not made the political agenda. Moreover, parallel to the existing ineffective market, a hidden one seems to operate, which increases private health spending and finally cancels the right of full coverage and challenges significantly the right to equal access. The preceding analysis argues that fundamental criteria for health policy, such as efficiency, effectiveness, equity, quality, and choice, are not fulfilled in the present Greek system.

To overcome the problems and deficiencies of the present system, some proposals are suggested. These proposals take into account the transitional problems of the Greek health system, the existing domestic tradition, and follow the international approach of managed competition that is based on the quasi-market principles of the Beveridgean model of health care. An agency (Alliance or Common Fund) on the demand side is suggested to be created from the four Sickness Funds, which provide mandatory health insurance and cover over 90% of the Greek population. This agency, functioning with branches at the local and regional level, would have a major advantage. Operating on behalf of almost the entire population, it can exercise monopsonistic power and force the existing providers, in both the public and the private sector, to compete for contracts. In other words, a regulated market that operates with two main protagonists that have different interests may direct the Greek health system to a desirable balance. Thus, many deficiencies of the system may be removed and to a great extent, the criteria of efficiency, equity, quality, and choice may have the possibility of being incorporated into Greek health policy.

REFERENCES

Abel Smith, B. Cost Containment in Health Care. London: Bedford Square Press, 1984.

Abel Smith, B., Calltrop, J., Dixon, M., Dunning, M., Evans, R., Holland, W., Jarman, B., Mossialos, E. Report of the Committee of Experts for Health Care in Greece. Athens: Farmetrica, Department of Health Welfare and Social Security, 1994 (in Greek).

Barr, N. The Economics of Welfare State. London: Weindenfeld & Nicolson, 1987.

Department of Health and Social Services. Practice Budgets for General Medical Practitioners. London: Her Majesty Statistics Office, 1989.

Economou, H. Primary health care in Greece: the health centres establishment. Soc Econ Health 3(2):83–95, 1994.

Eurostat. Review, CECA-CEE-CEEA. Bruxelles-Luxembourg, 1989.

Feldstein, P.J. Health Economics, 2nd ed. New York: Wiley, 1983.

Figueras, J., Normand, C., Roberts, J., McKee, M., Hunter, D. Karokis, A., Pope, C., Azene, G. Health Care Infrastructure Needs in Lagging Regions. London: London School of Hygiene and Tropical Medicine, 1992.

Filalithis, A.E. Health needs and the delivery of primary health care. In: Kyriopoulos, J.,

Niakas, D., eds. The Challenge of Competition in Health Care. Athens: Centre for Health and Social Sciences, 1993, pp 175–188 (in Greek).

Filalithis, A.E. The report of experts and the dialogue for the development of general practice in Greece. Prim Health Care 7(1):11–13, 1995 (in Greek).

Georgoussi, E., Gennimata, A., Drizi, L., Somarakis, M., Kyriopoulos, J. Users of outpatient care. Med Forum 16(3):25–31, 1991 (in Greek).

Kalapothaki, V., Kalantidou, A., Katsougianni, A., Trichopoulou, A., Kyriopoulos, J., Kremastinou, J., Hajikonstantinou, D., Trichopoulos, D. Health of the Greek population. Mater Med Greca 20(2):91–164, 1992 (in Greek).

KEPE. Health Program for 1976–1980. Athens: KEPE, 1976 (in Greek).

KEPE. Regionalisation of Health Services. Athens: KEPE, 1979 (in Greek).

KEPE. Program of Economic and Social Development. Athens: KEPE, 1983 (in Greek).

KEPE. An Estimation of the Hidden Economy in Greece. Study Group, Athens: KEPE, 1992 (in Greek).

Klein, R. Financing of health care: the three options. Br Med J 296:734–736, 1988.

Kyriopoulos, J., Niakas, D. Financing Health Services in Greece. Athens: Centre for Health and Social Sciences, 1991 (in Greek).

Kyriopoulos, J., Niakas, D. Economic and health policy issues in biomedical technology: the case of Greece. In: Malek, M., Rasquinha, J., Vacani, P., eds. Strategic Issues in Health Care Management. Chichester: Wiley, 1993, pp 57–64.

Lopez, A.D. Who dies of what? A comparative analysis of mortality conditions in developed countries around 1987. World Health Statist Q 43(2):105–114, 1990.

Matsaganis, M. Is health insurance in Greece in need of reform? Health Policy Planning 6(3):271–281, 1991.

Matsaganis, M. Know-how transfer and its perils: towards the introduction of family-doctor budgets in Greece. In: Kyriopoulos, J., ed. Health Policy at Crossroads. Athens: Themelio, 1995, pp 149–172 (in Greek).

Merkouris, M.P. Comments on the report of experts for health care in Greece. Prim Health Care 6(3):121–123, 1994 (in Greek).

Niakas, D. The need for change in health care finance method in Greece: confronting the issue. In: Kyriopoulos, J., Levett, J., eds. Financing and Delivering Health Care in Balkan Region. Athens: ASPHER-ASPH, 1992, pp 38–58.

Niakas, D. Health and Regional Development: Regional Health Policy in Greece. Athens: Centre for Health and Social Sciences, 1993 (in Greek).

Niakas, D. Are the proposals of the international committee of experts for the primary health care in Greece feasible? Primary Health Care 7(1):33–38, 1995 (in Greek).

Niakas, D. Health spending in Greece and the market for medical professionals: is there any relationship? In: Levett, J., Petsetakis, E., eds. Infrastructure Strengthening in Public Health. Athens: National School of Public Health, 1996, pp 31–41.

Niakas, D., Beazoglou, T. Is the development of alternative forms care for the aged in Greece necessary? In: Kyriopoulos, J., Georgoussi, E., Skoutelis, G., eds. Health and Social Protection in Ageing. Athens: Centre for Health and Social Sciences, 1994, pp 253–262 (in Greek).

Niakas, D., Kyriopoulos, J. Health spending in Greece and the national accounts: some necessary explanations. Soc Econ Health 3(1):18–29, 1994 (in Greek).

Niakas, D., Skoutelis, G, Kyriopoulos, J. Searching for the hidden activity in health care. Health Rev 1(6):42–45, 1990 (in Greek).

OECD. Financing and Delivering Health Care: A Comparative Analysis of OECD Countries. Paris: OECD, 1987.

OECD. Economic Survey, Greece. Paris: OECD, 1990.

OECD. The Reform of Health Care: A Comparative Analysis of Seven OECD Countries. Health Policy Studies 2. Paris: OECD, 1992.

OECD. Health Care Systems in OECD Countries: Facts and Trends 1960–1991. Health Policy Studies 3. Paris: OECD, 1993.

Pavlopoulos, P. The Hidden Economy in Greece: A Quantitative Determination. Athens: IOBE, 1987 (in Greek).

Rathwell, T. Market mania. Eur Health Reform 1(1):4–5, 1995.

Robinson, R., Le Grand, J., eds. Evaluating the NHS Reforms. London: King's Fund Institute, 1994.

Schulenburg, J.M. The German health care system at the crossroads. Health Econ 3(5): 301–303, 1994.

Simitis, C. Development and Modernisation of the Greek Society. Athens: Gnosis, 1989 (in Greek).

Sissouras, A. Health care systems and the challenge of 1992 in Europe, 2nd Health Meeting in Health Economics, Athens, mimeo, 1989 (in Greek).

Skoutelis, G. Social Security in Greece: from Development to Crisis. Athens: Centre for Health and Social Sciences, 1989a (in Greek).

Skoutelis, G. Unified health service. Proceedings of the 1st Greek Health Meeting in Health Economics. Athens: Centre for Health and Social Sciences, 1989b, pp 133–138 (in Greek).

Theodorou, M. The Outpatient Care of IKA. Athens. IMOSY, 1993 (in Greek).

Van Doorslaer, E., Wagstaff, A., Rutten, F. Equity in the Finance and Delivery of Health Care: An International Perspective. Oxford: Oxford University Press, 1993.

Williams, A. Priority setting in public and private health care: a guide through the ideological jungle. J Health Econ 7(2):173–183, 1988.

14

Health Care System in Turkey

Fahreddin Tatar* and Tevfik Dinçer
Hacettepe University, Ankara, Turkey

I. OVERVIEW

Turkey, founded in 1923 after the collapse of the Ottoman Empire, is situated in the southeast of Europe and bordered by the Mediterranean Sea, Iraq, and Syria on the south; Iran, Azerbaijan, Armenia, and Georgia on the east; the Aegean Sea and Greece on the west; and the Black Sea and Bulgaria on the north. The area is 779,452 km², of which 23,764 km² are in Europe (Thrace) and 755,688 km² in Asia (Anatolia).

Turkey's population was 62,510,000 in 1997 and it was estimated to reach 65,311,000 in 2000 and almost 70,000,000 in 2005. Although on the decline, the population is still growing at a high rate of 1.6% per annum. In comparison with the industrialized world the Turkish population is relatively young (35.8% of the population was under 15 and only 4.2% was 65 and over in 1990). In 1997, 35% of the population still lived in the rural areas.

Turkey, classified as a lower-middle-income country by the World Bank with a US$2500 GNP per capita in 1994 (UNICEF, 1996) suffers from health problems similar to those of other developing countries. High infant mortality rate (IMR) (52.6 per 1000 live births in 1996), high prevalence of preventable communicable diseases, together with cancer, circulatory diseases, and others, related both to development and underdevelopment, threaten the population (Sağlik Bakanliği et al., 1994). On the other hand, inequalities among different segments of the population and among regions exacerbate the problem.

The political system of Turkey is parliamentary democracy. The country is divided into 81 administrative units (provinces) each of which is headed by a

---

* *Current affiliation*: The Futures Group International/POLICY Project, Ankara, Turkey

governor representing the state authority at the provincial level. Provincial health administrations, the highest peripheral unit of the Ministry of Health (MoH) at the provincial level, are administratively responsible to the governor office.

The Turkish health care system can be described as "pluralistic" with numerous public as well as private health care institutions that provide and/or finance health care services. The process of fragmentation has, despite the adopted official policy directions, continued at an increasing pace since about the early 1980s. In recent years the government has seemed to abandon its long-standing policy direction to stop further fragmentation and instead began to boost further fragmentation of the health care programs.

Health care insurance (security) coverage is one of the most pressing problems faced by the Turkish health care system today. In 1994, 45.4% of the Turkish population had no health insurance coverage at all (Health Insurance Commission of Australia, 1995). Those who have coverage are not on the whole satisfied with the quality of the services rendered in the public health care institutions. Covert privatization through fee increases and preferential treatment for high direct out-of-pocket payments to public hospitals have in recent years increased with significant negative equity implications. A relatively recent attempt to provide the indigent population with health coverage through a scheme called "green card" has provided a proportion of the uninsured population with coverage.

The health care system in Turkey can be defined as one that falls in the category of welfare-oriented health care systems using Roemer's typology (Roemer, 1991). However, this is true if only judged by official documents and legislation. The system is increasingly being financed through direct out-of-pocket payments, which is also an evidence of the increasing role for the private sector and practices.

II. DESCRIPTION OF HEALTH CARE SYSTEM

A. Historical Development

Turkish health policy and the resulting health care system can be analyzed historically in three different phases. The first phase, 1923–1960, is the period commencing with the foundation of the Republic in 1923. The second phase, 1960–1980, is characterized by the introduction of socialization of health services. The current phase began in 1980 with the so-called "24 January 1980 (Economic) Decisions" that have since then radically reshaped the outlook of, among others, the health care sector.

The *first phase*, 1923–1960, can be regarded as a period characterized by intensive legislation efforts, aimed at establishing a framework for the health care system. In 1923, there were 86 hospitals with 6437 beds in the country for a total population of less than 13 million. Only three of these hospitals (950 beds) were owned by the central government; the rest were owned and operated by municipal authorities and the private sector, foreigners, and minority groups (Sağlik ve Sosyal Yardim Bakanliği, 1973). However, with the establishment of the MoH, the central government began to assume direct responsibility for health care provision and started to build its own facilities. This expansion took place by both building its own facilities and buying the existing facilities of local authorities and non-profit-making trusts (foundations). As a result of this policy, by 1963, the private sector had proportionately shrunk, in terms of hospital beds, compared to the massive expansion of the public sector in general and the MoH in particular (4.98% and 95.02%, respectively).

The dramatically increased role of the MoH during this period could be attributed to the prevailing socioeconomic conditions of the country. The statist character of economic and social policies during the first decades of the Republic required an overwhelming state involvement in every sphere of life including the health care sector.

The health policy during this period was characterized mainly by building hospitals especially in urban areas and vertical programs that were introduced to combat diseases such as malaria and tuberculosis. In 1946, a new health care delivery system based on the services of health centers in rural areas was introduced with the First Health Plan. However, although a number of health centers were built during 1950–1960, owing to difficulties in staffing and equipping these centers, no significant change was brought to the current system.

The *second phase* in the Turkish health care system commenced in 1961 with the Act of Socialization of Health Services, passed by the National Unity Committee of the 1960 military administration just before they left power.

The Act of Socialization was born out of an ambition to create an *egalitarian* health care system financed mainly out of general taxation with some user charges. The proposed system, which reflected the characteristics of the *basic health services approach* that was the convention in the 1960s, would enable the entire population to benefit from health care services along a hierarchical referral chain almost free of charge at the point of contact. The main emphasis in the new act was on provision of health care services to the entire population on the basis of equity. The system required the integration of both preventive and curative medicine, stressing the former more than the latter.

This act proposed a hierarchical referral system starting from *health posts* for around 2000–5000 people and staffed by a midwife. Primary aims of this unit were the provision of maternal and child health services, immunization, and health education concerning especially personal and environmental hygiene.

The second and most important unit brought by the act was *health centers*. The health center is defined as a social and medical institution that carries out its activities by following the principles of community medicine. It is responsible for 5000–10,000 people in a geographical area. Maternal and child health; malaria eradication; tuberculosis, syphilis, leprosy, and trachoma control; family planning; environmental health; health education; immunization; patient care; first aid and school health are among the major responsibilities of a health center in the area.

The third level in the organization model is a hospital serving a population of 50,000–200,000 people. Health centers are attached to these hospitals and they are supposed to work collaboratively in performing the tasks assigned by the act.

After the enforcement of the act, intensive efforts were made to cover the whole country. Despite its strengths on paper, the model did not achieve the intended aims for a host of reasons ranging from weak political support of successive governments to infrastructure problems, lack of financial support to professional resistance.

As a major health policy, socialization has officially never been scrapped. Even today, when all the fundamentals of socialization are clearly challenged and replaced, it still remains an official policy. The aim the system set to achieve was to provide people with free and equal health services. However, more than three decades after this noble aim was set, the citizens of the country on the whole are still without equal and free health services.

Turkish health care policy, around the mid-1980s, entered its *third phase* in line with the newly adopted economic development approach. The so-called "24 January Decisions," reflecting the structural adjustment and stabilization policies agreed with the International Monetary Fund and the World Bank, marked the beginning of a new era where the decades-long inward-looking development policy was replaced with an outward-looking (export-import-led) one. However, the decisions taken in 1980 have affected not only economic policy but also social policy in general and health care policy in particular. In this phase the relative role of the public sector vis-à-vis the private sector has been seriously questioned. The main contention seems to be that a public/private mix favoring the latter would be key to the solution of various health and health care problems. Since the late 1980s, intensive efforts have been made to carry out a health sector reform process geared toward the creation of a health care system where the role of the state as a provider and financier is reduced considerably, leaving a much larger role for the private sector to play. A detailed analysis of the reform proposals is presented later in this chapter.

B. Organizational Structure and the Health Care Delivery System

The Turkish health care system is characterized by a fragmented structure with multiple providers and financing institutions (Table 1). Though highly complex,

Table 1 Distribution of Hospitals and Hospital Beds by
Ownership, 1998

Institutions	Number of hospitals	Hospital beds	
		Number	%
Ministry of Health	698	82,032	49.8
Social Insurance Organization	115	26,279	15.9
Universities	37	23,828	14.5
Ministry of Defense	42	15,900	9.6
State Economic Enterprises	10	2,217	1.3
Other public	8	1,953	1.2
Private	210	12,678	7.7
Total	1120	164,887	100.0

Source: Sağlik Bakanliği, 1999.

it can be stated that health services are provided mainly by three systems quite
independent from one another: the MoH, the Social Insurance Organization
(SIO), and university hospitals. It must be pointed out here that MoH has historically been reluctant and unable to exert its authority over the remaining systems.

1. Public Sector

(a) The Ministry of Health. The MoH provides primary, secondary, and
tertiary care to the majority of the population through a network of health posts,
health centers, hospitals, and other facilities. At the periphery, the Provincial
Health Director is the main body responsible for organizing and delivering health
services under the responsibility of the MoH.

The MoH is by far the major provider of primary health care services. The
role the MoH plays in the provision of preventive health care services is more
clearly defined and visible in disease control programs identified and represented
by different vertical programs and directorates to conduct these programs. Examples include programs on tuberculosis, malaria, leprosy, and syphilis. However,
the MoH, despite its predominant role in the provision of preventive services,
is not the only actor in the field. Others, such as municipalities in especially
environmental health services and the private sector in family planning services,
also play a significant role (Price Waterhouse, 1990).

The MoH also plays a significant role in the provision of secondary and
tertiary health care services with 50% of all hospital beds in Turkey (Table 1).
The comparative performance of secondary and tertiary health care facilities and
general utilization figures are presented in Table 2.

Table 2 Selected Activities of Hospitals by Health Care Organizations, 1995

	MoH	SIO	Medical schools	Other public	Private	Total
Average length of stay	5.7	6.6	9.9	10.3	4.0	6.4
Bed occupancy rate, %	55.3	70.4	61.1	37.3	30.0	57.4
In-patients						
N	2,210,726	982,147	441,365	43,288	198,994	3,876,520
%	57.0	25.3	11.4	1.1	5.1	100.0
Out-patients						
N	41,578,790	26,112,437	5,276,810	1,328,198	1,574,533	75,870,768
%	54.8	34.4	7.0	1.8	2.1	100.0
Admissions per 100 population						6.3
Number of hospital beds per thousand population						24.6

Source: Ministry of Health, 1996a; Sağlik Bakanliği, 1996.

Insofar as health sector employment is concerned, the MoH is by far the largest employer for all categories of personnel except for specialist physicians, pharmacists, and dentists (Table 3).

(b) The Social Insurance Organization. As seen from Table 1, the Social Insurance Organization (SIO) is the second largest provider of hospital services with a sizable medical and nursing staff employment level (Table 3). The organization provides health care to the employees and dependents of formal employment sector outside the Civil Service. It is financed through employer and employee contributions. Premiums for health care to the SIO amount to 11% of the wage bill of which 5% is met by employees.

Despite originally being a (social) insurance, hence financing, organization, the SIO has chosen the direct method in the provision of health services operating its own facilities throughout the country. These institutions, mainly hospitals, are concentrated in areas with beneficiary concentration. SIO hospitals provide insured patients with curative health services free of charge at the point of contact. Apart from hospitals, the organization owns dispensaries, health stations, and centers for dental treatment and denture services. Owing to various reasons such as the lack of capacity, however, the SIO has been, at an increasing rate, buying health care services for its beneficiaries from other public and private providers. The organization also provides short-term medical and maternity benefits, employment-related accident and occupational disease benefits, and long-term benefits in terms of old age, disability, and survivors' pensions.

(c) University Hospitals. In 1998, there were 37 university hospitals with a total of 23,828 beds (Table 1). These hospitals not only function as teaching hospitals for their medical schools but also form a substantial part of the country's tertiary health care network with more than 18% of all specialist physicians available in the country (Table 3). Although it changes with varying degrees according to the region where the university hospital is established, sophisticated and new technology is the main characteristic of these institutions. These hospitals are overburdened especially with self-referred patients of whom a significant proportion could normally be treated at the secondary or even primary level.

(d) Other Public Providers. As can be seen from Table 1, apart from the aforementioned three, there are other organizations in the public sector that are involved in the provision of health care services. The most prominent of these is the Ministry of Defense, which, with its 42 hospitals and 15,900 beds, provides services to its military as well as civilian personnel and their dependents. The ministry also has its own medical school and training institutions for other personnel such as nurses and auxiliaries.

Table 3 Distribution of Health Human Resources, 1994

	Population per person	MoH		SIO		Universities		Other		Private		Total	
		N	%	N	%	N	%	N	%	N	%	N	%
Physician	929	34,405	52.3	6869	10.4	10,871	16.5	4562	6.9	9,125	13.9	65,832	100.0
Specialist	2220	9,737	35.3	4001	14.5	5,029	18.2	1655	6.0	7,142	25.9	27,564	100.0
Practitioner[a]	1599	24,688	64.5	2868	7.5	5,842	15.3	2907	7.6	1,983	5.2	38,268	100.0
Nurse	5340	35,348	62.8	6826	12.1	7,829	13.9	4038	7.2	2,239	4.0	56,280	100.0
Pharmacist	3331	1,193	6.5	944	5.1	358	2.0	560	3.0	15,311	83.4	18,366	100.0
Dentist	1986	2,171	18.9	465	4.1	469	4.1	602	5.3	7,750	67.6	11,457	100.0
Sanitarian	1087	22,678	73.6	2193	7.1	2,205	7.2	1730	5.6	2,005	6.5	30,811	100.0
Midwife	1718	33,038	92.8	1227	3.4	39	0.1	107	0.3	1,193	3.4	35,604	100.0

[a] Practitioner physicians are medical school graduates with no specialization.
Source: Ministry of Health, 1996a.

2. Private Sector

The private sector has a share of 8% of all hospital beds in the country (Table 1). However, this does not mean that Turkey has a small private sector. Private practice both within and without the public sector is widespread throughout the country. More than 50% of total physician time available in the country is widely believed to be devoted to private medical practice (Roemer, 1991). In a World Bank Report it has been stated that 40% of Turkish physicians are engaged in private practice. The majority of these physicians are normally employed by various public sector organizations but work in private solo or group practices on a part-time basis. According to the report, the number of doctors exclusively working in the private sector is quite small as the majority work on a part-time basis (World Bank, 1986, p. 36). Part-time physicians can refer their private patients to private hospitals as well as public hospitals where they are employed for further treatment or surgical operations. However, the share of the referrals from private surgeries to public versus private secondary and tertiary health care facilities is not known. With regard to dentists and pharmacists, the private sector seems to be the major employer. In 1994, 67.6% of dentists and 83.4% of pharmacists were working in the private sector (Table 3).

The MoH and other public sector hospitals have a small proportion of pay-beds. The proportion of pay-beds and the level of charges for such beds are higher in university hospitals than in those of the MoH. University hospitals allow their consultants to perform private outpatient services in their hospitals, too. This, when added to the overall size and capacity of all private sector operations, makes the private sector one of the largest providers of primary-level health care services in the country.

C. Financing of Health Care System

The share of GNP that Turkey devoted to health care was 4.06% in 1994. The share of the MoH budget, which has revolved around 4% of the state budget, is only around 0.81% of GNP. In 1995, the share of the MoH's budget within the state budget was 3.7% (Ministry of Health, 1996a). In the Health Master Plan Study of 1990 it was found that 34.1% of total health expenditures was from the general budget and 16.9% from insurance premiums whereas the direct out-of-pocket payments reached 49.0%. When the total health care expenditures are broken down by the type of health services, it has been found that 60.7% of the total expenditures was spent on primary-level medical care and 37.5% on hospital services. Only 1.8% of the expenditures were spent on preventive and promotive health services (Price Waterhouse, 1990).

Although not fully compatible with international standards, the available data on health care expenditures testifies to the complex and highly fragmented

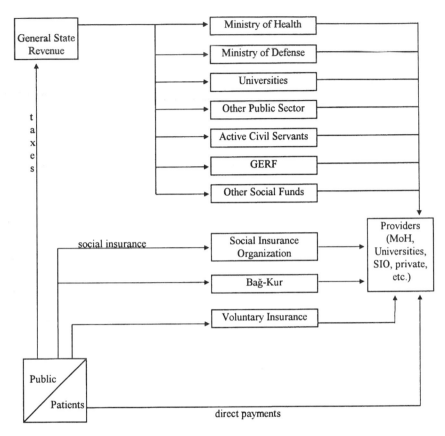

Figure 1 Structure of health care financing in Turkey. (From World Health Organization, 1996.)

financing structure of the health care system in Turkey (Fig. 1). Tables 4 and 5 show the aggregate sources of funding for health care services and expenditures.

As seen from Table 4, more than 42% of all health care finance comes from the state budget. The share of insurance funds is 21.77%. User charges account for 35.6% but this could not necessarily be treated as out-of-pocket payments made by patients since a significant proportion of that is met by employing organizations on behalf of their employees. Table 5, however, gives an idea of the minimum level of direct out-of pocket payments. According to Table 5, at least 18.5% of all health care expenditures are met by uninsured population as direct out-of-pocket payments.

Table 4 Aggregate Sources of Funding for Health Services and Expenditure, 1993 (in 1994 prices, trillion Turkish lira)

Source of funds	Use of funds					
	Public	%	Private	%	Total	%
State budget	69.0	66.0	0.5	0.86	69.5	42.63
Insurance funds	31.0	30.0	4.5	7.76	35.5	21.77
User charges	5.0	4.0	53.0	91.38	58.0	35.60
Total	105.0	100.0	58.0	100.0	163.0	100.0

Source: World Health Organization, 1996.

Table 5 Sources of Funds for Health Care, 1994 (in 1994 prices, billion Turkish lira)

Source	Turkish lira	% of grand total
Insured population		
Insurance payments		20.9
Social insurance	33,245	20.3
Private insurance	994	0.6
User charges	25,958	15.9
Civil servants and military personnel	3,966	2.4
others	21,991	13.5
Public finance	50,475	30.9
Civil servants and military personnel	32,425	19.9
others	18,050	11.0
Total (insured population)	110,671	67.7
Uninsured population		
User charges	30,231	18.5
Public finance (subsidy)	22,600	13.8
Total (uninsured population)	52,831	32.3
Grand total	163,502	100.0

Source: Health Insurance Commission of Australia, 1995.

Table 6 What the Money Is Spent On (in 1994 prices, billion Turkish lira)

	1992	%	1994	%	1996[a]	%
Hospital admissions	40,255	26.7	42,994	26.3	49,449	26.3
Ambulatory medical services	47,858	31.7	51,216	31.3	59,112	31.5
Pharmaceuticals	38,129	25.3	44,193	27.0	51,204	27.2
Other health services	21,185	14.1	21,573	13.2	24,126	12.8
Administration	3,360	2.2	3,526	2.2	4,063	2.2
Total	150,787	100.0	163,502	100.0	187,954	100.0

[a] Estimated figures.
Source: Health Insurance Commission of Australia, 1995.

It seems from Table 6 that in 1994 ambulatory medical services got the largest share of all health care expenditures (31.3%). This is followed by pharmaceuticals (26.3%) and hospital admissions (26.3%).

D. Reimbursement Mechanisms

Public hospitals are financed to a large extent from general budgetary allocations. However, third-party and direct out-of-pocket payments form a substantial proportion of all hospital income (almost one-third). Most public hospitals have their own revolving funds into which third-party payments flow. Hospitals use the revolving fund revenues toward meeting some recurrent as well as nonrecurrent expenditures. A significant proportion of revolving funds is used to supplement the salaries of especially medical personnel.

The centrally determined fee schedule does not reflect the actual costs. In fact, the level of fees is calculated to be around one-third of actual costs. This means that users of services rendered in public hospitals and their insurers are provided with significant subsidies. Third-party payers include GERF, SIO, Bag-Kur, and private insurance companies. For active employees and their dependents, the employing organizations also act as third-party payers. Government pays for the green card holders.

Physicians at primary health care settings such as health centers are salaried government employees. Those who work in private practices are usually paid on a fee-for-service basis.

Physicians in almost all public sector hospitals are remunerated on the basis of salary. However, there is a widespread practice where physicians receive a revolving fund allowance in addition to their salaries. The amount of revolving-fund allowances in especially large hospitals exceeds the actual salary levels.

E. Health Status of the Country: Basic Indicators

The health status of the country represents the characteristics of the majority of developing countries. High IMR, low life expectancy at birth, high maternal mortality rate, and high death toll from preventable infectious diseases, exacerbated by the contribution of malnutrition, epitomize a developing country with major health problems. Inequalities among different segments of the population and among regions further exacerbate the problem. However, attempts to elaborate these inequalities and to draw the general health status picture of the country are hindered by the lack or shortage of reliable data.

Life expectancy at birth, IMR, under-5 mortality rate, and maternal mortality rate are the most widely used indicators to elucidate health status of a country or region. Table 7 shows the comparison of Turkish health status indicators stated above by selected countries. Insofar as the life expectancy at birth is concerned, it can be seen from Table 7 that the global target of 60 years declared by WHO has already been attained. However, there is a long way to go to achieve the WHO's European Region's target of 75 years by the year 2000. Table 8 shows the health differentials in Europe in terms of life expectancy at birth.

Despite the fact that the IMR is on the decline (72 in 1992 and 52.6 in 1996), Turkey has the highest rate in Europe. Table 9 shows health differentials in Europe in terms of IMR.

On the other hand, geographical inequalities based on IMR should also be emphasized here. Table 10 below shows the huge gap between regions and urban versus rural IMR. The majority of these infants and children lose their lives from preventable diseases related to poverty in general. In 1990, it was estimated that

Table 7 Comparison of Turkish Health Status Indicators with Selected Countries

Countries	GNP per capita (US$1993)	Life expectancy at birth (1994)	IMR (1994)	Under-5 mortality (1994)	Maternal mortality (1992)
Turkey	2,970	66	47	55	150
China	490	68	35	43	95
Poland	2,260	71	14	16	11
Greece	7,390	78	8	10	5
United States	24,740	76	8	10	8
United Kingdom	18,060	76	6	7	8
Sweden	24,740	78	4	5	5

Source: UNICEF, 1996.

Table 8 Health Differentials in 27 Countries of Europe in Terms of
Life Expectancy at Birth (1989)

	Lowest	Turkey (1991)	Highest
Life expectancy at birth	66.4	66.8	78.2
Male/female differences in life expectancy	3.7	5.2	10.7

Source: World Health Organization, 1993.

Table 9 Health Differentials in Europe in Terms of IMR

	Lowest	Highest	Turkey
Infant mortality (per 1000 live births)	5.7	77.7	77.7
Neonatal mortality (per 1000 live births)	3.8	35.5	35.5
Post/neonatal mortality (per 1000 live births)	1.9	42.2	42.2
Maternal deaths (per 100,000 live births)	1.8	130.0	130.0

Source: World Health Organization, 1993.

Table 10 Adjusted Infant Mortality Rates (per
thousand) for 1985–1987

Place of settlement	Neonatal rate	Post neonatal rate	IMR
Urban	27.98	22.09	50.07
Rural	43.15	62.50	105.65
Region			
West	20.77	26.71	44.48
South	36.80	57.38	96.26
Central	53.33	36.67	90.00
North	a	a	b
East	36.36	66.67	103.03
Turkey	36.53	42.19	77.72

[a] Fewer than five observations.
[b] Fewer than 10 observations.
Source: Price Waterhouse, 1990.

35% of rural and 25% of child deaths and 35% of rural and 17% of urban deaths were from pneumonia (UNICEF, 1990). On the other hand, according to the MoH (Saḡlik Bakanliḡi, 1990), diarrhea accounted for 30,000 deaths annually among children under 5. Malnutrition as a contributing factor to deaths from causes such as pneumonia, diarrhea, or measles is especially a cause for concern. The major policy initiatives adopted to this end are to increase the immunization rate for preventable diseases and carry out special programs to attack diseases like pneumonia or programs like "oral rehydration" in the case of diarrhea.

As far as the morbidity statistics are concerned, as in many other countries, Turkey lacks reliable data. Despite this shortcoming, however, the general epidemiological outlook of the country can be outlined as follows (WHO, 1993):

in infancy: perinatal disease and infectious diseases,
in children aged 1–5 years: infectious diseases and their complications often associated with malnutrition,
in adolescence and the early 20s: accidents due to various causes,
in the 25–44 age group: heart disease and accidents,
in the 45–64 age group: heart disease and respiratory disorders associated with smoking.

It can be concluded that Turkey has a typical epidemiological profile of a developing country where infectious diseases and accidents prevail during childhood and where these are replaced by heart and circulatory diseases together with cancer for older age groups.

III. CURRENT HEALTH CARE SYSTEM ISSUES

A. Quality of Services

The Turkish health care system can be said to suffer from a wide range of quality problems at both macro and institutional levels. The problem of a high rate of uninsured population is further exacerbated by underinsurance. Though not documented, it is often proclaimed that even those with coverage have significant accessibility problems to health care services. The reason for this are manyfold but here a few of the most significant ones are briefly elaborated. The first one stems from the peculiar relations between the private and public practice in Turkey. As already mentioned, the size and scope of private practice in Turkey is much higher than it appears at first sight due mainly to widespread private practice within the public sector. The link between private surgeries of part-time physicians and the public hospitals they work for enables an environment where access to services in especially inpatient departments is secured (or secured faster) for those who first pay a visit to private surgeries. In public university hospitals full-timers are also allowed to practice privately in return for higher earnings for both the hospital and themselves. These practices have created a two-tier service: one for those who are able and willing to pay the charge and another for the worse-off people irrespective of their health care insurance coverage status.

The society in general can be said to be significantly dissatisfied with the health care system and this is evident from the complaints of patients that often make the headlines in newspapers as well as public statements made by politicians. However, the number and scope of studies on the quality of health care services rendered in both various public and private organizations are highly limited. Main exceptions are two surveys carried out in 1992 (Ministry of Health, 1995) and 1995 (Ministry of Health, 1996b). Both of these studies have revealed some significant insights, inter alia, on the quality of the health care services at the national level. The following section is based on the findings of these two surveys.

It seems that the general public, though not well familiar with the sector, has a low degree of favorability for the health care sector (around 2.2 on a scale of 2.0–3.4). Patients and service users are not very well acquainted with the sector but rate the sector higher than the general public. However, it is still low (less than 2.6 on the same scale). The most striking finding is that health personnel, as would be expected, are highly familiar with the sector but rate it very low (about 2.1 on the same scale). All these endorse the negative public image of the health care sector in general.

According to the majority of physicians (73%) the health care sector is in need of radical change. An additional 25% think that it could be improved. It seems that no one thinks that the health care sector is very good and only 2% of physicians believe that it is good. According to the survey findings, there are a host of reasons behind this highly negative picture. Accordingly, problems of planning, politicized rather than rational planning and management approaches, underfunding, lack of coordination, lack of a hierarchical referral system, and low level of personnel motivation due mainly to low salaries are the main underlying factors.

Health care facilities of different providers have varying degrees of favorability. SIO hospitals are the least favorable of all facility groups with about 2.0 points on a scale of 1.8–3.8. This is followed by MoH hospitals, receiving about 2.4 points on the same scale. University, the Ministry of Defense, and private hospitals, on the other hand, are more favorably regarded, with scores of 3.2, 3.4, and almost 3.8, respectively. When the services of the MoH are concerned, curative services are seen, by both general public and health personnel, to be the least favorable of all other service groups (just over 2.6 on a scale of 2.6–3.3).

A total of 23.2% of the population thought that the distance they covered or time spent to reach a physician was unreasonably long. Once they reached an institution, patients waited, on average, 69.2 ± 5.7 min to see the physician. The variation between geographical regions was significant ranging from 60 to 93 min. The differences between private insurance holders and those who were under social (public) security were highly significant being 17.8 and well over 70 min, respectively. The time waiting to see the physician was too long for 45% of people. In the case of private insurance holders only 16% were dissatisfied with the time waited. Time to see a physician was the longest in university hospitals where average duration was 129.5 min. Other major institutions lined up as follows: SIO hospitals (102 min), MoH hospitals (88.1 min), private surgeries (40.6 min), and so on. Insofar as medical examination time is concerned, there were some major differentials between groups of people and institutions. The general average medical examination took 16.6 ± 1.4 min. This varied between 9.4 and 24.1 min between geographical regions.

The findings indicate that about 61% of patients were satisfied with the information they received from their physicians. Private insurance holders were fully (100%) satisfied while the percentage satisfaction of the rest varied between 50 and 75. As far as overall satisfaction with medical examination is concerned, on average 19.2% of patients expressed dissatisfaction. However, this rate was zero for private insurance holders.

Patients were asked about their opinions on and satisfaction with various other aspects of hospitals they attended. These aspects included cleanliness, number of personnel, courtesy, adequacy of equipment, etc. It was found that the percentage of patients who were overall dissatisfied with the hospital ranged from 11.6 with MoH hospitals to 4.4 with private hospitals. Cleanliness was a particular problem especially for MoH and SIO hospitals whereas university and private hospitals were found to be expensive. Though not as significant as the above factors, lack of courtesy was also pointed out to be a problem.

B. Access to Services

Access to health care has always been regarded to be among the major problems of the health care system in Turkey. This is evident from the annual contact (utilization) rates with physicians, which was 2.44 ± 0.14 per capita in 1992 (Ministry of Health, 1995). This is well below the rates in industrialized societies (Roemer, 1991). This could be attributable to a host of reasons but financial problems would be the most prominent.

With regard to health care insurance (security) coverage, the population can be divided into two main groups. The first group, which formed 43% of the population in 1994, consists of people with no formal coverage (Health Insurance Commission of Australia, 1995).

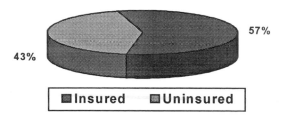

Figure 2 Health care financial coverage, 1994. (Based on data in Health Insurance Commission of Australia, 1995.)

The second group, i.e., those people whose health care expenditures are covered by one of the schemes, is divided into groups according to the scheme to which they are attached (Figs. 2 and 3).

First, there are active civil servants and their dependents, who enjoy free health services provided mainly by the MoH and universities. There are no formally set limits on the benefit package. Their expenses are met by their employers from the general budget allocations for that purpose. Services are virtually free of charge at the point of contact with the exception of prescribed drugs in outpatient departments, spectacles, etc. Patients, for instance, have to pay 20% of the total price of the prescription.

The second largest group with financial coverage for a full comprehensive range of services are active and retired members of the SIO including their depen-

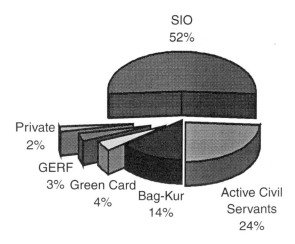

Figure 3 Health care security organizations and their beneficiaries, 1994. (Based on data in Health Insurance Commission of Australia, 1995.)

dents. As stated earlier, their expenditures are met out of premiums paid by both employees and employers. This group, too, pays toward prescription costs by 10–20%.

The Government Employees Retirement Fund (GERF), the third scheme, is responsible for the health care expenditures of the retired civil servants and their dependents. The GERF beneficiaries receive health care from public sector providers such as the MoH and university hospitals. The scheme is financed by the payroll contributions of the active civil servants as well as ad hoc government contributions.

The fourth scheme, Bag-Kur, is an insurance scheme that is open to merchants, artisans, and the self-employed including housewives. In fact, the scheme does not deny the population with no coverage of its membership so long as they enroll and pay the premiums. As in GERF, the organization provides health care benefits by contracting out its services to the MoH and SIO facilities or the University hospitals. However, the participation of beneficiaries to the health care insurance component of the scheme is quite low. It has been reported that of all 12 million Bag-Kur members only 4 million hold a health care insurance certificate (WHO, 1996).

The fifth and final public health care security arrangement is the green card scheme with the aim of providing health care to those indigent people with no insurance coverage. Once issued a card the holders can receive care from public sector hospitals free of charge provided they comply with the procedural requirements set in the legislation. Referral through a hierarchical chain, for instance, is a prerequisite under normal conditions. The expenses are met by the government and paid through local administrations directly to the provider of the services. The scheme has also a significant impact on the way that public hospitals are paid. Previously, the hospitals were expected to compensate for the expenses incurred due to the services provided to indigents from budgetary allocations for that purpose. Now, with the scheme, the indigents carry with them the financial resources needed for the hospital services (money follows the patient). The bills for the services rendered to the green card holders are based on a centrally set fee tariff (schedule), which is well below the real costs, but still this can be seen as a progressive step to considerably ease the financial as well as managerial burden of the hospitals.

The total number of people who were issued a green card in 1994 was reported to be 1,460,111 in 1994 (Ministry of Health, 1996a). As a result of annually conducted means tests, the number of people covered by the green card scheme fluctuates from one year to another. Although it has been widely credited for its equity implications, the scheme has also attracted a significant level of criticism. It is widely accepted that owing to the inherent inefficiencies in the system and difficulties in identifying "the indigent" it is not always the "most needy" who benefit from the system.

Finally, there is a relatively small group of people whose expenditures are covered by private funds mainly working for the banks and insurance companies. These generally purchase medical care from the private sector or university hospitals. The total number of people with private health care insurance policy is differently reported to be between 0.4% in 1996 (Kalkan, 1996) and 0.8% in 1995 (WHO, 1996). The proportion of those who also have public insurance coverage, however, is by no means clear. Apart from financial problems associated with access to health care, factors such as lack of adequate health personnel especially in rural areas and problems related to the geographical distribution and location of health care facilities also have a negative impact on access.

C. Cost Containment

Demand for health care is restricted for the uninsured population owing to financial barriers. For those who have insurance (security) coverage, however, there are usually long waiting lines and a perceived lack of quality in public practice. Those who are able and willing to pay often resort to private practice either within or without public premises. This seems to have, over time, created an environment where an increasing level of resources is devoted to private practice even within the public health care facilities. This has meant that most of those who would normally seek health care in public practice, too, are forced to pay private practice fees. This, with all its negative equity and health implications, must have depressed the demand serving cost containment purposes.

The government controls the capital construction of all state hospitals through the State Planning Organization. The state also controls the budgets of public hospitals, the purchase of high-technology medical equipment, the rates charged by hospitals, the price of drugs, and the margins of pharmacists, thus controlling the level of prices but not the volume of the services used, except by some cost-sharing mechanisms.

The number of personnel in public health care facilities is controlled by the state. Every health care facility has a specified number of beds and standards for staffing levels. A request for increasing the number of beds and/or personnel would have to be approved by the central authorities.

The number of places for medical as well as other health personnel is controlled by the state. The number of medical students has dramatically risen in recent years to fill the perceived gap in medical and health personnel throughout the country.

Outpatients with no coverage are required to pay the full price of all prescriptions. So far as these outpatients with coverage are concerned there is a 20% and 10% copayment, respectively, for active employees and retirees with the exception of the chronically ill. However, in recent years, owing to fierce competition, pharmacists have begun not to charge the copayment.

Physicians are not allowed to prescribe more than five items at a time for nonchronic illnesses. Physicians in some organizations such as the Ministry of Defense hospitals are required first to prescribe from the institutionally determined list of drugs. The SIO has relatively recently begun to use generic names instead of brand names. Physicians of the organization are required first to prescribe the drugs produced by the organization itself.

D. Current Health Care Reforms

As has already been stated, a radical health care sector reform process has been underway since the mid-1980s. The first major attempt during this period was made in 1987 with the passage of the Act of Basic Health Services. The act aimed at improving efficiency and effectiveness of especially public hospital sector through various initiatives. According to the act, hospitals would be transformed into the so-called *health enterprises* with considerable organizational (managerial and financial) autonomy. Hospital then would be highly independent to redefine their personnel regimes where they were allowed to recruit personnel on the basis of short-term contracts. The act and especially the planned cessation of an almost lifetime guaranteed employment status for hospital personnel created an unprecedented reaction from several quarters of which the medical associations seemed most vociferous. However, when the Constitutional Court canceled some of the crucial items of the act the government postponed its implementation.

A renewed and more systematic series of attempts began to be intensified in the early 1990s. The National Health Policy Document (the Document hereafter) prepared by the MoH as a result of these attempts was announced in 1993. This can be seen as a watershed in the health sector in that it was the first of its kind in Turkey where World Health Organization's Health for All policy approach and principles were incorporated in the national health policy-making process. The Document, a product of a long participatory process, has outlined the new direction that the Turkish health sector would take. The objectives of these reforms have been stated as follows (Ministry of Health, 1993):

Improved health status of the Turkish population,
Equity in health services,
Emphasis on preventive services, health promotion, and primary curative care; efficiency in service provision, purchaser provider split, and competition on the provider side,
Appropriate use of technology,
Community participation in decision marking,
Emphasis on multisectoral approach to health care,
Collection of effective, timely, and accurate information and information-based decision making,

Appropriate number and mix of human resources at right skill, right time,
and right place,
Transfer of decision-making authority to the individual service units.

According to the proposals, the MoH would, eventually, only formulate polices,
determine national quality standards, and monitor and evaluate the implementation of policies at the national level giving up its massive current role of direct
provision of health care services through a highly centralized organizational and
managerial structure.

The Document outlines a general national health policy framework and
contains chapters on health care policy issues such as finance, organizational
structure and management, and delivery system as well as other health policy
issues including life-styles and environment. The governments since then have
been working on the preparation of the legislative framework to implement the
approaches and principles outlined by the Document. The MoH has since been
working on reform legislation on the basis of findings of numerous national and
international studies. However, as of the beginning of 1997, despite the reiteration
of the commitment to the health care reform proposal by high echelons of the
government, this process has not been completed.

The current health care reform proposals, based on both the Document and
other official documents, fall under two main headings: provision and finance.

1. Health Care Provision

According to the reform proposals the *primary-level health care* is restructured.
The basics of the current arrangements for rural areas are to a large extent protected. *Health posts*, the most remote unit of the system, are staffed by a midwife
and serve a population of 500–1000. The next hierarchical health care unit to
which health posts are attached is *health centers*, serving a population of 3000–
5000. Health centers are staffed by at least one physician and an adequate number
of other allied health workers. The responsibility for the coordination of the health
posts and centers in a given district is given to the proposed *public health centers*.

Family practitioners (FPs), the newly developing medical specialty in line
with the proposals, would be responsible for the provision of primary curative
care and follow-up of their patients in secondary- and tertiary-level-care institutions. FPs are not government employees but independent contractors paid by
Provincial Health Authorities on the basis of a mixture of capitation and salary.
People are free to choose and change their FPs at specific intervals. FPs are to
act as gatekeepers in the envisaged hierarchical referral system.

Public sector hospitals are proposed to be transformed into the so-called
health enterprises. Public sector hospitals have long been accused of ineffectiveness, inefficiency, and low quality. The proposals attempt to correct these
problems by giving these hospitals a considerable level of organizational (mana-

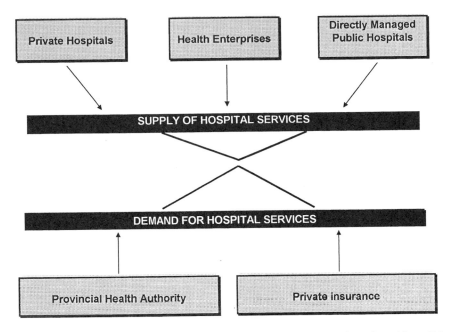

Figure 4 Proposed health care market for hospital services (purchaser/provider split).

gerial and financial) autonomy. Hospitals would, accordingly, be able to design their own personnel regime within a general framework. Financial self-sufficiency would force them to adopt the most efficient operational and managerial processes. Hospitals would no longer be administered but managed with a participatory approach. The top management would be formed by the participation of central and local government agencies as well as elected members of community organizations.

The main source of finance for health enterprises would be the revenues generated through the sale of hospital services. According to the proposed system, hospitals would compete for block service contracts offered by provincial health authorities (purchasing agency). Although not openly and clearly outlined, the proposals seems to lead toward the creation of a health care internal market in Turkey where both public and private hospitals compete with one another to gain contracts offered by a regional health care purchasing agency (Fig. 4). The regional health authority would act as a purchasing agency and would be responsible for the purchase of hospital services for the regional population with public sector health security/insurance plans. Given that the majority of the population would be covered by one of the public sector plans, the regional health authority would have a monopsonic power.

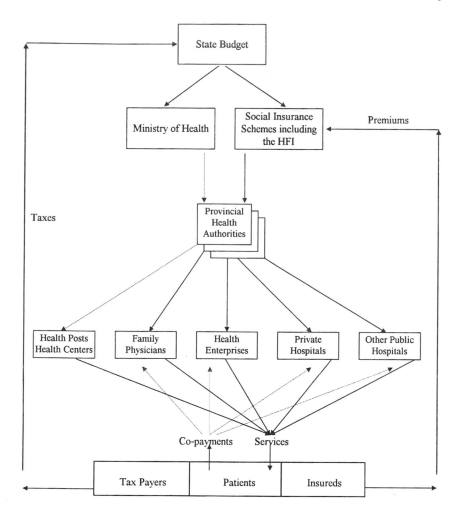

Figure 5 Proposed health care financing system and flows (except for private insurance arrangements). (From World Health Organization, 1996, with some minor adaptations.)

2. Health Care Financing

As stated in the account of the current state of the Turkish health care system, today an important portion of the Turkish population is without coverage for health care. The main emphasis made by the reform proposals is to include the entire population in social insurance schemes. To this end, the MoH planned to establish a new comprehensive General Health Insurance Scheme (GHIS) under which all existing social insurance schemes would be integrated. Later, however, owing mainly to the resistance of the SIO, this idea was abandoned. Now, instead, a new separate social insurance organization called the Health Financing Institution (HFI) is planned to be established to cover the existing uninsured population (Fig. 5). The main features of the GHIS (or HFI) can be stated as follows (Ministry of Health, 1995):

> The model is based on the principles of social insurance.
>
> Membership will be open to citizens of Turkey with no coverage under current status.
>
> Members will be entitled to a package of comprehensive services.
>
> Contributions will be related to ability to pay and will be zero for the very poor. The difference between the actuarial premium and the member's contribution will be met from the general tax revenues.
>
> GHIS will transfer its premium income to Provincial Health Directorates, which will be directly responsible for making contracts with service providers both public and private on behalf of the insured population.
>
> Some sort of copayment is recommended both to raise revenue and to limit unnecessary utilization.

According to the proposals, all financial resources from all sources, except for copayments, would be channeled to Provincial Health Authorities (Fig. 5). These authorities in turn would purchase secondary and tertiary health care services from competing public and private health care providers (Fig. 4).

IV. CONCLUSIONS

The Turkish health care system is under significant pressure to change. It seems that the population in general and its various segments such as patients, providers, and policymakers are not satisfied with the system. However, the health care scene since the mid-1980s has been dominated by intensive rhetoric but no action. The reforms that are designed to address the widely accepted ills of the system, such as gross inequities, inefficiencies at both macro and micro levels, and low quality, have taken a cue from some international tendencies. Reliance on market forces and processes such as competition in a controlled manner, the separation of purchasers and providers, regionalization in planning and management, and a greater emphasis on management rather than administration are the main pillars of the current health care reform proposals in Turkey.

The main challenge that faces the reforms, however, is to overcome the forces and processes that have over decades created the current health care system. It is clear that reform proposals would upset the balance of power. The expectations of those groups with a strong vested interest in the current health care system, including medical professionals, would have to be balanced against the interests of the entire population. This would undoubtedly require a strong government with matching political will and commitment to pursue the health care reforms. Whether Turkey would have a strong government with strong will and commitment to redress the current imbalances among various stakeholders in health care system for the *benefit of all* remains to be seen.

REFERENCES

Health Insurance Commission of Australia (1995). Final Health Financing Report. Policy Options Study for Turkey, Vol 1—Policy. Ankara.

Kalkan, N. (1996). Özel Sağlik Sigortasi Dosyasi (Private Health Insurance File). Milliyet 1 Mayýs.

Ministry of Health (1993). National Health Policy. Ankara.

Ministry of Health (1995). Health Services Utilization Survey in Turkey. Ankara.

Ministry of Health (1996a). Health Statistics 1995. Ankara.

Ministry of Health (1996b). Health Reforms Surveys—I. Ankara.

Price Waterhouse (1990). Health Sector Master Plan Study. Report on the Current Situation. Ankara.

Roemer, M.I. (1991). National Health Systems of the World. Vol Two. The Issues. New York: Oxford University Press.

Sağlik Bakanliği (1990). 2000 Yilinda Herkese Sağlik. Türk Milli Sağlik Politikasi. (Health for All by the Year 2000. Turkish National Health Policy). Ankara.

Sağlik Bakanliği (1996). Yatakli Tedavi Kurumlari İstatistik Yilliği 1995 (Statistical Yearbook of Health Care Institutions 1995). Ankara.

Sağlik Bakanliği, et al. ([Türkiye], Hacettepe Üniversitesi Nüfus Etütleri Enstitüsü ve Macro International Inc) (1994). Türkiye Nüfus ve Sağlik Arastirmasi 1993. (Turkey Demographic and Health Survey 1993). Ankara.

Sağlik ve Sosyal Yardim Bakanliği (1973). Sağlik Hizmetlerinde 50 Yil. (50 Years in Health Services). Ankara.

UNICEF. (1990). Analysis of Children and Mothers Situation in Turkey. Draft 2. Ankara.

UNICEF. (1996). The State of the World's Children 1997. Oxford: Oxford University Press.

World Bank (1986). Turkey Health Sector Review. Population, Nutrition and Health Development.

World Health Organization (1993). Highlights on Health in Turkey. Regional Office for Europe. Copenhagen.

World Health Organization (1996). Health Care Systems in Transition Turkey. (Preliminary Version). Regional Office for Europe. Copenhagen.

15

The Japanese Health Care System
Citizen Complaints and Citizen Possibilities

Rieko Yajima and Kazue Takayanagi
Nippon Medical School, Tokyo, Japan

I. OVERVIEW OF HEALTH CARE SYSTEM

The Japanese health care system is sometimes considered one of the best in the world, because it appears to have achieved universal coverage, high quality, and a comparatively low level of expenditure. But, under compulsory national health insurance and the uniform fee schedule that has worked well so far, various problems have occurred in Japan. A growing number of people believe some reforms or readjustments may be required.

A. Brief Review of the Japanese Health Care System

By 1961, the Japanese government required compulsory national health insurance. All health care insurance plans offer basically uniform sets of medical benefits. Insurance plans can be divided into three broad categories: employee health insurance, community health insurance, and health and medical services for the aged. The national and local governments pay for the administrative expenses; no plans are organized on a for-profit basis. In Japan, fees and the price of each health care procedure are fixed and itemized on nationally uniform fee schedules. Unlike the United States, physician fees and hospital fees are not separated. Medical institutes with more than 20 beds are designated as hospitals.

B. Insurance and Access

In Japan, insurance coverage is universal but access problems can arise due to the three-tiered structure of the health care system. This tiered structure consists of clinics, general hospitals, and special-function hospitals (university or large hospitals). Physicians theoretically refer patients to higher-level institutions if treatment can be improved upon. In practice, physicians are hired at the hospitals on a salary basis, except the director, and this has made physician-owned clinics preferred by practitioners. However, today there is a trend for young physicians to work at the hospitals. Consequently, the three-tiered structure of health care in Japan is disrupted by intense competition among clinics and hospitals. Even under universal coverage in Japan, the patient's cost-sharing arrangements and benefits are not the same among plans, producing citizen complaints of inequity.

C. Cost and Quality

In Japan, costs are low compared to many developed countries. However, the system has been criticized for failing to use the best available technologies. The increased age of the population and greater application of advanced medical technology have led to rising health care expenditures. About 6.92% of the gross domestic product was dedicated to health care in 1994. Unfortunately, negotiations on fees and prices take place within government institutions, and citizens do not have access to information inside these bodies.

D. The Physician–Patient Relationship

Physicians are traditionally held in high esteem in Japan. Under the fixed fee schedule, patients rarely talk frankly to physicians or criticize physicians' professional ability. In theory, all physicians are equally good. Yet, patients aggressively shop around for physicians, and this has produced a lack of continuity of care. Law and financial incentives encourage the utilization of a referral system.

In Japan, consumers do not clearly perceive the cost or benefits of services. Nevertheless, people have become more aware, seek more information, and desire better care standards. Culturally, the Japanese are less likely than Americans to register complaints, but they are likely to become more vocal as they become more knowledgeable about their health care system. Improvements in health care systems in Japan, as well as in the United States and other countries, will require more knowledgeable and vocal citizens.

II. DESCRIPTION OF THE HEALTH CARE SYSTEM

A. Historical Development

The Japanese health care system is sometimes considered one of the best in the world, because it appears to have achieved universal coverage, high quality, and a comparatively low level of expenditure. Few Japanese are concerned about premiums, and how much they pay to their physicians. They tend to trust the quality of health care in Japan.

Impressive indices of the health status of 125 million citizens also seem to support a high level of trust. According to the 1994 statistics, the perinatal mortality rate and neonatal mortality rate of 5.0 per 1000 persons and 1.7 per 1000 persons, respectively, are the lowest in the world. In 1995 the average life expectancy at birth for Japanese citizens is approximately 76.4 years for males and 82.8 years for females. This rate is comparably high among all nations, despite the fact that in 1935 the average life expectancy was 10 years shorter than in various countries in the West at 46.9 years for males and 49.6 years for females (Health and Welfare Statistics Association, 1996). Furthermore Japan's per capita utilization of computer-aided tomography (CAT) scans, and renal dialysis are among the highest of all advanced industrialized countries (Ikegami, 1991). The number of CAT scan terminals numbered 6400 in 1991, of which 900 were owned by clinics for outpatients only.

On many measures of health care or status, Japan ranks very high. Health care expenditures in 1994 amounted to 25.7 trillion yen, or approximately 6% of the GDP. This is a little more than half the percentage that the United States spends. However, health care expenditures have been increasing faster than in the United States since 1960, and this growth rate is exceeding the growth of Japan's GDP (Joseph et al., 1992; Wolfe and Moran, 1993). An increasing portion of spending is associated with Japan's aging population, which has exerted pressure upon Japan's health care economy. Health care expenditures are rising more rapidly than the cost of other Japanese goods and services, and the population is aging more rapidly than that of other industrialized countries.

Individuals over age 65 comprised 14.8% of the population (125 million) in 1995. This percentage is now quite similar to that of the United States. In contrast, the average number of children that one Japanese woman gives birth to in her life dropped from 4.5 in 1947 to 1.5 in 1994, according to the Annual Report on Health and Walfare (1996).

The demographic changes in the population have led to changes in the prevalence of diseases and illness. As the population ages rapidly, geriatric diseases and chronic diseases such as stroke, cancer, heart disease, and dementia have become more common. According to a tentative estimate made in June 1991, the elderly population in Japan will surpass 30 million in 2014, reaching

23% of the total population. It is also expected that significant increases in this segment of the population will continue into the future. In this changing scenario, more attention needs to be given to these new problems, which have historically been less prevalent. Currently, socioeconomic development and improvement in the infrastructure of health services are placing a growing emphasis upon quality of life issues and the need for quality improvement (Takayanagi and Iwasaki, 1992).

In addition to demographic changes, Japan is experiencing rapid social and environmental transformation. Air and water pollution, increases in traffic accidents, changed trends in eating habits (away from some traditional healthy foods), and work stress have contributed to increasing rates of "new" diseases that inflate health care expenditures. Many health care experts are concerned about the future of health care in Japan (Dentzor, 1991), believing that appropriate reform is required to adjust to the new health demographics and the availability of new technologies.

The Japanese health care system uses employment-based health insurance, patients choose health care providers, and physicians, who allegedly serve as patient advocates, make clinical decisions. The Japanese system attaches importance to advanced technology and is facing escalating health care costs. Yet, this same system has obtained virtually universal health care coverage through a combination of employer-based and government health insurance. The Japanese health care system offers lessons for how an industrialized, capitalist country can attain universal coverage, cost control, and a relatively good quality of care.

From the point of view of the Japanese, the American health care system is very complicated, particularly regarding the flow of funds. Nevertheless, the Japanese health care system is also exceedingly complex, which in turn tends to limit citizen participation in reform discussions. Despite differences in cultural systems and health care systems, calls for increased citizen participation in "reform" exist in both Japan and the United States. Informed participation in these discussions necessary for reform will require extraordinary effort and esoteric knowledge on the part of citizens. Truly, citizens in both countries can be said to be riding the backs of tigers: i.e., their health care systems.

B. Total Amount of Health Care Expenditures

The national health care expenditure for fiscal year 1994 was 25,791 billion yen, showing a trend of annual increases (Fig. 1), and the national health care expenditure per person was 206,300 yen. Although the growth rate has stabilized in recent years, it is increasing annually. The ratio of national health care expenditure to national income indicates the magnitude of medical care relative to the national economy. This ratio, which was 3% in 1961, rose to 6% in 1979, and has stayed at slightly above 6%. Since 1984 the Ministry of Health and Welfare has set a

billion yen

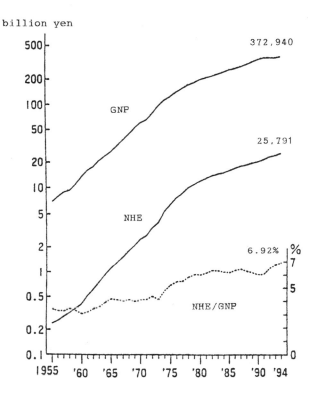

Figure 1 National health care expenditure (NHE) and gross national product (GNP). Source: "Estimates of National Medical Care Expenditure," Statistics and Information Department, Minister's Secretariat, MHW.

goal to maintain the increase in national health care expenditure within the scope of national income growth.

National medical expenditures have been regulated by controlling the cost of medical practice and account for 84% of the total health expenditures in Japan. The Central Social Insurance Medical Council is playing an essential role in this cost control. The medical fee schedule system was raised by 0.11%, 3.7%, and 5.0%, in 1988, 1990, and 1992, respectively (Shakai Hosho Junpo, 1993). Meanwhile, the standard drug reimbursement price was increased by 2.4% in 1988, but was reduced by 9.2% and 8.1% in 1990 and 1992, respectively (Tokyo Metropolitan Government, 1989). These price fluctuations, which have been instituted by the Ministry of Health and Welfare, are directed toward leading medical institutes in the interest of rectifying the excessive use of drugs. Similarly, drug tariffs should also reflect the actual market prices more appropriately.

C. Universal Health Care Insurance

The present Japanese health care system was developed based upon the laws of 1948, which are subsumed within the new constitution of 1947, established at the end of military occupation. Under the constitution, the government has the responsibility to guarantee all citizens minimum standards of wholesome and healthy living.

The Ministry of Health and Welfare is responsible for implementing health laws. By 1961, the Japanese government required compulsory national health insurance. Under universal insurance coverage, patients' choices have been unrestricted as to the type of health care facilities and the place of care. All health care insurance plans offer basic uniform sets of medical benefits, including medication, long-term care, dental care, and preventive care. Insurance plans can be divided into three broad categories: employee health insurance, community health insurance, and health and medical services for the aged.

The system of employer-based insurance includes some 1800 plans, consisting of five segments for workers and their dependents:

1. government-managed health insurance for workers in small companies of fewer than 300 employees,
2. insurance societies for workers in large companies,
3. the day laborer's insurance,
4. the independent seaman's insurance, and
5. mutual aid insurance for public-sector employees.

Premiums are deducted from employee payroll checks on the basis of income. For all plans under this system, employers and employees generally share the premiums. This type of insurance covers 65% of the population (Ikegami, 1992).

The system of community health insurance serves the self-employed, unemployed adults, employees of businesses that are too small for employer-based insurance, farmers, and their dependents. It is financed in part by premiums paid by covered persons on the basis of income, the number of individuals in the insured household, and assets. About 35% of the population utilize this type of insurance. Every local government (city, town, and village) must offer insurance under this system, and these local governments maintain a role in the financing, administration, and delivery of public health and social services. The national government provides financial assistance to the local governments for the costs of this public system.

A funding pool exists that pays all health care costs for the elderly (over 70 years of age). Copayments are waived, except for nominal fees at the receipt of health care services. The pool fund for medical benefits for the elderly is financed through both national and local governments, employer-based health insurance, and community-based health insurance, as mentioned above. Over time this system has required employers and employees to shoulder more of the burden of the costs of care for the elderly, and the national government also has needed to increase total health expenditures to maintain levels of support for the elderly.

These health insurance plans are further divided into more than 5000 units of insurers to carry out the operation. The numbers of insured persons is illustrated in Table 1. All Japanese must be covered by one of the above-mentioned plans. By the end of March 1994, the number of insured reached 124.98 million:

> 70.09 million covered by employees' health insurance (including 37.61 million covered by government-managed health insurance and 32.48 million by society-managed health insurance),
> 326,000 by seaman's insurance,
> 10.85 million covered under a mutual aid association, and
> 42.81 million covered through national health insurance.

The national and local governments pay for the administrative expenses of all of Japan's health insurance plans, none of which are organized on a for-profit basis. Private insurance exists for supplemental coverage, but it is strictly limited.

D. The Structure of Insured Medical Care

The insured person (the beneficiary of the insurance) regularly pays his or her contribution to the insurer (state, health insurance association; municipality, etc.) as shown in Step 1, Figure 2. When the insured person receives a consultation with a physician at Step 2, he or she must pay a partial cost-sharing fee, 10–30% accordingly at Step 3. These out-of-pocket payments account for about 12% of total health expenditure produced under social insurance (Tokyo Metropolitan

Table 1 Health Care Insurance Plan Enrollment in 1994

Kind of scheme	(1 unit: 1000)
Total	124,982
Total of employees' health insurance	82,171
Government-managed health insurance	37,704
Society-managed health insurance	32,475
Seaman's insurance	326
National public service employees' mutual aid association	4012
Local public service employee's M.A.A.	6838
Private school teachers' & employees' M.A.A.	816
National health insurance	42,811

Source: "Annual Operational Report," Social Insurance Agency, etc.

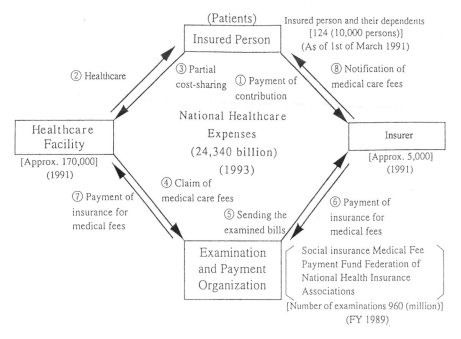

Figure 2 Structure of health care insurance.

Government, 1989). As shown in Figure 2, the health care facility submits the claim incurred for health care, deducting the amount paid by the patient, to the insurer via an examination and payment organization (Steps 4 and 5).

The services delivered (medical actions and medication administrations, etc.) are recorded on a statement of health care remuneration form. A screening committee composed of physicians in the examination and payment organization examines the statement as an audit to ascertain whether appropriate health care was administered. When the examined statement is sent to the insurer, the insurer pays the insurance for the medical care fees to the health care facility through the examination and payment organization (Steps 6 and 7). The insurer usually notifies the insured person about the health care fees paid from the health care insurance.

E. Resources

The source of revenue for health insurance is the insurance premium paid equally by the beneficiary and the employer, which is set at 8.2% of the salary of the beneficiary. A total of 16.0% of the amount is paid from the national treasury

System	Resources	Distribution	Ratio

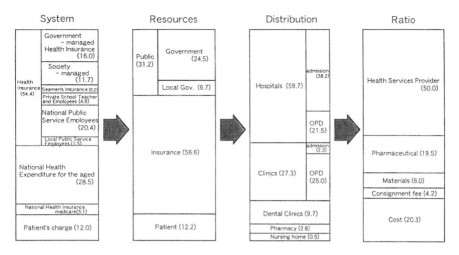

Figure 3 Structure of healthcare expenditure (HE) in 1991 (HE = 21,826 billion yen; HE per person = 176,000 yen).

(Fig. 3). On the other hand, both the insured and the municipal government pay the insurance premium of the National Health Insurance for nonemployees (of which the amount is set on a household basis), which amounted to 137,985 yen per insured person in 1991.

National health care expenses are paid by governments (31.2%), from insurance premiums (56.6%), and by patients (12.2%). As for the distribution of national health care expenses, general medical practice accounts for 87.0% (59.7% for hospitals and 27.3% for clinics), dental treatment for 9.7%, pharmaceutical practice for 2.8%, and facilities for the elderly at 0.5%. The national health care expenses are actually allocated to health services: provider cost (50.0%), pharmaceuticals (19.5%), medical material (6.0%), consignment fee (4.0%), and administrative cost (20.3%).

F. The Health Services Delivery System

In Japan, health providers are reimbursed on a fee-for-service basis. Fees and prices of each health care procedure are fixed and itemized on a nationally uniform fee schedule for the purpose of reimbursement. Fees are stringently regulated and determined regardless of the physician's experience, proficiency, or geographical location.

The number of physicians was 1.8 per 1000 population in 1994, with an average increase of 8000 physicians annually. This number was expected to increase to 2.2 per 1000 population in the year 2000. The Ministry of Health and Welfare's policy of 1.5 physicians per 1000 population was attained in 1983. It is now said that an Age of Excess Doctors has begun. Excess numbers of physicians will be an issue in health policies, but the physician-population rate is still considerably less than that of the United States, 2.3 per 1000 (Scieber et al., 1991).

The number of health facilities in Japan has been gradually increasing since World War II, supported by remarkable economic growth and the establishment of the universal health care insurance system. There were 152,532 facilities in 1994: 9731 hospitals, 85,588 clinics, and 57,213 dental clinics. The number of hospitals per 100,000 population was 8.0 in 1994, a rate four times higher than that reported in the United States (Shukan Shakai Hosho, 1994).

Unlike the United States, physician's fees and hospital fees are not separated in Japan. Historically, the Japanese health care system focused on clinic-based rather than hospital-based physicians owing to an emphasis on ambulatory care as opposed to inpatient treatment. A clinic is similar in many respects to the private office of an American physician, but some Japanese clinics are allowed to have beds for patients. Medical institutes with more than 20 beds are designated as hospitals. Although these medical institutes are not designated by function, they are generally distinguished from larger hospitals. Most large hospitals are public institutions, including university hospitals that have affiliations with medical schools. Most of the university hospitals are designated as special function hospitals. Although 81% of hospitals and 94% of clinics are operated privately and for profit, the level of profit is strictly regulated by the Annual Report on Health and Welfare (1994). Hospital administrators are required by law to be physicians, even if they are inexperienced or know little about hospital administration. Physicians who work in hospitals are employed on a salaried basis.

Most health care facilities in Japan must operate at their own risk, raising, collecting, and repaying capital on their own. In addition, there is no resource, except for medical profits, from which capital costs are paid. It is therefore necessary for hospitals to make profits large enough to ensure stable management. While the increased rate of labor costs, which accounts for about 50% or more of medical expenditures, is equal to that of the prices of commodities, the increase in points calculated by the medical fee schedule system of rating is kept lower than that of the prices for commodities. These conditions work against nonprofit hospitals. Virtually all hospitals in Japan are nonprofit. Nonprofitability of health care, which has been called for at the organizational level, was originally thought to reflect fairness in society. However, this concept has been influenced by historical precedent together with equality at the macro level, which means the standards of profession. Japanese people tend to think that all doctors do their job without regard to money or the profitability of their facilities. As a result, they assume that they can get the best-quality health care. However, this concept ends up creating misunderstandings, especially regarding profitability (Tanaka, 1993).

Table 2   Number of Hospitals and Beds in Industrialized
Countries

		Hospitals	Beds
Japan	(1992)	9,963 (0.80)	1,686,696 (135.53)
U.S.A.	(1991)	5,675 (0.22)	1,002,600 (39.68)
France	(1990)	3,830 (0.68)	702,184 (124.41)
W. Germany	(1989)	3,585 (0.46)	833,055 (105.88)
England	(1989)	1,646 (0.35)	270,334 (56.69)

Note: The numbers in parentheses denote the rate per 10,000 population.
Source: Shakai Hoken Junpo (1994).

The number of hospital beds in 1994 was 1,686,696 representing 13.6 beds per 1000 population. This figure represents 1.6 times more beds in Japan than in the United States. Thus, the quantitative improvement in the numbers of hospitals in Japan has advanced to a comparable level for other industrialized countries, in number of both hospitals and beds. These figures are presented in Table 2. Such levels, however, cannot be compared directly because the statistical definitions of hospitals and their substantial roles may differ from country to country (Shukan Shakai Hosho, 1994). The health care system in Japan has experienced a surplus of hospital beds. In response to this phenomenon, the number of beds is beginning to be limited by enforcement of the community health care plan.

III.   CURRENT HEALTH CARE ISSUES

A.   Insurance and Access

Since the Japanese health insurance system has developed from mutual aid associations, social insurance is predominant, which is strikingly different from the private health insurance system in the United States. The concept of a universal social insurance system was emphasized in the Council of Medical Security (1956). Within the Council it was noted that "as diseases are the biggest cause of poverty, the medical security should be regarded as important as the educational equality, if we show any respect for human life." Japan has been building its health care system around the backbone of social health insurance. Compulsory coverage and a single fee schedule simplify the claims processing system and insurers do not need to market their plans. As a result, the administrative costs of health care insurance are quite low and are reflected in lower health care costs.

However, the social insurance system has generated several problems. When the price patients have to pay for care is reduced because of insurance, total health expenditures may rise. Under insurance, people tend to visit physicians more frequently, and be less concerned about containing health care expenditures. Moreover, providers may resort to overtreatment since their fees are essentially paid by the third party and not by the patient. In addition, social insurance often fails to reward preventive care and health maintenance, since social insurance pays for treatments.

Under the Japanese insurance system, which in practice levies premiums according to income (an ability-to-pay principle), national funds can be distributed equitably, and even a high-risk group (e.g., those with AIDS) can be insured at a low premium. Even this system, which provides universal coverage, can be criticized on the ground that the patient's cost-sharing arrangements and benefits are inconsistent across plans, producing complaints of inequity.

Another criticism of the Japanese system is that there is a lack of choice among consumers regarding particular plans. The imbalance between risks and premiums obstructs the unification of various insurance plans, and as a result, the problem of moral hazard is magnified.

The provision of health care services in Japan was designed to have a three-tier structure. Unlike the United States, these tiers are not determined by income class but by function. Preventive health care is delivered at local and regional health centers, which provide checkups, immunization or vaccinations, health promotion including health education and exercise instruction, and environmental hygiene.

Secondary health care is delivered in clinics or at hospitals (large clinics) for minor ailments or diseases. If the doctors in clinics find the condition of patients to be too serious, or if they do not have the necessary equipment for diagnosis, they are supposed to send these patients to third-tier health care facilities, which are large hospitals including the national or university hospitals.

This system was intended to contain cost, avoid unnecessary high-technology treatment for minor ailments, and, if this system functioned properly, direct patients to nearby primary-care physicians. However, the system did not work as intended. Tertiary hospitals were completely open to all patients, regardless of their place of residence, whether they had a letter of admission from their primary doctor, or what type of insurance plan covered them. Patients had direct access to tertiary hospitals and medical specialists who practiced there: anybody could visit such facilities and be charged only a small copayment. Moreover, since physicians in clinics or small hospitals did not have direct access to practice in large tertiary hospitals, referral of patients to large hospitals might result in these physicians "losing" their patients. That is, once referred to a large facility, patients may prefer this setting to clinic-based physicians. Such a system might encourage primary physicians to underrefer to appropriate institutions and levels of care.

In Japan, differences between clinics and hospitals are narrow and loosely organized because one-third of clinics have some beds and large hospitals have outpatient departments where anyone can receive the same treatment as provided in clinics or small hospitals. Large hospitals, where high-technology and modern, costly equipment is available, attract patients. Newly graduated physicians are not attracted to practice in clinics, because they prefer to have a specialty. Moreover, as the cost of capital for newly opened clinics has increased owing to economic development and demand for modern technology, few clinics can support sophisticated new practices. The percentage of salaried physicians rose from 38% in 1965 to 59% in 1989 (Gray, 1989).

Differences in quality of care among clinics are not reflected within fixed fee schedules, which are approved by the Ministry of Health and Welfare. As a result, the three-tier structure, under which patients go to nearby physicians, has broken down.

To solve these problems, the medical care law was revised in 1993, and as a result, patient flow has been redirected, as presented in Figure 4. Patients requiring long-term hospitalization go to general hospitals accredited for long-term care. Beds for recuperation are equipped and staffed to support daily living and to provide appropriate medical care for patients who need long-term medical care. General patients in the acute stage will visit a secondary general hospital. Special-function hospitals have been specially accredited; they are well staffed and equipped for advanced medical care. References from clinics and other hospitals for the acceptance of patients are required. But this system does not function well and the decision of a health care setting still depends on the patient's preference.

However beneficial the uniform fee schedule may be for patients in reducing their worry about differences in costs between every clinic and hospital, such a payment system is inequitable among physicians. Moreover, as observed above, economic incentives for cost consciousness on the part of patients are minor at best. A uniform fixed fee schedule can lead to nonprice rationing of and restricted access to highly trained, prominent specialized medical personnel. Some physicians are reported to have taken gifts or money from patients. Gift giving is customary and frequent in Japan, and few people think it wrong in appropriate circumstances.

Insurers have no freedom to negotiate a fee schedule with providers or with the insured, since providers are prohibited from charging more or less than the fee schedule allows. Physicians can charge extra for only a few services, including private hospital rooms, new technologies that are not approved by the Ministry, and dental prostheses. The government of Japan can attempt to contain health care expenditures via the fee schedule, as any fee contraction applies to all insurers. They are starting to apply the fee-per-capita-service at hospitals for the aged.

Similarities noted above between clinics and hospitals produce intense competition. Patients themselves also compete aggressively for hospital rooms at "excellent" clinics where demand for beds may exceed supply. The alleged

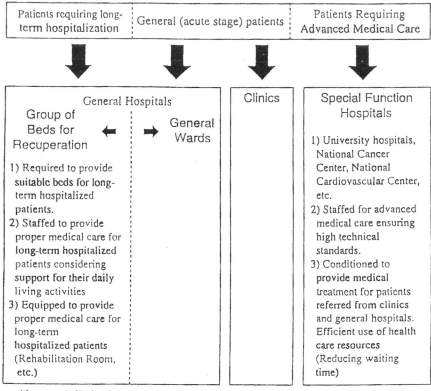

| Patients requiring long-term hospitalization | General (acute stage) patients | Patients Requiring Advanced Medical Care |

General Hospitals

Group of Beds for Recuperation ← | → **General Wards**

1) Required to provide suitable beds for long-term hospitalized patients.
2) Staffed to provide proper medical care for long-term hospitalized patients considering support for their daily living activities
3) Equipped to provide proper medical care for long-term hospitalized patients (Rehabilitation Room, etc.)

Clinics

Special Function Hospitals

1) University hospitals, National Cancer Center, National Cardiovascular Center, etc.
2) Staffed for advanced medical care ensuring high technical standards.
3) Conditioned to provide medical treatment for patients referred from clinics and general hospitals. Efficient use of health care resources (Reducing waiting time)

Notes: 1. Under the current law, hospitals (wards) are classified as general hospitals, psychiatric hospitals, tuberculosis hospitals, leprosy hospitals, and communicable disease hospitals. The function of general hospitals is not sufficiently defined.

2. The Revision Bill provides that, based on applications from general hospitals, the governors of prefectures approve the groups of beds for recuperation and the Minister of Health and Welfare approve the special functioning hospitals asking the opinion of the Council on Medical Service Facilities.

Figure 4   Redirected patient flow in the revised medical care law.

advantages of the three-tier functional structure of the health care system, such as cost containment and access, are being lost. This system generates inefficiencies and inequity in the delivery of health care services in Japan, different from those in the United States, but still of considerable concern to health care leaders and some citizens.

The inadequate distribution of doctors is more serious in rural areas, especially remote islands, secluded places in the mountains, and heavy-snow regions. Physicians seem unwilling to work in such places because they are concerned about lack of educational opportunities for their children and the likelihood of lesser financial rewards. National and local governments implemented "solutions" to inadequate distribution, but physicians in these regions are aging, and recent attempts to encourage physician relocation have not had encouraging results.

B. Cost and Quality

Since 1967, when Japan achieved universal coverage under present institutional arrangements, health care expenditures have continued to rise. Health care costs consumed 6.5% of Japan's GDP in 1990. However, Japan still ranked second lowest of the OECD countries after the United Kingdom, at 5.9% of its nominal GDP (Wolfe and Moran, 1993).

Primary contributors to increasing health care expenditures in Japan include the increased aging of the population (which has also changed the prevalence of illness), and greater application of advanced medical technology (see Table 3 and Figs. 5 and 6). Since the elderly need more medical care and social services than the nonelderly, expenditures on care for the elderly are rising rapidly. Medical treatment costs for the elderly in 1997 were 74,511 billion yen, 30.6% of total health care expenditures, according to the Annual Report on Health and Welfare (1996). Another reason for rapidly rising costs for the elderly is social change in Japan as women, who traditionally took care of older relatives, are entering the labor force and, as a consequence, a major source of care at home is disappearing. Care that was once provided in-kind is being "monetized" in GDP calculations and government budgets.

Nevertheless, the elderly are less likely to be institutionalized than in the

Table 3 Health Care Expenditure per Person in 1991

	Amount × 1,000 yen	Ratio
Average	153.1	1.00
0–14 years	50.9	0.33
15–44 years	70.6	0.46
45–64 years	191.4	1.25
> 65 years	509.8	3.33
>70 years	606.9	3.96

Source: "Estimates of National Medical Care Expenditure," Statistics and Information Department, Minister's Secretariat, MHW.

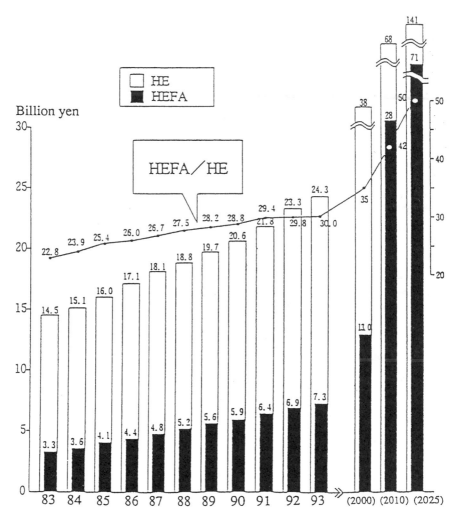

Figure 5 Health care expenditure shift and future estimation of HE and HE for aged (HEFA). Source: ''Estimates of National Medical Care Expenditure,'' Statistics and Information Department, Minister's Secretariat, MHW.

United States, and about 50% of them were living with their children as of 1990 (Ogawa and Retherford, 1993). Most Japanese elderly prefer to live with their children, and are accustomed to a traditional extended family system. Children, especially the first son and his wife, are still expected to be responsible for parents, including living with them and taking care of them.

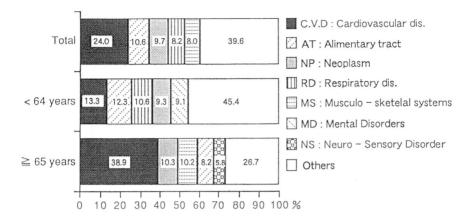

Figure 6 Health care expenditure by disease (percentage). Source: "Estimates of National Medical Care Expenditure," Statistics and Information Department, Minister's Secretariat, MHW.

The average length of stay in hospitals in Japan was 42.0 days in 1992, which is extremely long compared with other industrialized countries (Table 4), and it is approximately eight times that of the United States (Okamoto, 1992). The average bed occupancy rate is 82.2%, which is not enough to turn a profit or maintain a facility (Shakai Hoken Junpo, 1994). This figure is large because some hospitals have functioned as nursing homes. It is often difficult to distinguish between patients who need medical care and those who need custodial care. Increasing numbers of Japanese elderly (even those without acute medical problems) are construed as chronically suffering from diseases that increase hospitalization rates. These increased hospitalization rates also serve to lengthen average lengths of stay. Some believe that as a consequence of this system many nonmedical geriatric problems become *medicalized* in Japan. In other words,

Table 4 Average Length of Hospital Stay

		1970	1975	1980	1985	1990
Japan	(1992)	32.5	34.7	38.3	39.4	38.1
U.S.A.	(1991)	14.9	11.4	10.0	9.2	9.1
France	(1990)	18.3	15.0	16.8	14.6	12.4
W. Germany	(1989)	24.9	22.2	19.7	18.0	—
England	(1989)	25.7	22.9	19.1	15.8	14.5

Source: Shakai Hoken Junpo (1994).

these people are not hospitalized for the purpose of medical treatment but for daily care.

The free publicly financed medical service program for those aged 70 and over began in 1973. Over a decade, as access to the system was virtually unrestricted for the elderly, health expenditures grew rapidly, and some believe intergenerational inequities were created. In 1983, to restrain increasing health expenditures, the Ministry of Health and Welfare abolished public free medical services for the elderly. Under a new law, called the Geriatric Health Act, health expenditures for the elderly are now paid by a combination of public expenditures and pool funds of employer-based and community-based insurance. The elderly pay a nominal amount in out-of-pocket fees. Nevertheless, the rapid growth of health care expenditures for the elderly and others is expected to continue, especially public expenditures, which contribute to one-third of total health expenditures.

A change in society's concept of health care for the elderly is expected to reduce the average length of hospital stay. Japanese society is tolerant of the legitimization of ailments through admission to hospitals. Thus, there is a lack of self-reliant care and support for remodeling the patient's home living space. When the household composition of Japan is examined, the analysis shows a total of 40,270,000 households with nuclear families constituting 60% of the total, and three-generation households at 13.5% of the total. It is sometimes necessary to provide senior citizens residing at home with handrails, emergency buzzers, and other devices to help them lead a smoother daily life. Japan has to continue its efforts to expand these home care programs further, taking into account the nature of the revision in the medical services supply system, which is a salient point in the current proposed amendment to the Medical Care Law.

Levels of health care expenditures in Japan are remarkably low compared to most developed countries; however, the Japanese system produces other problems. Under uniform fee schedules, competition between physician-owned clinics and hospitals concentrates on the quantity of patients attended and not the quality of care provided. In other words, the number of patients seen determines income, and few controls have traditionally been exercised over quantity of services rendered or the intensity with which these services are provided. In Japan, it is tacitly agreed that no one criticizes physicians' professional abilities or academic credentials. No formal mechanisms for reviewing the quality of care exist in this setting, except inspection by an insurance fund's panel members.

Panels composed of physicians are authorized to deny payment when claims are false, excessive, or unnecessary. However, the effectiveness of this claim review inspection is dubious because of its apparent arbitrariness and the large amount of time-consuming work that would be required to check approximately 1.6 billion claims a year (Ikegami, 1991). Thus, the actual proportion of claims judged as providing excessive care is less than 1%, although the sentinel effect of this peer review may be greater than this figure suggests. Within this monitoring system, the assessment of underprovision or inappropriate care is difficult or impossible to appraise. Incentives exist to undersupply inputs for any service or procedure provided. Although the Japanese fee schedule approach can control health reimbursements effectively, it cannot influence physicians' actions appropriately.

Among advanced industrialized countries, prescribing and dispensing of drugs have been completely separated. However, Japan continues to be an exception to international norms. Almost all clinic-based physicians prescribe and dispense drugs within their medical settings. Even hospital-based physicians prescribe while the hospital pharmacy dispenses. Despite the efforts of the Ministry of Health and Welfare to regulate the separation of prescribing and dispensing and to cut drug reimbursements, per capita consumption of drugs (medications and injections) in Japan is highest among the advanced industrialized nations, constituting 30% of its $200 billion spending on health care (Fig. 7). This incentive for physicians to prescribe is sometimes referred to as the "pickling effect."

The Ministry approves new drugs, establishes drug prices on a fee schedule, and then regulates which drugs are to be prescribed. Unfortunately, physicians are widely recognized as having maintained their substantial incomes by prescribing high-priced drugs. This practice causes problems of side effects and microbial resistance, since powerful broad-spectrum antibiotics are often prescribed and consumed inappropriately (Iglehart, 1988). It is widely believed that methicillin-

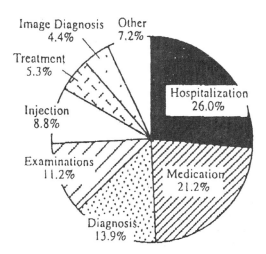

Figure 7 Medical care expenditure by type of medical action (fiscal 1990). Source: "Estimates of National Medical Care Expenditure," Statistics and Information Department, Minister's Secretariat, MHW.

resistant *Staphylococcus aureus*, which caused some patient deaths in health care settings, is one consequence of overprescribing antibiotics (Matsumoto, 1980; Endo et al., 1992).

Within the Japanese system, citizens do not participate in the process of setting fees directly; the process of setting fees is kept within the government bureaucracy and is not readily accessed. Japan's public policymaking process is highly centralized at the national level. The Ministry of Health and Welfare organizes the Central Social Medical Care Council, composed of 20 members who are representatives of providers, payers, and public interest groups (usually economists and lawyers), but they hardly represent consumers. Fee schedules are negotiated within this Council and the national government has put pressure on them to control fee schedules and to contain total health care expenditures. Citizen complaints or demands are muted, because negotiations within the Council are based upon technical and periodic surveys to which citizens do not have access. In addition, minutes of Council meetings are considered "internal proceedings" and are not available to the public.

The largest tax system in Japan is a direct tax, which is deducted from the working person's salary. Therefore, people are generally unaware of the income tax and are therefore disinterested in the distributions from this revenue source. Japanese citizens hardly say a word "as a taxpayer," and there are few complaints compared with other countries. The absence of cost-consciousness for health services is remarkable.

Moreover, since consumer rights movements have been muted in Japan, the status of patients as consumers is different from that of Americans. Patients in Japan, nevertheless, believe that hospitals offer superior-quality services compared to clinics, and consequently flock to them, resulting in overcrowding. In turn, this has placed continuing financial pressure on clinics to attract large numbers of patients or provide more services to current patients.

Meanwhile, even if high-quality health care is offered, it is not evaluated under the current payment system. Some reports say that high-quality health care is entirely too costly. For example, disposable products are used at the expense of the hospital. If a single-use product is used for meticulous infectious control during an operation, the hospital cannot demand payment from the payment funds for the extra cost or from the patient directly. There is not enough in the budget to spend on gloves for each handling of a patient, for each specimen, or for universal precautions. Under the current system, deficits are covered for public hospitals but not for private hospitals. Private hospitals have no choice but to pay for any deficits themselves or to make patients pay for the cost. With all health care being accessible to the public, there is a good chance that hospitals without high-quality health care may not be able to attract patients.

Thus, fee schedule systems and patient reactions to the system have brought about overcrowding and, perhaps, overconsumption at the high end of the medical-technological system. At the same time, pressure has been placed upon clinics to find more patients, prescribe more medications, and further reduce costs, which places them at a continual competitive disadvantage relative to hospitals, many of which are supported by government expenditures.

In comparisons of international health care expenditures, there is a tendency to exclude or underestimate expenses from public health services, medical education, and research. For example, in Japan, normal child delivery is not covered by health insurance, and expenditures are most likely underestimated. Private gifts and money to physicians from patients are also excluded from expenditure estimates, and it is impossible to estimate their size in Japanese health spending.

Various public health services play an important role in Japanese health care. After World War II, health centers were reorganized in individual regions based on population. There are now 852 prefectural or municipal health centers in Japan. National and local governments (Annual Report on Health and Welfare, 1996) finance these health centers, which emphasize services such as environmental health and safety, demographic statistics, and food hygiene, but include some primary health care services.

Public health centers have responsibility for all preventive health care. The most important work of health centers encompasses control of tuberculosis and other communicable diseases, but also extends to preventive health in cardiovascular disease, cancer, maternal and child health, mental health, and geriatric health. Universal maternal and child preventive care programs are provided in Japan through these health centers. Preventive services include checkups that are followed by individual counseling and health education, vaccination, and home visits of nurses. The vaccination rate has reached nearly 100% and maternal-child handbooks are given to all pregnant women. Both of these have contributed to promotion of the health of mother and child (Takayanagi, 1993). All costs of health centers are not included in estimates of total Japanese health care expenditures. The significance of public health centers in the Japanese system should not be underestimated.

The health of workers is protected through the Labor Standards Law. Under the Labor Standards Law and School Education Law, an annual health checkup in the workplace and in school is compulsory, and people can receive the service for a nominal fee.

These public health services have been intensifying the necessity to actualize a comprehensive service delivery system that encompasses daily health care, medical checkups, diagnosis, medical treatment, rehabilitation, and preventable illnesses. Medical checkup services are offered at hospitals or health centers; however, checkup service items vary from institute to institute. As a result, the quality of these services has never been evaluated.

Another factor sometimes overlooked is the health status of Japanese people. The reported number of acquired immunodeficiency syndrome patients was projected at only 1186 persons in 1996. Alcoholics and drug abusers are less prevalent than in the United States, and the Japanese diet has traditionally been a healthy one, with the exception of high levels of salt intake. These peripheral conditions help account for some proportion of relatively lower health care expenditures in Japan.

Also noteworthy is the literacy rate of 99.7%, as well as a high school enrollment rate of 93% in 1992, according to the Ministry of Education. Highly educated, professional women have an increased awareness of the need for maternal/child health care. However, the mortality rate among pregnant women is high (9.0 per 100,000 population in 1991) compared with other industrial countries by the National Health Trend/Health and Welfare Index (1992). Accessibility of care in Japan is very good, but the psychological access (acceptability) of care is extremely low.

C. Assessment System for Health Care

The only government scrutiny in the assessment system for health care delivery is financial audit by the payment organization. This organization reviews the procedures and medications administered, comparing them with the patient's diagnosis. However, this falls short of addressing the quality of these medical procedures. The lack of an effective assessment system is a problem.

Quality evaluations fall into four dimensions:

1. the medical level dimension,
2. the socioeconomic dimension (macrolevel health care quality),
3. the on-site health services dimension (microlevel health care quality), and
4. the individual quality dimension (consumer's satisfaction).

1. Medical Level Dimension

The jurisdiction of education is as follows: The Ministry of Education supervises undergraduate education, the Ministry of Health and Welfare controls postgraduate education, and academic societies control the training/learning of specialists. Postgraduate education is not obligatory. The titles of specialists are authorized only by the academic societies, except for anesthesiologists, who require recognition from the Ministry of Health and Welfare to claim their title. Academic societies take a leading role in the improvement of the quality of medicine. The payment funds control health services. The Ministry of Health and Welfare deals with extreme cases of malpractice through prefectural health centers. However, there is neither a system for peer review nor an organized evaluation system, by either the educational sector or the reimbursement/payment mechanisms.

The quality of medical treatment has long been defined by physicians as "quality of health care" itself. With strong professional autonomy, only the physician in charge has the power to make a decision regarding the patient's treatment. Neither the concept of "second opinion" nor referral systems between hospitals and physicians are popular. Besides, there is no mechanism that can check appropriateness of the treatment. This compels physicians to treat patients with diseases that may be beyond the physician's scope.

2. Socioeconomic Dimension

If the medical standards are enhanced by high-quality health care, unnecessary medical cost may be eliminated. For example, if an early diagnosis is made owing to an advanced technique, appropriate treatment can be given to the patient at a lower cost and thus the medical cost at the macroeconomic level can also be reduced. Repeated expensive and/or invasive examinations such as fiberscopy, catheterization, MR and CT have been done commonly by both the original hospital and the referring hospital for the same patient. The cost of examination is paid by the action without an evaluation of quality or necessity. So, repeated examination is at times required for "better quality." This is not only often hazardous to the patient but also costly. In such a case there is no cost control system. A system that utilizes comprehensive calculation measures and evaluation methods for quality of medicine at the macroeconomic level is necessary. Understanding quality of health care at the macrolevel and appropriate evaluation should be the first step in the right direction.

With regard to ties between health care and social welfare, Japan has not progressed much. In the face of an aging society, integration of these two components is necessary. The welfare plans for the twenty-first century have been submitted by the Ministry of Health and Welfare, and are aimed at improving welfare in Japan. The budget has been traditionally allocated to pensions, health care, and welfare with the ratio of 5:4:1. Change has been called for and the distribution may be shifted to 5:3:2. This suggests that more importance will be attached to welfare in financial terms.

With the increase in the population of elderly, it is becoming more evident that the current health care model will not be able to withstand the changing needs and demands of this segment of the population. In developing health policy, the Ministry of Health and Welfare, Ministry of Education, and Ministry of Labor all must participate. There is sectionalism among these ministries and even among offices inside the Ministry of Health and Welfare itself. In the aging society, implementation and/or coordination among them will be necessary.

3. On-Site Health Services Dimension

For delivery of minimal standards of health care, equality has always been a major principle of health care policy in Japan. The ''best health care'' defined by physicians certainly has the benefit of offering state-of-the-art medical treatment; however, it runs the risk of inappropriateness. It is often quite difficult to differentiate between necessities and appropriateness in health services, especially for patients. Though both physicians and patients seem to believe solely in state-of-the-art medical treatment, this is an inappropriate conception and must be rectified by raising awareness about true ''health care'' at a social level.

The problem in Japan is that all hospitals are nonprofit. Income for the hospital is basically from the strictly regulated medical fee schedule. On the other hand, the operating cost and fixed cost should be paid with slide to prices of commodities. Not only operating cost and fixed cost but also plant and equipment budgets should be paid from the revenues generated. Today most of the hospitals in Japan run a deficit (Takayanagi, 1993). Public hospitals may have some allowance, but not private hospitals. There are three types of hospitals in Japan: 40.6% are private organization-owned hospitals, 14.1% private individual-owned hospitals, and 20.9% public hospitals. There is some warning about the nonprofit hospitals changing to for-profit (Relman, 1991). According to the analysis of Chino public hospital in 1993, earning per cost was 86.6% in 486 moderate public general hospitals in 1991. The government should be intent on easing rules on hospital management to improve quality by quality assessment and/or marketing methods.

On the other hand, in the application of a fixed-fee-per-capita system at certain accredited hospitals for the aged, the medical fee per capita must be set high enough to take care of elderly patients. In particular, it must also be maintained at a high enough level to insure that the elderly can maintain a high quality of life instead of being bed-bound. However, the rate must also slide according to the price of the commodity. Flexibility must be encouraged for the use of health services with good incentives. Fee for service should be applied in part for the high-cost services for these senior patients, if necessary (Niki, 1994).

4. Individual Dimension

Introducing quality with patient-oriented care requires resources of both materials and manpower. With the progress of society, the importance attached to health care in Japan has shifted from rationing and maintenance of the minimum standards to providing high-quality health care. A healing environment is one of the important factors in proper patient care at any health services facility. One's physical environments affect one's mind. In that respect, it is to be desired that hospitals should offer hotel-like amenities in a warm and receptive atmosphere to promote healing.

The dignity of patients should be respected and an equal relationship should be established between physicians and patients. In many cases, neither consumers nor providers are aware of the acceptability of care. Proper informed consent and the patient's decision about choice of treatment are important factors. Patient self-care reliance and support systems that promote and reinforce this are necessary for independence from paternalistic health care.

The evaluation of the outcome basically deals with whether the patient has recovered or not, which, however, can be difficult to judge, since recovery processes vary depending on the patient's characteristics. The outcome of health care may positively influence the patient's cognitive and behavioral patterns, which, in turn, may enable successful rehabilitation or return to work. The quality of this whole process is defined as the quality of outcome. The general awareness of the Japanese patient regarding health care quality is low (Iwasaki, 1993).

Awareness of quality and the establishment of proper methods of evaluation are indispensable for the improvement of quality. It is a driving force for continuous efforts to be made to achieve this purpose. Evaluation in relation to society's needs is still in the stages of trial and error. After considering health care quality in Japan, we have become aware of the need for some fundamental changes in everyone's approach. For improving quality in Japan, recognition of quality and evaluation are the most important processes.

There is a movement to institute quality evaluation in the health care field. The Ministry of Health and Welfare and the Japan Medical Association set self-assessment standards in 1990. Recently, these two bodies announced the likelihood of establishing a foundation for health care quality assessment. The Japan Hospital Association also finalized its own guidelines for hospital standardization in late 1991, but both of these are to be self-assessed and not third-party evaluations. There is also a movement on the part of conscientious health care organizations to establish objective standards of assessment through voluntary associations such as the Japan Health Quality Assurance Society, founded in 1990. This independent nationwide project has begun on-site quality surveys of member hospitals on an experimental basis for third-party assessments, while also developing viable standards and conducting patient satisfaction surveys and research into outcome indicators used in health care quality analysis. This movement resulted in an organization for quality evaluation. The Japan Council for Quality Health Care was founded in 1995 for semiofficial quality evaluation to hospitals.

D.   Physician-Patient Relationship

Physicians are traditionally held in high esteem in Japan. On the other hand, the Japanese people are interested in health matters both as a part of traditional culture and out of a keen interest in science and technology. An increasing amount of information about diseases, fitness, and nutrition from books, magazines, and health manuals is available to the public, and this information supplements older health manuals and traditional or folk medicine. Accordingly, citizens believe they go to clinics armed with some knowledge about health and medicine. They want not only better care, but also knowledge about why and how they got their disease or illness. The health care received by patients should be in keeping with their personal values. Palmer calls this the "acceptability of care," or the degree to which health care satisfies patients (Palmer, 1991).

Yet, although people are becoming more informed, it is a tradition in Japan that physicians do not explain the details of procedures to patients. In addition, physicians have to see as many patients as possible under the fixed fee schedule to maintain income. Physicians argue that they do not have enough time to discuss problems with their patients even if they would like to. Furthermore, they do not have a rigid system of appointments, and patients come to them on a first-come-first-served basis. Medical social workers are busy with consultation about the choice of kinder physicians rather than social or financial consultations.

The fee-schedule assigns extremely low reimbursement for consultation, and it may not be assigned for consultation independent of the fee-scheduled service or procedure. Moreover, traditional aspects of Japanese society and the educational system have impeded the development of alternative, skilled sources of medical advice, such as nurses or nurse practitioners, who are unavailable in Japan.

Patients frequently tend not to talk frankly to physicians, and if they are not satisfied, they simply switch physicians. As a result, patients shop around for physicians to validate what they know or have read, which produces lack of continuity of care. Almost all the same tests and medical histories are retaken at the next clinic or hospital, and almost the same drugs are prescribed, resulting in duplication of high costs. Physician expenditures per capita in Japan are the second highest after the United States (Scieber et al., 1991). In Japan, record keeping for patients or the effective utilization of records has not been regarded as important. Patients do not have access to their own records. Drugs and laboratory tests constitute a larger ratio of revenue in primary versus tertiary care settings (Ikegami, 1991).

Patients are confused by freedom of choice of physicians, since under the universal fee schedule system information about which physicians are better than others is unavailable. Although Japanese society has the premise that all medical facilities provide the same level of care and this level is high enough for patients, patients do not always believe this. They are eager to consult health manuals, their friends, and relatives about their illness and physicians' reputations. Under these circumstances, it is necessary that we introduce patient-oriented principles and offer quality service to attract patients. Efforts have been made in the area of technique; however, little attention has been paid to comfortable equipment of health care settings and the relationship between patients and physicians. These areas have not been budgeted enough until now, either, which seems to be a cause of the complaints concerning quality of health care.

The Ministry of Education is in charge of the undergraduate education of physicians and nurses. The Japanese medical education system is primarily focused upon basic medicine and diagnosis; there are few practical courses, manuals, or standards of disease management at the undergraduate level. This means that there is a chance to receive excellent creative management or relatively poor care, depending on the physician. Basic pharmacology is more dominant than clinical pharmacology. Moreover, education in clinical settings places importance on the study of specialized areas and ignores education in primary care, which accounts for 80% of health care in Japan. Faculties in medical schools in Japan, despite the changing health care environment, have not changed their attitude, emphasizing research rather than education. There is no under- or postgraduate education about the course of patient-physician relationships or even interviewing methods. Therefore, the medical provider must develop clinical skills through on-the-job training. Technology-oriented postgraduate education without technology assessment is the current situation. A residency training program for specialists has just started but needs to be reviewed in terms of effectiveness.

On the other hand, medical lawsuits are very rare in Japan. Compared with the litigious American society, the Japanese society has fewer lawyers, and people tend to look down on malpractice suits. Physicians do not need to protect themselves from malpractice awards so far.

IV. DISCUSSION

A survey done by Harvard-Harris-ITF in 1990 compared public satisfaction with health systems in 10 nations (Blendon et al., 1990). In the survey of the Japanese, 29% said that ''on the whole, the health care system works pretty well, and only minor changes are necessary to make it work better'' (p. 188), which was 2.9 times the percent of similar American responses. Forty-seven percent of the Japanese said that ''there are some good things in our health care system, but fundamental changes are needed to make it work better'' (p. 188), while 60% of the Americans said so. Only 6% of the Japanese agreed that ''our health care system has so much wrong with it that we need to completely rebuild it,'' while 29% of the Americans thought so. Thus, this survey suggests that the Japanese people think that their health care system works well fundamentally, but minor changes are necessary to fine-tune the system.

On the whole, however, citizens are not satisfied with their health care systems in either Japan or the United States, and it seems that there are some differences in complaints of citizens between these two nations. The first difference is the financing system. Japanese health insurance is implemented through nonprofit health societies and local governments. On the other hand, insurance in the United States is entrusted to private insurance companies in a free, competitive market. Consequently, Japanese citizen complaints have focused on equity and equality while American citizens have focused on cost-containment and access.

Japan adopted a fixed fee schedule for the purpose of cost-containment, and national government intervention is unavoidable as long as the fee schedule and social insurance are heavily controlled by the government. As a result, in Japan, health care problems are visible political issues for the *national* government, which is the second difference between Japan and the United States. In Japan, historically almost all believe that the national government should be responsible for all kinds of health care systems. On the contrary, in a decentralized country like the United States, people have tried to avoid government intervention as much as possible.

Another difference between the two nations is their cultures, especially health "cultures." Compared to Americans, who are aggressive individualists in health and other matters, the Japanese tend to be more passive and conciliatory. Japanese accept government regulations, insurance plans, and physicians' medical advice, even if they are skeptical. Moreover, the Japanese try to solve problems domestically and regard their health problems as a personal responsibility. Nevertheless, in both nations, consumers find it increasingly difficult to comprehend the cost-benefit payoff of health services clearly because of market imperfections.

Japan has achieved universal coverage and a reasonable level of quality, and at the same time Japan has succeeded in keeping health care costs relatively low. The system structured through the laws of 1948 made health care accessible to one and all by increasing the number of physicians and insuring 100% of the population. Since 1948, Japan has come a long way on the path of economic development, and at the same time society has undergone rapid changes in employment, education, mass media, and scientific health care knowledge.

The Japanese are beginning to realize they will have to pay more for better-quality care including advanced technology and infrastructure, and to share the burden of health care costs of the growing elderly population. The rigid system that had worked well so far in Japan is showing cracks under today's different circumstances. As they pay more, Japanese citizens increasingly feel that they are not getting their money's worth, leading to strains in physician-patient relationships.

Patients want wider availability of advanced technology, less waiting, less travel time to medical settings, and better health care facilities where they can obtain more comfortable treatment and care. But, the fixed fee schedule and government insurance discourage change and innovation, and encourage heavy consumption of physician services and pharmaceuticals instead. This situation is reflected in complaints made by the Japanese in the 10-nation survey mentioned above.

Historically, the Japanese people are less likely than Americans to voice their complaints, but they are likely to become more vocal as they become more knowledgeable about their health care system. Citizens may form groups to collect information about quality of physicians, current medical research, price of treatment and drugs, and so forth. Patients are increasingly demanding ''informed consent'' and open debate, which traditionally has been very rare. If citizens become more vocal, physicians may become increasingly aware of their responsibilities, and at the same time the local and national governments may come to create a climate of more open debate. Recent changes in political party and coalition alignments in Japan may lead to the opening of new channels for citizen participation, including discussions of health care policies and regulations.

ACKNOWLEDGMENTS

The authors thank Dr. Arthur R. Williams for his support and advice on the chapter. The help of others at the Cookingham Institute of Public Affairs, Henry W. Bloch School of Business and Public Administration, and the University of Missouri–Kansas City is greatly appreciated. We also thank Professor Sakai Iwasaki, Chair, Department of Health Services Administration, for his helpful advice for the completion of this chapter.

REFERENCES

Blendon, R.J., Leitman, R., Morrison, I., Donelan, K. Satisfaction with health systems in ten nations. Health Affairs Summer:185–192, 1990.
Chino, T. Choice of the public hospital in services. Shakai Hosho Kenkyu 29(3):232–242, 1993.
Dentzor, S. The graying of Japan. US News World Rep September:65–73, 1991.
Endo, K., Taketsu, H., Shimoji, A., Matsumura, T. Attempts to control nosocomial *Staphylococcus aureus* infection. Jpn Inter Med 2(4):360–363, 1992.
Gray, C. Health care in Japan: challenged by an aging population. Can Med Assoc J 140: 946–949, 1989.
Health and Welfare Statistics Association. Health and Welfare Statistics in Japan. Tokyo, 1996.
Iglehart, J.K. Health policy report: Japan's medical care system, Part Two. N Engl J Med 319:1166–1173, 1988.
Ikegami, N. Japanese health care: low cost through regulated fees. Health Affairs Fall: 86–109, 1991.
Ikegami, N. The economics of health care in Japan. Science 258:614–618, 1992.

Iwasaki, S. The myth of Japan's health care model. Clin Perform Qual Health Care 1(2): 91–93, 1993.

Joseph, L.B., Richard, C.R., Stuart, A.W. Why We Spend Too Much on Health Care. Chicago: The Heartland Institute, 1992.

Matsumoto, K. MRSA innai-kansen to Kongo no taio, Nihon. Ishikai Zasshi 104(12): 1615–1618, 1980.

Ministry of Health and Welfare. Annual Report on Health and Welfare. Tokyo: Kosei Tokei Kyokai, 1996a.

Ministry of Health and Welfare. Estimates of National Medical Care Expenditure. Statistics and Information Department, Minister's Secretariat, Tokyo, 1996b.

Ogawa, N., Retherford, R.D. Care of the elderly in Japan: changing norms and expectations. J Marriage Fam 55:585–597, 1993.

Okamoto, K. Health care for the elderly in Japan medicine and welfare in an aging society, caring a crisis in long term care. Br Med J 305:403–405, 1992.

Palmer, H. Consideration in defining quality: striving for quality in health care. Health Admin 3–58, 1991.

Relman, A.S. Shattuck Lecture—The health care industry: where is it taking us? N Engl J Med 325, 1991.

Scieber, G.J., Pullier, J.P., Greenwald, L.M. Health care systems in twenty-four countries. Health Affairs Fall:22–38, 1991.

Shukan Shakai Hosho, 1793. International Comparison of Health Care Expenditure. Tokyo, 1994, pp 6–9.

Shukan Shakai Hosho, 1827. Report of Health Care Facility. Tokyo, 1994, pp 30–35.

Statistics and Information Department, Minister's Secretariat, MHW. Survey of Social Medical Care According to Action Taken. Tokyo, 1991.

Takayanagi, K. Health care quality in Japan: the pros and cons. Nihon Ishikai Zasshi 1(2): 94–96, 1993.

Takayanagi, K., Iwasaki, S. The Well-Being of Elderly People: Proceedings of the First International Symposium on Health Policy and Health Service System. Tokyo: Takusei Umenai, Mazaru Nishigaki, 1992.

Tokyo Metropolitan Government. Basic Study of Tokyo's National Health Insurance. Tokyo, 1989.

Wolfe, P.R., Moran, D.W. Global budgeting in the OECD countries. Health Care Financing Rev 14(3):55–76, 1993.

16

The Health Care System in Australia

Helen M. Lapsley
University of New South Wales, Sydney, New South Wales, Australia

I. INTRODUCTION

Australia has a pluralist health care system, with a history of government control, intervention, financing, and service provision combined with substantial private professional practice and private for-profit and not-for-profit institutional provision. The complexity of the sectors, complicated by a federal/state system of separate and overlapping responsibilities, has produced a health care system that one would hardly wish to replicate, yet it enjoys the support of the majority of the population. Early origins of the Australian population are historically British, with a small, dispersed Aboriginal population; recent European and even more recent Asian migration have contributed to a multicultural society, which has nevertheless retained and even expanded a British expectation of government provision and responsibility for delivery of heath care.

Many of the tensions and problems that are emerging within the health care sector are shared by other Western countries: an aging population, high community expectations, and a proliferation of technologies, pharmaceuticals, and therapies, which, without regulation and rationing, would result in soaring costs. Other problems are unique to Australia: the disparately low health status of the Aboriginal population; the tensions between federal and state funders, which have led to cost shifting, cost overlaps, and gaps in service delivery; and the problems of some health services being open-ended (the provision of medical services) while others are budget-capped (public hospitals). The role of the private health sector is interpreted and envisaged differently by the major political parties, although both acknowledge its continuing importance and the need for balance.

II. OVERVIEW

The Australian health care system, or at least the way in which it is organized and financed, appears to be in a constant state of change. While it is true that there continue to be many changes, these are predominantly incremental, and developmental. Some changes are a result of wider public sector policies of microeconomic reform, while others are a reflection of attempts to address the divided responsibilities between federal and state governments. Improvements in efficiency and increases in cost-effectiveness of the health care sector are the

Table 1 Australia—Levels of Health Services Responsibilities: Finance or Policy (Row A), and Service Provision (Row B)

| | | | Government | | Nongovernment | |
| | | | | | Voluntary | Private for |
Services		Federal	State	Local	nonprofit	profit
Community health	A	X	X	X	X	
	B		X	X	X	
Occupational health	A	X	X		X	
	B		X	X	X	X
Preventive health	A	X	X	X	X	
	B	X	X	X	X	
Environmental health	A	X	X	X	X	
	B		X	X		X
Health transport	A	X	X		X	
	B		X		X	X
Pharmaceuticals	A	X				X
	B		X			X
Public hospitals	A	X	X			
	B		X			
Private hospitals	A		X		X	X
	B				X	X
Medical services	A	X	X			
	B	X	X			X
Domiciliary care	A		X	X	X	X
	B		X	X	X	X

objectives of most recent changes. Table 1 illustrates the range of responsibilities for financing and service delivery across different levels of government and between different service providers.

Australia has achieved a relatively high health status and longevity for the majority of the population comparable with the United States and Canada, with the significant exception of the Aboriginal and Torres Strait Islanders, who comprise less than 2% of the total population. Of course, the health care system can take neither all the credit nor all the blame for health status; it must be shared with housing, education, and economic support services. In Australia, as with other developed countries, many of the public health gains have been achieved from clean water, sewerage and garbage disposal, work safety, and uncontaminated food—all factors that are no longer included as components of health care system expenditure. It would therefore be more accurate to describe Australian health care expenditure as the money that is spent on curative services, together with relatively small amounts on prevention, promotion, education, and research.

III. FINANCING

Over the last two decades the Australian health care system, particularly those parts concerned with financing personal care, has swung slowly to and fro on a pendulum between collectivism and individualism. Since February 1984 Australia has enjoyed the former, a universal health insurance system based on the principles of universality, equality, simplicity, and ease of access. It is an essentially tax-funded system known as Medicare providing, by agreement with the states and territories, free public hospital care for all Australians. In addition, the majority of the fee-for-service costs of generalist and specialist medical care and optometrical care are reimbursed by the commonwealth (federal) government. In addition, in 1998 approximately 30% of the population has some additional private health insurance coverage, although this percentage has been in gradual decline for several years.

After 10 years of Medicare, during which the cost of health care services has been contained at between 7.7% and 8.5% of GDP, and unchanged for the last 6 years (Australian Institute of Health and Welfare, 1998), a number of pressures are emerging (see Tables 2 and 3). Medicare is constructed in such a way that some degree of tension is inevitable, particularly in relation to those health care services, such as public hospitals, that are owned and managed by the states, but funded in part through federal government grants to the states. A brief review of ''hospital'' Medicare and ''medical'' Medicare should clarify some of the reasons for ongoing tensions.

Table 2 Total Health Services Expenditure, Current and Constant (average
1989–90) Prices,[a] and Annual Growth Rates, 1984–85 to 1996–97

	Amount ($m)		Growth rate over previous year (%)	
	Current	Constant	Current	Constant
1984–85	16,546	22,862	—	—
1985–86	18,586	24,180	12.3	5.8
1986–87	21,115	25,341	13.6	4.8
1987–88	23,333	26,287	10.5	3.7
1988–89	26,127	27,719	12.0	5.4
1989–90	28,800	28,800	10.2	3.9
1990–91	31,270	29,422	8.6	2.2
1991–92	33,084	30,203	5.8	2.7
1992–93	34,892	31,393	5.5	3.9
1993–94	36,587	32,589	4.9	3.8
1994–95	38,701	33,957	5.8	4.2
1995–96	41,308	35,716	6.7	5.2
1996–97[b]	43,204	36,768	4.6	2.9
Average annual growth rates				
1984–85 to 1987–88			12.1	4.8
1987–88 to 1992–93			8.4	3.6
1992–93 to 1996–97			5.5	4.0

[a] Health services expenditure for 1984–85 to 1996–97 is deflated to constant (average
1989–90) prices using specific health deflators.
[b] Based on preliminary AIHW and ABS estimates.
Source: AIHW Health Expenditure Database, Australian Institute of Health and Welfare,
April 1998.

IV. HOSPITAL MEDICARE

As part of the Medicare program, the federal government makes Medicare Compensation Grants to the states and the Northern Territory, which are designed to ensure that no state is financially disadvantaged through the operation of Medicare within the public hospital system. Through these financial arrangements with the states, all Australians are insured for public hospital services free at point of delivery. The federal government revenue for Medicare payments is financed primarily from general tax revenue, supported by a 1.5% levy on income tax, payable by all except very-low-income earners.

The grants from the federal government to the states and the Northern Territory comprise a base level of funding for public hospitals, together with an incen-

Table 3 Health Services Expenditure per Person, Current and Constant (average 1989–90) Prices,[a] and Annual Growth Rates, 1989–90 to 1995–96

	Amount ($m)		Growth rate over previous year (%)	
	Current	Constant	Current	Constant
1989–90	1,705	1,705	—	—
1990–91	1,823	1,716	7.0	0.7
1991–92	1,910	1,746	4.7	1.8
1992–93	1,990	1,790	4.2	2.5
1993–94	2,060	1,837	3.6	2.6
1994–95	2,168	1,911	5.2	4.0
1995–96[b]	2,294	1,986	6.5	4.0
Average annual growth rates				
1989–90 to 1995–96			5.1	2.6

[a] Health services expenditure for 1989–90 to 1995–96 is deflated to average 1989–90 prices using specific health deflators (see Table 2 for major deflators used).
[b] Based on preliminary AIHW and ABS estimates.
Source: AIHW Health Expenditure Database, Australian Institute of Health and Welfare, April 1998.

tives package. The calculation of the base-level funding is dominated by an age/sex-weighted population factor, while the incentives are for special service provision (e.g., AIDS, palliative care) and to encourage more efficient service provision (e.g., increased provision of day surgery, which occurs considerably less frequently in Australia than in the United States).

The role of the public hospital in Australia is somewhat in contrast to the United States. In Australia, public hospitals provide most of the hospital services to most people, regardless of income. While all Australians have public hospital insurance under Medicare, many of the 30% of Australians who also have additional private health insurance are admitted to public hospitals, but as private patients. Public hospitals, which include the major teaching hospitals and all the research centers of excellence, accounted for 73% of all hospital admissions in 1994 (Australian Institute of Health and Welfare, 1996).

The number of people in Australia with private health insurance has been steadily declining for several years. Private health insurance is not tax deductible, but since 1998, there is an additional taxation levy for high-income earners who do not have private health insurance. One reason why some people in Australia continue to maintain private health insurance is to have their own choice of physician within public hospitals. Medicare (public) patients are treated by the physician who is assigned by the public hospital. One of the anomalies of the present organizational arrangements, which has been identified in several inquiries and reviews, is that the federal government pays physicians on a fee-for-service basis for private patients in both public and private hospitals, while physicians providing services to public patients in public hospitals are paid by state governments, with a range of payment mechanisms that include fee-for-service, sessional fees, and salaries.

Owing to capped funding to all public hospitals, and despite a wide range of funding mechanisms and organizational structures throughout the states, many nonacute therapies and procedures have long waiting lists. The second and perhaps more important reason why over 30% of the population maintain private health insurance is to avoid the sometimes lengthy waiting times for nonacute procedures in public hospitals.

V. MEDICAL MEDICARE

Medical Medicare provides insurance on a fee-for-service basis for all services provided by medical practitioners, in public and private hospitals and all ambulatory settings. While there is some overall aggregate review of utilization patterns undertaken by the federal government, it is effectively an open-ended system. In an initiative that may appear curious from the perspective of other countries and other systems, the original Medicare legislation allowed for no private insurance for medical services. This 1984 legislation was amended in 1985 following a dispute between physicians and government in one state, to allow one concession: registered health insurance organizations were enabled to provide ''gap'' insurance to cover the difference between the Medicare benefit and the schedule fee for medical services provided to private patients in public and private hospitals. The Medicare Benefits Schedule fee is determined and updated through a consultation process between the federal government and representatives of the medical profession. There is a specific fee for every item of service, which is revised and amended as new procedures are developed and new technologies incorporated.

The federal government currently pays patients a rebate for medical services of 85% of the schedule fee, except for private patients in public hospitals, which has a 75% rebate, with the ''gap'' redeemable from the patient's private insurer. Physicians in private practice are able to direct-bill Medicare for all their patients and accept 85% of the schedule fee as full payment. This practice, popularly known as ''bulk billing,'' relieves physicians of accounting and billing processes, and has become the most frequently used method of payment for episodes of service by physicians. Direct billing has been increasing every year, and in 1996–1997, this method of payment was used for 71.8% of all medical services delivered and 80.6% of general practitioners' services (Health Insurance Commission, 1997).

Some physicians use direct billing only for pensioner and welfare recipient patients, whereas many others direct-bill for their whole practice. Other methods of payment, for physicians who do not direct bill, require the patient to either:

a. pay the full fee, and then claim 85% of the schedule fee from a Medicare office, or

b. take the physician's account to a Medicare office, which makes out a check to the physician for 85% of the schedule fee, and sends it to the patient, who then pays the balance.

Under this system, all physicians in private practice, both general practitioners and specialists, are allowed to charge patients whatever they wish, provided the service is not direct-billed. While direct billing to the federal government requires that there is no patient copayment, the other two methods of physician reimbursement allow higher charging. Some physicians charge the Australian Medical Association recommended fee for each consultation, which is a little higher than the Medicare schedule fee for most services, whereas others charge well in excess of the Medicare fee.

In Australia, the medical Medicare system reinforces the role of the general practitioner as the "gatekeeper" to the health care system. It is widely accepted that a visit to a specialist is accompanied by a referral from a general practitioner, and direct access to specialists is effectively discouraged through the payment of a considerably lower rebate for nonreferred specialist visits. This process, while inevitably duplicating many medical visits, ensures a more appropriate use of medical specialists, and maintains general practitioners in a family medicine role, including preventive and monitoring services. The relatively low rebate for general practitioner visits, and the direct billing of most visits, with no out-of-pocket patient costs, to some extent can be seen as a reflection of the oversupply of general practitioners in most parts of Australia.

While "fee for service" would not always be nominated as the preferred system of paying for medical services, the Medicare information base of general practice and specialist medical services provides a very rich resource for epidemiologists, policy analysts, service planners, and economists. Australia is now beginning to make use of these data relating to the provision and consumption of medical services. In addition to payments to medical practitioners, Medicare benefits are also payable for refraction testing by optometrists, based on a separate schedule of benefits. In 1996–1997, 96% of optometrical services were direct-billed.

Access is an important Medicare objective, but one that has not yet been fully realized. While there are no financial limitations to access to medical services, other limitations can also include knowledge of available services and the provision of culturally appropriate services, as well as geographical access. Also, the Medicare objective of universality that has been realized should not be confused with comprehensive availability of services. For example, dental services are not readily available, and those free at point of delivery are insufficient, and simply inaccessible to many people. Services such as physiotherapy, particularly for people with debilitating conditions, are insufficient and, for many, unaffordable.

VI. PHARMACEUTICALS

The federal government enables access to pharmaceuticals for nonhospital patients through the Pharmaceutical Benefits Scheme, which subsidizes a range of drugs prescribed by physicians and dentists. The objective of the scheme is to ensure access to cost-effective prescribed medicines at the lowest cost to government and consumers, consistent with reliable supply. A listing of safe, effective pharmaceuticals is maintained, and generic prescribing is encouraged. There are two levels of charges for prescriptions, one for the general public, and a considerably lower charge for welfare beneficiaries. There is also a safety net provision for the chronically ill or those who require large numbers of prescriptions. The charges and the safety net are indexed. Some items that are approved for sale or for prescription are not subsidized, and these can be purchased at pharmacies. Despite a relatively high level of consumption of pharmaceuticals, the federal government, as the only purchaser for many drugs, has been able to control total costs quite effectively.

VII. HEALTH OUTCOMES: WHAT DOES HEALTH CARE PRODUCE?

Australian health authorities frequently and publicly emphasize the role of social, economic, and environmental factors in contributing to health status, while not in any way reducing their claims for an increasing proportion of public expenditure on health care delivery. Whether the increases that are occurring in health expenditure (see Table 2) are reflected in appropriate improvements in health outcomes is an important question as yet without an answer.

There is now in Australia an increasing focus on and concern for preventable morbidity and premature mortality. From comparisons with other countries it can be learned how many premature deaths can be avoided. Professor Bruce Armstrong introduced the concept of an ''Arcadian normal,'' which he describes as the existence of disease levels that might reasonably be achieved if we had reasonable knowledge about the causes of the disease in question, and could apply this knowledge to practical programs in the community (Armstrong, 1990). Armstrong suggests that the Arcadian normal for each of the major groups of causes of death is the lowest age-standardized mortality rate for that category among 20 Western countries. Table 4 presents his estimates of the amount of disease that is preventable in Australia.

Armstrong (1990) discusses the potentially achievable reality, using a combination of primary and secondary preventive measures of known effectiveness. Some of these preventive measures are currently being applied, to a greater or

Table 4 Estimates of Potentially Preventable Mortality in Australia

Cause of death	Rate in Australia[a]	Country with lowest rate	% Rate in that country	% Preventable in Australia[b]
All causes	838.0	Switzerland	726.0	13.4
Infectious and parasitic diseases	4.3	Austria	4.0	7.0
All cancers	197.0	Greece	161.0	18.3
Cancer of the stomach	10.1	United States	6.0	40.6
Cancer of the lung	41.0	France	22.2	44.1
Cancer of the breast	21.2	Spain	19.0	10.4
Circulatory diseases	410.0	France	265.0	35.4
Ischemic heart disease	231.0	France	76.0	67.1
Cerebrovascular disease	95.6	Canada	57.5	39.8
Respiratory diseases	64.7	Austria	42.5	34.3
Chronic bronchitis, emphysema, and asthma	16.9	United States	8.3	50.9
Digestive diseases	29.0	Sweden	21.1	27.2
Chronic liver disease and cirrhosis	8.7	Ireland	3.5	59.8
Injury and poisoning	50.4	England and Wales	34.3	31.9
Road crashes	17.9	England and Wales	8.8	50.8
Suicide	11.8	Greece	3.9	66.9

[a] When compared with mortality rates obtaining in countries of northern, western, and southern Europe and other countries with populations of mainly European origin.
[b] Age-standardized mortality rate per 100,000 of the population.
Source: Armstrong (1990).

lesser degree, consistent with Australian values. For example, campaigns to reduce smoking have been extensively initiated and supported by federal and state
governments. Predominant among preventable morbidities are those cancers that
relate to tobacco. Policies to reduce smoking in Australia combine legislative,
public health, and fiscal measures, and are proving successful in reducing tobacco
consumption in all population groups except young females. Other preventive
policies that combine economic and public health strategies include those relating
to diet, alcohol, environmental factors, communicable disease, and road safety.
Australia is now supporting wider and more rigorous evaluation of alternative
policies to assess which are most effective in producing improved health outcomes.

Australia has had a long-standing and effective record in one important
area of prevention: infant and child health. All Australian mothers have access to
free neighborhood infant and early childhood services, which provide monitoring,
information, immunization, advice, and assistance. These ''well baby'' clinics
have provided equitable access and enable wide dissemination of sound public
health practices relating to infants and young children. However, despite this
access, the rate of fully vaccinated children in Australia has declined from 71%
at age 1 to 21.6% at age 6, showing that many children are not receiving the
follow-up inoculations required for full immunity (Australian Bureau of Statistics, 1996). These rates fall far short of the immunization goals of near-universal
coverage of children at school entry age, as illustrated in Table 5. A strategy

Table 5   Fully Immunized Children, 3 Months–6 Years, Condition by Age—April
1995

	Diphtheria/ tetanus %	Pertussis %	Polio %	Measles %	Mumps %	Rubella %	Hib[a] %
3–6 months	92.5	92.0	92.0	—	—	—	76.3
Total less than 1 year	84.0	82.7	83.1	—	—	—	55.4
1 year	88.5	86.2	86.3	85.5	84.7	79.6	62.3
2 years	63.0	57.5	86.9	91.4	90.1	81.1	52.4
3 years	61.5	55.6	87.9	92.8	90.7	79.7	54.7
4 years	64.5	57.4	86.9	93.9	90.7	77.6	57.8
5 years	77.3	68.4	86.5	93.7	92.2	72.5	43.2
6 years	45.2	17.2	60.2	91.7	88.4	62.8	26.6

Source: Australian Bureau of Statistics (1996). [a]Hemophilus influenza type b.

called *Immunise Australia* is currently being implemented, in an effort to improve immunization rates and data on immunization coverage.

VIII. MEASURING QUALITY

Quality information within the health care sector in Australia includes peer review, clinical audit, hospital and health services accreditation, university programs in quality of health care, and a number of associations of health care professionals focussed on identifying, measuring, assessing, and assuring quality. Despite all these initiatives, information relating to the quality of care provided in most health care environments is still inadequate, or simply lacking.

In Australia, one of the oldest but least formal quality assurance processes is the medical tradition of peer review activities, including mortality and morbidity meetings and grand rounds. While these have flourished in teaching hospital environments, they have not had the same influence on the process of care in other locations, particularly rural and remote areas, and there are no effective mechanisms to ensure that such knowledge is incorporated into best practice.

The Australian Council on Healthcare Standards (ACHS) was developed from the U.S. model, and has been in existence for over 20 years, providing an accreditation system for hospitals, nursing homes, community health centers, and day surgeries. Accreditation has remained a voluntary process for hospitals in the public and private sectors, with their only incentive to seek accreditation beyond government encouragement being a small premium from private health insurers paid to accredited private hospitals. Accreditation is only now beginning to require from hospitals evidence of the clinical quality and outcomes of care, in addition to their traditional focus on physical structure and the meeting of minimum standards.

The development of evidence-based guidelines, while gradual, nevertheless is an important factor in disseminating knowledge of best practice. The Quality of Care Committee was established in 1992, as a standing committee of the National Health and Medical Research Council (NH&MRC). Unfortunately this committee has now been abolished, and its role absorbed and combined with other NH&MRC activities. Through the committee and its working parties, a number of significant quality activities were undertaken, including the development and implementation of clinical guidelines, best practice for diagnosed breast cancer, the procedural and surgical management of coronary heart disease, and best practice for diagnosis and treatment of depression. The work of this committee was particularly influenced and assisted by the Clinical Practice Guidelines developed by the U.S. Institute of Medicine, and by the Clinical Guidelines produced by the Canadian Medical Association. While some of the quality issues are unique

Table 6 The Public's View of Their Health Care System in 10 Nations, 1990

	Minor changes needed,[a] %	Fundamental changes needed,[b] %	Completely rebuild system,[c] %	Per capita health expenditure (U.S. dollars)
Canada	56	38	5	1483
Netherlands	47	46	5	1041
West Germany	41	35	13	1093
France	41	42	10	1105
Australia	34	43	17	939
Sweden	32	58	6	1233
Japan	29	47	6	915
United Kingdom	27	52	17	758
Italy	12	46	40	841
United States	10	60	29	2051

[a] On the survey, the question was worded as follows: "On the whole, the health care system works pretty well, and only minor changes are necessary to make it work better."
[b] "There are some good things in our health care system, but fundamental changes are needed to make it work better."
[c] "Our health care system has so much wrong with it that we need to completely rebuild it."
Source: Blendon et al. (1990).

to Australia, especially the provision of high-quality health services to remote and isolated populations, others are those that are being addressed in other comparable countries.

Quality of service delivery is now included in the current federal/state Medicare agreements, and as case-mix payment systems for hospital services are introduced, they are being accompanied by specific service quality directives.

Consumer perception of and satisfaction with health services is an important measure used in conjunction with other measures of quality. While it is not possible to satisfy all demands, or enable everyone to have preferred options of health services without delay, a 1990 international survey (Blendon et al., 1990) showed that Australia is approximately the middle order of consumer satisfaction with the health care system. The data presented in Table 6 were obtained by survey, but as more effective and credible complaints mechanisms are developed, there are inevitably more consumer complaints. The increase in complaints may not be a measure of doing worse, but rather it may demonstrate better communication and greater consumer confidence in the effectiveness of the complaints process.

Blendon and his colleagues, in this 10-nation survey, found that Canadians were the most satisfied with their health system, and Americans were the least. America was the only survey country without universal health insurance coverage; it had the highest level of spending per person, and the lowest level of public satisfaction.

IX. RATIONING

The inevitability of rationing is generally accepted in Australia, although some still like to believe that improved payment mechanisms and more efficient practices will somehow avoid painful choices. Whatever payment mechanisms are used, health services already are rationed in Australia and will continue to be rationed. Rationing was previously implicit, and now is being made more explicit. Other countries are also acknowledging the need to ration, and increasingly making public the choices that are available. In Australia, there is an excellent opportunity to ensure that equity and access issues feature prominently in decision making. It would be naive to suggest that this process will ever be easy, or that it will ever be finally resolved. The choices and decisions are dynamic; as new therapies, treatments, and drugs become available, more alternatives present new questions, including those that address the value of life itself. ''Life at any price'' is a maxim that has to be seriously questioned. As the Australian population ages, quality-of-life measures must be included in choices. There are a number of examples of how explicit rationing occurs in Australia. Some therapeutic drugs whose price is considered by the Pharmaceutical Benefits Advisory Committee not to be justified by the evidence for efficiency and effectiveness are refused, and are not available under the Pharmaceutical Benefits Scheme. Australia is one of the few countries in the world to require drug companies to provide cost-effectiveness analysis together with clinical trial data with their applications for approval for use and subsidy.

Hospital services have always been rationed, inevitably first by location in a country with a small, widely scattered rural population. A range of access arrangements are available, one of the most widely known internationally being the Royal Flying Doctor Service (RFDS). This service provides routine and emergency visits to isolated settlements and aerial evacuation services. Despite such services, the rural population has considerably reduced access to medical services, and little or no access to the range of therapies and treatments provided by other nonmedical health professionals. An isolated patient transport scheme provides transport subsidies for travel to cities for treatment, which is an adequate arrangement for surgical procedures, but insufficient for ongoing treatments such as radiotherapy. It is acknowledged that such rationing does occur, but the resource requirements to provide more than marginal improvements are not available.

Hospital services, for elective and nonacute procedures, are rationed by waiting times, as already referred to in the discussion on hospital Medicare. Waiting lists are particularly prominent as a rationing tool for procedures that also involve expensive prostheses such as hip and knee replacements, as most public hospital budgets are insufficient to meet the public demand for these procedures. Access to chemotherapy and radiotherapy is also rationed by waiting lists, and this is one of the areas that is publicly being regarded as unacceptable, and is currently the focus of additional funding. Demand for these services is continuing to grow because of the aging of the population and the increasing incidence of cancer [Australian Health Technology Advisory Committee (1997)].

Domiciliary care is widely acknowledged to be insufficient, resulting in two alternatives, one very costly, and the other cost-shifting. In the first case, the lack of adequate domiciliary care for patients after hospital discharge sometimes results in unnecessarily long lengths of stay in expensive acute facilities. In the second case, informal caregivers and families provide extensive services, in a number of documented cases resulting in these carers leaving the paid workforce, and thus shifting costs to the welfare sector.

Explicit rationing occurs under Medicare, which is universal but not comprehensive. As already identified, Medicare provides reimbursement for medical and optometry services, though not for dental care, physiotherapy, or any of the services delivered by other health professionals in private practice. The large percentage of Australians without private health insurance must either go without, pay, or join long waiting lists to access the ambulatory nonmedical services provided by public hospitals. Not surprisingly, the dental health of Australians is closely correlated with income.

Implicit rationing is equally extensive. Clinicians' knowledge of the lack of hospital beds or insufficient therapeutic services lead to what are effectively rationing decisions being made on clinical grounds. For example, clinicians sometimes cite the existence of comorbidities as the reason for decisions against surgical interventions, when in fact clinical practices differ from areas where the supply of services is less constricted. Decisions relating to practice variations predicated entirely on service availability are essentially rationing.

Decisions made by clinicians to treat, to defer, or to deny treatment are made with the knowledge of bed supply, operating theater schedules, and waiting lists. Not enough is known about the ways in which clinical choices and rationing choices interact in Australia, but some indications are provided by comparison of rates of elective surgery between publicly and privately insured patients. The spread of diagnostic and therapeutic technologies has concerned the government funders in Australia, and the restrictions on, for example, the number of magnetic resonance imagers authorized for the federal government rebate are clearly mechanisms for rationing.

Restrictions on entry to medical schools can be regarded as rationing, although by international norms Australia already has a very high physician/population ratio, and a generous provision of nurses and other health professionals.

A method of making rationing more acceptable, and also more equitable, is being used by three Australian states, and considered by two others. This method involves a population-based formula, originally developed in the National Health System in the United Kingdom to redistribute services more evenly across the country. The versions that have been developed in Australia incorporate weightings for age/sex, standardized mortality ratios, population distance and dispersion, and aboriginality. The introduction of these funding formulas is enabling a more equitable, albeit often gradual, redistribution of resources from historically advantaged to more disadvantaged areas. These mechanisms do not avoid the need for rationing, but ensure that resource shortages are borne equally. The content and weightings of the resource allocation formulas vary slightly between the states; e.g., some states choose to allocate relatively fewer public resources where there are plentiful private facilities.

X. DISCUSSION

Australians have high expectations of their health care system, accompanied by a reluctance to accept that higher costs and more copayments may inevitably be associated with more and better. The role of the private sector continues to be debated. The private sector has always had a legitimate role in the provision of health care services, as an alternative to those services supplied by government. The "privatization" debate, however, is concerned with the conversion of public services, which were provided by the public sector, to provision by the private sector. The issues being considered when there is a shift from publicly produced services (e.g., from government-owned public hospitals to privately produced hospital services for public patients) include comparative efficiency, equity of access, quality measures, and disincentives to discourage overservicing. There is significant precedent for this; most nursing home beds in Australia are owned and managed by the private sector, while funding and regulation is supplied by the federal government. Open-ended bed-day payments to hospitals cannot be considered to provide sufficient incentives for efficiency relating to reducing length of stay, for increasing day-only procedures, or for greater provision of domiciliary services; yet it is widely acknowledged that all of these features need to be developed and encouraged more extensively.

Funder/purchaser/provider separation may encourage some of these desirable initiatives; it is hoped that Australian experimentation with such restructuring is introduced and evaluated cautiously and carefully. The introduction of case-mix payment is providing more efficient ways for paying hospitals for what they actually do, but still leaves the question open as to whether everything they do is what they should do.

The role of the voluntary sector within the health and welfare sectors has always been extensive although not always highly visible. In some cases the absence of a voluntary agency would mean that these services would have to be provided by government, for example, Red Cross blood services, Royal Flying Doctor health transport services, St. John Ambulance services, all of which are heavily subsidized by government. However, some voluntary agencies, such as the Multiple Sclerosis Society, the Royal Blind Society, and the Spastic Centers, provide services for people who may otherwise have no or insufficient provision specific to their needs. With increasing demands on existing government-provided services, and a reluctance or an inability on the part of government to provide more services, the nongovernment voluntary sector in Australia appears to be expanding in amount and range of service provision. This expansion has been facilitated through direct government subsidies and through tax-deductible donations. It may represent a response to the current recession, a policy shift toward smaller government and "economic rationalism," or both.

The increased reliance on the provision of essential services by nongovernment agencies raises issues of the monitoring and evaluation of equity and access provisions, quality of service standards, and efficiency of service delivery. There is a reasonable concern that the provision of a subsidy could be used to absolve government from further responsibilities, or to provide a scapegoat for inadequate or patchy service provisions. Consequently, the emphasis on quality in hospitals requires extension to all locations of care.

The inadequacy of health research funding in Australia has been identified frequently, relative to similar countries. Australian investment in research remains very low, despite its acknowledged quality and achievements.

Mental health remains somewhat of a "Cinderella," despite the significant improvement of a national mental health policy, and the eventual acknowledgment of federal government responsibility in this area. When Australia, along with other developed countries, shifted the focus in mental health from institutional to community care, equivalent funding was not made available, and there remain major gaps in service delivery. Many of the social costs of underfunding mental health are shifted to the welfare sector, to nursing homes and hostels, and to jails; the personal costs are borne by the unfortunate individuals and their families.

Where policies are effective, they are being strengthened, and applied more widely. The differences in organizational arrangements and structures of health services between the states have positive advantages. As methods of financing, reimbursement, and control are evaluated as being effective, they are adopted by other states. The overall federal control through financing provides an assurance of equity, while the states are able to introduce policies relevant to their own specific geographical and structural requirements.

In conclusion, despite the acknowledged inadequacies and gaps in service delivery, there are many very positive aspects of Australian health care policy. The underlying cultural values embody the concept of "a fair go for all," and this philosophy has ensured that the health problems and health needs of all groups are acknowledged, and that efforts continue to be made to ensure equitable access to health services. Economic and outcome evaluations are being developed to ensure that resources are more efficiently distributed, but it is difficult to believe, with increasing pressures as discussed, that the percentage of GDP currently spent on health care will be able to be held at the present level.

REFERENCES

Armstrong, B.K. Morbidity and mortality in Australia: how much is preventable? In: McNeil J., King, R., Jennings, G., Powles, J. A Textbook of Preventive Medicine. Melbourne & London: Edward Arnold, 1990.

Australian Bureau of Statistics. Children's Immunisation, Australia, April 1995. ABS Cat. No. 4352.0, Canberra, Australia, 1996.

Australian Health Technology Advisory Committee. Beam and Isotope Radiotherapy. National Health and Medical Research Council, Canberra., Australia, 1997.

Australian Institute of Health and Welfare. Australia's Health 1996: The Fifth Biennial Health Report of the Australian Institute of Health & Welfare. AGPS, Canberra, Australia, 1996

Australian Institute of Health and Welfare. AIHW Health Expenditure Database, April, AGPS, Canberra, Australia, 1998.

Blendon, R.J., Leitman, R., Morrison, I., Donelan, K. Satisfaction with health systems in ten nations. Health Affairs, 9(2):185–192, 1990.

Health Insurance Commission. Annual Report. Statistical Tables, Canberra, Australia, 1997.

17

A Health System in Radical Transition

The Experience of New Zealand

Laurence Malcolm
Aotearoa Health, Lyttelton, New Zealand

I. INTRODUCTION AND OVERVIEW

It is now widely recognized that New Zealand's recent and ongoing health reforms have been possibly the most radical of any OECD country. Set within the context of major reform of the state sector generally, health reforms proposed in 1991 and implemented in 1993 were based on the concept of an internal market and managed competition, similar to developments in the United Kingdom and the United States. There were strong expectations by government that market-style reforms would improve access and increase efficiency, especially in the hospital-based sector.

However, these expectations are now widely recognized to have been seriously, if not fundamentally, flawed. The 1996 election in New Zealand resulted in a significant shift from the political right to the center. The National/New Zealand First Coalition Government rejected the more extreme aspects of the 1993 health reform process and stressed collaboration rather than competition. Better health outcomes, rather than profit, became the overall goal of the hospital-based sector.

A further shift to the left occurred with the election of a Labour government late in 1999. A new system of population-based and funded district health boards (DHBs) is being implemented in 2001. There is to be full integration of purchasing and provision, of hospital and community care, primary and secondary, government and nongovernment, disability and public health services. It appears that this system may be the most integrated of any country. A population-based set of clinical service divisions within the DHB, rather than the traditional dominant hospital and weak community division, is likely to facilitate this integration.

The new DHBs are building upon the the most striking success story of the 1993 reform, the rapid progress toward integrated care initiated and largely driven by general practitioner/primary care physicians through independent practitioner associations (IPAs), more recently called primary care organizations (PCOs). PCOs now represent more than 85% of primary care physicians. Driven by professional rather than financial goals they have become accountable for quality and financial management of pharmaceutical and laboratory and other services within a broad clinical governance framework (Malcolm and Mays, 1999). They have established a wide range of joint venture relationships with secondary care providers in a move toward integrated care as extensive as in any country including the United States.

This chapter describes the historical background to these developments and discusses and analyzes the major policy issues underlying the changes and the lessons that have been learned from the reform process. Readers from a North American perspective will note that financing is considered to be only one aspect of the New Zealand system. The policy and organizational issues discussed are similar to many developments now widely labeled managed/integrated care in the United States and elsewhere.

II. NEW ZEALAND BACKGROUND

Table 1 shows some basic background information about New Zealand and its health and health services (Ministry of Health, 1999; Statistics New Zealand, 1998). Of particular importance from a population perspective is the indigenous Maori population constituting 15.2% by ethnic classification. Major developments, which have recognized the disadvantaged status of this population, not only in health but in many other aspects, have occurred over the last decade. There has been increasing recognition by the government of the 1840 Treaty of Waitangi signed between the British crown and the Maori people (James, 1992).

Health status measures such as life expectancy tend to be in the poorer half of the range for OECD countries, although significantly improving in recent years (Table 2). According to the World Health Report 2000 (WHO, 2000) New Zealand's overall health system performance rated only 41, below countries of a similar type. However, there are questions about the methods used to establish this rating. New Zealand's GDP per capita in 1998 at $US17,857 was in the lower half of the OECD range (Table 3). However, as will be discussed later, public sector restructuring and deregulation has led to a significant turnaround in New Zealand's economic performance with falling unemployment and recent

Table 1 Basic Background Information About New Zealand and Its Health and Health Services

Population 2001	3.848 million
Maori population 1998, %	15.2
Population over 65 years 1998, %	11.6
Life expectancy 1996–97, years	
Total male	74.3
Total female	79.6
Maori male	67.2
Maori female	71.6
Short-term beds/1000 population	2.1
Long-term care beds/1000 population over 65 years	16
Doctors per 1000 population	1.9

Source: Ministry of Health, 1999; Statistics New Zealand, 1998.

annual growth rates in GDP in the upper OECD range (New Zealand Government, 1998).

Health services are funded very largely from central government taxation, which, together with other sources of finance, e.g., social welfare, local authority, etc., add up to 77.5% being derived from government in 1998/99 (Ministry of Health, 2000). However, this represents a significant shift away from the 88.0% health expenditure from government in 1979/80 with a marked trend toward privatization of this expenditure during this period.

Table 2 Comparison of New Zealand's Health Statistics with Selected OECD Countries 1997

Country	Life expectancy males, years	Life expectancy females, years	Overall health system performance rating
Australia	76.8	82.2	32
Finland	73.4	80.7	31
New Zealand	73.9	79.3	41
Sweden	77.1	81.9	23
Switzerland	75.6	83.0	20
United Kingdom	74.7	79.7	27
United States	73.8	79.7	37

Source: WHO, 2000.

Table 3 Comparison of Health Financing Indicators for New Zealand as Compared with Selected OECD Countries, 1998($USPPP)

Country	GDP per capita, $US	Per capita health expenditure, $US	Health expenditure as percentage of GDP, %	Percentage publicly funded health expenditure of total, %
Australia	23,518	2,040	8.7	69.3
Finland	21,440	1,600	7.4	75.5
New Zealand	17,857	1,440	8.0	77.1
Sweden	21,117	1,820	8.6	83.0
Switzerland	26,774	2,740	10.2	70.3
United Kingdom	21,117	1,450	6.9	84.9
United States	30,579	4,270	14.0	46.7
OECD mean	—	—	7.9	74.4

Source: Ministry of Health, 2000.

A. New Zealand Health System Background from 1974 to 1984

Current health reforms in New Zealand must be seen against the background of organizational change that has been developing over a long gestational period (James, 1992; Malcolm, 1989, 1990, 1995). The conception of the current system may be considered to have been initiated in 1974 with the third Labour Government's White Paper (Department of Health, 1975). Given the close similarities between the New Zealand and the U.K. system it was not surprising that the government saw, as a model, changes taking place at that time in the U.K. national health system (NHS). What was proposed was essentially a bureaucratic structural model that sought to strengthen the public sector and to diminish and marginalize the private sector including the fee-for-service-funded general practitioners.

However, the consultative process took the emphasis away from a focus on institutions to services or programs as the organizational entities for the planning and eventually the management of the health system (Malcolm, 1990). This approach recognized the need to accommodate, in a pluralistic system, public, private, and voluntary services within this service or program framework. Area health boards, serving defined populations, would be responsible for all public sector services including those provided by the existing hospital boards and the public health functions of the Department of Health. They would also be responsible, as umbrella organizations, for the coordination of the activities of public, private, and voluntary sector services. Services, i.e., medicine, surgery, care of the elderly, mental health, etc., would provide the framework within which this integration would be achieved.

It was not until 1983, 9 years after this prolonged consultative process, in which progress was described as "glacial," that the Area Health Boards Act was passed. However, this merely permitted, rather than mandated, the formation of area health boards. At the same time, population-based funding of the existing hospital boards was introduced. This provided for the allocation of taxation-derived, central-government funding to the existing hospital boards, to provide hospital and related services for their geographically defined populations. The only significant exception to this was general-practice-related services subsidized centrally by fee-for-service payments, supplemented by targeted part charges.

Population-based funding led to a major redistribution of funds over subsequent years from overfunded to underfunded boards (Malcolm, 1989). The first area health boards were formed in 1985 but progress continued to be slow until 1989.

B. The Fourth Labour Government Reforms

Up until 1994, New Zealand's political system had been dominated by a conservative, purportedly right-wing national government for the best part of three decades. The political system had features of Eastern European countries with large and increasing government involvement in all aspects of the economy, which was heavily regulated. New Zealand, which in the 1940s had one of the highest per capita incomes in the world, had seen its prosperity gradually dwindle in comparison with other countries, a prosperity that was increasingly propped up by government borrowing (James, 1992).

In 1984, the fourth Labour government was elected and set about a vigorous transformation of the state sector. All commercial activities of government, i.e., post office, banks, etc., were corporatized and, in many cases, subsequently privatized (Boston et al., 1991). Financial markets were deregulated, wage and price controls scrapped, and almost all subsidies abolished. Major efficiencies were achieved in the provision of state sector services although at a cost of increasing unemployment (James, 1992).

Later in its 6-year term the government turned its attention to the core and social activities of government including health (Malcolm, 1989, 1990). In 1988, the State Sector Act, applying to all aspects of state services including health, legislated the implementation of general management, similar to the 1984 Griffith reforms in the NHS. It effectively abolished the "tribal" hierarchies of nursing, medicine, and business within existing boards and implemented general management at the top of the organization and service management at the operational level. In most areas one person was made accountable, at all levels, for the provision of services rather than the "triumvirate" of doctor, nurse, and administrator as existed previously.

In 1989, the associated Public Finance Act was passed, which shifted the focus of financing of government services from inputs to outputs and outcomes. The government, under the Act, became the purchaser of goods and services produced by different government departments. Thus the concept of purchasing rather than merely funding public services was legislated into government activity in 1989.

The area health board system with 14 boards, partly appointed and partly elected, was finally formed in 1989 from the amalgamation of 28 hospital boards and 15 health development or public health units of the Department of Health. Boards were expected in that year to cope not only with the massive amalgamation process, but also with major restructuring following the State Sector Act, as well as a 10% budget restraint. Furthermore, they were required to implement the New Zealand Health Charter, which, in line with the shift toward outcomes, specified the goals and targets area health boards were required to achieve to improve the health of their populations (Minister of Health, 1989; Beaglehole and Davis, 1992). Not surprisingly, such a massive change process was associated with a significant downside including major redundancies, lengthening waiting lists, decline in staff morale, and deferred maintenance and capital development.

C. The 1990 National Government Reforms

The new system was just beginning to settle down when New Zealanders, disillusioned with 6 years of a reforming Labour government, elected, despite election promises, an even more reforming National government. After 3 months in office it announced major slashes in benefit payments and set up, behind closed doors, a task force to report on further health sector reforms. Major motivating concerns were the massive government budget deficit and therefore a desire to cut government expenditure. Public support was sought on the grounds of lengthening waiting lists for elective surgery and the need for greater efficiency in health spending.

Major reforms were announced at the time of the July 1991 budget in the so-called "Green and White Paper" (Upton, 1991). Despite a massive decline in popularity in the polls, linked to other radical policies, e.g., major cuts to benefit payments, the government abolished all area health boards, appointing commissioners, in most cases existing chairpersons, to run the boards. The "green" or consultative aspects of the paper related to two issues. First, public opinion was sought on whether health services should continue to be funded by taxation or, alternatively, some form of social insurance. Second, public input was requested on the concept of core health services, i.e., those services that, in terms of community priorities, the government should continue to fund. Public submissions were strongly supportive of the continuation of taxation funding while there was little support for a narrow concept of core health services of the Oregon type.

The "white" part of the paper, i.e., explicit government policy, included the formation of regional health authorities (RHAs) to be established as integrated purchasers of all health services, public, private, and voluntary, funded by government. These authorities were to be established and operational by July 1, 1993. Purchasers would be split from providers in a model similar to that introduced in the U.K. reforms. The government proposed that the public health functions, as contrasted to the personal health functions, would be separated out in a Public Health Commission, which would purchase public health services through a public health agency. Health care plans would be set up as competing purchasers to keep RHAs "on their toes."

Three groups of providers were envisaged. First, there would be crown health enterprises, (CHEs), largely formed from existing area health boards. These would be owned by a Minister for Crown Health Enterprises thus completing the separation of purchasers and providers largely in the hospital-based system. Second, community trusts could be formed in which small rural communities could opt to manage their own hospital and related services. The third group of private providers, largely general practitioners, would have services purchased from them by RHAs instead of being passively funded centrally. Furthermore, and most controversially, part-charges based on family income were announced with an increase in the existing charges for general practitioner consultations and pharmaceuticals, and for the first time, they were applied to public hospital services.

D. Implementation of the 1991 Reforms

The government moved rapidly to follow the formidable timetable it had set for itself for the implementation of the reformed system. A top-level board, with a strong commercial emphasis, the National Interim Provider Board, was appointed to define the concept of the CHE, and to sound out the limits of competition and commercialization of these almost entirely publicly funded and owned services. It reported in 1992 recommending configuration of CHEs with each CHE having a strong competitive, commercial, or business-like emphasis in the way that it provided services, including making a profit despite being almost entirely government funded (National Interim Provider Board, 1992). The recommendations led to the formation of 23 CHEs from the subdivision of the 14 area health boards.

The four RHA establishment boards were appointed early in 1992 and by early 1993 had appointed staff and were developing a purchasing strategy within guidelines issued by government (Minister of Health, 1994). From July 1993 they became responsible for the purchasing of all health services for their regions.

The Public Health Commission was formed but the public health agency was dropped and the Commission largely purchased its services through RHAs. Health care plans, proposed as competing purchasers to the RHAs, were dropped.

E.   Modifications to the 1991 Health Reforms

The 1991 reforms, implemented in 1993, led to widespread continuing professional and public criticism. The first casualty of the new structure was the announcement by the government late in 1994 that the Public Health Commission, established to be responsible for national public health policy and the purchasing of public health services, would be abolished in 1995. The reasons for this abolition were twofold. First, the Commission, although successful in achieving a high profile for public health services and the publication of more than 20 policy advice papers, was seen to be fragmenting the formulation of national public health policy.

It thus appeared to be in conflict, in this role, with that of the Ministry of Health, which retained a significant responsibility for the regulatory aspects of public health. Another, and perhaps even more fundamental, problem was the fragmentation of the purchasing of public health services between the Ministry of Health with its regulatory responsibilities, the Public Health Commission, and the RHAs through which this purchasing function was in large part channeled (Malcolm and Barnett, 1994; Malcolm et al., 1996; Barnett and Malcolm, 1998).

With the abolition of the Commission, national public health policymaking was integrated at the national level and purchasing of public health services integrated at the regional level through RHAs. The provision of public health services remained largely integrated within CHEs.

Reservations continued to be expressed about the place of competition in the new system. Although competition, as part of the new market model, was expected to be the main incentive to efficiency, its scope remained limited and its downside, especially the focus on financial outcomes, was in conflict with the strong professional motivation of New Zealand's clinicians to whom patient care outcomes are the "bottom line." These and other problems, including a serious lack of public support for the reforms, led to further changes, which will be discussed in more detail below.

F.   Core Services and the National Health Committee

One of the important new structures in the 1993 reforms was the National Advisory Committee on Core Health and Disability Support Services. This committee reported directly to the Minister of Health. It was originally envisaged that the committee would define those services to which New Zealanders were entitled and therefore, by exclusion, those to which they we were not entitled and that this process might follow the Oregon model. However, after 2 years of consideration and much detailed work, the committee explicitly rejected the notion of a simple list of core services (National Advisory Committee, 1994). It was felt that it was not an appropriate way to describe people's eligibility or access to publicly funded health and disability support services. Such an approach did not have the capacity to tailor services to meet the needs of individuals and communities.

More appropriately, the committee decided that access to publicly funded services should be described in terms of the circumstances in which they should be publicly funded, that is: when they provide a benefit, when they are cost effective, when they are a fair and wise use of available resources, and when they are in accord with the values of communities (National Advisory Committee, 1994). The committee defined the range of core services to include broad categories such as primary care, mental health, disability support, secondary and tertiary medical and surgical services, etc. Within these broad divisions much of its work was focused on the development of guidelines for specific conditions such as the management of raised blood pressure, hormone replacement therapy, coronary artery bypass grafts, liver transplants, the treatment of drug and alcohol problems, etc.

With the rejection of the notion of a core list of health services and the abolition of the Public Health Commission, the Core Services Committee was restructured in 1995 to include a broader advisory role to the Minister on all aspects of health services including public health, personal health, and disability services. Given this wider function, the committee was renamed the National Advisory Committee on Health and Disability, or, in short, the National Health Committee. The committee continued its major focus upon advising the Minister on health and disability service priorities with a particular focus on the development of guidelines for a wide range of services.

G. The 1996/97 Coalition Government's "Reforms" of the Health Reforms

During 1996 it became apparent that there was widespread dissatisfaction, both public as well as professional, with the health reforms implemented in 1993. Despite government expectations that managed competition, at least between providers, would reduce costs and improve access, actual expenditure increased by 20–30%. Waiting lists had increased by 50% since 1993.

The reforms were not only failing to achieve their goals. They had failed politically in that health had become the top concern of the electorate. They had also failed professionally, with professional incentives, at least in the hospital sector, being replaced by commercial incentives. Physicians in hospital-based services were being marginalized in many situations to a mere technical role. The reforms were also failing organizationally in that competitive strategies were tending to fragment the collaborative relationships so essential in good health care. This experience, along with the recognition of the failure of competition generally, led the new government elected late in 1996 to discard managed competition in favor of managed collaboration (Ministry of Health, 1996a).

The key aspects of the 1997 reform process included the replacement of the four RHAs by a single national funder, the Health Funding Authority (HFA). The CHEs were replaced by Hospital and Health Services (HHSs). These bodies became more community focused and their primary goal was to improve the health status of the identified community they served.

H. The 1999/2000 Labour Government Reforms

A new Labour government elected in 1999 swept away the last vestiges of the reforms implemented in 1991. Modeled to some extent on the area health boards of the previous decade, the 2000 reforms are based upon a district health system. With two amalgamations the 23 HHSs have now become 21 district health boards

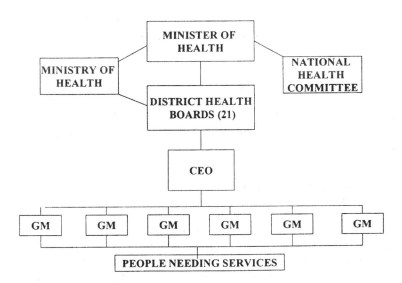

Figure 1 Basic structure of the New Zealand health system as being implemented in 2001 showing the relationships between the Minister of Health, the Ministry of Health, and the 21 district health boards. DHBs will be responsible for providing and funding of all health and disability services within their districts, both government and nongovernment. It is expected the chief executive (CEO) and general management (GM) structure will follow a population service model rather than a hospital framework orientation, as discussed in the text. This is much more likely to facilitate integration than the traditional hospital/community services division.

(DHBs). Boards will be partly elected and partly appointed. Funding will be based on their defined populations, which range from 30,000 to over 400,000. The Health Funding Authority was abolished at the end of 2000 and its funding of nongovernment services is being devolved to the DHBs. Thus the new DHBs appear to be the most integrated of district health systems of any country. They will be primarily responsible for the health status of their populations and for the provision of hospital and community services, primary and secondary care, personal and public, government and nongovernment, personal and disability services. The structure of the new district health board system, now being implemented, is shown in Figure 1.

Of particular importance in the new arrangements will be the integration of the primary health care sector through primary care organizations (PCOs). These are now well organized and significantly involved in the overall management of quality and cost in primary health care services (Malcolm et al., 1999).

III. HEALTH EXPENDITURE IN NEW ZEALAND

As an OECD country, New Zealand contributes to and conforms with OECD categories and definitions of health expenditure based upon the Abel-Smith classification developed for WIIO in 1963 (Ministry of Health, 1999). This includes within health expenditure all health services concerned with the promotion of health and the prevention, diagnosis, and treatment of disease, whether acute or chronic and whether physical or mental in origin, and the rehabilitation of people incapacitated by disease or injury.

Table 4 shows the sources of expenditure on health services in New Zealand comparing the years 1979/80 with 1998/99. The Abel-Smith classification divides sources into two categories, government and private. Within the government category the main source of expenditure is Vote:Health expenditure, which is taxation-derived and administered by the Ministry of Health. An increasing source of expenditure in the last decade has been the Accident Compensation and Rehabilitation Corporation (ACC) established in 1973 as a no-fault social insurance system for the payment of the health costs and compensation for accidents. ACC income is derived from employment sources and premiums paid by motor vehicle owners.

Other government expenditure includes health-related expenditure incurred by other government departments such as Social Welfare, Defence, Education, etc. The final government category is local government authority expenditure, which includes health protection activities such as water chlorination and fluoridation.

Private expenditure is divided into three categories: household, private out of pocket for pharmaceutical and medical equipment; health insurance covering

Table 4 Sources of New Zealand's Health Expenditure by Percentage Comparing 1979/80 with 1998/99

Government	1979–80, %	1997–98, %
Vote:Health	80.5	68.9
Accident Compensation (ACC)	0.7	4.7
Other government	6.6	3.2
Local authority	0.3	0.7
Total public/government	88.0	77.5
Private-nongovernment		
Household	10.4	15.9
Health insurance	1.1	6.2
Charitable	0.4	0.4
Total private-nongovernment	12.0	22.5
Total all sources	100.0	100.0

Source: Ministry of Health, 2000.

largely the cost of general-practice-related expenditure and elective surgery; and finally, expenditure raised by voluntary and charitable organizations for health related services.

Table 4 also shows the major trends in these categories of expenditure over the 17 years of the study period. There has been a major decline in direct government expenditure through Vote:Health, from 80.5% to 68.9% as progressive governments sought to control health expenditure. As a result there has been major cost shifting to other expenditure sources, especially the private sector and ACC. The increase in the latter costs can be attributed to significant cost shifting within the general practice sector, which, because of low government subsidies, succeeded in passing an increasing proportion of consultation costs onto ACC through problems associated with the "fuzzy" definition of an accident.

In the private sector, household expenditure, as a result of government controls on health costs, has increased significantly with major increases incurring in health insurance. However, as indicated above, this covers only a limited range of services and is still only 6.2% of total expenditure sources. The net result of these changes is a major decline in public expenditure from 88.0% to 77.5% over the period. This public/private mix is still slightly above the 1997 OECD mean of 74.4% with a range of 46.7% in the United States to 92.1 in the Czeck Republic (Ministry of Health, 2000).

New Zealand's total health expenditure in 1997, expressed in purchasing-power parities (PPP), was $US1,440 per capita constituting 8.0% of GDP. This figure has increased variably from 7.0% in 1980 and is now above the OECD

Table 5 Real (Inflation Adjusted) Trends in Total Health Expenditure 1979–1999

Financial year	Percentage increase over previous years
1979/90 annualized	1.8
1990/91	1.0
1991/92	3.7
1992/93	2.3
1993/94	5.9
1994/95	3.1
1995/96	1.5
1996/97	4.7
1997/98	6.6
1998/99	3.9
1990–1999 annualized	3.1

Source: Ministry of Health, 2000.

mean of 7.9%. Again, percentages vary widely from Turkey at 3.5% to the United States at 14.0% (Ministry of Health, 2000).

Trends in inflation-adjusted total health expenditure from 1979/90 to 1998/99 are shown in Table 5 (Ministry of Health, 2000)). The rate of growth in expenditure over the last 9 years has greatly exceeded that of the previous decade. This is associated with the health reform of the 1990s, which not only incurred significant costs but led to increasing community expectations. They were also associated with an improving economy allowing increases in health expenditure to cover a backlog of deferred maintenance of equipment and buildings as a result of rigid controls on hospital-related expenditure over the decade ending in 1993. A particular and continuing problem, as discussed later, has been the open-ended fee-for-service-related expenditure associated with primary medical care, especially for pharmaceutical laboratory services.

Table 6 shows categories of total health expenditure for 1998/99 divided into institutional, community, public health, and other categories of expenditure. Of this expenditure 35.6% was on public and 15.0% on private institutional care, totaling 50.6%. Community care totaled 42.8%. Attempts have been made to address this perceived imbalance over the years with some success, although progress has been much slower than desired. It has been exacerbated recently by significant increases in acute medical admissions, a problem that has also been noted internationally.

Table 6 Categories of Total Health Expenditure
1998/99 by Total ($NZ'000) and Percentage of Total

Category	Total, $m	Percentage
Institutional public	2981	35.6
Institutional private	1255	15.0
Community care	3585	42.8
Public health	227	2.7
Teaching and research	225	2.7
Total	8376	100.0

Source: Ministry of Health, 2000.

IV. ORGANIZATIONAL DEVELOPMENT AND FINANCING IN THE HEALTH SECTOR

It has already been indicated that it will be apparent to those from other countries, such as the United States, that New Zealand's health reforms have been focused more broadly than just upon how health services should be financed. These organizational developments have much in common with moves toward managed care in the United States. New Zealand's health care policymakers have recently been actively considering the concepts of managed care, or, more recently, integrated care, albeit within public sector financing.

Much more attention has therefore been given both in New Zealand and in this report to organizational issues and how the system should be managed. These issues have been considered from both a macro and a micro-organizational perspective. This section considers organizational development as well as the performance of providers both before and subsequent to the implementation of the most recent reforms.

New Zealand health providers may be categorized into four broad groupings the defining characteristics of which are summarized in Table 7 (Malcolm and Barnett, 1994). The first of these, and the one subject to most reform in recent years, may be broadly described as hospital and related services. The services provided by this group include all publicly owned hospital services complemented over the last two decades by an increasing range of community-based services. These services are almost totally both government-owned and government-financed.

An important and distinguishing characteristic of this grouping in New Zealand is that these services, although inclusive of hospital services, are almost entirely population-based; i.e., they serve a geographically defined population. As such, they were managed until 1993 by largely elected hospital or area health boards and financed on a population basis. This grouping is complemented by an entirely nongovernment-owned and -financed set of elective surgical and other specialist services.

The second broad grouping of health services in New Zealand is that of primary care/general practice and related services (Malcolm and Barnett, 1994; Malcolm, 1993; Malcolm et al., 1999). The scope of these services is essentially primary medical care together with associated investigations such as laboratory and radiology and the prescription of pharmaceuticals. The key provider in this grouping is the general practitioner together with practice nurses, midwives, pharmacists, physiotherapists, and, in a few situations, social workers.

The services provided within this grouping are all characterized, almost without exception, as privately owned but publicly subsidized to a widely varying extent. For example, general medical services (GMS) benefits, along with pharmaceutical subsidies, are subject to part-charge related to age and income. Financing is on a fee-for-service basis. These services are complemented to a varying extent by nongovernment agencies such as the Plunket Society, providing preventive child health services, and the Family Planning Association.

Apart from relatively minor changes in subsidy levels, this grouping has remained unchanged for decades. However, reform in these services is being seen, to an increasing extent, as the key to the current reform process with major developments toward budget holding and increasing accountability (Malcolm, 1995; Malcolm and Barnett, 1994; Malcolm and Powell, 1996; Malcolm and Mays, 1999; Malcolm et al., 1999)

The third broad grouping is disability services (Ministers of Health and Social Welfare, 1992). The defining characteristic of these services is that they provide long-term care, usually preceded by assessment and rehabilitation. Another important characteristic is that these services are provided by a wide range of agencies, both government and nongovernment, the latter including both private, or for-profit, and voluntary, or nonprofit. The government-owned hospital and related services sector described above overlaps to a some extent with services included in this sector, particularly long-term hospital care for the mentally ill and mentally handicapped.

A fourth grouping of health services are those that come under the heading of public health. These services, inclusive of health protection and health promotion, were largely provided until 1989 by the district offices of the Department of Health, when they were fully and largely successfully integrated into the area health board system. However, the 1993 reforms separated these out, at least contractually, under the purchasing role of the Public Health Commission (Barnett and Malcolm, 1997; Malcolm et al., 1996).

As will be discussed later, these divisions are being brought together at the district level through DHBs. However, the extent to which effective integration will be achieved will depend largely upon the quality of the relationships developed between clinicians in these divisions.

Table 7 Main Defining Features of the Four Health and Related Service Divisions ($NZ1 = $US 0.54, 1998)

Feature	Hospital and related services	Primary care services	Disability services	Public health
Scope	Hospital and community based services	General practice, pharmaceutical, and diagnostic	Assessment, rehabilitation, and long-stay care	Health protection and health promotion
Ownership	Mainly government but small private specialist component	Almost entirely private	Mixed government and nongovernment agencies	Mainly government
Source of financing	Almost entirely government, insignificant fee contribution	Largely government subsidized with one-third private fees	Mixed government and charitable donations	Almost entirely government
Type of financing	Capitation for geographically defined population	Fee-for-service but moving to capitation	Individual social welfare entitlement	Contracting with Public Health Commission
Annual government expenditure	$4.0 billion	$1.0 billion	$1.0 billion	$200 million

	Boards of governance	Individual entrepreneurs now working through primary care organizations	Mixed including boards of governance	Mostly within HHSs/DHBs
Organization	Boards of governance	Individual entrepreneurs now working through primary care organizations	Mixed including boards of governance	Mostly within HHSs/DHBs
Focus of service	Population served	Individual patient	Individual client	Population served
Main type of care	Acute	Episodic	Long-term	Public health
Community involvement	Significant	Increasing	High	High
Budgetary control	Tight with little growth in last decade	Continuing demand-driven fee-for-service but moving to capitation	Related to individual entitlement	Tight but expanding
Emphasis	Specialized medical treatment	Generalist	Maximizing independence and autonomy	Improving public health
Place of the hospital	Central but decreasing	Useful	Seen as threatening	Minimal
Preventive public health focus	Increasing	Important	Essential	Essential
Main barrier to access	Long waiting times	Financial	Lack of community services	Finance

Source: Based on Malcolm and Barnett, 1994.

A. Hospital and Related Services: Macro-organizational Development

Macro- organizational developments in this sector have been largely described above. The CHEs varied widely in the extent to which they followed the commercial model expected of them on the one hand, or continued the population-based community focus of the area health boards they replaced on the other. To a large extent this was dependent upon the attitudes of the boards and the CEOs appointed by these boards. Boards with little understanding of the "health business," and with CEOs from a commercial nonhealth environment, attempted to implement the more commercial market-orientated aspects of the 1993 health reforms. In attempting to follow a business model they sought to maximize the "products" they could sell to the purchasing RHAs. Some RHAs deliberately fostered such a commercial product-line approach based upon DRGs.

However, this led to fundamental conflicts. The first of these was that RHAs were funded on a capitation basis. They were thus incapable of responding to the business approach of CHEs, which focused upon expanding the business on a "fee for service" basis through a price/volume approach. These problems were compounded in almost all CHEs by a rapidly, and in some cases dramatically, increasing volume of acute admissions to which CHEs could only respond by cutting back on elective surgery even though they had been paid on a price/ volume approach for the undertaking of such surgery.

Other CHEs, more familiar with the "business of health," tended to follow the principles and practices developed from their predecessor area health boards. They were more sensitive to the need to involve professionals, especially physicians, in decision making through service management structures described below.

B. Intraorganizational Development

Of particular importance, not only from a New Zealand but also an international perspective, has been the extent of organizational change that occurred within the area health boards and continued through into some CHEs. This development is widely called service management, the decentralization of general management, not to the traditional divisions of hospital- and community-based services, but to service groupings such as medicine, surgery, mental health, elderly, primary care, etc. (Malcolm, 1989, 1990, 1991; Malcolm and Barnett, 1995; Malcolm and Mollett, 1992).

Progressive organizational development over the last decade, together with the area health boards' population-based approach to the provision of services, resulted in decentralization of the general management concept to the service level with institutions being largely replaced by services as the key organizational entities of the area health boards (Malcolm and Barnett, 1995). For example, in a 1993 survey of top managers of the area health board system, 60% agreed with the statement that "our hospitals are no longer organisational entities and services have replaced hospitals as the key organisational units" (Malcolm and Barnett, 1995). Only 22% disagreed.

Service divisions may be population-based with each service providing for the comprehensive care of a set of problems for a defined population. Thus each service can include both institutional and community aspects as well as developing relationships with services provided by the public, private, and voluntary agencies. Services managers are budget holders for achieving a balance between these various components. Furthermore, services may be accountability structures for quality assurance, team building between professional disciplines, involving doctors and other professionals in an accountability framework for the outcomes of their clinical decisions and for achieving service goals within a given budget (Malcolm and Barnett, 1994).

These arrangements were largely taken over and further developed by some CHEs as evidenced from a study of their organizational charts and a 1994 survey of chief executives (Barnett and Malcolm, 1997). Some CEOs indicated that they were no longer managing hospitals and that services had almost completely replaced hospitals as organizational entities. It appeared that the more commercial thrust of the CHEs was congruent with a greater degree of accountability such as is being achieved through service managers.

On the other hand, there was also a shift back toward a more controlling, managerialist posture from some top managers, in part because of their recent entry to the health sector and therefore a lack of understanding of the critical role of medical decision making and accountability. This was compounded by continuing financial contraints on CHEs, which reinforced a controlling management style. The most successful CHEs were those with a good working relationship between management and medical staff. Most of the commercial-sector CEOs appointed in 1993 left in the first 2 years. Many were disillusioned with their difficulties in managing the health sector for which their business experience had ill prepared them.

C. Financial Performance: Hospital and Related Services

A detailed study of the hospital sector in 1993 concluded that there had been no real increase in expenditure on this sector over the period 1983–1992 (McKendry et al., 1994). These results were not surprising. This sector of the health system was subject to progressive and, at times, major financial constraints over this period. Service management, as a strategy for involving medical staff in decision making about budgetary cuts, is considered by some to be a major factor in facilitating this reduction in expenditure (Malcolm and Mollett, 1992).

This overall financial restraint has had a powerful effect in restraining the growth in demand that has been a feature of health systems in other countries. There have been significant shifts in the balance of services from inpatient to day patient, outpatient, and community care. An important consequence, and one that has led to mounting public and political concern, has been the rise in the number of people on waiting lists for elective surgery. It has been argued, perhaps justifiably, that the progressive restraints on public hospital spending have been the major factor in this growth.

However, others, including the government in 1993, used the size of the waiting lists as the principal justification for the current reform process. They argued that the problem was more a matter of organization and management than resource availability. The debate relating to this issue continued around discussion papers produced by the National Health Committee.

D.   Performance and Organization of the Primary Medical Care Sector

Primary medical care type services are provided by about 3200 general practitioners, some solo, but the majority now in group practices. Although attempts were made, with the passing of the Social Security Act in 1938, to make these services a full charge on government, preferably by capitation, such moves were strongly resisted by the medical profession as being a threat to their independence. As a result, general practitioners remained free to charge their patients on a fee-for-service basis over and above the general medical services (GMS) benefit or subsidy.

By contrast with the hospital and related services sector, this sector has been largely uncontrolled in its expenditure and utilization over the decade to 1992 (Malcolm, 1993). Expenditure increased, on average, at a rate of 6.1% annually. In recent years large increases have continued to occur especially with pharmaceuticals and laboratory tests.

Table 8 shows the actual expenditure in 1997/98 associated with general practice, including the costs of primary medical care and associated services generated by each general practitioner and the cost per consultation and per registered patient (Malcolm et al., 1999). It will be noted that the cost for a consultation of $50.4 is heavily weighted with the prescription cost, $28.8. These figures are indicative of the levels of expenditure for which general practitioners are assuming responsibility as they move into budget holding.

This increasingly important sector of the New Zealand health system has remained almost totally unreformed for decades. However, the establishment of RHAs in 1993, with fully integrated budgets that include this sector, meant that a new and more decentralized negotiating body was available for general practitioners who wished to develop new initiatives.

Table 8 Government Expenditure $NZ on Primary Medical Care and Related Services for 1997/98 (GST exclusive)

Category	Total expenditure, $ million	Expenditure per consultation, $	Expenditure per capita, $	Expenditure per GP, $
General Medical Services	202.1	10.6	53.2	65,161
Accident Compensation Corporation	75.4	4.0	19.8	24,323
Laboratory	102.2	5.4	26.9	33,968
Pharmaceutical	546.6	28.8	143.8	176,323
Practice nurse	32.0	1.7	8.4	10,323
Total	958.2	50.4	252.2	309,097

Source: Malcolm et al., 1999.

A number of primary care pilot projects were established during 1991, most of which had a budget-holding approach to the management of primary care resources and were related to the GP fund-holding experience in the U.K. (Glennerster and Matsaganis, 1993). This led to the establishment of an increasing number of independent practitioner associations (IPAs) throughout the country (Malcolm and Powell, 1996, 1997). A survey was undertaken of these and other forms of general practice organization in 1999, described generically as primary care organizations (PCOs) (Malcolm et al., 1999). This showed that some 84% of general practitioners were members of 21 IPAs (2642 GPs), 10 contracting practices (86 GPs), two loose networks (389 GPs), and 28 community-owned services (60 GPs). PCOs have provided for the progressive buildup of collective accountability arrangements among general practitioners for the provision of their services. Included are alternatives to GMS such as capitation, fostering of age/sex registers and patient registration, accountability for quality-of-care issues, information systems, and progressive budget holding for laboratory, pharmaceuticals, maternity, and secondary care services (Malcolm et al., 1999).

An advanced example of this development is Pegasus Health in Christchurch. Including almost all general practitioners in the city in its 240 membership, it has been paying its members for GMS, immunization, and other related subsidies. It serves a population of some 280,000. Its goals are to build up standards and quality of general practice, to shift the balance of services from secondary to primary care, and to improve the health status of the people of Christchurch. It was successful in laboratory budget holding with 23% savings achieved and sustained over a 2-year period. Savings were put into alternative services for patients (Kerr et al., 1996). More recently it has moved to a global budget of over $80 million with a strong emphasis on reducing acute hospital admissions. Similar developments are occurring in other IPAs.

A range of other primary care initiatives have also been fostered and stimulated by the current reform process. These include contracting, including budget holding, by community groups and Maori organizations and the progressive empowering of communities both to provide and to contract for their own primary health care services (Malcolm et al., 1999). There is increasing evidence that Maori and the low-income populations are seriously underserved with primary and medical care and related services.

There is also increasing evidence that underutilization at the primary care level leads to overutilization at the hospital inpatient level, particularly for problems such as heart disease, asthma, and diabetes (Malcolm, 1996; Pomare et al., 1995).

E. Organizational Development in the Disability Sector

At the time of the publication of the Green and White Paper, the government called for wide debate as to where disability services, which include long-term care of the elderly, mental health, and physical and mental disability, were to be located in the new system. The government had made a firm decision that these services, provided by both health- and social-welfare-funded agencies, should be fully integrated under one authority, the options being either the new RHAs or, alternatively, under a social welfare umbrella. This was to follow the principle that there should be a single purchaser of these services that would be separate from the providers.

After a broad-based consultative process regarding these options the government announced late in 1992 that, on balance, RHAs would be in the best position to ensure that people obtained the most appropriate services and to make the most cost-effective choices. The government acknowledged the concerns of many disability agencies that integration into health might not be in the best interests of those who were disabled. This was on the grounds that the health sector was felt to be dominated by hospitals and those agencies with a sickness emphasis, rather than a normalization and autonomy emphasis. Integration was therefore to be phased in over a period of years and disability funding protected through "ring fencing" over this period.

The newly formed RHAs were given the responsibility of deciding how this integration could be best achieved. A major problem facing the authorities was the problem of purchasing an integrated or seamless service from among the multiplicity of providers including the CHEs, which dominated this service provision. Integration of purchasing did not guarantee integration of provision and seeking competitive bids from providers resulted in the RHAs purchasing fragments of care rather than an integrated seamless service. Furthermore, the need for assessment and rehabilitation prior to contracting out for the care of the disabled person could be adequately carried out by few agencies other than CHEs.

Although many CHEs were divesting themselves of long-term care for age-related disability, there was still the major problem of the dominant institutional mode of care in some CHEs for the mentally disabled, reinforced by strong staff resistance to institutionalization. The progress toward an integrated service concept of these services will be discussed later.

F. Organizational Development in the Public Health Sector

Reference has already been briefly made to this fourth category of health services in New Zealand public health services. An important focus of health care policy over the last two decades has been the desire to integrate services previously provided by hospital boards, largely secondary care services with some associated community services, with those provided by the Department of Health, again largely public health services, including health protection and health promotion (Barnett and Malcolm, 1998; Malcolm et al., 1996). The formation of area health boards during the 1980s, culminating in 1989, integrated at least under one organizational umbrella these two separate categories of services. With the promulgation of the New Zealand Health Charter and the 10 national health goals, it was expected that the area health boards would enable the operational integration of these two aspects of care. This would enable boards, through both personal and public health services, to improve the health status of New Zealanders focusing on the 10 national health goals.

To some extent this integration succeeded, although success varied widely within area health boards depending upon the interest of boards and their top management (Malcolm and Barnett, 1995). Improving the health status of the community was beginning to be seen as the business of both personal and public health providers. However, follow-up studies of this integration revealed a serious siphoning off of public health resources subsequent to the 1989 integration. This led the government, in the formation of the Public Health Commission, to separate the purchasing of public from personal health services within a defined public health service budget that would ensure its protection even though most public health services were to continue to be provided by the successors of the areas health boards, the CHEs.

A survey in 1994 of both CHE CEOs and public health service managers within CHEs indicated strong support from both groups for public health services remaining within the CHE organizational structure (Barnett and Malcolm, 1998; Malcolm et al., 1997). Of 21 CEOs of CHEs providing public health services the majority saw both health protection and particularly health promotion as being part of their core business. The majority also felt that personal and public health services should be integrated within CHEs although acknowledging that functional integration was still limited.

This organizational integration of public and personal health services appears to be unusual, if not unique, within health systems. For the most part public health services are provided by separate public health departments of state or local governments. While the importance of public health services and their contribution to improve health status and populations has been extensively discussed in the literature, there is relatively little analysis of the merits or demerits of their integration with personal health or treatment services (Barnett and Malcolm, 1998). The New Zealand experience over the last decade supports the necessary integration of public health policy formation at a national level and the integration of provision at the service level. With the formation of DHBs, and their primary goal of improving the health status of their defined populations, public health services are likely to find themselves more highly valued as part of an integrated provider system.

One of the developments emerging from the primary care sector is an increasing interest in public health services, particularly those services most closely associated with primary care services such as immunization, cervical screening, etc. This interest is being expressed by PCOs, community trusts, and other groups, especially Maori, who are deeply concerned about improving the poor health status of their people.

V. TRENDS IN HEALTH CARE POLICY

The above discussion and analysis of health provider organization and performance provides a background to the further consideration of major policy trends in health provision that have occurred, and are continuing to occur. This further discussion and analysis will be considered under the headings of health system goals, equity, financing, decentralization, integration, access, and accountability.

A. Health System Goals

Over the past two decades there has been a progressive shift toward improved health status for New Zealanders as the overall goal of the health system. However, the 1991 National Government's Green and White Paper saw some backtracking from the government being accountable for improving the health status of New Zealanders. It stated that the government "has an interest in effective public health activities because they reduce publicly-funded treatment costs" (Upton, 1991).

Events since then appear to have firmed up the government's commitment to improving health status as the overall goal of the health system.

The abolition of the Public Health Commission in 1995, with the integration of policymaking at the national level and of purchasing of public health services at the regional level, strengthened the importance of improvement in health status as the overall goal of the health system. This was again reinforced by an important publication of the Minister of Health late in 1995, *Advancing Health in New Zealand*, which indicated the government's firm commitment to this as the overall goal of the health system (Minister of Health, 1995).

This was further stressed by the 1996 Coalition Government's policy statement in which the health system, including CHEs, were to focus on improving health outcomes and achieving health gains. To an increasing extent PCOs have also indicated their commitment to improving the health of the populations they serve.

Provision of public health services will now be firmly located within the new DHB system. The integration of policymaking at the national level, and provision by DHBs in conjunction with their primary care services, will lead to a clearer definition of accountability for the achievement of improved health status at all levels of the system.

B. Policies Relating to Equity

Associated with policies toward improving health status there have been increasing policy directions about equity and a redirection of provider services, first, toward meeting the needs of disadvantaged groups, and second, shifting policy toward a more balanced health system (Minister of Health, 1994).

Of particular importance in recent years has been the increasing recognition of the disadvantaged status of Maori and the importance of the Treaty of Waitangi in empowering Maori to take responsibility for the provision of their own health services. Maori initiatives, started under the previous Labour Government, were continued and even strengthened under the 1990–1996 National government despite its apparent right-wing policies (Minister of Health, 1994).

All governments in recent years have been committed to a policy of shifting the emphasis away from hospital to community-based care and from secondary to primary care. However, progress toward this shift has been slow, and if anything, a reversal has occurred with the increasing demands for hospital-based services, particularly for acute care.

The development of PCOs has presented a new strategy for making this shift. Most PCOs are committed to not only the integration of primary care services but also the integration of primary and secondary care. They have an expectation that better access to and utilization of primary care will result in fewer referrals to secondary care and reduced admissions to hospitals (Malcolm et al.,

1999). A number of initiatives are now emerging in New Zealand to achieve this goal.

For example, discussions between Pegasus Health, representing most primary care physicians in Christchurch, and the geriatricians within the local hospital services led to the formation of Eldercare Canterbury, which brings all agencies providing care of the elderly services together into an integrating framework. This is only one of many primary and secondary care integration initiatives largely promoted by PCOs. DHBs are expected to promote the continued development of these initiatives as a key role in their integrating relationships.

C. Trends in Financing Policies

While in the 1970s hospital boards were funded on the basis of services provided, financing policies shifted in the early 1980s to financing on the basis of meeting the health service needs of their geographically defined populations. This led to progressive shifts toward equity in financing from over- to underfunded boards. This policy continued into the 1993 reforms. The RHAs were funded on a population and needs-related basis with fully capped budgets for the four sectors of the health system described above, including general practice and disability services, by the 1996/97 financial year (Minister of Health, 1994).

Thus RHAs were put at risk of having to contain demand-driven expenditure particularly related to general practice, e.g., pharmaceuticals. As a result there was a shift in RHA policy toward purchasing general practice and related services on a capitation and capped budget basis. Purchasing policy is also recognizing the importance of general practice/primary health care purchasing secondary services, also within a capped and capitated budget.

However, the attempt to finance CHEs on a contestable, price-volume basis led to a serious conflict of goals between the three groups of stakeholders. RHAs, and the HFA, were primarily concerned with containing expenditure within capped and capitated budgets. CHEs and their successor HHSs, in attempting to achieve government goals of being a successful business, sought to promote rather than contain utilization. The third major group of stakeholders, the clinicians, were primarily concerned with achieving better health outcomes and had relatively little interest in either commercial goals or cost containment. This serious conflict of goals had its most public expression in Canterbury Health leading to the Stent Report in 1998 (Health and Disability Commissioner, 1998).

The formation of DHBs, with integrated, population-based funding, and with a clear congruence of goals between all stakeholders, is leading to a resolution of the conflicts that plagued the New Zealand health system throughout the 1990s. There is now a clear commitment by government, and supported by PCOs, to population-based funding of primary care (Minister of Health, 2000a). The new government announced its primary care stategy in 2000, which focused strongly on capitated funding of PCOs. There has been strong support from the primary care sector for this strategy.

The major problem in financing now is not about the type of financing. It is about how to resolve the major inequities in funding between DHBs and, within DHBs, funding inequities within and between PCOs as they move to capitated, needs-based funding inclusive of the services listed on Table 8.

D. Decentralization

Decentralization of decision making has been a particular feature of most health systems, including New Zealand's. Within the New Zealand health sector, decentralization has paralleled that of the public sector generally.

Rondinelli (1981) describes four stages of decentralization, each a progressive distancing of decision making from government. The first, *deconcentration*, is intraorganizational with a shift of responsibility to lower levels within the organization. This has been particularly important in New Zealand within the hospital and related services sector, as discussed above, with service management, the shift of responsibility to clinical groupings with the objective of making health professionals, including doctors, more accountable for the outcomes of their decisions.

The second stage of decentralization is *devolution*, or political decentralization, the shift of responsibility to elected bodies, such as local government authorities. In New Zealand health services for many decades have been provided by elected hospital and area health boards. This responsibility has now shifted to the third stage, what Rondinelli calls *delegation* or, more appropriately within the New Zealand context, *corporatization*, a commercial model that has been generally applied widely throughout the state sector to the commercial activities of government such as forestry, post office, etc. The CHEs were an attempt to fit health services into this model with boards appointed by and financed by government, but required to operate as far as possible within a commercial mode.

The fourth and the most distancing of responsibility from government is *privatization*. This also has been a particular feature of the decentralization process in New Zealand as well as many other countries with the selling off of public assets to the private sector. New Zealand has been through an ongoing debate about the extent to which health services could be privatized particularly with the current reform process.

There has been a progressive shift toward privatization over many years in the long-term care of the elderly sector with hospital and area health boards. Most CHEs divested these services to the nongovernment sector where the evidence seems clear that such care is more efficient and more appropriately provided by nongovernment agencies with government subsidies. There is also a continuing policy shift in the provision of primary care services to community agencies, including Maori.

E. Integration

Integration of health services has been a particular policy trend in New Zealand as well as many other countries. Integration, which is based on the integrity of the health needs of individuals, families, and communities, seeks to achieve two goals, the provision of "seamless" care and the avoidance of cost shifting, which can be a particular problem when health services are financed from different sources.

Integration within the New Zealand health sector has been a progressive process over the last two decades (Malcolm, 1991). Integration has also been a particular feature of the current health reform process with the bringing together of all health and related funding, including general practice and disability services. New Zealand, with its RHAs, the HFA, and now DHBs, may well have one of the most integrated purchasing systems of any country. Of particular importance is the integration of primary and secondary care services with the development toward integrated care based upon primary care services. In this respect, New Zealand's integration of the purchasing function is probably more advanced than that of the U.K. NHS.

The service model including service management has been an important feature in the process of integration. The service view has been recognized by managers as being a fundamental framework for the integration of hospital and community-based services, personal and public services, of disciplines and of clinical services with resource management (Malcolm and Barnett, 1994). Service management in New Zealand, as compared with resource management in the United Kingdom, has focused more on service than resource outcomes.

The service framework has also been important in the integration of the government with nongovernment sectors. A particular problem of integration in other countries, including the United Kingdom, has been the attempt to integrate agencies, a process that has generally been unsuccessful. However, the service framework provides, not for the integration of agencies, but that part of agencies that identify with and claim ownership of common problems, share a common purpose, and use common resources, e.g., care of the elderly, mental health, etc. Although area health boards had not been particularly successful in this aspect of integration, where service management had been in operation, it was recognized widely to be an important framework for this process (Malcolm and Barnett, 1994).

Integration of the disability sector into health has been debated at some length over the last decade. It has been recognized that the service concept provides an important framework for such integration, e.g., all aspects of a mental health service to bring together the mental health services provided by different organizations, government as well as nongovernment, within a collaborative framework. Eldercare Canterbury, described above, in an important example of integration in the care of the elderly.

One of the important lessons over the past decade is that integration of purchasing may lead to disintegration of provision, especially if purchasing is based on a competitive model. Whereas disability services were becoming more integrated under the area health board system, they became seriously fragmented as a consequence of the commercially oriented purchasing functions implemented during the 1990s. The major challenge now facing DHBs is how to build relationships between the government and nongovernment sectors and to resolve the conflicts and barriers created by the commercial environment of the last decade.

Another concern of the disability sector is that DHBs, despite their population and health outcome orientation, are still largely hospital focused. Although the care of the elderly funding will be devolved to DHBs, there are uncertainties about how the services to the younger physically disabled will be funded.

The key next step in the process of integration is of primary and secondary care. The development of PCOs has provided the structure for integration of primary care providers, both primary care physicians with one another and now, for many PCOs, with other primary care professionals such as nurses and midwives. This integration is seen to provide the platform from which to begin the development of integrating relationship with secondary care professionals. DHBs now provide an appropriate structure through which PCOs, and other nongovernment sector services, can come together within an integrating framework. However, building relationships based on confidence and trust will be the major challenge in the immediate future, especially resolving the question of hospital dominance in DHB priorities (Malcolm, 2000).

F. Access

Improving access to health services has been an important policy goal of health systems in most countries including New Zealand. A primary motivating factor in the current reforms has been the problem of access, particularly to elective surgery, a problem increased by the continuing financial pressures on the hospital and related sector over the last decade. Access to the elected surgical services has been markedly improved in the last 2 years but more as a result of organizational strategies, including and developing systems for priority setting, and increased funding, rather than commercial approaches.

Access is also a problem for the primary-medical-care-related sector, limited more by financial barriers than availability. Access to more appropriately provided community services is the key access problem in long-term care and disability services. Of particular concern is the problem of access to primary and community services by disadvantaged groups including Maori. Recent evidence has confirmed that their utilization of primary care services is only a fraction of that of the average New Zealander (Malcolm, 1996; Malcolm et al., 1999). This almost certainly leads to a high and inappropriate use of hospital inpatient services. Although finance is only one aspect of the access problem, others being cultural, low expectations, and geographical barriers, the new government has announced a policy of providing free primary care services, including pharmaceuticals for children 5 years and under.

Budget holding also has the potential to improve access to primary care and related services. Already those PCOs in budget holding have used savings to reduce the cost of pharmaceutical charges and of access generally to primary care. Integrated care, built up from PCO budget holding, is now widely seen to be an important strategy for securing better access to both secondary and primary care and for ensuring a shift of resources currently tied up in institutional care to community-based services to improve this aspect of care in the disability sector. Pegasus Health in Christchurch, with its global budget (see above), is beginning to demonstrate the effectiveness of this approach.

G. Accountability

A key problem facing most health systems is the problem of the accountability of health professionals, particularly doctors. Decentralization of management to clinical groupings, such as medicine, surgery, mental health, etc., appears to have been more successful in New Zealand in comparison with other countries (Malcolm and Barnett, 1994, 1995). Furthermore, the model being implemented in New Zealand is a general management as well as a clinical directorate model (Malcolm and Barnett, 1995).

In the 1993 survey of top managers 71% said they were operating a general management model and only 9% a clinical directorate model (Malcolm and Barnett, 1995). The clinical directorate model appears to be more applicable to the subgroupings of medicine, surgery, etc., i.e., cardiology, orthopedics, etc. The formation of CHEs may have reinforced and further developed this model of accountability in that it appears to be congruent with the more business-like approach to management being adopted by CHEs. The 1994 study of the organizational arrangements, including interviews with CHE chief executives, confirmed that the service management structure had been widely adopted (Barnett and Malcolm, 1997). However, there are recent indications that real decentralization to service groupings has not been so widely implemented.

While the medical profession has been somewhat ambivalent about accepting this accountability, there is also an emerging recognition that there can be no power without accountability. With capped and, in most boards and CHEs, shrinking budgets, there has been a fear among doctors that decisions about priorities will be made without their involvement, a major threat to their power.

The main problem with service management, as perceived by clinicians, appears not to be the principle, which is well accepted. It is the reluctance of some general and service managers in practice to devolve real decision-making responsibility to clinicians. Part of the problem is also the inadequacy of the information systems to monitor expenditure and performance. Although New Zealand has made major progress with information system development in recent years, there is much to be done to implement effective systems at the operational level.

As already discussed, major progress is occurring toward greater accountability by primary care physicians for not only laboratory and pharmaceutical services but also other services including secondary care services. Primary care physicians have rejected not only risk sharing for such budget holding but also profit sharing. In other words, they see themselves as managing large and increasing amounts of public money for which they accept collective professional accountability. They are motivated by professional goals, i.e., to improve outcomes for patients through better management of public health resources, rather than being motivated by personal gain (Malcolm, 1997; Malcolm and Mays, 1999).

Each of the policy trends discussed above has been firmly built into the new Labour government's health policy. The New Zealand Health Strategy, announced by the government in 2000, strongly stresses health system goals, equity in access, capped population-based funding, and the decentralization of operational decision making to DHBs (Minister of Health, 2000b). There is a full commitment to integration and the DHB system is likely to be the most integrated of any national health system. The government has stressed accountability at all levels including of clinicians for the quality of the health care they provide.

VI. PURCHASERS, PROVIDERS, AND THE MARKET: DID IT WORK?

The short answer to this question is "no." In establishing a purchaser/provider split, the government sought to achieve two goals. The first was that the purchaser, not being the owner of its own health services, would be free to choose among competing providers as to where it could obtain the best value for the health and disability services dollar. Competition would be a significant spur to efficiency.

The second goal, and the perhaps of more importance, was that the RHAs, and the HFA as purchasers, would be in a better position to negotiate contracts with the independent general practitioners than either the Department of Health or area health boards, both bodies being seen by general practitioners as being unsympathetic to general practice.

There was widespread criticism of the performance of RHAs and the HFA from CHEs/HHSs, PCOs, and other nongovernment agencies and from the Ministry of Health (1995). Early criticism of the purchaser/provider relationship came from within the system. A letter to the Ministers of Health, Crown Health Enterprises, and Treasury from the Chair of the Crown Health Enterprises Chairs' Consultative Committee, comprised of the chairs of all the CHE boards, frankly criticized the dominant role of the RHAs. The relationship is described as a "master-servant" one, that "the nature of the relationship is evolving into a holding company subsidary type structure" (Malcolm and Barnett, 1994).

These views were supported from the 1994 interviews of CEOs (Barnett and Malcolm, 1997). Relationships, both professional and the performance of RHAs, were generally rated as less than satisfactory. There had been a centralization rather than decentralization of power with Treasury and the Ministry of Health continuing to play a dominant role in CHE decision making despite their independence as business entities, a concern also expressed by the above letter to the ministers.

IPAs/PCOs complained about the slowness of RHAs to come up with constructive policies. Progress toward greater accountability in general practice, including budget holding, has been delayed more by RHA and HFA intransigence than general practitioner interest in such developments. Nongovernment agencies including community groups have expressed similar concerns about difficulties in securing helpful, good working relationships from RHAs/HFA.

Evidence has already been advanced above to indicate that in few respects have the early expectations of the 1991 Green and White Paper and the structures and processes implemented in 1993 been achieved. The two primary goals of the 1993 reforms, better access at lower cost, have not been achieved. Rather, costs escalated to the same extent as the savings anticipated and access, as measured by the numbers on waiting lists for elective surgery, has increased by 50%.

With the emphasis upon the purchaser/provider split leading to confrontational rather than collaborative relationships between purchasers and providers it was not surprising that the main victims of the 1996 government's health policy were the RHAs. They were faced with implementing a fundamentally flawed philosophy, establishing a competitive market, which, by its very nature, diminished the collaboration so fundamental in good health care.

A primary goal of government with respect to RHAs, and hence of RHAs themselves, became cost containment. This was a view of RHAs expressed repeatedly by both providers and consumers. As new organizations, implementing a new policy, they could draw on little information and even less experience. They were faced with major risks in a new contracting relationship with well-established providers who had a great deal more political leverage.

On the other hand, RHAs made this task difficult for themselves including pursuing confrontational rather than a collaborative relationships with providers.

To protect themselves against risk RHAs entered into what is now recognized to have been grossly excessive and legalistic contracting processes resulting in protracted and intensely frustrating negotiations. The RHA's focus upon containing costs and reducing their risks led to a focus on immediate rather than strategic goals. They were required to consult on and purchase services to meet the needs of the communities they served. While more community consultation was undertaken than at any time in the country's health system history, this may have raised community expectations for services that, within strapped budgets, could not be delivered.

However, RHAs could claim some important achievements. Much better information became available about the health needs of communities and ways of addressing these health needs. A more business-like approach to contracting was established. There has been greater accountability of providers. The major developments in general practice through PCOs would not have occurred without the existence of RHAs. Entrepreneurial behavior had been encouraged. Despite claims of excessive bureaucracy, RHAs/HFA transaction costs amounted to only about 1.5% of total health expenditure, a small investment when it is considered that savings through PCOs and other new contracting relationships could well be 5–10% (Malcolm et al., 1999).

The HFA, formed in 1997, attempted to bring together the successes of RHAs and build upon what was achieved by RHAs within a national framework. But the first year of its operation was clouded by attempts to integrate what in many cases were widely divergent RHA policies. Many staff were losing their jobs and could therefore not be expected to function effectively. In 1999, the widely expected change of government and Labour's policy of abolishing the HFA led to further dysfunctioning. The limitations of the purchaser-provider split remained. With the election of the new government, and the abolition of the HFA, in late 2000, the fundamental flaws of the 1990s system have been finally discarded.

The major concerns within the health sector now center upon the extent to which the Ministry of Health, with its integrated policy and funding functions, will carry on some of the dysfunctionality of the HFA. Many of the staff of the HFA have been taken on by the Ministry of Health so that a culture of central control might persist. The new government's policy statements have indicated that it is prepared to devolve functions to DHBs to the extent that they demonstrate competence in managing the government sector together with their contracting relationships with nongovernment sector.

At present many questions remain as to how effective this new system will be. It appears that no other country has implemented a district health system that both provides government and funds nongovernment services. The potential conflicts are those that the purchaser-provider split was set up to avoid. But the success of the new system will depend largely on the quality of the relationships built between clinical health professionals at the district level. Important progress in this relationship building is leading to some optimism that the new BHB system will succeed.

VII. CONCLUSION

This chapter has described and analyzed the ongoing and escalating reform process within New Zealand's health system. It will be noted that some of these developments are similar to those occurring within the general concept of managed/integrated care within the United States. A population basis for health services delivery, integration of care, especially between primary and secondary, greater medical accountability, and incentives to promote such accountability are particular features of health policy development in New Zealand. This analysis has therefore considered issues broader than financing. It has also analyzed major policy themes of a health status orientation, access, decentralization, integration, access, and accountability.

If the hospitals, within the new integrated DHB system, can be replaced as organizational entities by services, a new framework for integration, accountability, and decentralization may emerge that would be appear to have international significance. Also important in the New Zealand experience is the shift away from fee-for-service to capitation and capped budgets. Related to this is the move toward a population focus with population-based funding and the provision of comprehensive services that are also population-based.

Of particular importance from the New Zealand experience has been recognition by physicians, especially in primary care, that accountability for costs as well as quality of care enables physicians to achieve savings within capped budgets and to use these savings for alternative services. This accountability, far from disadvantaging physicians, is seen to be a means of achieving real power in medical decision making. The importance of physician participation in the management of resources as well as quality of care is also emerging elsewhere as a key factor in health system reform (Shortell et al., 1995). The recent formation of CLANZ (Clinical Leaders Association of New Zealand) offers an important opportunity to develop clinical accountability for both clinical quality and cost in operational settings (CLANZ, 2000).

Also important has been the demonstrable failure of the commercial model with its financial incentives as a significant factor in improving health system efficiency and access. Integrated care with incentives based not on competition but on medical accountability and collaboration is becoming a significant factor in improving health system efficiency and access. Integrated care, with these incentives, could be the most effective solution to health system problems both in New Zealand and perhaps internationally (Berwick and Smith, 1995, Malcolm, 1997; Malcolm and Mays, 1999).

These developments may be more readily achievable in a small country. Shifts toward an integrated, population-based health system with organized and managed primary health care as a key service entity, which is developing well in New Zealand, could be of international significance in the search for more effective and efficient health systems.

REFERENCES

Barnett P, Malcolm L (1997). Beyond ideology: the emerging roles of New Zealand's Crown health enterprises. Int J Health Serv 27(1):89–108.

Barnett P, Malcolm L (1998). To integrate or deintegrate? Fitting public health services into New Zealand's reforming health system. Eur J Public Health 8:79–86.

Beaglehole R, Davis P (1992). Setting national health goals and targets in the context of a fiscal crises: the politics of social choice in New Zealand. Int J Health Serv 22(3): 417–428.

Berwick D, Smith R (1995). Cooperating, not competing, to improve health care. Br Med J 310:1349–1350.

Boston J, Martin J, Pallot J, Walsh P (1991). Reshaping the State. New Zealand's Bureaucratic Revolution. Auckland: Oxford University Press.

CLANZ (2000). Clinical Leaders Association of New Zealand, www.clanz.org.nz.

Department of Health (1975). A New Health Service for New Zealand. Appendix to the Journal of the House of Representatives. H-23. Wellington: New Zealand Government.

Department of Health (1992). Whaia te Ora Mot te Iwi: Strive for the Good Health of the People. Wellington: New Zealand Government.

Glennerster H, Matsaganis M (1993). The UK health reforms: the fundholding experiment. Health Policy 23:179–191.

Health and Disability Commissioner (1998). Canterbury Health Limited. Auckland.

James C (1992). New Territory: The Transformation of New Zealand Society 1984–1992. Wellington: Bridget Williams Books.

Kerr D, Malcolm L, Schousboe J, Pimm F (1996). Successful implementation of laboratory budget holding by Pegasus Medical Group. NZ Med J 109:354–357.

Malcolm L (1989). Decentralisation trends in the management of New Zealand's health services. Health Policy 12:285–299.

Malcolm L (1990). Service management: New Zealand's model of resource management. Health Policy 16:255–263.

Malcolm L (1991). Service management: a New Zealand model for shifting the balance from hospital to community care. Int J Health Planning Management 6:23–35.

Malcolm L (1993). Trends in primary medical care expenditure in New Zealand 1983–1993. NZ Med J 106:470–474.

Malcolm L (1995). Implementing managed care in New Zealand. In Jolt H, Leibovici M. Managed Care Principles and Practice. Philadelphia: Hanley & Belfus, pp 199–210.

Malcolm L (1996). Inequities in access to and utilisation of primary medical care services for Maori and low income New Zealanders. NZ Med J 109:356–358.

Malcolm L (1997). GP budget holding in New Zealand: lessons for Britain and elsewhere. Br Med J 314:1890–1892.

Malcolm L, Barnett P (1994). New Zealand's health providers in an emerging market. Health Policy 29:85–90.

Malcolm L, Barnett P (1995). Decentralisation, integration and accountability: a study of New Zealand's top health service managers. Health Services Management Res 8(2): 121–134.

Malcolm L, Barnett P, Nuthall J (1996). Lost in the market? A survey of senior public health service managers in New Zealand's ''reforming'' health system. Aust NZ J Public Health 20:567–573.

Malcolm L, Mollett J (1992). Implementing the post-hospital age. Health Services Management (June):17–21.

Malcolm L, Powell M (1996). The development of independent practice associations in New Zealand. NZ Med J 109:184–187.

Malcolm L, Mays N (1999). New Zealand's independent practitioner associations: a working model of clinical governance? Br Med J 310:1340–1342.

Malcolm L, Wright L, Barnett P (1999). The development of primary care organisations in New Zealand. Ministry of Health, Wellington, December, www.moh.govt.nz/publications/online.

Malcolm L, Barnett P, Wright L (2000). Emerging clinical governance: developments in independent practitioner associations in New Zealand. NZ Med J 113:33–36.

Malcolm L (2000). The organisation and management of primary health care in district health boards. Health Manager 7:8–11.

McKendry CG, Howard PS, Carryer BE (1994). New Zealand Hospital Sector Performance 1983–92. Ministry of Health, 1994.

Ministers of Health and Social Welfare (1992). Support for Independence for People with Disabilities: A New Deal. Wellington: New Zealand Government.

Ministry of Health (1995). Review of 1994/95 RHA Contracting. Wellington.

Ministry of Health (1996a). Health Policy Agreement, http//www.moh.govt.nz/policy.htm Wellington.

Ministry of Health (1996b). Sustainable Funding Package for the Health and Disability Sector. Wellington.

Ministry of Health (2000). Health Expenditure Trends in New Zealand 1980–99. Wellington.

Minister of Health (1989). New Zealand Health Charter. Wellington: New Zealand Government.

Minister of Health (1995). Advancing Health in New Zealand. Wellington: Ministry of Health.

Minister of Health (2000a). The Future Shape of Primary Health Care. Wellington, 2000, www.moh.govt.nz.

Minister of Health (2000b). New Zealand Health Strategy. Wellington, 2000, www.moh.govt.nz.

National Advisory Committee on Health and Disability Support Services. (1994) Core Services for 1995/96. Wellington: Ministry of Health.

National Interim Provider Board (1992). Providing Better Health Care for New Zealanders. Wellington: New Zealand Government.

New Zealand Government. (1998). Budget 1998, Wellington.

Pomare E, Keefe-Ormsby V, Ormsby C, Pearce N, Reid P, Robson B, Watene-Hayden N (1995). Hauora: Maori Standards of Health III: A Study of the Years 1970–1991. Wellington: Wellington School of Medicine.

Public Health Commission (1994). Our Health Our Future. Wellington.

Rondinelli DA (1981). Government decentralisation in comparative perspective: theory and practice in developing countries. Int Rev Admin Sci 47:133–145.

Shortell SM, Gillies RR, Devers KJ (1995). Reinventing the American hospital. Milbank Q 73:131–160.

Statistics New Zealand (1998). New Zealand in Profile 1998, Wellington.

Upton S (1991). Your Health and the Public Health. Wellington: New Zealand Government.

WHO (2000). World Health Report 2000, Geneva.

World Bank Group (1997). Health Nutrition and Population, Washington.

18

Health Care Financing
A Comparative Analysis

Khi V. Thai
Florida Atlantic University, Fort Lauderdale, Florida
Sharon M. McManus†
Macon State College, Macon, Georgia
Edward T. Wimberley
Florida Gulf Coast University, Fort Myers, Florida

I. INTRODUCTION

In the 29 Organization for Economic Cooperation and Development (OECD) countries, health care financing has become one of the major fiscal concerns of policymakers as health care expenditures became one of several major expenditure categories of the government budget, particularly when most OECD countries have struggled to control their budget deficits. This chapter focuses on health care financing in the OECD countries along two dimensions: (a) revenue sources and overall expenditures for health care, and (b) the mechanisms for reimbursement of hospitals and physicians. However, before addressing the above issues, difficulties and limitations of available health data will be discussed.

II. DIFFICULTIES IN INTERNATIONAL COMPARISONS

As pointed out by Schieber and Poullier (1989), international health care comparisons are difficult for the following reasons:

1. Data are not generally comparable.
2. Systems performance cannot be easily evaluated because of the inability to measure outcomes.
3. It is difficult to measure and control for social, medical, cultural, demographic, and economic differences across countries.
4. Transferability of policies across countries is problematic.

---

† Deceased

The above-cited difficulties are applicable to the OECD countries although they have many characteristics in common. Although all OECD countries are classified by the International Bank for Reconstruction and Development as industrialized and rich (Thai and Sekwat, 1994), per capita incomes differ significantly among OECD countries, ranging from $2807 (lowest) in Turkey to $44,360 (highest) in Luxembourg in 1998 (OECD, 2000). Similarly, life expectancies among OECD countries vary, ranging from 71 (lowest) in Turkey to 84 (highest) years in Japan for women, and from 66.4 (lowest) in Turkey to 77.2 (highest) in Japan for men in 1997 (OECD, 2000). These countries vary considerably, however, in some aspects such as wealth, size of land, languages spoken, and size of population. Moreover, despite their current level of industrialization, all countries have their own institutional and organizational arrangements, as well as their own history. These factors have all contributed to different developments of their health care systems and different ways their health care is financed. As discussed later, health care is financed differently among the OECD countries.

In addition, this study relies heavily on *OECD Health Data* (1994, 1995,2000). However, although OECD has time and resources for health data collections, data on a number of variables are incomplete. Several important variables needed for our comparisons are not available although they are listed in the above publications. General revenue and contributions and payroll taxes, for instance, are listed as two sources of health care financing but data are not available for most countries. In some other instances, data on some other variables such as health tax expenditures and private health insurance are available for a handful of countries and for only a few years, Finally, data on some variables such as total health care expenditures, public and private expenditures, and gross domestic products (GDP), which are relatively complete, are still missing for a few countries as well as a few years. Consequently, tables presented in this article will contain "na," indicating "not available." Those countries that have data for less than 3 study years will not be listed in the tables. These difficulties are described here so that the validity limitations of the data can be recognized.

Compounding the above problems is the lack of comparable data on health expenditures. Indeed, there is variation among the countries examined here regarding the array of health care services purchased or delivered. Some types of services occur in every country, for example, hospital services and physician services. However, some services are purchased through the health care system in a very small number of countries, for example, mental health or substance abuse services.

All countries include hospital services in their consideration of expenditures. The extent of those services and the ownership of the hospitals included do lead to differences. Some systems exclude private hospitals, but consider public hospitals, while others include both public and private facilities. Many countries consider hospital-based specialist physician services as part of hospital services, but some, like the United States, categorize some of these as physician services. In addition, some health care systems include long-term care/nursing home services into inpatient hospital services, for example, as occurs in Finland, Belgium, and the Netherlands, or in rural hospitals in Iceland (OECD, 1999). Other countries, like New Zealand, are encouraging hospitals to become more closely integrated with ambulatory care services and community health services (Malcolm, 1995). In Japan, very small clinics with fewer than 20 beds are considered part of community health care (OECD, 1994). Thus, there is considerable variation in the functions that comprise the term "hospital services," incorporating services at both the input and the output sides, as well as differentiating among the types of ownership of the organization. These differences in definition seem substantial, and increased specificity in terminology, or at least in the recording of which services are so categorized, appears indicated.

All countries also include physician services in expenditures, but as with hospital services, what is defined as physician services evidences variation across these health care systems. Hospital-based physician services are frequently included in inpatient hospital services, as, for example, in Canada (OECD, 1999). While in Japan, as noted above, clinics with fewer than 20 beds are considered as community health services. The differentiation among physician services, community health services, ambulatory care, and primary care may entail the same service but provided in a different location, or the same service delivered by a different type of health care professional (nurse or physician). These inconsistencies in the definition of physician services also render comparisons about expenditures for those services across the various health care systems very difficult.

Most of the OECD countries include pharmaceuticals or drugs within their health care expenditures. The majority of these countries also require some copayments or cost sharing on the part of the consumer in purchasing pharmaceuticals. In Canada, children and senior citizens have no cost-sharing requirements for drugs (OECD, 1999). In Greece, some copayments are required, but specified population groups are exempted from these requirements (OECD, 1999). It is unclear whether the discussions of expenditures for pharmaceuticals includes or excludes over-the-counter, nonprescription medications. Again, these variations in the definition of pharmaceuticals, specification of those included or excluded, and specification of exempted (or not) population subgroups renders the examination of those expenditures very difficult.

Long-term care is another component of health care system expenditures that many countries include. However, in Germany, Portugal, Czech Republic, Denmark, and the Netherlands, nursing home services are not considered as part of the health care system, but rather as part of social services, distinct from health care (OECD, 1999).

Many of the OECD countries provide public health and/or community health services. Here again is a diversity of services within these categories without a clear delineation or distinction between them. Preventive and curative services are included together. School health services, home nursing services, health centers, health clinics, primary care, ambulance services, environmental health, diagnostic services, rehabilitative services, and maternal and child health services all appear within the descriptions of these categories. Such a diverse array of activities within one or two types of expenditure impacts upon the meaning of any attempted comparison here.

Other types of health care services are also included in the determination of expenditures. Dental services are included for Switzerland, Ireland, and a few others, but not in Canada, where only dental services provided by oral surgeons in a hospital setting are included (OECD, 1999). Canada, Denmark, the Netherlands, and Spain include psychiatric or mental health services, and some substance abuse services. Denmark includes physiotherapists, chiropractors, and podiatrists; Switzerland includes physiotherapists and chiropractors; Norway includes physiotherapists (OECD, 1999). The United Kingdom, Canada, and Korea include expenditures for ophthalmic services (including eyeglasses) at least for some specified populations, while the Netherlands includes domiciliary care and services for the developmentally disabled population (OECD, 1999). And in a unique configuration, Finland includes employer-mandated occupational health services, which extends to primary care services (OECD, 1994).

Moreover, despite good efforts of OECD in data collections, data are not available, in some cases, for many countries, and in some other cases, for only some years of a single country. However, data documented by OECD are the most comprehensive source of health data for the OECD countries. This source, as will be presented later, provides useful information for those policymakers who are considering health care reforms.

III. HEALTH CARE FINANCING

In recent years the OECD has utilized a standard framework for comparing the health care financing systems of its member countries (OECD, 1992,1994, 1995,1998,2000). In 2000 this typology was modified to reflect the flows of financing and categories of expenditures. This typology is based upon two dimensions: sources of financing and method of reimbursement. There are two sources of financing: voluntary or private financing, and compulsory or public financing. Along with these, there are four methods of reimbursing providers: out-of-pocket by consumers without insurance; out-of-pocket by consumers reimbursed by insurance; indirectly by third parties through contracts; and indirectly by third parties through budgets and salaries within an organization that provides both insurance and care delivery. Reimbursement in the field of public finance typically means funding from the government; however, in health care, reimbursement generally refers to the funds delivered to the providers of services regardless of the source of those funds. The consumers with insurance may also be reimbursed by insurance if the consumer reimburses the provider directly.

The combination of these two dimensions, sources of financing and method of reimbursing providers, yields eight models as shown in Table 1.

No OECD country utilizes Model 2, as noted above. Moreover, most OECD health systems do not fall into a single model. The United Kingdom and Italy seem to fit Model 7 most closely. However, the Belgian system falls into Models 6 and 8 while the Canadian system fits Model 6 for physicians and Model 8 for hospitals. The French system fits Models 3, 5, and 8. The German system is

Table 1 OECD Framework for Health Care Financing and Reimbursement

Reimbursement	Financing	
	Private/voluntary	Public/compulsory
Out-of-pocket	Model 1	Model 2
Out-of-pocket with insurance reimbursement	Model 3	Model 4
Third-party contract	Model 5	Model 6
Third-party budgets and salaries	Model 7	Model 8

Model 1, voluntary financing with out-of-pocket payment to providers by consumers, where consumers pay providers directly and do not have health insurance.

Model 2, compulsory financing with out-of-pocket payment to providers by consumers, where consumers are taxed and pay providers directly. [This model is "hardly found in practice" (OECD, 1992, p. 19)].

Model 3, voluntary financing with reimbursement of consumers, where consumers who have health insurance pay providers and are reimbursed from the insurance source.

Model 4, public financing with reimbursement of consumers, where there is publicly funded insurance and consumers pay the providers and are then reimbursed by the insurance.

Model 5, voluntary financing and third-party payers or insurers contract with providers for direct payment, where services are usually free to the consumer and providers are reimbursed through contracts with voluntary insurance programs.

Model 6, public financing and insurers contract with providers for reimbursement, where services are usually free to the consumer and providers are reimbursed through contracts with the publicly funded insurance programs.

Model 7, voluntary financing with integrated insurance and provision of services within the same organization, where there are typically global budgets for hospitals and salaried physicians, services free of charge to the consumers, and financing is through voluntary insurance (as in a health maintenance organization).

Model 8, public financing with integrated insurance and service delivery, where there are usually global budgets for hospitals and salaried physicians, services are free of charge to the consumer, and financing is through a publicly funded insurance program.

Source: OECD (1992, 1994)

dominated by Model 6, supplemented by Models 5 and 7. The system in the United States is even more complex, encompassing Model 1 for the uninsured, Model 3 for the insured, and Model 6 for Medicare and Medicaid populations. Adapting the OECD framework, the remaining part of this chapter will examine two dimensions of health care financing in OECD countries: health care financing policy and methods of health care payment.

A. Private Versus Public Funding

OECD countries approach the funding of health services in a range of different ways. Regardless of the mix of these approaches, the public sector provides the majority of health care financing in every OECD country except the United States and Korea (Table 2), but the split between public and private funding has narrowed over the past three decades (OECD, 2000). In countries such as the United States, public financing has increased considerably (see Figure 1). Meanwhile, many countries with high public shares have experienced a slight decline, partly reflecting the widespread introduction of copayments and other forms of cost sharing.

Analysis of the levels of public and private funding of health care expenditures in the OECD countries reveals several important findings, as follows. In a framework of the pure public goods/pure private goods continuum in the theory of public finance, some goods such as defense and education are provided purely or wholly funded by government at one end of this continuum, and some goods such as household appliances are provided purely or wholly by the private sector or market at the other end of the continuum. In a pure communist system, where the market system does not exist, health care is considered as a pure public good, financed by the government and provided by the government. However, in OECD countries, this continuum does not exist since in no country is health care provided and funded wholly by government or by the private sector. In almost all OECD countries, health care is close to the pure public goods side of the continuum in terms of public/private funding. Indeed, in the last 33 years, except in Korea and the United States, health care expenditure in all the OECD countries was mainly financed by the public sector (Table 2). However, there is a great variation in the funding composition among the OECD countries. At the extremes are the United States and Luxembourg and the Czech Republic. In 1998, in the United States public expenditures for health care were at 44.7% of total U.S. health care expenditures while public expenditures for health care in Luxembourg and the Czech Republic were at 92.3% and 91.9% of total health expenditures, respectively (Table 2). High levels of public expenditures for health care can also be found in Belgium, where 89.7% of total health expenditures was publicly funded in 1998. In general, in all OECD countries, except the United States and Korea, over 50% of health care costs are covered by government (Table 2).

Table 2 Public Expenditure[a] on Health as a Percentage of Total Health Expenditure, 1970–98

Rank	Country	Public expenditure on health, % of total health expending				Absolute change in %
		1970	1980	1990	1998	1970–98
1	Luxembourg	88.9	92.8	93.1	92.3	3.4
2	Czech Republic	96.6	96.8	96.2	91.9	−4.7
3	Belgium	87.0	83.4	88.9	89.7	2.7
4	Iceland	81.7	88.2	86.5	84.3	2.6
5	Sweden	86.0	92.5	89.9	83.8	−2.2
6	United Kingdom	87.0	89.4	84.2	83.7	−3.3
7	Norway	91.6	85.1	83.3	82.8	−8.8
8	Denmark	85.2	87.8	82.6	81.9	−3.3
9	Japan	69.8	71.3	77.6	78.3	8.5
10	New Zealand	80.3	88.0	82.4	77.1	−3.2
11	Spain	65.4	79.9	78.7	76.9	11.5
12	Hungary	NA	NA	NA	76.5	NA
13	France	74.7	78.8	76.9	76.4	1.7
14	Finland	73.8	79.0	80.9	76.3	2.5
15	Ireland	81.7	81.6	71.7	75.8	−5.9
16	Germany	72.8	78.7	76.2	74.6	1.8
17	Switzerland	63.9	67.5	68.4	73.4	9.5
18	Poland	NA	NA	91.7	73.3	NA
19	Turkey	37.3	27.3	61.0	72.8[d]	35.5[d]
20	Austria	63.0	68.8	73.5	70.5	7.5
21	Netherlands	69.5	71.1	68.7	70.4	0.9
22	Canada	70.2	75.6	74.6	69.6	−0.6
23	Australia	67.4	62.5	67.4	69.3	1.9
24	Italy	86.9	80.5	78.1	68.0	−18.9
25	Portugal	59.0	64.3	65.5	66.9	7.9
26	Mexico	NA	NA	58.8	60.0*	NA
27	Greece	42.6	55.6	62.7	56.8	14.2
28	Korea	1.7	20.7	36.6	45.8	44.1
29	United States	36.4	41.2	39.6	44.7	8.3
EU unweighted average[c]		74.2	78.9	78.1	76.3	2.1
EU weighted average[c]		75.9	80.1	78.0	75.3	−0.6
OECD unweighted average[b,c]		69.4	73.4	74.8	74.4	5.0
OECD weighted average[b,c]		56.0	60.9	58.0	59.6	3.6

The heading of the first column reads "Rank in terms of large public share of 1998 total expenditure" with sub-columns "Rank" and "Country".

[a] Public expenditure on health includes general government (central, regional, and local) and social security programs.
[b] OECD averages exclude Hungary, Mexico, Poland, and Turkey, where data are not available for selected years.
[c] Total GDP converted to PPPs is used as weights in calculating weighted averages.
[d]

Source: OECD (2000).

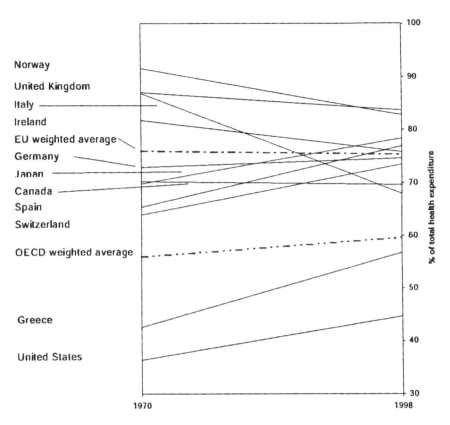

Figure 1 Public share of total health expenditure (1970–1998). Source: Organization for Economic and Co-Operation Development (2000) ⟨www.oecd.or⟩.

B. Trends in Public/Private Funding

From 1970 to 1998, four trends in the public funding share of health care expenditures (from among the then 29 members of the OECD) can be identified: significant increase and decrease, and moderate increase and decrease, as shown in Table 3. In general, Greece, Korea, Spain, and Turkey have increased significantly government share of health care expenditure while the Italian government reduced government share of health care costs. Moreover, nine of 27 countries reduced the government health care burden as a percentage of total health care expenditures.

Noting recent policy trends in several countries, Graig (1993) observed that the health care systems emphasizing government involvement have been moving toward more private sector involvement, while systems emphasizing the private

Table 3 Changing Public Health Care Spending of OECD Nations, 1970–98

Trend	Nations
Significant increase	Greece, Korea, Spain, Turkey
Significant decrease	Italy
Moderate increase	Luxembourg, Belgium, Iceland, Japan, France, Finland, Germany, Switzerland, Austria, the Netherlands, Australia, Portugal, United States
Moderate decrease	The Czech Republic, Sweden, UK, Norway, Denmark, New Zealand, Ireland, Poland,[a] Canada

[a] Estimated by the authors.
Source: Derived from OECD (2000).

sector have been experiencing increasing levels of government involvement. Examination of 11 countries with public share of over 80% of total health expenditure (Table 3) shows that eight countries reduced public share of their total national health care costs. These countries include the Czech Republic, Sweden, the United Kingdom, Norway, Denmark, New Zealand, Ireland, and particularly Italy.

Similarly, all health care systems that are more heavily funded by the private sector have experienced increasing levels of government funding involvement. All four countries (Greece, Turkey, Korea, and the United States) whose health care systems received the smallest shares of public funding in 1970 experienced increased shares of public funding (Table 2). As shown in Table 4, government in four countries (Greece, Turkey, Korea, and the United States) covered less than 50% of total health care costs in 1970, but in 1998, Korea and the United States were the only countries in the OECD where government share of total health care expenditures remained below 50%. Analyzing the trend of health care financing in Korea, it is expected that within a few years, more than 50% of health care costs will be covered by government.

C. Sources of Funding

What are the sources of public and private funding? Are there any significant changes in those financing sources in the past three decades among the OECD countries? In *OECD Health Data* (OECD, 2000) three sources of health care finance are cited: general government revenue, health payroll taxes, and private health insurance. In addition to the above sources, there are:

out-of-pocket payments by consumers who do not have health insurance, and

tax expenditures; that is, instead of directly financing health care costs, the government uses tax provisions to induce certain health care activities.

Table 4   Health Care Financing Funding (% Public Funding)

Tier	% of public funds	1970	1998
1	Over 90	The Czech Republic, Norway	Luxembourg, the Czech Republic
2	80–89.9	Luxembourg, Belgium, Iceland, Sweden, UK, Denmark, New Zealand, Ireland, Italy	Belgium, Iceland, Sweden, UK, Norway, Denmark
3	70–79.9	France, Finland, Germany, Canada	Japan, New Zealand, Spain, Hungary, France, Finland, Ireland, Germany, Switzerland, Poland, Turkey, Austria, the Netherlands
4	60–69.9	Japan, Spain, Switzerland, Austria, the Netherlands, Australia	Canada, Australia, Italy, Portugal, Mexico
5	50–59.9	Portugal	Greece
6	Below 50	Greece, Turkey, Korea, United States	Korea, United States

Source: Derived from Table 2 (OECD, 2000).

For example, employer-purchased health insurance for employees is not considered taxable income, and hospitals are able to finance their capital expenditures through tax-exempt bonds. These tax provisions result in tax losses, namely tax expenditures.

Although OECD has tried to compile health data for all OECD countries, data on funding sources are very incomplete. Information from only a limited number of countries and years is available for health payroll taxes and private health insurance (as shown in Tables 5 and 6). For information about general revenue for health expenditure, data from only one country (United States) are available. Thus, it is impossible to conduct a comprehensive analysis of revenue sources for health care funding.

As shown in Table 5, for those countries where data are available, Austria and Canada rely very much on health payroll taxes, which cover, during the 1965–93 period, between 71% and 81.3% of total health costs in Austria, and about 83% in Canada. However, in Ireland and the United Kingdom, where health care costs are heavily covered by government, health payroll taxes are not a major source of public revenue (about 8% or 9% of total health expenditure in Ireland and between 8% and 15% in the United Kingdom). The United States relies much more heavily on health payroll taxes (31.1% of total health expendi-

Table 5 Health Payroll Taxes as a Percentage of Total Health Expenditure

Country	1965	1970	1975	1980	1985	1990	1991	1992	1993
Austria	80	81.3	71.5	75.5	71.7	71.6	71	75	75.7
Canada	na	na	na	na	na	83.1	83.7	83.9	na
Ireland	na	na	na	na	na	8.4	8.4	8.9	na
Switzerland	na	na	na	na	58.5	60	58.8	na	na
UK	13	11	9	8	11	15	15	13	13
US	7.8	26.9	29	30.6	35.2	34.9	33.3	32.4	31.1

na = not available.
Source: OECD (1995), *OECD Health Data.*

ture) to pay its publicly funded health programs (which covered 44% of the total health expenditure in 1993). The gap of 13.9% (44.0% – 31.1%) in public funding is covered by other sources of revenues including general federal and state/local government revenues. Among the six OECD countries where data are available, there is no significant shift in the trend of this revenue source, except the United States, which faced a large increase during the period of 1965 and 1970 when two major publicly funded health programs were initiated, Medicare and Medicaid.

Table 6 Private Health Insurance as a Percentage of Total Health Expenditure

Country	1965	1970	1975	1980	1985	1990	1991	1992	1993
Australia	na	11.8	7.7	15.8	9.3	10.8	na	na	na
Austria	7.8	8.1	7.2	7.6	8.2	7.8	7.7	7.6	7.6
Belgium	na	0.3	0.6	0.8	1.2	1.6	1.6	1.7	na
Canada	na	na	0.7	0.8	1.1	na	na	na	na
Finland	1.1	1.2	0.8	0.8	1.2	1.7	1.5	2	na
France	na	1.4	2.4	1.4	2	2.8	2.9	3.1	3.3
Germany	6.6	6.2	4.6	5	5.2	na	na	na	na
Italy	na	na	na	0.2	0.5	0.9	0.9	1	1.1
Luxembourg	na	na	0.2	0.2	0.3	na	na	na	na
Netherlands	na	14.9	15.6	na	11.6	13.3	na	na	na
New Zealand	na	na	na	na	1.9	3.5	4.8	5.2	6.2
Spain	na	3.3	2.6	3.2	3.7	3.7	na	na	na
United Kingdom	0.6	0.9	0.9	1.2	2.5	3.3	3.4	3.5	3.5
United States	24.1	22.7	24.2	28.7	32.2	34	33.5	33.2	33.5

na = not available.
Source: OECD (1995), *OECD Health Data.*

In almost all the 14 countries for which data are available (Table 6), private health insurance has been an insignificant source of health care financing, except in the United States, where private insurance covers between 27.7% and 34.0% of total health care expenditure. As health care costs in Belgium and the United Kingdom are heavily funded by the public sector, private insurance covered less than 2% of total health expenditure and 4%, respectively, during the 1965–93 period. Private health insurance is also insignificant in Canada, France, Italy, Luxembourg, and Spain. Finally, private health insurance, while small, has been a very stable source of health care financing in the last three decades for these countries, except the United States.

IV. HEALTH CARE SPENDING

In general, there is great variation in total health expenditures and trends in health expenditure among the OECD countries (Table 7). As Table 7 illustrates, the longer history of health care expenditures in OECD nations clearly indicates that health care has significantly increased as a percentage of GDP since 1965. Essentially, health care expenses accounted for less that 4.7% of GDP in 1965 and then increased to the point where it consumed more than 8.3% of GDP by 1998, and for the United States had reached 13.6% of GDP.

A. Sizes or Levels of Health Care Expenditure

The average health care expenditure of 29 OECD countries was 8.3% of GDP in 1998, slightly increasing from 8.2% in 1995 after significant increases during 1965–95. The United States is still, by far, the largest spender on health care, both on a per capita basis and as a percentage of GDP (Table 7). Annual per capita spending on health in the United States amounted to $4178 in 1998, compared with an OECD average of $1891, calculated on a purchasing power parity basis, and a European Union average of $1768. Switzerland was the second highest spender per capita on health care, followed by Norway, Germany, and Canada, while four countries—the Czech Republic, Hungary, Poland, and Korea—each spent less than $1000 per capita on health care.

It is noted that in 1998, while the United States exhibited the lowest commitment to public funding (47.7%), health care expenditures were the highest of all OECD countries ($4178 per capita) (Table 7). According to country classifications in terms of the size of health expenditure as a percentage of GDP, no country falls in Tiers 1, 2, and 3 in 1970, and no country falls in Tiers 8 and 9 in 1998 (Table 8).

If tax expenditures for health care were included, the total health care expenditures of those countries using tax provisions to induce some health care activities would be much larger. Again, OECD (1995) provided very limited data on tax expenditures on health care, available for only six countries and, worse, very few studied years (Table 9). Although the data provided by six countries are not complete, it seems that tax expenditures were used more extensively in the United States and Greece than in Canada, Finland, Ireland, and New Zealand.

B. Trends of Health Care Expenditure

In general, health care expenditures increased rapidly in the OECD countries, from 4.7% of GDP in 1965 to 8.3% in 1998 (Table 7). Health care spending increased by 6.0% of GDP during 1965–70, from 4.7% GDP to 5.0%. It exploded during the period of 1970–80, from 5.0% of GDP to 6.9%, or an increase of 38%. Then, the growth of health spending increased during the decade of 1980–90, from 6.9% of GDP in 1980 to 7.6% in 1990, for an increase of 10.1%. Health care spending increased slightly in the first half of the 1990s, from an increase of 7.9%, from 7.6% of GDP in 1990, to 8.2% in 1995. In general, during the 30-year 1965–95 period, overall health care expenditures in the OECD, as a group of industrialized countries, grew faster than the economic growth. The share of health spending in GDP has stabilized since 1995. Health expenditures are rising in OECD countries at, on average, the same rate as gross domestic product (GDP). In 1998, the latest year for which comparative data are available, average health spending as a proportion of GDP in OECD countries was 8.3% (10.3% when countries are weighted according to the size of their economies), about the same level as in 1995 (Table 7). Between 1997 and 1998, the expenditure ratio was stable in most countries: it rose by 0.3 percentage points or more in only two countries (New Zealand and Norway) and fell by 0.3 percentage points or more in only three countries (Finland, Iceland, and Ireland).

Several common factors (OECD, 1987; Abel-Smith, 1984; Pfaff, 1990) account for the continuing increase in health care expenditures in the OECD countries:

> an expansion in the coverage of health insurance under public and private programs;
> demographic change, particularly the increasing population of elderly in the population;
> general economic inflation;
> increases in utilization of new technologies involving both higher capital expenditures and operational costs; and
> intensity of services as a result of the expansion of doctors per 1000 population.

In the OECD countries, while there are increased health care expenditures and common factors causing the continuing increase of health care spending,

Table 7 Health Expenditure[a] in 29 OECD Countries, 1965–1998

Country	Health expenditure as a percentage of GDP								Change (in %)	Per capita[b] 1998	Rank 1998
	1965	1970	1980	1990	1995	1996	1997	1998			
USA	5.9	7.1	8.9	12.4	13.9	13.8	13.6	13.6	7.7	4,178	1
Germany	5.1	6.3	8.8	8.7	10.2	10.6	10.5	10.6	5.5	2,424	4
Switzerland	3.8	4.9	6.9	8.3	9.6	10.1	10.3	10.4	6.6	2,794	2
France	5.2	5.8	7.4	8.8	9.8	9.7	9.6	9.6	4.4	2,077	10
Canada	6.0	7.0	7.2	9.2	9.5	9.4	9.4	9.3	3.3	2,312	5
Norway	3.9	4.5	7.0	7.8	8.0	8.0	8.1	8.9	5.0	2,425	3
Belgium	3.9	4.1	6.4	7.4	8.4	8.6	8.6	8.8	4.9	2,081	9
Netherlands	4.3	5.9	8.3	8.8	8.9	8.8	8.6	8.6	4.3	2,070	11
Australia	5.1	5.4	7.0	7.9	8.2	8.3	8.3	8.5	3.4	2,043	12
Italy	4.3	5.2	7.0	8.1	8.0	8.1	8.4	8.4	4.1	1,783	15
Sweden	5.5	7.1	9.4	8.8	8.4	8.7	8.5	8.4	2.9	1,746	16
Denmark	4.8	6.1	9.2	8.4	8.2	8.3	8.2	8.3	3.5	2,133	7
Greece	3.1	5.7	6.6	7.6	8.3	8.3	8.5	8.3	5.2	1,167	23
Iceland	3.9	5.0	6.2	8.0	8.2	8.1	7.9	8.3	4.4	2,103	8
Austria	4.7	5.3	7.7	7.2	8.9	8.9	8.2	8.2	3.5	1,968	13
New Zealand	na	5.2	6.0	7.0	7.3	7.3	7.6	8.1	2.9[d]	1,424	20

Portugal	na	2.8	5.8	6.4	7.7	7.7	7.6	7.8	5.0[d]	1,237	21
Japan	4.5	4.6	6.5	6.1	7.2	7.1	7.4	7.6	3.1	1,822	14
Czech Republic	na	na	3.8	5.0	7.3	7.0	7.1	7.2	na	930	24
Spain	2.6	3.7	5.6	6.9	7.0	7.1	7.0	7.1	4.5	1,218	22
Finland	4.9	5.7	6.4	7.9	7.5	7.7	7.3	6.9	2.0	1,502	17
Hungary	na	na	na	na	7.8	7.2	6.9	6.8	na	705	27
United Kingdom	4.1	4.5	5.7	6.0	7.0	7.0	6.7	6.7	2.6	1,461	18
Ireland	4.2	5.3	8.7	7.0	7.4	7.2	7.0	6.4	4.0	1,436	19
Poland	na	na	na	5.3	6.0	6.4	6.2	6.4	na	496	28
Luxembourg	na	3.7	6.2	6.6	6.3	6.4	6.0	5.9	2.2[d]	2,215	6
Korea	na	1.9	3.4	4.8	4.6	4.9	5.0	5.0	3.1[d]	730	26
Mexico	na	na	na	3.6	4.9	4.6	4.7	4.9[c]	na	766[c]	25
Turkey	na	2.4	3.3	3.6	3.3	3.8	4.0	4.1[c]	1.7[d]	233[c]	29
EU average	4.4	5.1	7.3	7.6	8.2	8.0	8.0	8.0	3.6	1,674	
OECD average	4.7	5.0	6.9	7.6	8.2	7.9	8.2	8.3	3.6	1,706	

[a] Total expenditure on health includes public and private spending.

[b] In $US and PPPs (purchasing power parities), a means of comparing health spending between countries on a common base. PPPs are the rates of currency conversion that equalize the cost of a given basket of goods and services in different countries.

[c] Estimated by authors.

[d] Change between 1970 and 1998, instead of 1965 due to unavailable data.

Source: OECD (1995, 2000).

Table 8 Health Expenditure Classified in Terms of Percentage of GDP, 1998

Tier	% of GDP	1970	1998
1	Over 10		Germany, Switzerland, United States
2	9–9.9		France, Canada
3	8–8.9		Norway, Belgium, Netherlands, Australia, Italy, Sweden, Denmark, Greece, Iceland, Austria, New Zealand
4	7–7.9	Canada, Sweden, United States	Portugal, Japan, Czech Republic, Spain
5	6–6.9	Germany, Denmark	Finland, Hungary, United Kingdom, Ireland, Poland
6	5–5.9	Netherlands, France, Greece, Finland, Australia, Austria, Ireland, Italy, New Zealand, Iceland	Luxembourg, Korea
7	4–4.9	Switzerland, Japan, Norway, United Kingdom, Belgium	Mexico, Turkey
8	3–3.9	Luxembourg, Spain	
9	Below 3	Portugal, Turkey, Korea	

Source: OECD (2000).

marked differences exist among individual countries. The limited space of this chapter does not allow further analysis of these differences. Briefly, the rising health care expenditures have been the one universal driver for health care reform. Industrialized countries all faced pressures to reform the finance and delivery of their health care systems.

Table 9 Tax Expenditures as a Percentage of GDP

Country	1965	1970	1975	1980	1985	1990	1991	1992
Canada	na	na	na	0.2	na	2	2.2	2.3
Finland	na	4.9	4.7	4.4	3.5	2.9	3	na
Greece	1.3	1.7	2.4	3.2	3.9	5.6	na	na
Ireland	na	na	na	0.7	2.2	2.9	2.9	2.9
New Zealand	na	na	na	na	na	1.5	1.4	1.4
United States	na	4.2	5	6.6	6.1	4.9	na	na

na = not available.
Source: (OECD) (1995), *OECD Health Data*.

V. MECHANISMS FOR HEALTH CARE REIMBURSEMENT

Now we turn to the second dimension of health care financing, the mechanisms for provider reimbursement. Various mechanisms for reimbursement are influenced and created by the context within which the flow of funds or fiscal transactions take place. None of the OECD countries is 100% publicly funded. Since hospitals and physicians are the primary health care service providers, they will be discussed separately here. The examples illustrate the dominant reimbursement mechanism present in that country.

A. Hospitals

Beginning with hospital services, there are several channels through which these institutions are reimbursed by the health care system. Most systems have both public and private hospitals, although the proportion of each varies. Japan forbids for-profit private hospitals (Yajima and Takayanagi, 1998). The first and most centralized reimbursement mechanism flows from the national government to a regional health authority, responsible for purchasing hospital services (and other services) for a geographically defined population. The authority is given a set budget, which may have the population size, age and other variables factored into the calculated amount, and services for that population are to be delivered within that budget. The United Kingdom, New Zealand, Italy, and Spain are examples of this approach (Maynard and Bloor, 1998; Malcolm, 1995; Taroni et al., 1998; OECD, 1994).

A second approach, the block grant, involves the national government dispersing a set amount of funds to state or provincial governments, usually based on size of population, and delegating responsibility for health care services to that level of government. Canada and Australia are examples of this approach. In Canada, the provincial government then negotiates with the provincial hospital association for reimbursement levels. In addition, the provincial governments can supplement the federal block grant through other sources of provincial revenues such as taxes (Manga, 1998; OECD, 1994). Australia renegotiates the federal block grants to the state governments every 5 years (Harris and Harris, 1998). In the United States, the Medicaid program follows a similar approach, with state governments setting reimbursement rates for that program. Although there are several mechanisms typically utilized by states, including prospective payment for Medicaid and other payers, prospective payment only for Medicaid admissions, selective contracting, and retrospective reimbursement (Thorpe, 1992), state government carries out this function. In several smaller countries, the county/municipality, rather than the state/province, sets the reimbursement. Denmark, Sweden, and Finland function in this manner (OECD, 1999).

A third approach evidences less direct government involvement and increasing private sector or quasi-governmental health insurance activity, but the focus remains at the national level. Here, the federal government determines a national fee schedule and all third-party payers reimburse a standard per diem rate for hospital services. Japan exemplifies this approach in which the set fees are negotiated between the federal government and a council of health care providers, payers, and consumers (Yajima and Takayanagi, 1998). Greece also functions in a similar manner with the federal government setting allowable fees (charges) and the third-party payers (insurance, sickness funds) then reimbursing hospital services on this per diem rate (Niakas and Petsetakis, 1995). In France, public and some private nonprofit hospitals receive global budgets but private hospitals are reimbursed through rates negotiated with the statutory insurers (OECD, 1992). In the United States, the Medicare program for those over the age of 65 years follows a similar approach, utilizing a set reimbursement amount for each client based upon diagnosis-related groupings.

A fourth approach provides for an increasing level of private sector activity and somewhat less government involvement, exemplified by Germany, the Netherlands, Belgium, and Switzerland (OECD, 1992,1994). Here, hospitals negotiate reimbursement fees with sickness funds and private insurers based upon prospective global budgeting for the hospital. In Germany, the sickness funds are largely independent of one another and both federal and state governments.

A fifth approach evidences a higher level of private sector, free-market-based activity, exemplified by the United States and, to some degree, also by Turkey and Austria (OECD, 1994). In the United States, private insurance typically reimburses on a percentage of the usual and customary charges by the hospital for that procedure. While private insurers are increasingly shifting to a fixed reimbursement form through a managed-care mechanism, setting reimbursement in advance for the enrolled population, there remains much more fluidity in what amounts hospitals can charge and in what third-party payers pay than in other health care systems. The government-funded insurance mechanisms reimburse hospital services through set fees determined either federally (Medicare) or at the state level (Medicaid). These insurance programs cover 34 million people (Moon, 1994) and 30 million people (Rowland, 1994) respectively. The large majority of the population, some 77%, is covered by private health insurance offered through some 800 private commercial companies and 73 Blue Cross/ Blue Shield plans (Whitted, 1993).

However, it is important to explore two other factors that influence these mechanics of hospital reimbursement: precisely what services are included in hospital services and charges, and does hospital reimbursement distinguish between capital expenditures and operating expenditures, and if so, how does this occur?

As described earlier, "hospital services" is not a consistent group of services across all countries under consideration here. Some countries combine acute care services and long-term care into hospital services. For example, both Japan and Italy include long-term care services in hospital services (Yajima and Takayanagi, 1998; Graig, 1993; Taroni et al., 1998). In New Zealand, hospitals are moving toward service management, an approach that combines hospital and community-based (outpatient, social, rehabilitative services) care (Malcolm, 1995). In Germany, all hospital, physician, and laboratory services are included in the hospital per diem (Graig, 1993), while in the United States, most of these services are billed separately. Thus, the definition of hospital services and what is included in the per diem charge or the global budget varies from system to system. To collapse all of these definitions for the purpose of comparing hospital expenditures or costs renders the comparison meaningless.

The distinction between hospital operating expenditures and capital outlays for service expansion or purchase of technology is another part of the lack of comparability in the definition of hospital services and their costs although it is beyond the scope of this analysis to elaborate further here.

Recent trends in reimbursement for hospital services demonstrate that the health care systems with more centrally controlled expenditures are building in some characteristics of free-market competition, while the least centrally controlled system is moving toward greater fixed and prospective reimbursement. For example, both the United Kingdom and Italy allocated fixed and capitated budgets to regional health authorities that are responsible for the purchase of hospital services to a geographically specified population (Maynard and Bloor, 1998; Taroni et al., 1998). Both countries have recently instituted mechanisms to promote competition between provider hospitals for reimbursement within regions in hopes that this will encourage greater efficiency. And in the United States, the majority of the private health insurance plans/third party payers are moving into managed care: a fixed and capitated reimbursement mechanism allowing (forcing) competition between providers in contracting with the payers to provide services to the plan's enrollees or subscribers.

In sum, each hospital receives a specified, set reimbursement amount from which it is to deliver the necessary services whether the mechanism is:

global budgeting, a fixed amount set in advance from the government (federal or state) or governmental agency (regional health authority) given to the hospital from which services are to be delivered for a specified population; or

managed care, a fixed amount set in advance from the private insurer given to the hospital under contract from which services must be delivered for a specified population; or

negotiated fees from sickness funds, a fixed reimbursement rate for the enrolled or covered population.

Only two countries appear to allow an "escape hatch" for potential failure to remain within the prospective budget or estimated cost projections. In Greece, if a nonprofit hospital is unable to cover its costs from the per diem charges set by the Ministry of Health, it becomes eligible for direct government funding. According to Niakas and Petsetakis (Chapter 13), such hospitals are now under direct government control. In addition, some large private hospitals are not dependent upon sickness funds and set their own rate to attract the self-pay or privately insured consumer (Niakas and Petsetakis, 1995). And in the United States, if a hospital (whether public, for-profit private, or not-for-profit private) is unable to cover the cost of services from the fixed reimbursement sources (Medicare, Medicaid, managed care plans), it shifts those costs to the nonfixed sources of reimbursement, standard indemnity health insurance plans and direct-pay clients, by charging these groups of consumers higher prices.

B. Physicians

There are also several channels through which physicians are reimbursed by the health care system, again varying in the degree of centralization and government involvement. The emphasis here will be upon primary care physicians or general practitioners, those physicians who tend to be the consumers' first contact or point-of-entry to the health care system.

The most centralized and direct approach involves the federal or national government employing or contracting directly on a full-time basis with the physician. The clearest example of this mechanism occurs in the United Kingdom. Here, general practitioners contract with the National Health Service (NHS) and the physicians' salaries are comprised of three components: (a) a base salary, which covers practice costs, (b) a capitation rate based upon the number of clients who have "signed on" with the physician, and (c) fees received from services to clients such as tests and immunizations (Graig, 1993; Potter and Porter, 1989; OECD, 1992). Specialized physicians can be employed (a) full-time in the NHS, which allows up to an additional 10% of their NHS salary to be earned in private work, or (b) part-time in the NHS, whereby these specialist physicians can also deliver unlimited private sector services (Graig, 1993). Such a centralized and direct physician reimbursement approach also occurs, although on a much smaller scale, in the United States with federal government salaried physicians in the Veterans Administration, the military, and the Public Health Service.

In Italy, a similar approach has been taken. The regional Local Health Offices (USLs) have contracts with the federal government for the purchase of health care services for a specified geographical region. From a national list of ambulatory services, the USLs set the maximum fees to be paid to physicians. General practitioners are self-employed but contract with the government to provide regular and comprehensive care to clients who have registered with them.

Primary care physicians act as gatekeepers for referrals to specialists. The USLs purchase, on a fee-for-service basis, services from the general practitioners. Thus, with mandatory client registration with physicians, the physicians' annual per capita fee is based upon the number of clients on his/her list (Taroni et al., 1998; OECD, 1994). A similar mechanism is utilized in New Zealand where four Regional Health Authorities with capped and capitated budgets purchase services from primary care practitioners (Malcolm, 1995; OECD, 1994). Other countries with a similar approach include Finland, Iceland, Ireland, Norway, Portugal, and Spain (OECD, 1992,1994).

A second approach decentralizes government authority away from the federal level to the state or provincial level. This mechanism is exemplified by the Canadian approach where the provincial governments, operating within the parameters of the federal block grant and the provincial global budget for health services, negotiate physicians' fees with the provincial physicians' association (e.g., Manga, 1998; OECD, 1994). From these negotiated provincial fees, physicians are reimbursed on a fee-for-service basis, with, for the most part, few controls on volume of services. There are provincial variations on volume limits or reimbursement limits; especially notable in this regard is the province of Quebec (Evans et al., 1989; OECD, 1994). State determination of physician reimbursement also occurs in the United States within each Medicaid program, the insurance program for the low-income population. State governments individually set the reimbursement rates they will pay for the federally specified services included in Medicaid. Related to this approach is the decentralization of these functions to the county or municipality (local) level. Examples of this approach are Denmark and Sweden (OECD, 1994).

A third approach to physician reimbursement involves the federal government setting a national fee schedule for physician services. This can be seen in Australia, Japan, and Greece. The Australian national health insurance, Medicare, sets fees for both general practitioner and specialist services and reimburses 85% of the "schedule fee" (Harris and Harris, 1998; OECD, 1994). There is no limit on the volume of services that can be provided. In Japan, all insurers within the mandatory, universal health insurance system reimburse on the basis of a national, fixed, and itemized fee schedule. Physicians are then reimbursed on a fee-for-service basis from the appropriate insurer. There are no limits on volume of services. In addition, hospital and physician services are not separated and physicians not only prescribe but also dispense drugs (Yajima and Takayanagi, 1998; OECD, 1994).

It is useful to note that in the United States, a national, set reimbursement mechanism for physicians is utilized by the Medicare program, an insurance program for those over the age of 65 years. There is a Medicare reimbursement rate for physician services with fixed, set fees determined through a Resource-Based Relative Value Scale (RBRVS). Calculation of the reimbursement to a physician involves physician work, practice expense, malpractice insurance, and a single national value conversion factor. The final reimbursement amount is a geographically weighted sum of the three components times the conversion factor (Koch, 1993; Hsiao et al., 1988a, 1988b; Grimaldi, 1991).

A fourth approach involves less government activity in physician reimbursement, whether at the national, state/provincial, or local level. Luxembourg, Austria, Belgium, Switzerland, France, Germany, and the Netherlands exemplify this avenue with funding sources negotiating with physicians regarding fees. Government is involved either as a party in the negotiations or with governmental approval of the negotiated agreement being required. In Germany, the sickness funds negotiate with associations of physicians for reimbursement rates (Graig, 1993, Henke, 1990; OECD, 1992). Physicians (general practitioners) must accept sickness fund reimbursement as full payment (Graig, 1993).

Physicians send vouchers for services delivered to their clients to regional physician associations of reimbursement. These associations then reimburse the physicians, based upon the negotiated amounts from the sickness funds, and they also monitor the volume of services delivered by each physician. Physicians providing services in hospitals and those who serve outpatient and ambulatory populations are two distinct groups and provide services in either the hospital or outpatient setting only (Stone, 1980; OECD, 1994). While private insurance exists, it usually is purchased by the affluent as a supplement to sickness funds. this insurance reimburses physicians at much higher rates than the sickness funds (Graig, 1993).

A similar approach to the German system has been developed in the Netherlands; however, the Dutch federal government is a more active participant in negotiations with physicians about reimbursement levels. The government and physicians negotiate a "norm income," or income range, which then becomes one of three factors utilized in calculating physician payment levels with sickness funds (Graig, 1993; Kirkman-Liff, 1989). The other two factors are the "norm patient-list size" (a standard negotiated practice size) and the "norm practice costs." These three factors determine the sickness fund's monthly capitation rate to the physician (Graig, 1993; Kirkman-Liff, 1989). Private insurance is also present in this health care system and physicians who contract with private insurers are reimbursed at a fixed rate for specified services. Most general practitioners treat clients covered by both types of insurance and are reimbursed on a capitation basis for those covered by sickness funds and on a fee-for-service basis for those covered by private insurance. Specialists are paid from a separate fee schedule.

The fifth approach involves little or no direct government involvement and is exemplified by the United States' free-market-based insurance system. The approach exhibited in Turkey is similar (OECD, 1994). In the United States, for the majority of physicians' services, physicians are reimbursed on a fee-for-service basis by private and independent insurance companies for services delivered to insured beneficiaries. Insurance typically reimburses approximately 80%

of the charges with the client or beneficiary (recipient of the physician service) paying the remainder. The independent insurance companies reimburse on the basis of ''UCR,'' or usual, customary, and reasonable fees. Here, ''usual'' means that the fee is usual in that doctor's practice, ''customary'' means customary in that community, and ''reasonable'' means reasonable in terms of the distribution of all physician charges for that service in that community (Koch, 1993). Increasingly, as insurance companies move toward managed care in efforts to control costs, the reimbursement mechanism for physicians is shifting away from UCR to a capitation-based mechanism, or some combination of capitation and discounted fee-for-service.

Most countries considered here, regardless of the dominant approach to reimbursement, allow physicians to ''earn more'' either through no limits on volume of services, and additional percentage of salary from service delivery, or extra charges over the set reimbursement fee. Many of these systems, except Canada, also have imposed user fees or copayments by the consumer. Japan and Greece have additional cultural mechanisms whereby physicians can earn more. A traditional ''gift giving'' to physicians can enhance the likelihood of being served and of lessening waiting times for services (Yajima and Takayanagi, 1998; Niakas and Petsetakis, 1995).

Recent reforms in several health care systems have encouraged competition between physicians. In the more centrally controlled systems, the United Kingdom and New Zealand for instance, physicians with larger practices (or client lists) are able to become ''budget holders.'' In this approach, the Regional Health Authority pays the general practitioner a set sum of money for services they provide to clients, as well purchasing laboratory services, specialist physician services, and hospital services for his/her clients. The budget-holding general practitioner ought to seek out the ''best'' prices from the providers of those services. Here, the physician is at risk financially and the reimbursement mechanism promotes competition among specialist physicians, hospitals, laboratories, etc. (Maynard and Bloor, 1998; Malcolm, 1995; OECD, 1992). In Italy, the USLs set the maximum fees that the region is willing to pay for the national list of ambulatory services, promoting competition among the providers (Taroni et al., 1998). In the United States, as noted above, private insurance companies are increasingly moving toward managed care mechanisms with either prepayment of services or discounted fee-for-services for a defined and enrolled population (Williams and Torrens, 1993). Managed care physician reimbursement incorporates several mechanisms including salary, discounted fee-for-service, and capitation, often with incentive compensation based upon the profits generated by the plan and/or productivity of the physician. It is assumed that as managed care mechanisms enroll and thus control a larger portion of the population, providers will become more competitive and efficient. These recent trends are perceived by Graig (1993) as moving more health care systems toward greater similarity. OECD has also noted some convergence among health care systems, while point-

Table 10   Reimbursement Mechanisms for Hospitals and Physicians

	Providers	
Reimbursement authority	Hospitals	Physicians
1 Government sets funding and reimbursement		
a. Federal/national	Iceland, Ireland, Italy, New Zealand, Norway, Portugal, Spain, United Kingdom	Finland, Iceland, Ireland, Italy, New Zealand, Norway, Portugal, Spain, United Kingdom
b. State province	Australia and Canada	Canada
c. County/municipal	Denmark, Finland, Sweden	Sweden, Denmark
2 Government sets re-imbursement	France, Greece, Japan	Australia, Greece, Japan
3 Private/social insurance funding sources, negotiates with providers		
a.	Belgium, Germany, Luxembourg, the Netherlands, Switzerland	Austria, Belgium, France, Germany, Luxembourg, Netherlands, Switzerland
b.	Austria, Turkey, United States	Turkey, United States

ing out that dissimilarities continue to exist (OECD, 1999). The dominant mechanism for the reimbursement of hospitals and physicians in the OECD countries is summarized in Table 10 (OECD, 1995).

C.   Health Care Performance: Satisfaction and Reforms

There is no agreement on a good indicator to measure the quality of health care systems of the OECD countries to determine whether there is a correlation between health care costs and quality and to comparative analysis of health care quality of all OECD countries. According to OECD (2000), OECD health systems are under increasing pressure to improve their performance. Successful performance measurement and management involves, typically, a series of related actions, including: specifying the objectives of the health system; measuring key aspects of the structure, process, and outcomes of the health system against these objectives; analyzing the data collected to distinguish between controllable and uncontrollable variations; identifying suitable benchmarks; publishing the comparisons and benchmarks; and, if appropriate, implementing management action to raise performance levels toward the chosen benchmarks. Many OECD countries have now developed national performance frameworks and have implemented reforms aimed at improving the performance of their health systems.

There has been also growing interest in international benchmarking of performance. OECD has annually published health data, providing statistical data on many health care variables of its member countries, including health expenditure, life expectancy, lengths of hospital stays, and mortality. In addition, OECD's Health Policy Unit has devoted its efforts to these themes. In particular, work is underway to review examples of the development of performance frameworks and performance management in OECD countries. In addition, various projects are being undertaken to investigate international variations in health system performance across the OECD and to explore the causes of these variations (OECD, 2001).

In general, a health care system's performance is measured on three dimensions: cost, access, and quality. In terms of health care quality, OECD's health data shows that people are becoming healthier in the OECD area. In the past three decades, premature mortality, a key indicator for a country's overall health performance, has more than halved across OECD countries and continues to decline (OECD, 2000). While premature mortality declined more rapidly for women than for men between 1960 and 1990, since 1990 the decline for men has been roughly the same on average as for women. In the United States, however, premature mortality is 20% higher than the OECD average in the case of men, and 11% higher for women, suggesting that the United States still has some way to go to catch up to the healthiest OECD countries. In Mexico, Hungary, Poland, and the Czech Republic, meanwhile, death rates are still relatively high among populations under 70 years of age (OECD, 2000).

In terms of costs, OECD data show that health care costs have escalated in the past three decades (Table 7). In addition, many countries have problems with health care access, including the lack of health care coverage in the United States and long waiting for many types of health care in many other countries.

One indicator of quality is the level of satisfaction expressed by consumers. In the last several years, comparative studies of selected OECD countries were conducted by Blendon et al. (1990,1991,1996), and Mossialos (1997). According to these studies, in nine of 15 countries, over a half of their citizens were very and fairly satisfied with their health care system (Table 11). Denmark and Finland have the most satisfying health care systems. Meanwhile, only less than 20% of citizens in Italy, Greece, and Portugal were very and fairly pleased with their health systems while health care cost were relatively high in those countries (Table 11).

Moreover, there is no association between the expenditures and the quality of the health care system. In the United States and Germany, where health care

Table 11 Health Care Costs and Quality/Satisfaction of Sixteen OECD Countries, 1996

Country	Public satisfaction		Health expenditure			
	Rank	% of population satisfied with their system	Rank most costly	% of GDP	Publicly funded (as % of total health spending)	Privately funded (as % of total health spending)
Australia	9	63.3	7	8.3	66.6	33.4
Belgium	5	70.1	6	8.6	88.8	11.2
Denmark	1	90.0	7	8.3	82.4	17.6
Finland	2	86.4	11	7.7	75.9	24.1
France	8	65.1	3	9.7	76.3	23.7
Germany	7	66.0	2	10.6	78.3	21.7
Greece	14	18.4	7	8.3	58.7	41.3
Ireland	10	49.9	13	7.2	72.5	27.5
Italy	15	16.3	10	8.1	67.8	32.2
Luxembourg	4	71.1	16	6.4	92.8	7.2
Netherlands	3	72.8	4	8.8	67.7	32.3
Portugal	13	19.9	11	7.7	66.7	33.3
Spain	12	35.6	14	7.1	78.5	21.5
Sweden	6	67.3	5	8.7	84.8	15.2
United Kingdom	11	48.1	15	7	83.7	16.3
United States	na	na	1	13.8	45.5	54.5

[a] Funding as a percentage of total health expenditure.
Source: Derived from OECD (2000), *OECD Health Data*, and OECD (2001) "Satisfaction with health care systems" (http:www.oecd.org/els/health/sources/Satisfac.htm).

was the most expensive among the 15 surveyed countries (ranked first and second, respectively in terms of percentage of GDP), the German health care system was ranked number 7, as measured by satisfaction, while Denmark's health care system is the most satisfying among OECD countries although its health care expenditure ranked seventh as measured by percentage of GDP. The British health care system, which cost the least among the 16 countries listed in Table 11, was ranked eleventh in terms of quality/satisfaction (only 27% of the population felt that it worked pretty well), while the Dutch health care system was ranked the third best and cost the fourth lowest among the 15 studied countries.*

---

* Using per capita health expenditure as a measure of health care cost, Blendon et al. (1990, p. 189) found that there is an association between the quality of health and the health care cost—the higher cost the better satisfaction—if the United States and Sweden were excluded from the analysis.

Table 12 Citizens' Perceptions About Health Care Reforms, 1996

Country	Runs quite well (%)	Minor changes needed (%)	Fundamental changes needed (%)	Rebuild it completely (%)	Other (%)
Austria	40.2	33.5	18.0	3.3	5.0
Belgium	41.7	34.0	16.5	2.9	4.9
Denmark	54.4	37.2	5.7	1.8	1.0ᵛ
Finland	38.9	51.6	7.7	0.6	1.2
France	25.6	40.9	24.6	5.0	3.9
Germany	36.9	38.5	16.7	2.2	5.7
Greece	3.8	25.5	44.2	25.0	1.6
Ireland	19.4	30.7	25.6	16.9	7.4
Italy	3.4	15.1	43.8	33.1	4.5
Luxembourg	31.9	43.9	13.3	2.5	8.4
Netherlands	31.0	46.0	17.6	3.5	1.9
Portugal	3.6	19.4	38.3	31.8	6.9
Spain	14.1	30.4	34.0	13.5	7.9
Sweden	28.5	44.1	21.8	3.4	2.2
United Kingdom	14.6	27.4	42.0	14.0	2.0
United States[a]	na	17.0	46.0	33.0	

na = not available.
[a] Based on 1998 survey.
Source: OECD (2001), based on Mossialos, E. (1997), "Citizens' view on health systems in the 15 member states of the European Union," Health Econ 6:109–116; and Eurobarometer survey.

Finally, there is no association between the quality of a health care system and the size of public funding or private funding. In the United States, where the private sector comprised the largest portion of health care expenditure (57.5%) as compared with other surveyed countries, the American health care system left over 40 million Americans without health coverage.

D. Health Care Reforms

Dealing with escalating health care cost, health care systems in many countries have been subject to constant reform pressure. According to various recent surveys, the majority of citizens in all studied countries, except Denmark, believe that their health care systems need reforms, either minor or major (Table 12). Reflecting their dissatisfaction, Italians, Portuguese, and Greeks believe that their health care systems need to be reformed, and so do Americans. Seventy-nine percent of Americans, 77% of Italians, and 69% of Greeks believe that their health care systems need fundamental changes or need to be rebuilt completely (Table 12).

VI. CONCLUDING COMMENTS

One final dimension to the examination of health care expenditures pertains to the "value" of those expenditures. More attention is being given to the final outcome or the result of the expenditures in health care. One frequent index or measure of the value of health care expenditures is the health status of the population. While recognizing that many more factors other than or in addition to the purchase of health care services impinge upon the health status of a population, indices such as life expectancy and infant mortality rate are utilized to compare the result of health care expenditures across countries. It is assumed that spending funds on health care will, or at least ought to, improve life expectancy (lengthen) and diminish infant mortality. A further assumption or thesis might be advanced that if one country spends more funds on health care than other countries, that country ought to demonstrate increased life expectancy and lowered infant mortality than countries that spend less on health care. Again recognizing that there is not a clear causal relationship between these variables, the United States spends far more per capita than other OECD countries, yet evidences lower life expectancy and higher infant mortality than other countries that spend far less per capita.

A second component of outcome is customer or client satisfaction with the health care system. In a widely publicized study of satisfaction with 10 health care systems, Blendon et al. (1990) examined this issue, as discussed above. These authors noted that in the United States and Italy, respondents indicated a higher degree of dissatisfaction than in other countries, while in Canada, respondents indicated a higher degree of satisfaction with the health care system.

Discussion of health care reform or altering the health care system in many OECD countries has been taking place, as noted by several authors (e.g., Graig, 1993; Roemer, 1991; OECD, 1992, 1994). Certainly, changing the health care system in the United States has been a prominent topic in the political arena for some time. However, before comparisons can be made on the basis of expenditures, it is important to examine not only the sources of those expenditures, but also what is being purchased, and how the providers are being reimbursed. The variations among these factors are influential in the overall expenditure level.

REFERENCES

Abel-Smith, B. (1984). Cost Containment in Health Care. London: Bedford Square Press.
Blendon, R.J., Leitman, R., Morrison, I., Donelan, K. (1990). Satisfaction with health systems in 10 nations. Health Affairs 9(4):185–192.

Evans, R.G., Lomas, J., Barer, M.L., Labelle, R.J., Fooks, C., Stoddart, G.L., Anderson, G.M., Feeny, D., Gafni, A., Torrance, G.W., Tholl, W.G. (1989). Controlling health care expenditures—the Canadian reality. N Engl J Med 320(9):571–577.

Graig, L. (1993). Health of Nations: An International Perspective on U.S. Health Care Reform, 2nd ed. Washington, DC: Congressional Quarterly, Inc.

Grimaldi, P.L. (1991). BRBVs: How New Physician Fee Schedule Will Work. Healthcare Financial Management 45(9):58–75.

Harris, M.G., Harris, R.D. (1998). Australian health system: continuity and change. J Health Hum Serv Admin 20(4):442–467.

Henke, K-D. (1990). "Federal Republic of Germany." In: OECD. Health Care Systems in Transition: The Search for Efficiency. Paris: OECD.

Hsiao, W.C., Braun, P. Yntema, D., Becker, E.R. (1988a). Estimating physicians work for a resource-based relative-value scale. N Engl J Med 319(13):835–841.

Hsiao, W.C., Braun, P., Dunn, D., Becker, E.R., DiNicola, M., Ketcham, T.R. (1988b). Results and policy implications of the resource-based relative value study. N Engl J Med 391(13):881–888.

Kirkman-Liff, B. (1989). Cost containment and physician payment methods in the Netherlands. Inquiry 26(4):468–482.

Koch, A. (1993). Financing health services. In: S.J. Williams, and P.R. Torrens, eds. Introduction to Health Services, 4th ed. Albany, NY: Delmar Publishers, Inc., pp 299–331.

Malcolm, L. (1995). Radical health reform in New Zealand: towards managed care. Public Budgeting Financial Management 7:89–121.

Manga, P. (1998). Avoiding fundamental reform: current cost containment strategies in Canada. J Health Hum Serv Admin 20(4):468–501.

Maynard, A., Bloor, K. (1998). Universal coverage and cost control: the United Kingdom National Health Service. J Health Hum Serv Admin 20(4):423–441.

Moon, M. (1994). The role of Medicare in reform. In: E. Ginzberg, ed. Critical Issues in Health Care Reform. Boulder, CO: Westview Press, pp 171–189.

Niakas, D., Petsetakis, E. (1995). Problems and perspectives in health care policy in Greece. Public Budgeting Financial Management 7:251–278.

Organization for Economic Co-operation and Development (1987). Financing and Delivering Health Care. Paris: OECD.

Organization for Economic Co-operation and Development (1992). The Reform of Health Care: A Comparative Analysis of Seven OECD Countries. Paris: OECD.

Organization for Economic Co-operation and Development (1994). The Reform of Health Care Systems: A Review of Seventeen OECD Countries. Paris: OECD.

Organization for Economic Co-operation and Development (1995, 1998, 1999, 2000). OECD Health Data. Paris: OECD.

Organization for Economic Co-operation and Development (2001). Satisfaction with health care systems. www.oecd.org/els/health/sources/Satisfac.htm, 3/10/2001.

Organization for Economic Co-operative and Development (2001). News release. www., oecd.org/media/publish/pb00-15a.htm. 3/1/2001.

Potter, C., Porter, J. (1989). American perceptions of the British National Health Service: five myths. J Health Politics Policy Law 14:341–365.

Roemer, M.I. (1991). National Health Systems of the World. Vol. 1. The Countries. New York: Oxford University Press.

Rowland, D. (1994). Lessons from the Medicaid experience. In: E. Ginzberg, Critical Issues in Health Care Reform. Boulder, CO: Westview Press, pp 190–207.

Schieber, G.J., Poullier, J.-P. (1989). Overview of international comparisons of health care expenditures. Health Care Financing Rev (annual supplement):1–7.

Stone, D. (1980). The Limits of Professional Power: National Health Care in the Federal Republic of Germany. Chicago: University of Chicago.

Taroni, F., Guerra, R., D'Ambrosio, M.G. (1998). The health care reform in Italy: transition or turmoil? J Health Hum Serv Admin

Thai, K.V., Sekwat, A. (1994). Recent developments in public financial management in the European community: a comparative analysis. Public Budgeting Financial Management 6:310–356.

Thorpe, K.E. (1992). Health care cost containment: results and lessons from the past 20 years. In: S.M. Shortell, U.E. Reinhardt, eds. Improving Health Policy and Management: Nine Critical Issues for the 1990s. Ann Arbor, MI: Health Administration Press, pp 227–274.

Whitted, G. (1993). Private health insurance and employee benefits. In: S.I. Williams, P.R. Torrens, eds. Introduction to Health Services, 4th ed. Albany, NY: Delmar Publishers, Inc., pp 332–360.

Williams, S.J., Torrens, P.R. (1993). Managed care: restructuring the system. In: S.J. Williams, P.R. Torrens, eds. Introduction to Health Services, 4th ed. Albany, NY: Delmar Publishers, Inc., pp 361–373.

Yajima, R., Takayanagi, K. (1998). The Japanese health care system: citizen complaints, citizen possibilities. J Health Hum Serv Admin 20(4):502–519.

Index